COMMUNICATING ABOUT HEALTH

COMMUNICATING ABOUT HEALTH

CURRENT ISSUES AND PERSPECTIVES

2nd Edition

Athena du Pré, Ph.D.
University of West Florida

Boston Burr Ridge, IL Dubuque, IA Madison, WI New York
San Francisco St. Louis Bangkok Bogotá Caracas Kuala Lumpur
Lisbon London Madrid Mexico City Milan Montreal New Delhi
Santiago Seoul Singapore Sydney Taipei Toronto

The McGraw-Hill Companies

COMMUNICATING ABOUT HEALTH: CURRENT ISSUES AND PERSPECTIVES

Published by McGraw-Hill, a business unit of The McGraw-Hill Companies, Inc., 1221 Avenue of the Americas, New York, NY, 10020.

This book is printed on acid-free paper.

4 5 6 7 8 9 0 FGR/FGR 0 9 8 7 6

ISBN 978-0-07-286294-2
MHID 0-07-286294-7

Publisher: *Phillip A. Butcher*
Senior Sponsoring editor: *Nanette Giles*
Developmental editor: *Joshua F. Hawkins*
Senior marketing manager: *Leslie Oberhuber*
Project manager: *Ruth Smith*
Senior production supervisor: *Carol A. Bielski*
Designer: *George Kokkonas*
Lead media project manager: *Marc Mattson*
Photo research manager: *Brian Pecko*
Cover design: *Adam Hoff*
Interior design: *Kay Fulton*
Typeface: *10.5/12 Minion*
Compositor: *GAC Indianapolis*
Printer: *Quebecor World Fairfield Inc.*

Library of Congress Cataloging-in-Publication Data

du Pré, Athena,
Communicating about health : current issues and perspectives / Athena du Pré.--2nd ed.
p. cm.
Includes bibliographical references and index.
ISBN 0-07-286294-7 (softcover : alk, paper)
1. Communication in medicine. 2. Medical personnel and patient. 3. Health education.
4. Health promotion. I. Title.
R118.D87 2005
613--dc22 2004044981

www.mhhe.com

Brief Contents

Part One. ESTABLISHING A CONTEXT FOR HEALTH COMMUNICATION 1

CHAPTER 1. *Introduction* 3

CHAPTER 2. *History and Current Issues* 25

Part Two. THE ROLES OF PATIENTS AND CAREGIVERS 55

CHAPTER 3. *Patient–Caregiver Communication* 57

CHAPTER 4. *Caregiver Perspective* 84

CHAPTER 5. *Patient Perspective* 115

CHAPTER 6. *Diversity Among Patients* 140

Part Three. SOCIAL AND CULTURAL ISSUES 171

CHAPTER 7. *Social Support* 173

CHAPTER 8. *Cultural Conceptions of Health and Illness* 203

Part Four. COMMUNICATION IN HEALTH ORGANIZATIONS 235

CHAPTER 9. *Culture and Diversity in Health Organizations* 237

CHAPTER 10. *Leadership and Teamwork* 270

Part Five. HEALTH IN THE MEDIA 303

CHAPTER 11. *Health Images in the Media* 305

CHAPTER 12. *Planning Health Promotion Campaigns* 338

CHAPTER 13. *Designing and Implementing Health Campaigns* 365

Contents

Preface xxi

Part One. **ESTABLISHING A CONTEXT FOR HEALTH COMMUNICATION 1**

CHAPTER 1. *Introduction* 3

WHAT IS HEALTH COMMUNICATION? 5
Defining Communication 5
Process 5
Personal Goals 6
Interdependence 7
Sensitivity 7
Shared Meaning 8
Defining Health Communication 8
Implications 10

MEDICAL MODELS 10
Biomedical Model 10
Biopsychosocial Model 11
Implications 12

IMPORTANCE OF HEALTH COMMUNICATION 12
Six Important Issues 12
Implications 15

CURRENT ISSUES IN HEALTH COMMUNICATION 15
Medical Cost-Cutting 15
Prevention 18
Patient Empowerment 18
Global Health Needs 19
Changing Populations 21
Technology 21
Implications 22

SUMMARY 22

KEY TERMS 23

REVIEW QUESTIONS 23

CLASS ACTIVITY: Review Your Own Experiences 24

BOXES: Box 1.1 Perspectives: True Stories About Health Communication Experiences 6
Box 1.2 Theoretical Foundations: The Basis for Health Communication 9
Box 1.3 Perspectives: A Memorable Hospital Experience 13
Box 1.4 Ethical Considerations: An Essential Component of Health Communication 16
Box 1.5 Resources: Opportunities for Further Exploration 20

CHAPTER 2. *History and Current Issues* 25

MEDICINE IN ANCIENT TIMES 25
Imhotep 25
Hippocrates 26
Implications 28

MEDIEVAL RELIGION AND HEALTH CARE 28
Medical Spiritualism 28
Barber Surgeons 29
Science and Magic 29
End of an Era 30
Implications 30

RENAISSANCE PHILOSOPHY AND HEALTH CARE 30
Principle of Verification 31
Cartesian Dualism 31
Implications 33

HEALTH CARE IN THE NEW WORLD 33
Health Conditions 33
Hippocrates' Influence 34
Women's Role 34
Implications 34

THE RISE OF ORTHODOX MEDICINE 35
Population Shifts 35
Germ Theory 35
Research and Technology 36
Campaign of Orthodox Medicine 36
Flexner Report 37
Decline of Sectarian Medicine 37
Implications 38

TWENTIETH CENTURY HEALTH CARE 38
Specialization 38
Medicine and Free Enterprise 39
Implications 39

ADVENT OF MANAGED CARE 39
Health and Wealth 40
Problems 40
Reform Efforts 41

Managed Care 41
Consumers' Perspective 44
Caregiver's Perspective 46
Organization's Perspective 47
Pros and Cons 48
Implications 50

SUMMARY 50

KEY TERMS 52

REVIEW QUESTIONS 53

CLASS ACTIVITY: Health in the News 53

BOXES: Box 2.1 The Hippocratic Oath 27
Box 2.2 Perspectives: Sick in the Head? 32
Box 2.3 Theoretical Foundations: Kaleidoscope Model of Health Communication 42
Box 2.4 Resources: More About Managed Care 46
Box 2.5 Managed Care at a Glance 48
Box 2.6 Ethical Considerations: Classroom Debate on Managed Care 51

***Part Two.* THE ROLES OF PATIENTS AND CAREGIVERS 55**

CHAPTER 3. *Patient–Caregiver Communication* 57

PHYSICIAN-CENTERED COMMUNICATION 58
Assertive Behavior 59
Questions and Directives 60
Blocking 60
Patronizing Behavior 61
Power Difference 63
Criticism of Physician-Centeredness 63
Implications 66

COLLABORATIVE COMMUNICATION 66
Climate for Change 68
Communication Skill Builders: Cultivating Dialogue 69
Nonverbal Encouragement 69
Verbal Encouragement 70
Implications 71

ENVIRONMENTAL RESTRUCTURING 72
Mobility and Involvement 74
Soothing Surroundings 75
Implications 76

COMMUNICATION TECHNOLOGY: TELEMEDICINE 76
Advantages to Consumers 77
Advantages for Caregivers 78
Disadvantages 78
Implications 79

COMMUNICATION SKILL BUILDERS: TIPS FOR PATIENTS 80

SUMMARY 81

KEY TERMS 82

REVIEW QUESTIONS 82

CLASS ACTIVITY: Redesigning the Doctor's Office or Hospital 83

BOXES: Box 3.1 Stepping Over the Line 62
Box 3.2 Ethical Considerations: Therapeutic Privilege 64
Box 3.3 Theoretical Foundations: Communication as Collaborative Interpretation 67
Box 3.4 Perspectives: A Mother's Experience at the Dentist 72
Box 3.5 Doorknob Disclosures 74
Box 3.6 Resources: More About the Planetree Model 76
Box 3.7 Resources: Health Communication Journals 80

CHAPTER 4. *Caregiver Perspective* 84

MEDICAL SOCIALIZATION 85
Theory of Socialization 85
Selection 88
Curriculum 89
Nursing 89
Dentistry 89
Diverse Caregivers 90
Physicians 90
Socialization Process 91
Loss of Identity 92
Privileged Status 92
Overwhelming Responsibilities 93
Withdrawal and Resentment 93
Effects of Socialization 94
Medical School Reform 94
Implications 95

PROFESSIONAL INFLUENCES ON CAREGIVERS 96
Time Constraints 96
Competition 97
Loss of Autonomy 97
Implications 98

PSYCHOLOGICAL INFLUENCES ON CAREGIVERS 99
Maturity 99
Self-Doubt 103
Satisfaction 103
Implications 105

STRESS AND BURNOUT 105
Causes 107
Conflict 107
Emotions 108

Communication Deficits 108
Workload 109
Other Factors 109
Effects 109
Communication Skill Builders: Tips for Avoiding Burnout 109
Implications 110

COMMUNICATION TECHNOLOGY: KNOWLEDGE COUPLING 111
Implications 111

SUMMARY 112

KEY TERMS 113

REVIEW QUESTIONS 113

CLASS ACTIVITY: Doctors in the Movies 114

BOXES: Box 4.1 Theoretical Foundations: Talking Like a Doctor 86
Box 4.2 Resources: More on Communication Training for Caregivers 91
Box 4.3 Ethical Considerations: Privacy Regulations Incite Controversy 100
Box 4.4 Managing Medical Mistakes 104
Box 4.5 Perspectives: Blowing the Whistle on an Impaired Physician 106

CHAPTER 5. *Patient Perspective* 115

PATIENT SOCIALIZATION 115
Voice of Lifeworld 116
Feelings Versus Evidence 118
Specific Versus Diffuse 118
Implications 119

PATIENT CHARACTERISTICS 119
Nature of the Illness 120
Patient Disposition 120
Communication Skills 121
Implications 121

SATISFACTION 122
Attentiveness 122
Information 123
Convenience 123
Moderation 123
Implications 124

COOPERATION AND CONSENT 124
Reasons for Noncompliance 125
Caregivers' Investment 126
Informed Consent 126
Implications 130

ILLNESS AND PERSONAL IDENTITY 130
Reactions to Illness 132
Narratives 132
Implications 136
SUMMARY 136
KEY TERMS 137
REVIEW QUESTIONS 137
CLASS ACTIVITY: Informed Consent in Current Events 138
BOXES: Box 5.1 Perspectives: The Agony of Uncertainty 116
Box 5.2 Resources: More About Patient Communication Skills Training 122
Box 5.3 Cash for Cooperation? 127
Box 5.4 Ethical Considerations: Patients' Right to Informed Consent 128
Box 5.5 Theoretical Foundations: Integrative Health Model 134

CHAPTER 6. *Diversity Among Patients* 140
STATUS DIFFERENCES 140
Misunderstandings 140
Health Literacy 141
Communication Skill Builders: Surmounting Status Barriers 143
GENDER DIFFERENCES 143
SEXUAL ORIENTATION 144
RACE 146
Different Care and Outcomes 146
Explanations 147
Distrust 147
High Risk, Low Knowledge 147
Access 148
Patient–Caregiver Communication 148
LANGUAGE DIFFERENCES 149
DISABILITIES 155
Communication Skill Builders: Interacting With Persons Who Have Disabilities 156
AGE 158
Children 158
Communication Skill Builders: Talking With Children About Illness 159
Older Adults 159
Effects of Ageism 161
Communication Patterns 161
Promising Options 164
Communication Technology and Older Adults 164
Communication Skill Builders: Reaching Marginalized Populations 165

SUMMARY 166

KEY TERMS 168

REVIEW QUESTIONS 168

CLASS ACTIVITY: Overcoming the Self-Consciousness of a Disability 169

BOXES: Box 6.1 Resources: More About the Health Literacy Initiative 143
Box 6.2 Ethical Considerations: Who Gets What Care? 150
Box 6.3 Perspectives: Language Barriers in a Health Care Emergency 152
Box 6.4 Perspectives: "My Disability Doesn't Show" 157
Box 6.5 Theoretical Foundations: Communication Accommodation 162
Box 6.6 Resources: Health Communication and Older Adults 165
Box 6.7 Resources: More on Serving Marginalized Communities 166

Part Three. **SOCIAL AND CULTURAL ISSUES 171**

CHAPTER 7. *Social Support* 173

CONCEPTUAL OVERVIEW 174
Coping 174
Crisis 175
Normalcy 176

COPING STRATEGIES AND SOCIAL SUPPORT 176
Action-Facilitating Support 177
Nurturing Support 177
Esteem Support 177
Communication Skill Builders: Supportive Listening 178
Emotional Support 178
Communication Skill Builders: Allowing Emotions 178
Social Network Support 179
Communication Skill Builders: Keeping Social Networks Active 180
Support Groups 181
Communication Technology: Virtual Communities 182
Implications 183

LAY CAREGIVING 184
Lay Caregivers' New Role 184
Profile of the Lay Caregiver 185
Stress and Burnout 185
Caring for Caregivers 188

DEATH AND DYING EXPERIENCES 188
Life at All Costs 189
Death With Dignity 190
Advance-Care Directives 191
Coping With Death 191

Communication Skill Builders: Coping With Death 194
Implications 195

OVERSUPPORTING 195
Overhelping 196
Overinforming 196
Overempathizing 198
Implications 199

SUMMARY 199

KEY TERMS 200

REVIEW QUESTIONS 201

CLASS ACTIVITY: Comforting a Friend 201

BOXES: Box 7.1 Resources: More About Coping and Social Support 184
Box 7.2 Perspectives: A Long Goodbye to Grandmother 186
Box 7.3 Ethical Considerations: Do People Have a Right to Die? 192
Box 7.4 Resources: Insight About Dying Experiences 196
Box 7.5 Theoretical Foundations: Theory of Problematic Integration 197

CHAPTER 8. *Cultural Conceptions of Health and Illness* 203

WHY CONSIDER CULTURE? 204
Implications 207

THE NATURE OF HEALTH AND ILLNESS 208
Health as Organic 208
Health as Harmony 210
Implications 211

SOCIAL IMPLICATIONS OF DISEASE 212
Disease as a Curse 213
Stigma of Disease 217
The Morality of Prevention 218
Victimization 218
Implications 219

PATIENT AND CAREGIVER ROLES 219
Mechanics and Machines 222
Parents and Children 223
Spiritualists and Believers 223
Providers and Consumers 226
Partners 227
Implications 228

CULTURAL COMPETENCE 228

COMMUNICATION SKILL BUILDERS: DEVELOPING CULTURAL COMPETENCE 229

SUMMARY 230

KEY TERMS 231

REVIEW QUESTIONS 231

CLASS ACTIVITY: How It Was—How It Could Be 231

BOXES: Box 8.1 Perspectives: Zackie Achmat Fights for AIDS Care in Africa 206
Box 8.2 Resources: More About Culture and Health 209
Box 8.3 Theoretical Foundations: Theory of Health as Expanded Consciousness 214
Box 8.4 Perspectives: Thai Customs and a Son's Duty 220
Box 8.5 Ethical Considerations: Physician as Parent or Partner? 224

Part Four. COMMUNICATION IN HEALTH ORGANIZATIONS 235

CHAPTER 9. *Culture and Diversity in Health Organizations* 237

ORGANIZATIONAL CULTURE 238
- Cultural Integration 239
- Advantages of Diversity 239
- Implications 245

HISTORICAL PATTERNS OF ACCEPTANCE 246
- Female Physicians 246
- Building Equity 247
- Communication Styles 248
- Minorities in Medicine 248
  - *History* 248
  - *Current Representation* 249
  - *Communication Effects* 249
- Implications 251

DIVERSE TYPES OF HEALTH CARE 252
- Nurses 252
  - *Nursing Shortage* 252
- Nurse Practitioners and Physician Assistants 254
- Implications 254

ALTERNATIVE AND COMPLEMENTARY CARE 255
- Definitions 255
- Popularity 257
- Advantages 257
- Drawbacks 258
- Implications 259

MANAGING CONFLICT 259
- Definitions 260
- Conflict of Interest 261
- Violent Conflict 262

Communication Skill Builders: Defusing Violent Situations 263
Nurses' Role Conflict 263
Implications 265

COMMUNICATION SKILL BUILDERS: INTEGRATING DIVERSE EMPLOYEES 265

SUMMARY 266

KEY TERMS 267

REVIEW QUESTIONS 268

CLASS ACTIVITY: Inventory of Personal Beliefs 268

BOXES: Box 9.1 Perspectives: Cultural Transformation at Delnor Hospital 240
Box 9.2 Theoretical Foundations: Model of Multiculturalism 244
Box 9.3 Ethical Considerations: Is Affirmative Action Justified or Not? 250
Box 9.4 Alternative and Complementary Medicine at a Glance 256
Box 9.5 Resources: More on Conflict Management 263

CHAPTER 10. *Leadership and Teamwork* 270

CURRENT ISSUES 271
Consolidation 271
Competition 274
Consumerism 276
Staffing Shortages 278
Implications 278

CHALLENGING THE BUREAUCRACY 278
Hierarchies or Partnerships? 279
Advantages 279
Disadvantages 280
Opportunities for Change 280
Communication Skill Builders: Training New Leaders 281
Authority Rule or Multilevel Input? 282
Advantages 282
Disadvantages 283
Opportunities for Change 283
Communication Skills Builders: Managing by Collaboration 284
Specialized Jobs or Mission-Centered Expectations? 284
Advantages 285
Disadvantages 285
Opportunities for Change 285
Communication Skill Builders: Promoting a Shared Vision 285
Strictly by the Rules . . . or Not? 286
Advantages 286
Disadvantages 287

Communication Skill Builders: Evaluating the Rules 287
Implications 288

TEAMWORK 288
Advantages 289
Difficulties and Drawbacks 291
Communication Skill Builders: Working on Teams 292
Implications 292

ROLE OF COMMUNICATION SPECIALISTS 293
Reducing Uncertainty 293
Bridging Boundaries 293
Providing Social Support 294
Building Skills 294
Working With the Media 295
Managing Crises 296
Communication Skill Builders: Crisis Management 296
Promoting Community Outreach and Health Education 296
Marketing 297
Advocating for Patients 297
Researching Health Communication 298
Implications 298

SUMMARY 299

KEY TERMS 299

REVIEW QUESTIONS 300

CLASS ACTIVITY: Mending a Breach of Trust 300

BOXES: Box 10.1 Perspectives: Leaders Communicate With Purpose 272
Box 10.2 Ethical Considerations: Should Health Organizations Advertise? 276
Box 10.3 Resources: More About Adapting to Changes in Health Care 278
Box 10.4 Theoretical Foundations: A Model for Innovative Leadership 290
Box 10.5 Resources: More About Careers in Health Communication 299

***Part Five.* HEALTH IN THE MEDIA 303**

CHAPTER 11. *Health Images in the Media* 305

ADVERTISING 306
Nutrition 307
Obesity 307
Effects on Children 308
Activity Levels 308
Alcohol 308
Source of Knowledge 309

Glamorized Images 309
Programming Content 312
Body Images 312
Health Effects 313
Eternal Hope 313
Implications 314
NEWS COVERAGE 314
Accuracy 315
Sensationalism 318
Advantages 320
Communication Skill Builders: Presenting Health News 320
Communication Technology: Interactive Health Information 321
Advantages 322
Drawbacks 322
Communication Skill Builders: Using the Internet 323
Implications 324
ENTERTAINMENT 324
Portrayals of Health-Related Behaviors 324
Mental Illness 324
Disabilities 325
Sex 325
Violence 326
Portrayals of Health Care Situations 327
Medical Miracles 327
Entertainment and Commercialism 327
Entertainomercials 327
Product Placement 328
Pro-Social Programming 329
Impact of Persuasive Entertainment 330
Implications 332
MEDIA LITERACY 332
Teaching Media Literacy 333
Implications 334
SUMMARY 334
KEY TERMS 335
REVIEW QUESTIONS 336
CLASS ACTIVITY: Building Media Literacy 336
BOXES: Box 11.1 Theoretical Foundations: Cultivation Theory and Social Comparison Theory 310
Box 11.2 Resources: More About Media Effects on Children 314
Box 11.3 Perspectives: Media Relations at the CDC 316
Box 11.4 Resources: Learning Opportunities for Health Journalists 321
Box 11.5 Ethical Considerations: Is the Entertainment Industry Responsible for Health Images? 330

CHAPTER 12. ***Planning Health Promotion Campaigns* 338**

BACKGROUND ON HEALTH CAMPAIGNS 339
Motivating Factors 339
Exemplary Campaigns 342
Go to the Audience 342
Take Action 343
Measure Your Success 343
Encourage Social Support 344
Implications 344

PLANNING A HEALTH CAMPAIGN 345
Step 1: Defining the Situation and Potential Benefits 345
Benefits 345
Current Situation 346
Diverse Motivations 346
Step 2: Analyzing and Segmenting the Audience 347
Data Collection 347
Segmenting the Audience 350
Audience Profiles 352
Step 3: Establishing Campaign Goals and Objectives 356
Step 4: Selecting Channels of Communication 358
Channel Characteristics 358
Communication Technology: Using Computers to Narrow Messages 359
Multichannel Campaigns 360

SUMMARY 362

KEY TERMS 362

REVIEW QUESTIONS 363

CLASS ACTIVITY: Focus Group Exercise 364

BOXES: Box 12.1 Perspectives: Gross! Wash Your Hands 340
Box 12.2 Resources: Careers in Health Education and Promotion 350
Box 12.3 Ethical Considerations: The Politics of Prevention—Who Should Pay? 354
Box 12.4 Theoretical Foundations: The Knowledge Gap Hypothesis 357
Box 12.5 Resources: More on Tailored Health Communication 361

CHAPTER 13. ***Designing and Implementing Health Campaigns* 365**

THEORIES OF BEHAVIOR CHANGE 367
Health Belief Model 367
Social Cognitive Theory 371
Embedded Behaviors Model 372
Theory of Reasoned Action 373
Transtheoretical Model 373
Implications 375

DESIGNING AND IMPLEMENTING A CAMPAIGN 377

Step 5: Designing Campaign Messages 377
Choosing a Voice 377
Designing the Message 381
Step 6: Piloting and Implementing the Campaign 384
Step 7: Evaluating and Maintaining the Campaign 386
Evaluation 386
Maintenance 387

SUMMARY 388

KEY TERMS 389

REVIEW QUESTIONS 389

CLASS ACTIVITY: Evaluating Messages 390

BOXES: Box 13.1 Perspectives: Unselling Drugs with Madison Avenue Know-How 368
Box 13.2 Theoretical Foundations: Synopsis of Behavior Change Theories 376
Box 13.3 Ethical Considerations: Three Issues for Health Promoters to Keep in Mind 378
Box 13.4: Resources: More About Designing Health Campaigns 385
Box 13.5 Resources: More About Assessing the Impact of Health Campaigns 388

References R-1–R-59

Credits C-0

Author Index I-1–I-9

Subject Index I-10–I-18

Preface

I had no idea when *Communicating About Health: Current Issues and Perspectives* was first published how many readers would call and write me about the book. It has been an extraordinarily rewarding experience hearing from people in the United States and around the world. Your enthusiasm makes it a genuine pleasure to present this second edition with updates and additional features.

Like the first edition, this one is designed to provide an insightful, rich, and thorough overview of health communication. My goal is to provide up-to-date information, broad enough to show the depth and diversity of health communication, yet grounded enough to illustrate how communication occurs in actual health-related settings. I hope for readers to come away with a sophisticated understanding of health communication and useful suggestions for communicating more effectively and ethically about health.

■ MY APPROACH

Health communication encompasses everything from the way we talk about health concerns around the dinner table to patient-caregiver interactions, leadership and teamwork in health care organizations, and health images in the media. Because health is so dynamic, complex, and interdependent, it is important to understand current issues and how the various components interrelate. For example, it is essential for patients to understand something about media campaigns and for physicians to understand marketing issues. Likewise, everyone must be attentive to changing public opinions, cultural diversity, and opportunities to improve the health care system.

Effective communication is not merely a nicety or fringe benefit of health transactions. It is an absolute necessity. In many ways communication is synonymous with maintaining and restoring health. Through communication we define what it means to be healthy or well, describe our concerns, determine what behaviors are personally and socially acceptable, educate ourselves and others, and work together to promote good health.

I believe the most effective health communicators are committed to lifelong learning. They are attentive to their environments and aware of current issues. They are good listeners who consider health from multiple personal, professional, and cultural viewpoints. And they present ideas in ways that inspire and motivate others. All of these are communication skills. In *Communication Skill*

Builders sections throughout the book, you will read experts' tips for communicating effectively in a wide range of health-related situations.

■ INTENDED AUDIENCE

This book is designed primarily for people pursuing careers in the health industry and those with a research interest in health communication. This includes caregivers, public relations professionals, media planners and producers, public health promoters, marketing professionals, human resources personnel, health care administrators, researchers, educators, and others.

It may seem that such a diverse audience could not be served by the same text, and that is true to some extent. People in each of these professions will benefit by continuing their education beyond this book, to pursue more detailed instruction in communication skills specific to their interests. However, this book provides something that career-specific texts cannot—a revealing overview of how various professions, cultures, and current concerns converge in health care. I believe that, where health is concerned, understanding the big picture is as important as mastering a particular skill set.

■ MY BACKGROUND

I have a professional and a theoretical interest in health communication. In recent years, I have devoted myself to teaching health communication, studying health transactions, consulting with health care organizations, and writing books and articles on the subject. Earlier in my career, I covered health news for newspaper and television audiences and served as public relations director for a large medical center. In these capacities, I wrote news stories, directed public health campaigns, designed advertising, produced a monthly television program about health issues, assisted in strategic planning and marketing efforts, and worked alongside health caregivers and administrators.

As a former journalist, I understand the difficulties in keeping the public informed, and I am uncomfortably aware that unethical practices sometimes degrade the value of what the media has to say. My experience in a health care organization reminds me how challenging it is to maintain morale, encourage open communication, and adjust to market pressures. As a scholar and researcher, I appreciate more than ever how important (and difficult) it is to manage the multiple goals and diverse influences on health communication.

Together, these experiences make me especially sensitive to the weaknesses and strengths of health communication. It is impossible to observe (and be part of) health communication efforts and believe they are all good or all bad. You will notice throughout the book that issues are described in terms of their potential advantages and drawbacks. For instance, public health promotion is an immensely valuable way to inform and motivate people. However, promoters must be careful to avoid stigmatizing ill persons and making people unnecessarily anxious. I believe communicators are most effective when they have given careful thought and ethical consideration to the communication strategies available to them.

Another result of studying and working in the health industry is my immense respect for the diverse people who comprise it. I am frustrated by scholars who criticize the actions of health professionals and patients without also acknowledging what they are up against—time limits, stress, overwhelming emotional demands, and so on. I believe health communication can be improved in many respects, but it is naive to call for reform or expect it to happen without understanding and modifying the factors that influence it. This book provides insight about many of those factors.

FEATURES IN THE NEW EDITION

I have preserved features that were popular in the first edition. For example, while updating information in every chapter I have continued to integrate research evidence, real-life examples, suggestions for practical application, and current issues. Each chapter again includes an *Ethical Considerations* box with current issues, suggested sources, and discussion questions. Readers will find even more theories and communication strategies than before, and chapters still include key terms, review questions, and class activities.

One of the most notable changes is an additional chapter about patient diversity. Throughout the book, you will also see more references to global health issues. Following is a list of new features that appear throughout the book, followed by a description of material in each chapter:

- A ***Theoretical Foundations*** box in each chapter showcases an important theory relevant to health communication.
- ***Resources*** boxes suggest articles, books, movies, websites, organizations, and other means to continue exploration of key communication issues.
- ***Perspectives*** boxes in each chapter describe actual episodes of health communication as described by patients, professionals, family members, health care leaders, and others.
- ***Communication Skill Builders*** present practical strategies for communicating with patients and caregivers, avoiding burnout, talking to children about illness, listening, facilitating social support, talking about death, developing cultural competence, stimulating teamwork, designing public health campaigns, and more.
- ***Communication Technology*** features describe the impact of virtual communities, telemedicine, tailored health messages, and the Internet.

Part One: Establishing a Context for Health Communication

The first two chapters provide an introduction to health communication suitable for students in any discipline. Chapter 1 describes the nature of health communication, current issues, and important reasons to study health communication. It also provides tips for making the most of features such as *Ethical Considerations* and *Theoretical Foundations* boxes that appear throughout the book.

Chapter 2 provides an account of how health has been shaped by centuries of philosophy and scientific discovery. Understanding these issues allows for deeper appreciation of topics described in the rest of the book. Chapter 2 culminates with a description of current issues in health care. The section on managed care is particularly important.

Part Two: The Roles of Patients and Caregivers

Part Two focuses on interpersonal communication between patients and caregivers. Chapter 3 describes patient–caregiver communication in terms of who talks, who listens, and how medical decisions are made. It includes an expanded discussion of power differences and a new feature on health communication as a collaborative interpretation. This chapter features updated information about innovative approaches in telemedicine.

In Chapter 4, readers view health from the perspective of professional caregivers. The chapter describes the rewards of caregiving as well as the stress, competition, time limits, and self-doubt that often influence how caregivers communicate. The chapter describes recent research about the way physicians are socialized to think and act "like doctors," outlines the controversy surrounding new privacy regulations, and reveals patients' (mostly favorable) reactions to knowledge coupling whereby physicians use computers to help with diagnosis and treatment recommendations.

Chapter 5 looks at health communication through patients' eyes, considering what motivates patients, what they like and do not like about health care, and how they express themselves in health encounters. This edition looks more closely at how communication is influenced by the nature of an illness, patients' dispositions, and threats to personal identity. It includes information about communication skills training for patients.

The popular segment on patient diversity in the last edition has been expanded into a full chapter (Chapter 6), including information and tips on communicating effectively with patients who differ in terms of social status, gender, sexual orientation, race, language, ability, and age. This chapter includes a new discussion of health literacy and tips for better serving marginalized populations. Case studies describe the experiences of a Spanish-speaking woman in an English-speaking hospital and a college student coping with a physical disability.

Part Three: Social and Cultural Issues

Part Three focuses on the influences of cultural and social issues on health. Chapter 7 illustrates the importance of social support and provides tips for supportive communication. This edition features expanded coverage of lay caregiving, death and dying experiences, and virtual communities.

Chapter 8 describes social conceptions of health and healing. It describes the increasing importance of focusing on global health as evidenced by the outbreak of Severe Acute Respiratory Syndrome (SARS), AIDS, and severe health threats in developing countries. The chapter highlights the importance of cultural competence, examines culturally diverse ways of defining health, and describes different roles patients and caregivers may be expected to play. It includes a new feature about the theory of health as expanded consciousness and suggestions for communicating more effectively across cultural lines.

Part Four: Communication in Health Care Organizations

Part Four investigates communication in health organizations. This unit emphasizes the impact that organizations have on caregiver attitudes, patient satisfaction, who receives medical care, and how care is provided.

Chapter 9 focuses on communication as a medium for creating and reflecting organizational cultures. It includes a new case study about a hospital where employees redesigned the culture to be more patient-centered, the latest figures on gender and racial equity in medicine, the role of communication in addressing the current nursing shortage, and emerging issues about alternative/complementary care. The chapter also includes a description of conflict in health organizations and suggestions for using communication to manage conflict and diversity effectively.

Chapter 10 has been substantially updated to focuses on vigorous changes in the way health care agencies operate. It describes how health care organizations are using communication to become more patient-centered, more adaptive and competitive, and more pleasant places to work. Experts share advice on training new leaders, managing by collaboration, promoting a shared vision, working in teams, and rewriting the rules by which health care organizations operate. This chapter includes an expanded discussion of career opportunities for people with expertise in health communication.

Part Five: Health in the Media

Part Five explores the media's influence on health. Chapter 11 provides the latest about health images in advertising, news, and entertainment. It features a new section about health care advertising and a feature by Vicki Freimuth, former Media Relations Director at the Centers for Disease Control and Prevention. The chapter includes tips for reporting health news, using interactive media to present health information, and developing media literacy.

Chapters 12 and 13 guide readers through the creation and evaluation of public health campaigns. Both chapters have been substantially revised and updated to include more examples of outstanding health campaigns, more theories about the impact of health messages, and additional tips for developing effective campaigns.

STRENGTHS OF THE BOOK

Communicating About Health offers several advantages. For one, it offers up-to-date coverage of issues and research. It describes how managed care, telemedicine, financial reform, the Internet, and other factors are changing the nature of health communication.

Second, this book offers an in-depth look at diversity in health care. It describes culturally diverse ways of thinking about health and healing, and reveals how such factors as gender, age, and race influence health communication. Readers are able to look at health care through the eyes of caregivers, patients, administrators, health promoters, and others who contribute to the process.

Third, *Communicating About Health* is a useful guide for people interested in improving their health-related communication skills. It includes suggestions for encouraging patient participation, providing social support, listening, developing cultural competence, working in teams, designing health promotion campaigns, and more.

Fourth, this text situates health communication within the contexts of history, culture, and philosophy. This gives a depth of understanding and allows readers to better grasp the significance of health communication phenomena. For instance, evidence that doctors tend to dominate medical transactions takes on added significance when readers understand the influence of science and technology on medicine. By the same token, managed care comes into focus in light of the way health care has evolved in the United States.

Fifth, this book is designed to promote critical thinking and discussion. It poses ethical considerations, discussion questions, and class activities to encourage active involvement with the material. Additionally, case studies and interviews with health professionals bring health communication to life.

In summary, *Communicating About Health* is much more than a literature review. It explores the diverse perspectives of people involved in health communication and shows how they blend and negotiate their ideas to create communication episodes. The book integrates research, theories, current issues, and real-life examples. This blend of information enables students to understand the implications of various communication phenomena. At the same time, readers learn how they can contribute to health communication in a positive way as professionals, patients, and researchers.

GETTING THE MOST FROM THE BOOK

A key appeal of health communication is that everyone is involved with it in some way—as patients, professionals, leaders, or so on. The information presented here becomes more meaningful and useful when students are encouraged to integrate the information with their own ideas and perspectives. If you have time, break the chapters into units and allow active discussion about the material.

The philosophy that diversity should be celebrated and explored carries over into the classroom when students are encouraged to respect a variety of viewpoints. It is important to realize that, where health is concerned, ignoring or minimizing differences can have unhealthy and even deadly consequences.

People may respond differently to the ethical dilemmas and discussion questions presented within chapters. I encourage you to explore a variety of perspectives without establishing any one viewpoint as dominant. The object is not to find the one right answer, but to gain experience discussing and reflecting on the immense responsibilities of communicating about health.

Finally, keep in mind that actual practice is less linear than the written word. Although Chapters 1 and 13 are far apart, that does not mean the issues covered are remote from each other in the actual scheme of things. I point this out periodically and ask readers to keep in mind that the different aspects of health communication are interrelated.

ACKNOWLEDGMENTS

A great number of people have contributed to the creation of this text. My first thanks are to McGraw-Hill Senior Sponsoring Editor Nanette Giles; Developmental Editor Josh Hawkins; and Project Manager Ruth Smith, who have done an extraordinary job suggesting which topics and viewpoints should be included in the book and bringing it to fruition. I am also grateful to reviewers who suggested ideas for the second edition: Mary L. Brown, University of Arizona; Rajiv N. Rimal, Johns Hopkins University; Monique Mitchell Turner, University of Maryland; and Gust A. Yep, San Francisco State University. I also remain indebted to the editor and reviewers of the first edition: Holly Allen, Rebecca Cline, June Flora, Stephen Hines, Katherine Miller, Donna Pawlowski, Claire F. Sullivan, Teresa Thompson, and Gust A. Yep.

I would also like to thank colleagues and students who have contributed ideas, narratives, and feedback, most notably Ron Belter, Jennifer Terry, Susanne Fillmore, Dawn Murray, Praewa Tanuthep, Beverly Davis Willi, Jennifer Seneca, Lori Juneau, Stefanie Howell, Melanie Barnes, Amy Jenkins, Bridget King, Micah Nickens, Samantha Olivier, and Gwynné Williams. I owe heart-felt thanks to Ken Brown, M.D., who served as my advisor on medical details, managed care, and many aspects of health care administration.

As always, I am indebted to mentors Sandy Ragan, Sonia Crandall, Jon Nussbaum, Betty Adams, Cris Berard, and the late Jung-Sook Lee. Finally, many thanks to members of my family (Jordan, Hannah, Ginger, Ed, and Sarah) who accommodated the many hours devoted to this project and provided endless support. I am grateful.

Part One

ESTABLISHING A CONTEXT FOR HEALTH COMMUNICATION

CHAPTER 1

Introduction

When my 9-year-old daughter came home from her grandparents with a rash from poison ivy, I wasn't alarmed. She'd had it before. I smeared her with sticky white ointment from a tube promising to "soothe minor rashes and skin irritations." A few days later, however, Hannah awoke with one eye nearly swollen shut. The inflamed rash had spread to her face. I felt I had failed miserably as Dr. Mom.

I called the HMO and learned our regular doctor was out, but another doctor could see us at 11 a.m. In the meantime, I called Hannah's school to explain and brought her to the university with me. In the hallway, a colleague stopped to ask in horror, "Is that poison ivy!? You better get her to a doctor. It can cause blindness around the eyes like that." I felt even more frightened and guilty. The only comfort was that Hannah said it didn't itch much.

In the car, I mentally rehearsed what I would say to this doctor I didn't know: "The ointment worked last time. . . . She wasn't this bad last night. . . . Maybe I should have brought her in sooner. . . . I'm a good mom!" My guilt escalated when I realized these statements sounded more like a courtroom defense than an explanation of my daughter's symptoms. I wondered if my little girl was going to be all right and why I was feeling such a mixture of emotions.

How many instances of health-related communication can you identify in this real-life example?

You might have counted five or more, including the ointment label, the call to the doctor's office, the call to school, the colleague's frightened warning, and my daughter's comments. All of these fall within the domain of health communication.

In addition, the story hints at several factors that influence health communication—emotions, expectations about good parenting, effects of health maintenance organization (HMO) membership, the Dr. Mom image from commercials, and so on. All this before we even reached the doctor's office!

Episodes like the one described illustrate that health communication is a part of everyday life. Everyone is involved in some way. Our ideas about health are influenced by health care professionals, friends, family members, co-workers, educators, advertisers, entertainers, public health promoters, and many others. Television medical dramas may influence what people expect from actual doctors and nurses. At the same time we influence the people around us with our own actions and thoughts about health.

One reason health communication is so dynamic and interdependent is that health itself is dynamic and interdependent. The World Health Organization (WHO) defines **health** as "a state of complete physical, mental and social well-being and not merely the absence of disease or infirmity" (WHO, 1948). This definition, unchanged for more than 50 years, reminds us that *healthy* is not the opposite of *sick*. Being healthy means more than that. It is a state of harmony and equilibrium between many aspects of life. Health involves inner feelings, physical abilities, and relationships with others. Throughout the book, you will be exposed to diverse theories about the nature of health and its relation to communication.

A central theme of this book is that one aspect of health communication affects others. To be effective in any arena, you must understand how various components of the health care system rely upon and influence each other. For example, a well-meaning campaign director unfamiliar with cultural ideas about health may create messages that are unappealing or offensive to the audience he or she is trying to reach. A marketing/public relations director who does not understand the dynamics of patient–caregiver communication is unable to help shape and promote services that meet the needs of internal and external shareholders. A caregiver ignorant about health care administration misses out on leadership opportunities and has relatively little chance to influence how organizations are run. Moreover, caregivers who do not communicate well between themselves can confuse patients with contradictory information.

Knowledge gaps are understandable, even among people who have been in health-related careers for some time. Ideas about health, health care, and prevention are changing rapidly. Whereas specialization was once encouraged, now effective health care scholars and practitioners are attuned to broader contexts. They consider situations from many perspectives. They understand the historical, cultural, and market pressures that influence health. They are skillful at encouraging feedback, listening, analyzing, experimenting with new communication techniques, and selling their ideas to others.

In Chapter 2 you will learn more about current issues in health care by going back in time. Following the evolution of medicine from ancient Egypt to 21st century managed care reveals a lot about where we are today. When you understand the philosophy and events that have shaped the modern system you are in a better position to decide what has worked well, where we went wrong, and where we should go from here.

Perhaps the most rewarding aspect of studying health communication is putting what you know to good use. Throughout the book, Communication Skill Builder sections present practical tips for communicating more effectively about health. Based on research evidence, you will learn about effective ways to communicate with diverse patients, present your concerns as a patient, avoid burnout, stimulate cultural diversity, manage conflict, work in teams, design health campaigns, and more.

It is an exciting and challenging time to be involved with health. Perhaps more than ever before, health care leaders are open to innovative ideas. They are also facing critical challenges—to control costs, attract clients, earn employees' loyalty, and more. The changes are both destabilizing and exciting. In Richard T. Pascale's (1999) terms, it can sometimes feel like "surfing the edge of chaos" (p. 198). The good news is that disequilibrium opens the field to new ways of thinking and behaving. People involved with health care today have the potential to reshape and improve the system. In Chapters 9 and 10 you will learn about innovative ways health care organizations are pursuing these goals.

The remainder of Chapter 1 is divided into four sections. The first defines health communication. The second section introduces two approaches to health care—the biomedical and the biopsychosocial models. The third outlines the importance of studying how (and why) people communicate as they do about health. The chapter concludes with a look at current issues that underline the importance of understanding health communication.

WHAT IS HEALTH COMMUNICATION?

Health communication is shaped by many influences including personal goals, skills, cultural orientation, situational factors, and consideration of other people's feelings. The definitions presented in this section emphasize the interdependence of these factors. As you will see here and throughout the book, communicators influence—and are simultaneously influenced by—the people and circumstances around them. They rely on others to help them meet goals, develop a satisfying awareness of self and others, and make sense of life events.

Defining Communication

To attempt a conversation with someone who does not understand you is usually neither satisfying nor productive. There is more to effective communication than putting thoughts into words. Understanding other people's perceptions and clearly expressing your own are important aspects of communication. The definition of **communication** offered by Judy Pearson and Paul Nelson (1991) underscores these concerns: "Communication is the process of understanding and sharing meaning" (p. 6). The significance of this definition becomes clear when we examine communication in terms of process, personal goals, interdependence, sensitivity, and shared meaning.

Process Defining communication as a process recognizes that people are involved in an ongoing effort to understand each other and the world around them. Meaning is interpreted in light of past, present, and future expectations.

Box 1.1 PERSPECTIVES
True Stories About Health Communication Experiences

In Perspectives boxes you will read about the real-life experiences of people involved with health communication. These true accounts represent the viewpoints of patients, loved ones, caregivers, executives, social activists, health campaign managers, and others. They provide insight about how people of different races, cultures, ages, languages, abilities, sexual orientations, and education levels experience health communication. See Box 1.3 for the first in a series of Perspectives boxes that appear throughout the book.

Some factors that influence communication are set in motion before a word is ever spoken. Consider the scenario at the beginning of this chapter. As I chatted with my daughter on the way to the doctor's office I was already wondering what would be said during the visit. The physician also approached the transaction with assumptions and expectations. In many ways, the groundwork for communication episodes begins to take form long before the participants even meet.

Just as communication has no set beginning, it has no definite ending either. People may reevaluate the meaning of a conversation long after it has ended. For instance, you might say to a friend: "When I began physical therapy, I thought my therapist was mean. But now I realize he was doing me a favor by making me work so hard."

As a process, communication is influenced by its placement in the ongoing stream of life and events. Good communicators realize that it is often helpful to know what people expect going into a communication episode and how they feel about it later. In health care situations this may mean collecting information about events leading up to an illness or health care visit and making follow-up phone calls or visits to answer any questions or concerns that arise later. In Chapters 3 through 5 we will explore the nature of patient–caregiver communication and look at health through the eyes of professional caregivers and patients.

Personal Goals Researchers have found that participants approach health encounters with a range of goals and expectations. The main goal of caregivers is presumably to maintain or restore patients' health, but caregivers may have other goals as well, such as saving time, preventing burnout, displaying their knowledge, and so on. Likewise, patients may have many goals including the need to vent emotions, to be forgiven, to be reassured, or simply to be healed.

As I drove my daughter to the doctor, my confidence as a parent was shaken. I craved reassurance that I had not made her condition worse.

Although I didn't take my colleague's warning about blindness too seriously, it did escalate the anxiety I felt about my child. These concerns influenced my goals for the encounter. Emotions and identity are tied to how people behave in medical settings.

One measure of effective communication is how well participants feel their goals have been met. Knowing what people expect from a health encounter is a useful way to increase participants' satisfaction.

Interdependence Although it is important to consider personal goals, communication ultimately relies on how well people work together to coordinate their goals and establish common understandings. Defining communication as "understanding and sharing" emphasizes that no one communicates alone. Communicators are **interdependent;** that is, they rely on each other and exert mutual influence on communication episodes.

Communication is a process of acting, reacting, and negotiation. For example, if the waiting room receptionist seems curt and unfriendly, patients are likely to feel defensive. This may affect their willingness to be open about embarrassing or frightening concerns.

In contrast, pleasing communication can alter a health care encounter for the better. In the poison ivy episode the receptionist who greeted us was friendly and sympathetic. She showed my daughter a rash on her own arm, caused by poison ivy in her garden. The waiting room was quiet and pleasantly decorated, and it was not long before a nurse called Hannah's name. The nurse smiled and joked with us, greatly easing the anxiety we felt. By the time the doctor entered the examination room, my daughter and I were much less anxious than before.

Being friendly and receptive in health care encounters will encourage others to be friendly and open in return. It is unrealistic to expect people to be honest, trusting, and friendly when they feel discouraged by the behavior of people around them. Interdependence also serves to emphasize that everyone involved in the communication has some influence on it. Patients, family members, receptionists, and others often affect health communication as much as doctors do.

Sensitivity Many theorists consider that the best communicators are sensitive to other people's feelings and expectations. Sensitivity enhances health communication on many levels. Research shows that public health campaigns are most effective when they are designed with the audience's concerns and resources in mind (Murray-Johnson & Witte, 2003). By the same token, people are usually most satisfied with physicians who listen attentively and seem to understand what they are feeling (Grant, Cissna, & Rosenfeld, 2000; Tarrant, Windridge, Boulton, Baker, & Freeman, 2003).

Being sensitive means looking and listening carefully. It also means interpreting the cues offered by other communicators. Whether Hannah and I realized it or not, we were probably presenting a number of cues that we were anxious about the visit. My arm around her shoulders, her hesitant smile, our tone of voice—all of these might have cued the staff that we were apprehensive. They were sensitive to the cues and responded in a way that was culturally appropriate and pleasing to us personally.

Sensitivity is more difficult when communicators do not share the same cultural expectations. In a different culture, a well-intended joke might seem offensive rather than kind. Interpreting subtle cues and responding to them in a sensitive way requires an awareness of **cultural display rules** (ways of showing emotions in different cultures) and an understanding of personal preferences and cultural expectations. To be effective, health communicators must be concerned enough to pay close attention to people's behavior and knowledgeable enough to recognize cultural and personal preferences that make people different.

Shared Meaning What an action means depends on the people and the circumstances involved. For instance, trading friendly put-downs with a friend means you like each other, but the same put-downs from someone you barely know might make you angry. Meaning exists in the participants' mutual interpretation of it. In other words, meaning is shared.

So how do people know if they are sharing the same meaning? Usually, they can tell by the way other people respond. A nod of the head, a smile, an angry look, or a question may signal how a conversational partner is interpreting the conversation. People send and receive messages constantly, although they may not be aware of it. Hannah and I were not trying to look anxious, but we probably showed that emotion in several ways. Likewise, our willingness to engage in humor and light conversation was displayed when the receptionist held out her arm and we both smiled, moved closer, and relaxed our rigid posture. Had we behaved differently, the receptionist would probably have treated us differently.

Because communication is a cooperative process, it is inappropriate to blame one partner or the other when communication between them is unsatisfactory. In the past, scholars often blamed doctors for being insensitive to patients' wishes. However, theorists such as Teresa Thompson (1984) and Gary Kreps (1990) caution that patients should not be considered the underdogs in health situations. Patients are active agents who can influence the way health communication is conducted. For example, doctors are sometimes criticized for doing most of the talking in medical encounters. At the same time, however, patients are known to be particularly submissive around doctors. Whether patients realize it or not, they may contribute to the very dynamic they dislike.

Defining Health Communication

Kreps and Barbara Thornton (1992) define **health communication** as "the way we seek, process and share health information" (p. 2). People are actively

Box 1.2 THEORETICAL FOUNDATIONS
The Basis for Health Communication

He who loves practice without theory is like the sailor who boards the ship without a rudder and compass and never knows where he may cast.

—*Leonardo da Vinci*

As we explore the field of health communication, theories connect the dots just as constellations reveal patterns in the stars. Good theories make sense of diverse information and help us to get our bearings. They help us know, in advance, where we are headed and what paths are available to us. A Theoretical Foundations box in each chapter showcases a theory relevant to health communication. These theories address such issues as these:

- What is health?
- How do we make sense of health crises?
- What behaviors enhance and compromise coping efforts?
- How do interpersonal relationships influence health?
- How does multiculturalism influence health and health care?
- How can health care organizations stimulate teamwork and innovation?
- In what ways do the media influence our health?
- How do people respond to public health campaigns?
- What factors influence people to become more knowledgeable and proactive about their own health?

Each Theoretical Foundations box poses questions that invite you to analyze the theory as it applies to your experiences and beliefs. You will also find a list of resources to help you continue your exploration of the ideas presented.

involved in health communication. They are not passive recipients of information. Instead, people seek and share messages and mingle what they hear and see with their own ideas and experiences. A great deal of health communication involves professional caregivers such as doctors, nurses, aides, therapists, counselors, and technicians. But we serve as caregivers for friends and loved ones as well. Chapter 7 demonstrates the value of social support when we are ill, healthy, and even (perhaps especially) when we cope with death and dying.

Implications

Communication, then, is an ongoing process of sharing and creating meaning. The challenge is not merely to put thoughts into words, but to cooperate with others in developing a shared understanding of what is happening and what it means. This perspective has implications for the study of health communication.

First, it is important that participants in a health episode strive to understand the expectations they bring to bear on the encounter. Whether they communicate face to face or through mass media, their expectations reflect personal experiences, emotions, and cultural beliefs.

Second, whether communication is effective or not depends on circumstances and the participants' goals. It is impossible to present communication skills that work in every situation. Instead, becoming a better communicator requires developing a range of communication strategies and using them appropriately.

The following section introduces two approaches to health care that are fundamental to considering how and why people communicate as they do about health.

MEDICAL MODELS

What causes ill health? If your answer is germs you have probably been influenced by the biomedical model, which is not surprising considering that it has been the basic premise of Western medicine for the last 100 years. But if you believe illness is caused by a variety of factors, including a person's frame of mind, your views more closely reflect the biopsychosocial model, which is gaining favor in today's health care system. Following is a description of each model and its impact on health communication. By way of illustration we will return for a final time to the poison ivy episode to see what the doctor said.

Biomedical Model

The **biomedical model** is based on the premise that ill health is a physical phenomenon that can be explained, identified, and treated through physical means. Biomedicine is well suited to a culture familiar with engines and computers. "Repairing a body, in this view, is analogous to fixing a machine," writes Charles Longino (1997, p. 14). Physicians are like scientists or mechanics. They collect information about a problem, try to identify the source of it, and fix it. For instance, while the doctor was examining my daughter's poison ivy reaction, he asked these questions: "When were you exposed to the poison ivy?" "When did you first notice the rash?" "Does it itch?" "Is it spreading?"

Health communication influenced by the biomedical model is typically focused and specific. Doctors' questions require only brief answers (i.e., "Last weekend." "Sunday." "No." "Yes."). Patients may have little input, and talk is largely restricted to physical signs of illness (Roter et al., 1997).

At its best, the biomedical approach is efficient and definitive. Medical tests and observations may yield evidence that can be logically analyzed and treated with well-established methods. One criticism of the biomedical model, however, is that it marginalizes patients' feelings and social experiences, sometimes to the extent of treating people as impersonal collections of parts or symptoms. As you will see Chapter 5, people are often dissatisfied when caregivers do not listen to their concerns surrounding an illness, and they may not trust diagnoses if they feel the doctor did not fully understand the problem.

Biopsychosocial Model

The **biopsychosocial perspective** takes into account patients' physical conditions (biology), their thoughts and beliefs (psychology), and their social expectations. From this perspective illness is not solely a physical phenomenon but is also influenced by people's feelings, their ideas about health, and the events of their lives.

Caregivers influenced by the biopsychosocial model are likely to be concerned with patients' thoughts and emotions as well as the physical conditions of their illnesses. For example, consider this dialogue.

Doctor: That must really itch. Is it driving you crazy?

Child: (giggling) Not really.

Parent: I thought the ointment would help, but the rash seems to be getting worse.

Doctor: That was a reasonable treatment. I'm not sure why it didn't help. At any rate, I can put your mind at ease . . .

With his comments the doctor addressed Hannah's (itchy) feelings and my concern. His reassurance that the ointment was "a reasonable treatment" did not take long but was immensely comforting to me. Hannah and I left feeling that the doctor had respectfully addressed the situation *and* our feelings. Plus, we had a prescription for medicine that cured the rash overnight. The biopsychosocial approach is supported by evidence that people's thoughts and emotions have an influence on their overall health. Researchers have long known that emotional stress tends to elevate people's heart rates and blood pressure. They are now finding that excessive stress reduces the body's resistance to disease (Goodkin, Fletcher, & Cohen, 1995) and can cause depression and mood changes (Herbert, 1997). On the bright side, health is enhanced by good humor, a positive attitude, and social support (Fontana & McLaughlin, 1998; Goodkin et al., 1995).

The biopsychosocial approach is appealing for its thoroughness and personal concern. The case study in Box 1.3 points out how grateful people can be to caregivers who go beyond strictly physical concerns. However, implementing a biopsychosocial approach is no easy task. At a time when health professionals are conscientiously conserving resources, broadening the scope of medicine may seem unrealistic (Crawford, Taylor, Siepert, & Lush, 1996). Some health professionals feel it is too time consuming to evaluate all aspects of a patient's well-being. You will read more about caregivers' concerns in Chapter 4.

Implications

The biomedical model establishes a narrow focus on physical manifestations of disease. It assumes there is a specific cause of ill health that can be identified and treated. The biopsychosocial model is broader in scope and includes physical, social, and psychological aspects of health. As you will read in Chapters 6 and 8, cultural ideas about health influence how we define well-being and what we expect from health care efforts.

Although it is a useful shorthand to speak of medical models, it is important to remember that models are only prototypes. As such, they are open to interpretation and blending. Few patients or caregivers operate solely within one model, nor would most people wish the entire health care system to adopt a single model. Ultimately, the best option may be the awareness that health can be approached in different ways and the versatility to use different aspects of these models appropriately.

■ IMPORTANCE OF HEALTH COMMUNICATION

Health communication is important to individuals, organizations, and society overall. It is crucial to meeting medical goals, enhancing personal well-being, saving time and money, and making the most of health information. Following are six reasons to study health communication. Each of these is addressed more fully in the chapters that follow.

Six Important Issues

First, *communication is crucial to the success of health care encounters.* Without it, caregivers cannot hear patients' concerns, make diagnoses, share their recommendations, or follow up on treatment outcomes. "Health communication is the singularly most important tool health professionals have to provide health care to their clients" according to Kreps & Thornton (1992, p. 2). Patients who take an active role in medical encounters are more likely to be satisfied with their doctors, trust diagnoses, and carry out treatment regimens (Cecil, 1998; Frankel & Beckman, 1989; Young & Klingle, 1996).

Interpersonal communication is crucial considering that about 90 million people—roughly 1 in 2 adults in the United States—suffer from low health

Box 1.3 PERSPECTIVES
A Memorable Hospital Experience

In my short 27 years I have visited hospitals in four states, and only one stands out in my memory, St. Jude Children's Research Hospital in Memphis, Tennessee. My family spent nearly 2 years of our lives walking in and out of the doors of St. Jude while my sister was being treated for leukemia.

Walking into the administrative office the first day we arrived was like being in grandma's house seated by a warm, open fireplace. During those first hours of our shock and fear over my sister's diagnosis, the hospital staff worked quickly on her paperwork without making us feel the least bit rushed. The warmth and tone of their voices was like that of a family member. We were assured we could always reach them—if not at work, at home! They were our new family.

The doctors at St. Jude stopped and spoke with families and patients and answered any questions they were asked. The doctors were not the only gems in the hospital, though. I remember two very special nurses, Jackie and Mary. One night my parents and I went to eat and were late getting back (it was shrimp night!). We found Mary, who had gotten off work 1½ hours earlier, reading to my sister. Jackie assisted my sister with manicuring her nails even though it was not part of her technical duties. The nurses at St. Jude stepped out of their textbook roles to accommodate the needs of their patients.

Members of the housekeeping and dietary staff were always helpful too. When my sister thought she had an appetite for a hamburger or macaroni and cheese, they always did their best to get some up to her before she realized she did not want anything at all.

The last person I recall from the support staff was Mrs. Fran, our social worker. She was a dream, not just a friend you could talk to but one you could count on to take care of the little things you naturally forget in situations such as ours. When my sister died, Mrs. Fran was there for my family and made all the arrangements to get us back home to Louisiana.

There were many difficulties in dealing with the death of a loved one, and my sister was only 15. However, my parents and I feel an incredible debt to St. Jude. We have founded a fundraising chapter for St. Jude in Baton Rouge and I hope to pursue a career to help caregivers, families, and the public understand the importance of interpersonal communication skills in hospitals and other health care centers.

—Gwynné Williams

literacy, meaning they find it difficult to read medical directions and research and use health information ("Health Literacy," 2003). Experts estimate that low health literacy accounts for about $73 billion a year in avoidable medical costs ("Financial Impact," 2003), and the loss in productivity and quality of life is immeasurable. Effective interpersonal communication can offset these tragic and costly consequences. You will learn more about health literacy and relevant communication strategies in Chapter 6.

Second, *communication is an important source of personal confidence and coping ability.* Health professionals are less likely to experience burnout when they are confident about their communication skills (Ramirez, Graham, Richards, Cull, & Gregory, 1996). Likewise, patients cope best when they feel comfortable talking about delicate subjects like pain and death, and people involved in support groups often cope better and even live longer than similar persons who are not members.

Third, *effective communication saves time and money.* Caregivers who listen attentively and communicate a sense of caring and warmth are less likely than others to be sued for malpractice (Nichols, 2003). Likewise, patients who communicate clearly with their caregivers have the best chance of having their concerns immediately addressed (Cegala & Broz, 2003), which is likely to improve their health and save time and money.

Fourth, *communication helps health care organizations operate effectively.* By communicating well with clients and potential clients, organizations are better able to evaluate their effectiveness and develop plans for improvement. Communication skills are also useful in motivating employees, establishing innovative teams, and raising performance standards (Vestal, Fralicx, & Spreier, 1997). Survey results show that supervisors' communication skills are one of the most important determinants of nurses' job satisfaction and their intention to stay on the job (Thorpe & Loo, 2003).

Fifth, *wise use of mass media can help people learn about health and minimize the influence of unhealthy and unrealistic media portrayals.* Health promoters use communication skills to assess public needs, inform people about health issues, and encourage them to behave in healthy ways. Media consumers—especially those who rely on newspapers, magazines, and computers—are likely to be well informed about health issues and actively maintain their own health (Rowe & Toner, 2003; van der Pal-de Bruin et al., 2003). However, the media is also filled with glamorous images of people engaging in unhealthy behaviors, making media literacy especially important. Researchers have found that media literate individuals are less likely than others to believe unrealistic images of eating, drinking, using drugs, and being unnaturally thin (Singer & Singer, 1998). In Chapters 11–13 you will learn more about health images in the media, media literacy, and how to create effective health campaigns.

Sixth, *health communication may be important to you because the health industry is rich with career opportunities.* A background in health communication is an asset in a range of careers including clinical care, public relations, marketing, health care administration, human resources, education, community outreach, crisis management, patient advocacy, and more. What is more, health communication researchers are needed to investigate the issues described here and propose workable solutions.

To get an idea of how large and dynamic the health industry is, consider these statistics. In the United States, health care accounts for $1,200,000,000,000 in domestic spending per year. That's $1.2.trillion (Centers for Disease Control, 2002). More than 11 million people are employed in healthcare, and the demand is growing substantially. The U.S. Bureau of Labor Statistics (2003b) reports that 9 of the 20 fastest growing occupations are health-related. Demand is expected to increase for many types of caregivers and for health service managers (people able to market, coordinate, plan, and supervise health care services). As you will learn, communication skills are a valuable asset no matter what aspect of health care interests you.

Implications

Health communication is important for a number of reasons. Communication is an important means of providing health care and assessing people's needs and concerns. Interpersonal communication provides a way to cope with stressful events and offset the devastating effects of low health literacy. By facilitating effective health care, communication can save patients and caregivers time and money. Communication can also help health care organizations run more efficiently and be better places to work. Knowledgeable use of media can help people become more informed about health and be less vulnerable to unhealthy suggestions in the media. Finally, communication skills are an asset when pursuing careers relevant to health care.

CURRENT ISSUES IN HEALTH COMMUNICATION

The chapter concludes with a brief overview of current issues in health care. The effects of these topics on health communication will be discussed in detail throughout the book.

Medical Cost-Cutting

For years, medical care in the United States seemed to have an unlimited budget. Insurance companies paid for medical services almost without question. However, a backlash occurred. Insurance premiums became too costly for many people to afford them. By the 1990s, U.S. census data revealed that about 40 million Americans had no health insurance. By that point the need to rein in health care costs had become undeniable.

Managed care is one result of cost-cutting efforts. Consumers pay a set fee to managed care organizations in return for medical services. The

Box 1.4 ETHICAL CONSIDERATIONS
An Essential Component of Health Communication

Our customers routinely bare their bodies, as well as their souls, within our organizations. I can think of no other enterprise in our society where so much is placed in the hands of others.

—*Larry Sanders, Chair of the American College of Health Care Executives*

Sanders (2003) advises those who provide and study health care: "One of the most significant ways we can demonstrate how much we care about those we serve is to visibly display our personal commitment to operating with extraordinary integrity, ethics and morality each and every day" (p. 46).

It is imperative that people involved with health care understand the ethical implications of their actions and conduct themselves with honor and integrity. They must also be aware of others' perceptions. If people perceive—rightly or wrongly—that health-related professionals are not ethical, they may experience stress, avoid medical care, lie to health care providers, or withhold information to protect themselves.

I once studied a hospital unit in which several of the patients had AIDS but were afraid to tell their caregivers about their diagnosis. The caregivers were justifiably angry that they might become infected because they were not aware which patients were contagious. However, the patients had a good point as well. They felt their diagnosis would not be kept confidential, and they were probably right. Patient records were often left open on the counter of the nurses' unit, posted outside patients' rooms, and handled by more than a dozen employees including clerks, secretaries, pages, and more. There was no reasonable assurance of confidentiality. Consequently the caregivers distrusted the patients, and the patients distrusted everyone in the organization.

Many of the ethical dilemmas that people in health care face are essentially matters of communication. Issues frequently arise concerning honesty, privacy, power, conflicts of interest, social stigmas, media images, advertising, and persuasive messages about health. In most cases,

organizations' objective is to manage their resources well enough to provide care and still make a profit. Optimistically, managed care may cut costs and make it feasible for more people to have health coverage. However, many people worry that health organizations will skimp on services to save money (Eastman, Eastman, & Tolson, 1997). We will discuss these issues more in Chapter 2.

In another effort to economize, many hospitals and clinics have formed alliances or been purchased by large corporations. The danger with large there is more than one option, but no simple solution. What seems right in one situation may be wrong in another. Personal preference and culture, among other factors, shape what people want and expect. Even so, there is value in thinking through the implications and exploring diverse reactions with others.

An Ethical Considerations box in each chapter presents an ethical dilemma and a list of discussion questions and additional resources. I encourage you to discuss and debate these issues, eliciting diverse viewpoints. Do not be afraid to change your mind or argue both sides of an issue. It is usually easier to behave ethically if you have thought the issues through *before* you find yourself in a real-life dilemma. Following are some questions you might ask yourself as you consider your options concerning ethical challenges posed in this book and elsewhere:

- Is this option legal?
- Is it honest? Is deception or omission of the truth involved?
- Who will be hurt? Who will be helped?
- Will the decision benefit me personally but hurt others?
- Are the results worth the hardship involved?
- Is it culturally acceptable?
- Will my decision compromise people's privacy or trust?
- Will my decision be demeaning or degrading to anyone?
- Is it fair? Will my action unfairly discriminate against anyone?
- Is the action appropriate for the situation?
- Have I considered all the options?
- How would I wish to be treated in the same situation?
- How would I feel if my decision or action were published in tomorrow's newspaper?

organizations is that centralized decision making will make them less sensitive to individual and community needs. In Chapter 10, you will learn how some health care organizations are balancing the need to contain costs with the need to provide top-quality care.

In this climate of change and consolidation communication specialists can help assess community needs, market new services, keep people informed about changes, and facilitate team efforts to design high-quality, affordable care systems. Caregivers, administrators, and researchers who wish to influence the transformation of health care will need a range of communication skills to express their ideas and work together.

Prevention

Prevention has become a health priority for two main reasons: It increases people's quality of life, and it is less costly than medical treatment. Although the first reason has always been true, the second has become an important concern in recent years. S. Reneé Gillepsie (2001) observes that the dual pressures of competition and cost-containment have created "a new conceptualization of the patient as both valued customer and dangerous consumer of health care resources" (p. 99). Within this framework, recruiting the "right" patients (e.g., those who do not require expensive care) may keep a health care organization in business. However, patients with expensive health needs can drain the organization's resources.

Prevention is cost-efficient because it is usually less expensive to prevent diseases and injuries than to treat them. For example, it costs less to provide cardiovascular exercise programs than to perform open-heart surgeries. Prevention efforts are often led by interdisciplinary teams of physicians, nurse practitioners, physician assistants, and dietitians (Longino, 1997). Chapters 9 and 10 focus on diverse caregivers and interdisciplinary teamwork.

Complementary or alternative medicine is also becoming popular. Four in 10 Americans now use alternative therapies such as chiropractic, acupuncture, and relaxation therapy (Barrett, 2003). These are relatively inexpensive and are geared toward prevention and long-term health maintenance. As you will see in Chapter 9, compared to conventional practitioners, alternative and complementary therapists often spend more time talking with patients about lifestyle choices and emotional well-being. As complementary therapies gain acceptance, people may develop new ideas about health care and the nature of patient–caregiver communication.

In summary, prevention efforts have several consequences for health communication. First, prevention is less specific than biomedical care. It is more likely to involve interdisciplinary teams of caregivers and to focus on issues relevant to people's lifestyles, attitudes, and social networks. This makes the ability to collect information and to communicate in teams especially important.

Second, communicating well with patients and the public is at the heart of prevention efforts. Whether communication occurs through conversations, brochures, news stories, or mass media campaigns, strategies are needed to motivate people to adopt and continue healthy behaviors. Information must be presented in ways that are useful, accurate, interesting, and motivational.

Patient Empowerment

It is easier than ever to be knowledgeable about health. Health is the subject of cable television channels, magazines, best-selling books, news programs, advertisements, and extensive computer databases. Network news programs devote about half their coverage to health issues ("Health Ranks Fifth," 1998), and the Internet provides information to more than 655 million users worldwide ("UN Report," 2002).

It is said that knowledge is power, and that may be the case in health care. The current Information Age coincides with a move toward **patient empowerment**. Empowerment means patients have considerable influence in medical matters. Their ideas count. They ask questions and state preferences, and they may visit doctors or other caregivers, not because they are ill, but because they would like information or feedback on a health issue.

Patient empowerment is also encouraged by increased competition in the health industry. People are now courted by health plans and medical centers vying for their business. Advertising appeals make it plain that health care agencies are not simply a source of assistance but are part of an industry that relies on consumers.

Increased knowledge and the awareness that health agencies need patients' business may reduce the status difference between patients and their caregivers. As Tom Ferguson (1997) puts it:

> As we move farther into the Information Age, health professionals will do more than just treat their patients' ills—they will increasingly serve as their coaches, teachers, and colleagues, working side-by-side with empowered consumers in a high-quality system of computer-supported, low-cost, self-managed care. (paragraph 34)

It will be interesting to see if (and how) patients and caregivers adapt to the idea that they are well-informed partners working toward common goals. On the one hand, patient empowerment relieves some of the pressure on caregivers to "fix" people who do very little to maintain their own health (Kaplan, 1997). On the other hand, patient empowerment dispels the notion that people should simply follow doctors' orders. It is no longer enough (if ever it was) to simply tell patients what to do. Empowered patients want information and the right to make their own decisions. Changing expectations require new communication skills and different styles of interaction on the part of patients and caregivers.

Global Health Needs

In today's environment, travel, immigration, and the international exchange of food and products mean that diseases are continually carried across national borders. The outbreak of severe acute respiratory syndrome (SARS) in 2003 provided a striking example of how quickly a communicable disease can spread around the globe. Within 100 days, the disease that began in southern China had killed more than 100 people in 20 countries (WHO, 2003c).

The world health community was able to contain the outbreak of SARS within a few months largely because international agencies such as WHO had

Box 1.5 RESOURCES
Opportunities for Further Exploration

This book is designed to give you a rich and current overview of health communication. We will visit a number of locations (e.g., social settings, doctors' offices, board rooms, movie theaters) and look at health through different people's eyes. My hope is that, as you explore each perspective, your appreciation of the nuances that influence health and health communication will increase. Along the way you will probably want to know more than I could fit into the book, so I provide Resources boxes in each chapter that include information about relevant websites, organizations, publications, movies, and more.

To get you started, here is a list of organizations and websites you might wish to pursue for more about health communication:

- American Association for Health Education: www.aahperd.org
- American Communication Association: www.americancomm.org
- Centers for Disease Control and Prevention's Health Communication Key: www.cdc.gov/od/oc/hcomm/hcomm_about.html
- Central States Communication Association: www.csca-net.org
- Eastern Communication Association: www.ecasite.org
- Health Communication Around the World: www.sla.purdue.edu/HealthCOMM
- International Association of Business Communicators: www.iabc.com/index.htm
- International Communication Association: www.icahdq.org
- National Communication Association: www.natcom.org
- Public Relations Society of America: www.prsa.org
- Southern States Communication Association: ssca.net
- Western States Communication Association: www.westcomm.org

already established working relationships between people from many countries and cultures. WHO leaders credit a spirit of teamwork and "international solidarity" with saving lives around the world (World Health Organization, 2003c).

The AIDS epidemic has been far worse. People in 200 countries have been diagnosed with the life-threatening virus (World Health Organization, 2003a). The situation is especially critical in Africa. Of the 42 million people known to be infected worldwide, 30 million live in sub-Saharan Africa (Abrams, 2003). In Chapter 8 we will focus more on international teamwork and the intercultural competence needed to work toward global solutions.

Changing Populations

Population shifts are also changing health care needs in the United States. One shift is toward an older society. It is estimated that 1 in 4 Americans will be older than 85 by the year 2050 (U.S. Bureau of the Census, 1997). Although many elderly persons are healthy, they are more likely than others to have chronic diseases, which will increase the need for medical care, assisted living facilities, social services, and home care (Kadushin & Egan, 1997).

The racial and ethnic makeup of American society is also expected to change. Within 50 years, people of color will make up the majority of the U.S. population (Voelker, 1995). Unfortunately, they will still have comparatively few social opportunities, meaning that the number of low-income individuals in this country will rise (Kadushin & Egan, 1997). Less educated, underprivileged individuals are typically most in need of health care, but are least likely to be informed about health issues and to utilize health services (Bochner, 1983; Williams et al., 1995). Thus, there will be an added imperative for programs that promote healthy behaviors and fund care for needy persons. The challenge is to provide affordable care to the people who need it and to use prevention efforts to keep people as healthy as possible. This will require a cooperative effort between health care professionals and members of the public.

Furthermore, diversity among health care workers is not expected to keep pace with the overall population. Currently, minorities comprise less than 6.6% of physicians and 12% of nurses although they account for more than 25% of the U.S. population (American Medical Association, 2001b; "HHS Awards," 2003; U.S. Bureau of the Census, 2000). The odds are that caregivers will find themselves dealing with patients who differ markedly from them (and from each other) in terms of knowledge, need, and cultural beliefs. Communication is a valuable tool for meeting this challenge. It is important to understand and appreciate culturally diverse views of health and illness and to become skillful at intercultural communication.

Technology

Technology may address many of the issues just described. The ability to communicate with health care clients across great distances may avail people of medical care they would not otherwise receive. Access to information can empower patients and increase opportunities for social support. Health messages can be broadcast around the world or tailored (narrowcast) to meet the needs of specific individuals. Technology has become a powerful communication tool in medicine. But questions concerning privacy, quality, cost, and access remain to be resolved. For example, some people worry that technology will make it even more difficult for low-income and undereducated persons to use and understand medical resources. In Communication Technology sections throughout the book you will learn more about the issues surrounding telemedicine, knowledge coupling, virtual communities, narrowcasting, and more.

Implications

Although it may seem that the average person is not affected by changes in the health industry, that is far from the case. As shown here, changes are affecting the type of caregivers people are apt to see, what services are available, and what role individuals play in maintaining their own health. People who work in the health industry are likely to experience the stress and promise of change, the pressure to save money, the imperative to use new technology, and the need to communicate effectively with a variety of people and to include them as partners in their own care and disease prevention efforts. We are all influenced by health issues, not only in the United States, but around the world.

SUMMARY

Effective health communication involves an extensive number of people. Physicians often seem to call the shots, but they are affected by a range of factors themselves, including budget limitations and public expectations. Doctors do not work alone; nurses, therapists, technicians, counselors, and others also influence what goes on in health care situations. In the larger scope of things, health care administrators, media professionals, and public health promoters play important roles. Furthermore, everyday citizens affect the process more than they may realize.

In a context of rapid change, the most effective people are those who keep the larger picture in sight, are open to new ideas, and work with others to identify and implement options that serve multiple goals at the same time. The emphasis is on communicating as leaders and team members.

Communication about health issues is achieved within a complex array of influences. It is partly the result of individual action and partly the result of social contexts and expectations. Participants in health care must strive not only to attain their personal objectives but also to maintain the good faith of those around them, without whom they cannot achieve long-term success. As we acknowledge that physicians are not solely responsible for people's health, we must also acknowledge that patients should share the responsibility. What patients feel, do, and think are important to the process of care and to their overall states of health.

With this philosophy it seems important to emphasize that, if health communication is good (or bad) we have a host of people to thank (or blame). Almost always we are among those people. We influence the process throughout our lives, as patients, caregivers (professional or otherwise), citizens, and conversationalists who help pass along information and ideas about health. We all have something to gain by understanding the process, and hopefully, something to contribute as well.

There are different ways of looking at health. Two of the most popular perspectives are the biomedical model, which assumes that disease is best understood and treated in physical terms, and the biopsychosocial model, which treats health as a broad concept including social, personal, and physical factors.

Health communication is important for several reasons. It allows patients and caregivers to share concerns and establish trust. Effective communication also helps people cope and builds their self-confidence. Communicating well saves time and money and helps health care organizations solicit, organize, and implement new ideas. Finally, media messages have the potential to improve or discourage healthy habits. Part of effective communication is discerning between helpful and harmful information.

Health communication is especially important now as the industry and the public work toward a more affordable health system, disease prevention, patient empowerment, and treatment for a diverse population. The current health care system is quickly evolving amid diverse global pressures, making the nature of medicine and the importance of health communication a dynamic and important consideration in the 21st century.

KEY TERMS

health
communication
interdependent
cultural display rules
health communication
biomedical model
biopsychosocial model
patient empowerment

REVIEW QUESTIONS

1. Why is it important for people in one aspect of health (e.g., campaign management, public relations, clinical care) to be knowledgeable about broader issues relevant to health?
2. What is the significance of defining communication as a process?
3. How do personal goals, interdependence, and sensitivity affect the communication process?
4. How do communication partners establish shared meaning?
5. What are the implications of describing health communication in terms of seeking, processing, and sharing information?
6. Have you ever felt like the underdog in a health care encounter? What contributed to this feeling? Is there anything you or other people might have done differently?
7. Why is it important to study theories in conjunction with research about health communication?
8. How are the biomedical and biopsychosocial models different? How are they alike?
9. Do you believe health is affected by moods and communication with others? Why or why not?

10. Have your health care experiences been characterized more by the biomedical or the biopsychosocial approach? How? Which do you prefer and why?
11. What do you think of the case study about St. Jude Hospital (Box 1.3)? How have your experiences with hospitals been similar or different?
12. What are six reasons to study health communication?
13. Why is it especially important that people involved in health care maintain high ethical standards?
14. What questions might you ask as you evaluate the options presented by an ethical dilemma?
15. What role can communication specialists play as health agencies strive to cut costs?
16. How is the emphasis on disease prevention likely to affect health communication?
17. How does patient empowerment affect health communication?
18. What shifts are expected in the U.S. population over the next 50 years? How will these changes affect health care and health communication?
19. Why should we be concerned about health crises around the world? What role does communication play in striving for global health?

CLASS ACTIVITY

Review Your Own Experiences

Take a few moments to remember a health care experience. Write down how you behaved in that experience and how the others around you behaved. Consider the following questions as a class or in small groups:

1. How satisfied were you with the experience?
2. What were your goals? For instance, were you interested in getting a physical cure, being reassured, or avoiding embarrassment? (People almost always have multiple objectives.)
3. What were the goals of the other people involved? Were your goals the same as theirs or different?
4. In what ways were the participants affected by their feelings, the situation, and one another's behavior?
5. Did the encounter reflect the biomedical or the biopsychosocial model more?
6. How would you improve the communication in a similar situation?

CHAPTER 2

History and Current Issues

> *The dignity of a physician requires that he should look healthy, and as plump as nature intended him to be; for the common crowd consider those who are not of this excellent bodily condition to be unable to take care of others. Then he must be clean in person, well dressed, and anointed with sweet-smelling unguents that are beyond suspicion.*

This quote is attributed to Hippocrates, a Greek physician and educator who lived several hundred years before the birth of Jesus (Fabre, 1997). Hippocrates was influential in establishing the role of physicians in society and the ethics of Western medicine. A journey through history shows how some ideas (some ancient, some modern) influence the way people think and talk about health today. You may be surprised to find that your assumptions about health care have roots in the philosophies of ancient Egypt, medieval Europe, or colonial America.

To understand why health communication has evolved as it has, this chapter sketches the history of medicine. It depicts health care during ancient times, the Middle Ages, and the European Renaissance to create an appreciation and understanding of health communication in the 21st century.

MEDICINE IN ANCIENT TIMES

Many westerners date medicine to ancient Greece and think of Hippocrates as the first physician. This would make medicine about 2,000 years old, a period during which tremendous change has taken place. However, the first doctor in history was actually Imhotep of ancient Egypt, who lived about 2,000 years before Hippocrates was born.

Imhotep

As the first known physician, **Imhotep** was part of an ancient medical community that is still admired for its vast knowledge. Translations of early texts suggest Egyptians were aware of blood circulation and the actions of bodily organs thousands of years before the Western world attained that knowledge. A learned observer of archeology once remarked that the accomplishments of ancient Egypt would make citizens of the modern world "blush for shame" (Thorwald, 1962, p. 15).

Imhotep was not only a healer but a priest, sculptor, and architect as well. He designed the first stone pyramid, which was built for King Zoser about 2600 B.C. In the centuries after his death, Imhotep attained godlike status. Some legends portrayed him as the son of Ptah, the Egyptian god of architecture. Others revered Imhotep as a medicine god and evoked his name in healing ceremonies.

The ancient Egyptians took a **religio-empirical approach** to medicine, combining spiritualism and physical study. Healers were holy men such as Imhotep, but the ancients also recognized a physical component of illness (Thorwald, 1962). They developed an impressive variety of instruments including surgical appliances, sutures, drugs, and immobilizing casts. Mummies show that the ancient Egyptians were prone to many disorders that plague people today, including dental ailments, cancer, and arteriosclerosis (hardening of the arteries).

It is believed that Imhotep was the basis for the Greek god Aesculapius, whose name is mentioned in the famous Hippocratic Oath (Garrison, 1929). In fact, historians believe Hippocrates was strongly influenced by the writings of ancient Egypt.

Hippocrates

Hippocrates (460–370 B.C.) is often considered the founder of scientific medicine and Western medical ethics. Perhaps his most enduring legacy is the oath that bears his name.

The **Hippocratic Oath** (Box 2.1) established a code of conduct for physicians that has influenced the Western world until the current day. In a collection of succinct sentences, the oath says a great deal about medical ethics then and now. For centuries medical students took the Hippocratic Oath when they received their degrees. The tradition has largely been abandoned, but most doctors are familiar with the oath and continue to be influenced by the ethical framework it presents.

Parts of the Hippocratic Oath—particularly the appeal to medicine gods Apollo and Aesculapius—seem archaic today. More remarkable, however, are the issues that remain current. The oath's edict to "give no deadly medicine" is relevant to modern debates over physician-assisted suicide. Likewise, the mention of abortion and sexual misconduct could be straight from 21st century headlines, as could issues of patient confidentiality.

The oath's pledge not to "cut persons labouring under the stone," but to leave such work to specific practitioners, reflects the distinction in Hippocrates' day between medicine and surgery. It is believed that this passage refers to bladder and kidney stones, which were then extracted by surgeons but not by physicians (Edelstein, 1967).

Hippocrates' views on the nature of disease are as important as the oath that bears his name. At the time Hippocrates lived, many people believed disease was God's punishment, and they were shamed by it (Amundsen & Ferngren, 1983). Hippocrates' ideas helped dispel this notion. In place of

Box 2.1 The Hippocratic Oath

I swear by Apollo the physician, and Aesculapius and Hygeia, and Panacea, and all the gods and goddesses, that according to my ability and judgment, I will keep this oath and its stipulations—to reckon him who taught me this art equally dear to me as my parents, to share my substances with him, and to relieve his necessities if required; to look upon his offspring in the same footing as my own brothers; and to teach them this art if they shall wish to learn it, without fee or stipulation, and that by precept, lecture, and other mode of instruction, I will impart a knowledge of the art to my own sons, and those of my teachers, and to disciples bound by a stipulation and oath according to the law of medicine, but to none other.

I will follow that system of regimen which, according to my ability and judgment, I consider for the benefit of my patients, and abstain from whatever is deleterious and mischievous. I will give no deadly medicine to anyone if asked, nor suggest any such counsel; and in like manner I will not give to a woman a pessary to produce abortion. With purity and holiness I will pass my life and practice my art. I will not cut persons laboring under the stone, but will leave this to be done by men who are practitioners of this work. Into whatever houses I enter, I will go into them for the benefit of the sick, and will abstain from every voluntary act of mischief and corruption; and, further, from the seduction of females or males, of freemen and slaves. Whatever, in connection with my professional practice, or not in connection with it, I see or hear, in the life of men, which ought not to be spoken of abroad, I will not divulge, as reckoning that such ought to be kept secret.

While I continue to keep this Oath unviolated, may it be granted to me to enjoy life and the practice of this art, respected by all men, in all time. But should I trespass and violate this Oath, may be the reverse be my lot.

—This version of the Hippocratic Oath was published in 1910 by P. F. Collier and Son in Harvard Classics *(Vol. 38). It was placed in the public domain in June 1993.*

spiritual explanations he presented a rational/empirical model of medicine. From a **rational/empirical approach,** disease is best understood by careful observation and logical analysis.

Hippocrates promoted the idea of health as a harmonious balance between many factors including diet, contact with nature, relationships, and physical strength. He also advocated a balance between different body fluids, which he called body humors—blood, phlegm, yellow bile, and black bile (Moore, Van Arsdale, Glittenberg, & Aldrich, 1987). Thus, although Hippocrates strengthened the notion that physical factors are a significant part of disease, he acknowledged social and personal influences as well. In this way Hippocrates' philosophy was an early forerunner to the biopsychosocial approach.

The treatment of body humors had a substantial impact on the practice of medicine, forming the basis for bloodletting and other purging practices. Bloodletting involved lancing a vein or applying leeches to allow a portion of the patient's blood to drain from the body. It was believed this would purge impure blood or balance blood levels with other humors. Other purging practices including vomiting, sweating, and the use of laxatives.

Implications

Modern medicine has roots in ancient Egypt. Imhotep's popularity helped establish physicians as people worthy of awe and respect. Although not much detail is available about Imhotep's life, historians believe his legendary views on illness inspired Hippocrates, whose ideas are well documented and have had a substantial influence on Western medicine.

Hippocrates' views have had several effects on health communication. By establishing medicine as rational and empirical, Hippocrates helped shape the role of physicians as scientists and intellectuals rather than as spiritualists. As a result, medical talk began to focus on physical, social, and personal factors. If the rational/empirical perspective had never taken root, you might now visit a minister rather than a doctor when you become ill. By the same token, treatment and diagnosis might involve spiritual exploration more than physical remedies.

Although Hippocrates' ideas enjoyed popularity for a time (and were revived centuries later), they were overshadowed when early Christianity brought about a resurgence of spiritualism in Western Europe.

■ MEDIEVAL RELIGION AND HEALTH CARE

Christianity dominated the course of Western medicine for hundreds of years during what is known as the Middle Ages or medieval period (A.D. 500–1450). Medical spiritualism, which waned but never fully died under Hippocrates' influence, was renewed with vigor.

Medical Spiritualism

As Donald Bille (1981) defines it, **medical spiritualism** is the belief that illness is governed by supernatural forces such as gods, spirits, or ghosts. Medical spiritualism was supported by the belief that Jesus performed healing miracles. Healing was so closely tied to Christianity that monks were the principle physicians during much of the Middle Ages (White, 1896/1925).

As the only recognized religion in medieval Europe, the Catholic Church was involved in making laws, allocating land and resources, and caring for the sick and homeless. As such, it had immense influence over people's well-being and way of life.

The church's ideology affected the nature of health communication. From a spiritualist perspective, disease was treated through prayer and faith and, sometimes, through application of natural (God-given) substances such as plants. Illness was thought to be manifested differently in each person (Thompson, 1990). As a result, patients' thoughts and feelings, faith, and behaviors were directly relevant to the subject of healing.

During a portion of the Middle Ages, the church banned the practice of secular medicine, particularly surgery. Surgeons were often regarded as sorcerers, butchers, and atheists (White, 1896/1925). Because the soul was believed to inhabit a person's entire body, to cut into the body (before or after death) was to interfere with God's work.

Barber Surgeons

During the Middle Ages, health care was provided mostly by monks and by a limited number of secular practitioners, most of whom did not perform surgery. Barbers began offering surgical procedures in addition to hairstyling because they had the sharp instruments and public facilities necessary. **Barber surgeons** were called upon to perform simple surgeries, bloodletting, and tooth extractions (Douglas, 1994). It is believed that the modern barber pole was derived from the image of white and blood-stained bandages swirling in the wind as they dried outside barber shops. If these images sound harrowing by today's standards, consider that during the time of barber surgeons people were still unaware of germs and had no effective anesthesia!

Although it is easy to regard the church as antiprogressive for discouraging secular medicine, it is perhaps understandable considering how dreadful surgery seemed at that time. As medical historian John Duffy (1979) describes it, prior to the 1860s surgery was "a grim and bloody business" requiring the surgeon "to be a strong, fast, forceful operator, ruthlessly immune to the screams and struggles of the patient" (p. 130).

Science and Magic

Monastic medicine varied from the scholarly to the superstitious. It was, in turn, praised and condemned.

In cathedral schools such as Salerno in southern Italy, the clergy studied medical theory. These institutions became models for European medical schools to follow. The church founded the first hospitals as we know them and staffed them with its own learned practitioners, forming what Darrel Amundsen and Gary Ferngren (1983) laud as a "vast charitable institution" (p. 15).

In contrast to this academic atmosphere, however, was the exercise of **Christian magic,** bizarre ceremonies and exorcisms condoned by the church

(Amundsen & Ferngren, 1983). In an effort to disgust evil spirits into leaving a patient's body, for instance, the patient might be instructed to eat toad livers or drink rats' blood (White, 1896/1925). (In fairy tales to come, of course, these ingredients made up the imaginary contents of witches' brew.)

The church also became involved in selling fetishes and hosting miracles, some of which were later exposed as hoaxes. **Fetishes** were holy relics said to protect those who purchased them from calamities such as shipwreck, fire, lightning, and difficult childbirth (White, 1896/1925). Those who could afford to buy fetishes or visit holy sites made lavish offerings to the church in trade for divine intervention.

End of an Era

Ironically, as medicine advanced with the monks' practice of it, their work began to seem disturbingly secular and altogether overwhelming. The very technology and pharmacology they developed were at odds with the church's position on healing by faith and were diverting the monks from other spiritual pursuits (Ackerknecht, 1968). In 1311 the church forbade monks to practice medicine any longer.

Implications

A return to medical spiritualism accompanied the rise of Christianity. As with any enterprise of such vast duration and involvement, the church's role during the Middle Ages had both positive and negative aspects. The church has been criticized for profiting from its caregiving role and for suppressing the development of secular medicine. At the same time, it is lauded for helping establish a compassionate perspective toward the ill and founding institutions of care and learning that served as a model of Western medicine. Today, this influence is reflected in the existence of church-funded and other nonprofit medical centers devoted to public service.

Although spiritual leaders are no longer the principle caregivers in medicine, religion still has a role in health care. It is common to pray for ill persons and for members of the clergy to visit ill persons and be present at the time of death. The presence of spiritualism has endured to some extent, even in the context of high-tech biomedical care.

■ RENAISSANCE PHILOSOPHY AND HEALTH CARE

From one extreme to another, the religion-oriented thought of the Middle Ages was followed by the intellectual skepticism of the European Renaissance. The Renaissance began in the 1300s (overlapping with the Middle Ages) and continued into the 1600s.

Confronted with the age-old question, "What is real?", artists and philosophers of the Renaissance looked to mathematics and matter for answers. Their theories changed the Western worldview, including the nature of medicine.

Partly in reaction to the religious dominance of the Middle Ages, Renaissance thinkers tended to be skeptical about anything they could not prove. **René Descartes** (1596–1650), an influential philosopher and mathematician of the time, introduced his method of doubt, prescribing that the thinker systematically doubt the existence of all things until that existence could be verified. (Such a method eventually led him to doubt his *own* existence until, realizing he had to *exist* to be *doing* the doubting, he reached the famous conclusion, "I think, therefore I am.")

Principle of Verification

The **principle of verification**—do not believe it if you cannot prove it—changed the nature of health communication. No longer were people considered ill based solely on their feelings. Instead, physicians and others began to look for verifiable signs of illness (a perspective consistent with today's biomedical approach).

Surgery and autopsies became acceptable. In fact, not only physicians but artists became interested in human dissection (Dowling, 1997). Renaissance artists including Michelangelo and Leonardo da Vinci studied the human body inside and out to make their representations of it more precise. Mathematical precision and a knowledge of anatomy became mainstream in both science and art.

The principle of verification affected health communication. If illness is physically verifiable it follows that people may believe they are ill even though they really are not. This idea is still pervasive in Western medicine. You know this if you have ever gone to the doctor feeling ill and been told that tests confirm you are "just fine." In fact, some people avoid going to the doctor because it seems a sign of weakness to complain about something that (medically speaking) is trivial or does not exist. (See Box 2.2.) My experience producing health campaigns bears this out. I once directed a campaign to encourage people to go to an emergency room if they experienced chest pains. The campaign was spurred by evidence that people were dying of heart attacks because they were afraid to go to the emergency room and find out (to their embarrassment) that they had nothing more than indigestion.

Cartesian Dualism

Renaissance thinkers were challenged to explain the relationship between body and soul. As mentioned, during much of the Middle Ages, the soul was considered to inhabit the entire body. Descartes proposed an alternative in the form of a mind–body dualism.

Box 2.2 PERSPECTIVES
Sick in the Head?

After two months with a 101-degree temperature but no real discomfort, a 21-year-old woman presented her concerns to a doctor. "From the beginning, I got the feeling he really didn't want to see me," she remembers. "I waited 4 hours in the waiting room."

During a brief consultation, the doctor scolded the woman for smoking and prescribed two medications. "Those were to relieve the congestion in my chest (which I didn't have) and strep throat (which I also didn't have). We paid and left. I knew I didn't have strep throat, and I wasn't sick from smoking, but I took the medicine because it might help, and he was a doctor," says the woman.

The medicine made her feel worse, and the woman eventually went to a physician assistant who diagnosed a urinary tract infection and prescribed medication that provided immediate relief. Looking back, the woman muses: "I wondered why the first doctor was so incompetent. He came highly recommended. I guess he figured I was a young hypochondriac. I didn't really spend that much more time with the physician assistant, but she believed I was sick, where the other doctor obviously didn't."

This true story brings up an interesting question. What makes an illness real? Is it symptoms, lab tests, a certain look or demeanor? A byproduct of organic medicine is the belief that an illness is not real unless it is physically verifiable, and society frowns on those who complain of "imaginary" conditions.

The phrase "sick in the head" is typically a put down, an insult that suggests one is crazy or out of touch with reality. Yet in reality there is strong evidence that what people think does affect how they feel, germs or no germs.

What Do You Think?

1. How do you feel if a doctor tells you there is nothing wrong, but you feel sick?
2. If you feel sick, but the doctor can find nothing wrong with you, are you sick?
3. How would you feel if you were told your illness was "all in your head"?
4. What would you do if you thought the doctor's diagnosis was incorrect?

Cartesian dualism (named for Descartes) contends that people have both souls and bodies, but the two are not the same. Descartes felt that the soul dwells only temporarily in the human body, a belief based on the conviction that the soul lives after the body dies (Cottingham, 1992). Furthermore, Descartes theorized that the soul was seated in the human brain (other animals being presumably soulless). Thus, in Descartes' view, the soul is most closely associated with the mind, not spread throughout the body.

The medical implications of Cartesian dualism are profound, including the separation of medicine into two branches, one for the mind and one for the body. From this perspective, disease (a physical condition) is distinguishable from illness (the condition as it is experienced). Of course, this distinction goes only so far. Few people would argue that the mind and body have no influence on each other. Nevertheless, dualism was (and still is) accepted as a general principle. For the most part, medical doctors (i.e., internists, cardiologists, neurologists) consider it their primary function to treat physical ailments. Mental health is more the domain of psychiatrists, psychologists, social workers, and the like.

Implications

During the Renaissance, emphasis on observable signs of illness overshadowed more "invisible" influences such as spiritual, social, and psychological factors. Based on the principle of verification, people may believe they are ill when, from an empirical perspective, they are not.

Cartesian dualism established significant boundaries for health communication. Western physicians' traditional reluctance to discuss matters of emotion or faith is rooted in the dualism model. This is especially true of the biomedical approach.

■ HEALTH CARE IN THE NEW WORLD

Near the end of the Renaissance, European settlers began inhabiting North America. For the most part, the New World was not a healthy place, physically or emotionally.

Health Conditions

The relatively good health enjoyed by Native Americans before 1600 was replaced by widespread epidemics after European settlers began arriving, and the early settlers fared little better. James Cassedy (1991) reports that 80% of the settlers in Virginia died between 1607 and 1625, and contact with settlers resulted in the death of 90% of the Native American population. The settlers suffered from exhaustion, malnutrition, and very often, severe depression. In addition, both settlers and Native Americans were threatened by exposure to diseases uncommon in their homelands. Without the immunity that might have resulted from previous exposure, many died of conditions such as measles, dysentery, malaria, and influenza.

Health care consisted mainly of family efforts and home remedies. Caregivers were diverse, including physicians as well as folk therapists specializing in herbs, hypnosis, acupuncture, phrenology (based on the size and shape of the skull), and other forms of treatment. Many of these folk remedies remained quite popular until the late 1800s (Cassedy, 1991).

Hippocrates' Influence

People nostalgic for the age of humble country doctors may not wish to turn time back quite so far as the 1700s. Physicians in colonial America adhered largely to Hippocrates' idea of body humors. Believing that illness was the result of an imbalance of humors or a contamination of them, standard practice was to aggressively purge the body. Early accounts describe patients who died after being induced to vomit 100 times or enduring days of sweating and bleeding (Cassedy, 1991). Cotton Mather, a Boston minister and healer, spoke out against such aggressive treatments. He once wrote:

> Before we go any farther, let this Advice to the Sick, be principally attended to: *Don't kill 'em!* . . . If we stopt here, and said no more, this were enough to save more *Lives* than our *Wars* have destroyed. (as cited in Duffy, 1979, p. 35)

It is no wonder that people preferred more gentle folk remedies and often summoned doctors only as a last resort.

Women's Role

In colonial America women played an important but unofficial role in health care. Most care was provided in the home, and women were expected to nurse ill family members. Schools of nursing had yet to be established. During the Civil War, female nurses and a small number of unlicensed women physicians were accepted as military medics, but the prevailing assumption was that most women were too delicate and uneducated to be doctors (Bonner, 1992). We will explore the role of women and minorities more in Chapters 6 and 9.

Implications

Folk medicine was popular in colonial America because it was gentler than the aggressive purging favored by physicians. Most health care was provided in the home with assistance from family members. Health communication was influenced by the assumption that family members would be involved in caring for their loved ones. Another assumption was that illness could be treated in a variety of ways, by different types of medical practitioners. As you will see, the ideology of health care was about to change.

THE RISE OF ORTHODOX MEDICINE

The Industrial Revolution was made possible by mass production and diverse power sources available in the United States by the late 1800s. The revolution brought people to urban centers to work in factories and made health care a booming business. This dramatically widened the schism between what Cassedy (1991) calls **orthodox practitioners,** who were educated in medical schools, and **sectarians,** who practiced folk medicine taught to them by friends and family members.

Folk medicine had long been popular as a safer and less painful alternative to orthodox medicine (also referred to as conventional medicine). However, these advantages were diminished by the introduction of anesthesia and sterilization in conventional medical centers, medical research and technology, medical school reform, and a campaign to wipe out disease through orthodox medicine. Together these factors contributed to the decline of sectarian medicine.

Population Shifts

Industrialization increased the demand for medical care. The number of crippling injuries rose with the introduction of heavy machinery in factories and on farms (Cassedy, 1991). Contagion was also a threat in dense population centers, a factor aggravated by inadequate drainage and waste disposal.

Medicine became more lucrative, but also more demanding. Larger patient-to-physician ratios made house calls impractical and required physicians to develop more intricate methods of keeping records. Hospitals and clinics were opened to bring patients and doctors together. The image of the solitary, traveling country doctor gave way to that of the physician situated at the hub of an overwhelming number of patients, professionals, and technical facilities.

Germ Theory

At about the same time, a scientific breakthrough helped hospitals and medical centers become safer and more appealing than in the past. That breakthrough was germ theory, which became widely accepted in the late 1800s through the work of Louis Pasteur.

Simply put, **germ theory** states that disease is caused by microscopic organisms called germs (Twaddle & Hessler, 1987). The ramifications of such a simple notion are astounding. An awareness of microscopic agents has allowed communities to remove the threat of many contagious diseases, reduce the incidence of infection, and develop inoculations against smallpox, measles, polio, and other diseases. Based on germ theory, Joseph Lister revolutionized surgery by sterilizing medical instruments and environments (Raffel & Raffel, 1989).

Hospitals began cleansing their instruments and separating people with contagious diseases from other patients.

Research and Technology

Medical centers made it possible to systematically collect patient data and acquire expensive technology. As research and technology advanced, so did the demands on health professionals to expand their knowledge, increase their patient loads, and track the health of a diverse population (Raffel & Raffel, 1989). With so many demands, it was necessary for physicians to limit the time they spent with each patient, promoting the idea that medical communication should be brief and to the point.

Medical developments also made it important for doctors to be well trained. Physicians increasingly gained legitimacy through attendance at medical schools, membership in medical societies, contributions to professional journals and research, and eventually through laws requiring doctors to be state licensed. The American Medical Association (AMA) was organized in 1846 to unite doctors across the continent and to speak on their behalf.

Campaign of Orthodox Medicine

In his book *The Silent World of Doctor and Patient,* Jay Katz (1984) makes a case that conventional practitioners in the early 1900s sought to distinguish themselves as the legitimate guardians of people's health. In Katz's view, this campaign was not entirely self-serving. Many people believed scientific knowledge and technology could be used to eradicate disease. Whether conventional medicine was more concerned with this goal or with attaining professional dominance, the effect was the same. Folk medicine was largely discredited as quackery, and "orthodox" medicine gained a virtual monopoly over health care. As Katz describes it, this monopoly seemed to eliminate the need for physicians to explain or justify their actions:

> Since they no longer had to defend themselves against the criticism of rival groups, doctors asserted more adamantly, and now without fear of contradiction, that laymen could not judge medical practices and had to comply with medical orders. (p. 39)

Physicians' authority was considered unquestionable. Doctors were not expected to express doubts or uncertainties, and they were not to be influenced by the opinions of people (including patients) less educated than themselves.

The image of physicians as all-knowing authorities inspired public trust. But defining medical professionalism in terms of certainty and scientific expertise discouraged doctors from showing emotions or admitting doubts or mistakes (Katz, 1984). At the same time, patients and others were effectively silenced into submission. Soon, many patients and others were too trusting or intimidated to speak freely to their doctors (Katz, 1984).

Flexner Report

One part of the campaign to promote scientific medicine took the form of medical school reform. Prior to 1900, most medical schools in the United States were run as private businesses, oriented more toward profit than rigorous education (Cassedy, 1991). Such schools produced thousands of physicians with little knowledge of biology or physiology.

Disturbed by the low scientific standards in these schools, the AMA commissioned Abraham Flexner of the Carnegie Foundation to evaluate U.S. medical schools and make recommendations. The **Flexner Report,** published in 1910, was a stinging indictment. It charged that all but a few medical schools in the country—the notable exceptions were Harvard, Johns Hopkins, and Western Reserve—were lax in their coverage of biology and other sciences. The report also criticized medical schools for not offering more supervised, hands-on experience with patients.

Of the 155 medical schools he evaluated, Flexner recommended that all but 31 cease operation (Raffel & Raffel, 1989). In fact, nearly two thirds of U.S. medical schools did close, unable to meet the reform standards (Twaddle & Hessler, 1987). Most of the schools that remained open were incorporated within universities.

The chief model for reform was Johns Hopkins Medical School, with its alliance to Johns Hopkins Hospital (both located in Baltimore, Maryland). The staff at Johns Hopkins incorporated the most up-to-date knowledge of healthy ventilation, efficiency, and infection control. They emphasized science, laboratory and research experience, and clinical experience with actual patients (Raffel & Raffel, 1989). Following this example, medical schools across the country became more demanding and began to focus intensely on organic aspects of disease as well as clinical and laboratory experience.

Decline of Sectarian Medicine

For the most part sectarian healers were not prepared to fight the emerging dominance of conventional medicine. Americans were enamored with science and technology—both of which were firmly rooted in the camp of conventional medicine by the early 1900s. Moreover, there was little to unite diverse healers, and because their treatments promised gradual and long-term effects, outcomes were hard to isolate and measure (Cassedy, 1991).

Osteopathy and chiropractic were among the only sects to maintain popularity. Other forms of therapy such as acupuncture and herbal remedies faded from significance for several decades, at least in the United States. Interestingly, the very reasons that led to their decline—long-term results, low-tech methods—are now contributing to a resurgence of popularity as people seek to reduce costs and prevent ill health. You will read more about that in Chapter 9.

Implications

As the United States entered the 20th century, public confidence became firmly invested in conventional medicine, with its emphasis on science and technology. The nature of health care was changed by increased demand for services and by higher patient-to-caregiver ratios. Physicians began to treat people in hospitals and clinics rather than in private homes. The time patients and caregivers could spend together was limited, and patients' input was given less significance in light of evidence that disease was caused by microscopic germs.

Technology and research made demands of their own, requiring doctors to become skilled in the sciences. Medical school reform, based on the Flexner Report, urged science and research in medical schools across the country. In the midst of this, most forms of sectarian medicine dwindled or were abandoned altogether.

TWENTIETH CENTURY HEALTH CARE

Medicine began to depend even more on technology, and by 1900 physicians were using X-rays to see inside the body. High-powered microscopes identified a long list of diseases including malaria, influenza, pneumonia, tuberculosis, and more (Reiser, 1978). With the new technology a small vial of blood could be the basis for dozens of diagnostic procedures. The phrase "a battery of tests" became common. The efficiency of technology, combined with Americans' confidence in it, made technology an appealing option in medical care.

People's confidence in medicine grew, but this confidence was accompanied by a corresponding feeling of alienation as they found themselves in unfamiliar surroundings and felt less qualified to treat themselves and their family members. As medicine became high tech, it lost some of the intimacy to which people were accustomed. Emotional concerns seemed out of place in the sterile, scientific atmosphere of clinics and hospitals. Caregivers trained in the sciences were not necessarily prepared to deal with emotional aspects of illness. Added to this, doctors were so greatly outnumbered by their patients it became difficult to establish close relationships with them all.

Social conditions affected medicine as well. Racial segregation continued well into the 20th century. African-American patients and caregivers were not allowed into most hospitals in the United States until the 1960s (a topic to be covered more thoroughly in Chapter 9). Even as the United States was building one of the most respected medical systems in the world, its benefits were not available to all citizens.

Specialization

The immense growth in medical knowledge and technology spawned an era of **specialization** in which doctors focused on particular aspects of health.

Neurologists, allergists, radiologists, cardiovascular surgeons, and oncologists—to name a few—began limiting their practices to specific concerns. A patient with an ailment in any of these categories could see an expert rather than a generalist, a prospect that was appealing but expensive. Before long it became more prestigious and profitable to be a specialist than a general practitioner. As you will see, this trend eventually led to a critical shortage of general practitioners. It also changed the nature of health communication. Talk about broader concerns often seems out of place when seeing an expert who focuses on a specific body part or system.

Medicine and Free Enterprise

As health care evolved over the course of U.S. history, it came to be treated largely as a free-market commodity. That is, consumers, commanding what buying power they could, were soon able to choose between a range of caregivers who charged fees for the care they provided. This fee-for-service system included the opportunity to buy health insurance.

Insurance became particularly important in the United States as health care costs rose to cover the expenses of medical technology, education, specialization, staffing, and facilities. The premise of insurance is to pool resources so that expenses are spread over a great number of people, saving any one subscriber from overwhelming debt. This premise assumes that most people will not require more than they contribute and that enough people will subscribe to establish an adequate treasury.

Implications

In the early 1900s science and technology made it possible for conventional practitioners to curtail the spread of germs and treat disease in new ways. Knowledge grew so quickly that caregivers began to specialize in particular types of medicine.

The emphasis on expert knowledge and technology affected health communication. As confidence in medicine grew, people seemed less qualified to care for family members at home. At the same time, talk between patients and caregivers was overshadowed by an emerging reliance on physical tests. For the most part, medicine continued to become increasingly high tech and (as you will soon see) expensive.

ADVENT OF MANAGED CARE

The success of the U.S. medical system was phenomenal. The strength of the United States after World War II made it a model for rebuilding countries, many of whom received medical aid from the United States. In this section, we discuss the financial crisis surrounding health care that has given rise to managed care.

Health and Wealth

By the mid 1900s Americans who could afford health insurance had access to specialists and facilities as superb as any in the world. It seemed for a while that no expense was too great, especially when the government or insurance companies were footing the bill.

The emphasis on individuality and the value of human life in the United States fostered the expectation of equal treatment for all and immense expenditures for the sake of single individuals (Balint & Shelton, 1996). In practice, of course, the system fell far short of that ideal. Discrimination has never been fully abolished, and the poor have always been underserved. Nevertheless, the ideology of individualism justified using every resource available for any patient deemed to be in need of it.

Problems

Eventually, the rising cost of health care became more than Americans could afford. As medical care and safer living conditions increased the average life expectancy, the U.S. population increased. Diseases once fatal became treatable, allowing people to live many years, albeit sometimes with expensive treatment all the while (Larson, 1998).

It became clear by the late 1960s that health care was becoming too expensive. Health insurance rates began to climb out of the reach of many Americans. Before long, tens of millions of U.S. residents were uninsured (McDermott, 1995).

As Americans were forced to drop their insurance coverage, insurance treasuries decreased, leading to steep rate hikes for those who continued to subscribe. Government-sponsored health programs forecast bankruptcies, unable to keep up with rising medical costs and growing numbers of uninsured and needy people. Critics charged that doctors and hospitals had been overutilizing medical resources, assuming insurance companies would pay whatever price they asked.

The United States also began to experience a shortage of primary care doctors, especially in rural and low-income areas. This was particularly lamentable because primary care physicians are valuable in tracking and monitoring people's overall care. Without primary care, the uncoordinated efforts of various specialists led to treatment duplications and unforeseen drug interactions. Moreover, systemic illnesses were more apt to go undetected by doctors with a very specific focus. Finally, many patients became discontented because specialists were not focused on them as whole persons. As the kaleidoscope model of health communication (Box 2.3) suggests, health is a complex and dynamic interplay of many factors. Specialists are valuable, but generalists are needed as well.

Reform Efforts

Beginning in the late 1970s, several measures were taken to curb costs and improve medical care. One was increased surveillance. Utilization review boards began to review patient records to identify treatment duplications and to see if costs were justified. Second, funding agencies (government and private insurers) began to require that patients see specialists only with referrals from primary care physicians.

Finally, funding agencies established specific reimbursement rates for health services. For example, **diagnosis-related groups (DRGs)** establish in advance what the funding agency will pay hospitals for certain procedures or the treatment of specific ailments. One effect of set reimbursement rates is that funding agencies have substantial control over the market value of health services. A major player in this process is the U.S. government. Although the U.S. health system is ostensibly private rather than state run, the government has substantial influence because it establishes the reimbursement rates for Medicaid and Medicare, government-funded programs that pay for health benefits provided to the elderly, underprivileged mothers and children, and persons with disabilities (Felty & Jones, 1998). Medicare covers more than 40 million Americans, including 90% of the elderly ("Medicare," 2003).

Some people worry that reimbursement rates will limit the care health agencies are willing to provide, especially if the rates are too low. If reimbursement rates are too low, health organizations may discontinue services or stop treating Medicaid patients. Especially worrisome is funding for diagnostic tests, prescription drugs, AIDS treatment, and care for dying individuals. Reimbursement restrictions have had several effects besides influencing what services are marketable. First, health care organizations are under pressure to keep their costs below reimbursement rates. If their expenses fall below reimbursement rates, they get to keep the difference. However, if their expenses exceed reimbursement rates, they take a loss. Furthermore, paperwork to justify expenses has increased, and physicians accustomed to professional autonomy may chafe under the scrutiny of third parties who may second-guess their judgments.

Managed Care

Another response to cost containment was the creation of managed care. About 93% of U.S. residents and about 95% of U.S. physicians now participate in managed care plans ("Employment Status," 2001; "Trends and Indicators," 2002).

Managed care organizations essentially coordinate the costs and delivery of health services. Whereas health decisions used to be made almost entirely by caregivers and patients, managed care organizations now recruit patients, match them up with caregivers and facilities, and monitor expenses. As such,

Box 2.3 THEORETICAL FOUNDATIONS
Kaleidoscope Model of Health Communication

If someone were to ask you, "Which is more important—your personality, your loved ones, or your health?" you would probably not have an easy answer. They are all important. Moreover, they overlap. It is difficult to imagine enjoying good health without the support of loved ones or losing your identity but keeping your health. Consistent with this awareness, Mary Anne Fitzpatrick and Anita Vangelisti's (2001) **kaleidoscope model of health communication** portrays well-being as a dynamic and interactive mosaic. The components of health communication (and health itself) are depicted as changing and interrelated. Although we may focus on one factor ("a fragment of glass"), its influence is never static or isolated.

The kaleidoscope model depicts health as the core, around which concentric circles of influence revolve. (See Figure 2.1.)

- *Social identity* (outer tier) includes ethnicity, social class, race, age, gender, and the interplay of these identities.
- *Social context* (second tier) arises from communication within social, professional, and family relationships.
- *Coping* (third tier) involves how people respond to illness cognitively, emotionally, and behaviorally.
- *Patient outcomes* (inner tier) are defined partly by satisfaction and a commitment to perform health-enhancing behaviors.
- *Health* (core) is defined as an individual's quality of life.

The kaleidoscope metaphor is based on several premises. One is that interpersonal communication is central to health and health management. Fitzpatrick and Vangelisti (2001) explain:

> *To predict and explain health through interpersonal communication processes may seem at first glance either a naïve or futile undertaking. Whereas we agree that no amount of talk between caregiver and patient will cure end stage Oates cell carcinoma, interpersonal communication may prolong life and certainly will affect the quality of life for the affected individual. And, communication may prompt another individual to give up smoking or comply with a treatment recommendation and thus prevent the disease from occurring. (p. 505)*

A second assumption is that health communication is not a linear process in which Behavior A naturally and predictably leads to Outcome B. Instead, complex processes interact in cyclical ways to influence health and how we communicate about it. "It is often impossible to know which comes first, as most of the processes are mutually reinforcing" (Fitzpatrick & Vangelisti, 2001, p. 507). For example, a friend may encourage you to

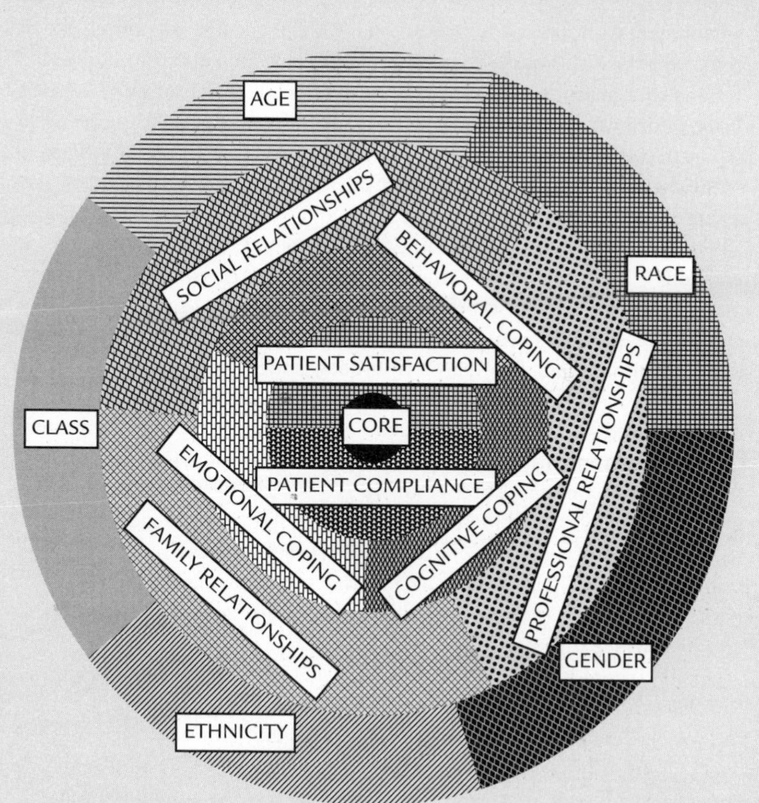

Figure 2.1 Kaleidoscope Theory of Health Communication. In the kaleidoscope model, concentric rings of influence interact to define health communication. From the broadest to the most immediate, the rings include social identity (outer tier), social context (second tier), coping (third tier), and patient outcomes (inner tier). The core represents health and quality of life.

Source: Copyright 2001 © by John Wiley & Sons. Originally published in The New Handbook of Language and Social Psychology. *Reproduced by permission from John Wiley & Sons Limited and the authors, Mary Anne Fitzpatrick and Anita Vangelisti.*

join a gym. Your health (quality of life) may improve, not only because you are burning calories but also because you are pleased by the friend's interest and the increased time you have together, you eat better to preserve your fitter physique, you begin to think of yourself as a healthier

continued

Box 2.3 THEORETICAL FOUNDATIONS
Kaleidoscope Model of Health Communication, *continued*

person, you work off stress, and so on. One thing leads to another; the circle of influence is more powerful than any one factor.

A third assumption is that the processes overlap. For example, it is difficult to draw a clear line between coping ability and social support or to separate the influence of gender and ethnicity. Although it is helpful to name these factors, in the kaleidoscope model they are not meant to represent distinct and separate entities.

Fourth, the processes are "multiply determined" (Fitzpatrick & Vangelisti, 2001, p. 507). That is, influence is exerted by several tiers at once. We know that underprivileged segments of the population have the greatest health risks because of a number of interrelated social, cultural, and personal factors. Compared to others, underprivileged individuals typically have poorer diets, are less knowledgeable about health matters, have less access to medical care, experience the stress of daily discrimination, and are more likely to suspect that health professionals value them less than other people (Roter et al., 1997; Cooper-Patrick et al., 1999). In many ways, the same factors that place underprivileged individuals at risk (e.g., illiteracy, discrimination, poverty) reduce their chances of getting quality care. Thus, their health status is multiply determined by a number of factors. (For more on the link between socioeconomic status and health, see Chapters 6 and 8.)

Finally, there is no one right or best way to address health concerns. Results can be reached in any number of ways. "The kaleidoscope model views health communication as changing, complex, teeming, and dynamic" (Fitzpatrick & Vangelisti, 2001, p. 507). Conditions continually change, even within the same person. As Fitzpatrick and

managed care represents the influence of people (or entities) other than patients and caregivers. By "managing" resources such as money, labor, technology, and facilities, managed care organizations seek to make health care more efficient and affordable.

It is easiest to understand managed care (and how it compares to traditional health insurance) if we look at it from the consumer's perspective, the provider's perspective, and the perspective of health organizations.

Consumer's Perspective Imagine that Sam is trying to decide between traditional health insurance and a managed care organization.

- *Traditional Insurance* First, he meets with an insurance agent. The agent asks how much money Sam is willing to pay from his own pocket each year for health services. Let's say Sam is willing to pay $500 per year (an

Vangelisti put it, health experiences are reconfigured "with every spin of the dial" (p. 507).

What Do You Think?

1. Do you agree that interpersonal communication has profound effects on people's health? Why or why not?
2. In what ways is your own health influenced by social identity, social context, and coping?
3. What factors influence your satisfaction with medical care and your willingness to follow medical advice?
4. If there are multiple paths to the same goal, what are some different ways we might address the dilemma that underprivileged people tend to have higher health risks but fewer resources for managing them?

Suggested Sources

Cooper-Patrick, L., Gallo, J. J., Gonzalez, J. J., Vu, H. T., Power, N. R., Nelson, C., & Ford, D. E. (1999). Race, gender, and partnership in the patient-physician relationship. *Journal of the American Medical Association, 282*(6), 583.

Fitzpatrick, M. A., & Vangelisti, A. (2001). Communication, relationships, and health. In W. P. Robinson & H. Giles (Eds.), *The new handbook of language and social psychology* (pp. 505–530). Chichester, England: John Wiley & Sons.

insurance deductible). The insurance company agrees that if Sam's expenses exceed his deductible it will pay 80% of the remaining medical bill. (Keep in mind that numbers vary.) Based on this agreement, Sam will pay the insurance company a set amount of money per month (an **insurance premium**). He may choose his own caregivers.

- *Managed Care* Next, Sam meets with an agent from a managed care organization. This organization offers to pay all of Sam's medical expenses if he agrees to pay a set amount each month. This amount is less than the monthly insurance premium Sam was been quoted, there is no deductible, and Sam is not obligated to pay a percentage of his medical bill. Beyond the monthly payment, all he will pay is $15 every time he requires care (a **co-payment**). (Again, numbers vary.) With this plan, Sam must see caregivers affiliated with the managed care organization.

Box 2.4 RESOURCES
More About Managed Care

- American Association of Health Plans: www.aahp.org
- American Association of Managed Care Nurses: www.aamcn.org
- *American Journal of Managed Care*: www.ajmc.com
- Managed Care Information Center: www.themcic.com

From a consumer's perspective, the most visible difference between traditional insurance and managed care is financial. The equation looks something like this:

> *Sam's Expenses With Traditional Insurance:*
> Monthly premiums + Deductible + 20% of bills over the deductible
>
> *Sam's Expenses With Managed Care:*
> Monthly payments + Co-payments

There is also a difference in choice. Sam's choice of caregivers is more limited with managed care. (As you will see later in the chapter, there are other underlying differences between managed care and traditional insurance as well.)

Caregiver's Perspective Now let's compare traditional insurance and various managed care options from a physician's perspective. (The same scenario could apply to a range of caregivers.) This section describes options with fee-for-service, health maintenance organizations (HMOs), and preferred provider organizations (PPOs). (HMOs and PPOs are the main types of managed care organizations, although new variations continue to emerge.)

- *Fee-for-Service* Imagine that Dr. Green treats patients covered by traditional health insurance. When she treats these patients, they pay her directly unless their bills exceed their insurance deductibles. In that case the patients pay the doctor a portion of the bill, and their insurance companies pay her the rest (called **reimbursement**). It is called **fee-for-service** when patients or insurance companies pay the customary fee for health care services. All in all, the more care Dr. Green provides under a fee-for-service agreement, the more money she makes.
- *HMO* A **health maintenance organization (HMO)** may offer to hire Dr. Green and pay her salary. If so, it will provide an office and administrative and support staff (receptionists, nurses, and so on). The advantages are stability, fewer administrative duties, and better working hours because Dr. Green will share the patient load with other caregivers in the

organization. The disadvantage is less independence (and possibly a moderate decrease in income). She may only treat patients who are HMO members, and the organization will monitor the care Dr. Green provides and what it costs (motivating her to stay within budget).

- *Capitation* Another alternative is for the HMO to offer Dr. Green a set amount per patient, regardless of the care each patient ultimately needs. This is called **capitation.** If she enters a capitation agreement, Dr. Green will receive a set amount for each patient she agrees to serve (usually calculated as per patient/per month). From this money she will pay for operating expenses, medical costs, and so on. The advantage is that she receives money whether care is needed or not. The disadvantage is that if the patient requires care that costs more than the payment provided, Dr. Green must provide care anyway, and therefore she loses money.
- *PPO* A **preferred provider organization (PPO)** will offer Dr. Green a different deal. She will continue to practice in her own office and run it as she always has. She may treat patients outside the plan, but she must agree to provide care for PPO members at a discount rate (lower than what she would normally charge). The PPO will not pay Dr. Green a salary or a capitated fee. Instead, it will pay her a discounted fee for each service she provides. The advantages are that Dr. Green is assured a relatively stable patient load and she will continue to remain fairly independent. The disadvantage is that she will probably make less money per service than she would under a fee-for-service agreement. In summary, Dr. Green's payment options look something like this:

Income With Fee-for-Service:
Deductible + Reimbursement (for services provided)

Income With HMO:
Salary or capitated fee (regardless of care provided)

Income With PPO:
Reduce fee for each service provided

From a caregiver's perspective, managed care offers a relatively stable patient load and income. The caregiver may be spared some of the expense of maintaining facilities and staff. But the trade-off is a loss of professional independence and, in some cases, increased financial risk. Capitation is especially risky because providers receive a set fee no matter how much care is needed. (Managed care itself is based on capitation, with members contributing a set amount to the organization each month.)

Organization's Perspective Managed care also affects hospitals, medical centers, treatment and diagnostic centers, and other organizations in the health care industry. These organizations may contract with managed care agencies to provide care for their members and/or offer their own managed care plans.

Box 2.5 Managed Care at a Glance

Managed Care: A health care system in which income, resources, and health services are supervised by a managing body such as a health maintenance organization or preferred provider organization. Patients pay the organization a set fee each month to receive health services.

Health Maintenance Organization (HMO): A managed care organization that offers enrollees a variety of health services for a set monthly fee. Caregivers may receive salaries or capitated fees. They usually provide services only to HMO members.

Preferred Provider Organization (PPO): A managed care organization that pays caregivers a discounted fee for each service they provide to patients enrolled in the organization. Caregivers may provide care in their own offices and may also treat patients not enrolled in the PPO.

Capitation: A set fee paid to cover a person's health needs, regardless of the care actually required.

Either way, their income is increasingly governed by the terms of managed care, with its reliance on discounts and capitated fees.

To illustrate, hospitals used to make more money if the beds were full than if they were empty. More patients meant more income. Now health care professionals must be mindful that the costs of providing care may exceed the money they receive for it. Having all the beds full can be disastrous unless they are managing their resources carefully.

Capitation, discounted fees, DRGs, and other cost-curtailment efforts may be especially hard on nonprofit medical organizations. These organizations are granted tax exemptions in return for their pledge to provide care for needy persons and to reinvest the money they earn in the organization rather than paying owners or stockholders (Bruck, 1996). In short, nonprofit medical organizations are obligated to provide free care to patients who cannot afford to pay and do not have health coverage. This means these organizations must be especially frugal and must stretch the income from paying consumers over a wider area. Even with tax exemptions, limited reimbursements and capitated fees may hit nonprofit organizations especially hard. (For a synopsis of managed care terms see Box 2.5.)

Pros and Cons There is an upside and a downside to managed care. Here are a few considerations both ways.

On the bright side, managed care is designed to make health care more affordable. Even if insurance pays 80% of medical bills, a long-term or serious illness can cost a patient thousands of dollars. Membership in a managed care organization curbs that risk because subscribers pay set fees regardless of their medical needs. These benefits may be especially valuable to people with chronic illnesses who benefit from regular treatment and effective health maintenance (Nussbaum, Ragan, & Whaley, 2003).

Second, by uniting caregivers and sharing resources, managed care may help health care organizations run more efficiently and effectively. Everyone will benefit if resources are used to the fullest (Emanuel & Dubler, 1995). Moreover, physicians relieved of some of the administrative demands of running a medical practice may have more time to spend with patients (Rabinowitz, 2003). (The actual research on this is mixed.)

Third, managed care has an incentive to keep patients well. Organizations make more money if people do not require costly treatments. Patients may benefit if managed care organizations are willing to provide preventive services and information. (As you will soon read, this potential has not been well fulfilled so far.)

Unfortunately, the potential disadvantages of managed care are numerous. A nationwide poll shows that public opinion was favorable toward managed care in 1995, but dissatisfaction has steadily increased since then ("While Managed Care," 2002).

One cause of discontent is the cost. Managed care premiums have risen as much as 20% a year (Marshall, 2003). Managed care organizations say premium hikes are necessary because health expenses are rising and the population is getting older. Analysts charge that managed care organizations could curb spending if they put more effort into preventing widespread health risks such as obesity. "I think that [the rising cost of premiums] is primarily due to the short-sighted nature of many of the for-profit companies," said a managed care executive on an anonymous survey. "The managed care plans don't think it's worthwhile to invest in prevention programs when people change their plans frequently, trying to get lower costs" ("Health Economics," 2003).

Another concern is that, in an effort to save money, managed care organizations may undertreat patients. Journalists have coined the phrase "death by HMO" to refer to instances in which people's health was hurt or destroyed when their managed care organizations refused to authorize expensive treatments. It is a common practice to offer cash incentives to managed care physicians who contain costs, and to withhold a portion of their salaries to be awarded only if the care they provide costs less than a set amount (Eastman, Eastman, & Tolson, 1997). Some people worry that these incentives will interfere with caregivers' professional judgment.

Third, patients in managed care lose some of the ability to choose or switch caregivers. To receive full benefits, they are limited to providers who participate in their care plans, and they may be forced to switch providers if they change employers or if their employers change their managed care affiliations. Such disruptions may compromise the quality of patient–caregiver relationships (Emanuel & Dubler, 1995).

Fourth, medical information becomes less confidential when patient records and caregiving decisions are scrutinized by members of a managed care organization. Some 80% of physicians surveyed said they might divulge sensitive information (such as drug abuse) to other members of a health maintenance organization, even if patients asked them not to tell (Eastman et al., 1997).

Fifth, a great deal of energy in managed care is diverted to paperwork, authorizations, and procedures. Many caregivers say it is nearly impossible to do their jobs well and meet the increased demand for paperwork. Patients are frustrated by the red tape as well. Says one managed care Medicaid patient:

> It's hard to get a doctor who takes Medicaid. They send out a list of doctors who'll see us, but they don't tell you that only a few'll take new patients. Nobody wants Medicaid patients. The doctors hate dealing with us, the insurance is such a pain in the butt. (Gillespie, 2001, p. 109)

Finally, critics are troubled that patients may be kept in the dark about matters that concern their care. For instance, they may be unaware that their doctors are being paid to minimize the cost of their care. Even more worrisome are so-called **gag rules** that prohibit physicians from telling patients about treatment options not covered by the health plans in which they participate (Brody & Bonham, 1997). For example, if the doctor believes a cancer patient might benefit from a certain treatment but the treatment is expensive or not covered by the health plan, the doctor would be disciplined for even mentioning it to the patient. Although the AMA and the federal government have banned the use of gag rules, many suspect they are at least implicitly enforced. About 31% of managed care physicians surveyed say they have avoided mentioning useful medical procedures to patients because those procedures are not covered by the health plan (Wynia, VanGeest, Cummins, & Wilson, 2003). Physicians worry that patients' mistrust is damaging their professional reputations and diminishing how much patients trust their doctors (Gorawara-Bhat, Gallagher, & Levinson, 2003). (To debate the managed care issue yourself, see Box 2.6.)

Implications

Health care is in a state of transition, no doubt both for better and for worse. In an effort to stop spiraling costs, funding agencies have implemented stricter review processes, referral systems, and reimbursement guidelines. The industry has responded to these guidelines by cutting costs and developing new delivery systems such as managed care.

Managed care organizations assume the financial risk of providing patient care. Managed care is useful to the extent that it promotes health and conserves money. However, many people worry that there is a conflict of interest between saving money and providing optimal care.

■ SUMMARY

A historical perspective suggests why patients and caregivers communicate as they do and why they devote themselves to certain topics but not to others.

The ancient Egyptians established a basis for considering health in both spiritual and physical terms. About 2,000 years later, influenced partly by

Box 2.6 ETHICAL CONSIDERATIONS Classroom Debate on Managed Care

Managed care is currently the most controversial issue in health care. You have already been exposed to several viewpoints about it. Some people fear managed care will lessen the quality of medical decisions by limiting what doctors can say and do. Others favor the managed care emphasis on wellness and applaud the effort to cut health care costs. There are other issues, both pro and con. Read up on the managed care debate (a few sources are listed below) and develop your own viewpoint.

Hold a classroom debate. Divide the class into four groups: (a) those in favor of managed care, (b) those who support a return to fee-for-service, (c) those who propose specific alternatives, and (d) those who are undecided. Appoint team captains or have the instructor moderate. One group at a time should present its arguments, with time after each argument for questions and challenges. (Make sure talking time is fairly divided among the participants.)

As the debate progresses, people may change their minds. If so, they should get up and move to the group that best represents their viewpoints.

Suggested Sources

Dean, V. C. (1997). Physician satisfaction reflects changes in health care landscape. *Journal of Family Practice*, *45*, 319–321.

Hall, M. A., & Berenson, R. A. (1998, March 1). Ethical practice in managed care: A dose of realism. *Annals of Internal Medicine, 128,* 395–402.

Holleman, W. L., Holleman, N. C., & Moy, J. G. (1997, February 1). Are ethics and managed care strange bedfellows or a marriage made in heaven? *The Lancet*, *349*, 350–351.

La Puma, J. (1998). *Managed care ethics: Essays on the impact of managed care on traditional medical ethics*. New York: Hatherleigh Press.

Peeno, L. (1998, March 9). What is the value of a voice? *U.S. News & World Report*, *124*, 40–44.

Rodwin, M. A. (1998, March). Conflicts of interest and accountability in managed care: The aging of medical ethics. *Journal of the American Geriatrics Society*, *46*, 338–341.

Shapiro, R. S., Tym, K. A., Eastwood, D., Derse, A. R., & Klein, J. P. (2003). Managed care, doctors, and patients: Focusing on relationships, not rights. *Cambridge Quarterly of Healthcare Ethics*, *12*(3), 300–307.

Ulrich, C. M., Soeken, K. L., & Miller, N. (2003). Ethical conflict associated with managed care: Views of nurse practitioners. *Nursing Research*, *52*(3), 168–175.

Egyptian ideals, Hippocrates of ancient Greece proposed a rational/empirical model for medicine. Within that model, illness was believed to reflect people's physical well-being as well as their harmony with nature and other people. Parts of the Hippocratic Oath continue to influence Western medical ethics.

During the Middle Ages, illness was assumed to be a spiritual matter, to be treated with prayer and holy redemption. Patients' spirituality and behaviors were central to talk between patients and caregivers. In the centuries that followed, a fervor for accuracy and physical proof characterized the European Renaissance. Talk of faith or emotions was treated as inappropriate (even misleading) to scientific analysis. Cartesian dualism strengthened the separation of mental and physical factors. Its basic assumption (which continues to influence medicine) is that patients' thoughts and feelings are largely separate from their physical conditions. A more contextual viewpoint is offered in the kaleidoscope model of health communication.

Today, the United States is renowned for its scientific, high-tech medical system. However, spiraling costs and overutilization have made it necessary to allocate health resources with care. Managed care, which has grown from the need to rein in medical costs, has spawned new concerns about the quality of care Americans will receive from organizations that have a vested interest in saving money.

KEY TERMS

Imhotep
religio-empirical approach
Hippocrates
Hippocratic Oath
rational/empirical approach
medical spiritualism
barber surgeons
Christian magic
fetishes
René Descartes
principle of verification
Cartesian dualism
orthodox practitioners
sectarians
germ theory
Flexner Report
specialization
diagnosis-related groups (DRGs)
managed care organizations
kaleidoscope model of health communication
insurance deductible
insurance premium
co-payment
reimbursement
fee-for-service
health maintenance organization (HMO)
capitation
preferred provider organization (PPO)
gag rules

REVIEW QUESTIONS

1. Why was medicine in Imhotep's time referred to as religio-empirical?
2. How did Hippocrates' ideas about medicine affect the role of physicians and the nature of health communication?
3. How did the medical spiritualism of the Middle Ages affect health communication?
4. For what reasons (spiritual and practical) did the church ban surgery during the Middle Ages?
5. What role does religion play in modern health care?
6. Based on the principle of verification, how do you know if you are ill? Who is better able to know the state of your health, you or a doctor?
7. Do you agree with Cartesian dualism that the mind and body are separate? What effect has dualism had on health care and health communication?
8. How did Hippocrates' ideas influence health care in colonial America?
9. What was women's role in health care in colonial America? What factors led to the rise of orthodox medicine in the United States?
10. Based on the kaleidoscope model of health communication, what factors influence our health? On what five premises is the model based?
11. How have reimbursement restrictions affected the health care industry?
12. How does managed care compare to traditional health insurance from a consumer's perspective? From a care provider's perspective?
13. What are potential advantages and disadvantages of managed care?

CLASS ACTIVITY

Health in the News

Have class members clip or record a news items concerning health care. Discuss the items in class. These questions may help guide the discussion.

1. What ethical questions are presented by the issue?
2. Can you identify the historical roots of the topic you chose? Does it reflect a spiritual approach to illness? A scientific approach? Does Cartesian dualism apply?
3. Does the issue reflect under- or overutilization of medical resources?
4. Do you see evidence of tension between conventional medicine and complementary (sectarian) forms of care?
5. Does the issue involve managed care or other changes in the health care industry?

Part Two

THE ROLES OF PATIENTS AND CAREGIVERS

CHAPTER 3

Patient–Caregiver Communication

Ben noticed a lump in his breast just after his 58th birthday. Embarrassed about the problem, he avoided mentioning it to his wife for several months, thinking it would probably go away on its own. When she learned about it, his wife encouraged, then begged, Ben to see a doctor. In the next few months other family members joined her entreaties. Finally, Ben made a doctor's appointment.

On the day of the appointment the family was anxious to hear what the doctor said. Imagine their surprise when Ben returned and said the visit went "just fine," but he did not tell the doctor about the lump. When the shocked family asked why, Ben shrugged and said, "He didn't ask."

This story illustrates some of the complex factors that affect patient–caregiver communication. Although it may sound foolish not to tell a physician about your health concerns, research suggests that episodes like Ben's occur quite frequently. In a classic study of 800 visits to a pediatric emergency clinic, 26% of the parents said they did *not* tell the doctor what concerned them most (Korsch & Negrete, 1972). Their explanations were similar to Ben's. Most said the doctor did not encourage them or even give them a chance to share the information. Physicians may see the matter differently, wondering why patients seem to play guessing games with them rather than coming straight to the point. Recent evidence suggests that patients and caregivers continue to experience this impasse (Young & Flower, 2002).

This chapter examines what happens during medical transactions—who talks, who listens, and how people behave. Communicating well is important for a number of reasons. Researchers suggest that patient–caregiver communication has an impact on how well patients recover, how they tolerate pain, how much stress they experience (Morse & Proctor, 1998), and whether people follow medical advice (Beckman & Frankel, 1984).

Moreover, doctors are less likely to be sued for malpractice if their patients consider them good communicators—friendly, funny, likable, and open (Boodman, 1997). Doctors who have never been sued are observed to spend more time with patients, use more humor, and solicit patients' participation more often than doctors who have been sued (Levinson, Roter, Mullooly, Dull, & Frankel, 1997).

Because patient–caregiver communication is so important, researchers and others tend to judge it by high standards. As you read about (and experience) patient–caregiver communication, you may be tempted to blame one party or another if the communication seems insensitive or ineffective. One of my students, when asked to sum up health communication literature, declared quite candidly, "What I get is that doctors are mean and patients are dumb." Few people might be so blunt, but experts and students alike are often guilty of similar assumptions.

Resist the urge to draw simplistic conclusions. Keep in mind that patients and caregivers work together to shape their communication patterns. Communication is a transactional process. No one communicates alone, and participants are not completely at liberty to behave as they might wish (Rawlins, 1989, 1992; Watzlawick, Beavin, & Jackson, 1967). Relational or **transactional communication** means that communicators exert mutual influence on each other such that the approach one participant takes suggests how the other might respond. For instance, if a physician acts like a parent, the patient is encouraged to behave in the complementary role of a child (and the other way around). Patients sometimes become frustrated with their caregivers' parent-like behavior, unmindful that they have encouraged it by adopting meek and submissive roles themselves (Pendleton, Schofield, Tate, & Havelock, 1984). Stephen Bochner (1983) urges people not to consider patients and caregivers as adversaries but as "reasonable people of good will, trying to exchange views with other reasonable people of equally good will" (p. 128) in circumstances that are sometimes very challenging.

The chapter is divided into five sections. The first two describe physician-centered and collaborative communication, including communication skill-builders for caregivers. The next two describe environmental restructuring and the impact of telemedicine on patient–caregiver communication. The chapter concludes with communication tips for patients who wish to take an active role in medical encounters.

■ PHYSICIAN-CENTERED COMMUNICATION

Medical transactions in the United States have traditionally utilized **physician-centered communication** in which doctors do most of the talking, choose conversational topics, and begin and end communication episodes. This is also true of nurses to some extent, but most research shows nurses to be more patient centered (Beyers, 1996; Drass, 1988).

The disproportionate power granted to physicians is partly a result of cultural expectations. Westerners tend to regard doctors as scientific experts with the unique ability to understand and treat disease. Consequently, patients may feel unqualified to take an active role in medical encounters.

Medical tradition and medical education also contribute to physician-centered talk. Katz (1984) describes the long-standing belief that physicians should act on their own authority "without consulting their patients about the decisions that need to be made" (p. 2). He observes that, traditionally, doctors felt it was wrong to "confuse" patients with medical details or "burden" them with making medical decisions.

Added to the conviction that doctors know best is the conventional belief that patients will waste time describing irrelevant details unless doctors keep a tight rein on medical interviews. Medical schools have traditionally taught doctors to keep interviews brief and to the point. Doctors tend to assert themselves verbally and nonverbally, ask focused questions, and block discussion of highly emotional topics. In extreme cases, doctors may treat patients as if they are ignorant or childlike.

Assertive Behavior

Physicians often communicate more assertively than patients. In patient interactions studied by Richard Street, Jr., and Bradford Millay (2001), only about 2% of physicians' talk was devoted to partnership building and supportive communication. Patients rarely asserted themselves as active participants. Less than 7% of patients' talking time was devoted to asking questions and assertively conveying their concerns. Patients in the study were more apt to actively participate when physicians encouraged them to do so.

Doctors touch more, pause more, and use more gestures than patients do (Street & Buller, 1987, 1988). It is commonly accepted that doctors can touch patients, even in ways that are typically regarded as intimate, but patients do not have license to touch doctors. As such, intrusions on patients' personal space are permitted, but patients' behavior is highly restricted (Northouse & Northouse, 1985). Although no one would argue that patients should touch doctors in any way they choose, the difference in what doctors and patients are allowed to do points out the asymmetrical nature of patient–caregiver communication.

Doctors' interruptions also display their control over medical encounters. A common occurrence is that a doctor enters the examination room and asks, "What seems to be the problem?" That may seem like an easy question, but try answering it in 18 seconds or less! In 74 doctor's office visits studied by Beckman and Frankel (1984), most patients talked for less than *a third of a minute* before the physician interrupted them and began asking specific questions. (None of the patients who were allowed to keep talking took more than 2 ½ minutes.) Patients tend to perpetuate this cycle by quickly yielding the floor when doctors speak. Frankel (1984) reports that, in 15 out of 16 interruptions he studied, patients did not resume talk they abandoned when their physicians began speaking. A number of studies support that patients yield the floor to their doctors and rarely tell their doctors when they disagree or are dissatisfied with them (Scherz, Edwards, & Kallail, 1995; Street, 1990, 1992).

In a study of 72 patient visits with a family physician, Kandi Walker and colleagues (2002) noted that the patients displayed a general willingness to let the physician guide the encounter, and in various ways the physician conveyed that her understanding of health conditions was superior to the patients' (Walker, Arnold, Miller-Day, & Webb, 2002). For example, when a patient who had had kidney infections before said she recognized the symptoms of a current infection, the physician responded, "Let me take a look. Since I am the doctor here . . ." (Walker et al., p. 52). The patient briefly objected that she was sure of the diagnosis without an exam but then acquiesced and was relatively submissive during the remainder of the medical visit.

Questions and Directives

Doctors use their talking time mostly to ask questions and issue **directives** (instructions or commands). In office visits studied by Candace West (1993), physicians asked 91% of the questions and were less apt to answer questions than patients were. Other studies have shown that physicians ask mostly closed questions such as "Where does it hurt?" and "How long has it been bothering you?" This questioning style offers little opportunity for patients to explain themselves or introduce additional concerns.

Doctors may keep medical conversations focused to save time and prevent patients from rambling. Researchers suggest that patients tend to stammer and stutter, especially when they are afraid the doctor will disapprove of their behavior (du Pré & Beck, 1997). Ironically, these stutters and stammers, which may sound like wasted time, are often signals that something especially important is about to be said. The doctor who too quickly diverts the conversation may lose an important opportunity to learn what is on the patient's mind.

Blocking

Research on nurse–patient communication often refers to **blocking,** a process by which nurses steer talk away from certain subjects. Through topic shifts or questions, nurses are sometimes observed to block complaints or avoid patients' emotional disclosures (Jarrett & Payne, 1995).

Physicians sometimes avoid emotional disclosures as well. They may change the subject when patients hint at emotional concerns (Suchman, Markakis, Beckman, & Frankel, 1997). In one conversation studied by Suchman et al., the patient asked, "You know how you get sorta scared?" and the physician responded, "How long were you on the estrogen?" Traditionally, only about 10% of physicians' speech has been devoted to partnership-building behaviors such as asking for patients' opinions (Roter, Hall, & Katz, 1988).

The contrast between blocking statements and supportive ones is well illustrated by Greene, Adelman, and Majerovitz (1996). They quote dialogue from a medical visit during which an 80-year-old patient said she was "Very nervous. Very nervous" and told the doctor she had recently suffered the sudden death of two friends and watched her husband committed to an intensive care unit. The physician's reply was, "Do you smoke?" (p. 270).

On the flip side, Greene et al. (1996) quote an encounter with a different doctor during which an 84-year-old patient told the doctor she was being pressured to provide care for a mentally ill family member. "They've been putting a lot of pressure on me and it's made me very nervous," the patient said. The physician responded, "Maybe there's a way I can help. Well, I can see [by] what you said that you have a lot of things on your mind. An awful lot of pressure and tension" (p. 273). The doctor wrote a letter that resolved the dilemma, and he received effusive thanks from the patient. Greene and coauthors point out that the doctor in this episode acknowledged the woman's feelings, offered specific assistance, and reassured her that he was concerned.

Patronizing Behavior

Because of physicians' high social status and their extraordinary ability to influence people's lives, patients may be reluctant to protest their actions. It follows that patients of relatively low social status will feel this effect most strongly. The powerlessness of women and minorities in medical situations is well documented and sometimes quite shocking. Studies show that some doctors treat medical conditions differently depending on their opinion (usually stereotypical) of the patient (Fisher, 1984; Paget, 1993; West, 1984, 1993).

Critical theorists such as Alexandra Todd point out ways in which some doctors **patronize** patients (treat them as if they are inferior) by withholding information, speaking down to them, and shrugging off their feelings as childish or inconsequential. Many of these episodes involve **transgressions,** which are episodes in which a doctor or patient acts inappropriately (Farber, Novack, & O'Brien, 1997). For example, Todd (1984) describes an examination she witnessed during which the gynecologist exclaimed, "This is all girl" while examining a patient's breast for lumps. When the patient did not respond, he repeated, "I *said,* this is all girl." After the exam, the physician told the women to "get dressed like a good girl" and he would give her some "happy pills" (birth control pills) (p. 182). (See Box 3.1 for tips on handling transgressions.)

More recently, Christina Beck (Beck, Ragan, & du Pré, 1997) describes her panic and frustration when a doctor refused to take her seriously. Previously diagnosed with a hormone deficiency that had already caused one miscarriage, Beck pleaded with her new doctor to begin hormone replacement therapy at the beginning of her next pregnancy. Calling her "honey" and telling her "don't worry," the doctor declined do so. Within weeks Beck suffered another miscarriage. Writing of the experience, she expresses regret that she, "a normally assertive, intelligent, and well-educated woman," did not take a firmer stand or switch doctors.

Episodes such as these point to the pitfalls of a power inequity between patients and doctors. Although most caregivers do not abuse the power difference, when they do, patients may perceive that they have little recourse.

Box 3.1 Stepping Over the Line

It is sometimes difficult to establish what behaviors are appropriate between a patient and a caregiver. Touch, personal disclosures, and body exposure usually reserved for intimate relationships are often required in medical settings.

Usually both parties recognize the boundary between intimacy (a unique sense of closeness, interdependence, and trust) and detached concern (the effort to understand another person, but with restricted emotional involvement). However, patients and caregivers sometimes cross the line. Farber et al. (1997) call actions that cross the line between intimacy and professionalism *transgressions* (from the Latin phrase meaning "to step across").

Transgressions frequently have painful and confusing results. Feelings of heartache, disappointment, guilt, and loss of reputation may result. Patients, typically in positions of lesser power, may feel violated or forced into behaving against their wishes. Professionals may feel harassed or embarrassed and may face legal action and loss of professional privileges.

Sexual contact is an obvious transgression, but other behavior can be inappropriate as well. Doctors say patients sometimes transgress by demanding more time than the caregiver can afford, asking for money or favors, being overly flirtatious or seductive, giving frequent or expensive gifts, and even by being verbally abusive (Farber et al., 1997). Zook (1997) describes how hospital nurses are sometimes harassed by patients who grab them and make suggestive comments. Caregivers may transgress by making sexual advances, asking unnecessary personal questions, insulting patients, or sharing confidential information with others.

Researchers propose that transgressions may result from patients' vulnerability, their need for assurance, and the trust they place in their caregivers. Caregivers, too, may experience strong feelings (either positive or negative) in relation to patients, feelings that may be heightened by a sense of isolation from family and friends.

Farber et al. (1997) and Zook (1997) suggest these steps for avoiding or terminating transgressions:

- Take stock of personal needs and social expectations that may motivate a transgression (loneliness, need for approval, etc.).
- Establish clear boundaries for touch and talk.
- Be careful not to send ambiguous or mixed messages.
- Seek the counsel of support groups, friends, and colleagues.
- Have others present during transactions.
- Acknowledge transgression attempts and discuss them in a calm way with the other person.
- If inappropriate behavior does not stop, let the other person know you intend to take formal action. If it still does not stop, contact the health care management or the local medical society.

This situation is particularly unfortunate for patients of low socioeconomic status, who may feel the effects of discrimination more than others but may not be at liberty to choose or switch doctors.

Power Difference

To a large extent, caregivers establish how people should and should not behave as patients. Caregivers are typically granted a great deal of influence by virtue of their expertise, their high social status, and their ability to perform important services for people. In this way, they are a powerful socializing force. By contrast, patients have traditionally been rather powerless.

It is true that people do not have to do what the doctor says. But because people have traditionally sought medical care when they are ill or hurt, they may not be in much of a position to argue. Throughout history, patients (who are quite literally weak) have relied on their caregivers to be strong. In the current political climate in which doctors are criticized for being domineering, it is easy to forget that society expected them to be dominant for many generations.

It is important to consider that power is granted to physicians by others. Doctors do not have license to treat patients without their consent, nor can they require them to follow medical advice. They cannot even require patients to show up for exams. However, patients may not perceive that they have much choice in these matters, based on the alternatives.

People usually describe "good patients" as those who do not complain, who follow advice, and who improve as expected (Pettegrew & Turkat, 1986; Taylor, 1982). These expectations imply that good patients are obedient and nonassertive. Cultural expectations, combined with the desire to stay in caregivers' good graces, may be enough to silence patients into the appearance of submission whether they eventually follow doctors' advice or not.

Criticism of Physician-Centeredness

Not everyone is satisfied with physician-centered communication. One reason for the criticism is that social expectations are changing as people become more educated and more actively involved in their own health (Ferguson, 1997). Many people are no longer content answering questions and following doctors' orders. They wish to discuss options and participate in medical decision making.

Second, it is difficult to satisfy patients if they do not make their expectations known. Researchers suggest that doctors are often unable to accurately assess patients' priorities and satisfaction levels. In one study, nurses, receptionists, and technicians understood patients' priorities more clearly than physicians did (O'Connor, Shewchuk, & Carney, 1994). Physicians overestimated patients' concern with technical and environmental aspects of health care, whereas other employees were more likely to perceive that patients' true priorities were the responsiveness and understanding of their caregivers.

Box 3.2 ETHICAL CONSIDERATIONS
Therapeutic Privilege

Although Anna (age 68) is seriously ill, she feels relatively well and her spirits seem high. She often remarks to those around her that she is feeling much better and she is eager to talk of future plans. However, it is obvious to her caregivers and to her family that she will not live more than a few months. The family has asked Anna's physician not to tell her she is dying. They argue that she probably knows she is dying but that her behavior implies a request that people not bring up the issue. They feel that Anna's current happiness is what really matters at this point and they are reluctant to impose bad news upon her, particularly when there is nothing than can be done about it.

Therapeutic privilege is the prerogative sometimes granted physicians to withhold information from patients if they feel that disclosing the information would do more harm than good. For many years doctors withheld information from patients if they thought patients would be unable to understand it or would be distressed by it (Katz, 1984).

Robert Veatch (1991) argues that therapeutic privilege is indefensible because it is counter to the goal of making patients informed partners in their own care. Charles Lund (1995) takes a more moderate view. He asserts that physicians should almost always tell patients the truth, but he warns that blunt honesty is not always the kindest method of disclosure.

In some cultures, people prefer to shield family members from distressing news about their health. In Japan, for example, although people typically want to know the truth about their own health, they often insist that physicians shield family members from distressing diagnoses (Kakai, 2002). Based on cultural ideas about illness and death, they are afraid of destroying their loved one's hope and fearful that talking about adverse outcomes might lead to their occurrence (Kakai, 2002).

What Do You Think?

1. If you were Anna's physician, would you tell her she does not have long to live? Why or why not?
2. If physicians feel certain regimens will help patients, but patients are likely to refuse the treatment if they know everything about

One reason it is difficult to know what patients want is because their expectations differ according to anxiety level, age, education, and familiarity with the caregiver (Street, 1990). The caregiver trying to ascertain the presence and effects of these varied factors may have a difficult time doing so, particularly because patients tend to be nonassertive with doctors.

A third criticism is that physician-dominated communication, although it seems efficient in the short run, is actually counterproductive. Researchers the diagnosis, are the physicians justified in withholding the information?

3. If physicians withhold information, should they go so far as to lie if patients ask outright about their prognosis?
4. How do you respond to the argument that physicians can never be sure about patients' odds of recovery, so it is sometimes better to withhold information that might diminish patients' hopes?
5. What if you were the physician and a patient told you, "If this condition is terminal, don't tell me"? Would you withhold information even if it meant making treatment decisions on the patient's behalf?
6. What if patients do not say, "Don't tell me" outright but their actions seem to suggest that they do not want to know if the news is bad? Would you tell them?
7. Is it ever permissible to give a patient's family information without telling the patient? If so, under what circumstances?
8. If you were the patient, are there any circumstances in which you would wish information to be withheld from you?

Suggested Sources

Gostin, L. O. (1995). Informed consent, cultural sensitivity, and respect for persons. *Journal of the American Medical Association, 274,* 844–845.

Kakai, H. (2002). A double standard in bioethical reasoning for disclosure of advanced cancer diagnosis in Japan. *Health Communication, 14*(3), 361–376.

Katz, J. (1984). *The silent world of doctor and patient.* New York: The Free Press.

Lund, C. C. (1995). The doctor, the patient, and the truth. In J. D. Arras & B. Steinbock (Eds.), *Ethical issues in modern medicine* (pp. 55–57). Mountain View, CA: Mayfield.

Veatch, R. M. (1991). *The patient–physician relation: The patient as partner, Part 2.* Bloomington: Indiana University.

have found that patients who feel they have been belittled or who have been unable to share important information are less likely than others to follow treatment advice. At the same time, doctors who discourage patients from talking may miss important information.

Finally, some people worry that doctors and patients will buy into the dominant–submissive dynamic supported by physician-centered communication. Patients may believe they are helpless and ignorant, and doctors may believe they know what is best, even to the extent of deceiving patients or withholding information (see Box 3.2).

Implications

Researchers conclude that doctors have traditionally been more assertive than patients—talking more, interrupting more, asking more questions, and choosing what topics will be discussed. Sometimes physicians go so far as to make patients feel belittled and helpless. Patients, in turn, are relatively passive and accommodating, at least while they are with their doctors.

Physician-centered communication is consistent with the cultural belief that doctors have superior skills and knowledge. Both patients and caregivers typically consider it the physician's responsibility to create an environment of trust and support (Cegala, McGee, & McNeilis, 1996). This assumption supports the illusion that doctors are solely responsible for what is communicated, although the basic tenets of communication suggest that transactions are mutually managed. All in all, patients probably play a greater role than they realize in establishing the tenor of communication with their caregivers.

Physician-centered communication has come under criticism partly because it is inconsistent with patient empowerment. Research shows that some misunderstandings and dissatisfaction might be avoided if doctors were less assertive—and patients were more forthcoming—in medical interviews. In the next sections, you will learn about a collaborative style of patient–caregiver communication that places patients and caregivers on more equal footing.

COLLABORATIVE COMMUNICATION

Medical communication continues to be predominantly physician centered, but interest has shifted in recent years toward empowering patients. In light of that interest, some practitioners and researchers have begun searching for ways to establish greater equity between patients and their caregivers.

Collaborative communication establishes patients and caregivers as peers who openly discuss health options and make mutually satisfying decisions (Balint & Shelton, 1996; Laine & Davidoff, 1996). Although collaborative communication is consistent with patient empowerment, it is neither entirely patient centered nor caregiver centered. Instead, participants work together as partners. (See Box 3.3 for more about the collaborative interpretation model of health communication.)

This section describes developments in the health industry that make collaborative communication appealing. It also describes communication techniques that may be used to encourage patients' active participation in medical dialogues.

Box 3.3 THEORETICAL FOUNDATIONS
Communication as Collaborative Interpretation

> *Michelle, a 15-year-old caring for her 5-month-old daughter, seeks emergency care for excessive menstrual bleeding. Although Michelle was hospitalized 2 weeks earlier for asthma and suspects that the asthma and her current problem are the result of stress, she does not mention either the hospitalization or stress to her doctors.*

This true story, described by Amanda Young and Linda Flower (2002), illustrates what they call a "rhetoric of passivity" supported by participants' assumption that patients should go along with what caregivers say and do. The medical student caring for Michelle asks leading and close-ended questions that do not encourage her to share her concerns. For her part, Michelle makes only brief replies and is not assertive about sharing her concerns. Consequently, Young and Flower report:

> *Michelle leaves the hospital with a referral to see a gynecologist with no discussion of what she thinks is causing her problem—a list of stressors that would boggle the mind of a middle-class adult, let alone a 15-year-old single mother in the inner city. (p. 82)*

Young and Flower (2002) propose an alternative model of communication based on a "rhetoric of agency" that recognizes patients as coagents in health encounters. Their **model of collaborative interpretation (CI)** proposes that health communication is most effective when patients actualize the roles of decision makers and problem solvers and caregivers function as counselors or friends who work alongside patients to help them achieve shared goals. This rhetorical shift relies on the mutual efforts of everyone involved. It cannot work if patients are unwilling to share their stories and take an active role in health care transactions. Nor will it work if caregivers perpetuate the paternalist notion that they know what is best for patients. With the CI model, patients and caregivers are coagents who establish shared goals and work collaboratively to pursue them.

Importantly, the CI model does not privilege either patients or caregivers. Instead, as Young and Flower (2002) describe it, the goal is "an experience that validates the expertise of both patient and provider and that dignifies the patient's needs" (p. 89). Such a model can be difficult to create, especially since it is a new idea for many people. As a helpful guide, Young and Flower present a list of criteria that define collaborative interpretations. Here are a few criteria on their list:

- Patients and caregivers draw on each other's expertise by asking for details about past experiences with the health concern.

continued

Box 3.3 THEORETICAL FOUNDATIONS
Communication as Collaborative Interpretation, *continued*

- Discussion includes the patient's views about how the health concern influences his or her lifestyle and physical, mental, and emotional health.
- The patient and caregiver explicitly discuss their interpretations of the health concern and the impact it may have on life, work, and relationships.
- Participants openly share their goals and expectations.
- Patients and caregivers develop a mutual sense of control by identifying strategies that are beneficial, practical, and acceptable.

Suggested Sources

Emmanuel, E. J., & Emmanuel, L. L. (1995). Four models of the physician-patient relationship. *Journal of the American Medical Association, 267,* 2221–2226.

Smith, D. H., & Pettegrew, L. S. (1986). Mutual persuasion as a model for doctor-patient communication. *Theoretical Medicine, 7,* 127–146.

Young, A., & Flower, L. (2002). Patients as partners, patients as problem-solvers. *Health Communication, 14*(1), 69–97.

Climate for Change

In an issue of *Health Communication* devoted to "The Patient as a Central Construct," Robert Kaplan (1997, p. 75) forecast a move away from the "find it—fix it" biomedical model to an "outcomes model" that emphasizes long-term quality of life. The goal of the outcomes model is to minimize people's reliance on medicine and maximize the importance of their everyday health and fulfillment.

Significantly, Kaplan's outcome model (and others similar to it) requires a wide-angle focus, extending far beyond organic indications of illness. Diet, exercise, emotional health, attitude, and similar factors become issues of immediate concern. Caregivers such as nutritionists, exercise physiologists, counselors, and others are more prominent partners in patients' health efforts.

As caregivers' roles change, so may patients'. The very term *patient* becomes problematic when the emphasis shifts to everyday well-being. *Patient* connotes a person in ill health who seeks the services of a care provider. Some theorists suggest that the terms *health citizen* or *health decision maker* are preferable because they acknowledge that people are involved in health care all the time—not just when they seek professional assistance (Rimal, Ratzan, Arnston, & Freimuth, 1997).

As health becomes a way of life, not just an occasional excursion to the doctor's office, many people feel it is insensible to treat patients as passive or incidental components of the process. Patricia Geist and Jennifer Dreyer (1993) apply Eisenberg and Goodall's concept of dialogue to medical encounters. A **dialogue** is a conversation in which both people participate fully and equitably, each influencing the encounter in ways that make it a unique creation. When conversational partners engage in dialogue, they do not simply adopt ready-made roles; they create them to suit their own situations and preferences (for more, see Eisenberg & Goodall, 2004). Researchers suggest that patients and caregivers are typically more satisfied with dialogues than with one-sided conversations but they may be afraid dialogues will take too long or that others will not wish to take part in them (Geist & Dreyer, 1993). Those who take the risk may enjoy profound rewards. For example, even people who are highly phobic about dental care respond well when dentists show a genuine interest in them and work hard to earn their trust (Kulich, Berggren, & Hallberg, 2003).

Some patients and caregivers have always maintained collaborative relationships. For the majority, however, communicating in a collaborative way about health is a relatively new idea. Here are several communication techniques that are useful for initiating and maintaining medical dialogues.

Communication Skill Builders: Cultivating Dialogue

Although these techniques may be used by patients or caregivers, the majority of the literature is addressed to caregivers, recognizing, perhaps, that patients are traditionally more likely to follow their caregivers' cues than the other way around.

Nonverbal Encouragement Researchers have noted several nonverbal ways caregivers can encourage patients to take a more active role in medical encounters.

- *Look interested.* Patients respond well when caregivers show interest in what they are saying. In a study of 337 consultants with 15 general practitioners, patients spoke more freely and disclosed more to physicians who looked at them as the patients spoke (Bensing, Kerssens, & van der Pasch, 1995). Gaze was also positively associated with both parties' efforts to reach agreement and the physicians' sensitivity to psychosocial problems.
- *Touch (cautiously).* People may interpret touch in a number of ways. Subjected to physical contact and proximity usually reserved for intimate relationships, some patients may feel defensive or violated (Northouse & Northouse, 1985). Others may regard touch as a sign of comfort or esteem. Nursing home residents perceived nurses who touched a patient's arm to be more affectionate and immediate than other nurses (Moore & Gilbert, 1995).

- *Pay attention to nonverbal displays.* Partly because patients are so nonassertive verbally, physicians may use nonverbal cues to gauge patients' feelings as well as the severity of their symptoms (Pendleton et al., 1984). Patients tend to be more satisfied with physicians who are skillful at understanding body language and are able to display their own emotions nonverbally (DiMatteo, 1979).

Verbal Encouragment The challenge has sometimes been to get patients to open up and share concerns. Suchman and colleagues (1997) lament lost opportunities for caregivers to display emotions, asserting that "the feeling of being understood by another person is intrinsically therapeutic" (p. 678). However, many patients feel inhibited, fearing they will seem inappropriate if they share their feelings with a doctor. Some caregivers have overcome patients' inhibitions using open questions, treating people as equals, encouraging self-disclosure, coaching patients, and using humor. These techniques are discussed next.

- *Use open questions.* Branch and Malik (1993) propose that skillful communicators can address patients' concerns in intense but brief discussions. They observed how five physicians invited patients to expand the scope of medical talk with open questions such as "What else?" By listening attentively, the physicians were able to hear the patients' concerns in 3 to 7 minutes. The patients were satisfied, and the doctors have won accolades as some of Massachusetts's most outstanding general physicians.
- *Don't rush.* Give patients a reasonable amount of time to express their concerns.
- *Avoid abrupt topic shifts.* If you suddenly change the subject patients may wonder if they have offended you or if you have really been listening. To reduce misunderstandings, strive for smooth transitions, such as: "I appreciate your sharing these things; we're going to have to shift gears now and I'll ask you some different types of questions about your symptoms" (suggested by Smith & Hoppe, 1991, p. 464).
- *Determine the real issue* before *the exam.* Keep in mind that patients often work up to their main concerns. Do not launch into a physical exam until you are sure of the main point of the visit. ("Is anything else on your mind today?")
- *Listen for distress markers.* Patients often stutter and stammer when they are working up to an important disclosure. Do not change the subject before you know what it is. Your reassurance will help them speak openly.
- *Ask for the patient's feedback.* Most patients will not interrupt you to let you know they cannot follow your advice. You must ask.
- *Reassure patients.* Keep in mind that patients seek medical attention for many reasons—to be reassured, forgiven, comforted, cured. Words mean

a lot ("You needn't feel embarrassed about this." "It's not your fault." "I understand.")

- *Treat people as equals.* Status differences often inhibit open communication. For example, one family physician studied earns patients' trust (and gratitude) by disclosing some of her own feelings and reassuring patients who seem nervous or unsure (du Pré, 2002; Smith-du Pré & Beck, 1996).
- *Coach patients.* After patients were briefly coached on how to read their medical charts and express their concerns and questions, they were typically more involved in medical interviews and felt they were better able to get the information they wanted (Finney et al., 1990; Greenfield, Kaplan, & Ware, 1985). Greenfield et al. report that coached patients also experienced greater health benefits than others.
- *Consider using humor.* The use of mild, respectful humor seems to be a particularly effective means of minimizing status differences between patients and caregivers (Beck & Ragan, 1992; du Pré, 1998; Ragan, 1990) and helping family caregivers relieve stress (Bethea, Travis, & Pecchioni, 2000). Playful transactions emphasize that the participants have similar feelings, lessening the social distance between them.

For an example of especially pleasing patient–caregiver communication read the mother's story in Box 3.4.

Implications

Collaborative communication between patients and caregivers may further several goals of modern health care, including the desire to treat patients in a holistic way, encourage people to actively maintain their own health, and save money. Theorists speculate that patients will become more active in medical encounters under three conditions: (1) they are well informed about medical matters; (2) they are assertive about asking for information, setting agendas for medical encounters, and participating in medical decisions; and (3) they make rational choices even when that involves *not* following doctor's orders (Brashers, Hass, & Neidig, 1999). John Balint and Wayne Shelton (1996) assert that involved, well-informed patients save the health care system money by maintaining their own health more effectively.

Dialogues allow patients and caregivers to take an active role in communication episodes. Other techniques that encourage participation include gaze, touch, nonverbal sensitivity, open questions, peer-oriented talk, self-disclosure, coaching, and gentle humor.

Keep in mind that terms such as *physician-centered* and *collaborative* communication are merely guideposts. No one is always physician oriented or collaborative, nor would one style be effective in every situation. The most effective communicators are able to adapt and mix different communication strategies to suit different goals and different people.

Box 3.4 PERSPECTIVES
A Mother's Experience at the Dentist

When I first took Kathryn to the dentist she was very apprehensive. She had never been to one before due to lack of dental insurance and money, and she only went to the doctor when she was really sick, which was once every two years or so. Most illnesses we handled at home, and the idea of preventive care was foreign to her. I knew she needed to go. I knew she wasn't brushing as good as she should, and I also knew that sometimes she lied to me about brushing at all. I couldn't watch her every minute.

When I remarried last year, we were finally fortunate enough to have dental insurance, only we found out there was a 1-year waiting period for anything other than cleanings. So I waited.

Finally, the year was up, and in July, I took Kathryn to the dentist for the first time in her life. I tried in advance to make her understand that it was all right to be scared, but that did not mean that it was all right to whine, cry, and generally throw a fit. I told her again and again that I would never take her to anyone I didn't trust or anyone I thought would harm or hurt her unnecessarily.

On a Saturday morning we drove 40 miles to the dental center. Right away, the staff tried to make Kathryn feel at home. The receptionist greeted me and Kathryn by name and asked Kathryn if she was tired from getting up so early on a Saturday. But as I filled out the forms, Kathryn hid behind me, and she spent a lot of time trying to hug me and kiss my cheek. She always does this when she is nervous.

I found I was nervous as well. Not only could I not ease Kathryn's fears, but I found myself feeling like I was a bad parent for not bringing her to the dentist until she was 8. I wasn't sure, as nice as the receptionist was, if she would understand things like no money and no insurance. So we didn't talk about the fact that Kathryn should have been to the dentist years ago, we just talked about easy things like the nice weather and my wedding pictures.

Soon it was time for Kathryn to go back. After taking X-rays the hygienist led us back to an examination room and found me a small stool to sit on so that I could stay in the same room. She was very friendly and made me feel comfortable. She was also nice to Kathryn and didn't put us down for not coming in sooner.

■ ENVIRONMENTAL RESTRUCTURING

People are affected not only by words and gestures but also by elements of their physical environment. Early research shows that environments have a significant influence on health-related communication. Kreps and Thornton (1992) describe the subduing effect of confined spaces (small rooms, low

The cleaning was a little nerve-wracking, since it was a bit uncomfortable, and Kathryn has a wonderful gag reflex. But the hygienist never seemed to get upset, and she even talked to Kathryn as though she understood, asking her questions like, "It's a little scary at first, isn't it?" and "Are you okay? We can wait a minute if you want to, but if we go ahead, we'll be done sooner." It was great that she was so understanding.

By this time, Kathryn was less apprehensive about me leaving the room for a few minutes. The dentist and I walked to the other end of the hall where he explained that Kathryn had a lot of cavities. He recommended a series of four brief appointments to help Kathryn become more at ease as they repaired her teeth. He made me feel at ease, telling me what a pretty girl Kathryn was. Then he got serious and let me know he understood my concerns about not bringing her in sooner, but not to worry. The cavities were not severe, they were all in baby teeth, and although there were several, they would be easy to fix.

I collected Kathryn and stopped by the front desk, where the receptionist pulled out a surprise box and let Kathryn pick out what she wanted. The next visits were not as bad as Kathryn thought they would be. Every time she was a little happier and not so apprehensive about what would happen. Once she had been through the routine, she knew what to expect, and that helped. She said she liked everyone at the dentist's office. Once I brought a newspaper article I had written about Kathryn's school with her picture in it. The staff insisted on reading the whole thing and remarked what a good writer I was and how pretty Kathryn was. They also insisted on seeing my wedding pictures. It wasn't just something to be nice, they really wanted to see them.

I feel good taking Kathryn there because I know, no matter what, we will get the best treatment. Not only that, but we have established friendships with these people that will last. They truly believe they are there to serve, and they show that in everything they do. Just ask Kathryn. She'll tell you.

—*Donna*

ceilings) versus the stimulation of open spaces and windows. du Pré (1998) observes that communication in a doctor's office tends to be quieter and more private than in the open-air arrangement of most physical therapy units, where conversations are often loud and invite participation from anyone in earshot. With the goal of improving communication and emotional well-being, health practitioners and researchers are beginning to examine, and in

Box 3.5 Doorknob Disclosures

The instant intimacy demanded in medical situations is tricky to manage. The physician may wish to get right to the point, but the patient may consider it extremely risky (or even rude) to disclose information in the first few seconds of the conversation. However, delaying disclosures or beating around the bush can waste valuable time, often at the expense of other people.

While studying interactions in a family practice office a few years ago, I noticed that patients often began with small concerns, not their main worries. One woman said initially that she was suffering from a sore throat. Only halfway through the medical visit did she admit that depression was her biggest problem. In fact, she eventually told the doctor she had tried to commit suicide several days earlier. Many other patients blurted out their main concerns just as the physician was leaving the room. These so-called **doorknob disclosures** occur at what seems to be the last instant of the medical visit. The physician in such a situation can postpone the main concern until another time, or as more often happens, launch what is in effect *another* medical interview with the patient. Remember this the next time you curse the physician for keeping you waiting!

many cases reshape, the environments in which patients and caregivers communicate. This section examines efforts to improve communication by altering the physical environment of medical settings.

Mobility and Involvement

Some medical centers are making environmental changes to encourage collaborative care. For instance, a hospital staff may rethink the traditional expectation that all patients should stay quietly in bed.

Many patients are quite lucid, not contagious, and anxious to feel somewhat in control of their circumstances. In recognition of this, medical centers such as Griffin Hospital in Derby, Connecticut, now allow patients to see their medical charts and even add comments of their own (Weisman & Hagland, 1994). **Co-authoring,** as this practice is called, places patients in a central position, no longer excluded from details of their own health or forbidden to comment on it an official way. Patients capable of doing so may also manage their own medication in the hospital, getting prescriptions from an on-site pharmacy and taking them as recommended.

Although it was long assumed that patients would only be frightened or baffled by medical details, they are now being encouraged to learn about their own health and treatment. Reference libraries are open to patients and their families in some medical centers, and some hospitals now routinely hold admit conferences during which the patient, family members, and key caregivers discuss expectations and procedures ("Feeling Comfortable," 1995). These changes alter the traditional expectation that patients are merely passive recipients in the health care process.

Soothing Surroundings

For the most part, medical settings have been characterized as intimidating and sterile. The quarters are usually cramped and the furnishings austere. Some medical centers have begun to change the atmosphere, however. The idea is that environments that soothe and uplift can reduce stress (thus reducing pain), keep people's spirits up, and facilitate better communication.

The effort to restructure medical environments is led most notably by **Planetree,** a nonprofit organization designed to help medical centers establish pleasing and empowering surroundings. Planetree was founded in California in 1978 by Angelica Thieriot, who was dismayed by how "cold, impersonal and lonely" she found U.S. hospitals compared to those of her native Argentina (Schwade, 1994, paragraph 23). (Planetree is named after the type of tree under which Hippocrates is said to have mentored medical students.)

Hospitals influenced by the Planetree model often offer hotel-style rooms with accommodations for overnight visitors. Patients are encouraged to wear their own clothing, and soothing colors and adjustable lighting help reduce the cold sterility common to clinical settings (Voelker, 1994). Rooms are equipped with thermostats so patients can control the temperature. Treatment rooms are often designed so patients can gaze at colored glass or soothing displays as they undergo procedures.

Large windows are another Planetree feature, allowing access to sunlight and a view of plants, flowers, and fountains. At some hospitals "healing gardens" provide living displays of plants honored through the centuries for their curative properties (complete with labels describing the significance of each).

The Bergan Mercy Medical Center in Omaha, Nebraska, has adopted the Planetree model to "humanize and demystify" its emergency services department (Lumsdon, 1996). An administrator remembers that the caregiving staff was initially indignant when it was proposed that they institute patient-centered care. They felt they were already patient centered. But soon, says the administrator, they became excited about ideas they had never considered before. Now the hospital staff keeps clinical equipment in handy closets (not out in the open) whenever possible, plays Disney movies to soothe frightened children, and uses dimmer switches to adjust room lighting. The hospital received only 2 patient complaints the year after changes were implemented compared to 37 the year before (Lumsdon, 1996). (See Box 3.6 for more about Planetree.)

Box 3.6 RESOURCES
More About the Planetree Model

- Frampton, S., Gilpin, L., & Charmel, P. (Eds.) (2003). *Putting patients first: Designing and practicing patient-centered care.* San Francisco: Jossey-Bass.
- Gearon, C. J. (2002). Planetree (25 years older). *Hospitals & Health Networks, 76*(10), 40–43.
- Planetree website: www.planetree.org

Implications

The environment sometimes says as much as words do about a health experience. Patients' input is encouraged by recent efforts to allow hospital patients to move around, visit the in-house library, get and take their own medication, and add comments to their medical records. In addition, the Planetree philosophy that people are more relaxed in the presence of sunlight, living plants, and soothing colors may have a significant impact on the way people behave in those settings.

Early evidence suggests that patients in specially designed healing environments require less pain medication, go home sooner, voice fewer complaints, and are generally more satisfied. Morale is also higher among staff members.

Sometimes people in different environments communicate long-distance about health issues. The following section describes how telemedicine is influencing patient–caregiver communication.

COMMUNICATION TECHNOLOGY: TELEMEDICINE

From her living room a physician looks in on patients in the hospital. They are able to see each other and converse through two-way interactive television. A small keyboard allows the doctor to check her e-mail messages, review patient charts, order prescriptions, examine diagnostic information, and read the latest research. This is not science fiction. It is David Bates and Anthony Komaroff's (1996) vision of telemedicine in the not-so-distant future.

The technology is already available to make Bates and Komaroff's vision come true. **Telemedicine** is the process of communicating across distances for health-related purposes. (*Tele* is Greek for *far.*) It may involve the use of telephones, pagers, computers, facsimile (fax) machines, electronic mail, voice mail, Internet links, interactive video, and more.

A good example of telemedicine is the program at East Carolina University (ECU) School of Medicine. In the early 1990s, the ECU staff began offering long-distance medical consultations to inmates at Central Prison, 100 miles from campus (Whitten, Sypher, & Patterson, 2000). The patients and caregivers interact via a teleconference link that allows them to see and talk to each other. Medical personnel at the university and prison work together to conduct exams and discuss medical information. Digital cameras and digital stethoscopes transmit detailed information to the off-site physician. Since beginning the program, ECU has expanded it to serve people in rural communities where specialists are not available.

As with all telemedicine programs, there are advantages and disadvantages to the ECU program. Communication scholars have long been aware that messages may be interpreted differently depending on how they are conveyed. Communication is affected by response time, the amount of nonverbal information that is conveyed, and how comfortable people feel with each other and with their means of communication. Here are some advantages and disadvantages of telemedicine.

Advantages to Consumers

Many people are optimistic that telemedicine will conserve money and resources. Communication technology offers a number of benefits to patients, especially those who do not live near major medical centers.

First, technology may enable patients and caregivers to communicate more often and more openly, which may improve the quality of care. Balas et al. (1997) found that callers to professionally staffed health information hotlines typically reported better health outcomes and fewer visits to the hospital than others. Likewise, patients whose caregivers keep in touch with them via telephone are more apt to follow through with treatment regimens and to schedule recommended exams. Patients may also be willing to disclose information via long-distance technology (particularly through e-mail) that they would be uncomfortable sharing face-to-face (Baur, 2000).

Second, technology may allow people in underserved communities access to the types of doctors and technology usually reserved for big city dwellers. Doctors, particularly specialists, are disproportionately located in densely populated areas and are relatively scarce in rural ones. With telemedicine a person could conceivably contact a health professional anywhere in the world by phone, e-mail, voice mail, or computer (Woottin, 1996). Participants in the ECU program report that telemedicine has made medical care available to people who would not otherwise have access to it.

Third, better care can mean less expense. Telemedicine reduces the need for each small town to have its own set of medical specialists. Patients in smaller markets can stay close to home rather than transferring to major medical centers. Plus, easier access may mean identifying and treating illness before it becomes severe and more costly to treat (Whitten et al., 2000).

Fourth, patients may become better educated about health matters through long-distance consultations and access to computer databases. The online Medline database, updated daily by the National Library of Medicine, provides information from more than 12 million journal articles.

Finally, people may enjoy therapeutic support via long-distance communication with others. Computer users can converse electronically with health professionals and laypeople who share their concerns (Galinsky, Schopler, & Abell, 1997). We will talk more about virtual communities in Chapter 7.

Advantages for Caregivers

Caregivers may benefit from telemedicine as well. First, being able to communicate with patients and colleagues in other locations reduces travel time and the demands on office space and staff.

Second, vital information can be transmitted from one location to another instantly or with only a brief delay, amplifying opportunities for immediate response and medical teamwork (Harrison, Clayton, & Wallace, 1996). A cardiologist, for example, can monitor a patient's heart activity and direct paramedics' efforts even before the patient arrives at the hospital. Sixty-four percent of the caregivers in the ECU study say they have learned valuable skills and information while participating in exams with other doctors and specialists (Whitten et al., 2000).

Third, diagnostic images and patient records can be electronically stored and quickly retrieved, even by people in different locations (Chamberlain, 1994). Caregivers may be able to access the medical charts of patients they are seeing for the first time. This could save time in emergencies and allow different caregivers to coordinate their care more effectively.

Disadvantages

With so many advantages it may seem puzzling that telemedicine is not more prevalent. Although the technology continues to improve, much of it has been available for years.

One reason for the slow beginning is cost. Technology is expensive and quickly outdated. Even staff members at ECU wonder what will happen when their start-up grant expires (Whitten et al., 2000). "When the grant money is done, if we haven't done our homework right, the whole system will collapse," says a physician at ECU. "If we have done our homework right, it will fit right into managed care" (Whitten et al., p. 121).

A second concern involves scheduling. Nearly half of the ECU participants studied said it is a hassle to schedule two teams of medical caregivers (one onsite and one remote) to take part in telemedicine consultations (Whitten et al., 2000).

A third reservation concerns privacy. Some people worry about electronic eavesdropping and the possibility that hackers (computer enthusiasts) could gain access to confidential patient records. To restrict access, medical networks now rely on encryption (secret coding) and electronic "firewalls" designed to stop unauthorized users from reaching confidential data banks (Pasternack, 1997).

Fourth, it is unclear how caregivers can or should be compensated for services rendered long-distance. Should they charge for phone conversations, e-mail correspondence, and the like? If so, how should those rates compare to the cost of face-to-face visits? Reservations about this issue, and the fear of being inundated by patient messages and questions, may make some caregivers leery of opening up new lines of communication.

Fifth, it is still unclear how medical licensing and malpractice laws (both of which are governed by individual states) will apply to medical care that spans state lines (Parednia & Allen, 1995).

Sixth, greater use of technology may widen the gap between the well served and the underserved. The cost and complexity of technology suggest that it will proliferate in the households of well-educated and affluent people first, increasing access to those already known to use health resources, and systematically excluding underprivileged individuals.

Finally, some worry that telemedicine will become a less effective substitute for face-to-face communication. No one expects (or even wants) telemedicine to entirely replace face-to-face medical visits. Still, the limits of technology may restrict what patients and caregivers are able to convey to each other (Baur, 2000). Some worry that medical decisions will be made on the basis of incomplete or misleading information. Chamberlain (1994) cautions that high-tech methods cannot make up for poor communication: "No amount of technology is going to compensate for an ill-conceived or ill-designed message. The buck stops there . . . with the communicator" (paragraph 4).

Implications

With telemedicine patients and caregivers can communicate through more channels than ever before. New technology has the potential to quicken responses and encourage medical teamwork, keep patients and caregivers well informed, conserve medical resources, and reduce costs (at least in the long run). As Street (2003) points out, communication technology such as e-mail offers simultaneous benefits and drawbacks. People have greater access to caregivers, even those who are far away, but they lose some of the immediacy and feedback of face-to-face interaction. There is little doubt that telemedicine will become increasingly prevalent. Issues remain to be resolved, however, concerning the cost of technological investments, scheduling challenges, confidentiality, legal issues, professional compensation, patient access, and communication quality.

Box 3.7 RESOURCES
Health Communication Journals

Here is information on the leading journals in health communication.

- *Health Communication*, edited by Teresa Thompson, PhD, of the University of Dayton, has been published since 1989. It presents up-to-date research about a broad range of health communication topics. For more about the journal, visit the website at www.erlbaum.com/journaltitles.htm
- *Journal of Health Communication*, edited by Scott D. Ratzan, MD, MPA, specializes in coverage of domestic and international issues relevant to health. Visit the website at www.tandf.co.uk/journals/titles/10810730.html

Following are some tips for improving patient–caregiver communication whether the participants are in the same location or not.

COMMUNICATION SKILL BUILDERS: TIPS FOR PATIENTS

This chapter looks at health communication from many angles, from the traditional to the futuristic. But the bottom line is that patients and caregivers cannot succeed—in communicating or healing—without mutual effort. Earlier in the chapter, we reviewed ways caregivers can stimulate collaborative communication. Here are a few suggestions for patients:

- *Write it down.* Write down your main concerns and questions as well as any medications you take and any dates that may be important to the diagnosis.
- *Think it through.* Assess your emotions and physical sensations in advance. Rehearse how to state your goals for the interview in a concise and straightforward way (preferably within 1 minute).
- *Prepare for the standard questions.* Be ready with answers to such questions as What does it feel like? When? Where? For how long?
- *State your goals.* Be as clear as possible when making the appointment so the caregiver knows your concerns and expectations. ("I'm experiencing sharp abdominal pains" or "I'd like an overall physical and a chance to ask some questions.")
- *Talk to the nurse.* Odds are you will speak with a nurse before you speak with the doctor. Let the nurse know your concerns. He or she can help facilitate your visit.

- *Get to the point.* Use the first minute of a medical interview to suggest what you would most like to cover.
- *Acknowledge reservations.* If something prevents you from speaking frankly with a caregiver, let that person know ("I'm embarrassed," "I'm afraid," etc.).
- *Be assertive.* When dissatisfied, few patients express negative assessments in front of their doctors (Korsch & Negrete, 1981). If your questions have not been answered or you do not agree with the advice given, state your feelings in a clear and respectful way. Walking away dissatisfied helps no one.
- *Be succinct.* Caregivers have a legitimate need to keep transactions within reasonable time frames.

SUMMARY

The traditional power difference between patients and physicians is manifested in conversations in which patients tend to acquiesce and physicians to dominate. Most studies show that doctors do the majority of the talking and ask most of the questions (questions that stipulate brief responses). Unwittingly or not, patients collaborate in the lopsided nature of these medical conversations by speaking hesitantly and abandoning topics when interrupted.

Some caregivers, far from being anxious to abuse the power granted them, are frustrated by the barriers it creates. They attempt to empower patients through the use of encouraging words and nonverbal gestures, humor, and more comfortable medical settings.

Recognizing that environmental constraints have an effect on the way people communicate, some medical centers are restructuring their health care units. In some cases patients are allowed to visit the pharmacy, do research in the library, and review their own records. Amenities inspired by the Planetree model make health care settings more pleasant in an effort to improve the way people feel and behave.

Technology expands the options and the challenges for health communication. Patients and caregivers may have access to more information and more means of message transmission than ever before, but the rules and expectations for telemedicine are still forming.

No matter what the medium or setting, communication between patients and caregivers is most effective when both sides are sensitive to each others' goals. For their part, patients can strive to communicate more clearly and assertively. Caregivers can show that they are sensitive to the challenges patients face in communicating about issues that are personal, fearful, and uncertain.

KEY TERMS

transactional communication
physician-centered communication
directives
blocking
patronize
transgressions
therapeutic privilege
collaborative communication
model of collaborative interpretation
dialogue
doorknob disclosures
co-authoring (medical records)
Planetree
telemedicine

REVIEW QUESTIONS

1. What factors contribute to the prevalence of physician-centered communication?
2. Traditionally, physicians have had more control over medical conversations than patients. How do physicians' communication behaviors contribute to this power imbalance? How do patients' behaviors contribute to it?
3. Why might patients and caregivers commit transgressions? What are some methods for handling transgression attempts?
4. What are some reasons for the power difference between patients and caregivers?
5. In your opinion, should doctors and patients work toward greater equity in medical conversations? If so, what could patients do? What could caregivers do?
6. Why is physician-centered communication criticized?
7. What is therapeutic privilege? What guidelines would you suggest for using this privilege?
8. Contrast a "rhetoric of passivity" with a "rhetoric of agency."
9. Based on the model of collaborative interpretation, describe effective patient–caregiver communication. What criteria define collaborative interpretation?
10. Do you feel the term *patient* is accurate when describing well people seeking to maintain their own health? Brainstorm some other terms we might use.
11. Compare the assumptions of physician-centered and collaborative communication. How is the caregiver's role different in each model? How is the patient's role different?
12. How can caregivers use nonverbal communication to encourage patients' communication?
13. How can caregivers use verbal communication to encourage patients' communication?

14. How could patients and caregivers lessen the likelihood of doorknob disclosures?
15. How are some health centers restructuring their environments?
16. In your experience, does the physical environment affect patient–caregiver communication? Why or why not? If so, how?
17. What advantages does telemedicine offer to consumers? To caregivers?
18. What are the potential disadvantages of telemedicine?
19. Would you communicate with professional caregivers via e-mail given the chance? Why or why not?
20. Would you communicate with professional caregivers via two-way interactive television? In what ways might your communication be different than if you were in the same room?
21. What are some tips for better communication on the part of patients?

CLASS ACTIVITY

Redesigning the Doctor's Office or Hospital

Imagine you have the opportunity to redesign a doctor's office or hospital to be more patient friendly. At the same time you can change the staff's routines. What would you do? Consider these questions:

- What would patients see when they walked in the door?
- To whom would they speak first?
- Would there be a receptionist area? A waiting room? If so, what would these areas look like?
- Can you improve on the take-a-magazine-and-wait routine?
- Do colors, windows, carpets, and lighting matter?
- Would you change the color of examination rooms, treatment rooms, or patients' rooms?
- Would you change the way doctors, nurses, receptionists (or others) act? How?
- What changes might put patients more at ease?
- What changes might increase caregiver satisfaction?

CHAPTER 4

Caregiver Perspective

I was asked to see Mrs. B, who had just been diagnosed with pancreatic cancer. . . . Her husband asked numerous questions about the toxicity of the treatment regimen and about difficult quality-of-life issues. I answered his questions, then turned to Mrs. B and asked for her thoughts and feelings. To my surprise, she was engrossed in filing her fingernails and watching television. When she saw me looking at her, she said, "I'm sorry. I wasn't listening to your conversation. What did you say?" (Urba, 1998, paragraph 13)

After feeling surprised by the woman's conduct, physician Susan Urba (1998) realized what was happening. The patient was overwhelmed by the information, unable to listen any more. "She was too polite to ask us to leave, so she protected herself the only way she could. With her fingernail file and remote control" (Urba, 1998, paragraph 14). In this encounter and others like it, Urba says she has learned a valuable lesson, reflected in the title of the article, "Sometimes the Best Thing I Do Is Listen." Urba reflects that "the most important healing is done by the patient, and the physician can only have a small role in that process" (last paragraph).

Dr. Urba's experiences bring to mind the privileges and pressures of working every day with human life. This chapter looks at medicine from the caregivers' perspective. Understanding the way caregivers are socialized and the demands and rewards of caregiving provides insight into why caregivers communicate as they do.

The chapter is divided into five sections. The first three describe medical socialization, professional influences on caregivers, and psychological influences on caregivers. As you learn more about the way caregivers are trained and the immense pressures they experience, the communication patterns described in Chapter 3 are more understandable. Although caregivers may wish to give more time and attention to each patient, many factors make that hard to accomplish. The fourth section focuses on stress and burnout among caregivers and reveals the important role communication plays in keeping caregivers healthy. The last section explores a high-tech process called knowledge coupling that may change the way patients and caregivers communicate.

As you read this chapter and the next one on the patients' perspective, remember that, although it is a useful device to examine one perspective at a time, health communication is ultimately shaped by the way diverse perspectives come together. No one perspective explains the entire process.

MEDICAL SOCIALIZATION

Becoming a caregiver is not strictly a matter of acquiring technical expertise. It is also a process of **socialization** (learning to behave appropriately within a specific community).

By entry into their chosen fields, most health care professionals are expected to be proficient in what Harvard University medical professor Elliot Mishler (1984) calls the **Voice of Medicine.** As the vocabulary of traditional biomedicine, this voice is characterized by carefully controlled compassion and a concern for accuracy and expediency.

The Voice of Medicine does not provide caregivers with much of a vehicle for sharing their emotions or soliciting emotional responses. Instead, it is characterized by medical terminology and attention to physical details. For the most part, patients' individuality is treated as less important than their physical conditions. However impersonal it may sound, the Voice of Medicine answers to the extraordinary demands of time and emotion exacted from caregivers and suits society's image of caregivers (physicians especially) as stoically objective and in control. Let's look at the socializing forces in caregiver education, particularly in medical school.

Theory of Socialization

A person is said be socialized when he or she can behave with relative ease and appropriateness within a community. But the socialization process is never complete. People and communities change, requiring constant adaptation, and there is no such thing as being perfectly appropriate. (Ironically, it is inappropriate to always be appropriate. People are expected to be unique and break the rules sometimes.)

Communication theorists (i.e., Miller & Jablin, 1991) posit that newcomers to a culture attempt to fit in (assimilate) while still maintaining a sense of their own individuality. They learn what is expected of them (including when to misbehave) through official rules and informal conversations. They also witness, and are subject to, rewards and penalties. Rewards may take the form of raises, awards, promotions, friendly behavior, popularity, and so on. However, violators may be regarded as weak, stupid, crazy, or rude, and may even be expelled from the community.

As you will see, medical students who do not measure up to expectations may fail or be judged negatively. This may seem a particularly dreadful possibility considering how much they have invested emotionally and financially. Considering these factors, students may go to unusual extremes to meet community standards. (See Box 4.1 for a theoretical look at "talking like a doctor" versus "talking like a student.")

A **speech community** refers to a group whose members share a common set of expectations (Hymes, 1962). Even within one neighborhood, there may be several speech communities with varying degrees of overlap.

Box 4.1 THEORETICAL FOUNDATIONS
Talking Like a Doctor

"Being" a doctor is more than using medical jargon and wearing a white lab coat. A large part of professional socialization is learning to talk as doctors talk. Lorelei Lingard and coauthors (2003) studied medical faculty and third-year medical students at a hospital in Canada (Lingard, Garwood, Schryer, & Spafford, 2003). They found that different communication patterns were associated with "thinking as a Student" versus "thinking as a Doctor." These differences were evident in the way students and doctors conducted themselves during **case presentations,** episodes in which health care professionals meet to share information and evaluate the progress of their patients. The communication patterns the researchers observed present theoretical implications about the way doctors are socialized and how communication shapes their identities and attitudes.

Students Versus Doctors

Although students in clinical practice function much like doctors, that is not their only concern. They must also take care to prove themselves and to fit in. Therefore it is no surprise that they dread seeming incompetent or unprepared. One student in Lingard and colleagues' (2003) study said, "To point out things you don't know is sort of shooting yourself in the back" (paragraph 33).

The students employed a range of face-saving strategies when faced with uncertainty. For example, when a doctor asked them questions they could not answer or challenged decisions they had made, the students typically attempted to (a) emphasize information they *did* know rather than dwell on what they did not know, (b) ask their instructors to provide assistance or suggestions, or (c) deflect criticism by using disclaimers, apologies, and explanations. Lingard et al. (2003) conclude, "For the most part, students in our study approached uncertainty as a condition to be avoided at all costs and, when not avoidable, to be disguised" (paragraph 27).

By contrast, the physicians seemed comfortable acknowledging the uncertainties of medical care. Perhaps because they could admit uncertainty without losing credibility, the doctors spoke openly about the imprecise art of making diagnoses and prognoses. They challenged students to defend their actions and judgments, perhaps to test and develop the students' confidence. However, in larger discussions the same physicians admitted that even experienced professionals often disagree and that scientific evidence is fallible. In short, the physicians communicated in ways that showed them to be both more confident and more tolerant of uncertainty than the students.

Another difference emerged in the students' response to information supplied by patients and their loved ones. The students typically accepted this information as valid and accurate. For example, one student defended a medical judgment by saying, "Well, the mom being an MD gave me some terms I took at face value" (Lingard et al., 2003, paragraph 39). In the doctor's eyes, however, even a medical degree did not give the mother unquestionable credibility, as evidenced in his response, "well Mom may not know" (paragraph 39). In other instances as well, the physicians displayed skepticism about what their patients told them.

Assimilation

Students' communication patterns are understandable considering the tenuous position in which they find themselves. As Lingard and colleagues (2003) note: "Students are balancing on the threshold of a profession, with one foot inside and one foot outside its activities" (paragraph 23). In that context, owning up to limited knowledge is a risky enterprise. Furthermore, the new students may not be confident (or jaded) enough to question the credibility of physicians or clients.

The students' communication changed, however, as they became more experienced members of the medical community. Their talk began to sound more like doctors' in four ways (Lingard et al., 2003):

- They learned to sound confident even, sometimes, when they did not feel confident.
- They begin qualifying information conveyed by nonmedical sources (e.g., "The parents claim . . . ").
- They filtered information and presented their interpretations rather than simply relaying what they have seen and heard.
- They began acknowledging greater levels of uncertainty without losing confidence (e.g., saying "I don't know" without a disclaimer).

In short, as students gained experience they began to speak more like doctors. But perhaps more importantly, they began to think and act differently as well. Lingard et al. (2003) reflect that the students had not conquered uncertainty; they had just become more confident in the midst of it. And the students did not just *say* they were more skeptical of patients' accounts. They based their actions on that skepticism. Changes in their communication were matched by changes in their behavior.

As with any form of assimilation, accepting a new identity involves both gains and losses. Explore your reactions to this study by answering the following questions.

continued

Box 4.1 THEORETICAL FOUNDATIONS
Talking Like a Doctor, *continued*

What Do You Think?

1. What are the implications if doctors adopt more confident communication styles? How might this influence their chance of success? How might it influence their interactions with patients? How might their nonphysician colleagues be affected? (Try to think of positive and negative effects within each type of relationship.)
2. In what ways is it advantageous for doctors to be skeptical about what patients tell them? In what ways is it disadvantageous?
3. What are some strategies you might use for managing the immense uncertainties surrounding a person's health status and care?

Suggested Sources

Lingard, L., Garwood, K., Schryer, C., & Spafford, M. (2003). "Talking the talk." School and workplace genre tension in clerkship case presentations. *Medical Education, 37*(7), 612–620.

Ogawa, T., Taguchi, N., & Sasahara, H. (2003). Assessing communication skills for medical interviews in a postgraduate clinical training course at Hiroshima University Dental Hospital. *European Journal of Dental Education, 7*(2), 60–65.

The distinction between speech communities and geographical communities helps explain why patients and caregivers may seem to have divergent expectations although they transact so frequently. They may live and work in close proximity but be part of different communities by virtue of their expectations. Based on the notion of speech communities, keep a few ideas in mind as you read the following description of medical socialization. First, no two communities are exactly alike; medical schools differ as well. The generalizations given here do not apply equally to all programs. Second, people are active agents in the process. Therefore, even people in the same community may be affected differently. Third, community standards may seem unfair or unreasonable to outsiders, but they usually have a rational basis within the community.

Selection

An important part of medical socialization is selecting who gets to take part. Those whose abilities and ideals are inconsistent with the caregiver community may be systematically excluded from it, for better or worse.

Entrance requirements may be as simple as a high school diploma for medical aides and nontechnical assistants. Technicians (such as radiology techs) may be required to have specialized training, serve apprenticeships, and be licensed. Other positions may require college degrees or even postgraduate education.

High rank is usually associated with greater focus on science and technology, such that medical school applicants are evaluated mostly on the merits of their scientific knowledge (Bryan, 1991). Few people question the value of biology and physiology, but some people feel medical schools should be equally concerned about the ethics and social skills of prospective doctors.

Sanford Brown (1995) contends that, far from encouraging social skills, the medical school process actually *inhibits* social development. The pressure to be scientifically competitive discourages premedical students from pursuing a broader education in courses such as philosophy, art, and history. Individuals who are highly driven to succeed are apt to do well in medical school, but they may be impatient and domineering in dealing with others. Moreover, the rigors of medical school further inhibit students from developing life experience, social interactions, and personal growth. Ironically, Brown argues, these are probably as important as science to doctors' personal well-being and success with patients.

Curriculum

Largely as a result of medical school reform in the early 1900s (covered in Chapter 2), science is the core of most caregiver education programs today. Except for nursing programs, very little attention is given to communication and relationship building (Bryan, 1991).

Nursing Nursing schools, which got their start in the United States about the time medical schools were becoming more science based, place considerable emphasis on such subjects as pathology (the study of diseases), epidemiology (occurrence and distribution of diseases), and pharmacology (drug therapy). However, they have traditionally operated from a more patient-centered and biopsychosocial philosophy than physician-education programs (Drass, 1988). Nursing schools typically offer courses in communication, family life, social issues, and public health. As future nurses, students are encouraged to preserve patients' sense of self and help them resume normal and independent lives (Robertson, 1996).

Dentistry Dentists, like medical doctors, are primarily trained to deal with physical ailments. Although 80% of dentists surveyed felt they were well trained to treat and diagnose physical conditions, only about half (52%) rated their communication training in dental school to be good or excellent (DiMatteo, McBride, Shugars, & O'Neil, 1995).

Diverse Caregivers Training programs for other types of caregivers offer varied (but usually minimal) amounts of communication instruction. As you might expect, at the high end are social work and psychology programs; at the low end, technician training. Diverse therapists (i.e., respiratory, physical, occupational, speech) usually fall in the middle, but few training programs offer extensive instruction on patient–caregiver relationships. Moreover, little attention has been given to receptionists and other personnel who typically receive no training as caregivers but transact with patients in frequent and influential ways.

Physicians The medical school curriculum is extensively invested in scientific knowledge. Lectures and laboratory experience focus on physiology, anatomy, biochemistry, microbiology, pathology, and immunology. Most people support the notion that doctors should be knowledgeable about science. The more troubling issues are whether the science curriculum is dehumanizing and whether science is taught in a useful way.

Critics such as Alan Bonsteel (1997) maintain that "cold, clinical physicians" result from medical education that concentrates on science but neglects interpersonal communication, social issues, and ethics. In traditional medical schools, students learn about the human body mostly by using cadavers rather than living individuals. This process is valued as a means of educating students and toughening them up. Cadavers provide valuable opportunities for exploring the human body. But Bonsteel argues that an overreliance on cadavers encourages medical students to regard the body as an inanimate object. There is no need to communicate with a cadaver, treat it gently, or wonder about its feelings. Bonsteel urges medical schools to stop portraying people as impersonal "biological systems" and to treat them as individuals with feelings and emotions.

Other critics charge that science is not taught effectively within the traditional medical school curriculum. Traditionally, medical students have been required to learn massive amounts of scientific material in their first 2 years. Pressed for time, students may memorize the information without understanding it, a process called **rote learning** (Regan-Smith et al., 1994). These students may do well on multiple-choice exams but be incapable of applying the information to actual situations. Among students in traditional medical curricula, about half (49%) said they did not understand the scientific information they learned for tests (Regan-Smith et al., 1994). One student said that studying science was like memorizing a chant "yet not comprehending a word of it" (paragraph 7).

Another criticism of the traditional medical school curriculum is that textbook science is taught in the first 2 years followed by 2 years of clinical experience. A study by the Robert Wood Johnson Foundation recommends that science and clinical experience be integrated through all 4 years of medical school (Marston, 1992). This would mean less pressure to cram textbook information into 2 years and more opportunities to understand scientific

Box 4.2 RESOURCES
More on Communication Training for Caregivers

- Gadacz, T. R. (2003). A changing culture in interpersonal and communication skills. *The American Surgeon, 69*(6), 453–458.
- Kagawa, S. M., & Kassim-Lakha, S. (2003). A strategy to reduce cross-cultural miscommunciation and increase the likelihood of improving health outcomes. *Journal of the Association of American Medical Colleges, 78*(6), 577–587.
- Ogawa, T., Taguchi, N., & Sasahara, H. (2003). Assessing communication skills for medical interviews in a postgraduate clinical training course at Hiroshima University Dental Hospital. *European Journal of Dental Education, 7*(2), 60–65.
- Winchester, T. A. (2003). Teaching communication skills to nursing home certified nursing assistants. *Geriatric Nursing, 24*(3), 178–181.

information within the context of actual patient care. The report also encourages medical schools to add more social, ethical, and psychological information to their curricula.

One promising means of reform is the implementation of **problem-based learning (PBL).** Problem-based learning challenges students to apply information to actual scenarios, rather than simply memorize it. For instance, students may be presented with a case study and asked to analyze the patient's condition and identify factors relevant to the patient's health. Regan-Smith and associates (1994) found that only 6% of students in PBL curricula learned by rote.

Another useful technique is videotaped role playing. Students conduct interviews with mock patients, practicing their responses to realistic symptoms and emotional concerns these "patients" present. Usually, students review the videotapes with communication specialists and the mock patients involved. (For additional information on communication training for caregivers, see Box 4.2.)

Socialization Process

When students complete their fourth year of medical school, they officially become medical doctors (MDs) or doctors of osteopathy (DOs). But in most cases (depending on their state of residence and medical specialty), they will not be licensed to practice medicine until they then complete a 1-year internship and 2 to 7 years of medical residency. Thus, people who enter medical school at age 22 cannot expect to begin licensed medical practice until they are at least 29. In the intervening years, they are surrounded by information and issues foreign to most people. It is no surprise that most doctors are said to leave medical school with a significantly different perspective than when they began.

Medical school has been called the "longest rite of passage in the Western world" (Bonsteel, 1997, paragraph 3). Few other experiences are so extensive and life altering. The intensity, uniqueness, and isolation of medical education make it an especially hospitable arena for socialization. In the next section we will examine some of the ways the medical culture is established in medical school.

Loss of Identity Medical school has been compared to military boot camp in that newcomers are apt to feel stripped of their previous identity and doubtful about their self-worth. Like the military, medical school has a strict hierarchy, and those at the lowest levels are reminded in many ways of their lowly status.

The phrase "medical student abuse" appears frequently in published literature. Henry Silver and Anita Glicken (1990) define **abuse** as negative acts or words unnecessarily harmful, injurious, harsh, or insulting. Tales are told of medical students being cursed, slapped, kicked, punished, and worse. One student told of having his knuckles struck until they bled while trying to master the techniques of suturing.

Statistics suggest harsh treatment is widespread. Of third-year medical students surveyed, 85% reported they had been yelled at or shouted at in humiliating ways during their training, and 73% had been reprimanded with curse words (Sheehan, Sheehan, White, Leibowitz, & Baldwin, 1990). Nearly one fourth (23%) had been threatened with physical harm (most often by hostile patients), and 16% had been physically attacked (in equal numbers by faculty, residents and interns, and patients). Similar results are echoed in many studies.

Medical students performing clinical duties are subservient to higher ranking interns and residents, who are themselves subservient to practicing physicians. Those of lower rank are reminded of their place with public pop quizzes in which personnel of higher status can publicly challenge them to answer medical questions or make diagnoses (Sheehan et al., 1990). Novices are also called upon to do **scut work,** menial chores no one else wants to do. It is commonly accepted that some of these chores are assigned mainly to punish or humiliate the novices, who are referred to in derogatory terms such as "scut monkeys" (Sheehan et al.). However, even as they are being cast as peons within the system, medical school students are induced to see themselves as superior to those *outside* it.

Privileged Status Doctors in the United States are typically granted extraordinary power, prestige, and money. In addition, they witness marvels and horrors unknown to most people.

To be granted access to wonders seldom witnessed can be a rewarding experience. Perri Klass, who published her medical school memoirs in a book called *A Not Entirely Benign Procedure* (1987), recalls a heady sense of wonder dissecting cadavers, reflecting that she was doing something "normal people never do" (p. 37). Klass compared the sensation to initiation into a priesthood.

Others remember the elation of being addressed as doctor for the first time. This usually occurs during clinicals, when students are less than halfway through medical school. Although they are years away from medical licensing, they are called "doctor" by most patients, who tend to view them as bona fide professionals. In this way, students get an early dose of the prestige, but also the formidable responsibilities, that go with the title.

Overwhelming Responsibilities Medical school is often overwhelming in terms of the amount of work and its critical nature. Nearly half (44%) of medical students surveyed felt they had been placed in dangerous situations (such as drawing blood from AIDS patients) before they were adequately trained to do so (Sheehan et al., 1990). The expectation that students will expeditiously move from observers to participants is reflected in the clinical battle cry, "Watch one, do one, teach one" (Conrad, 1988, p. 326). Learning on the job can be a frightening experience when human lives (including your own) are at stake.

Heated competition in the high-pressure environment of medical school sometimes leads people to desperate actions. About 39% of medical students surveyed say they have witnessed classmates cheating, and 66.5% have heard about cheating (Baldwin, Daugherty, Rowley, & Schwarz, 1996).

Sleep deprivation is also common. Bonsteel (1997) reports that residents are often required to work 36-hour shifts and may log 90 to 120 work hours in a week. Sleep deprivation typically causes irritability and interferes with people's ability to make decisions, remember details, and solve problems (Lamberg, 1996; Olson & Ambrogetti, 1998). These deficits can lead to deadly mistakes in medical settings. In one survey 97% of medical students said they had provided substandard care as a result of sleep deprivation (Sheehan et al., 1990). However, socialized to regard sleep deprivation as a normal part of medical training, 68% of the same students felt it was an "unfortunate but necessary" part of their education.

Withdrawal and Resentment Confronted by overwhelming demands, it is not surprising that medical students often begin to regard patients as enemies. Phillip Reilly, author of *To Do No Harm* (1987), remembers the extreme exhaustion during his residency that led him to resent the neediness of a comatose patient: "He was an enemy, part of the plot to deprive me of sleep. If he died, I could sleep for another hour. If he lived, I would be up all night" (p. 226).

Persuaded by the curriculum (and often by mentors) that disease is best understood in physical terms, it becomes acceptable to depersonalize patients. Who would *not* find it more manageable to think in terms of "the kidney transplant in Room 406" than of the kindly woman whose daughter is weeping at her bedside? Focusing on specific, organic concerns is more familiar and less emotionally exhausting than thinking in terms of unique individuals.

Effects of Socialization

It is natural to feel somewhat incensed by the traditionally harsh customs of medical school, particularly from an outside perspective. By the standards of many other speech communities, treatment described as "medical student abuse" would be considered unconscionable. Indeed, efforts are underway at some universities to curtail the number of hours required of students, interns, and residents. However, the conditions described here are still common.

Whether justified or not, medical school customs endure partly because they serve several functions. First, the high-pressure environment may prepare students for the actual demands of medical practice. Medicine requires great patience, endurance, and emotional control (Knight, 1981). Students put to the test early may be better prepared to handle immense pressure later.

Second, a clearly established chain of command may help medical teams make decisions and carry them out. Emergencies are handled most efficiently with decisive leadership, and centralized decision making reduces the likelihood that caregivers' efforts will be disorganized and uncoordinated (Knight, 1981).

Third, the hardships of medical school may strengthen group membership. Shared activities help shape members' attitudes and unite them in common experience. The result is often an enduring sense of camaraderie.

Fourth, medical school may indeed serve as a long **rite of passage** (a challenge that qualifies one for advancement). Medical students may feel an extraordinary sense of accomplishment as they qualify for higher rank by surviving the harsh years as an initiate (Conrad, 1988). They may feel more entitled to the privileges of medical practice than they did upon entering medical school.

Medical School Reform

Reform efforts are underway in some schools to broaden the scope of caregiver education. Most medical schools now require some training in psychological and social aspects of illness (Laine & Davidoff, 1996), and some schools are expanding their curricula to include communication skills training, management and business, end-of-life care, and ethics.

An innovative program at Harvard Medical School requires students to participate in a 3-year course on doctor–patient relationships (Branch et al., 1991). The program is designed to create "humanistic physicians" who appreciate social and psychological aspects of illness and embody ethics, warmth, and sensitivity. The course makes use of small-group discussions to help students explore their own feelings and philosophies and work together to develop their communication skills. Additionally, some schools now pair medical students with trained mock patients who give the students feedback about their bedside manner (Mangan, 1996).

New rules are also being drafted to limit the hours medical interns and residents are on duty. The National Accreditation Council for Graduate Medical Education has decreed that interns should work no more than 80 hours per week for no more than 4 weeks without a day off (Cooney, 2003). This is still a grueling schedule, and schools are not forced to comply. However, medical schools who require interns to work up to 100 hours per week, as in the past, may not qualify for accreditation in the future.

Professionals have mixed reactions to reform efforts. One medical professor I know asserts that working around the clock is important because it allows interns to see how patients' conditions change over time. He argues that clocking in and out will give interns naïve, snapshot images of illnesses. By contrast, some professionals applaud reform efforts. Both sides agree that curricular and clinical reforms will not be easy. Many medical systems rely on staffing by interns, and the medical curriculum is already immense. At some point, experts say, it may be necessary to choose between more instruction in science and more instruction in people skills. Many find that a hard call to make.

Implications

Today's caregiver education programs are primarily science based. Students usually spend a small proportion of their time actually studying how and why people communicate as they do. However, they are continually engaged in activities that model how communication is to be done.

The intense and isolating nature of medical studies reinforces the "realities" within the system and largely insulates students from people outside it. Medical students may perceive an important distinction between insiders, who have experienced medical school, and outsiders, who have not. Doctors may come to identify with each other more than they identify with their patients. Nursing, while science based, devotes a larger percentage of instruction to establishing relationships with patients and understanding their lifeworld concerns.

Several implications may be derived from the medical school experience. First, it implies that admission to the medical arena is not to be granted lightly. Medical schools pride themselves on admitting an elite portion of applicants, and once admitted, testing their endurance in many ways before authenticating them as doctors. Second, the experience implies that physicians' authority is unquestionable and subordinates should comply with it. Third, it implies that doctors should be stoic and self-sacrificing.

These assumptions may profoundly affect doctors' communication with others. For instance, applying the hierarchy of medical school to professional encounters, doctors may regard the people around them as subordinates. Thus, doctors may be especially sensitive to questions and comments that seem to challenge their authority. This assumption sometimes leads patients and co-workers to label doctors as arrogant and bossy. It is more likely, however, that doctors are simply acting according to assumptions instilled in medical school.

Nevertheless, people who expect to be treated as peers may take offense at doctors' attitudes. Others may be intimidated into silence (Ely, Levinson, Elder, Mainous, & Vinson, 1995). When people always defer to physicians' judgment, there is room for avoidable errors, and heavy responsibility is placed on doctors' shoulders.

Doctors may also push themselves to extremes that hurt them personally and damage their relationships. Based on the arduous demands of medical school, physicians may feel they should work long hours and stifle personal emotions and discomfort (Haug, 1996). Anything less may seem weak or inappropriate. However, such a schedule can quickly lead to burnout and loss of family and social interaction. With excessive work and minimal opportunities to relax or vent emotions, physicians may be in worse shape than their patients. When patients' suffering is (or seems to be) less severe than the physicians', doctors may conclude that patients are weak and overly demanding.

Of course schools differ, as do people's reactions. Moreover, some medical schools are implementing reforms to increase students' awareness of psychological and social factors and to reduce the overwhelming demands of scientific and clinical training.

PROFESSIONAL INFLUENCES ON CAREGIVERS

Once they join the ranks of medical professionals, today's caregivers are influenced by a range of factors, including time constraints, competition, and limits on professional autonomy. Overshadowing it all is managed care, which may either aggravate professional tensions or soothe them.

Time Constraints

Caregivers are often very busy, and expediency may be the only alternative to turning away patients in need. Time is in short supply. Even adding a few minutes to each patient visit soon adds up. Consider that a doctor who spends 15 minutes with each patient can see 32 patients in an 8-hour day. If the doctor adds just 5 minutes to each visit, however, the number of patients drops to 24 per day. In one month, the doctor will be about 172 patients behind. In one year, 2,064 fewer patients can be seen *by that doctor alone.* Figures like these are used by doctors who insist they must get right to the point if they are to see all the patients requiring treatment.

Caregivers who are employed by hospitals and medical centers face time constraints as well as they try to keep up with a myriad of patient needs and unpredictable caseloads. Short-staffing and emergencies sometimes make it necessary to work long hours under stressful conditions.

Time constraints may affect the amount and type of information patients and caregivers share. Pressed for time, caregivers may seem rushed and impatient. Although it is tempting to blame the caregivers for this less-than-hospitable demeanor, researchers have found that caregivers do not like time constraints any more than patients do. Doctors rate themselves more satisfied when they have adequate time to talk to patients (Probst, Greenhouse, & Selassie, 1997).

Research indicates that physicians worried about time constraints often limit talk to specific physical indicators (Ben-Sira, 1990). Doctors may reason that people have numerous sources of emotional support—friends, family members, clergy, counselors, and others—but physicians are the only ones qualified to diagnose physical conditions and prescribe treatments. Doctors may devote the brief time available to the physical concerns they are uniquely qualified to assess and treat.

Interestingly, although they may consider the biomedical approach a means of saving time, physicians are typically not satisfied with interviews that focus on strictly biological indicators. Most doctors studied preferred to cover a range of topics and have patients take an active role in medical interviews (Lepper, Martin, & DiMatteo, 1995; Roter et al., 1997). Doctors' dissatisfaction may reflect evidence that strictly biomedical visits seemed to accomplish fewer goals, led to more follow-up visits, and resulted in poorer health outcomes (Roter et al.).

On the bright side, discussing emotional concerns may not be as time consuming as it seems. A range of studies suggests that patients' emotional concerns can often be addressed in a brief amount of time (Branch & Malik, 1993; du Pré, 2002; Smith & Hoppe, 1991). An extensive study of medical visits revealed that biomedical visits took about 20.5 minutes each, whereas biopsychosocial visits took about 19.3 minutes (Roter et al., 1997).

Competition

As the health industry looks for ways to save money, some caregivers fear for their jobs. Independent fee-for-service practitioners, especially, are finding it more difficult to compete with large health agencies.

Competition may have positive or negative effects on patient–caregiver communication. One possibility is that caregivers will become especially concerned with patient satisfaction, hoping to maintain a loyal clientele. That might bode well for patient–caregiver relationships. However, another possibility is that caregivers may be so anxious that they communicate less effectively and resent it when patients switch doctors or question their judgment.

Loss of Autonomy

Loss of autonomy is an issue with managed care and fiscal reform. **Professional autonomy** means caregivers work independently, making decisions without much supervision. Traditionally, physicians have had considerable autonomy, and other caregivers such as nurses, pharmacists, and therapists have had limited input about treatment decisions. With managed care, even doctors are likely to have supervisors, and their decisions are subject to administrative review and financial oversight.

Research suggests that about two thirds of doctors feel they have lost autonomy in recent years, mostly as a result of managed care ("Public, Physicians," 1996). The loss of autonomy may explain, in part, why HMO doctors are typically less satisfied with their jobs than physicians who work on a fee-for-service basis (Schulz, Scheckler, Moberg, & Johnson, 1997). Specialists are particularly sensitive to the effects of managed care since they must rely on referrals from primary care physicians.

Caregivers may also feel constrained by economic pressures. They must answer, not only to their employers, but also to funding agencies and patients who have strong (but often conflicting) interests in medical decisions.

Health communication may suffer if doctors become discouraged by institutional demands. An Israeli study suggests that salaried physicians (like those employed by hospitals and some HMOs) are more apathetic than others. Salaried physicians surveyed were less likely than other doctors to instigate talk about patients' lives and emotions (Ben-Sira, 1990). The physicians said their outlook would turn around if the organizations for which they worked allowed them adequate time for patient visits, reduced administrative demands, and gave them more authority to make decisions about patient care.

Changing government regulations also influence the way that caregivers practice, adding additional layers of oversight. See Box 4.3 for information about the impact of new privacy regulations.

A loss of autonomy is not necessarily bad. Some feel caregivers will perform better with closer oversight. Moreover, some caregivers welcome the fellowship and teamwork possible with HMOs. Studies show that many primary care physicians (Schulz et al., 1997), pharmacists (Muirhead, 1994), nurse practitioners, physician assistants, and counselors (Freeborn & Hooker, 1995) appreciate the camaraderie, working hours, and professional support of managed care settings.

Some people are optimistic that caregivers and managed care organizations will work out a pleasing compromise between professional authority and financial considerations. Val Dean, a physician and managed care executive, asserts in a (1997) editorial that HMOs are becoming more sensitive to doctors' concerns at the same time doctors are becoming more comfortable with group practice. Sharing administrative responsibilities and patient care is a prospect that appeals to some doctors, Dean says, especially new doctors, who may not expect the same autonomy as doctors did in the past.

Implications

The way caregivers communicate is, in part, a reflection of professional pressures. Patients may be quick to assume that caregivers do not want to spend time with them, when caregivers may have little say in the matter themselves. Indeed, time constraints seem to bother doctors as well as patients.

Increased competition can create stress among caregivers of all types. Although doctors may prefer to remain independent, competition with managed care organizations may leave them little choice but to take part. It remains to be seen if professional competition will improve or damage patient–caregiver relationships.

Professional autonomy is typically lessened by participation in managed care organizations. Doctors accustomed to making their own decisions may be required to follow new guidelines, cut spending, and justify their actions. The added scrutiny may add to job stress at the same time it diminishes loneliness.

PSYCHOLOGICAL INFLUENCES ON CAREGIVERS

Medicine is an emotional minefield, and research suggests caregivers are woefully ill prepared for it. As a result, they may act in ways that puzzle or wound others, even as they are themselves reeling under the pressure. Caregivers' thoughts and feelings, although invisible to most patients, help explain why caregivers communicate and cope as they do. In this section you will learn how caregivers are affected by emotional maturity, self-doubt, and satisfaction.

Maturity

Medical schools have been criticized for allowing students little time to develop and mature as individuals. The intense workload can isolate students from the normal activities and emotional development of young adulthood. As a result, say Wayne Weston and Mack Lipkin, Jr. (1989), many students progress through medical school "in the throes of delayed adolescent turmoil" (p. 46).

Patients look to caregivers not only for technical advice but also for wisdom and understanding. However, young doctors may have less everyday life experience than the patients who turn to them for guidance. As Weston and Lipkin (1989) put it, a physician "may know precise drug treatment but stand empty-handed and mute before the patient who desperately needs counsel and support" (p. 45).

Doctors may avoid emotional matters or offer stiff platitudes (such as "I'm sure it will all be fine"). Patients are likely to sense doctors' insincerity and feel their concerns have been brushed aside as unimportant. Seldom do patients realize that doctors may not *know* how to respond, having never experienced or been prepared for the situation at hand.

Caregivers may have emotional "hot buttons." When one of these sore spots is touched, the emotional response can surprise the doctor and the patient, although neither may understand it (Novack et al., 1997). For example,

Box 4.3 ETHICAL CONSIDERATIONS
Privacy Regulations Incite Controversy

In recent years people have been outraged to learn that health care providers have sold or carelessly leaked their "confidential" medical information to others. For example, a Florida state worker was able to download the names of people diagnosed with AIDS (Barnard, 2003). Companies including Eli Lilly pharmaceuticals and CVS Pharmacy have been charged with selling the names of patients on Prozac and other drugs (Ho, 2002; "Medical Records," 2001). The problem has grown since the advent of computer databases that make it easy to transmit medical data that was once stored only in doctors' filing cabinets (Conan, 2002).

New federal regulations about patient privacy went into effect in 2003. The Health Insurance Portability and Accountability Act, better known as HIPAA, provides patients increased access to their own medical records and regulates who else may see them. The new regulations—which present a number of implications for health communication—have provoked a good deal of controversy.

One area of controversy involves the mandate to inform patients of privacy regulations. HIPAA requires health care providers to give every client a written copy of the organization's privacy policies. As a consumer, you have probably encountered this in the form of *HIPAA Alert* or *Patient Privacy* statements that doctors, health plans, dentists, and others ask you to sign. On the surface, this seems like a positive measure. Patients are informed up front about the measures being taken to protect their privacy and their right to file a grievance if the rules are not upheld. However, the process is less than perfect.

For one thing, the forms can be lengthy and difficult to understand, especially for people with limited reading skills. Compounding this is the implied or explicit demand that patients sign the forms whether they understand them or not. According to the U.S. Department of Health and Human Services, it is not necessary for patients to sign this form to receive care or services (Health Privacy Project, 2003). However, based on confusion about HIPAA standards (the act is about 400 pages long) and fear of incurring costly fines for noncompliance, a number of health care providers have refused to treat patients who do not sign the privacy notices.

The most serious complaint about the privacy notices is that they do not give patients a choice about how their medical information will be used. Early on, legislators envisioned the forms as consent letters. Patients could say yes or no to receiving information about the latest drugs or treatment options associated with their medical needs. For example, if you are on a drug commonly used to treat AIDS, you might appreciate receiving updates and promotional information about related drugs. However, you might feel that putting such information in the mail is a violation of your privacy. Says one physician, "When my postman knows what diseases my wife has, that's not appropriate" (Barnard, 2003, paragraph 19). Others worry that, if these mailing lists are in circulation, the information will be used to unfairly discriminate against them. One man, who mistakenly receives information meant for people with hepatitis C, wonders:

> *What happens now with—my wife and I are going to be refinancing our house, and what if somehow the erroneous information that I have hepatitis C finds its way from an insurance company or a pharmacy, a manufacturer, something like that, into someone's financial database and they say, "Well, jeez, we don't want to lend money to someone who has hepatitis C?" (Conan, 2002, transcript p. 7)*

Under HIPAA regulations, health care providers cannot sell their mailing lists to others. However, they can accept money to send information to patients themselves as long as the information is health related. Either way, the information is in the mail. Janlori Goldman, director of the Health Privacy Project, says: "They don't have to tell the customer they're doing it, and they don't have to give the customer the chance to opt out" (Goldman quoted by Conan, 2002, transcript p. 6).

There is not room to outline all the provisions of HIPAA or to describe the pros and cons of each, but here are a few of the mandates:

- Health care clients must be assured of confidential environments.
- Health care clients around the country now have the right to see their medical records and suggest changes. (This right was already guaranteed in some states.)
- People who feel their medical privacy has been violated can now register a complaint with the U.S. Department of Health and Human Services. Some people feel this regulation should have included the provision for patients to sue for breaches of confidentiality. That right is not guaranteed under HIPAA.
- HIPAA requires that health care providers adopt a standardized set of codes, train staff about privacy regulations, and appoint a staff member to oversee implementation of HIPAA. The benefits are that medical information will be easier to share and compare and privacy will be a top agenda item. The drawback is that the transition

continued

Box 4.3 ETHICAL CONSIDERATIONS
Privacy Regulations Incite Controversy, *continued*

is costly and time intensive. Some medical professionals say the regulations allow even less time for patient care in already short-staffed medical units.

What Do You Think?

1. Have you been asked to sign HIPAA Alerts? Did you understand the information provided? Did you feel you had to sign?
2. Under what circumstances, if any, would you like to receive health-related information through the mail? Do you feel it is important that people have an opportunity to opt out of such mailing lists?
3. Have you ever felt that you had to discuss confidential medical information within earshot of others (e.g., at a pharmacy counter or during a medical visit)? Do you feel this is a serious problem? If so, what would you do to fix it?
4. Some people feel the private environment regulations are too strict. For example, an orthodontist who previously encouraged patients and families to move throughout the clinic and get to know staff members issued an HIPAA Alert saying, "We must now regretfully restrict all patients and friends to the reception seating areas only." What is your opinion of this?
5. How far do you think the federal government should go to enforce privacy regulations? Do you agree with adding additional staff members, more paperwork, and oversight committees? Would you suggest other or additional measures?

Suggested Sources

Barnard, A. (2003, January 22). Doctors brace for changes on patient privacy. *Boston Globe,* National/Foreign, p. A1.

Conan, N. (2002, April 12). Medical privacy. National Public Radio's Talk of the Nation. Retrieved online August 31, 2003, from LexisNexis.

Health Privacy Project. (2003). Myths and facts about the HIPAA privacy rule. U.S. Department of Health and Human Services. Retrieved online August 31, 2003, from www.healthprivacy.org

Ho, D. (2002, January 18). Eli Lilly settles charges of violating the privacy of Prozac patients. Associated Press, Business News. Retrieved online August 31, 2003, from LexisNexis.

Medical records; the growing threat to patient privacy. (2001, November 28). *San Diego Union-Tribune,* p. B-8.

Caregivers want many of the same things patients do. Doctors studied were most satisfied when they did not feel rushed, when they felt knowledgeable, and when they felt they had communicated well (Probst et al., 1997). Like patients, caregivers are discouraged by the loss of long-term patient–caregiver relationships. Doctors often feel betrayed or cheated when patients switch doctors. (Ironically, at the same time patients cry that doctors should not make decisions based strictly on costs, patients themselves are now likely to switch doctors based on that very consideration.) Physicians interviewed by Geist and Dreyer (1993) said they were gratified by patients who remained with them even when less expensive medical plans were offered to them.

Nurses are most satisfied when they have a reasonable workload and feel a sense of personal satisfaction (Robertson, 1996). Because nurses tend to be more involved than doctors with patients' everyday functioning, they are often more frustrated with minor setbacks and patient idiosyncrasies (Robertson, 1996). Nurses are also sensitive to issues of autonomy and respect. Many report feeling dissatisfied because doctors or supervisors do not give their opinions much credence (Bucknall & Thomas, 1996; Smith, Droppleman, & Thomas, 1996).

Implications

Many behaviors that seem to indicate caregivers are indifferent may actually stem from factors related to emotional maturity, self-doubt, and satisfaction. Medical school often deprives students of family, personal, and social time. Shielded from life experience of this sort, physicians may have a difficult time understanding their patients or reacting to them with patience and wisdom. Sometimes a gruff demeanor hides a caregiver's feelings of uncertainty and self-doubt.

Doctors' satisfaction seems to hinge on the amount of time they have, patients' input, and a sense of accomplishment. Nurses' satisfaction is linked with rewarding patient contact and the sense that their ideas are valued by others.

STRESS AND BURNOUT

Health care is emotionally demanding, as evidenced by high substance abuse and suicide rates among professional caregivers. Doctors, psychologists, and pharmacists are more likely to commit suicide than members of any other profession (Pincus, 1995). The suicide rate for doctors is nearly three times the national average (Jahn, 1997), and they suffer from higher-than-average rates of drug abuse and eating disorders (Bonsteel, 1997). When medical professionals abuse drugs, it may be difficult for co-workers to know what to do. (See Box 4.5 for a true story about one staff member's response to a physician's substance abuse.) Nurses are also prime candidates for burnout, as you will see in this section, which focuses on stress and burnout among health professionals.

Box 4.5 PERSPECTIVES
Blowing the Whistle on an Impaired Physician

As manager of a small community clinic, having to identify an impaired physician was not on my agenda. Clinic operations were going smoothly and patients seemed to like the clinic and the physician, Dr. Havard (not his real name). I knew things about Dr. Havard, such as his turbulent relationship with his ex-wife and his constant financial difficulties. However, he seemed to be a caring and sensitive doctor. Several months into his employment at the clinic, I started noticing strange behavioral changes in Dr. Havard, such as being chronically late for work and his inability to account for missing narcotic samples.

I thought Dr. Havard's actions were suspicious, but did not know they were signs of an impending problem until I received a phone call from a representative of an Internet pharmaceutical company. The woman on the other end of the phone explained to me that large quantities of a prescription narcotic had been ordered for the clinic. I explained to her that the physician does not dispense narcotics on the premises because of the potential of robbery. After several similar phone calls from various companies, I approached Dr. Havard with the information. He said, "It's all a mistake. I'll take care of it."

I knew that he was not going to resolve the situation, and the phone calls become more frequent, demanding payment in excess of $20,000. I notified the clinic administrator, whose office is in a neighboring city. When I originally reported the problem, the administrator told me to "watch and listen." A week later, while working in my office, I received a phone call from a local pharmacist, who explained to me that a clinic patient presented a prescription for the same narcotic with authorization for three refills from Dr. Havard. She called because she knew it was rare for Dr. Havard to write prescriptions for such a large quantity of narcotics. When I asked for a description of the patient, she

Stress refers to physical and psychological responses to overwhelming stimuli. Stress is considered a major cause of burnout among caregivers, but other factors (like boredom and feeling unappreciated) also contribute.

Burnout is actually a combination of factors. In her 1982 book *Burnout: The Cost of Caring,* Christina Maslach describes burnout as emotional exhaustion, depersonalization, and a reduced sense of personal accomplishment. In Maslach's words, **emotional exhaustion** is the feeling of being "drained and used up" (p. 3). People experiencing emotional exhaustion feel they can no longer summon motivation or compassion. **Depersonalization** is the tendency to treat people in an unfeeling, impersonal way. From this perspective, people may seem contemptible and weak, and the individual experiencing burnout may resent their requests. A **reduced sense of personal accomplishment**

described Dr. Havard to a "T." After my initial shock, I called the administrator back and explained the situation. The next day, the administrator confronted Dr. Havard and asked if he had written the prescription. He denied it and said he didn't know who the patient was. I was given the "go ahead" to treat the prescription as stolen and contact the Sheriff's Department.

Soon after the incident, Dr. Havard was drug tested and suspended from employment because he tested positive for narcotics and could not produce a legitimate prescription. When sheriff's deputies caught up with him, he confessed to writing the prescription for a "relative." He was offered assistance through the state's impaired practitioners' program. The program offers confidential counseling and assistance, and the chance to resume practice.

I felt that I was ruining Dr. Havard's career by turning him in. However, I had an ethical and moral obligation to report him to his superiors to protect his patients.

—*Denise*

What Do You Think?

1. If you discovered your doctor was abusing narcotics would it change your opinion of him or her?
2. Do you believe patients should be informed if their doctor is found to have a drug addiction, or should this information be kept confidential? Why?
3. Would you want the doctor to undergo counseling and have a second chance to practice medicine? Why or why not?

involves feeling like a failure. People who feel this way may become depressed, experience low self-esteem, and leave their jobs or avoid certain tasks.

Causes

There are several common causes of stress among health care employees. As you will see, stress is a major cause of burnout, but it is not the only cause.

Conflict Stress can result from many factors, including competing and ambiguous demands. Nurses report feeling stressed when they must work holidays or weekends or when their efforts are frequently interrupted by phone calls and various demands (Ray, 1983). Nurses also report a high degree of stress when they are required to carry out treatment decisions they believe to be inappropriate or harmful to patients (Albrecht & Halsey, 1991). These situations place caregivers in a **doublebind,** meaning there are negative consequences no matter which option they choose. Employees who must choose between family time and work are apt to feel a loss either way. Likewise, nurses who believe their actions are hurting patients' health are likely to feel badly, but they may be reprimanded or lose their jobs if they do not carry out orders. (This topic is covered more fully in the discussion of organizational conflict in Chapter 9.)

Emotions Intense emotions can cause stress and lead to emotional exhaustion. Although caregivers work in an emotionally charged atmosphere, they are expected to remain calm most of the time (Pincus, 1995). It can be difficult to be caring and compassionate yet keep personal emotions in check. Caregivers often develop what Lief and Fox (1963) call **detached concern,** a sense of caring about other people without becoming emotionally involved in the process. Some degree of detachment is useful to keep from feeling overwhelmed. However, the expectation that health professionals will squelch or avoid their own emotions may lead them to become apathetic, cynical, or confused about their feelings (Novack et al., 1997).

Ironically, the very qualities that make people seek careers in health care may make them especially prone to burnout. The **empathic communication model of burnout** proposed by Katherine Miller and associates suggests that health care is appealing to people who are concerned about others and are able to imagine other people's joy and pain (Miller, Birkholt, Scott, & Stage, 1995; Miller, Stiff, & Ellis, 1988). These people are typically responsive communicators (able to communicate well with people in distress), but they may easily feel overwhelmed by constant exposure to emotional situations. Regrettably, caregivers typically receive little instruction on how to care for themselves or manage their own stress and burnout.

Communication Deficits Communication plays a significant role in stress and burnout. Caregivers are affected by the amount of information they receive, their confidence as communicators, and how involved they are in decision making. Too much information can make people feel overwhelmed. Too little information can make them worried and uncertain (Maslach, 1982). For example, mental health nurses report feeling stressed about changes in the health industry and the perception that their employers do not keep them well informed (Fagin et al., 1996).

Other evidence suggests that people are more susceptible to burnout if they do not feel they are skillful communicators. Among physicians surveyed, those who felt their communication skills were below par were more likely than others to treat people in impersonal ways and to perceive a low sense of personal accomplishment (Ramirez et al., 1996).

Nurses' stress seems largely rooted in communication as well. They typically rate their greatest stressor to be conflict with supervisors and physicians

(Hanlon, 1996). Other sources of nurses' stress include lack of autonomy and limited opportunities to use their talents on the job (Anderson, 1996). Researchers suggest that burnout is more likely among nurses who are excluded from decision making (Ellis & Miller, 1993).

Workload An excessive workload, or a highly monotonous one, can cause stress. Sharon Dreidger (1996) describes modern nursing as "quicker and sicker" than in the past. Overnight hospital stays are usually limited to people who are very sick or badly hurt. As a result, nurses may be continually involved in difficult, intense situations. Conversely, Dow (1996) describes the stressful monotony of repeating the same tasks day after day as a radiology technician. (He says he finds relief in focusing on people rather than monotonous routines.)

Other Factors Stress does not affect everyone in the same way, nor does it always lead to burnout. People are able to tolerate different levels of stress before they experience burnout (Fagin et al., 1996; Ray, 1983). Studies show that stress is more bearable if people feel they are appreciated and are performing important services. A British study (Ramirez et al., 1996) found that surgeons had higher stress levels than most doctors. But because surgeons were highly satisfied and publicly respected, they were far less likely to experience burnout than other professionals such as radiologists. Radiologists were the least stressed, but also the least satisfied of those surveyed. They experienced the highest burnout rate, apparently because they felt isolated and unappreciated.

Effects

Stress and burnout affect people physically and emotionally. Physically, people may suffer from sleeplessness, fatigue, weight changes, digestive disorders, headaches, and more (Hanlon, 1996). They also are at high risk for heart disease and other stress-related conditions (Ornish et al., 1998). Psychological symptoms include reduced self-esteem, depression, defensiveness, irritability, and a tendency toward accidents, anger, and emotional outbursts (Hanlon, 1996). Burnout also affects organizations, making it more likely that employees will be apathetic, miss work, and quit their jobs (Ellis & Miller, 1993; Miller et al. 1988).

Communication Skill Builders: Tips for Avoiding Burnout

Caregivers adopt several strategies to deal with or avoid burnout. Understanding these strategies (even the ineffective ones) can help people better understand the motives of their caregivers. Novack et al. (1997) and David Baldwin (1995) offer the following suggestions to minimize burnout:

- Reserve time for family and social events.
- Take part in (or organize) support groups of other professionals.

- Write down your experiences and feelings.
- Get to know yourself better. Spend some time in personal thought and expression.
- Put yourself in other peoples' shoes so you do not lose sight of the challenges that face those around you.
- Take "one-minute vacations"; for example, walk outside or flip through a magazine.
- Surround yourself with souvenirs and photos of loved ones.
- Take brief phone breaks to call loved ones.
- Set clear rules for patients concerning appointment times, phone calls, and cancellations.
- Congratulate yourself on successes, even little ones.

Sometimes the most tempting reactions to burnout are not the most effective ones. Caregivers all too often seek relief by abusing the drugs that are their stock in trade (Miller, 1997). It is believed that between 6% and 20% of nurses abuse drugs and alcohol (Cantanzarite, 1992). In addition, nurses report that they would like to withdraw from their patients and co-workers when they feel stressed, but withdrawal usually does not help as much as prayer, talk with friends, and physical activity (Albrecht, 1982). Finally, caregivers may try to conserve their emotional energy by discouraging patients from talking about their feelings or from making requests the caregiver may be unable to fulfill (Branch & Malik, 1993; Candib, 1994). Patients may misunderstand the caregivers' intent and feel dehumanized or ignored by these tactics.

Factors that seem to mitigate stress and burnout include participatory decision making and positive esteem from others. Participation in workplace decisions seems to be especially important. Hospital employees who participated in decisions were significantly less likely than others to experience stress and burnout (Ellis & Miller, 1993; Miller, Ellis, Zook, & Lyles, 1990). They were also more satisfied with their jobs and more pleased with their personal accomplishments. The authors of this research suggest that participatory decision making is important because it reduces employees' uncertainty and increases their sense of control. Miller et al. (1990) also found that burnout was mitigated by supportive communication from bosses and co-workers. This was especially true among hospital support staff such as food service, clerical, and housekeeping personnel.

Implications

Stress and burnout threaten to deplete caregivers' energy and reduce their capacity for compassion. Burnout causes people to feel emotionally exhausted, unmotivated to help others, and discouraged about their own abilities. Stress is likely to be intense among medical professionals, who may have to manage conflicting demands and be continually involved in emotional situations. The empathic communication model of burnout suggests that people who are compassionate and sensitive are drawn to medicine, but are particularly susceptible to the effects of stress and burnout.

Burnout can be devastating for health professionals, the people around them, and the organizations for which they work. Sometimes, people assume caregivers are indifferent or unfeeling, when they are actually dealing with, or trying to avoid, emotional overload. A range of strategies—many of them involving communication—are available to help professionals reduce stress and avoid burnout.

COMMUNICATION TECHNOLOGY: KNOWLEDGE COUPLING

By now, many people are getting used to an additional presence in the exam room—a computer. **Knowledge coupling** is a form of medical informatics in which patient information is entered into a computer data bank where it is matched (coupled) with extensive information about diagnoses, treatment options, the latest research, and more (Weaver, 2003).

Here is how knowledge coupling works. When someone makes a doctor's appointment, the computer generates an extensive list of questions relevant to the patient's health concerns. The lengthier questionnaires include hundreds of items covering much more information than a patient could convey during a regular medical visit (Weaver, 2003). The patient fills out the questionnaire and submits it prior to the medical visit. The medical staff enters the information into the computer database and reviews the result—a descriptive report that suggests what additional questions to ask; what physical factors to investigate; what risk factors, disease, or illnesses seem to be indicated; and possible therapies to help the patient.

The process will not make doctors or medical visits obsolete. With knowledge coupling—instead of spending a majority of the medical visit collecting health information—patients and caregivers can use their time together to "interpret, discuss, and evaluate" the results suggested by the computer (Weaver, 2003, p. 63). In other words, the computer finds and presents relevant information, but the decisions are still left up to the people involved. Their job is to "weigh the pros and cons associated with various options; and to agree to a plan to address the problem" (Weaver, 2003, p. 63). Information and decisions from the medical exam are entered into the computer and patients leave with a printout of "office notes" describing the information and decisions reached.

Implications

Although some people are put off by the use of computers in patient care, an early study by Robert Weaver (2003) suggests the majority of patients respond favorably. They like the thoroughness of the questionnaires, which often ask for information they might not have supplied during a doctor's visit. "They help me think that things aren't being missed," reported one respondent (Weaver, 2003, p. 66). Patients also report greater confidence with diagnoses and treatment recommendations, and they appreciate leaving medical exams with a written record they can study and share with others.

Some patients felt it was distracting for the doctor to type information into a computer during the medical visit, but others felt that, by doing its job, the computer freed them up to spend more time being "heard and understood" by their doctors (Weaver, 2003, p. 74).

SUMMARY

People dissatisfied with health communication may assume that caregivers do not know how or do not care to communicate well. However, it is probably much closer to the mark to say that caregivers are sometimes overwhelmed, unsure, exhausted, or oriented to different goals than their patients.

Medical school serves as a powerful socializing agent, preparing students to accept the immense privileges and responsibilities of medical practice. As students become professionals, they typically adopt the communication styles, logic, and attitudes of their mentors. In many ways they begin to think and talk like the professionals they model. This can have positive and negative consequences for communication.

Researchers suggest that the extraordinary demands placed on medical students and physician residents encourage them to see patients as weak and contemptible. Overall, caregiver-education programs are considered more successful at instilling technical competence than at preparing caregivers to deal with the diverse emotions and personalities they will encounter. The academic emphasis on physical matters, for instance, often persuades students to think of patients as adversaries or as mere bodies to be fixed. This may reduce the emotional burden on caregivers, but it may be very unsatisfying to patients.

Nursing schools typically emphasize a patient-centered approach, but other types of caregivers are likely to receive very little instruction on communicating with patients. This is particularly regrettable because communication competence is important in avoiding stress and burnout. Changes in the industry, health care legislation (such as HIPAA), work demands, involvement in medical decisions, and personal characteristics also play a part in stress and burnout.

In short, caregivers find themselves managing a host of demands that are often at odds with each other. They are expected to be quick but thorough, strong but emotionally accessible, always available but never tired, and honest but infallible. Understanding these conflicting demands may help people understand why caregivers communicate as they do. Considering the pressures they face it is no wonder caregivers experience higher than average rates of suicide and substance abuse. It is vital that we identify healthy solutions.

Knowledge coupling makes it possible to collect extensive information about a patient and couple it with the latest medical data. This may relieve caregivers of the pressure to know everything there is to know about medicine. It remains to be seen how widespread knowledge coupling will become and whether this will free patients and caregivers to engage in better informed partnership behaviors.

In the next chapter, you will look at health communication through the eyes of patients. As you explore health care from another perspective, remember what you know about caregivers. The richest insights come from understanding several angles at once.

KEY TERMS

socialization
Voice of Medicine
speech community
case presentations
rote learning
problem-based learning (PBL)
abuse
scut work
rite of passage
professional autonomy
stress
burnout
emotional exhaustion
depersonalization
reduced sense of personal accomplishment
doublebind
detached concern
empathic communication model of burnout
knowledge coupling

REVIEW QUESTIONS

1. How is a speech community different than a geographical community?
2. Compare the communication patterns of students and physicians in Lingard et al.'s (2003) study. In what ways did the students become socialized to think and communicate as doctors? In what ways are these changes positive? In what ways are they negative?
3. How is science taught in traditional medical school curricula? How does rote learning differ from problem-based learning?
4. What activities typically make up medical student abuse?
5. How does sleep deprivation typically affect people?
6. What are four main effects of medical school socialization?
7. How are some medical schools reforming their curricula?
8. What are some implications of the way physicians are socialized?
9. How might time constraints affect patient–caregiver communication?
10. How might increased competition in the health industry affect the nature of patient–caregiver communication?

11. Describe the provisions of the Health Insurance Portability and Accountability Act (HIPAA). What are the implications for health communication?
12. What are emotional "hot buttons," and how might they influence patient–caregiver communication?
13. How do physicians typically feel when they make medical mistakes? What factors might discourage doctors from revealing their mistakes?
14. What factors are most linked to caregiver satisfaction?
15. What factors contribute to stress and burnout among caregivers?
16. Does high stress always lead to burnout? Why or why not?
17. What are the effects of stress and burnout among caregivers? What are some techniques for reducing stress?
18. How does knowledge coupling work? In what ways is knowledge coupling appealing to you? In what ways is it unappealing? What are the implications for health communication?

CLASS ACTIVITY

Doctors in the Movies

Watch all or part of the following movies and discuss how the information in this chapter applies to the characters.

Making of a Doctor (Parts 1 and 2), produced by NOVA, follows the progress of seven Harvard Medical School students through medical school and into their first years of practice. Excellent insight about the demands and ethical dilemmas of studying and practicing medicine. See the NOVA website (http://www.pbs.org/wgbh/nova) to order videos and free teachers' guides.

The Doctor, released in 1991 by Touchstone Pictures, follows a physician diagnosed with throat cancer who suddenly finds himself experiencing medicine from a patient's perspective. Recommended by doctors as very realistic. (Rated PG-13)

Gross Anatomy, released in 1989 by Touchstone Pictures, shows the experiences of a group of medical students struggling to adjust to anatomy lab, their own relationships, and the high-pressure environment of medical school. A funny but eye-opening look at the medical school experience. (Rated PG-13)

CHAPTER 5

Patient Perspective

I remember, as a child, the distinct smell of the doctor's office. It is different than any other odor, and it leaves a lasting impression. The smell of rubbing alcohol, the smell of medicines, and the smell of antibacterial soap on the doctor's hands. As a child, you don't know what to make of it.

These musings by a college student evoke vivid images of patienthood. Whatever else people may remember of childhood, most will never forget the sensory alert of waiting anxiously to be seen by a doctor.

Being a patient can be a frightening experience, even as an adult. Uncertainty is guaranteed, and pain is a strong possibility. At the same time, though, there is the promise of relief, a cure, or a reassuring health assessment. (See Box 5.1 for a true story about one patient's experience managing uncertainty.)

This chapter looks at health care situations through patients' eyes. It examines the socialization process that helps patients learn how to behave appropriately. It also describes what patients like and dislike about caregivers and what motivates people to follow (and, just as often, to ignore) medical advice. The chapter concludes with a discussion of illness and personal identity and a survey of diversity among patients.

PATIENT SOCIALIZATION

As you will see in this section and the next, patients are expected to behave in particular ways, and those who defy expectations may be considered whiny, crazy, annoying, stupid, or so on. With their very well-being hanging in the balance, people are loath for caregivers to view them in these ways.

How is it, then, that people come to understand what behaviors will distinguish them as "good" patients? Unlike caregivers, patients are usually in medical situations only briefly and occasionally. Moreover, while caregivers are allowed, even required, to watch other caregivers, patients seldom get to observe other patients, and few training programs are available to patients about communicating in medical settings (Cegala & Broz, 2003). Thus, socialization into patienthood is an imprecise process. Patients may feel they have been thrust center stage but do not know the script.

People apply their everyday knowledge to the patient role and generally display all the hesitancy you might expect. This section describes the Voice of

Box 5.1 PERSPECTIVES
The Agony of Uncertainty

It all began one day when I was in eighth-grade physical education class. As the class began to warm up and stretch, I noticed a knot on my knee. A month passed and the knot did not go away. In fact it grew from the size of a pencil eraser to the size of a quarter. My mother made an appointment with our family doctor, and I began to panic. I personally gave myself one year to live.

During my appointment the doctor asked questions like "Have you fallen down recently?" I was so distraught I felt like screaming, "I did not come in here for a bump and scrape!" But I just said no.

After ordering X-rays, the doctor said he could not tell if the knot was a cyst or a tumor and referred us to a bone and joint specialist. I was beyond scared. I was only 13 and had never had anything worse than the flu. I had so many questions, but there wasn't much chance to ask them. Every question I asked got a brief response, when what I really wanted was a full explanation and, above all, reassurance. The conversation went something like this:

Doctor: It looks like you have a cyst or a tumor. I'm going to refer you to a specialist.

Me: What does that mean?

Doctor: It means he will look at your knee and figure out what is going on.

Me: Is it serious?

Doctor: That's what he'll be able to determine.

Me: Well, OK.

I wasn't sure about the difference between a cyst and a tumor, and both sounded horrible. I was afraid the doctor would laugh if I said I was afraid of having cancer. Or had he just told me I *did* have cancer? I left not knowing, and I had to wait a month to see the specialist.

On the day of the appointment with the specialist, Dr. Benze, we waited $2\frac{1}{2}$ hours to see him. However, his personality and gentle

Lifeworld, the typical power difference between patients and caregivers, and the dilemma patients face when they disagree with caregivers' advice or assertiveness.

Voice of Lifeworld

Quite naturally, patients interpret their health within the arena most familiar to them—everyday life. In contrast to the scientific Voice of Medicine that manner made up for the wait. Dr. Benze compassionately and carefully told me the lump (now the size of a small orange) was a tumor. When I began to cry, he explained that not all tumors are cancerous. He arranged to surgically remove the tumor in two days, and he promised to tell me everything about the surgery in advance and to share the lab results with me as soon as he received them.

On the day before surgery my mother and I visited the hospital to make arrangements. The admitting attendant was detached and unfriendly, but the nurses and doctors were wonderful. They tried to make me feel comfortable and relaxed. An outpatient nurse sat down with us and described in detail what would happen before, during, and after the surgery. I felt comfortable asking every question I did not feel safe asking the first doctor.

Suffice it to say that the surgery went well. The tumor was not cancerous, and I have had no more tumors. Overall, the experience was a positive one. The worst part was leaving the first doctor's office with so many fears and questions I never got to voice. Although the surgery was frightening, I felt better once people starting telling me what was going on.

—Sarah

What Do You Think?

1. Do you think the first doctor could have communicated more effectively with Sarah? If so, how?
2. Do you think Sarah could have communicated more effectively? If so, how?
3. Sometimes doctors feel they will alarm or confuse patients (especially young patients) by giving them medical details. Do you agree?
4. How can patients help ensure that they get the information they want?

physicians use, patients speak what Mishler (1984) calls the Voice of Lifeworld. The **Voice of Lifeworld** is concerned with health and illness as they relate to everyday experiences. For example, a physician may understand back pain in terms of specific discs and muscles, but from a lifeworld perspective, the main issue is that the pain interferes with a person's ability to pick up a child or perform tasks at work. Patients are usually most concerned with how they feel and how their health affects their regular activities. When asked by a doctor what is wrong with them, patients typically describe sensations and events, as in, "I get a horrible pain behind my eyes when I try to read the newspaper. It really scares me."

As the following analysis shows, the Voice of Lifeworld and the Voice of Medicine differ in two main ways: One is primarily oriented to feelings and the other to evidence, and one is precise and the other specific.

Feelings Versus Evidence Doctors and patients tend to have different philosophies about health. That is, they make sense of it in different ways. Patients "know" they are sick (or healthy) based on how they feel. Through experience, comparisons with others, and gut instinct, they distinguish between feeling well and feeling ill (Mishler, 1981, 1984).

Physicians, however, are taught to be empirical. Science teaches that feelings can be distorted and unreliable. Doctors "know" someone is sick based on observation and tests. You may recall from Chapter 2 that this emphasis on physical indicators has roots in the Renaissance principle of verification, the 19th century discovery of germs, and scientific means of detecting illness using microscopes and other technology.

As a general principle, patients trust feelings, but physicians trust evidence. Depending on which perspective the participants take, health care encounters may sound very different. Predictably, lifeworld talk is more emotional, social, and contextual, while medical talk is more technical.

Howard Waitzkin (1991) proposes that lifeworld concerns can be problematic from a medical perspective. Lifeworld troubles may seem irrelevant to the medical condition, they may be relevant but outside the physician's power to control, or they may be uncomfortable to discuss. "Under these circumstances, doctors typically interject questions, interrupt, or otherwise change the topic, to return to the voice of medicine" (Waitzkin, p. 25).

Specific Versus Diffuse One result of their disparate philosophies is that doctors are often precise while patients are diffuse. To illustrate, a doctor hears "pain behind the eyes" and wants to know exactly where, how strong, how long. Patients, however, may be concerned with surrounding issues such as the scariness of the pain (Will I die? Can I still be a good parent? Am I going blind? Do I have a tumor? What have I done to deserve this?). Although both mean well, doctors may be frustrated when patients "go on and on," and patients may feel rebuffed when doctors seem uninterested in their feelings.

Patients are also more diffuse in their perception of what causes illness. Unlike doctors, who typically strive to find the cause of an illness, patients often perceive that it has multiple causes, common among them stress and relationship issues (Helman, 1985). Consequently, physicians' scientific specificity may seem sorely deficient in explaining illnesses as patients perceive them. People may leave exams wondering if their doctors really understood their problems at all.

Patients may also have numerous goals, which sometimes take precedence over purely physical healing. They may wish to vent emotions, confess, or be reassured, forgiven, or comforted during a medical visit. These goals may be in direct opposition to doctors' efforts to eliminate situational factors and focus on measurable ones.

All in all, patients tend to interpret illnesses in the broad context of everyday life, whereas physicians are taught to reduce diseases to their simplest, most measurable parts. Of course, the differences described do not hold true for all patients or all medical professionals. Some caregivers are very sensitive to their patients' emotions and life experiences, and some patients are able to identify specific signs of illness even when they experience no symptoms. Even so, understanding that patients and caregivers have traditionally been socialized to regard illness differently may help both sides understand each other better.

Implications

Different viewpoints about health give rise to conflicting expectations. Patients typically speak with the Voice of Lifeworld, which emphasizes the personal and social effects of illness. Their concerns are typically more emotional and more diffuse than the biomedical focus usually taught in medical school. Even when patients are willing to abandon their lifeworld agendas, they may have a hard time understanding or living up to their doctors' expectations. Patients may find themselves trying to get to the biological point when they do not know what the biological point is.

There is some indication that the Voice of Medicine and the Voice of Lifeworld may change if medicine's goal becomes preventing disease and injury rather than just treating them. Prevention is a diffuse topic involving an array of risk factors and lifestyle decisions. Furthermore, talking about prevention is usually not as emotionally intense as talking about existing illness. The result of prevention-oriented talk may be the emergence of a third voice that is both diffuse and informative. To the extent that communication is built on shared meaning, a mutually satisfying philosophy of health might enhance patient–caregiver relationships.

PATIENT CHARACTERISTICS

Although patients would like to maintain their caregivers' positive regard, they may have goals that are at odds with their caregivers' preferences. For instance, a patient may doubt the validity of a diagnosis or wish to reiterate information the caregiver has dismissed as unimportant. Other patients may not be well educated, assertive, or skillful enough to participate as they would like to in health care transactions. In this section we look at factors that influence patients' communication patterns.

Nature of the Illness

A patient whose condition is chronic or hard to define may feel like a nuisance to the doctor. Situations like these present a dilemma. The patient must either risk the caregiver's disapproval or leave feeling that nothing much was accomplished. Either choice has negative consequences.

What do most patients do? Researchers suggest they usually abandon or delay pursuit of their own goals rather than challenge caregivers (Scherz et al., 1995). This may be because a damaged identity is hard to mend, but specific goals can usually be pursued at a later date. Whatever their rationale, patients may hint at their feelings, but seldom do they assert them. Instead, dissatisfied patients are known to switch doctors or to come back again and again, perhaps hoping for the right conditions in which to accomplish their goals. All the while, physicians may be unaware of the patients' dissatisfaction.

The problem is especially difficult for people with multiple concerns. A patient with depression may feel that other concerns are brushed aside as psychosomatic even when they are legitimate physical conditions. Gillespie (2001) describes the frustration of low-income patients experiencing depression and chronic health problems:

> They resented feeling as though they had to prove or stress how sick they "really" were, especially since they felt this account might also label them as neurotic. They had to hide their upset because showing it only lent further evidence to potential neuroses. (p. 109)

Patient Disposition

Patients' backgrounds and personalities also influence how they communicate in medical settings. After reviewing patient–caregiver literature, Jeffery Robinson (2003) concluded that a number of factors may persuade patients to temper their participation in medical dialogues:

- Patients may think it is appropriate to be passive.
- They may be too fearful or anxious to be assertive.
- They may not know or understand enough to participate in medical discussions.
- They may be discouraged by caregivers' communication styles.
- Socioeconomic factors such as education level may influence how actively patients participate.
- The nature of the medical visit (routine or symptom-specific) may influence their behavior.
- The length of the visit and the people present may influence patients' involvement.

A number of studies support these ideas. Better educated patients are typically more assertive than others (Street, Voigt, Geyer, Manning, & Swanson, 1995).

Likewise, extroverted individuals tend to participate more actively in medical exams, giving and requesting information and asking for what they want (Eaton & Tinsley, 1999). Jill Kroll and colleagues (2000) found that, among women experiencing menopause, those who are more confident and more determined to participate in medical encounters exercise more control during medical interviews and are more satisfied with the care they receive (Kroll et al., 2000).

Communication Skills

As you have seen, even when patients want to engage their caregivers and have important things to say, they may have a hard time putting their ideas into words or gauging the appropriateness of their communication. This dilemma is often complicated by mixed messages from their doctors. Doctors frequently ask patients to explain themselves and then quickly interrupt the explanations. This is illustrated by the finding that doctors tend to curtail patients' accounts but consider it important that patients provide clear and thorough descriptions of their concerns (Cegala et al., 1996).

Patients may benefit from skills training programs that prepare them to communicate effectively with medical providers. Although the results are mixed and patient education programs are scarce, there has been modest success in this area. During training sessions, patients are usually instructed and encouraged to ask questions, provide information, and verify their understanding of information (Cegala & Broz, 2003). One reason skills training has not been more effective is that, even if patients are trained *how* to pose questions, they may not know *what* to ask. Donald Cegala and Stefne Broz (2003) reflect:

> Most patients do not formulate questions until they have had time to process what the physician has said or do not realize their lack of understanding until they try to follow the recommended treatment or explain their illness to someone. (p. 10)

Nevertheless, Cegala and Broz (2003) conclude that even modest improvements can enhance medical care and reduce the length of medical visits. (See Box 5.2 for additional resources on this topic.)

Implications

Patients are in a difficult position when they do not have the knowledge, confidence, or disposition to assert their ideas in the presence of medical professionals. Communication skills can help to some extent, but even well-educated patients with good communication skills may find themselves out of their depth conversing about medical topics on the spot. As a result, caregivers may not even know that patients are dissatisfied or are reluctant to accept what they hear. The next two sections examine factors that contribute to patient satisfaction and patient–caregiver cooperation.

Box 5.2 RESOURCES
More about Patient Communication Skills Training

- Cegala, D. J., Post, D., & McClure, L. (2001). The effects of patient communication skills training on the discourse of elderly patients during a primary care interview. *Journal of the American Geriatrics Society, 49,* 1505–1511.
- Cegala, D. J., McClure, L., Marinelli, T. M., & Post, D. M. (2000). The effects of communication skills training on patients' participation during medical interviews. *Patient Education and Counseling, 41,* 209–222.
- McGee, D. S., & Cegala, D. J. (1998). Patient communication skills training for improved communication competence in the primary care medical consultation. *Journal of Applied Communication Research, 26,* 412–430.

SATISFACTION

Patients seem to have many grievances about medical care, but they are quite satisfied overall. Studies suggest that 75% to 90% of patients are satisfied with their doctors, yet the same patients have a number of serious complaints ("How Is Your Doctor," 1995; "Public, Physicians," 1996). Some researchers speculate that patients believe the care they receive, while not optimal, is as good as can be expected.

Patients have strong opinions about doctors and nurses. They know what they like—attentiveness, lots of information, and no hassles. They want to know they can speak freely, and they want to feel confident their doctors will not turn against them if they seek second opinions (Jadad & Rizo, 2003). These preferences are embodied in communication behaviors such as listening, asking questions, informing, and encouraging. This section examines what patients like and dislike about health care experiences. It concludes with evidence that the most satisfying, effective care embodies moderate amounts of the qualities patients like most.

Attentiveness

Patient satisfaction is more closely linked to caregivers' communication than to their technical skills (Tarrant, Windridge, Boulton, Baker, & Freeman, 2003). This may be because it is harder to judge technical skills and because patients automatically assume caregivers are technically competent. It may also reflect how important communication skills are to diagnosis and treatment.

People like doctors who seem to take them seriously and like them back (Grant, Cissna, & Rosenfeld, 2000). This impression is enhanced when doctors are nonverbally expressive, maintain eye contact, and encourage patients to participate in medical conversations (Conlee, Olvera, & Vagim, 1993). Patients evaluate nurses by similar criteria, preferring those who seem genuinely sensitive and caring (Williams, 1997).

Physicians also get high marks for listening attentively and acknowledging patients' emotions without trying to control them (Grant, Cissna, & Rosenfeld, 2000). Conversely, patients are displeased when doctors shrug off their emotional concerns (Laitinen, 1994; Street, 1992) and do not ask for their viewpoints ("How Is Your Doctor," 1995; "Public, Physicians," 1996).

Satisfaction may vary by health concern. The least satisfied patients surveyed are those with chronic, hard-to-cure conditions such as headaches and back pain (Charles, Goldsmith, Chambers, Haynes, & Gauld, 1996; "How Is Your Doctor," 1995). By contrast, obstetric, cancer, and heart patients are more satisfied than average, perhaps because these conditions are treated by doctors as more serious and legitimate than some others.

Information

In an article titled, "I Am a Good Patient, Believe It or Not," Alejandro Jadad and Carlos Rizo (2003) describe a series of interviews with patients. They conclude: "In most cases it would not take fancy technology, extra time, or increased costs to satisfy what patients 'want.' It would take only an assertive patient and a confident health care provider who is willing to listen" (paragraph 6).

Patients like to be well informed and seem to feel a disquieting lack of control when they are not. They are twice as likely to be satisfied with doctors they choose themselves (Quesenberry, 1997). Likewise, patients react negatively when they do not know what to expect. Hospital patients most frequently complain that no one person seems in charge of their care, different caregivers give conflicting information ("How Is Your Doctor," 1995), and caregivers do not explain procedures and daily routines fully (Bowker, 1996; Charles et al., 1996).

Convenience

Finally, patients like it when things run smoothly. Satisfaction is enhanced when there is good news about their health, when the wait is not long, and when their health plan is covering the costs (Probst et al., 1997). Hospitals in recent years have begun efforts to streamline paperwork and admitting procedures, realizing that patient satisfaction relies on more than skillfully performed medical procedures.

Moderation

There is some evidence that moderate doses of pleasing behavior work better than extreme amounts. Patients do not like doctors to be extremely dominant, but they are also dissatisfied when they are extremely passive (Cardello, Ray, & Pettey, 1995). Either way, patients perceive the doctors to be disinterested.

Furthermore, although patients prefer doctors to be friendly, it may be a good idea to moderate friendly behaviors when giving patients serious information. Evidence suggests that patients take doctors' warnings less seriously when the doctor speaks in a friendly, rather than an aggressive, manner (Burgoon & Burgoon, 1990). When male physicians seemed aggressive but sincere, patients were satisfied and they were highly motivated to comply with the doctors' advice (Burgoon & Burgoon, 1990). In a similar study, infertility patients tended to underrate the risks explained to them by a friendly doctor, but took the same risks seriously when they were explained in an authoritarian manner (Witte & Zmuidzinas, 1993).

Implications

Communication skills are at the top of patients' wish list for doctors and nurses. (Unfortunately, there is little research about patients' satisfaction with other caregivers.) Patients seem to assume that caregivers are competent in technical and scientific matters. They like them or not based on whether they seem respectful, friendly, and interested. Patients also appreciate being fully informed and, like everyone, enjoy convenience. Finally, caregivers may do well to note that friendliness can sometimes put patients too much at ease, leading them to underestimate the severity or importance of crucial advice.

COOPERATION AND CONSENT

Even more important than medical visits is what happens between visits. Although patients are not likely to challenge their doctors' advice in person, statistics show that patients are often unlikely to follow the advice once they leave the doctor's office. Only 50% to 60% of patients follow medical advice completely or most of the time. About 1 in 5 prescriptions goes unfilled, and half of the prescriptions that are filled are taken incorrectly (Ringel, 1997). These numbers are not limited to certain types of patients either. Compliance rates are similar among patients of different ages, sexes, and education levels (Burgoon & Burgoon, 1990).

As Michael Burgoon and Judee Burgoon (1990) observe, it is curious that patients do not follow medical advice more closely, considering that patients pay for the advice, presumably stand to benefit from it, and typically revere the expertise of medical professionals. The next section explores some of the reasons patients may not follow through with medical regimens. It also describes caregivers' stake in getting patients to perform medical regimens, and policies concerning informed consent.

Reasons for Noncompliance

People who do not follow medical advice are not necessarily lazy or indifferent about their health. A number of more legitimate concerns may affect their decisions.

For one, medical recommendations may be impossible or impractical to carry out considering patients' circumstances. They may be unable to afford prescribed medication or be physically incapable of performing suggested routines (Frankel & Beckman, 1989). For example, patients who miss hemodialysis treatment often report that no one is available to drive them to and from appointments (Gordon, Leon, & Segal, 2003). Medical professionals may be frustrated when patients continue to expose themselves to "avoidable" health threats. However, poor patients may have little choice. As Gillespie (2001) describes it:

> Low income families live in older homes filled with lifetimes of dust and molding timber. They breathe the air polluted by factories that never cease production and by the cars of daily downtown professionals who sleep in clean, suburban air each night. Often depressed, they are more likely to smoke and less likely to eat well. Many sleep on the floor, knowing that the asthma this triggers could kill them, but afraid that a stray bullet shot through the window will do so sooner. (p. 114)

In other situations, recommended regimens may be so foreign to patients that they cannot integrate them into their lifestyles. For instance, some people consider it inconceivable to completely remove red meat from their diet.

Second, patients may not agree with the doctor's assessment or treatment recommendations. Research suggests patients are apt to distrust diagnoses and thus ignore medical advice if they are unable to describe their concerns during the medical visit (Frankel & Beckman, 1989). People may also deny diagnoses that threaten their self-images. It may be difficult to admit obesity, hearing loss, depression, sexually transmitted diseases, and the like.

Third, patients may stop medical routines prematurely if they perceive no effect or if their symptoms cease (Ringel, 1997). It is difficult to get people to remain on treatment for conditions like high blood pressure because they cannot directly perceive that the medicine has any effect.

Finally, patients may stop taking medication if they experience unpleasant side effects (Löffler, Kilian, Toumi, & Angermeyer, 2003). Rather than contact the physician for alternate instructions, they may try other methods or conclude that the cure is worse than the disease.

These factors are exacerbated when physicians do not encourage patients to express their concerns and reservations at the time medical advice is given. Evidence suggests many people leave their doctors' offices knowing they cannot or will not follow through with advice given, but they do not feel free to say so. Doctors who assume that patients should follow orders regardless of their circumstances may be discouraged when treatment outcomes are less than optimal.

What is more, patients who do not feel comfortable talking with the doctor in person may be reluctant to be honest about treatment failures later on.

Caregivers' Investment

It may be tempting to assume that, if patients do not follow medical advice, they have only themselves to blame. But caregivers may (justly or unjustly) be blamed as well. Effective communication and patient–caregiver cooperation are important to caregivers for several reasons.

First, lack of patient–caregiver cooperation can waste time and frustrate everyone involved. Ineffective communication is a leading cause of caregiver burnout (Maslach, 1982; Ramirez et al., 1996). Furthermore, patients who feel discouraged from voicing their concerns are typically less communicative and less cooperative (Frankel & Beckman, 1989; "How Is Your Doctor," 1995). Patients may even lie. Gynecology patients interviewed by Todd (1984) said they sometimes lied to their doctor about contraceptive use rather than suffer his disapproval. Ironically, as patients and caregivers become anxious, they are even less likely to communicate skillfully (Kreps, 1990), causing a negative spiral with potentially serious consequences.

Second, caregivers' careers may be damaged by excessive treatment failures. Hospitals may refuse to grant doctors privileges, and medical groups may deny them admittance. Their reputation among patients may suffer as well.

Finally, a persuasive reason to improve cooperation involves money. With capitation and restricted reimbursements, doctors may lose money on patients who do not improve as expected. Conversely, they may save money when communication is effective. Research suggests good communication can avert health disasters and reduce expenditures for unnecessary procedures. In the United States, improper use of prescription medication results in hospital stays totaling about $8.5 billion per year ("How Is Your Doctor," 1995). Bill Clements (1996) estimates that a managed care agency saves about $210 each time it avoids an unnecessary emergency room visit, $85 to $115 when it avoids an unnecessary referral, and about $20 for each unnecessary office visits it avoids. Multiplied by hundreds of patients, the savings could be substantial. Clements concludes: "Make no mistake about it: Bad communication costs you money" (paragraph 3).

Considering these factors, how far should caregivers go to gain patients' compliance? Some doctors are trying cash rewards (see Box 5.3). Others are trying to involve patients more in medical decision making. As the next section illustrates, over time, public policy has changed concerning patients' role in medical decisions.

Informed Consent

For centuries physicians considered it wise to tell patients only as much as they could understand (in the doctor's opinion), and nothing that might dissuade

Box 5.3 Cash for Cooperation?

Communication is important, but can it stack up to cold hard cash? Maybe not. Some medical centers are having success with innovative cash-for-compliance programs that reward patients for healthy behavior.

An overview of 11 programs suggests prizes and coupons may work well and actually save health agencies money (Giuffrida & Torgerson, 1997). Incentives include cash or cash coupons (usually $4 or $5 or a chance to win from $25 to $100) for keeping appointments, maintaining healthy blood pressure (for hypertensive patients), reaching weight loss goals, immunizing children, or abstaining from drug abuse. In all but one program, cash incentives were more successful than reminder phone calls and warnings. Incentive programs were even more successful than a program to offer more convenient appointment times.

Program sponsors say it is less expensive to offer cash prizes than to pay staff to work overtime or call patients, and everyone stands to gain if incentives reduce unnecessary care and keep serious health concerns from escalating. It is not clear, however, if patients will develop motivation to continue the behaviors without the rewards.

them from following medical advice. For example, if a doctor judged that the potential advantages of a drug outweighed its possible side effects, the doctor might not tell the patient about side effects for fear the patient would not take the drug (Katz, 1995). Likewise, although doctors have always been required to get patients' permission before they operated on them, they have not been required to tell patients about the risks involved.

In most cases physicians were presumably following their best judgment, even though they withheld information from patients. In some cases, however, patients were subjected to risk, even to deadly medical experiments, without their knowledge. One example is the **Tuskegee Syphilis Study** conducted in Alabama (Box 5.4).

Public outrage over the Tuskegee Syphilis Study and others like it led the U.S. government to pass informed consent laws. **Informed consent** means patients must be (a) made fully aware of known treatment risks, benefits, and options; (b) deemed capable of understanding such information and making a responsible judgment; and (c) aware that they may refuse to participate or cease treatment at any time (Ashley & O'Rourke, 1997). When patients are children or are otherwise unable to make decisions, close family members may be allowed to consent on their behalf.

Informed consent is a victory for patient empowerment. However, the terms are sometimes hard to apply even when people try hard to do so. For example, a long list of complications (many of them extremely unlikely) might result from a simple procedure. It may be impractical or impossible to list every possible outcome. However, physicians may be accused of negligence if

Box 5.4 ETHICAL CONSIDERATIONS
Patients' Right to Informed Consent

During the infamous Tuskegee Syphilis Study, which began in 1932, some 600 African-American men were enrolled without their knowledge in a medical experiment. They were patients of the Public Health Service in Macon County, Alabama, and the experiment was conducted by the U.S. government (through the Tuskegee Institute in Alabama).

Although medical researchers knew that 399 of the men had syphilis, the men were not told. Doctors simply told all the men they had "bad blood" and provided them with medicine, meals, and burial expenses. However, the medicine was not really medicine at all. It was a harmless but ineffectual placebo.

The study was designed to help medical researchers learn more about the effects of syphilis among African Americans. Syphilis is a sexually transmitted disease that affects the bones, liver, heart, and central nervous system. In advanced stages, it can cause open sores, heart damage, tumors, blindness, insanity, and death. When the study was begun, there was no effective treatment for syphilis. However, by 1940 penicillin was known to be very effective at treating and even curing it.

The syphilis patients in the Tuskegee experiment were not given penicillin. Instead, researchers continued to watch the disease progress until the experiment was called off in 1972, some 40 years after it began.

When details of the Tuskegee study were made public, there was an angry outcry. Some likened it to the Nazis' medical experiments on Jewish prisoners during World War II. The courts eventually ordered the federal government to pay the men and their families a total of $10 million for the injury and indignity they had suffered. Twenty-five years after the experiment (in May 1997) President Bill Clinton publicly apologized for the government's behavior.

Now, before patients are given medical treatment (experimental or otherwise), they must be fully informed, give consent, and be aware that they can cease treatment at any time. It is hoped that informed consent will prevent atrocities such as the Tuskegee Syphilis Study. But informed consent is sometimes hard to apply in more routine cases.

What Do You Think?

1. Sometimes the scientific basis for medical research is difficult to fully understand. How do you establish if the consenting person is fully knowledgeable?

2. Some people, like those with terminal illnesses, are willing (even anxious) to try untested therapies. Researchers may not know what results to expect, and may even anticipate negative outcomes. Who should decide whether the patient undergoes untested therapies? Should public money be used in these cases?
3. Is it ever justified to deceive people (as in giving placebos) to make sure they are not just responding to the power of suggestion? If so, under what conditions?
4. Sometimes it is in the best interest of society or health care workers to know if a person has a contagious disease (such as AIDS). If the person does not consent to a test for that disease, is it permissible to perform the test without the person's knowledge? (A vial of blood may be used for a variety of tests without the patient's knowledge.)

(For related information, see the Class Activity at the end of the chapter.)

Suggested Sources

Angell, M. (1997, October 28). Tuskegee revisited. *Wall Street Journal,* pp. A22W, A22E.

Ashley, B. M., & O'Rourke, K. D. (1997). *Health care ethics: A theological analysis* (4th ed.). Washington, DC: Georgetown University Press.

Gillioti, C. M. (2003). Medical disclosure and decision-making: Excavating the complexities of physician-patient information exchange. In T. L. Thompson, A. M. Dorsey, K. I. Miller, & R. Parrott (Eds.), *Handbook of health communication* (pp. 163–181). Mahwah, NJ: Lawrence Erlbaum.

Katz, J. (1995). Informed consent: Ethical and legal issues. In J. D. Arras & B. Steinbock (Eds.), *Ethical issues in modern medicine* (4th ed., pp. 87–97). Mountain View, CA: Mayfield.

Shelton, D. L. (1997, April 15). Mistrust of doctors lingers after Tuskegee; many blacks remain wary—and underserved—a quarter-century after infamous syphilis study. *Washington Post,* p. WH8.

an unlikely outcome results and the patient was not warned about it in advance. Partly because complete disclosure is so difficult to define, the courts have been somewhat reluctant to hold physicians responsible for informed consent violations except in clear-cut cases (Katz, 1995).

Implications

All in all, effective cooperation between patients and caregivers is immensely important. Patients stand to benefit when they are able to carry out treatment options, and favorable outcomes reflect well on physicians. Moreover, when patients and caregivers work together, they may avoid expensive, unnecessary care later.

However, research suggests that patients follow medical advice only about half the time. This may be because they are not capable of following the advice, they do not agree with the diagnosis or recommended treatment, the advice or treatment are culturally or personally disagreeable, or they do not perceive a benefit.

Informed consent requirements are designed to allow patients enough information so they can make knowledgeable judgments about their own care. Some theorists believe health care should go even further toward including patients in treatment decisions. As early as 1973, medical analyst Harold Walker predicted that doctors would become less authoritarian and more persuasive. The difference is subtle but important. From an authoritarian perspective, patients are expected to *comply* with doctors' orders. From a persuasive perspective, however, patients take an active role in decision making. They *cooperate* in the process as informed and influential participants.

If patients are included in decision making, it may be possible to overcome or accommodate many of the factors that now keep them from following medical advice. The caregiver aware of a patient's financial and physical limitations, cultural reservations, denial, or discouragement is better able to negotiate more acceptable options with the patient or provide information that may assuage the patient's reservations. Patients who take an active role in medical encounters are typically more committed to carrying out the decisions made (Cecil, 1998; Young & Klingle, 1996). At the very least, patients and caregivers can establish outright what each is willing to do. This may ultimately be less frustrating than allowing their differences to go unspoken.

Acknowledging that patients make decisions based on a number of factors outside formal medical settings, the next section examines how illnesses can affect people's sense of identity.

ILLNESS AND PERSONAL IDENTITY

To understand the effects of illness on personal identity, consider for a moment who *you* are. A few words might come to mind: student, son, daughter, parent, athlete, kind, smart, energetic, and the like. To the extent that you and the people around you agree on these roles and descriptions, they make up your identity. They define who you are, and you are not likely to change in unforeseen, significant ways. **Personal identity** is a relatively enduring set of characteristics that define a person.

At first consideration, having an identity may seem easy. You simply are who you are. However, the deeper reality is that you work hard to "be" who you are. People generally want to be viewed favorably and to feel good about themselves. Therefore, they act in ways that are consistent with the positive image they wish to portray (Goffman, 1967). Like other people, you are probably invested in maintaining the qualities and talents that make you unique. Very often, this requires a great deal of work (studying, listening, practicing, rehearsing, exercising, etc.). These behaviors are not "you," but they do support the identity that helps you and others understand you.

What if you were suddenly unable to maintain the behaviors that seem to make you who you are? What if you lost your memory and could no longer pass a test? What if your looks or your ability to talk or walk changed substantially? These are extreme examples, but even minor illnesses and injuries can interfere with people's ability to "be" who they are. If the effects are short-lived, people probably do not experience a serious crisis of identity. However, long-term effects can change how people see themselves and how others treat them (Vanderford, Jenks, & Sharf, 1997).

In addition to personal identities, we also have **social identities** characterized by perceived membership in societal groups such as "teenagers," "Hispanic Americans," or "retired persons" (Harwood & Sparks, 2003). Based on the groups with which we identify, we may expect ourselves (and others like us) to think and behave in particular ways. For example, we may be surprised when a youthful friend reveals she has a serious heart condition and we may thereafter view her as "older" than her peers (Kundrat & Nussbaum, 2003).

When we are diagnosed with an identity-threatening illness, it may become part of our identity as well. Jake Harwood and Lisa Sparks (2003) call this a **tertiary identity**—a label that simultaneously defines the illness and one's alignment toward it. For example, during a recent leadership retreat, a colleague of mine recently introduced herself to the group as, among other things, a "breast cancer survivor." The group responded with applause and hugs. Surviving cancer was treated as courageous and admirable, and I believe group members felt a sense of intimacy that she had shared this news with them. Harwood and Sparks propose that a number of tertiary identities are available to people with the same health conditions. For example, my colleague might have said, "I'm a cancer victim" rather than a "survivor." I believe the crowd would have been sympathetic, but their reaction (and their image of her) would have been somewhat different. Perhaps even more important, different wording would reflect something important about the way she viewed her *own* circumstances.

This section examines how people manage their identities in the life-altering circumstances of ill health. It reviews common responses to illness and describes the role of patient narratives.

Reactions to Illness

Patients' reactions to illness may be surprising and unexpected, even to the patients themselves. Kathy Charmaz (1987) has studied the way people with long-term illnesses seek to reconcile their previous identities with the changed circumstances in which they find themselves. She has identified four stages common to the process. First, people take on a **supernormal identity,** determined not to let the illness stop them from being better than ever. This stage is usually followed by a sense of **restored self,** when people are not quite as optimistic, but typically deny that the illness has changed them. The third stage is **contingent personal identity,** when people admit that they may not be able to do everything they could previously do and begin to confront the consequences of a changed identity. The final stage, **salvaged self,** represents the development of a transformed identity that integrates former aspects of self with current limitations. Of course, not everyone goes through every stage or spends the same amount of time in each stage. However, Charmaz's model illustrates that illness and identity are sometimes intertwined, and that people actively try to manage their identity when illness threatens their ability to behave as they normally would.

Sometimes people's abilities are not substantially altered by their health condition, but they may be surprised or horrified to have a condition that seems to clash with their established beliefs. For instance, an unmarried high school teacher may be horrified to learn she is pregnant and may wonder if her pregnancy will affect students' image of her or cost her her job.

It can be useful to ascertain whether people consider their health conditions to be identity threatening and how they react to that possibility. Weston and Brown (1989) write that patients may feel determined, ashamed, victimized, or even relieved by diagnoses. Some respond to illness with a zealous determination to "beat" it, as if it were an enemy. Others interpret illness as punishment. For some, it is comforting to have a name for the illness, and perhaps a plan for dealing with it.

These diverse reactions can be informative. Patients who lash out at others may feel their illness is degrading or is unfair punishment. Patients who seem very upbeat may be said to "be taking it well" or be "very strong," but in some instances they are hiding deeper feelings or harboring unrealistic expectations. Patients who seem relieved may have expected something worse (it might be helpful to know what), or they may simply be glad to escape part of the dread and uncertainty of not knowing. In the case of extended illnesses, reactions are likely to vary considerably even within one person.

Narratives

People are natural born storytellers. One person tells another what it was like to undergo surgery, have a baby, go on a blind date, and so on. Nearly any time people gather, even for a few moments, they tell stories of this sort.

According to narrative theorists (i.e., Beach & Japp, 1983; Fisher, 1984), people tell stories for some very compelling reasons. (A **narrative** is a story.) At a surface level, narratives are informative. They tell people of specific goings-on and perhaps prepare them to take part in similar circumstances. But at an even deeper level, narratives shape interpretations and viewpoints—some would say they shape reality.

The essence of narrative theory is that people use storytelling to help establish common values and interpretations. An example may help to clarify this idea. A 58-year-old cardiac patient told his doctor:

> It's been tough. I've gone from being a man who is really healthy and has no problems to having a bad heart attack and a big operation and being a real weight watcher. It has been a big change, and it has had its tough moments, but I'm alive and I guess that is what matters. (Brown, Weston, & Stewart, 1995, p. 39)

In this simple account, the man suggests an identity for himself. Despite the unusual occurrence of his ill health, his words imply that he is by nature a strong man, physically and emotionally. This characterization sums up a series of events and may shield him from being typified as self-pitying or sickly.

People may not be fully aware of what their narratives imply. The cardiac patient might say he was just telling his story as he saw it, with no particular intention of creating an image for himself. Nevertheless, stories tend to leak cues about people's viewpoints, and they are often persuasive in suggesting certain interpretations. Especially when different narratives reinforce the same themes and morals, they help solidify expectations about the world and shape people's identities.

Narratives are important to health communication for two reasons. First of all, patients frequently speak in narrative form (Eggly, 2002). They describe and explain (except when they are limited to answering closed questions). Patients are typically more satisfied with medical care when they express concerns in their own words (Putnam, Stiles, Jacob, & James, 1985). Second, narratives are loaded with information. A sensitive listener can detect cues to a person's hopes, fears, doubts, future intentions, and more. Particularly since patients are often nonassertive about expressing these feelings, caregivers may find that narratives offer valuable insights (Smith & Hoppe, 1991). Subtle cues may be the only indications that a patient is dissatisfied, in despair, reluctant to cooperate, overly anxious to please, or so on. All of these factors can be directly relevant to the success of medical care.

If the move toward patient empowerment continues, narratives are likely to become more influential components of patient–caregiver communication. Geist and Gates (1996, p. 221) describe the trend toward patient-centered care as "movement from biology to biography." Narratives reveal much about a person's identity and viewpoints. Patients typically describe their health concerns within a sequence of events they consider relevant. When caregivers listen and ask open-ended questions, they can learn a great deal—not only about patients' physical conditions, but also about their expectations and values (Eggly, 2002). How relevant are such factors to personal health? Very relevant, according to the integrative health theory, which proposes that health is not an isolated condition, but alignment between multiple factors (see Box 5.5).

Box 5.5 THEORETICAL FOUNDATIONS Integrative Health Model

Health cannot accurately be reduced to a failure of body, identity, or behavior, say the creators of integrative health theory (Lambert, Street, Cegala, Smith, Kurtz, & Schofield, 1997). Instead, **integrative health theory** proposes that health is alignment between interpretive accounts (assumptions and explanations), performance (activities and behaviors), and self-image (understanding of one's own identity).

Ideally, alignment is stable and enduring (the person is healthy), but a change in any one force can upset the alignment. Lambert and colleagues (1997) present the example of a man who feels healthy despite undiagnosed high blood pressure. However, once his condition is diagnosed and he begins taking medication for it, the man experiences a side effect (impotence). His interpretive account—that as a healthy male and husband (his self-image) he should have a sexual relationship with his wife—is threatened by his inability to engage in sexual activity (performance). In short, "the impotence is a resistance that destabilizes his healthy alignment," write Lambert and associates. "When he realizes he is impotent, he no longer feels healthy" (p. 34).

Lambert and colleagues (1997) use the term **resistance** to describe factors that threaten alignment. The effects of resistance are not predictable or universal. The man in the previous example might respond by altering his self-image, redefining his ideas about being a good husband, or resuming sexual activity by ceasing the medication (Lambert et al.).

People may have a difficult time adjusting to resistance factors that seem small to others. By the same token, over time, people sometimes achieve alignment others would not think possible. Marianne Brady and David Cella (1995) describe the resiliency with which some cancer patients ultimately adapt to their illness: "Many even say they are strengthened by the experience and note an improved outlook on life, enhanced interpersonal relationships and a deepened sense of personal strength" (paragraph 13). Although their physical abilities may be compromised by the disease, these people apparently adjust other factors to achieve a new (even an improved) sense of alignment.

The integrative health model presents several implications for health communication. For one, it sets aside the centuries-old question of whether health is fundamentally a matter of mind or body. By rejecting reductionistic notions, it provides an inclusive definition of health that relies more on alignment between factors than isolation of any one element. From this perspective, a health examination would not be focused on identifying the "cause" of a health concern but in considering how it is situated within broader contexts.

Another implication is that restoring alignment may be simple or complex. Sometimes there is primarily one form of resistance. Lambert and coauthors (1997) give the example of an appendectomy that restores a young woman to full health. In her case alignment is disrupted, but quickly restored. In other situations, however, focusing on one resistance point may not help (or may even worsen) overall alignment. For example, amputating a foot may remove physical danger but plunge the patient into personal crisis. Considering this, the biomedical model may be appropriate for some medical encounters but woefully insufficient for others.

A third implication is that outcomes are neither static nor definitive. Lambert and colleagues (1997) write: "It is never known in advance which accommodations will be successful, nor is it known whether accommodations will themselves lead to the emergence of new resistances" (p. 35). Even when alignment is present, there is no guarantee it will stay that way. In fact, it almost certainly will be challenged. Because of this, health is viewed more productively as a process, as a temporal emergence, than an outcome.

Finally, in the midst of this complexity, Lambert and colleagues (1997) argue that there is one constant: The patient is always central in the process. As an individual involved in the ongoing work of balancing identify and performance, a "patient is at the center of the aligned elements" and is "also the one doing the work of interactive stabilization" (p. 31).

What Do You Think?

1. In what ways do your daily activities support your self-image? How would you feel if you lost the ability to perform these activities?
2. Think of the last time you felt unhealthy. What resistance factors were involved? Was alignment restored? If so, how?

Suggested Sources

Integrative health is based on the collective ideas of a number of theorists. For the rich background behind this theory, see the following.

Charmaz, K. (1987). Struggling for a self: Identity levels of the chronically ill. In J. Roth & P. Conrad (Eds.), *Research in the sociology of health care* (pp. 283–321). Greenwich, CT: JAI Press.

Corbin, J., & Strauss, A. L. (1988). Experiencing body failure and a disrupted self image. In J. Corbin & A. L. Strauss (Eds.), *Unending work and care: Managing chronic illness at home* (pp. 49–67). San Francisco: Jossey-Bass.

Goffman, E. (1974). *Frame analysis: An essay on the organization of experience.* New York: Harper Colophon.

Pickering, A. (1995). *The mangle of practice: Time, agency, and science.* Chicago: University of Chicago Press.

Implications

Health is not something people simply have or do not have. To a large extent, health reflects the interplay of many factors. The way individuals interpret their health may affect how they react to it, how they describe their experiences, and how they feel about themselves. Diverse reactions to illness are common, and they are not always negative. Sometimes people are relieved or grateful for illness experiences.

People may deal with chronic illness in stages, at first denying that it will affect their lives, then considering the effects it might have, and perhaps developing "salvaged selves" that integrate elements of their former identity with conditions imposed by the illness.

As everyday storytellers, people act as narrators of their own lives. Narratives are ongoing biographies influenced by the storyteller's perspectives and the reactions of listeners. Such narratives provide a means of interpreting illnesses and orchestrating society's treatment of them. Integrative health theory emphasizes that health is alignment between self-image, performance, and interpretive accounts. Thus, health cannot be assessed in isolation. It must be considered within the context of individual experience.

SUMMARY

In contrast to the well-established ways caregivers are socialized, people learn how to be patients mostly through life experience and watching others (including their caregivers). Patients often communicate in hesitant and nonassertive ways, probably because they are uncertain what is expected of them and are afraid to seem rude or ignorant.

Although a caregiver may see health as a biological phenomenon to be identified by its physical manifestations, patients usually interpret illnesses in light of their effects on everyday activities. The Voice of Lifeworld is concerned with feelings and events. Patients' communication is influenced by a variety of factors including the nature of their illnesses, their personalities, and communication skills. Patient satisfaction is often based more on how caregivers listen and empathize than on perceived technical competency. Interestingly, patients tend to have serious complaints but still consider themselves satisfied overall with their doctors' care.

Patients' compliance with medical advice is notoriously low for a range of reasons. The imperative to use caregivers' time and resources to their fullest benefit has some theorists searching for new ways to increase cooperation between patients and caregivers. The expectation that patients should make informed decisions about their own care supports an image of patients and caregivers as cooperative partners.

Illness can affect people's very identity. Evidence suggests that people work to maintain their identities, even when illness changes their patterns of behavior. Narratives are a key component of patient talk and may reveal much more than factual details. Storytellings usually reflect how people view the world, how they see themselves in relation to others, and what events are most significant to them. Information of this sort can give caregivers valuable insight.

Patients may respond to illness in many ways—from relief to terror—and may experience changes in their personal identity as a result of illness. The integrated health theory describes the importance of alignment and resistance in maintaining good health.

Now that you have an overview of patient issues, read Chapter 6, in which you will learn how health and health communication are influenced by diversity in age, race, income, ability, sexual orientation, and more.

KEY TERMS

Voice of Lifeworld
Tuskegee Syphilis Study
informed consent
personal identity
social identities
tertiary identity
supernormal identity
restored self
contingent personal identity
salvaged self
narrative
integrative health theory
resistance

REVIEW QUESTIONS

1. What is the Voice of Lifeworld?
2. How is patients' philosophy of health and illness traditionally different from doctors'?
3. Why have patients traditionally been powerless? In your opinion, should they try to get on more equal footing with doctors? If so, how?
4. Have you ever found yourself unable to tell a doctor what you wanted to say? If so, what held you back? What factors would make it easier for you to communicate openly?
5. How do patients typically behave when their goals are different than their doctor's?
6. What factors are linked with patient satisfaction?
7. What reasons might patients have for not following medical advice?
8. Have you ever ignored medical advice? If so, why?
9. Would you be more likely to follow medical advice if you would get a cash prize for doing so?
10. How does patient–caregiver cooperation affect caregivers?
11. What are the stipulations of informed consent?

12. What are the four stages in Charmaz's (1987) model of identity management during chronic illness?
13. Why are narratives important to health communication?
14. Describe integrative health theory. What is meant by *alignment*? By *resistance*?

■ CLASS ACTIVITY

Informed Consent in Current Events

In 1997 a group of U.S.-sponsored researchers sought permission to conduct an experiment in Africa. Women who were both pregnant and HIV-positive were eligible to participate. A portion of the women (selected randomly) would be given AZT, an experimental drug scientists hoped would prevent unborn babies from getting HIV from their mothers. For comparison purposes, other women in the study would receive only placebos. All participants would receive prenatal medical care (which was otherwise unavailable in the women's community).

There was fierce debate about the research proposal. On one hand, it met the guidelines for informed consent. No one would be included except those women who agreed to take part after being fully informed about the study. On the other hand, some people felt the stakes were too high, and it was indefensible to withhold treatment from some women that might reasonably be expected to save their babies' lives.

The researchers maintained that the study might show whether or not AZT is a more successful way to save babies in the future. Furthermore, they said, every woman who participated would benefit, because without the researchers to provide prenatal care and HIV-prevention therapy of some sort, none of the women were likely to get medical care at all.

What Do You Think?

As a class, or in small groups, discuss your responses to the following questions.

1. Would you have approved the study or not? What are your reasons?
2. Is it OK to place some people at risk so that others may benefit? If so, under what conditions?
3. What do you think of the argument that all research participants would benefit from the study because it would offer more care than they would receive otherwise?
4. Is it acceptable for American researchers to conduct research on citizens of other countries? Why do you think they did not perform the study in the United States?

For more on this topic, see these sources:

Angell, M. (1997, September 18). The disputed editorial (reproduced online from the *New England Journal of Medicine*). ABCNEWS.COM (Online). Available at www.abcnews.aol.com/sections/living/Daily News/nejmedit1015.html

Joseph, J. (1998, February 19). The ethics of an AIDS study. ABCNEWS.COM (Online). Available at www.abcnews.aol.com/sections/living/Daily News/aidspregnant_0218.html

P.S. Wondering what happened? The study was approved amid great controversy. However, when AZT trials elsewhere rendered promising results, researchers began giving AZT to all the women in the African study. The issue of medical experimentation with citizens of developing countries is still being debated.

CHAPTER 6

Diversity Among Patients

She was in a motorized wheelchair that she controlled with her only usable finger. I could not understand her guttural speech or her facial contortions. She could not consistently hold her head up or control her drooling. After a few desperate moments, I asked her if she knew how to use a typewriter. She managed to make me understand a "yes" answer, and I ran out of the room to locate a typewriter on a movable stand. Pleased with my ingenuity, I stood next to her expecting some limited request. My smugness gave way to sheer awe as she painstakingly, letter by letter, tapped out with her left fourth finger the question: "What are the risks for me taking the birth control pill?" (Candib, 1994, p. 139)

In this account, Lucy Candib (1994) recalls a young woman who taught her to respect each patient as an individual. In the scope of health care, it is easy to categorize patients in impersonal categories. However, there is extraordinary diversity among the people who seek health care. This chapter explores patient diversity in terms of status, gender, sexual orientation, race and ethnicity, language, disabilities, and age. As you will see, each has an impact on health communication. Skill Builder sections provide tips on overcoming status barriers, interacting with people who have disabilities, talking to children about illness, and reaching members of marginalized populations.

STATUS DIFFERENCES

A basic law of communication is that people who are similar are likely to understand each other better. This presents particular difficulties when high-status caregivers communicate with poor and illiterate patients. Their life experiences are likely to be so different that they have a hard time understanding and warming up to each other. Patients of low socioeconomic status are consistently less satisfied with medical care than other patients (Becker & Newsom, 2003). As I use the term here, **socioeconomic status (SES)** is a combined measure of such factors as income, education, and employment level.

Misunderstandings

Research supports that misunderstandings occur for several reasons when doctors interact with low SES patients. First, low SES patients have historically asked fewer questions than others and revealed less about their conditions (Bochner, 1983). This occurs despite evidence that they are typically more fearful about their health than most people and are less able to judge the severity of their illnesses themselves (Ben-Sira, 1990).

Second, doctors tend to use a strictly biomedical model with poor and minority patients (Roter et al., 1997) and involve them less in decision making (Cooper-Patrick et al., 1999). The influence probably goes both ways. That is, caregivers take a biomedical approach because patients do not bring up other concerns, and patients keep quiet because doctors use the biomedical model.

Third, low SES patients are less likely than others to benefit from written materials and media presentations. In some inner-city hospitals as many as 82% of the patients are functionally illiterate (Williams et al., 1995). Illiteracy is especially high among elderly and non–English-speaking patients, many of whom cannot read medical consent forms or instructions on a medicine bottle. Unlike other patients—who may be exposed to health information via pamphlets, cable television, newspapers, computers, and other means—poor and illiterate patients are apt to rely strictly on their doctors and advice from people they know.

Fourth, prejudice is a stumbling block to communication between caregivers and low SES patients. Medical students' regard for impoverished patients tends to diminish between their first year of study and their last. Fourth-year medical students are less likely than others to believe all people should receive medical care even if they are poor (Crandall, Volk, & Loemker, 1993).

Finally, although low SES patients are more likely than others to follow doctors' advice, they may be receiving guidance about the wrong subjects (Taira, Safran, Seto, Rogers, & Tarlov, 1997). Taira and associates found that doctors often mistake the health risks facing low and high SES patients. For example, low-income patients are more at risk for obesity. However, doctors more frequently discuss diet and exercise with high SES patients, perhaps because they assume those patients are more interested.

Health Literacy

Low literacy is associated with poor health. Considering that about 90 million people in the United States suffer from low health literacy, it is clearly a problem for individuals and communities ("Health Literacy," 2003).

Health literacy involves reading and understanding health information, but it is more than that. As defined by WHO, **health literacy** "represents the cognitive and social skills which determine the motivation and ability of individuals to gain access to, understand and use information in ways which promote and maintain good health" ("Health Promotion Glossary," 1998, p. 10). This definition emphasizes that it is not enough to read and write. To be literate about health, people must also

- Understand the language in which information is conveyed (be it English, Spanish, statistical jargon, legal talk, or some other language variant).
- Have access to reliable and relevant information.

- Be interested in health-related information.
- Have the social skills to discuss health matters with others.
- Understand how to apply the information.
- Be willing and capable of putting health information to effective use.

Regarded this way, it is clear that none of us is entirely health literate. Medical information is often baffling, even to well-educated individuals. Moreover, just because we can understand the words does not necessarily mean we can or will put the information to good use. But for many Americans, the problem is worse than that. About 1 in 5 Americans is unable to read a prescription bottle (AMA, 2003a). Other people are able to read but other factors—such as low proficiency with English or vision impairments—may make it difficult for them to understand and use health information.

Low literacy is masked by embarrassment. People are often too ashamed to admit they are unable to read or understand medical information (Bernhardt & Cameron, 2003). Friends and family members may not even realize the problem. At a briefing to launch the AMA's new health literacy initiative, physician David W. Baker said:

> We find that a lot of people have gone through their lives and listen to the radio, watch television and don't read their newspapers too often but can get by pretty well with minimal reading skills. . . . They come into the health care setting and they are all of a sudden faced with medications and instructions and all of this information written at too high a level for easy comprehension. (AMA, 2003a, paragraph 7)

Embarrassment and frustration may discourage people from pursuing medical care and may lead them to take medicine incorrectly, overlook health risk factors, and miss out on important information.

All of this leads to worse health problems and higher expenses. It costs about $12,974 per year to care for an individual who reads at a second-grade level or lower, compared to about $2,696 per year for a person with greater reading skills (Bresolin, 1999).

Rather than spending billions to treat health conditions that might have been avoided, the AMA and cosponsors have launched an effort to minimize the literacy gap. Part of the effort is *Ask Me 3*, a simple program that encourages patients to ask questions and seek clarification when they talk with medical professionals. Patients are encouraged to ask their doctors, nurses, and pharmacists these three questions:

- What is my main problem?
- What do I need to do?
- Why is it important for me to do this?

Simple and attractive *Ask Me 3* materials reassure people that, "Everyone wants help with health information. You are not alone if you find things confusing at times." Handouts suggest options for patients who feel confused. For example,

Box 6.1 RESOURCES
More About the Health Literacy Initiative

To obtain a health literacy kit, copies of *Ask Me 3* materials and information about state health literacy initiatives, and to view the AMA health literacy video, log onto the American Medical Association website at www.ama-assn.org.

if they do not understand answers to the suggested questions, patients are encouraged to say, "This is new to me. Will you please explain that to me one more time?" (For more about the Health Literacy Initiative, see Box 6.1.)

Communication Skill Builders: Surmounting Status Barriers

The unfortunate result of status-related communication barriers is that the neediest people receive the least amount of information and attention. Experts offer the following ideas for improving communication between caregivers and patients with low health literacy.

- *Caregivers: Be attentive and respectful.* Try to identify patients' needs and respect their contributions. Double-check illiterate patients' understanding of verbal information, listen attentively, and do not be put off by patients' colloquialisms. In an article titled "All I Really Need to Know About Medicine I Learned From My Patients," physician Dwalia South (1997) says most patients do not have large medical vocabularies. They describe unfamiliar lumps and bumps as "hickeys" and "doodads." Nonetheless, people know a lot about their own bodies, and smart caregivers take patients' knowledge seriously.
- *Caregivers: Let patients know what is expected.* Bochner (1983) suggests that low SES patients may be tongue-tied by intimidation or may simply be unaware what is expected of them. He encourages doctors to socialize patients into the medical context by explaining routines and encouraging them to participate in discussions.
- *Patients: Be explicit about feelings and questions.* Do not assume caregivers understand your concerns (Bochner, 1983). Instead, make an effort to express your feelings and questions. You can improve communication by overcoming your reluctance to speak up.

GENDER DIFFERENCES

It is naive to assume that all women or all men communicate in the same way. Neither are males and females always different in how they communicate. Studies do indicate some general differences and similarities, however.

Females tend to be more nonverbally expressive in health care situations, talk more than men, engage in more partnership-building behaviors, and reveal more personal information about themselves (Gabbard-Alley, 1995, 2000). Females in the United States are also more knowledgeable than males about health issues. This may be because women are most often targeted as consumers, utilize medical services more than men, and typically feel more responsible for the health of family members ("Women Most Active," 2003).

Health professionals in the United States tend to share more information with females than with males, perhaps because women ask more questions. However, the literature suggests that health professionals typically take men's concerns more seriously than women's (Beck et al., 1997; Gabbard-Alley, 1995). The paucity of medical research about women's health concerns has became a topic of heated debate in the last decade, prompting legislation to include more women in clinical trials and to devote more money to research women's health issues such as breast cancer (Waalen, 1997).

Research indicates only slight differences between males' and females' preferences as patients. Men typically have no strong preference considering the sex of their doctors, but women favor female physicians ("How Is Your Doctor," 1995), and they prefer women's clinics to traditional clinics (Bean-Mayberry et al., 2003). In at least one study researchers have found that patients' age and sex are not relevant to their satisfaction with caregivers (Williams, 1997). Whether male, female, young, or old, patients tend to want the same things, namely, caring and respect.

In the next section we discuss the dangers of **heterosexism,** the assumption that people's romantic relationships involve members of the opposite sex.

SEXUAL ORIENTATION

In an article called "Do Ask, Do Tell," physician Jennifer E. Potter (2002) asserts that gay and lesbian patients often receive substandard care because doctors are not aware of, or misunderstand, their sexual orientation and behaviors. Potter recalls her own experience as a teenager when, after telling her family physician she was attracted to girls, he laughed off her confusion as a "phase a lot of girls go through" (p. 341). Later, a psychiatrist tried to "cure" her of homosexual tendencies, and doctors urged her to use birth control, never considering that she might be sexually active with women rather than men. Although Potter regarded the prescription for the pill "absurd," previous experience told her to keep the truth to herself. Even as a student at Harvard Medical School, Potter was encouraged to keep her lesbianism a secret.

Fear of social rejection can rob homosexual individuals of comfort and acceptance. Potter (2002) describes the temptation to "pass" as heterosexual: "On the face of it, maintaining silence makes almost everyone happy" (p. 342). But pretending to be heterosexual felt like lying by omission. She writes that pretending to be something she wasn't eroded her self-respect, unwittingly put her in cahoots with people who wished to ignore and invalidate homosexuality, and made her feel isolated. She could not introduce her long-term partner to friends or invite her to professional and social gatherings. Now, although Potter is open with her close friends and associates, other people still make erroneous assumptions about her lifestyle. Although it may seem inappropriate or awkward to reveal her sexual orientation to them, misunderstandings can make people feel embarrassed or deceived. Potter reflects that "Coming out is a process that never ends. Every time I meet someone new I must decide if, how, and when I will reveal my sexual orientation" (p. 342).

Discrimination is a particularly threatening possibility when one's health is at risk. For example, some homosexual women with cancer say they fear they will receive substandard care if they reveal their sexual orientation to their doctors (Matthews, 1998). However, keeping quiet presents risks as well. Although a vaccination against Hepatitis A is recommended for men who have sex with men, a study in Birmingham, Alabama, revealed that only 34% of gay African-American men there have been vaccinated (Rhodes, Yee, & Hergenrather, 2003). The researchers found that men who had open communication with their caregivers were more likely to be aware of the hepatitis risk and to seek the vaccination.

The tell-or-not dilemma may be especially difficult for older adults. A Canadian study reveals that homosexuality among older adults is largely ignored by society and by health care providers (Brotman, Ryan, & Cormier, 2003). Moreover, older adults who are homosexual may be especially sensitive to societal stereotypes and lack of acceptance although they may be in long-term relationships that are important to their happiness.

In the United States (although not in other countries), a disproportionate number of HIV/AIDS cases have occurred among homosexual males, adding to the stigma and stress they may already feel. In a study of homosexual couples in which one or both partners has HIV/AIDS, Haas (2002) found that primary relational partners provided the majority of support during the illness, followed by friends and family members. Ignoring or minimizing the importance of these relationships can have serious consequences for people's coping abilities.

Caregivers who avoid talking about sexuality are not necessarily prejudiced against it. They may be embarrassed or uncomfortable with the subject or feel that it lies outside their expertise. Richard Gamlin (1999) proposes that nurses should strive to become more comfortable with their own sexuality and should use role-playing to gain experience talking about sexuality with patients. Caregivers who are comfortable discussing sexuality are more likely to help patients feel comfortable. In one study, adolescents said they think it is important for their caregivers to know their sexual history, and they are most comfortable revealing this information when the caregivers asks about sexual issues directly (Rosenthal et al., 1999).

In summary, like everyone else, homosexual individuals are adversely affected when they feel they cannot be open with their caregivers. As you will see in the next sections, a similar fear of discrimination influences people of different races.

■ RACE

Racism can make you sick. That is the conclusion of studies linking race to everyday well-being, medical care, and life expectancy. As this section shows, people of color are at a disadvantage where health and longevity are concerned.

Racism is discrimination based on a person's race. People belong to a certain race if they share a hereditary background or common descent such as European or African (Merriam-Webster, 1999). Practically speaking, people often judge race by visible characteristics such as skin color. Because the Black/White distinction is so visible, it is the basis for a great deal of racism, with direct and indirect effects on health.

In the United States race is associated with life expectancy. The average life span of an African-American male is 68.2 years—nearly 7 years shorter than the average White male ("National Vital Statistics Report," 2002). Likewise, African-American women live an average of 74.9 years—5.1 years shorter than most White women.

Research shows that the link between health and race is social rather than biological. In other words, people of minority status do not suffer ill health because of the genes they are born with but because of what occurs during their lifetimes (Bhopal, 1998).

Different Care and Outcomes

Some researchers suggest that people of color receive different medical care than others. For example, among children ages 6 to 17, White children are twice as likely to receive prescription medications as African-American and Hispanic children (Hanh, 1995). Among adults, White patients are three times more likely than African Americans to undergo cardiac procedures (Daumit, Hermann, Coresh, & Powe, 1999).

Furthermore, some studies show that African Americans experience less favorable outcomes than White patients following medical procedures. One group of researchers charted the conditions of patients who received cardiopulmonary resuscitation (CPR) in the hospital (Ebell, Smith, Kruse, Drader-Wilcox, & Novak, 1995). African-American patients were resuscitated as successfully as White ones, but they were less likely than White patients to survive until discharge from the hospital. The researchers speculate that the difference may lie in how closely African-American patients were monitored following CPR, the severity of their illnesses, or a preference among African-American patients to request "do not resuscitate" orders following a CPR episode.

Only slightly more promising is evidence that Black patients in one study lived about as long as White patients (about 6 years) following their first hospitalization for heart failure (Croft et al., 1999). However, the Black patients were typically younger than the White patients, so although their response to initial treatment was roughly the same, they experienced ill health sooner in their lives and died at early ages.

Explanations

There are several explanations why people of different races seem to receive different medical care and may respond differently to it. Overall, differences seem rooted in distrust, high risk, lack of knowledge, limited access, and ineffective patient–caregiver communication.

Distrust One explanation for the link between race and health is that people of color are less likely to pursue medical attention because they distrust the medical establishment. Based on historic patterns of discrimination (like the Tuskegee Syphilis Study described in Chapter 5), members of minority races may distrust medical personnel (Gamble, 1997).

In one study, African-American mothers who perceived racism in the community overall were dissatisfied with the medical care their chronically ill children received (Auslander, Thompson, Dreitzer, & Santiago, 1997). Accustomed to being treated as inferior, these mothers worried more than others that their children were not receiving the best medical care possible.

Distrust may cause people to underutilize health services and to doubt the validity of medical advice (Ferguson et al., 1998). This could contribute to the comparatively low number of medical interventions among African Americans and Hispanics. They may be approved for prescriptions they never fill or may decline to undergo medical procedures if they distrust their doctors' judgment. Or, they may never see a doctor at all.

High Risk, Low Knowledge A second explanation is that members of minority races are not well informed about health issues, despite the fact that they are often at high risk for disease. African-American men are significantly less knowledgeable about prostate cancer warning signs than White men (Barber et al., 1998), although African-American men are twice as likely to die of prostate cancer ("Prostate Cancer," 1993). Members of minority races may be at high risk for disease because a disproportionate number of them are of low socioeconomic status (Carter, Schill, & Wachter, 1998). With limited resources, they may suffer from poor living conditions, unhealthy diets, and insufficient access to health information and health services (Baldwin, 2003).

There is also evidence that everyday discrimination threatens people's health. A survey of Black, White, and Hispanic individuals shows that ill health is higher among people who are subjected to everyday discrimination such as poor service, insults, and being treated as inferior or stupid (Williams, Yan,

Jackson, & Anderson, 1997). African Americans were twice as likely as White Americans to report "fair" or "poor" health and twice as likely to report ongoing discrimination. The researchers conclude that the stress of dealing with negative social feedback takes a significant toll on people's health. This viewpoint is supported by evidence that African Americans are twice as likely as White Americans to have stress-related disorders such as hypertension (high blood pressure) (Croft et al., 1999).

Despite their high-risk status, members of minority races may be relatively unaware of health issues because they do not use or trust mainstream media as much as White audiences or because many health messages are not designed to appeal to minority audiences (Engelberg, Flora, & Nass, 1997; Yep, 1992, 1993). Individuals who are not well informed about health services and disease warning signs are more likely than others to become seriously ill before they seek medical attention (Ferguson et al., 1998). If African Americans are sicker than others when they seek medical care that might explain (in part) why they do not respond to treatment as well and why they do not undergo the same procedures as other patients.

Access A third explanation is that minorities have comparatively low access to advanced medical facilities. Low-income individuals may not qualify for care in high-tech medical centers, and such centers are not likely to be located within low-income, minority neighborhoods (Flores, Abreu, Olivar, & Kastner, 1998). Canadian researchers report that residents of affluent neighborhoods usually get quicker ambulance service than people in poor neighborhoods and the best paramedic crews are dispatched to rich neighborhoods (Govindarajan & Schull, 2003).

Once they are admitted to a particular hospital, patients receive fairly equitable treatment regardless of race (Diminitz, 1998; Leape, Hilborne, Bell, Kamberg, & Brook, 1999). However, care may vary from one hospital to another, and because of location and insurance limitations, poor patients are less likely to end up in hospitals that offer advanced-care treatments such as bypass surgery and chemotherapy (Leape et al., 1999). This is unfortunate because African-American men have the same chance of surviving prostate cancer as White men *if* they have equal access to medical care (Optenberg et al., 1995). In short, low-income individuals may receive less advanced care because the medical facilities available to them do not offer it.

Patient–Caregiver Communication Finally, medical care may differ because of poor communication across racial lines. Patients and caregivers may be uncomfortable with people of other races, may misinterpret communication cues, or may allow stereotypes to interfere with their judgment. Studies show that the families of African-American patients sometimes feel that medical personnel are reluctant to implement costly procedures they might use to treat other patients (Krakauer & Truog, 1997). Patients who are the same race as their doctors are more likely than others to be involved in medical decision making, with the consequence that African-American patients are involved in decision making less often than White patients are (Cooper-Patrick et al., 1999).

The idea that stereotypes affect physicians' judgment is supported by a study published in the *New England Journal of Medicine* (Schulman et al., 1999). For the study, researchers videotaped actor/patients who described their symptoms (involving chest pain) using the same words and gestures, wearing identical clothing (hospital gowns), in the same setting. The patients differed only in terms of age and race. Doctors who viewed the tapes were significantly more likely to recommend heart catheterization for male and White patients than female or Black patients. This suggests that—all other things being equal—racial and sexist stereotypes do influence physicians' judgments. These stereotypes are likely to affect how doctors perceive patients' conditions and the treatment they recommend. (See Box 6.2 for a discussion of ethical principles when allocating health resources.)

In summary, research shows that racism affects health and health care in varying degrees depending on the level of patients' trust, their knowledge and health risk, access to medical information and services, and stereotypes affecting patient–caregiver communication. Many of these issues can be addressed with more effective communication. Verbal and nonverbal signs of acceptance are appreciated. In one study, African-American and Latino-American patients said they felt more comfortable with caregivers who had culturally sensitive artwork, reading material, and music in their offices (Tucker et al., 2003).

LANGUAGE DIFFERENCES

It is especially difficult to ensure that patients are fully informed concerning their medical options when the patients and their caregivers speak different languages. Nearly 25 million adults in the United States do not speak English proficiently ("Demograhics," 2002). Non-English speakers are less satisfied with medical care than are Caucasians or members of ethnic and racial minorities (Weech-Maldonado et al., 2003). At one inner-city hospital, more than one-fourth of Latino parents said language barriers discourage them from using medical facilities (Flores, Abreu, Olivar, & Kastner, 1998). These parents felt that the scarcity of Spanish-speaking physicians led to their children being misdiagnosed or given the wrong medicine. (Box 6.3 describes the experiences of a Spanish-speaking woman in a U.S. hospital.)

Language barriers can be frustrating for patients and caregivers. Among patients at an urban children's hospital in the United States, 68% of residents surveyed spoke little or no Spanish, yet most of them cared for patients with limited English proficiency "often" or "every day" (O'Leary, Federico, & Hampers, 2003). Most of the residents felt that Spanish-speaking families understood the diagnosis only "sometimes" or "never," and 80% of the residents

Box 6.2 ETHICAL CONSIDERATIONS Who Gets What Care?

"Doctor, do everything you can!"

Is it ever justified for a doctor to do less than everything possible? Conventional American wisdom says no. Americans have come to expect that physicians will provide the best possible care, cost notwithstanding (Morreim, 1989). However, it has become too expensive to do everything possible for every person (Malinowski, 1996).

Many people feel that, if the U.S. health system is to survive, it is necessary to make some judgments about who gets what care. Health care is being called on to eliminate excessive and unnecessary procedures. The question is: Where is the line between necessary and unnecessary?

One option is to provide care to those people who can afford to pay for it. This option places underprivileged persons at a disadvantage and may create a deeper schism between people of high and low socioeconomic status. All in all, few people are willing to allow low-income citizens to suffer in ill health.

Another option is to give priority to procedures that are known to have high success rates. For instance, a procedure that gives patients a 30% chance of survival may be granted priority over one with a 20% survival rate. This seems logical, but it is difficult to allow patients to go untreated when there is even a 1 in 5 chance of saving their lives. As Norman Levinsky (1995) points out, statistics are merely generalizations, and every patient is unique. There is no guarantee that a risky procedure will fail or that a tried-and-true one will succeed. Moreover, statistics vary, and sticking with well-established procedures diminishes the chances of developing new, better treatments.

Still another option is to provide care for people who are likely to enjoy the highest quality of life as a result. From that perspective, it might be more important to fund expensive treatment to help a young child walk than to help an 85-year-old use his legs again following a stroke. Levinsky (1995) warns that such judgment calls are likely to lead to unfair discrimination. He wonders how it is possible to judge people's quality of life, and warns that such judgments are likely to be biased against people who hold values different than the medical decision maker's.

As you can see, deciding how health resources will be allocated is no simple matter. To get an idea of how difficult it is, try answering the following questions.

What Do You Think?

1. If one person can afford expensive treatment but another cannot, is it OK to refuse care to the less affluent person?

2. If there is a slight chance that an expensive experimental drug will prolong a dying person's life, should the insurance company or health organization pay for use of the drug?
3. If two patients suffer from the same condition, should they be treated differently?

   What if one is a child and one is very old?

   What if one is famous and the other is unknown?

   What if one is homeless and the other is a community leader?

4. If you could fund only two of the following procedures, which would you choose? On what criteria would you base your choices?
   - *a.* Surgery to help an infertile couple conceive a child.
   - *b.* Plastic surgery to improve the appearance of a person born with a facial deformity.
   - *c.* Chemotherapy for a very sick person.
   - *d.* Drug therapy that might prevent a person from getting AIDS.
5. Who should decide which care will be funded? Doctors? Funding agencies? Community members? Patients? Legislators?
6. If research is able to develop improved treatment options, but the cost of the research significantly raises health care costs, should the system continue to fund research? What if higher costs mean some people will lose their insurance?
7. Doctors say one reason they overtreat patients is because they may be sued for malpractice if they do not do everything possible. How would you resolve this dilemma?

Suggested Sources

Clancy, C. (1995). Managed care: Jekyll or Hyde? *Journal of the American Medical Association, 273,* 338–339.

Council on Ethical and Judicial Affairs, American Medical Association. Ethical issues in managed care. (1995). *Journal of the American Medical Association, 273,* 330–335.

Levinsky, N. (1995). The doctor's master. In J. D. Arras & B. Steinbock (Eds.), *Ethical issues in modern medicine* (4th ed., pp. 116–119). Mountain View, CA: Mayfield.

Malinowski, M. J. (1996). Capitation, advances in medical technology, and the advent of a new era in medical ethics. *American Journal of Law & Medicine, 22,* 331–360.

Morreim, E. H. (1989). Fiscal scarcity and the inevitability of bedside budget balancing. *Archives of Internal Medicine, 149,* 1012–1015.

Box 6.3 PERSPECTIVES
Language Barriers in a Health Care Emergency

Picture yourself in Mexico at a hospital trying to get someone, anyone, to help make a terrible pain in your stomach go away. You hear: "Tu no hablas Espanol, y nadien te puede entender." In other words, "You don't speak Spanish, and no one can understand you." Finally, you find a first-year English student, a schoolboy, who attempts to translate. Next, you find yourself in a room, half-clothed, wearing a hospital robe, wondering: Did the boy understand you? Did the doctors understand him? What is wrong with you? What is happening?

Perhaps this will give you some idea what it is like for Spanish-speakers in the United States health care system. This is a true story about my mother (Maria) and her mother (Consuelo), Cuban Americans trying to deal with the frustrations, anxieties, and fears of communicating with medical professionals who speak a different language.

The Story

Consuelo had been showing symptoms for some time before finally agreeing to see a doctor. Now that she had moved to a new city with little to no Hispanic culture, she wondered fearfully if she would be able to communicate with doctors. But this time the pain was intense, and at least she had her daughter, Maria, to help her communicate. Consuelo wanted very much to be understood, and maybe this time she would be. That thought finally gave her the courage to see a doctor.

At the doctor's office Consuelo could tell something was wrong. She was now in her early 60s and knew her diabetes was not getting any better. She understood enough of the conversations between the doctors and her daughter to gather that she needed a heart catheterization. Maria was not giving her all the details, but Consuelo could sense from her body language that the procedure was serious. She was right. A few moments later she found herself being wheeled off to the operating room for an emergency catheterization—without Maria. Now she felt more scared and afraid, knowing she had no means of communicating with the people around her and unsure what they were doing or why.

Before the procedure the surgeon needed Consuelo to understand the process and answer some questions. This was no easy task. Once again, as Consuelo had feared, she was unable to communicate. By this time, she began feeling extremely anxious and frustrated that neither the surgeon nor any of his assistants could understand what she was saying. Finally, after what seemed decades, the surgeon summoned Maria to the operating room after finding no one else who could translate.

For Maria, the experience involved mixed emotions. She had accompanied her mother many times before to the hospital, but had never been allowed inside the operating room. Now that she was there, she felt more anxious than ever. First, she wanted to do a good job because she felt her mother's life depended on it. Second, she felt uneasy being in the room because she was unfamiliar with the environment. Consequently, Maria did not know how she should act, what she should say, or what was expected of her. She also had to fight her emotional reactions at seeing her mother on the operating table. However, Maria was relieved to be able to be with her mother and decided to concentrate on positive feelings to get them both through the experience.

When Consuelo was back in a hospital room after the procedure, the doctor broke the news that Consuelo needed open-heart surgery and would soon be transferred to a larger hospital. Once again, Consuelo could tell something negative was being conveyed, but knew she would have to wait until the conversation was over to get the full story from Maria. Waiting only added to her anxiety. A few times, Consuelo tried to interrupt, but was only chastised by Maria for interfering with her efforts to understand the implications of what the doctor was trying to tell her.

Unfortunately, although the larger hospital was located within a predominantly Hispanic community, few doctors and nurses there could speak Spanish. That meant that Maria, and her husband, Jesus, would have to take turns staying at the hospital to translate for Consuelo. But the difference in Consuelo's outlook was remarkable. After only a few hours in the new hospital, she started to feel better about herself and less depressed. This was because the new physicians, regardless of whether they spoke Spanish or not, attempted to speak to her in Spanish and to understand what she was saying. Consuelo recalled one young physician who would walk into her room saying, "Buenos dias," bringing a smile to her face, and then leave saying, "Buenas noches" despite the time of day, making her laugh. These small gestures made all the difference to Consuelo.

Maria noticed that her mother began to light up whenever a doctor entered the room. She also noted that the doctors were no longer looking at her, but talking directly to her mother. Maria was still translating, but she was no longer the focus of their conversation. In return, she noticed that her mother seemed more attentive and willing to follow the doctors' advice. A few times, Consuelo even answered the physicians in English with responses such as "yes" when she understood what they were saying. This in turn would make them laugh and rub her hand as a sign of acceptance and reward. And if this were not enough, Consuelo was introduced to a Spanish-speaking nurse at the hospital who would occasionally visit, making her feel even more at home.

continued

Box 6.3 PERSPECTIVES
Language Barriers in a Health Care Emergency, *continued*

The surgery went well, but following it, Consuelo was paired with a therapist who could not speak Spanish and made no effort to communicate with her. She began to feel depressed and frustrated again. But she learned to get over this new obstacle quickly after talking about her feelings with her family. They found a way to make her realize that her good experiences at the new hospital far outweighed the bad ones, and soon Consuelo was able to ignore the therapist's behavior and move on with her treatment.

Consuelo was in the hospital for about a month. In that time she learned a lot about what she liked and did not like. As a result, she asked Maria to help her look for doctors who would be as attentive with her as the hospital doctors had been. Now Consuelo has at least one doctor she likes very much who speaks Spanish.

—*Marie*

What Do You Think?

1. How might you have acted if you were Consuelo? If you were Maria?
2. Do you think hospitals should do more to accommodate non-English speakers? Why or why not?
3. How could Consuelo have eliminated some of her anxiety?
4. What could the first surgeon have done to help both Maria and Consuelo feel more at ease?
5. Researchers have found that people are more fearful about medical visits if they feel socially alienated and disconnected from their environments. What might we do to ease these feelings?
6. Have you ever been in a situation in which you have had to communicate with someone who did not speak the same language as you? How did you handle the situation?

said they avoided caring for these patients whenever possible. Despite the frustrations and perception of poor communication, they used interpreters only about 58% of the time.

In a similar study, non-English-speaking patients and primary care physicians in California made do without trained interpreters 94% of the time although they felt trained interpreters significantly increased the quality of health communication when they were used (Hornberger, Itakura, & Wilson, 1997). In some cases, family members or bilingual employees were used as untrained interpreters, but in 11% of the cases, no interpreters were used at all although the patient and physician spoke different languages. One physician reported that members of the housekeeping staff do most of the interpreting although they usually speak English poorly themselves and have little knowledge of medical terminology. As in the other study, doctors said they try to avoid seeing non-English-speaking patients.

The roadblocks to providing interpreters are common ones: time and money. Physicians may do without interpreters to save time or protect the patients' privacy. They may also be hesitant to incur the expense because guidelines for reimbursement of interpreter services are unclear.

More optimistically, some organizations are reporting success using trained interpreters and communication technology. Community members trained to understand basic medical goals and terminology can often help bridge the language gap between patients and caregivers (Woloshin, Bickell, Schwartz, Gany, & Welch, 1995). They may also be in a position to help both sides better understand the cultural and status differences that affect them. Likewise, patients are typically satisfied with medical interactions in which trained interpreters participate via telephone or videoconference technology (Jones, Gill, Harrison, Meakin, & Wallace, 2003).

DISABILITIES

Individuals with disabilities are often confronted with frustrating dichotomies. For one, people tend to either treat their disabilities as the most important thing about them or to self-consciously avoid the issue entirely. Health professionals have typically not received much training on how to communicate with disabled persons. Consequently, when treating these individuals, physicians often focus on the disability and ignore medical concerns that are not directly related to it (Braithwaite & Thompson, 1999). On the other hand, well-meaning acquaintances may consider it taboo to talk about the disability. A woman described by Dawn Braithwaite and Lynn Harter (2000) said she initially appreciated it when her future husband did not make a big deal about her disability when they met. But after several months of getting to know each other, she was exasperated that he never even mentioned the subject. Eventually, she brought it up to end the awkward silence.

Another dichotomy concerns the way persons with disabilities are regarded by society. Sally Nemeth, a health communication scholar who is blind, reflects that people with disabilities are often cast "either as heroic super crips or as tragic, usually embittered and angry, unfortunates worthy only of pity and charity" (Nemuth, 2000, p. 40). The reality is that people with disabilities are much like anyone else.

It is frustrating to be treated as helpless or unsophisticated. Health professionals (and others) tend to treat individuals with disabilities as if they are childlike—speaking slowly and loudly to them even when that is not necessary and giving instructions rather than asking for their opinions (Harper &

Wadsworth, 1992). Topics such as sexuality are often avoided. I remember attending the wedding of a friend, Melissa, who had been deaf since age 6. Although Melissa was well into her 20s when she married, her family realized on the eve of her wedding that she knew nothing about birth control. The school Melissa attended did not provide sexual education to students with disabilities, and her parents had always considered her too "sheltered" to need such information.

People whose disabilities are invisible to others may encounter unique difficulties. A study of people with heart disease revealed that they consider themselves older than their same-age peers, largely because of physical limitations and attention to end-of-life issues typically associated with older people (Kundrat & Nussbaum, 2003). Those with invisible illnesses face the dilemma of either keeping their illnesses a secret or revealing them to others and risking a changed social identity. Some individuals, particularly men, may be loath to admit disabilities they think will make them seem dependent or pitiful (Moore & Miller, 2003). For more about the frustration of invisible disabilities, see Box 6.4.

These challenges have an effect on health communication. Individuals with disabilities are typically less satisfied with managed care providers than doctors they choose themselves, mostly because doctors on a provider list may not be knowledgeable or comfortable dealing with disabilities (Kroll, Beatty, & Bingham, 2003). And because of the need for trust and familiarity, it may be particularly stressful for persons with disabilities to change doctors (O'Connell, Bailey, & Pearce, 2003). On the bright side, even brief training sessions may help people interact more sensitively with people who have disabilities (Harper & Wadsworth, 1992). Following are some tips for communicating effectively.

Communication Skill Builders: Interacting With Persons Who Have Disabilities

- Talk to people with disabilities directly, not to their interpreters or companions.
- Remember to identify yourself to sight-impaired persons.
- Treat adults with disabilities as adults.
- When a person with a disability is difficult to understand, listen attentively, then paraphrase to make sure you heard correctly.
- Whenever possible, sit down when speaking to people in wheelchairs so you can communicate at eye level.
- Relax! For example, do not become embarrassed if you accidentally say, "See you later," to a blind person.
- Do not insist on helping people with disabilities. If they do not ask for help, or if they decline your offer of assistance, respect their wishes (Soule & Roloff, 2000). Keep in mind that it is discouraging to regularly

Box 6.4 PERSPECTIVES
"My Disability Doesn't Show"

Dear Editor,

Since receiving my handicapped hangtag two years ago, I have been rudely approached by so many people that I've lost count.

I am a 44-year-old female, tall, thin, and do not walk with a cane, nor am I in need of a wheelchair. My handicap is internal, from two major back surgeries, and although I do have pain while walking, I walk with confidence. By simply looking at me, one would not know that I have a handicap.

Since using my handicapped hangtag, I have been rudely approached by not only people off campus, but from just as many students on campus. I have heard it all from, "You sure look handicapped," or "You must really be handicapped from driving a car like that (a 1992 Firebird)," to "How can I get one of those (a handicapped hangtag)?" These comments not only hurt my feelings but are truly insulting, especially since I received my back injuries from serving my country while in the military, and the scar on my back extends from my neck to my buttocks.

I would like to educate everyone on campus, as well as people off campus, that not all handicaps are visible. Not everyone with a handicap is over 60, nor do they have to walk with a cane, nor do they have to be in a wheelchair.

In order to receive a handicapped hangtag, the Department of Motor Vehicles requires that one must have limitations of walking because of arthritic, neurological or orthopedic (which I have) conditions, and one must have a disability rating of 50 percent or greater. My disability rating is 80 percent and is permanent.

The last comment came January 28th by a student getting into his blue truck, which was parked next to me in front of the campus police station. The young man made the normal comment that I did not look handicapped. Normally I usually just tell people if they have a problem with me to take my license plate number and report me, but this time, I lost it and told this guy to mind his own business, and added a few explicit words to boot.

I would like to see people stop stereotyping others based on their looks and think before they inadvertently insult someone, because it really does make me feel bad, and I have every right to use my handicapped tag.

—Beverly Davis

"owe" people gratitude for their assistance, especially when the assistance is unnecessary. (It is okay to extend the same common courtesies you would offer an able-bodied friend, such as holding a door open.)

- Heed the wisdom of Thuy-Phuong Do and Patricia Geist (2000), who remind us: "Everyone is othered to some extent; we all possess disabilities, whether visible or invisible" (p. 60).

As you are probably gathering by now, the concept of being "othered," treated as if you do not belong, is demoralizing in everyday life and particularly in medical transactions. As the following section shows, age can be a source of "othering" as well.

AGE

Age can have an impact on how people communicate with their caregivers and the people around them everyday. This section focuses briefly on children and more extensively on older adults. As you will see, both groups use health care services a great deal, and their communication is profoundly affected by the assumptions of people around them.

Children

Communicating with children can be challenging because their perceptions may be different than adults'. For example, children may perceive that painful medical treatments are a means of punishment (Hart & Chesson, 1998). Moreover, children may be unsure how to express their feelings or afraid to speak freely in front of people they do not know.

Parents can be both a help and a hindrance in caring for young patients. Many times, parents have valuable information about their children's conditions and are able to comfort them as no one else could. Parents may become especially frustrated if their concerns are not taken seriously, or if they do not feel well informed about their children's health needs (Kai, 1996). And rightly so. Parents are the children's principle caregivers, and their responsibility does not end at the doctor's office or hospital. However, it can be difficult for caregivers to attend to young children *and* manage the complex emotions of their parents. Parents tend to be especially anxious, guilty, and uncertain where their children's health is concerned (Kai, 1996).

When children are hospitalized, parents and professional caregivers may have conflicting ideas about what care each of them should provide (Adams & Parrott, 1994). It may be unclear who is to feed the child, change bandages, and perform other tasks. With nurses' input, Adams and Parrott drafted a list of tasks parents should perform for their hospitalized children. By sharing the list with parents (orally and in writing), the nurses were able to reduce parents' uncertainty and their own. As a result, the nurses were more satisfied with their jobs, and the parents were more confident in the care their children received.

Communication Skill Builders: Talking With Children About Illness

Bryan Whaley, who has conducted extensive research about children in health situations, offers this advice for explaining illnesses to children:

- *Let children set the tone.* Determine what the child wants and needs to know before launching into explanations the child may find incomprehensible, distressing, or simply irrelevant to his or her concerns (Nussbaum, Ragan, & Whaley, 2003; Whaley, 1999).
- *Pay attention.* Notice how the child conceives of illness and medical care. Ask questions and invite children to describe (and perhaps draw) their images of medical care and illness (Whaley, 2000).
- *Go easy on medical terminology.* Usually, children are more interested in how an illness will influence their lives and activities than the precise germs, tests, and scientific names involved. As Whaley (1999) puts it, "Disease and etiology appear inconsequential or of negligible concern to children" (p. 190).
- *Talk about illness as something normal.* Children are typically reassured to know their illnesses are normal and manageable. Speaking of an illness as a crisis or mystery may interfere with the child's coping ability (Whaley, 1999).

Buchholz (1992) adds that children benefit from honesty. Like adults, children usually cope better if they have a realistic idea what to expect from health care experiences. Adults should also keep in mind that prior experience with medical procedures may not diminish children's fear and anxiety (Buchholz, 1992). Experienced patients may be all too aware of how frightening and painful procedures can be.

Older Adults

Experts predict that, between 1996 and 2030, the number of people over age 65 will double. By 2050 they will make up one fourth of the U.S. population (U.S. Bureau of the Census, 1997). Population shifts will likely change health care needs and transform our understanding of the aging process. Jon Nussbaum and colleagues write:

> This aging of America has spawned many myths centered on the notion that the process of growing old cannot possibly be a positive experience and surely will be a time of great sadness, depression, and failing physical capacities. (Nussbaum et al., 2003, pp. 187–188)

These ideas are based more on stereotypes than reality. A **stereotype** is a belief that all members of a group are alike in some way (i.e., sad, fun, weak, jovial). **Ageism** is discrimination based on a person's age. It occurs when people judge others by preconceived notions about their age group, as when managers refuse to hire employees over age 65 because they believe people of that age are not productive.

Ageism results from negative stereotypes of the elderly, which are common among U.S. residents of all ages. Young adults who listened to old-sounding voices judged the speakers to be sour, unfriendly, cranky, gloomy, displeasing, and pessimistic (Mulac & Giles, 1996). What's more, people are apt to maintain those stereotypes even as they get older. Middle-aged individuals and elderly people themselves often have stereotypical ideas about being old (Hummert, Gartska, Shaner, & Strahm, 1995; Hummert, Gartska, & Shaner, 1997; Hummert, Nussbaum, & Wiemann, 1992). Elderly women are portrayed in a particularly negative light (Hummert et al., 1997).

Ageism is reinforced by media portrayals of the elderly as lonely, unhappy, and irritable (Nussbaum, Thompson, & Robinson, 1989). People with ageist beliefs are unlikely to regard elders as unique individuals who can change, learn, react, and grow physically stronger (Ryan & Butler, 1996; Solomon, 1996). Instead, they tend to patronize the elderly by speaking very slowly to them, using baby talk, and restricting conversations to happy subjects (Hummert & Shaner, 1994). They may even avoid communicating with older adults (Giles, Ballard, & McCann, 2002).

Despite Western society's cynical views about aging, many older adults enjoy good health, rewarding relationships, and a positive outlook on life (Nussbaum et al., 2003). As the Baby Boomers enter their 50s and 60s, they are likely to change society's ideas about growing older. Already physicians report that Baby Boomers have different health needs than their parents. For instance, because they are more athletic, today's middle-aged patients have more sports injuries than prior generations ("Getting Old," 2003).

Not all older adults accept ageist beliefs about their health. My grandmother, for one, once stomped angrily from a doctor's office after being told she "was just getting old." As she left, she declared, "I don't owe you a cent. I knew how old I was when I came in here!" James McCague, a columnist for *Medical Economics,* uses his 85-year-old aunt as an example of changing attitudes among older adults. When his aunt insisted on having a bypass despite her age, her doctor told her she was "quite functional" for an 85-year-old and was not a candidate for the surgery. To this she retorted, "I am the sole caretaker of my 90-year-old sister. I can't be just 'functional.' I want to be as healthy as I can be" (McCague, 2001, p. 104). The physician finally performed the procedure, and McCague reports that last time he checked, his aunt was out applying for a passport! A physician himself, McCague reflects on changes among elderly patients:

> The elderly patient does not report symptoms with resignation; the questions ask for a solution. The elderly patient does not want his questions taken within the context of his age, and more important, is angry when the physician does so. Elderly patients today see medicine like everyone else—as a commodity to which they have the right to equal access. . . . That hope, that wonderful "great expectation" of the human species, is the crux of the

demand of the elderly and, while we physicians need to moderate or shape it, we must never ignore or ridicule it. (p. 104)

Effects of Ageism Despite changing trends, reconciling Western society's negative view of aging with new ideas about getting older is still a challenging enterprise with numerous implications for health communication. (See Box 6.5 for more on communication accommodation and overaccommodation.)

For one, elderly persons are usually treated by caregivers who are significantly younger than they are. Relatively unfamiliar with the diversity among older adults, young people are likely to rely on stereotypes. They may lump elderly persons into simplistic categories such as frail, mild-mannered grandparents, or worse, cantankerous grumps.

Second, people may not try very hard to maintain or restore older people's health. Research indicates that people expect elderly persons to be ill and confused. This expectation is common even among doctors and the elderly (Nussbaum et al., 1989). As a result, people tend to shrug off elders' illnesses and emotional distress as unavoidable and untreatable. In short, because they do not believe older people can change, many people do not try to help them (Solomon, 1996).

Third, studies support that treating people as if they are helpless encourages them to believe it. Margaret Baltes and Hans-Werner Wahl (1996) found that, at home and in nursing homes, caregivers encouraged elders to be dependent by being attentive and supportive when the elders needed help, but caregivers discouraged or ignored them when they seemed independent. The authors conclude that caregivers are sometimes overresponsive in ways that encourage learned helplessness among older adults.

Fourth, caregivers tend to underestimate older patients' desire for information. The elderlys' biggest complaint about hospital care is that they are not fully informed about what to expect in terms of pain, specific procedures, daily routines, and follow-up care (Charles et al., 1996). Caregivers may assume elderly patients are not interested in medical details, are incapable of understanding them, or will be unduly frightened by risk factors. However, research suggests older adults generally are interested and are capable of understanding and assessing risks (Majerovitz et al., 1997; Smith, 1998).

Communication Patterns Although older adults are not as different as caregivers (and others) may imagine, it is worth noting several communication patterns that distinguish their behavior in medical contexts.

One is older adults' typical reluctance to ask questions and assert themselves with doctors despite their desire to participate and be well informed (Nussbaum et al., 2003). Older adults' silence may mask their desire for complete information.

Second, caregivers may be put off by the presence of loved ones who often accompany older adults to medical visits. According to Nussbaum and coauthors (2003), "The companion will ask more questions, will cause the medical

Box 6.5 THEORETICAL FOUNDATIONS Communication Accommodation

When people believe (rightly or wrongly) that older adults have diminished capacities, they tend to change their behavior toward them. For instance, people may speak more loudly to accommodate a hearing loss or move closer to accommodate an elder's shortsightedness. To **accommodate** is to adapt to another person's style or needs.

In some cases, accommodation is useful and appreciated. According to **communication accommodation theory,** people tend to mirror each other's communication styles to display liking and respect (Coupland, Coupland, & Giles, 1991). It is called **convergence** when partners use similar gestures, tone of voice, vocabulary, and so on. On the other hand, **divergence** is acting differently than the other person, as in whispering when the other shouts. Divergence implies that the partners are socially distant. They may be asserting uniqueness, pursuing different goals, or displaying that they do not understand or do not like each other.

To illustrate, patients who are baffled by their doctors' rapid explanations may converge by speaking rapidly themselves or by being silent to accommodate the physicians' speech. However, patients may diverge by paraphrasing the explanations more slowly to make sure they understand them. Socially speaking, divergence is risky in that it shows the participants to be somewhat out of sync. Extreme divergence may seem disrespectful or rude.

People often mirror the behaviors of their conversational partners without really thinking about it, especially if they like each other. Accommodation can spiral, however, so that feedback encourages people to escalate their behaviors toward each other. For instance, when a dear friend speaks loudly and slowly to an elderly person, the elder may respond in a similar way, which may reify the friend's belief that the elder is a bit slow and hard of hearing. In turn the friend may accommodate even more, and so on. Thus, what was intended to be accommodation has become **overaccommodation,** an exaggerated response to a perceived need.

Especially if the overaccommodation is pervasive (everybody seems to do it), elderly individuals may begin to believe they are indeed of diminished capacity, and they may behave in line with that expectation (Ryan & Butler, 1996). In short, they start to "do" being old, as society has defined it.

Elderly individuals usually have no control over the cues that suggest to others that they are aging. Indeed, they may have a hard time dealing with these cues themselves, although the cues may not be signs of significantly reduced ability at all (Nussbaum, Pecchioni, Grant, & Folwell, 2000; Ryan & Butler, 1996).

An older-sounding voice is one example. In one study people whose voices sounded old were perceived by others to be older than their contemporaries, and even perceived *themselves* to be older (Mulac & Giles, 1996). An "old" voice is quivery and breathy, with prolonged vowel sounds and extended pauses between words. These characteristics are certainly not signs that the speaker is less intelligent or is physically impaired in any significant way, but they may be enough to spur accommodation and overaccommodation.

Ironically, a great number of accommodating behaviors are unnecessary. Contrary to the assumption that older people are worse communicators than others, they are sometimes better. Mark Bergstrom and Jon Nussbaum (1996) found that respondents over age 50 handled conflict more cooperatively and productively than young adults, who were apt to be confrontational and judgmental.

Older adults' physical abilities are not as compromised as people suspect, either. Significant hearing loss only occurs in about one third of people ages 65 to 74 and in about one half of people over age 85 ("Hearing and Older," 1998). Likewise, only 1 in 4 people experiences significant vision loss by age 75 (Desloge, 1997). These conditions are worth note, and they are more prevalent among elderly persons than others, but they by no means apply to *all* older adults. In fact, 62% of elderly persons who live at home have no limitations that prevent them from living ordinary lives (Joyce, 1994). This means that accommodating behaviors are largely unnecessary.

What Do You Think?

1. To test the effects of communication accommodation, try altering your speech and observing how your conversational partners react. Do they converge (e.g., whisper if you whisper) or diverge?
2. How would you react if everyone started speaking unusually slowly or loudly to you?
3. Do you tend to change your communication patterns around older adults?

encounter to last significantly longer, and will expect more information regarding the health of the older patient than the older patient normally seeks" (p. 192).

Finally, the fast pace of medical contexts may be incompatible with older adults' health needs, which (although they are not necessarily debilitating) are likely to be more numerous and chronic than younger patients', making it infeasible to cover them during a quick visit (Nussbaum, Pecchioni, Grant, & Folwell, 2000).

Promising Options Training sessions have been effective in dispelling ageist assumptions held by medical students (Intrieri, Kelly, Brown, & Castilla, 1993) and caregivers (Baltes & Wahl, 1996). Although not yet widespread, such educational programs may help change the way elders are treated in medical situations.

Technology provides another resource. The next section discusses communication technology as it affects older adults. Afterward, the chapter concludes with communication skill builders for reaching marginalized populations.

Communication Technology and Older Adults Advanced technology can be a benefit or a liability for older adults. From one perspective, access to online health information and interaction expands opportunities for adults with limited mobility. On the other hand, older adults who do not keep up with technology may have difficulty finding and keeping jobs and staying in the mainstream of a technology-savvy society (McConatha, 2002). There is some evidence that older adults are rising to the challenge.

"It's clear that older adults, like their younger counterparts, don't want to be left behind on the information highway," writes Donald Lindberg (2002, p. 13). Individuals over age 55 are the fastest growing segment of Internet users (Lindberg, 2002).

Older adults who are proficient at using online resources may benefit from a greater sense of control over their environment and personal fate. They may also feel less isolated and more informed about choices and options. Based on these ideals, Douglas McConatha (2002) proposes what he called the **e-quality theory of aging:** that older adults benefit as both teachers and learners when they "use, contribute to, influence, and express themselves" in electronic environments (p. 38).

Based on experience working with older adults in an assisted living facility, David Lansdale (2002) says residents experienced a new sense of freedom when they learned to use an online computer made available to them. Lansdale applies the metaphors of "driving" and "going back to school." He writes:

> *Driving* is the antidote to helplessness. One of the most exciting events in adolescence comes with access to the keys to the car, and the freedom it promises. At the other end of life's continuum, an elder is often forced to relinquish the keys, often one of the more trying transitions of a lifetime. (p. 135)

Lansdale says older adults who began using the computer were free again to "go" where they pleased and choose their own paths and experiences. At the

Box 6.6 RESOURCES
More on Health Communication and Older Adults

- AgePages sponsored by the National Institutes on Aging and the National Library of Medicine: www.healthandage.net/html/min/nih/entrance.htm
- Coupland, N., Coupland, J., Giles, H., & Coupland, D. (2003, March). *Language, society, and the elderly: Discourse, identity, and aging* (Language in Society, No. 18). Malden, MA: Blackwell.
- Hummert, M. L., & Nussbaum, J. F. (Eds.). (2001). *Aging, communication, and health*. Mahwah, NJ: Lawrence Erlbaum.
- Morrell, R. W. (Ed.). (2002). *Older adults, health information, and the World Wide Web*. Mahwah, NJ: Lawrence Erlbaum.
- Nussbaum, J. F., & Coupland, J. (Eds.). (2004). *Handbook of communication and aging research* (2nd ed.). Mahwah, NJ: Erlbaum.
- Nussbaum, J. F., Pecchioni, L. L., Robinson, J. D., & Thompson, T. L. (2000). *Communication and aging* (2nd ed.). Mahwah, NJ: Lawrence Erlbaum.
- Sparks, L., O'Hair, H. D., & Kreps, G. L. (Eds.) (in press). *Cancer communication and aging*. Creskill, NJ: Hampton Press.
- WHO Active Ageing: A Policy Framework 2002: www.who.int/hpr/ageing/Active Ageing PolicyFrame.pdf.
- Williams, A., & Nussbaum, J. F. (2001). *Intergenerational communication across the life span*. Mahwah, NJ: Lawrence Erlbaum.

same time, they could relieve their boredom and feel like they were participating in life beyond the facility's borders. Similarly, by "going back to school" via the Internet, older adults found pleasure in expanding their knowledge and skills. This provides a striking contrast to the view of aging as a steady decline in intellect and abilities. (For more resources about health communication and older adults, see Box 6.6.)

Communication Skill Builders: Reaching Marginalized Populations

As this chapter has shown, people may be marginalized on the basis of many factors including status, gender, race, sexual orientation, language, disability, and age. All have implications for health and health communication. Leigh Arden Ford and Gust A. Yep (2003) offer the following suggestions for understanding and improving health-related communication with members of marginalized populations:

Box 6.7 RESOURCES
More on Serving Marginalized Communities

- Association for Community Health Improvement: www.hospitalconnect.com/DesktopServlet
- Braithwaite, D. O., & Thompson, T. L. (Eds.). (2000). *Handbook of communication and people with disabilities: Research and applications.* Mahwah, NJ: Lawrence Erlbaum.
- Gay and Lesbian Medical Association: www.glma.org/home.php3
- Minority Health Project: www.minority.unc.edu
- WHO's Healthy Cities/Healthy Communities Project provides a template for initiating community-based health efforts at www.well.com/user/bbear/hc_articles.html

- *Do not impose your worldview.* Instead, seek to understand and work within the worldview of the people involved. Allow for multiple meanings.
- *Establish open dialogues in which people can communicate openly and honestly.* Strive for understanding. Allow meanings to emerge.
- *Strive to communicate in culturally acceptable ways.* Develop new skills and awareness.
- *Listen to people rather than telling them what do or think or how to act.* Seek opportunities for open-ended interviews, focus groups, and casual interactions.
- *Empower people to use their own skills and resources.*
- *Allow members of the population to emerge as leaders of the health effort.*
- *Help to unite community groups into broad-based coalitions.*

See Box 6.7 for more resources on this topic.

SUMMARY

Patients are quite diverse. It is tempting to stereotype what is unfamiliar, but categorizations are often barriers to communication. Status differences can intimidate people into silence, outmoded ideas about old age can typecast the elderly as grumpy and sick, and language differences can create frustration and misunderstanding. In other ways as well, stereotypes contribute to inequitable patterns in which people may be undervalued and misunderstood.

Patients of low socioeconomic status are typically more fearful and less informed than others, but they talk less during medical exams and are likely to be treated within a strictly biomedical model. Status differences often have serious consequences for health and health communication. Low health literacy is an enormous problem, influencing 1 in 2 American adults and resulting in billions of dollars of avoidable expense. Communication may help overcome the ill effects of status differences. Patients and caregivers can most effectively bridge the status gap if they develop trust, acknowledge and reconsider stereotypes, make the most of face-to-face communication rather than printed materials, and encourage questions and open dialogue.

Men in the United States tend to utilize medical services less than women, and are less likely to accompany loved ones to medical visits or provide in-home care for them. Doctors tend to give male patients less information than they give females, but evidence suggests that doctors and society overall have traditionally taken men's health concerns more seriously than women's.

Sexual orientation can be a difficult subject for both patients and caregivers. Caregivers may feel out of their depth discussing sexual issues, although ignoring them may compromise medical care since some health risks are related to sex and close relationships are crucial to coping. Patients may be reluctant to bring up the issue for fear of rejection.

Although members of racial minorities are often at high risk for disease, their health may suffer because they do not trust doctors and because they have limited access to medical facilities. Some evidence suggests that doctors treat African Americans and Hispanics differently than White patients.

People who do not speak English may wish to bring a friend or relative along to medical visits to help interpret, since interpreters are not often available otherwise. Patients baffled by language differences may agree to procedures they do not understand or be so frustrated they do not return for further care. Caregivers can be frustrated also and may be held liable if adverse outcomes result. The good news is that community interpreters and long-distance interpretation services have mostly pleasing results if they are used.

Many people treat individuals with disabilities as if they are childlike or incapable of contributing to conversations and decisions. These assumptions may seriously limit communication between individuals with disabilities and their caregivers. Moreover, the same attitudes can make it difficult to cope on a daily basis. Although people mean well, their actions may stigmatize and isolate individuals with disabilities. Suggestions are presented to make communication more equitable and respectful.

Children frequently undergo routine exams and emergency care, but they may have a difficult time dealing with the foreign atmosphere, strangers, and threat of pain that medical care poses. Parents can help, but their role is somewhat ambiguous. Caregivers may either feel parents are too demanding or are not helpful enough.

Finally, older adults may be typecast in ways that affect their personal identities and the health care they receive. Ageist assumptions that older people are less healthy and less intelligent than others may cause people to write off legitimate health concerns as unavoidable signs of old age. Communication accommodation behaviors are often unnecessary and can be stigmatizing, especially if carried to extremes.

KEY TERMS

socioeconomic status (SES)
health literacy
heterosexism
racism
stereotype
ageism
accommodate
communication accommodation theory
convergence
divergence
overaccommodation
e-quality theory of aging

REVIEW QUESTIONS

1. Why might misunderstandings occur between patients and caregivers of different socioeconomic status?
2. How prevalent is low health literacy in the United States? What are the consequences?
3. Describe the AMA's *Ask Me 3* program.
4. What are some tips for improving communication between patients and caregivers of different socioeconomic status?
5. How is patient–caregiver communication usually different for men and women in the United States?
6. Why is discussion of sexual orientation important in medical transactions?
7. What are some explanations why people of different races seem to receive different medical care?
8. What guidelines do you suggest when deciding who gets medical care (see Box 6.2)?
9. Why are multilingual interpreters important to health care? Are they often used? Why or why not? What are some promising options for bridging the language gap?
10. What are two frustrating dichotomies that people with disabilities often face?
11. What are some tips for communicating more effectively with people who have disabilities?
12. What are some tips for communicating more clearly with patients who are children?
13. How do ageist assumptions affect health communication?
14. Describe communication accommodation theory.

■ CLASS ACTIVITY

Overcoming the Self-Consciousness of a Disability

The following comments were filed anonymously on an Internet bulletin board for people with disabilities. Read the letter, then consider the discussion questions either alone or in groups.

> There are a lot of things out of our control—this I know. I experience the joy of inaccessible buildings, pitying smiles, and the "supergimp" or "wondercrip" mentality. ("Wow, I can't believe that you are in college. You must find it so hard! That's amazing!") every time I venture outside to get things done in my life. Inaccessible buildings can cut us off from socialization. So can people's attitudes toward us, be they parents, doctors, therapists, or potential partners. . . . Just as our attitudes of others affect us, our attitudes affect other people. . . . I didn't get on a loudspeaker and say, "I'm insecure about my walking! Please watch me and how bad I am at it!" I just thought about it. Too much. And it came across in the way I carried myself, how loud I spoke, and what I did. . . . So think positively. Even if you feel insecure about your disability, which many of us do—including me, in certain situations—force yourself not to think about it. . . . If you are not thinking about your disability, chances are neither will they.

What Do You Think?

1. Have you ever been challenged to live with a disability (even a temporary one such a broken leg)? If so, what was most difficult about it?
2. How do you feel when you encounter people with physical disabilities? With intellectual disabilities?
3. Is your attitude toward people with disabilities different depending on how they act? If so, how?
4. Sometimes people are afraid of doing or saying the wrong thing. Consequently, they avoid novel situations, such as asking a classmate with a disability to join them for coffee. Would you be comfortable including a person with a disability in your social circle? Why or why not?

Part Three

SOCIAL AND CULTURAL ISSUES

CHAPTER 7

Social Support

Struggling to be strong after the death of his young daughter, Alonzo is hurt and mystified when friends' first question is, "How is your wife?"

Margie misses the normal times, when people talked to her about the weather, boys, and school. Now they just hold doors for her and try not to stare at her wheelchair.

Everyone knows Drew's illness is very serious, but no one speaks of it to him. Drew wonders how he is supposed to cope with such an emotional topic in silence.

Lucy spends two hours each morning and three hours each evening caring for her three children and her elderly mother. In between, Lucy maintains a full-time job outside the home. She is glad she can help, but she wonders how many years it will be before she can take a vacation or spend a quiet day alone. Such thoughts make her feel sad and guilty.

Mario is pleased with life and himself. Things have not been easy, but he appreciates the pleasures of life like never before. Friends and loved ones are closer and he is at peace with himself. He marvels that dying has brought about some of the best days of his life.

As these scenarios suggest, the majority of communication about health does not occur in a doctor's office or hospital. It occurs at home, at the grocery store, on the telephone, and in other settings of everyday life. Spouses, children, friends, and co-workers often have as much influence as doctors and nurses.

Social support includes a broad range of activities, from comforting a friend after a romantic disappointment, to listening while a grieving father tells and retells his story, to performing an Internet data search, to acknowledging that a handicapped individual is a normal person.

Most people perform more supportive behaviors than they realize, and as a consequence, have positive effects on people's health and moods. Research shows that supportive communication can help speed healing, reduce symptoms and stress, lessen pain, and build self-esteem (Cohen & Wills, 1985; Metts & Manns, 1996). And the benefits go both ways. People who provide social support often feel an increased sense of worth and personal strength themselves (Ferguson, 1997).

This chapter is divided into three sections. The first provides a conceptual overview of coping and social support. The middle sections examine social support in two contexts—lay caregiving and death and dying experiences. The final section cautions that, although social support is invaluable, inappropriate or excessive amounts of it can be counterproductive.

CONCEPTUAL OVERVIEW

In the simplest sense, **social support** is people helping people. Melanie Barnes and Steve Duck (1994) define social support as "behaviors that, whether directly or indirectly, communicate to an individual that she or he is valued and cared for by others" (p. 176). Some theorists (i.e., Albrecht & Adelman, 1987) consider that the central function of social support is increasing a person's sense of control. Their viewpoint is substantiated by research (covered in this chapter) that people cope best when they feel well informed and actively involved. This section describes different coping mechanisms and the role social support plays in helping people through crisis situations.

Coping

To understand social support, it is useful to begin with the phenomenon of **coping**. As Sandra Metts and Heather Manns (1996) define it, coping is "the process of managing stressful situations" (p. 356).

Everyone is affected by stressful situations, which range from everyday hassles to life-threatening occurrences. There is some evidence that people's everyday coping skills are more important to their moods and their health than the way they cope with major crises (Burleson, 1994).

Coping usually involves two efforts: changing what can be changed (**problem solving**) and adapting to what cannot be changed (**emotional adjustment**) (Tardy, 1994). Of course, it is not always easy to know when to problem solve and when to adjust. The options vary according to the people and the circumstances involved. Often, coping strategies depend on how much control people believe they have over their situation.

When people believe they can manage their health successfully, they are said to have **health self-efficacy** (Bandura, 1986). Efficacy is derived from the Latin term for "change-producing." People with high self-efficacy are more likely than others to maintain healthy lifestyles. A sense of self-efficacy may be fostered by positive experiences in the past, encouragement from others, and a cultural belief that people control their own destinies. This is called an **internal locus of control.** Locus of control is more general than health self-efficacy, although the two are often related. Many North Americans have an internal locus of control. As a result, they are change oriented and hard working, but they may be frustrated by failure and may feel baffled and betrayed when things do not work out as they had planned (Marks, 1998). People who believe they control their own fate may be reluctant to ask for help and may believe they are responsible for what happens—both good and bad. Faced with ill health, they might ask, "What did I do to cause this?" Even assured that no one is to blame, these people may feel guilty and ineffectual.

By contrast, people who do not believe they can change their health for the better have low health self-efficacy. This is common in cultures in which people believe events are controlled mostly by outside forces. This is called an **external locus of control.** Because of their belief in fate, these people are sometimes characterized as *fatalistic.* They are likely to regard events as God's will or the natural order of things. People with low health self-efficacy may not be motivated to take personal action regarding health matters. For example, even if they are aware of healthy dietary recommendations, they may not change their diet because they do not feel they have control over their health (Rimal, 2000). In fatalistic cultures people may reason: "It makes no sense to change my lifestyle. I will die when it's my time, no sooner or later," or "I'm sick because God willed it. Therefore, it is not right to seek a medical cure." As you might expect, adolescents with an external locus of control are more apt to "follow the crowd" and smoke if their friends do (Booth-Butterfield, Anderson, & Booth-Butterfield, 2000).

Coping strategies may be affected by cultural beliefs and perceptions of self-efficacy. People with high self-efficacy are typically problem solvers, highly motivated to protect their own health. However, they may be at a loss when illness reduces their sense of control. In some situations people are powerless to change their health status or to repay their caregivers' kindness (Metts & Manns, 1996). This may be especially demoralizing for people who have always believed they could control their health. In these situations, a belief in fate may help people accept what they cannot change. All in all, effective coping seems to combine elements of both problem solving and acceptance.

Crisis

A **crisis** is an occurrence that exceeds a person's normal coping ability. The first sign of crisis is usually a sense that events are out of control. This may give rise to panic or denial. For example, the parent of a seriously ill child remembers: "I didn't want to talk about it because it was something I wanted to shut in the back of my mind and have go away" (Chesler & Barbarin, 1984, p. 123).

People in crisis are also likely to feel that things have changed, perhaps forever. During difficult times, people often yearn for the simple routines that characterized everyday life (Wartik, 1996). It may seem that life can never be that way again. Following a death, grieving loved ones may wonder how they will ever resume daily activities when they feel so sad and disconnected to the things that used to seem normal. It is common for people in intense grief to momentarily forget how to perform simple routines such as using an automated teller machine or driving from one place to another (Wartik, 1996).

A major crisis may serve as a turning point or dividing line. People affected by serious illnesses often feel their life has two parts, before the diagnosis and after it (Buckman, Lipkin, Sourkes, Toole, & Talarico, 1997). Circumstances are so radically altered that nothing seems the same. The change is not always negative. People who learn to cope with terminal illnesses or near-death experiences sometimes say they are happier than before, appreciating pleasures they used to disregard (McCormick & Conley, 1995). A cancer survivor interviewed by Anderson and Geist Martin (2003) reflects on the strength and courage she has discovered while undergoing surgery and radiation treatments:

> I wear my scar as a badge of courage but I've never thought of myself as a courageous person. But I am, I am a courageous person. People notice the scar. But you know I don't mind the scar. Years ago, I decided that I wanted to change my name, to pick out who I wanted to be. Ivy came to mind because I liked the plant. It's a vine, it is strong, you can cut it down and it comes back. There's a lot of strength in Ivy. (p. 138)

Normalcy

A sense of crisis does not usually abate until it seems that life is normal again. **Normalcy** is essentially the sense that things are comfortable, predictable, and familiar. Being normal is not always as easy as it sounds. It requires the cooperation of other people, even strangers (Barnes & Duck, 1994). Consider the plight of individuals with physical disabilities. Often, their toughest challenge is not learning to use wheelchairs or other appliances. Their toughest challenge is resuming a sense of life as usual. Without this, they are trapped in a crisislike state, excluded from the comfortable give and take of everyday transactions with people (Braithwaite, 1996). Persons with disabilities may be inundated with people willing to help them, but very few who engage them in casual conversation or friendly debates over politics or sports. When people behave as if individuals with disabilities are unlike other people (even by being unusually kind or helpful toward them), they perpetuate a sense of crisis and alienation (Braithwaite, 1996).

While doing research about support groups, I once heard a young woman who had recently become blind say she longed to do favors for friends again. As she put it: "You appreciate people's help, but it's not the way life really is. You want to help back and no one lets you do that." In short, it is hard to lead a normal life when everyone treats you as if you are abnormal.

■ COPING STRATEGIES AND SOCIAL SUPPORT

Coping strategies and social support often look very much alike. For instance, people may cope with stress by taking steps to improve their situation, learning more about it, seeking the company of loved ones, having a good cry, or talking it out. These activities fall in two main categories, which also characterize the two main types of social support. As Carolyn Cutrona and Julie Suhr (1994) describe it, social support may be categorized as **action-facilitating support** (performing tasks and collecting information) or **nurturing support** (building self-esteem, acknowledging and expressing emotions, and providing companionship). Here is a description of social support based on Cutrona and Suhr's categories.

Action-Facilitating Support

Two types of action-facilitating support are performing tasks and favors and providing information. For instance, people might support someone trying to lose weight by sharing fitness information, buying healthy foods, and serving as exercise companions.

Tasks and favors are called **instrumental support** (Cutrona & Suhr, 1994). Research shows that instrumental support is most appreciated when care receivers feel they are active participants and are involved in decision making (Bottorf, Gogag, & Engelberg-Lotzkar, 1995).

Informational support might involve performing an Internet data search, sharing personal experiences, passing along news clips, and so on. Information can help people increase their understanding and make wise decisions. As Kreps (2003) points out, "information is the primary process for promoting cancer prevention" (p. 164) and an important part of coping effectively with cancer as well. Even when people cannot change their circumstances, those who are knowledgeable about what is happening usually feel more in control, experience less pain, and recover more quickly than others (Roter & Hall, 1992). In a book about her experience as a breast cancer survivor, Susan Ryan Jordan (2001) described the quest for information that made the disease seem less fearful, reflecting that "fear is worse than death."

Nurturing Support

Nurturing typically involves three types of support: esteem, emotional, and social network. These are not directly oriented to task goals, but rather to helping people feel better about themselves and their situations.

Esteem Support **Esteem support** involves efforts to make a distressed individual feel valued and competent. Encouraging words may ease feelings of helplessness and despair (Wills, 1985). People often report that unconditional approval is the most helpful form of support. Statements like, "We're behind you no matter what you decide," are comforting reminders that loved ones will not leave just because the situation is difficult to handle. Being supportive involves listening effectively (Brady & Cella, 1995). Studies show that most distressed individuals are not looking for advice; they just want to talk and be heard (Lehman, Ellard, & Wortman, 1986).

Communication Skill Builders: Supportive Listening Brant Burleson, a leading authority on social support, offers the following tips for being a supportive listener (based on Burleson, 1990, 1994):

- *Focus on the other person.* Give the person a chance to talk freely. Focus on what he or she is saying rather than your own feelings and experiences.
- *Remain neutral.* Resist the urge to label people and experiences as good or bad. Likewise, encourage the speaker to describe experiences rather than label them.
- *Concentrate on feelings.* Focus on feelings rather than events. It is usually more supportive to explore why someone feels a certain way than to focus on events themselves.
- *Legitimize the other person's emotions.* Statements like, "I understand how you might feel that way," are typically more helpful than telling the other person how to feel (or how not to feel).
- *Summarize what you hear.* Calmly summarizing the speaker's statements can help clarify the situation and help the distressed individual understand what he or she is feeling. As Burleson (1994) explains: "Due to the intensity and immediacy of their feelings, distressed persons may lack understanding of these feelings" (p. 13).

Emotional Support **Emotional support** includes efforts to acknowledge and understand what another person is feeling. This support is particularly valuable when people must adapt to what they cannot change (Albrecht & Adelman, 1987). In a health crisis it is common to feel angry, baffled, afraid, depressed, or even unexpectedly relieved or giddy.

Emotions are a natural part of coping with health crises, yet many people are not comfortable with emotional displays (theirs or others people's). They may be afraid to appear weak or be reluctant to upset others (Zimmermann & Applegate, 1994). The result is that people tend to present the appearance that things are going well, even when they are not.

No one can deny the power of positive thinking. But problems may arise when people find themselves feigning a cheerfulness they do not feel or avoiding subjects they actually wish to discuss. Suppressing emotions commonly leads to depression and moodiness (Metts & Manns, 1996). When asked, people (patients, caregivers, and others) often say they avoid sensitive topics because they do not wish to distress the people around them (Gotcher, 1995). However, when interviewed individually, the same people usually express the private wish that those topics be brought into the open. In the long run it is usually easier to cope when emotions can be brought into the open.

Communication Skill Builders: Allowing Emotions

- *Do not assume people are "OK" because they do not seem emotional.* Quiet people are at greatest danger for being ignored and misunderstood.

When people are quiet or apprehensive about communicating, people around them are less likely to share concerns with them and less apt to understand their feelings (Ayres & Hopf, 1995). In interviews, fathers of children with cancer said they were reluctant to discuss their feelings because they might be overcome by emotion (Chesler & Barbarin, 1984). These fathers received less emotional support than the mothers did and were often expected to act "strong" when others were emotional.

- *Keep in mind that people usually benefit from opportunities to talk openly and honestly.* Cancer patients who feel they can talk about subjects like death and pain with their loved ones cope better than people who consider those topics taboo (Gotcher, 1995).
- *People in grief often find it insensitive and unhelpful when others try to minimize their losses or get them to cheer up* (Lehman, Ellard, & Wortman, 1986). Ivy, the cancer survivor interviewed by Anderson and Geist Martin (2003), put it this way:

> The emotions went up and down, up and down. I talked to Jack and he listened. There was a point where Jack's optimism got to me. It was like stop, you're not listening to me. I could die, stop. (p. 137)

- *In Western cultures, seriously ill patients typically appreciate honesty.* A participant in Thomas McCormick and Becky Conley's (1995) study said: "That's one of the things that I like my doctor for, because he was plain with me that I was incurable" (paragraph 38). She explained that people who do not know they are dying cannot prepare for it emotionally or practically. They lose the chance to settle financial affairs, communicate with loved ones, set new priorities for their limited time, and adjust emotionally to what is occurring. (As you will see in Chapter 8, members of some cultures prefer to shield people from negative prognoses, believing that talking about adverse outcomes will bring bad luck.)

All in all, it is important to remember that emotions are a natural part of the coping process, and the person who displays strong and even conflicting emotions may be coping more effectively than the one who keeps a stiff upper lip. Keeping conversations light and cheerful may discourage people from coping effectively.

Social Network Support **Social network support** involves ongoing relationships maintained even when no crisis exists. Companionship of this sort helps people feel valued and is a reassuring reminder that friends' support is always available (Barnes & Duck, 1994).

Strong networks can enhance our confidence and coping abilities. For example, teens are most likely to negotiate safe-sex options with their partners if they come from families that display a problem-solving orientation. However, teens accustomed to conflict avoidance are more reluctant to bring up safe sex and subsequently put themselves (and their partners) at greater risk (Troth & Peterson, 2000). Likewise, eating disorders such as bulimia are often associated with low levels of perceived support from family and friends (Grissett & Norvell, 1992), but teenage girls who regularly engage in mutually satisfying conflict resolution with their fathers are less likely than other girls to develop eating disorders (Botta & Dumlao, 2002).

Some evidence suggests that strong social networks can even help us live longer. For example, elderly men with strong social networks are likely to live longer and manage job stress more effectively than other men their age (Falk, Hanson, Isacsson, & Ostergren, 1992). When interviewed, older adults who have experienced the death of a spouse recommend that the best coping strategy is to keep busy and interact with others (Bergstrom & Holmes, 2000). They say the worst strategy is to isolate yourself at home.

Research shows that social networks are more or less supportive depending on the number of people involved, how often they interact, the level of conflict during interactions, and the communication skills of those involved (Grissett & Norvell, 1992; Haring & Breen, 1992). People usually benefit most from having a number of friends and family members who stay in close contact, display liking and respect, and handle conflict effectively.

Communication Skill Builders: Keeping Social Networks Active Common sources of social support include family members, friends, professionals, support groups, virtual communities, and self-help literature. Each source is likely to provide a somewhat different form of assistance. Here are some suggestions for facilitating social support in a variety of contexts.

- *People need social support even when they seem OK.* Although women give and receive more social support than men (Chesler & Barbarin, 1984), men may need it just as much. Likewise, people with limited education usually receive more support than highly educated individuals, probably because people assume highly educated people are self-sufficient (Choi, 1996).
- *Friends are important.* Friends' attention is flattering because it is so freely given (family members are more obliged). Friendship also offers a pleasing sense of continuity, entertainment, and a gentle reminder that other people have joys and concerns too (Rook, 1995). In some instances, friends are even more helpful than family members. When people studied by Metts and Mann (1996) told loved ones they had HIV or AIDS, friends were typically more supportive than family, perhaps because the family members were more overwhelmed by their own emotions.
- *Emotional support can be as important as doing favors or running errands.* A study of people with chronic fatigue syndrome (CFS) revealed that emotional support was more helpful than favors and tangible assistance, even though people with CFS are often too weary to do much on their own (Kelly, Soderlund, Albert, & McGarrahan, 1999).

- *Even simple gestures mean a lot.* Experts suggest that friends drop by for brief visits and make their willingness to help known. When uncertain what to do, they can provide services like mowing the lawn or leaving a casserole without fear of being in the way.
- *Keep family members well informed.* When a loved one is in the hospital, family members may be especially anxious if they do not feel well informed. This is hard on the families, and it may compromise their ability to provide support and share important information about the patient (Cross et al., 1996).
- *Make family members and loved ones feel welcome.* Presbyterian Hospital Matthews in Matthews, North Carolina, has expanded its critical care unit so that a family room adjoins each patient room (Daniels, 1996). Every family room is equipped with soothing artwork, a sofa bed, recliner, telephone, and a window to provide a view of nature and allow in sunlight. A kitchen and showers are also available to guests. Nurses report that patients are less agitated and experience fewer symptoms of stress and anxiety when loved ones are near. The arrangement also gives nurses a chance to educate patients' families and answer their questions. (The hospital requests that each family choose a spokesperson so nurses are not flooded with the same questions from different people.)
- *Health professionals can assist with communication strategies as well as treatment regimens.* Because of their regular experience with health dilemmas, health professionals may be able to suggest strategies people would not think of on their own. Consider the dilemma of people who have had unprotected sex while cheating on their romantic partners. Health counselors in Marifran Mattson and Felicia Roberts' (2001) study helped people find acceptable ways to insist on condom use while they awaited the results of HIV tests. The counselors first encouraged clients to be honest with their partners, but if it became clear that clients would rather expose their unsuspecting partners to a health risk than admit their infidelity, the counselors sometimes helped people devise stories to tell instead. In one instance, a counselor suggested a man could tell his girlfriend he had urethritis ("kind of like a male yeast infection") and must use a condom for several months (at which point results of the HIV test would be available). Such deceptions may seem questionable, but the alternative (risky sex) may be worse.

Support Groups

Support groups are comprised of people with similar concerns who meet regularly to discuss their feelings and experiences. As defined by Schopler and Galinsky (1993), the term *support group* includes a range of formats, from informal self-help groups (with an emphasis on shared concerns and minimal intervention by the facilitator) to treatment groups (providing a form of psychological therapy with active guidance by a trained professional). In recent years, online support groups and virtual communities have joined the list.

In their various forms, support groups are popular around the world. More than 26,000 Al-Anon/Alateen group meetings are conducted in 30 languages in 115 countries (Al-Anon.Org, 2003). Type the search term "HIV/AIDS Support Groups" into Google and you will have access to more than 580,000 online resources. There are also support groups for people dealing with grief, codependence, an enormous variety of illnesses and addictions, and other concerns.

The effort may be justified. There is evidence that support group members tend to experience fewer symptoms and less stress and may even live longer than similar people who are not members ("Living With Cancer," 1997; Wright, 2002). Similarly, involvement in support groups has been shown to reduce depression and anxiety among cancer patients (Evans & Connis, 1995).

Support groups have several advantages. Being around similar others may make people feel that they are not alone or abnormal. Similar others can also give firsthand information on what to expect and how to behave. At the same time, support group members may feel better about themselves because they are able to help others (Taylor, Falke, Mazel, & Hilsberg, 1988). Another advantage is the convenience and low cost of support groups. Because they are made up mostly of laypersons, there are few or no fees and (for the most part) members can schedule meetings where and when they wish.

The greatest dangers are that support groups will become counterproductive gripe sessions or that members will develop an us-versus-them viewpoint (Fisher et al., 1988). They may begin to feel that no one outside the group understands them as well as they understand each other (a form of oversupport described later in the chapter).

Communication Technology: Virtual Communities

Communication technology has expanded the options for supportive relationships. Telephones and computers have given rise to **virtual communities,** groups of people with similar concerns who communicate via information technology.

People can communicate with others online, look up information, correspond with experts, and even take part in support groups facilitated by health professionals. There are now than 1 million health-related sites on the World Wide Web. Although some criticize the Internet for publishing misleading information, Ferguson (1997) found that people were remarkably savvy about distinguishing between reliable and questionable health news.

Online support groups allow people to communicate about key issues, sometimes with the guidance of professional facilitators. Expertise in communication technology is becoming a useful skill for health professionals. A survey of social workers indicated that most of them were interested in facilitating computer-mediated support groups but did not feel confident using the technology (Galinksy et al., 1997).

Ferguson (1997) surveyed therapists to gauge the quality of advice typically offered on computer bulletin boards. In one instance a grieving man who shared his story online received dozens of immediate replies. People said they understood how he was feeling and advised him to continue therapy, find solace in his religious faith, be kind to his wife, accept others' help, and resist any temptation to abuse drugs. The therapists Ferguson surveyed applauded the people's kind efforts, and most said they would not have been able to help the man in such an "immediate, compassionate, and practical way" themselves (paragraph 8).

There is mixed evidence about the impact of virtual communities. Communicating through technology is a plus for people who are short on time or transportation, have disabilities or responsibilities that prevent them from leaving home, or find comfort in the relative anonymity of technology-mediated conversations (Braithwaite, Waldron, & Finn, 1999; Galinsky et al., 1997). People with HIV/AIDS who make use of Internet information are found to have greater knowledge of the condition, more success coping, and larger support networks than similar people who do not go online (Kalichman et al., 2003).

However, overreliance on technology-mediated communication may prevent people from developing relationships in their own communities, ultimately robbing them of the types of social support that cannot be transmitted via fiber optics. Other disadvantages include difficulty using and obtaining technology, potential threats to privacy, lost nonverbal cues, and hurtful remarks people might *not* make were they face-to-face (Galinsky et al., 1997).

Implications

Coping and social support go hand in hand. Social support is essentially a concerted effort to help people cope with difficult circumstances. Even a relatively minor health event can constitute a crisis if the people involved do not have adequate skills or resources to cope with it. During a crisis, people usually perceive that their lives have radically changed and they do not have control over what is happening.

People cope with crises in different ways, some by developing a peaceful acceptance, others by actively changing their situations. Especially when their usual coping strategies do not work, people may need assistance developing new strategies or expanding their efforts. Sometimes people are comforted by the reinstatement of normal routines and everyday communication. People also rely on others to help them manage tasks, emotions, esteem, and knowledge. Social support is conveyed largely through communication. The most effective communicators are sensitive to the wishes of people they are trying to comfort.

People usually cope more effectively when they can discuss sensitive topics than when they feel compelled to feign cheerfulness. Do not assume that individuals are coping well because they are quiet or do not display much emotion. Research suggests these people often receive less support than others, although they probably need it just as much.

Box 7.1 RESOURCES
More About Coping and Social Support

Here are some additional sources of information about supportive communication.

- Green, J. O., & Burleson, B. R. (Eds.) (2003). *Handbook of communication and social interaction skills.* Mahwah, NJ: Lawrence Erlbaum.
- Lewis, M., & Haviland-Jones, J. M. (Eds.) (2000). *Handbook of emotions.* New York: Guilford Press.
- Miller, J. F. (2000). *Coping with chronic illness: Overcoming powerlessness.* Philadelphia: F. A. Davis.
- Reinhardt, J. P. (Ed.) (2001). *Negative and positive support.* Mahwah, NJ: Lawrence Erlbaum.
- Ryff, C. D., & Singer, B. H. (Eds.) (2001). *Emotion, social relationships, and health.* New York: Oxford.
- Stroebe, M. S. (Ed.) (2001). *Handbook of bereavement research: Consequences, coping, and care.* Washington, DC: American Psychological Association.

Virtual communities and support groups expand the opportunities for communicating with people who have similar concerns and experiences. (For more about coping and social support, see Box 7.1.)

The following sections describe social support in two contexts: lay caregiving and death and dying experiences.

LAY CAREGIVING

It is important to remember that patients are not the only ones in need of social support. Loved ones and caregivers experience grief, uncertainty, and exhaustion as well, and their needs are frequently overlooked in concern over the ill individual. This section focuses on **lay caregivers,** nonprofessionals who provide care for others. Lay caregivers are an important source of social support, but they also need support themselves.

Lay Caregivers' New Role

The number of lay caregivers has risen in recent years, mostly because the elderly population is growing and because hospital stays are shorter than they used to be. Many surgeries are now conducted on an outpatient basis. Patients recuperate at home rather than in the hospital. This is good news and bad news. As Donna Laframboise (1998) puts it: "Good news! You can go home from the hospital tomorrow. Bad news! You'll have to do everything yourself, even though you're still on crutches or full of stitches" (p. 26).

Someone must help ill or hurt individuals while they are at home. Home health professionals provide a portion of this care, but researchers estimate that two thirds of all home health is provided by family members for free (Joyce, 1994).

Profile of the Lay Caregiver

Most lay caregivers in the United States are women (average age 46), and most care receivers are elderly relatives (average age 77) (Kate, 1997). Women's influence as lay caregivers is well documented. Married men tend to live longer than single men, and men's health is likely to decline if their wives die (Norcross, Ramirez, & Palinkas, 1996). This is true largely because women monitor their husbands' health and encourage them to seek medical attention when needed. Women do the same for their friends and children.

Lay caregivers' time is in demand like never before. More than half of American women now work outside the home ("Comprehensive Survey," 1998). Additionally, a growing number of men and women are entering the Sandwich Generation, a popular term for people who provide care for both their parents and their children. By some estimates, young adults today will spend more time caring for their elderly parents than they will spend raising their own children.

Stress and Burnout

Caregiving is no simple task. In addition to providing medical care and assistance, lay caregivers are frequently responsible for maintaining the household and budget, working at a career outside the home, and providing information and support to others. Many women caregivers report spending at least 35 hours a week earning a paycheck and at least 10 additional hours a week providing care for loved ones in need (Jenkins, 1997).

Legislation was passed in the 1990s to help career people provide care for needy family members. The **Family and Medical Leave Act of 1993** guarantees that people can take up to 12 weeks off work to care for ailing family members, seek medical care themselves, or bring new children into their families (through birth, adoption, or foster parenting). However, the act does not require that employers *pay* workers while they are on leave, and it does not apply to all companies or all employees. To be eligible, employees must have worked at the company at least 1 year for an average of 25 hours (or more) per week. Only companies with at least 50 employees are obligated to provide medical and family leave.

Although most people juggling careers and caregiving feel good about what they do overall (Scharlach, 1994), it is easy to feel stressed, exhausted, and resentful at times. Said a 31-year-old caring for her ill mother: "Your parents have given you so much that the last thing you're ever going to do is not help

Box 7.2 PERSPECTIVES
A Long Goodbye to Grandmother

A few years ago, I lost my grandmother to Alzheimer's disease. Until she died, I saw my grandmother every week of my life. We had a very close relationship.

Alzheimer's is not a disease that just appears one day and kills you. It causes gradual deterioration of a person's memory and sense of being. Minutes and days and years all seem the same or don't exist at all. My grandmother's condition started about 1 year before her death.

Before Grandma got Alzheimer's, our extended family was fairly close. No one wanted to put Grandma in a nursing home, but caring for her was not going to be easy. Her three daughters (including my mother) decided Grandma would stay with each of them for 1 week at a time.

Grandma and I had always enjoyed playing Scrabble and working crossword puzzles together. She always tried to get me to use my thinking skills. My favorite times were when she would tell me stories about when she was a young girl or a teenager. She was a very flirty girl, although she had a prissy attitude as an elderly person.

As Grandma's forgetfulness worsened, she often forgot what year it was. She would also forget to eat. Soon, she could no longer remember conversations we had had. I could answer a question and 5 minutes later, she'd ask it again. I would tell her every week why and where I was going to school. We would talk about the world now compared to the world in her day. Sometimes she would talk out loud to her parents, who had been dead 50 or 60 years.

Her worst times were at night. She stayed up most of the night talking to people she thought were there. As much as I loved Grandma, I would get aggravated with her during those nights of constant talking. Several times a night, we'd go into her room to comfort her. She'd whine and cry like a child. It was difficult for me to deal with this. I started distancing

them out. But at the same time, it's so hard. I get resentful sometimes" (Laframboise, 1998, p. 26).

Part of the strain is emotional. Caregivers may grieve over future plans that no longer seem possible. A 76-year-old woman caring for her ailing husband lamented: "This isn't how we planned to spend our retirement years. . . . Why did this happen to us?" (Ruppert, 1996, p. 40).

It is also painful to see a loved one suffer or change. The progression of Alzheimer's disease is particularly heart-wrenching to witness. Caregivers may watch sadly as the individual's personality and awareness gradually change. Sometimes Alzheimer's patients become belligerent or unable to recognize the people around them (see Box 7.2). To make matters worse, caregivers may feel myself from her during the day because she made me angry with the things she did at night. Even though I knew she had no idea what she was doing, it still aggravated me.

The stress starting wearing on other family relationships as well. The daughters started finding fault with each other. No one said anything out loud, but the frustration was there under the surface. I was sad to see relationships start to disintegrate. I asked my grandmother to forgive me even if she didn't quite understand why.

Over the months, Grandma's condition deteriorated. She lost touch with reality and she lost trust in her family. One day she and I were home by ourselves and I got her a glass of water. When I gave it to her, she smelled it. Then she looked at me and said, "I never thought you would do this." I asked what she meant, and she said, "Of all people, I didn't think you would poison me. I expected the others, but not you." This hurt me very much. I took the glass of water and poured it down the sink and let her watch me pour a new glass. But she continued to believe I was trying to kill her.

By the time she died, Grandma weighed less than 95 pounds. The times that I could talk with her were over. She stayed with us for the last month of her life. She was in such bad condition we didn't want to move her. The night of her death my mom and dad left for church and I stayed behind. I read her the Bible and sang her some songs while I played my guitar. As I did this she began to cry a little. I didn't expect her to respond, but that was a special moment. About 5 hours later, she died in her bed with her family in the room with her.

—*Nicholas*

guilty about their own frustration and resentment. It may feel wrong to be angry with a person who is ill and needy (Moynihan, Christ, & Silver, 1998).

Lay caregivers may also feel unprepared to perform the tasks delegated to them. Although they now perform many services once carried out by health professionals, lay caregivers often receive only minimal instruction on what to do and what to expect (Ruppert, 1996). As a result, they may feel overwhelmed and may worry that they will do something wrong or miss important warning signs. When a loved one's life is at stake, the pressure can be as exhausting as the physical demands of caregiving.

Caregivers may jeopardize their own health if they overextend themselves. People are like elastic, says Geila Bar-David of the Caregiver Support Project in

Toronto (Laframboise, 1998). If they are stretched too thin for too long, they will lose strength and may even snap. Caregivers who are reluctant to leave their posts may need reminding that they will be of no use unless they remain healthy (emotionally and physically) themselves.

Caring for Caregivers

Community resources are expanding somewhat to serve the needs of people who care for loved ones at home. Many medical centers now sponsor lay caregiver support groups and skills-training programs. A program at Salem Hospital in Salem, Oregon, helps lay caregivers establish diet and exercise regimens and teaches them skills such as how to move patients without hurting themselves (Ruppert, 1996). Members also learn about caregiver stress and emotions and have a chance to express their feelings. Good communication skills can help. In a study of 76 older adults and lay caregivers, Jim Query, Jr. and Kevin Wright (2003) found that participants with high communication competence were less stressed and more satisfied with the social support they received.

Friends and families remain the most promising source of support for lay caregivers. In a particularly striking example of social support, 40 people in Fairfax, Virginia, organized themselves to help a dying friend and her family ("What Her Friends Did," 1997). Lynn Mazur was inspired by the book, *Share the Care* (Capossela, Warnock, & Miller, 1995). She organized a group effort to help her friend, Karen Hills, who was dying of cancer at age 34. Mazur called everyone in the Hills' family address book and found 40 people anxious to help out. They met at the Hills' home and filled out questionnaires suggesting what they could each contribute to the effort. Team captains were chosen, and soon volunteers were in place to drive Karen's young daughter to school, clean house, prepare meals, read to Karen, help with her physical therapy, and so on. The assistance allowed Karen and her husband and child to spend more relaxing time together. The tasks were simple and quick enough that burnout was not a problem. In fact, Mazur says, people were relieved to know they could help, and caregivers turned to each other for support when they were tired or sad.

All in all, it is important to remember that caregivers need care too. Assistance can sweeten the rewards of caregiving and lessen the demands.

DEATH AND DYING EXPERIENCES

Death is an unpleasant topic to people in many Western cultures. "Death is un-American. It doesn't square with our philosophy of optimism, of progress," wrote Herbert Kramer, a terminally ill cancer patient (Kramer & Kramer, 1993, paragraph 21). Nevertheless, dying is inevitable, and it marks a stage of life during which social support is crucial. Because communication figures so prominently in social support efforts, an understanding of death and dying is crucial to the study of health communication.

To some people, the phrase "a good death" seems like an oxymoron. They do not believe there is any such thing. However, many people argue that dying can be a special (albeit emotional) experience with many positive aspects. This section analyzes these two perspectives, characterized as "life at all costs" and "death with dignity." It also explains advance-care directives and offers experts' advice on dealing with death.

Life at All Costs

Have you ever happened to walk past a hospital morgue? Probably not. Most hospitals locate the morgue (where dead bodies are kept) in an out-of-the-way area where people will not chance upon it. What's more, the morgue staff may be regarded as somewhat weird and eccentric based on their choice of occupation.

This may seem perfectly understandable if you grew up in a society in which death was regarded as something gross and ghoulish. Death may seem even worse if you are a caregiver pledged to maintain life. To you, death may be more than creepy; it may represent failure (Hyde, 1993).

Medicine's dedication to preserving life has many benefits. Caregivers' devotion and talent, along with their access to medical technology, has helped to increase the average American's life expectancy by 60% in the last century ("By the Numbers," 1995). Few Americans lived beyond 47 in 1900. Now the average lifespan is 76.3 years.

Caregivers have several reasons to keep patients from dying. For one, caregivers are typically trained to preserve life, not allow it to end. Moreover, death is frightening, even to professionals who have encountered it before (McCormick & Conley, 1995). Saving a life is usually a rewarding experience, whereas a patient's death may bring feelings of guilt and grief. Finally, caregivers (doctors especially) may be harshly criticized or sued if a patient dies. Physicians' decisions are often intensely scrutinized by family members, lawyers, insurance companies, quality assurance and risk management personnel, administrators, and others (McCue, 1995). Jack McCue attests: "It is little wonder that physicians engage in inappropriately heroic battles against dying and death, even when it may be apparent to physician, patient, and family that a rapid, good death is the best outcome" (paragraph 2).

There are downsides to the life-at-all-costs perspective. As McCue (1995) proposes, "a rapid, good death" is sometimes preferable to a prolonged, painful end. Prolonging life sometimes means prolonging death. Furthermore, this perspective does not account well for the needs of patients with terminal illnesses. Dying individuals often feel forgotten and ignored because their caregivers are uncomfortable with death, reluctant to become emotionally involved, and uncertain how to act around dying people (Hyde, 1993).

Finally, the opportunity to die peacefully among loved ones is sometimes lost in the confusion of tubes, wires, monitors, and hospital restrictions (Cohn, Harrold, & Lynn, 1997). It is hard for loved ones to be present, and difficult to maintain a sense of intimacy and individuality, in an institutional setting like a hospital. Communication scholar Sandra Ragan reflects on the difference between her father's death and her sister's:

> Dad's death was a conflicted one: he died in a hospital, connected to various machines, and in constant fear, until his last 48 hr when he entered a morphine-induced semi-consciousness, that his doctors would not give him adequate medication. (Ragan, Whittenberg, & Hall, 2003, p. 219)

In contrast, her sister died at home under Hospice care:

> Sherry died peacefully in her own home with no medical intervention other than oxygen, a catheter, and the blessing of morphine and ativan. Her family and loved ones surrounded her, and throughout her last night, she was cradled by her daughter and her beloved cocker spaniel. (Ragan et al., pp. 219–220)

Death With Dignity

The motto of death with dignity is attributable mostly to **Hospice,** an organization that provides support and care for dying persons and their families. About half of all dying patients in the United States now receive Hospice care (Emanuel & Emanuel, 1998).

Hospice is designed to help people feel as comfortable and satisfied as possible during the last stage of their lives. Central to Hospice's philosophy is the belief that death is a natural part of life, thus personal and unique (McCormick & Conley, 1995). People are encouraged to die as they have lived, surrounded by the people and things they love most.

Hospice volunteers and professional caregivers visit with terminally ill individuals and their loved ones to talk with them about death, make sure the dying person is not in pain, encourage spiritual exploration, and provide many forms of assistance. In this effort, Hospice is more oriented than orthodox medicine to personal expression, emotions, spirituality, and social concerns. Loved ones are considered important participants in the dying process.

Beth Perry, a Hospice nurse, recalls an especially rewarding experience helping a dying patient. "Roman, a handsome man in his mid-50s, seemed too well to be a patient on a palliative care unit," she remembers (Perry, 2002, paragraph 5). But Roman *was* dying, and he was bored and tired of the process—ready for the tedium to end. Although Roman's caregivers knew his death was near, they sought a way to rekindle his sense of purpose. Someone remembered that he and his wife had bought a new home just before he became ill, and the grounds were not yet landscaped. They suggested that the couple plan the garden and grounds together. "The result was amazing," writes Perry (paragraph 7):

> The next time we visited the pair, gone was the stony silence, the painful watching of time tick by. Instead, we found the two of them with their noses

> in the same magazine, eagerly debating annuals versus perennials, tulips versus delphiniums.

Although Roman did not live to plant the garden, his last days were filled with enthusiasm rather than boredom. Julie, another nurse caring for Roman, says, "People can take almost anything, but they can't take being forgotten. They want to know that something they have done will live on after they die, and sometimes it is part of my role to help them" (quoted by Perry, 2002, paragraph 8).

Advance-Care Directives

Advance-care directives describe in advance the medical care a person wishes to receive (or not receive) if he or she becomes too ill to communicate. These directives take some of the pressure off caregivers and loved ones, who might otherwise be forced to make those decisions on their own.

Despite the advantages, the majority of U.S. residents have not written advance-care directives or even conveyed their wishes about end-of-life care to their physicians. In one study, more than half of the patients surveyed had not discussed their preferences regarding end-of-life care with their doctors (Hofmann et al., 1997). Of those, about 25% revealed to researchers that they would not wish to be kept alive with artificial life support.

Advance-care directives have become more specific through the years. When they were first conceptualized as "living wills" in the 1960s, they typically referred in vague terms to "heroic" life-saving measures (Emanuel & Emanuel, 1998). This presented obvious difficulties in interpretation (e.g., Is a feeding tube heroic? Is intravenous therapy heroic?). It is now common for advance-care directives to include a person's preferences regarding specific procedures and circumstances, to endow someone with decision-making authority, and to describe the person's philosophy of life and death to help guide decisions during unanticipated circumstances. (See Box 7.3 for a discussion of the right-to-die issue.)

Coping With Death

One positive aspect of death is that it draws people together. Loved ones who may not have seen each other in years unite again with a common concern. Death also provides an occasion for contemplating life and the purpose of living. A sense of insight and spirituality often surrounds death (McCormick & Conley, 1995). Moreover, by sharing in loved ones' deaths, people may become less fearful of death themselves. Joyce Dyer, who wrote *In A Tangled Wood* (1996) about her mother's 9-year experience with Alzheimer's disease, reflected after her death:

> I want to remember every moment I had with my mother, including every second of the last nine years. I want to remember her toothless grin, her

Box 7.3 ETHICAL CONSIDERATIONS
Do People Have a Right to Die?

In 1997, Oregon made history by legalizing physician-assisted suicide for terminally ill patients. Under the law, a doctor may help a person commit suicide if at least two physicians verify that the person has less than 6 months to live and the patient requests help with suicide at least once in writing and twice verbally with at least 15 days between requests ("Oregon Begins," 1998).

Physician-assisted suicide refers to instances in which, at the request of a terminally ill person, a doctor provides the means for that person to end his or her own life (Krug, 1998). This is different from **euthanasia** (also called mercy killing), in which a physician or family member intentionally kills the patient to end his or her suffering. The distinction lies in who does the killing—the patient or another person.

The person most commonly associated with physician-assisted suicide is Jack Kevorkian, a physician who, by his own estimate, has assisted in the suicides of 130 people since 1990 (Robertson, 1999). Kevorkian was tried for murder five times, but he was not convicted until the fifth trial, which concluded in April 1999. Kevorkian was declared guilty of second-degree murder by a Michigan jury and sentenced to 10 to 25 years in prison. The conviction was based on an assisted suicide that Kevorkian videotaped and allowed to be broadcast on *60 Minutes* (Willing, 1999). Kevorkian argues that he is motivated by compassion for people dying slow, painful deaths. His opponents charge that he is a medical "hitman" operating outside the law (Robertson, 1999).

Controversy over physician-assisted suicide is likely to continue for quite some time with people vigorously arguing both sides of the issue. Proponents of physician-assisted suicide include Dax Cowart, who was badly burned in an explosion in 1973 (Cowart & Burt, 1998). Two thirds of Cowart's body was burned in the accident, and he lost his eyesight and his fingers. For more than a year Cowart begged doctors to let him die. Despite his pleas, medical teams continued to treat his burns. The treatment kept Cowart alive and eventually helped him regain the ability to walk. But for more than a year he was in nearly unbearable agony. He recalls: "The pain was excruciating, it was so far beyond any pain that I ever knew was possible, that I simply could not endure it" (paragraph 21). Cowart supports physician-assisted suicide. However, even if a law like Oregon's had been in place when his accident occurred, he would not have qualified for lawful physician-assisted suicide because he was not dying.

Cowart is now an attorney in Corpus Christi, Texas, and describes himself as "happier than most people." But he maintains his conviction that people should not be forced to undergo treatment they do not wish, even if that treatment is needed to keep them alive (Cowart & Burt, 1998). Faced with the same ordeal again, he feels he would wish to die and should be allowed to do so. Cowart's views are captured in his videos *Please Let Me Die* and *Dax's Case*.

On the other side of the issue, some argue that people in intense pain and grief may not see things clearly enough to make life-ending decisions. They point out that Cowart has changed his mind about living with his disabilities. Although he initially felt life would be empty, he now is happy and successful (Cowart & Burt, 1998). Other critics say ill (even terminally ill) patients may request death for the wrong reasons. They may be afraid about the future, feel out of control and scared, or believe they are a burden to loved ones (Muskin, 1998). For these reasons, they feel it is wrong to help someone commit suicide, even if the person requests it.

What Do You Think?

1. Under what circumstances, if any, do you feel patients should be assisted in killing themselves?
2. Should it make a difference whether a patient is terminally ill or not?
3. If you were in Dax Cowart's place, do you feel you would want to die? What would you have done if you were Cowart's caregivers and loved ones?
4. What do you think of the argument that people who are scared and in pain may be not thinking clearly enough to make life-or-death decisions?
5. What do you think of the counterargument—that people should not second-guess the patient's wishes because they cannot fully understand the extent of his or her personal suffering?

Suggested Sources

Cowart, D., & Burt, R. (1998). Confronting death: Who chooses, who controls? *The Hastings Center Report, 28,* 14–24.

Kenny, R. W. (2001). Toward a better death: Applying Burkean principles of symbolic action to interpret family adaptation to Karen Ann Quinlan's coma. *Health Communciation, 13*(4), 363–385.

Kenny, R. W. (2002). The death of loving: Maternal identity as moral constraint in a narrative testimonial advocating physician-assisted suicide. *Health Communication, 14*(2), 243–270.

Krug, P. (1998). Where does physician-assisted suicide stand today? *Association of Operating Room Nurses Journal, 68,* 869.

Muskin, P. R. (1998). The request to die: Role for a psychodynamic perspective on physician-assisted suicide. *Journal of the American Medical Association, 279,* 323–328.

Robertson, T. (1999, March 26). Michigan jury gets Kevorkian case: Defendant cites civil rights leaders. *Boston Globe,* p. A3.

Willing, R. (1999, April 14). Kevorkian sentenced to 10–25 years. *USA Today,* p. A1.

> screams, her growing fondness for sweets and then for nothing at all, the bouquets of uprooted flowers she picked for me from her unit's patio, the way she tried to fold her bib, the rare pats on my cheek that meant everything, her last words, her last party, her last dance. And I want to remember what I learned from aides and nurses, from volunteers and cleaning staff, from my mother's own sick friends. I don't want to forget a single thing. (Dyer, 1996, p. 136)

People may be surprised by the mixture of emotions they feel about death. Most of us are not sure what to expect, and consequently we are often uncertain how to act around dying individuals. One nurse described her initial discomfort when a young man in her care joked that he had to live quickly because he would not live long (Erdman, 1993). The nurse was eventually able to laugh with the young man when he quipped that he was watching movies on fast forward and bathing his dog in the drive-through carwash to save time. Writes Erdman: "The nurse was at first caught off guard by the patient's comments, but the humor opened the door to further communication about death" (p. 59).

Caregivers may take a patient's death especially hard. Janice Rosenberg (1996) writes that a doctor is typically regarded as "super-scientist, able to confront death and beat it every time" (paragraph 3). Even physicians may expect themselves to be superhuman, and they may feel guilty and sad when outcomes are less than perfect. To make matters worse, doctors may consider it unprofessional to feel or show emotions (Haug, 1996).

Usually, whether a death is good or bad depends on the emotional coping resources of the people surrounding it. Supportive gestures are especially helpful, but insensitive actions are especially hurtful. McCue (1995) recommends assistance and social support for caregivers and loved ones. Often, he asserts, elderly individuals accept their own deaths as deeply personal and spiritual, but they are adversely affected by the fear and dread of well-meaning others. Supporting caregivers and families is important for their sake and for the patients' sake.

Communication Skill Builders: Coping with Death

Here are some techniques for dealing with death suggested in the literature.

- *Develop a realistic perspective.* The first step in coping with death is to develop a realistic understanding of the process. Based on news reports and movies, people typically imagine death as violent and scary. However, the majority of deaths are nothing like that. Colin Parkes (1998) describes the typical death as a "quiet slipping away" without pain or horror.
- *Talk about death.* The second step is to make death and relevant issues acceptable topics of conversation. Bringing issues like pain, death, and cancer into the open can reduce the horror that seems to lurk around them (Parkes, 1998). Such discussions benefit the dying person as well

as others. People who work with dying individuals often say they are more peaceful about death because of it and are grateful for the lessons dying people have shared with them (Sadler & Marty, 1997).

- *Accept emotions.* Finally, accept that emotions are a natural and legitimate part of coping with death. It is normal to feel a range of intense emotions when dealing with death and dying.

In her book *On Death and Dying,* Elisabeth Kubler-Ross (1969) describes death as occurring in five stages: denial and isolation, anger, bargaining, depression, and acceptance. Not everyone experiences all five stages, or in the order given, but dying individuals and the people around them are likely to experience many of these phases. Although with enough time and support, many people eventually feel peaceful about death, they may at times refuse to believe what is told them, or they may feel angry, overwhelmed, sad, or hopeless. Often, people feel their god has let them down, and they react by showing anger or attempting to bargain for mercy. It may be reassuring to remember that these stages are common and legitimate components of the coping process.

Implications

As the need for lay caregivers has risen, the demands on lay caregivers' time have increased as well. The traditional expectation that women will provide care for loved ones continues, but American women are more likely than ever to have careers outside the home. Americans are living longer, and intergenerational relationships are becoming more extended, with the accompanying benefits and stress. Support groups, skills-training programs, and the assistance of family and friends are promising sources of support for lay caregivers.

Although most people would prefer to avoid death for as long as possible, the process does have some positive aspects. Medicine has traditionally considered death a failure to be avoided at all costs, but groups such as Hospice promote the philosophy that there is such a thing as a good death. For the most part, a good death unites people in a sense of peace and comfort. Treating it in a realistic and open way can help. (For more information about death and dying experiences, see Box 7.4.)

OVERSUPPORTING

Before closing this chapter on social support it is important to acknowledge that there can be too much of a good thing. Some attempts at social support hurt more than they help. Especially if "supportive" efforts are offered inappropriately or profusely, they can impair people's coping abilities. This section looks at **oversupport,** defined as excessive and unnecessary help (Edwards & Noller, 1998). Following is a discussion of three types of oversupport: overhelping, overinforming, and overempathizing.

Box 7.4 RESOURCES
Insight About Dying Experiences

For insightful and compelling insight about the dying process, I recommend these programs:

- *Like Rembrandt Draperies: A Portrait of Cathy Tingle,* an unforgettable documentary about a woman's experience with cancer, the oncologist who became her friend, and the sometimes frustrating experience of struggling for control when medical professionals refused to listen to her. Available for purchase through LifeWorks Video at www.lifeworksvideos.com. Not rated.
- *Wit,* starring Emma Thompson as a professor who finds out she has advanced-stage ovarian cancer. The 99-minute movie shows the frustrations and rewards of interacting with medical professionals. Produced by Warner Home Video. Rated PG-13.
- *On Our Own Terms: Moyers on Dying,* a four-part series in which Bill Moyers chronicles the experiences of dying individuals, their loved ones, and health care professionals. Produced by *Films for the Humanities, Inc.* for the Public Broadcasting System. Not rated. Available at www.shop.pbs.org.

Overhelping

Overhelping is providing too much instrumental assistance. This can make people feel like children or shield them from life experiences. People who are overhelped may become needlessly dependent on others, feel left out of life activities, and begin to doubt their own abilities (Goldsmith, 1994).

Helen Edwards and Patricia Noller (1998) found that some women's take-charge attitude led them to be overly domineering in caring for their elderly husbands. Couples in this situation reported high conflict and low morale. Their relationships and their attitudes suffered.

Overinforming

Forcing information on people when they are too distraught to understand it or accept it (**overinforming**) may only heighten their stress. Philip Muskin (1998) calls this "truth dumping" and warns people against it. Health-related information can be confusing and frightening. Facts change and outlooks vary. People may shy away from the truth, preferring to preserve hope or minimize their confusion. The theory of problematic integration describes how people make sense of ambiguous, contradictory, and complex information. (See Box 7.5 for more about this theory.)

Box 7.5 THEORETICAL FOUNDATIONS Theory of Problematic Integration

Imagine that you will go through life knowing with relative certainty what to expect and how to feel. Perhaps you will graduate, establish a rewarding career, stay healthy and fit until retirement, and enjoy your later years with the money you have wisely saved along the way. At least this is what you expect and what you hope for.

The theory of problematic integration is based on the idea that we orient to life in terms of *expectations* (what we think will probably happen) and *evaluations* (whether occurrences are good or bad) (Babrow, 2001). However, our expectations and values are challenged almost constantly in large and small ways. (Although this sounds regrettable, the challenges are actually opportunities for greater development, a point to be discussed presently.)

As defined by Austin Babrow and colleagues, the **theory of problematic integration** describes a process in which communication serves to establish a relatively stable orientation to the world, but also to challenge and transform that orientation (Babrow, 1992; Brashers & Babrow, 1996; Ford, Babrow, & Stohl, 1996). *Problematic integration* (PI) occurs when expectations and evaluations are at odds, uncertain, changing, or impossible to fulfill. The disruption may be relatively minor (perhaps a setback that delays graduation) or major (someone close to you is diagnosed with a life-changing illness). Whatever the case, communication will play a pivotal role at every stage of your experience. As Babrow (2001) puts it:

> *Communication shapes conceptions of our world—both its composition and meaning, particularly its values. [Problematic integration theory] also suggests that communication shapes and reflects problematic formulations of these conceptions and orientations to experience. (p. 556)*

In recognizing that communication helps to define, challenge, and transform our experiences, Babrow (2001) makes the point that uncertainty is not inherently bad or good, and we are not always able to extinguish uncertainty by dousing it with information. Sometimes uncertainty exists because we have too little or too much information, or because we are not sure what to make of the information presented us. Furthermore, resolving one uncertainty may produce others. Babrow writes that "PI permeates human experience" (p. 564) although it is difficult to predict when and how uncertainties will arise. Going back to Babrow's first point, the notion of uncertainty is not necessarily undesirable. Indeed, he suggests that uncertainty presents an "opportunity for self-exploration" (p. 563). (For exploration of a similar idea, see the feature on health as expanding consciousness in Chapter 8.)

continued

Box 7.5 THEORETICAL FOUNDATIONS
Theory of Problematic Integration, *continued*

Consider the example of advance-care planning provided by Stephen Hines (2001). Medical professionals have typically been disappointed by patients' disinclination to specify what care they wish to have (or forgo) should they become too ill to express their wishes. Hines suggests that people shy away from the issue because health care professionals, in their desire to reduce their own uncertainty in end-of-life situations, have not been very sensitive to the uncertainties experienced by prospective patients and their loved ones. In short, people may neglect to file advance-care directives—not because they are indifferent or stubborn—but because the uncertainty they present feels unmanageable.

This brief review does not encompass all the facets of problematic integration theory, but hopefully it does illustrate something about the way people constitute, challenge, and transform their understandings, particularly in health-related crises.

Suggested Sources

Babrow, A. (2001). Uncertainty, value, communication, and problematic integration. *Journal of Communication, 51*(3), 553–573.

Babrow, A. S. (1992). Communication and problematic integration: Understanding diverging probability and value, ambiguity, ambivalence, and impossibility. *Communication Theory, 2,* 95–130.

Bradac, J. J. (2001). Theory comparison, uncertainty reduction, problematic integration, uncertainty management, and other curious constructs. *Journal of Communication, 51*(3), 456–476.

Ford, L. A., Babrow, A. S., & Stohl, C. (1996). Social support messages and the management of uncertainty in the experience of breast cancer: An application of problematic integration theory. *Communication Monographs, 63,* 189–208.

Hines, S. C. (2001). Coping with uncertainties in advance care planning. *Journal of Communication, 51*(3), 498–513.

Overempathizing

Overempathizing is actually something of a misnomer, because it applies only to a particular type of empathy, called emotional contagion. In a general sense, **empathy** is the ability to show that you understand how someone else is feeling. Miller and colleagues (1995) have identified two components of empathy: **Empathic concern** is an intellectual appreciation of someone's feelings; **emotional contagion** involves actually feeling emotions similar to the other person's. Research shows that the second kind, emotional contagion, can be overdone.

One drawback of emotional contagion is that it can be exhausting. Miller and colleagues (1995) identified a link between emotional contagion and emotional exhaustion among people who work with homeless individuals. As you may recall from Chapter 4, emotional exhaustion is a component of burnout characterized by reduced motivation and compassion.

Taken to extremes, emotional contagion can also be detrimental to support receivers. Some of the literature on support groups warns that members sometimes empathize so much with each other that they perceive people outside the group to be ignorant and uncaring. Jeffrey Fisher and co-authors noted this effect among HIV/AIDS support group members (Fisher, Goff, Nadler, & Chinsky, 1988). The perception that others are less empathic may discourage group members from developing social networks with diverse people.

Another danger is that people may hesitate to express themselves to listeners who are likely to become upset. In Eric Zook's (1993) case study, a man who cared for his dying partner at home remembers: "As long as I was kind of detached and logical about it, he would take it [his declining health] very well" (p. 117). The perceived need to seem unemotional and in control can make it seem that people do not need social support, when in fact they do. Men, particularly, may be uncomfortable with emotional displays (Chesler & Barbarin, 1984), and may prefer to confide in people who will remain calm.

Finally, some people find emotional empathy overwhelming or belittling (Goldsmith, 1994). They may avoid scenes in which others seem to pity them. Wayne Beach (2002) describes the "stoic orientation" adopted by a father and son discussing the news that the mother was diagnosed with cancer. The son received the news calmly. Rather than reacting emotionally, he initially responded with a series of "OKs" and technical questions such as "That's the one above her kidney?" (p. 279). Beach speculates that this factual, stoic orientation saved the father and son from immediately "flooding out." In this way, they were able both to maintain composure and to display that they were knowledgeable and capable of coping with the news.

Implications

Although social support is usually positive, excessive or inappropriate efforts can have negative consequences. Overhelping restricts care receivers' activities and may diminish their self-confidence. Overinforming, or truth dumping, can destroy people's hope and make them feel overwhelmed. Likewise, when listeners become overly emotional about speakers' concerns, they may inadvertently discourage them from sharing their feelings.

SUMMARY

A diverse number of behaviors make up social support. Support is useful in everyday life and in times of crisis. What is most supportive depends on the nature of the situation, the people involved, and their perception of health self-efficacy. Sometimes problem solving is the most effective coping strategy. In those instances, instrumental and informative support are likely to be appreciated. When the situation calls for emotional adjustment, nurturing support may be a useful way to help people feel better about themselves, express their emotions, and feel that others will stand by them in times of trouble.

Being normal sounds easy, but to members of society viewed as abnormal, achieving a sense of normalcy can seem as impossible as it is desirable. People do well to remember that individuals who are disabled or ill do not usually benefit from being treated as if they are childlike or helpless.

Communication is most supportive when it allows distressed individuals to express themselves as they wish and to set the pace for talk and action. Supportive listeners are attentive, nonjudgmental, and able to help people understand their own emotions.

Sometimes efforts that are meant to be supportive hurt more than they help. Too much assistance can make people feel helpless and dependent. Too much information or ill-timed disclosures can tax people's coping ability, and emotional contagion can be exhausting and can discourage people from describing their feelings.

Lay caregivers are an important source of social support, but they too need support, especially considering the many demands placed on at-home caregivers. Likewise, death and dying experiences represent important opportunities for social support. When people are able to cope effectively, death may bring people together and help them overcome their fears.

KEY TERMS

social support
coping
problem solving
emotional adjustment
health self-efficacy
internal locus of control
external locus of control
crisis
normalcy
action-facilitating support
nurturing support
instrumental support
informational support
esteem support
emotional support
social network support
support groups
virtual communities
lay caregivers
Family and Medical Leave Act of 1993
Hospice
advance-care directives
physician-assisted suicide
euthanasia
oversupport
overhelping
overinforming
theory of problematic integration
empathy
empathic concern
emotional contagion

REVIEW QUESTIONS

1. What two efforts are usually involved in coping?
2. How is a sense of normalcy related to social support?
3. What are two types of action-facilitating support?
4. What are three types of nurturing support?
5. What are some tips for supportive listening?
6. In what ways is support group involvement typically beneficial? In what ways can it be harmful?
7. What are the advantages and disadvantages of virtual communities?
8. Describe provisions of the Family and Medical Leave Act of 1993.
9. What factors typically contribute to stress and burnout among lay caregivers?
10. Have you experienced the death of a loved one? How did it compare to the process described in "A Long Goodbye to Grandmother" (Box 7.2)?
11. In your opinion, is there such thing as a good death? If so, how would you describe a good death?
12. Why might caregivers adopt a life-at-all-costs perspective?
13. What are the potential disadvantages of a life-at-all-costs perspective?
14. What role does Hospice play?
15. What is your opinion of the right-to-die issue (Box 7.3)? Why?
16. What are some tips for coping effectively with death?
17. In what ways can people be oversupportive? What are the likely outcomes of different types of oversupport?
18. What does the theory of problematic integration suggest about the nature of uncertainty and how we manage it?

CLASS ACTIVITY

Comforting a Friend

Tom has just learned that Marcos, a high school friend, has died in a car accident. Fighting back tears, Tom says to you, "I can't believe it. Marcos called me a couple weeks ago and I never got around to calling him back. Now he's gone forever."

Decide what you would do to comfort Tom (a few possibilities are listed below) and compare notes with your classmates. Keep in mind that there is no perfect way to provide social support. The options you choose may reflect different personal preferences and cultural assumptions.

Which (if any) of these strategies would you adopt, and why?

- Distract Tom so he doesn't think about the death too much. Suggest a movie or game of tennis to take his mind off things.

- Tell Tom he shouldn't feel guilty about not calling Marcos back.
- Tell Tom you know just how he feels.
- Tell Tom you can understand why he feels sad and then listen quietly if the feels like talking.
- Try to put Tom's grief in perspective. Tell him about the time you lost two good friends in one year.

CHAPTER 8

Cultural Conceptions of Health and Illness

Unaware that the patient believes her soul will remain where she dies, the physician is frustrated by a woman's wish to leave the hospital when her condition is critical (Orr, 1996).

An Asian immigrant to the United States reports a perplexing set of symptoms including a sense of heaviness and insomnia. Physical tests can detect nothing wrong. The patient attributes his illness to "too much wind" and "not enough blood," conditions resulting from his past immoral behavior. He is simultaneously being treated by a folk healer with meditation and herbal therapies. The American physicians eventually conclude that the man's condition exists "only in his head" although he vigorously denies any emotional upset (Kleinman, Eisenberg, & Good, 1978).

A patient unfamiliar with institutional medicine is disappointed when she is not cured by the X-rays ordered by her doctor (Uba, 1992).

Deeply committed to the healing power of positive thinking, a Navajo man becomes upset when his doctor describes the negative outcomes that may result from an upcoming surgery (Jecker, Carrese, & Pearlman, 1995).

Diverse beliefs about health and illness profoundly affect health communication. Everyone is involved in various ways with making sense of health experiences. The way you talk about health, how you describe your aches and pains, the reasons you seek medical care or encourage others to—all these go beyond physical manifestations of illness. Moreover, you are apt to find yourself sharing health concerns with someone from a different culture more than once during your lifetime.

As the population becomes more diverse, it is especially important to appreciate culturally diverse ways of viewing health and illness. Misunderstandings can occur when people have different ideas about the nature of disease, how people are supposed to act in health care situations, and how illness reflects on people in the community. For example, doctors who do not understand that Eastern cultures consider mental illness dishonorable may be frustrated when Asian patients seem to be depressed but vehemently deny it (Kleinman et al., 1978). If these patients refuse counseling, their caregivers may assume they are indifferent or obstinate. As a result patient–caregiver relationships may suffer, and these people may avoid medical care in the future. This chapter examines evidence that cultural ideas influence health and shape the way people experience health and illness.

Culture refers to a set of beliefs, rules, and practices that are shared by a group of people. Cultural assumptions suggest how members should behave, what roles they are expected to play, and how various events and actions should be interpreted. In some cases one culture disdains what another reveres. For example, in some Russian cultures, patients assume that doctors are incompetent if they do not wear lab coats and behave in a formal manner (Goode, 1993). Conversely, many Americans like doctors who seem casual and friendly. It may be helpful for the doctor treating a Russian immigrant to understand that person's cultural expectations.

This chapter is divided into five sections. The first addresses the question, Why consider culture? The next three sections present different ways of conceptualizing health and illness, the social implications of disease, and diverse roles patients and caregivers play. The final section presents tips for developing cultural competence. As you will see, health is defined partly by social values and assumptions. From different perspectives, the very definitions of being well, sick, or cured are different.

WHY CONSIDER CULTURE?

Considering cultural differences is not merely an exercise in curiosity. It is an important prerequisite for working toward better health around the world. Consider the following statistics:

- Every day about 24,000 people die from conditions that could have been cured with basic medical care. The yearly total is equal to the population of New York City (Donnelly, 2003).
- In India each year, an average of 10,700 children die of cancer, whereas about 350 children die of the same disease in the United Kingdom ("Children," 2003).
- In Tanzania, Africa, 2 of every 10 children will not live until age 5 (Spear, 2003).
- Around the world, about 11 million children die every year because of preventable conditions such as malnutrition and unsafe air and water ("About 11 Million," 2002).
- In developing countries, 1 in 16 women will die during childbirth, compared to 1 in 4,600 in the United Kingdom (Eaton & Dyer, 2003).
- Although the United States is the wealthiest country in the world, 24 countries outrank Americans in terms of life expectancy. This is primarily because the gap between rich and poor is larger in the United

States than in any other developed country ("Health and Income Equity," n.d.).

- About 29.4 million people in Africa have HIV or AIDS. In 1996, 7.6 million of the 9 million people who died of AIDS lived in Africa ("Expert Group Stresses," 2003).
- About 950,000 people in the United States have been diagnosed with HIV or AIDS (WHO, 2002b). Another 400,000 to 500,000 are infected but do not yet know it ("AIDS Conference," 2002).

These statistics are not as remote as they may seem. The world population is changing in ways that will affect us all. By 2050, 80% of people over age 60 will live in developing countries (WHO, 2002a). As mentioned in Chapter 1 the outbreak of SARS, AIDS, and other communicable diseases makes it clear that health is a global phenomenon, and addressing global health concerns requires a commitment to open communication and understanding.

Another reason to study culture is its affect on health-related behaviors. This is especially true concerning sexual practices and the risk of HIV/AIDS. In many parts of Africa, men's privilege to demand sex, even from women they do not know, contributes to an environment in which women can do little to protect themselves from AIDS. Gregory Kamwendo and Olex Kamowa (1999)—both of the University of Malawi in southern Africa—describe Malawian customs that put people at risk for sexually transmitted diseases. These customs include raids in which boys and men sneak into adolescents' girls huts during the night and have intercourse with them, ritual "sex education" in which *fisis* (anonymous male tutors) have sex with girls to test their readiness for marriage, exchanges in which men swap wives for sexual episodes, and spousal inherences in which a man "inherits" his brother's widow or his wife's sister. Underlying these customs is the belief that women cannot refuse sex or insist on condom use. Kamwendo and Kamowa (1999) write:

> In Malawi, women have no power to negotiate for safe sexual practices with their partners because sex is a taboo subject even between husband and wife, and a woman who discusses sex openly is viewed as ill-mannered and promiscuous. (p. 172)

In Malawi, HIV/AIDS is more prevalent among married women than any other demographic group. (For information about a courageous effort to improve HIV/AIDS treatment in Africa, see Box 8.1.)

In Mexico, men are often admired for having many sexual partners and for fathering many children (Pick, Givaudan, & Poortinga, 2003). Marital infidelity among men is as least implicitly tolerated. Women are expected to be chaste, but it is common practice for young women to use premarital sex to get men to marry them (Pick et al., 2003).

In India and China, girls and young women may be recruited to work as sex workers or "hospitality girls" (Liao, Schensul, & Wolffers, 2003). Often,

BOX 8.1 PERSPECTIVES
Zackie Achmat Fights for AIDS Care in Africa

While in some areas of the world, the medical community urges people to seek care for HIV/AIDS, in parts of Africa there is little available to them even if they visit a doctor. On a continent in which more than 29 million people have HIV or AIDS, the price of treatment is too expensive for many people to afford ("Expert Group Stresses," 2003).

Adurrazack "Zackie" Achmat is trying to change that. Achmat is himself HIV-positive, but although supporters have offered to pay for his treatment, he refuses to take any medication not made available to all South Africans. He is founder and chair of the Treatment Action Campaign (TAC) to get better care for African citizens with HIV/AIDS. TAC leads the call for better treatment and has provided funding for more than 60 AIDS-related organizations.

Achmat charges that international drug companies overprice needed drugs and that the African government has turned its back on poor citizens who are dying by the millions from AIDS. In protest, Achmat once bought generic AIDS medication in Thailand for one-hundredth of what it costs in Africa. He brought back a shipment large enough to treat 700 people (Hawthorne, 2003). Upon returning he turned himself over to the police, who were seeking him on charges of smuggling. Although Achmat voluntarily submitted receipts for his purchases to the police, he refused to turn the drugs over. Instead he submitted a videotape detailing the needs of people in South Africa.

Achmat also organized protests against 39 international drug companies that he said have charged South Africans exorbitant rates while offering similar drugs for a fraction of the price in other countries. The companies eventually agreed to lower their drug prices somewhat, but Achmat says it may not be enough.

In a part of the world known for civil rights violations, Achmat has been an activist nearly all his life. As a teenager in the 1970s he participated in student demonstrations and burned his school down to protest racial segregation in Cape Town. An acknowledged homosexual, he also led awareness campaigns on behalf of gay and lesbian groups.

they do not have strong family backgrounds or economic means, and therefore they have little opportunity to escape situations in which they are likely to be exposed to (and pass on) sexually transmitted diseases.

In India, sex is such a taboo subject that the government largely refuses to acknowledge AIDS as an issue, and HIV/AIDS outreach workers are often harassed by police officers (Chatterjee, 2003). This is especially troublesome since much of the population is illiterate and unaware how AIDS is transmitted (Chatterjee, 2003).

In an interview with *Currier International,* Achmat declared:

> *I think that to let people die because they do not have money, it is politically and morally an error. In South Africa, after the end of apartheid, we had obtained our freedom and we wanted to [eradicate] poverty and to give better living conditions to all. But, suddenly, we found ourselves in a situation where 3 to 4 million people, or more still, can die because of AIDS in the next three years, simply because they cannot buy the drugs. ("Interview," 2003)*

Despite the grim outlook, Achmat remains optimistic. In June 2003, TAC suspended civil disobedience protests in hopes that government relief was forthcoming. Achmat typically wears a t-shirt with "HIV Positive" in large letters across the front and encourages others to do the same, whether they are infected are not. The t-shirt is a way to acknowledge the millions of people with AIDS in Africa and to suggest that "positive" action is underway. (For updates, visit the TAC website listed below.)

In 2003 Achmat, along with fellow activitist, Frenk Guni, was awarded the prestigious Jonathan Mann Award by the Global Health Human Rights Council. *Time* magazine honored him as one of 35 Heroes of 2003 in the magazine's European edition.

Suggested Sources

Hawthorne, P. (2003, April 20). Dying to get AIDS drugs to all. *Time Europe.* Retrieved online July 27, 2003, from www.time.com/time europe/hero/zackieachmat.html

Hope, K. R., Sr. (Ed.) (1999). *AIDS and development in Africa: A social science perspective.* New York: Haworth Press.

Interview: Zachie Achmat. (2003, July 25). *Currier International.* Retrieved online July 25, 2003, from www.courierinternational.com/interview/avec/Achmat.htm

Treatment Action Campaign website: www.tac.org.za

Implications

As interdependent citizens of the world it is imperative that we seek to understand the perspectives of people who may be very different from ourselves. In a lecture titled "The Small World of Global Health," physician and public health specialist, J. P. Koplan (2002), said:

> As diseases and risk factors converge around the world, we will have to recognize our interdependencies and look to each other for solutions. We know

> that a nipavirus outbreak in Malaysia has implications for hog farms in North Carolina. Effective tuberculosis control in India and Mexico affects TB rates in the United States, as does Dengue fever control in Mexico and the Caribbean. Foodstuffs contaminated with pathogens or pesticides can originate abroad and appear on your kitchen counter. (p. 297)

The solution is not merely to protect the United States from what occurs abroad, even if that were possible. Koplan (2002) says we must also consider how U.S. exports and cultural messages affect people in other countries:

> Our pressure on the tobacco industry here in the United States has immediate ramifications for the health systems and economies of developing countries. The impact of violent American television programming is felt all over the world. (p. 297)

The following section examines cultural ideas about health on a more fundamental level by describing the way that health and healing are defined in cultures in the United States and around the world.

THE NATURE OF HEALTH AND ILLNESS

Cultures conceptualize health in various ways. Some consider that disease is manifested differently within each person. Others see disease as something objective and independent, outside patients' control and beyond their understanding. This section establishes two basic ways of viewing health—as an organic phenomenon and as a harmonious balance.

Health as Organic

In many Western societies germs or physical abnormalities are typically taken as signs of ill health. In the absence of these factors, a person is generally considered to be healthy. This perspective is consistent with the biomedical approach. The **organic perspective** assumes that health can be understood in terms of the presence (or absence) of physical indicators.

One strength of the organic perspective is its emphasis on scientific knowledge. Based on scientific principles, caregivers and researchers keep detailed patient records, conduct studies and experiments, identify risk factors, and link diseases to their causes (Marwick, 1997). This effort to learn and accumulate knowledge has led to remarkable advances in medicine. Medical research is responsible for pain remedies, diagnostic tests, a variety of vaccines, diverse treatment options, and numerous forms of medical technology.

Medical research has led to the development of **evidence-based medicine (EBM),** the practice of making treatment decisions based on the results of scientific studies (Levin, 1998). EBM is being adopted in many medical schools and hospitals as a means of avoiding medical waste and making effective decisions (Levin, 1998; Marwick, 1997).

BOX 8.2 RESOURCES
More About Culture and Health

To learn more about cultural ideas concerning health visit the following websites:

- Center for Research on Ethnicity, Culture, and Health: www.sph.umich.edu/crech
- Ethnomed: www.ethnomed.org
- Transcultural Nursing Society: www.tcns.org
- University of California at Los Angeles Center for Culture and Health: www.npi.ucla.edu/cch/index.htm
- University of North Carolina Program on Ethnicity, Culture and Health Outcomes: www.echo.unc.edu

Physical evidence does not explain everything, however. A weakness of the organic model is its inability to account for conditions that cannot easily be verified. People who perceive illnesses that are not scientifically identifiable are often viewed with suspicion or labeled hypochondriacs. Patients with undetectable conditions such as chronic fatigue syndrome sometimes say the worst part is that so many people regard their condition as "not real" (Komaroff & Fagioli, 1996). Western society's faith in the observable survives despite evidence that science is imperfectly equipped to understand all aspects of the human body. Mental illnesses, long considered less real than physical illnesses, gained legitimacy in the 1950s as medicine began to recognize a chemical basis for them (Byck, 1986). The difference is science's ability, not the illnesses themselves.

The organic approach can seem cold and impersonal, especially to people who are accustomed to a different style of care. African Americans have traditionally been dissatisfied with health care, partly because they feel snubbed by caregivers who seem disinterested in them as individuals (Levy, 1985; Spector, 1979). African-American communities have traditionally placed great emphasis on community and religion. Compared to the personal concern of community members, clinical care can seem indifferent and unfeeling.

Furthermore, classifying people as either healthy or sick satisfies the logic and precision of scientific thought, but such simplicity may be at odds with human experience. As Charles Rossiter (1975) points out, *sick* and *healthy* are inadequate to describe all aspects of the human condition. There are varying levels of sickness and varying levels of health. Moreover, some people seem to be unhealthy although they do not have specific diseases.

Another drawback of either–or thinking is that people may assume that if they are not sick, they are perfectly healthy. Not so, argue some theorists.

They propose that true health is not only physical, but reflects a harmonious balance between many aspects of life. This perspective is discussed in the following section.

Health as Harmony

As you may recall from Chapter 1, the idea of health as harmony is supported by the World Health Organization, which defines health as "a state of complete physical, mental, and social well-being and not merely the absence of disease or infirmity" (WHO, 1948). From this perspective, health is cultivated through personal beliefs, contact with other people, physical strength, and other factors. From the **harmony perspective,** health is not simply the absence of physical signs of disease; rather it is a pleasing sense of overall well-being. The perspective is in keeping with the biopsychosocial perspective.

Traditional Navajo cultures believe the best way to remain healthy is to maintain a balance between physical strength, social interactions, and spiritual beliefs (Bille, 1981). From their viewpoint, concentrating on only one factor can upset the delicate balance. For example, striving for physical strength without also seeking spiritual growth is not healthy, and a person may become ill because of the imbalance. This is not to say that Navajo deny the existence of germs. They accept that germs cause some diseases. But they also observe that some people are less vulnerable than others to germs. If several people are exposed to a contagious disease, some of them are likely to get sick, but others may not. Based on Navajo beliefs, people who live balanced lives are more likely to remain well, even when exposed to physical threats.

Members of the Odawa and Ojibway aboriginal communities in Canada believe that health is based on harmony with the environment, or Mother Earth (Wilson, 2003). As one member of the culture explained:

> She (Mother Earth) is something that heals you if you let it. You don't always feel it. You have to be thinking about it. You can't just go out for a walk and feel it. You have to be spiritually connected to feel her. (Wilson, third section, paragraph 8)

Within this belief system it is therapeutic to live in harmony with the environment.

Members of some Asian cultures think of health in terms of balanced energy (Uba, 1992). According to the Chinese Tao, **yin** and **yang** are polar energies whose cyclical forces define all living things. Yin is associated with coolness and reflection, and yang with brightness and warmth. Cycles and combinations of yin and yang define human life and are a common element uniting all forms of existence. Within this belief, one's central life energy is called **chi** (pronounced *chee*). Illness and even death may result if the chi is wasted or if yin and yang are not balanced. Life energy is sustained and balanced by awareness, rhythmic breathing, physical regimens, and meditation. The importance of energy may lead members of some Asian cultures to resist undergoing surgery or receiving immunizations, believing these procedures will interfere with their life energy and the rhythms that define their well-being (Uba, 1992).

Across cultures, folk healing is typically oriented to lifeworld concerns. Usually, a folk healer's role is to integrate social support with spiritual faith and physical treatment. The curanderos of Mexican-American cultures and the hand-tremblers of some Native-American cultures are good examples. These folk healers are usually well-known members of their communities (Bille, 1981). As such, they are familiar and accessible, without institutional boundaries or technical jargon. Curanderos and hand-tremblers take extensive personal interest in their patients and preside over rituals that bring members of the community together. In this way, healing involves a show of moral support and a sense of peace and belonging.

Health care that includes patients' lifeworld concerns has been praised as realistic and compassionate (Friedman & DiMatteo, 1979; Thompson, 1996). There is evidence that some people perceive more improvement when treated by folk practitioners than with conventional medicine (Kleinman et al., 1978). The discrepancy may amount to the distinction between healing and curing. McWhinney (1989, p. 29) calls *healing* a "restoration of wholeness," which includes spiritual and moral consideration, as opposed to purely physical *curing*, which he says may still leave a patient in "anguish of spirit" about the causes, effect, and fears associated with the illness.

One drawback of the harmony perspective is that it produces gradual and ambiguous results. Unlike organic medicine, which is devoted to analysis and comparison, attempts to establish harmony may be difficult to evaluate and measure (Cassedy, 1991). If immediate and measurable results are needed, the harmony perspective alone may seem insufficient. This is especially true for conditions like cancer and broken bones, which have traditionally responded well to organic treatment. Harmony may help people resist disease and injury and recover more quickly. But most people would agree that, for some ailments, nothing beats a trip to the Emergency Room or hospital.

Implications

Cultural ideas about health vary from intensely personal to purely physical. The two perspectives presented here—the organic and the harmonious—reflect different ways of conceptualizing health. These models are roughly equivalent to the biomedical and biopsychosocial medical models, but the terms *organic* and *harmonious* are used here to include a broader array of cultural viewpoints than the medical models might commonly encompass. For example, yin and yang have existed far longer than the modern concept of biopsychosocial medicine, and although the Tao is compatible with biopsychosocial care, it is not synonymous with it.

From an organic perspective, patients' beliefs and social practices are not central to the topic of health. Instead, disease is regarded in physical terms.

Medicine has flourished under the assumption that medical knowledge should be carefully recorded, analyzed, and shared. The downside of the organic approach is that its definition of health is fairly narrow, largely excluding social, spiritual, and psychological factors that are sometimes relevant to illness episodes.

Conventional practitioners have traditionally adhered to an organic model of illness. Partly as a result, they are typically reluctant to bring up spiritual concerns during medical visits (Todd, 1989). In fact, they are likely to avoid such issues, perhaps because it is time consuming to be so inclusive or because patients have such diverse beliefs it is difficult to understand or comment on them.

The organic perspective lends itself to scientific and statistical analysis, whereas the harmony perspective recognizes illness as a phenomenon that occurs for different reasons in different people. Health is believed to reflect harmony between all aspects of a person's life. From this perspective, personal viewpoints, habits, and social networks are considered integral parts of the health equation. Thus, communicating with the patient is central to identifying and treating illness. Some conventional practitioners focus on harmony in their patients' lives, but the harmony perspective is more common among alternative medicine specialists and folk healers.

The organic and harmony perspectives are not necessarily at odds with each other. As mentioned, physical health is a significant component of both perspectives. Moreover, each model may be appropriate in different situations, and sometimes they are both appropriate. Few people would argue that some conditions—like cancer, appendicitis, or traumatic injury—are well served by an organic approach (Pachter, 1994). However, other conditions—like high blood pressure, headaches, and fatigue—seem to defy understanding in purely physical terms. Depending on the nature of the illness, a person might seek an organic remedy, a harmonizing one, or both. In some cases, conventional practitioners are actively teaming up with folk healers. Amos Deinard, a pediatrician at the University of Minnesota Hospital, says, "Our attitude is, you bring your shaman and we'll bring our surgeon and let's see if we can work on this problem together" (Goode, 1993, paragraph 7).

SOCIAL IMPLICATIONS OF DISEASE

One function of culture is to make sense of the world. Cultural assumptions act as guides to interpretation, indicating why things happen and what significance should be attached to various events (Garfinkel, 1967). For instance, death might be interpreted as a glorious ascension to the afterlife or as a tragic and regrettable occurrence. Illness may be regarded as an unfair or random affliction or as a valuable opportunity for renewed awareness. (See Box 8.3 for a description of the theory of health as expanded consciousness.)

It is often difficult to make sense of disease. Some cultures honor scientific explanations. But even in those cultures, scientific accounts sometimes seem inadequate. At different times in history, epilepsy, cancer, tuberculosis, mental illness, AIDS, and other ailments have been viewed so negatively that people with these conditions were shunned or even imprisoned (Friedman & DiMatteo, 1979). Sick people may be regarded as a threat to the moral order because behaviors associated with their conditions (e.g., homosexual contact) are considered immoral, or because their conditions seem contagious or frightening.

Many times, public reaction is not based on facts, but on fears or cultural assumptions. Prior to 1950, people were so fearful of cancer they typically avoided telling anyone outside the family if a loved one was diagnosed with it (Holland & Zittoun, 1990). They often chose not to tell the patient either. That has changed since the public has accepted that cancer is not contagious.

Social taboos have long surrounded the issue of mental illness as well. In 16th- and 17th-century England public horror over insanity was so great that the mentally ill were incarcerated as criminals, after which they were brutally treated and denied the right to marry or own property (MacDonald, 1981).

Even cultures steeped in organic definitions of disease may react with fear and loathing when confronted with certain disorders. It is common to blame ill persons for their conditions. This section considers the social effects of diseases regarded as threatening to the moral order. It surveys a variety of ideas about illness, including the notion of disease as a curse, the social stigma of some illnesses, moral issues of prevention, and the implications of referring to patients as victims. These ideas represent different (sometimes overlapping) ways of considering health and illness within the context of cultural beliefs.

Disease as a Curse

Blaming someone is one way of making sense of frightening illnesses, write D. Nelkin and S. L. Gilman (1991) in a book about plagues. People may reason that disease is the result of curses inflicted by God or witches. It may be especially tempting to blame gods or witches when science and other explanatory models fail. White (1896/1925) proposes that as long as people cannot explain illness by natural law they attribute its cause and cure to the supernatural. As he puts it, "In those periods when man sees everywhere miracle and nowhere law . . . he naturally ascribes his diseases either to the wrath of a good being or to the malice of an evil being" (p. 1).

During the bubonic plague of the 14th century, more than one third of the European population died (Slack, 1991). Struggling to make sense of this devastating epidemic, people killed tens of thousands of women, accusing them of using witchcraft to make their neighbors ill (Nelkin & Gilman, 1991). Others attributed the plague to God's wrath over women's fashions, blasphemy, drunkenness, improper religious observances, and other behaviors (Slack, 1991).

Box 8.3 THEORETICAL FOUNDATIONS Theory of Health as Expanded Consciousness

The majority of us spend our lives trying to stay healthy, and when we get sick, want nothing more than to be well again. We may be missing the point. According to Margaret Newman's **theory of health as expanded consciousness,** a health crisis is not necessarily negative or undesirable (Newman, 2000). Instead, health events are integral parts of life that provide opportunities for growth and change.

Newman was influenced by David Bohm's (1980) concept that our everyday life is influenced by underlying patterns that characterize who we are and what we experience. Bohm conceived of two types of order—the **explicate order,** made up of the tangible elements of our existence, and the **implicate order,** comprised of patterns beneath the surface. Although the tangible elements of our lives may seem like the "real thing" because we can see, hear, taste, and feel them, the meaning of what we do often lies within the underlying, implicate order. Bohm compares the dual nature of life to waves on the ocean. We can see the waves, but we will not really understand what causes them unless we explore the underwater currents that give rise to them.

Within this metaphor, a health event makes waves. It disrupts what might otherwise seem to be a peaceful, unremarkable existence. As nurse and a nurse educator, Newman (2000) observes:

> *The thing that brings people to the attention of a nurse is a situation that they do not know how to handle. They are at a choice point. Each of us at some time in our lives is brought to a point when the "old rules" do not work anymore, when what we have considered progress does not work anymore. We have done everything "right" but things still do not work. (p. 99)*

You might ask, and this is a *good* thing? According to Newman, yes. In her view, life is a process of attaining greater levels of understanding and awareness. When things stop working well, we experience a sense of chaos. But, she says, if we "hang in there" through the uncertainty and ambiguity a health crisis may become a means of seeing underlying patterns and transcending previous limitations. This can be a richly rewarding and liberating experience (Newman, 2000).

Imagine a person who has worked throughout her life to support others. She has devoted her energy and time to doing well at work, caring for her family, running errands, serving on committees, cleaning the house and yard, and so on. She is lauded with thanks and awards. Meanwhile, she appears less physically fit than she used to. Her hair and clothing are not carefully groomed and tended. But this is nothing compared to is happening within her. In fulfilling so many outward "obligations" she neglects her own spiritual and emotional growth. Although she interacts frequently with people, she does not share much of herself or appreciate the uniqueness of the people around her.

Suddenly (or what appears to be suddenly) the woman comes down with the flu and must cancel her commitments for several days. Faced with this prospect, she might put all her energy into fighting the illness, frustrated that it has interrupted her life. Or she might look for a deeper level of meaning. What does the illness (an outward manifestation) suggest about what is happening within her? And at an even deeper level, what does this disruption signal about the underlying pattern of her life? Perhaps this is an opportunity to reevaluate a pattern that appears virtuous on the surface but is harmful to her and others in the larger scheme of things. Perhaps understanding the pattern will allow her to restructure her life in a way that is more functional and adaptive, allowing her to develop her inner self as well as perform helpful tasks in the tangible world. Or perhaps she will ignore the underlying currents until they give rise to a much bigger, harder-to-ignore "wave" such as a stroke or heart attack.

Seen this way, health events are opportunities for developing higher levels of understanding and more effective interactions with our environments. Greater harmony between inner and outer levels of existence provides the means for seeing beyond one's self and transcending old habits and assumptions. As Newman learned from her mentor, Martha Rogers, "health and illness should be viewed equally as expressions of the life process in its totality" (Newman, 2000, p. 7).

Newman coaches nurses to help people find the meanings and patterns revealed by their health experiences, whether or not their diseases are eradicated. She writes:

> *Transcendence of the limitations of the disease does not necessarily mean more freedom from the disease; it does mean more meaningful relationships and greater freedom in a spiritual sense. These factors are considered an expansion of consciousness. (Newman, 2000, p. 65)*

Furthermore, a health crisis is not merely a senseless or regrettable circumstance. Newman (1986) writes that, since she began to regard health as the expansion of consciousness,

> *Illness and disease have lost their demoralizing power. . . . The expansion of consciousness never ends. In this way aging has lost its power. Death has lost its power. There is peace and meaning in suffering. We are free from the things we have feared—loss, death, dependency. We can let go of fear. (p. 3)*

continued

Box 8.3 THEORETICAL FOUNDATIONS
Theory of Health as Expanded Consciousness, *continued*

What Do You Think?

1. Have you ever learned something valuable about yourself as the result of a health crisis?
2. What can caregivers and loved ones do to help people evaluate their life circumstances when an illness occurs?
3. In what ways are your health and outward, everyday life (explicate order) influenced by underlying factors (implicate order)?

Suggested Sources

Bohm, D. (1980). *Wholeness and the implicate order*. London: Routledge & Kegan Paul.

Coward, D. D. (Fall 1990). The lived experience of self-transcendence in women with advanced breast cancer. *Nursing Science Quarterly, 3*(3), 162–169.

du Pré, A., & Ray, E. B. (in press). Comforting episodes: Transcendent experiences of cancer survivors. In L. Sparks, D. O'Hair, & G. L. Kreps (Eds.), *Cancer communication and aging.* Cresskill, NJ: Hampton Press.

Malinksi, V. M. (Ed.). (1986). *Explorations of Martha Rogers' science of unitary human beings.* Norwalk, CT: Appleton-Century-Crofts.

Newman, M. A. (1995). *A developing discipline: Selected words of Margaret Newman*. New York: National League for Nursing Press.

Newman, M. A. (2000). *Health as expanding consciousness* (2nd ed.). Boston, MA: Jones & Bartlett.

Rogers, M. E. (1986). Science of Unitary Human Beings. In V. M. Malinski (Ed.), *Explorations of Martha Rogers' Science of unitary human beings* (pp. 3–14). Norwalk, CT: Appleton-Century-Crofts.

Today, some African tribes attribute AIDS to the work of witches. Many of the Goba, who live in a rural area of Zambia, Africa, believe that death only occurs naturally in old age (Yamba, 1997). In all other cases, it is attributed to the work of witches in the community. (According to Goba beliefs, a person may be a witch and not even know it.) The Goba use the same word (*ng'anga*) to refer to healers and to witchfinders. When a young person dies, suffers an injury, or is unable to conceive children, the family is expected to hire a witchfinder to identify, and often to kill, the witch believed to be responsible. Supposed witches are publicly challenged to survive impossible feats (such as drinking poison). If they do not survive, their guilt is assumed. Yamba reports that the tribe members maintain their belief in witches partly because they are unsatisfied with biomedical explanations of illness. If witchcraft is not involved in sexually transmitted diseases, "why else, they argue, would two men be exposed to the same woman and yet one would become infected while the other would not?" (paragraph 8).

All in all, people may suspect that supernatural forces are at work when rational explanations fail to make sense of illness episodes. One result of treating illness as a punishment or curse is that ill persons may be shunned, and supposed witches may be accused and even killed. In light of this, people may not admit they are ill, and treatment may be withheld in the name of religion. In Europe in the 1700s some people refused the smallpox vaccination because it was regarded as interference with God's way (Nelkin & Gilman, 1991). For similar reasons, some Southeast Asians regard medical care as fruitless or a sign of weakness (Uba, 1992). Likewise, Kashmiri men in India, although at high risk for diabetes, frequently decline treatment or lifestyle changes because they feel the disease is Allah's will and they should enjoy life (including eating what they want) until it is their fate to die (Naeem, 2003).

Stigma of Disease

Even when illness is not regarded as a supernatural curse, a culture may consider people with certain diseases to be corrupt or immoral. As Erving Goffman (1963) uses the term, **stigma** refers to a type of social rejection in which the stigmatized person is treated as dishonorable or is ignored altogether.

Social theorists compare HIV and AIDS to a plague in that infected persons are often avoided and seen as dangerous and unprincipled. Numerous studies tell of HIV and AIDS survivors who have been fired from their jobs and abandoned by their families and friends (Adelman & Frey, 1997; Cawyer & Smith-duPré, 1995). Stigmatized in this way, people with HIV and AIDS must often choose between two forms of isolation. Either they keep the diagnosis a secret (eschewing potential support) or tell others and risk being shunned and avoided by them (Cline & Boyd, 1993).

One effect of social stigma is that people's individuality, even their humanity, is overshadowed by the discrediting characteristic. A participant in Rebecca Cline and M. Faye Boyd's (1993) study of HIV survivors says:

> I am finding it harder and harder to get away from AIDS . . . I am angry at people, society, for not looking at me as a normal person with a normal disease, putting labels on me and trying to isolate me, putting shame and guilt on me. (pp. 137 & 139)

For those whose conditions stir society's fears and prejudices, disease is plainly more than a physical phenomenon. Some people die of embarrassment, too afraid or ashamed to seek care for medical conditions stigmatized by society. Others may keep their diagnoses secret for fear of retribution.

Sometimes people avoid medical evaluations because they are afraid of being stigmatized by the results. For example, although they are predisposed to breast cancer, highly religious Jewish women is Israel are less likely than others to seek genetic testing (Bowen, Singal, Eng, Crystal, & Burke, 2003). Given the history of persecution against Jewish people, these women are especially wary of being stigmatized as genetically "different" or "at risk" (Bowen et al., 2003). As the following section shows, moral issues are often applied to illness, even when health is regarded as an organic phenomenon.

The Morality of Prevention

The news is filled with health warnings and risk factors. Such information enables people to make healthy choices, enhancing their own well-being and assuring themselves of long, healthy lives. At least that is one implication—take care of yourself and there is no reason you should become ill. Prevention information is enabling to an extent, but taken too far it may lead to prejudice against ill persons (Brody, 1987). One backlash of the prevention movement is that people may have so much confidence in prevention that they believe illness always results from laziness or indifference. The rationale is that, if illness can be prevented, ill people have not tried very hard to stay healthy.

"Why isn't it possible to just get sick without it also being your fault?" asks physician/essayist Paul Marantz (1990, p. 1186). Marantz describes the smug comments surrounding a young friend's unexpected death from heart failure. A medical resident minimalized the man's death by dubbing him "a real couch potato" (Marantz, p. 1186). Marantz was angry that onlookers would judge his friend, even to the extent of making his premature death seem OK or deserved.

The fallacy that only the lazy or indifferent get sick compounds the hardship of being ill (Marantz, 1990). People fall ill for reasons that are difficult to explain, even though they have worked hard to stay healthy. Marantz and others propose that suffering is often made worse by the assumption that ill persons engineer their own misfortunes.

One alternative to blaming ill persons is to see them as victims of circumstances beyond their control. As you will see, however, there are social implications to playing the victim role as well.

Victimization

As the average lifespan has increased, so has the duration of chronic diseases. Many people survive and lead relatively normal lives with serious diseases. This has created a semantic dilemma. These people are not accurately described as "patients." So what do you call a person with AIDS or cancer or emphysema? A common practice is to call them victims, as in "AIDS victims" or "cancer victims." However, many people so described resent the implications of that characterization.

A participant in Cline and Boyd's (1993) study declares: "I'm HIV positive but I'm not a victim! I'm a *survivor!*" (p. 144). Another participant in the same study concurs: "I hate that word. I'm not a victim because I'm not allowing AIDS to victimize me. The word 'victim' really ticks me off. And 'innocent victims' implies that there are 'guilty victims'" (p. 145). These people's reactions attest to the power of cultural metaphors. Words and images imply values and judgments with serious implications for those involved.

Implications

Diseases and their implications are open to cultural interpretation. Particularly when great uncertainty surrounds a disease or when medicine can do little to stop it, people are apt to assume supernatural forces are at work. Society may also stigmatize people who have dreaded diseases as being menacing and contemptible.

It seemed for a time that reframing disease in scientific terms would shield sufferers from moral judgment. Ironically enough, Western society has attributed a moral quality to science, with the effect that people who get sick are often considered to be lazy or appallingly ignorant.

People presumably do not wish to be stigmatized or blamed for their illnesses; neither do most people want to be characterized as helpless victims. The lesson overall is that cultural characterizations carry social implications. As cultures attempt to make sense of health and illness, they apply their value systems to the task. As a result, health is a topic loaded with social importance and values.

Consistent with this viewpoint is the idea that people involved in health episodes are expected to act in culturally appropriate ways. The following section examines different ways of conceptualizing patients' and caregivers' roles.

PATIENT AND CAREGIVER ROLES

Culturally speaking, there are right and wrong ways to "do" and to "treat" illness. That is, some behaviors are rewarded, whereas others bring social penalties. For example, some cultures expect patients to cry out when they feel pain (Nyinah, 1997; Wood, 1979). Others consider this weak and unseemly, even a sign that the patient has been evil in the past. Members of traditional Hispanic cultures typically believe pain should be endured stoically because it is God's wish (Duggleby, 2003).

Likewise, people might be expected to remain "respectfully" quiet in medical encounters or to take a "responsible" role by sharing their thoughts. The rules for being a good patient and a good caregiver may be contradictory and confusing. Nevertheless, with people's health hanging in the balance, health care participants may fervently wish to behave correctly. (See Box 8.4 for more about Thai customs regarding family members' role as health advocates.)

Box 8.4 PERSPECTIVES
Thai Customs and a Son's Duty

Absolutely nothing in Thai culture is as important as a son's duty to take care of his elderly parents. My paternal grandmother came to live with my family when I was 15 years old. She left Chonburi, a small city in the eastern part of Thailand, and moved to Bangkok after my grandfather died of a heart attack. Grandmother Kim had been paralyzed for 20 years because of a bad fall, so my father insisted she must come to live with us so we could take proper care of her and so she wouldn't be lonely.

Grandmother Kim was 91 years old then, but she still had a great memory, especially about finances. Even though she had no expenses of her own, she insisted that my father give her a monthly allowance. She kept perfect mental notes on the status of her money so that she could distribute it as she pleased. For example, every day before I left for school, Grandmother gave me some money to give to the monk she watched on television each day. She was looking after her future by buying merit enough to go to heaven when she died. Grandmother also gave me money for myself each morning, and she gave other people money as well.

Although she required a lot of care and assistance, Grandmother was not depressed. Instead, she seemed happy and content with her financial projects and with providing advice to our family. Still, my mother and I watched over her constantly and we hired a private nurse to help take care of her. My mother was a very skillful and competent caregiver since she had taken classes at the hospital to prepare her to take care of Grandmother Kim.

After I graduated from high school, I pursued a bachelor's degree at a university far from home. I would go back every weekend, however. When she was 95, Grandmother began to get weak. The doctor said she might have lung cancer. I didn't think she had any diseases; instead, I believed it was her time to go to heaven. My father didn't think she had lung cancer, either. He was convinced her lungs were perfect because she had no symptoms of any lung problem. No matter how strongly my father opposed the doctor's opinion, the doctor insisted on a lung biopsy as soon

This section examines different roles patients and caregivers are expected to play. A **role** is a set of expectations that applies to people performing various functions in the culture. For example, people may play the roles of patient, doctor, sister, friend, employee, or parent. Each role is guided by a set of culturally approved rules. Typically, one role exists in relation to another:

as possible. We agreed not to tell my grandmother about any suspicion of cancer, since we thought it might be too hard for her to know. We agreed to only tell her she had suffered a stroke. As we waited during the surgery, my father confided in me that he was unsure he had made the right decision to let the doctor do a biopsy.

When the results came back, my grandmother didn't have cancer. After she came home, everyone expected her to feel better. Unfortunately, Grandmother got worse. We took her to another doctor who said that, since a biopsy could make an elderly patient weaker, it had been inappropriate to do the procedure. My father asked the doctor how much time his mother had left in this world. He told us that Grandmother could not be expected to live longer than one year. She died within several weeks.

Although I was away at the university when Grandmother died, I quickly returned. It is Thai custom that kin and family have to see the dead person before the body is placed in the coffin. Therefore I had a chance to see her for the last time in the mortuary. As my mother and I got her dressed and cut her hair, I noticed that Grandmother's body was small and cold. I told my mother that Grandmother had kissed me and told me to be a good girl the last time I saw her. Up to this day, I still remember every single word she told me. I think she knew her time to go was close. However, she didn't show any signs that she was afraid of death.

My father blamed the first doctor for his mother's death, but he blamed himself most of all. He thought that, if he had insisted the doctor not perform the biopsy, she would have stayed with us longer. My mother and I both tried to comfort Father. I thought the best way to relieve him of some of his sorrow was to tell him that it was time for Grandmother to go. She had stayed longer than most other people could; also she had suffered from a stroke and had been paralyzed for a long time. However, I do understand my father's feeling because he is a son, and his responsibility is to do everything to keep his mother alive and healthy.

—Pem

patient–caregiver, student–teacher, parent–child, and so on. A role may lose meaning without its counterpart (e.g., a teacher is not a teacher without students). Therefore, role playing is a collaborative endeavor, and people usually adjust their performances to form meaningful combinations. This can be so compelling that people sometimes feel forced into roles they would rather not assume. For example, if your conversational partner adopts a parental role, you may feel like a child, and you may act that way—even if you would rather not. To do otherwise might seem uncooperative and rude.

As you will see in this section, patients and caregivers often play complementary roles—as mechanics and machines, providers and consumers, parents and children, and so on. Keep in mind that these roles are collaborative achievements, supported by participants' mutual efforts. This does not mean that the participants always like the roles they assume. They may be motivated by a sense of cultural appropriateness or the perceived need to "play the scene" as the other person is playing it.

Mechanics and Machines

From one perspective caregivers are similar to mechanics and patients to machines. The implication is that the patient is relatively passive, and the caregiver is expected to be analytical and capable of fixing the problems that are presented.

This perspective does not encourage emotional communication between patients and caregivers. The focus is more on identifying physical abnormalities and fixing them (Todd, 1989). When caregivers take on a mechanic role, they are typically more concerned with what they can observe and change than what the patient might be feeling.

Some people feel that scientific medicine is relatively mechanistic. That is, when caregivers take on the role of scientists, they are much like mechanics—concerned with the orderly physical functioning of the human body. As mechanics or scientists, caregivers are expected to be objective, value-neutral, and capable of collecting information, diagnosing the problem, and fixing it. From this perspective, it may seem inappropriate for caregivers to display emotions or call into play such intangible notions as faith or spirituality. Eric Cassell (1991) puts it this way: "Adjectives like warm, tall, swollen, or painful exist only for persons but, ideally, science deals only with measurable quantities like temperature, vertical dimensions, diameters" (p. 18).

One advantage of the mechanic/scientist role is that it reduces the emotional drain on caregivers. If patients are like machines who simply need fixing, emotions need not become part of the process (Bonsteel, 1997). At the same time, the confidence that people can be fixed may seem comforting and neat.

Of course, patients may not appreciate being treated like machines. Some argue that ignoring patients' descriptions and considering them passive in their own care amounts to a mechanized form of medicine in which the patient is treated as little more than a set of parts. Richard Swiderski's (1976) analysis of medicine through the ages concludes that doctors have often considered patients less relevant than their pulse rates, blood, and urine. This is an image the public has embraced as well, as evidenced by patients' disappointment when their physicians do not run tests or prescribe medications. One reason for overuse of antibiotics is patients' insistence that treatment be embodied in some physical form, even when pharmacology suggests it will have no effect (Fisher, 1994).

Parents and Children

The popular expression "doctor's orders" suggests a relationship in which physicians issue directions patients are expected to obey. This approach is referred to as **paternalism,** reflecting the idea that patients are like children and caregivers are like parents.

Members of some cultures carry this to an extreme. For instance, many South Africans (Herselman, 1996) and Asians (Uba, 1992) show respect for physicians' authority by outwardly agreeing with anything their doctors say, even when they do not understand the information or have reservations that will prevent them from following the medical advice.

David Hufford (1997) tells of a tragic case in which a 14-year-old Asian immigrant to the United States felt ashamed for complaining about abdominal pain after her doctor said it was normal menstrual cramping. She refused further medical care for a year, until the liver cancer that had gone undiagnosed was so advanced she died. Hufford points out the tragic consequences of stereotyping a young girl's condition, on the one hand, and adhering to cultural expectations that suffering be endured without complaint, on the other.

One implication of the paternalism model is that patients may be regarded as naive or incapable. There is a historical precedent for regarding patients as ineffectual, even as bungling intruders, in matters of their own health. In an 1871 commencement address at Bellevue Hospital College, the famous physician/poet/novelist Oliver Wendell Holmes (1891) warned graduates: "Your patient has no more right to all the truth you know than he has to all the medicine in your saddlebags . . . He should only get so much as is good for him" (p. 388). Holmes advised the graduates to adopt the habit of "shrewd old doctors" who keep a few stock phrases to quiet "patients who insist on knowing the pathology of their complaints without the slightest capacity of understanding their scientific explanation" (p. 389).

Another implication is that doctors may be expected to know what is best for their patients. Some theorists (e.g., Emanuel & Emanuel, 1995) feel this is a risky assumption because patients may have many feelings and desires unknown to their doctors. Expecting physicians to anticipate and act upon patients' wishes may place an unrealistic burden on doctors and unfairly rob patients of opportunities to make their own decisions. (See Box 8.5 for more on this issue.)

Spiritualists and Believers

Caregivers also may be cast as spiritualists who use their powers on behalf of faithful patients. The image of caregivers as spiritual figures (and even as gods) was established thousands of years ago. As discussed in Chapter 2, the

Box 8.5 ETHICAL CONSIDERATIONS
Physician as Parent or Partner?

Medical ethicist, Robert M. Veatch (1983), reflects that physicians are often criticized as being "aloof and unconcerned" rather than concerned and attentive as people would like them to be. In short, physicians often act like strangers when patients wish they would act like friends or family members.

Paternalism (the idea that doctors are like parents) is a long-standing tradition. The Hippocratic Oath, written approximately 2,500 years ago, beseeches physicians to use their best "ability and judgment" on each patient's behalf. This presumes that physicians are well acquainted with medicine *and* with the particular needs and preferences of each patient. Paternalism is also based on the belief that physicians are more capable of making medical decisions than patients are.

Some people feel paternalism is outdated. Veatch (1983) points out that it is difficult to know patients well in the current age of large patient loads, specialization, and emergency and outpatient care. These factors make it unlikely that doctors will understand the unique needs and preferences of each patient. The paternalistic model is also criticized as inconsistent with patient empowerment, which presumes that patients are knowledgeable and active agents in their own health care (Emanuel & Emanuel, 1995).

What Do You Think?

1. Do you feel it is realistic or preferable for health caregivers to know their patients' feelings and values?
   a. If so, how might they accomplish this?
   b. If not, what alternatives would you suggest?
2. Can you think of circumstances in which you would want your physician to know your feelings and life circumstances?
3. Can you think of circumstances in which you would rather your physician did not know you well?
4. Do you feel patients are capable of making decisions about their own care?

Suggested Sources

Emanuel, E. J., & Emanuel, L. L. (1995). Four models of the physician–patient relationship. In J. D. Arras & B. Steinbock (Eds.), *Ethical issues in modern medicine* (4th ed., pp. 67–76). Mountain View, CA: Mayfield.

Reilly, D. R. (2003, Winter). Not just a patient: The dangers of dual relationships. *Canadian Journal of Rural Medicine, 8*(1), not paginated.

Veatch, R. M. (1983). The physician as stranger: The ethics of the anonymous patient–physician relationship. In E. E Shelp (Ed.), *The clinical encounter: The moral fabric of the patient–physician relationship* (pp. 187–207). Dordrecht: D. Reidel.

Egyptian physician Imhotep was eventually granted the status of a god. Jesus has been called "the great physician," and is revered for legendary acts of curing the sick (Moore et al., 1987). Throughout history, physicians are described as "little Gods," a celestial metaphor that extends to nurses, often portrayed as "angels of mercy" (Moore et al., 1987, p. 232).

Anthropologists have compared the doctor's role to that of a priest, a powerful and somewhat mysterious authority figure. This awe-inspiring image may be strengthened by patients' reverence and physicians' displays of power. Pendleton and colleagues (1984) point to doctors' laboratory coats, specialized vocabulary, and honorific titles as supporting props in this image. They also suggest that the image is bolstered by an information imbalance that makes physicians' knowledge seem all the more marvelous. They write: "Powerful rituals, such as examining and prescribing, are the more charismatic in the absence of adequate explanations" (p. 9).

Among the most well known healer/spiritualists are the shamans of traditional Native-American cultures. A shaman is believed to coax a patient's disease into his or her own body, then expel it through strength of will (Swiderski, 1976). The assumption is that illness is an invasion of magical or supernatural forces. The faithful believe shamans can communicate with beings beyond the physical world, an ability that gives them magical abilities and healing powers.

The success of a spiritual ceremony is often said to rely on the patient's faith in the healer and the greater spiritual force that has accepted the healer as a medium. One result of this assumption is that failure to recover may be construed as an indication of the patient's insufficient faith (Kearney, 1978). For this reason, patients may be particularly trusting and may benefit from the power of positive thinking. However, if their conditions do not improve, they may be loath to admit it.

Another spiritualist group is the Christian Science Church, whose members believe that conventional medicine is anti-Christian. "They are taught that 'illness is an illusion' and can be cured only through prayer," explains Andrew Skolnick (1990, paragraph 5). Christian Scientists believe that orthodox medical care makes illnesses worse. Thus, they do not use drugs or surgery, and they refuse even simple home treatments like heating pads, ice packs, or back rubs. Christian Scientists' refusal to allow medical care has raised controversy across the nation, especially when children's lives are involved (Skolnick, 1990). Some courts hold that it is child abuse to deny children the medical care that might save their lives. Others feel that requiring medical care would violate the Christian Scientists' right to worship as they choose.

A belief in the supernatural also characterizes the health beliefs of some Southern Appalachians (Bille, 1981). In that culture, spiritual ceremonies involving faith healing and glossolalia (speaking in tongues) are believed to restore health. **Faith healers** are expected to channel the curative power of the Holy Spirit, which they pass to believers through ceremonies known as the laying on of hands. **Glossolalia** involves a trancelike state during which a worshiper seems to speak in a foreign language. It is believed that the language is known only to God or that it is a foreign tongue known to some, but unknown to the worshiper except through divine inspiration (Lippy & Williams, 1988).

Even scientists acknowledge the power of faith (although they are not likely to regard it as the central focus of their work). Evidence supports that people who expect to be cured sometimes *are,* even when the "treatment" is an inactive **placebo** such as flavored water or sugar. Placebo effects are so common that medical researchers routinely give some research participants an actual treatment and give other people placebos. If the treatment group does not experience greater effects than the placebo group, the researchers cannot be sure they are measuring anything more than the power of suggestion. Sometimes placebo effects are unintentional. When thermometers were introduced in a British hospital in the 1800s, some patients assumed they were curative and seemed to spontaneously recover before the treatment could be administered (White, 1896/1925). The reverse is sometimes true as well. People who have no confidence in a treatment may be unaffected by it. These examples do not prove that all disease can be reduced to the effects of faith and emotions. However, they do suggest there is more to disease than meets the (microscopic) eye.

A religiouslike faith in caregivers serves multiple goals. It inspires confidence (on the part of patient and caregiver), which may be an important part of healing. It also honors the extraordinary role caregivers play in managing life and health.

There is a downside, though, in dashed hopes and exorbitant malpractice claims. With the expectation that medicine can work miracles if done correctly, people may feel particularly angry when things do not go well, and may rightly or wrongly charge that their caregivers are incompetent (Kreps, 1990).

Providers and Consumers

It has become popular to describe health care in terms of consumerism. Patients are regarded as shoppers or clients who pay doctors primarily to provide information and carry out the patients' wishes (Roter et al., 1997). Some theorists predict that competitiveness will make caregivers more mindful of patient satisfaction (Lombardo, 1997). This could be an advantage. However, caregivers who have traditionally seen themselves as serving a higher purpose than profit margins find the marketplace metaphors disturbing.

Howard Friedman and M. Robin DiMatteo (1979) caution that consumerism may be a risky conceptualization for all involved. If the customer is always right, they wonder, will medical centers that respect patients' treatment decisions later be held liable if adverse outcomes result? Friedman and DiMatteo also worry that pleasing patients may sometimes be at odds with helping them. Considering that the most effective medical options are sometimes the most unpleasant, how far will caregivers go to avoid upsetting their patients?

Similarly, consumerism seems to place cost as a top priority. Richard Glass (1996) is concerned that physicians may choose less aggressive treatment options if they are forced to be more mindful of cost than care. A physician himself, Glass maintains that patients "rightly expect something different from their doctors than from consumer goods salespersons" (p. 148). He argues that a marketplace mentality may have "perverse effects" on medical care, and he beseeches health care management not to interfere unduly in medical decision making.

Partners

Only as partners do patients and caregivers assume roughly the same role. Of course, they each bring something different to the encounter in terms of experiences and expertise. But as partners, they are directed toward the same goals and expected to act as peers. The partner role is consistent with collaborative medical talk.

As partners, patients and caregivers are expected to use a vocabulary they both understand and to make decisions together. The success of health care managed in this way hinges largely on the quality of patient–caregiver relationships. In 1996, the *Journal of the American Medical Association* introduced a regular column called "The Patient–Physician Relationship." In an article launching the new feature, Glass (1996, p. 148) proclaimed the doctor–patient link to be the "center of medicine," a covenant not to be compromised by impersonal reliance on technology or profit-oriented decisions. This emphasis underscores the importance of trusting communication between patients and caregivers.

Retired physician Francis Lombardo (1997) writes that he earned patients' trust by being a respectful listener. As he describes it: "Once a patient has sized you up as someone who won't hassle or ridicule him, he'll feel much freer to bring up those touchy topics himself, like the fact that he thinks he might be gay" (p. 121).

Some people find the partnership model appealing because it allows both patients and caregivers to have influence over medical decisions, as opposed to being strictly patient-centered or doctor-centered (Beck et al., 1997; Smith & Hoppe, 1991). Hufford (1997) attests that patients have important and relevant statements to make about their own health. "Sick people, it turns out, often do know exactly what has been happening to them, what it feels like and when it happens, and there is nothing fictional about it" (Hufford, p. 118).

Few people criticize the idea of patients and caregivers as partners. However, this may be a difficult transition to make. Patients and caregivers have traditionally upheld the expectation that doctors will guide medical discussions and patients will be relatively quiet and passive in their doctors' presence (see Chapter 3 for a review of this literature). A shift is possible, but it will require change and cooperation on both sides.

Implications

Cultural expectations help establish the roles patients and caregivers are expected to play. Patients are cast as machine-like when caregivers act like mechanics or scientists concerned predominantly with identifying physical problems and fixing them. The paternalistic model portrays patients as children, and caregivers as wise and helpful parents. As spiritualists, caregivers are awe inspiring, and patients are expected to be faithful and trusting. As consumers, patients are courted, but medical rigor may be sacrificed. As partners, patients and caregivers act as peers invested in attaining mutually satisfactory results.

CULTURAL COMPETENCE

It is challenging to develop cultural competence, but the effort is often rewarded. Richard Weingarten (2003) recalls his experiences as a Peace Corps volunteer in Brazil in 2001:

> Brazil's lively Latino culture served as a healthy antidote for my tendency to be reserved and often depressed . . . What seemed like emotional and intellectual "excess" to me, was easily accepted by my Brazilian friends. I felt much more myself interacting with Brazilians and connected to a larger sense of self I developed in Brazil. (p. 303)

Experiences such as these remind us of the value of acceptance and diversity in understanding ourselves and others.

Researchers have reported mixed results teaching cultural competence in medical schools. A class called Physicians, Patients & Society at a Canadian medical school left little impression on students (Beagan, 2003). According to Beagan, students who completed the course still felt there were no significant differences among people relevant to race, class, gender, culture, and sexual orientation. Melanie Tervalon (2003) argues that awareness will lag until medical schools integrate diversity throughout the 4-year curriculum. Delese Wear (2003) suggests it will be useful not to teach about particular cultures, but to help medical students build awareness about disparities of "power and privilege" in all society (p. 549). Sonia Crandall and colleagues have had success using mock interactions to help medical students develop cultural competence (Crandall, George, Marion, & Davis, 2003; Morell, Sharp, & Crandall, 2002).

Influenced by training and personal experiences, health care workers respond to diverse patients in different ways and, consequently, provide different types of care to those patients. Sherly Kirkham (1998) observed that nurses in a Canadian hospital offered either resistant care, generalist care, or impassioned care.

- *Resistant Care:* Nurses who provide resistant care rely heavily on stereotypes and insist that people conform to mainstream cultural standards. They are typically not interested in learning about diverse types of people and are frustrated when people behave in ways they consider inappropriate or ignorant.

- *Generalist Care:* Generalists believe in offering respectful care to all individuals. Although they might not be highly knowledgeable about different races or cultures, generalists try to accommodate patients' personal preferences.
- *Impassioned Care:* Nurses who offer impassioned care demonstrate a high commitment to learning about other cultures and honoring diverse ways of thinking and behaving.

These categories are useful for understanding the various perspectives people may have when communicating with diverse patients.

COMMUNICATION SKILL BUILDERS: DEVELOPING CULTURAL COMPETENCE

Although it is useful to be aware of overall cultural differences, be careful about assuming cultural beliefs based on people's appearance or ancestry. For example, Hispanic Americans may have roots in Central America, South America, or the Caribbean—all of which have different customs (Murquia, Peterson, & Zea, 2003). To recognize cultural and individual differences, Betty Pierce Dennis and Ernestine Small (2003) suggest that caregivers consider the following questions when getting to know people from other cultures:

- How do the client and family members identify themselves? For example, do they call themselves American, Jamaican, Puerto Rican, Russian-American, or Ghanaian?
- Are the caregivers' questions answered by the client or by another family member?
- Is there a family member who always speaks first? Who makes decisions?
- Do they speak with the caregiver in English and to each other in another language?
- Will you need an interpreter? Is so, select one that fits the family structure. For example, if only men respond to interview questions, a child or a female would not be an appropriate interpreter.
- Determine how respect is shown. Ask what titles should be used. First names may be regarded as disrespectful.
- Here in the United States maintaining eye contact shows interest and involvement. Is it the same or different in their culture?
- Food is very cultural. What are the food choices of the client? Are ethnic dishes preferred? Can arrangements be made with the family based on the medical needs of the client?

■ SUMMARY

Social desirability and cultural modes of expression influence the way people think about health and illness. As we strive to become better communicators it is important to understand cultural diversity for a number of reasons: (1) cultural beliefs and customs influence health-related behavior, (2) in today's global environment health concerns in one country or ethnic group have repercussions for everyone, and (3) surmounting cultural barriers enhances our ability to work together for better outcomes.

To some, disease is an organic phenomenon, and what shows up under a microscope may be more to the point than the patient's subjective experiences. Consistent with the biomedical model, this perspective is apt to consider undetectable conditions less real than physically verifiable ones.

Other people believe health is affected by harmony among such factors as relationships, spiritual forces, the environment, behavior, and energy fields within the body. This broader definition is contextual and aims for more than physical well-being.

The premises that underlie diverse beliefs may be more similar than they seem. Even staunch supporters of the organic approach admit that stress and attitude affect healing. And diverse religions may acknowledge an organic element, as well as a spiritual element, to disease. The theory of health as expanded consciousness proposes that a health disruption can be a valuable opportunity for reflection and change. Cultures may make sense of illness in different ways. Especially when a disease seems to defy explanation, people may believe it is caused by witchcraft or divine intervention. One effect of viewing illness as a spiritual manifestation is that ill persons may be stigmatized as immoral or dishonorable. Science is essentially a cultural viewpoint, based on assumptions about the causes of disease and people's control over their own health. When people assume that they can control their health by behaving wisely, they may consider that people become ill mostly because they were ignorant or negligent. At the other extreme, people may regard ill individuals as victims.

Cultural values and assumptions are embodied in the roles patients and caregivers play. How one interprets illness has an effect on the type of healing process preferred. If disease is regarded as a physical phenomenon, patients may be like passive machines and caregivers like mechanics or scientists. Patients may be considered incapable if they are cast as children seeking the guidance of parent-like caregivers who know what is best.

Caregivers have long been deified to varying extents. Even orthodox practitioners who pride themselves on scientific care are regarded with awe for their extraordinary ability to understand and treat illness. In some cultures, healers are spiritual leaders, expected to channel supernatural powers for the benefit of faithful patients. Considering patients and caregivers to be consumers and providers is more enabling, but some people worry that medical care may suffer if it is forced to uphold the rules of the marketplace. Finally, as partners, patients and caregivers work to build mutually satisfying relationships and care procedures.

By becoming more culturally competent we increase our understanding of ourselves and others. The next chapter expands the discussion of diversity to organizational culture and diverse types of health-related professionals.

KEY TERMS

culture
organic perspective
evidence-based medicine (EBM)
harmony perspective
yin and yang
chi
theory of health as expanded consciousness
explicate order
implicate order
stigma
role
paternalism
faith healers
glossolalia
placebos

REVIEW QUESTIONS

1. Describe Zackie Achmat's campaign for better AIDS care in Africa. Do you think civil protests are merited? Why or why not?
2. What are the strengths and weaknesses of the organic approach?
2. What are the strengths and weaknesses of the harmony approach?
3. Can you think of times when your health was affected by organic factors? By issues of harmony? By both?
4. Describe the principles of the theory of health as expanded consciousness. What is the role of the explicate order? The implicate order? What role do nurses (and other caregivers) play in helping people cope with health episodes?
5. What are the implications of regarding illness as a curse?
6. Why might members of a society stigmatize ill individuals?
7. How can an emphasis on prevention lead to prejudice against ill people?
8. What are the different roles patients and caregivers might play?
9. Which of these roles have you played as either a patient or caregiver? Which roles appeal to you most? Why?
10. How is each role set described likely to affect health communication?

CLASS ACTIVITY

How It Was—How It Could Be

This exercise is based on the following excerpt from an actual doctor–patient conversation (quoted by Greene et al., 1996, p. 270). (The words are exact but some details surrounding the case have been modified.)

PT: And I'm so very nervous. Very nervous.

MD: Why are you very nervous?

PT: Well, I have a husband that's ill, but he's up, you know, he's with me. And, ah . . . then I went . . . Well, it really started with two sudden deaths of friends that were very close to me.

MD: I see.

PT: Very close. And then my husband was taken to the hospital. He was on intensive care . . . right after that. That's the reason why I never got back to Dr. V.

MD: I see.

PT: It was a little bit too much.

MD: Do you smoke?

In pairs or small groups:

1. Read the excerpt carefully.
2. Discuss how both participants might have expressed themselves more clearly and considerately.
3. Assign one person to play the patient and another to play the doctor. Recreate the conversation in your own words, adding to it so that you achieve the objectives listed below. (Use your imagination to supply missing details.)
    a. Acknowledge the patient's feelings.
    b. Assess the impact of her emotions and recent experiences.
    c. Go over her health concerns (she has three):
    - A "cold" that has lasted 2 weeks. (Examine her throat and ears. Prescribe antihistamine.)
    - "Tightness" in her legs. (What does she mean by *tightness?* Check her blood pressure.)
    - "Palpitations" and chest pains (What does she mean by *palpitations*? This could signal heart trouble. Does she smoke? Is her diet high in fats and salt? Does she exercise? Does she have a family history of heart trouble?)
4. Rehearse the conversation out loud (and share with other class members if you wish).
5. The entire exam can last no longer than 10 minutes—the average length of an HMO visit.

What Do You Think?

1. Consider the conversation as you revised it:
    a. How well did your (role play) conversation acknowledge and explore the patient's feelings?

   b. How well did it assess the impact of recent life events?
   c. How well did it cover physical concerns?

2. Did the conversation as you redesigned it focus more on organic elements of disease or harmony in the patient's life?
3. Was there adequate time to cover all goals for the encounter? If not, what would be a reasonable time frame?
4. If you had to eliminate some portions to make the exam shorter, which would you eliminate?
5. How would you describe the roles of the doctor and patient in the excerpt quoted? In the conversation as you redesigned it?
6. Did this activity give you any insights into the challenges facing doctors and patients?

Part Four

COMMUNICATION IN HEALTH ORGANIZATIONS

CHAPTER 9

Culture and Diversity in Health Organizations

About 150 years ago, a father received a letter from his daughter, saying she wished to become a physician. He replied: "If you were a young man I could not find words in which to express my satisfaction and pride . . . but you are a woman, a weak woman; and all I can do for you now is to grieve and to weep. O my daughter! Return from this unhappy path." (as cited in Bonner, 1992, p. 11)

Well into the 1900s, it was generally believed that women lacked physical strength and intelligence and were too emotionally unstable to practice medicine (Bonner, 1992). Furthermore, it was considered scandalously immodest of women to touch and see portions of other people's bodies.

There was not much room in medicine for minorities either. Until the 1960s, African Americans were refused entrance to U.S. clinics and hospitals. Black doctors were forced to open their own hospitals because they were not allowed to practice alongside white practitioners (Cassedy, 1991). As you will see, health organizations are much more diverse than in the past, but they still do not reflect the amount of diversity in the overall population.

This chapter describes the role of culture and diversity in health organizations. **Health care organizations** provide products, services, and information to help people maintain health and manage illness and injuries. Some types of health organizations are pharmacies, doctors' offices, clinics, diagnostic centers, long-term care facilities, managed care organizations, fitness and wellness centers, counseling services, home health agencies, insurance companies, nonprofit agencies such as the American Heart Association, and more.

Health care organizations have a powerful impact on health communication. Organizational members create the environments in which health care is provided and are largely responsible for the tone, quality, and timing of health care transactions. We would all like to think of health care organizations as centers of excellence in which members are professional, compassionate, and devoted to their work. Whether this is the case or not depends largely on the culture of the organization—what is expected, how members define their roles, and what actions and attitudes are valued.

This chapter examines the culture of health care organizations and the diverse professionals who comprise them. As you will see, organizational members and clients differ most visibly in terms of race and sex. But even more importantly, they differ in terms of job duties, occupations, skills, and experiences. You will read about health care organizations that top the charts in patient and employee satisfaction. You will also learn more about efforts to bring more women and minorities into medicine. The chapter showcases professional diversity by spotlighting communication issues that influence nurses, nurse practitioners, physician assistants, and alternative/complementary care providers. You will read about the advantages of diversity in terms of personal growth and innovation and the challenges of working with people with different visions and ideals. Making the most of diversity requires skillfully handling the conflict that naturally arises from our differences. We will look at various kinds of conflict common in health organizations and tips for successful conflict management.

ORGANIZATIONAL CULTURE

During the Industrial Revolution, it was popular to think of organizations as smooth-running machines (Hawkins et al., 1997). However, a general shift in ideology has occurred since the 1970s. Now organizations are more likely to be viewed as cultures. As defined by Edgar Schein (1986), an **organizational culture** is comprised of members' basic beliefs and assumptions about the organization and its place in the larger environment. In Schein's view, organizational culture has a "taken-for-granted" quality. That is, established ways of thinking and acting are accepted so thoroughly that members rarely question them.

Organizational culture is important because it represents a common set of assumptions that help guide people's actions and interpretations. For example, it is commonly assumed in medical organizations (and society overall) that physicians will be referred to as "Doctor." However, nurses are not usually addressed as "Nurse." If Maria Brown is a doctor, she is probably called Dr. Brown. If she is a nurse, she is probably called Maria. Scholars of organizational culture examine conventions such as these to see what values they imply.

To illustrate, Campbell-Heider and Hart (1993) propose that doctors' expertise is emphasized by addressing them in terms of their medical degrees. They are treated as distinctly different from other people. (For many years, nurses were taught to stand when a doctor entered the room.) By contrast, calling nurses by their first names, with no honorific title, suggests they are "everyday people" not much different than patients, clerks, or others who also go by first names. This may put patients at ease because nurses seem more casual and friendly, less intimidating than doctors. At the same time, however, it may make nurses seem significantly less powerful and educated in the eyes of patients, doctors, and supervisors. Nurses may even buy into the low-status image themselves, displaying meek subordination even when it is in patients' interest and their own to speak up (Campbell-Heider & Hart, 1993). In Schein's (1986) view of culture, people do not intentionally address doctors and nurses differently. They have simply come to accept "normal" ways of behaving and may not be fully aware that their actions support cultural values.

Cultural Integration

The significance of regarding organizations as cultures is that people are not regarded as mere cogs in a machine, as in the industrial metaphor. Instead, they are individuals whose thoughts and values help define the organization and shape its activities. Organizational cultures are accomplished through communication. As Charles Conrad (1994) writes: "Cultures are communicative creations. They emerge through communication, are maintained through communication, and change through the communicative acts of their members" (p. 31).

Schein (1986) suggests it is important to consider how the organization's philosophy is embodied in rules, goals, and the physical environment. It is also important to consider whether people in the organization share the same philosophy about their work, what customs they observe, how their personal expectations mesh with the organization's, how they communicate with each other, and what motivates them (Schein, 1986).

Organizational cultures are influenced by the broader cultures in which they operate and by members' personal preferences. People within an organization have preexisting assumptions about the community, the world, and their place in it. These may be more or less consistent with their co-workers' beliefs and with the organizational culture. An **integrated organization** is one in which members share a common language and set of assumptions (Schein, 1986).

Sometimes people seek to intentionally alter an organization's culture. When the staff of Delnor Community Hospital in Geneva, Illinois, decided to redesign the corporate culture, they began at the top. "We knew the leaders had to display a passion for excellence or other people wouldn't pick up on it," says Brian Griffin, director of marketing and public relations. Then they focused on employee satisfaction, reasoning that patients would not get top quality care if staff members were discontent or uninvolved. In 2002, Delnor was ranked number one in the nation in terms of employee satisfaction in hospitals its size. (For more on the Delnor story, see Box 9.1.)

Advantages of Diversity

It may be tempting to hire people whose ideas conform to organizational beliefs and to develop highly unified beliefs among employees. It is certainly advantageous when organizational members commit to pursuing the same

Box 9.1 PERSPECTIVES
Cultural Transformation at Delnor Hospital

When Linda Deering assumed the role of chief nurse executive at Delnor Community Hospital in Geneva, Illinois, she had a few ideas. "Being the new whippersnapper, I was frequently in the president's office telling him what was right and wrong with his organization," she says laughing. "Bless his courage, he listened. He challenged me that, if I thought I could do something about it, go to it."

Deering was inspired by research evidence that caregiver relationships influence patient outcomes. "That grabbed me," Deering recalls. "Before we were forever spending our time on clinical skills and education. Those are important, but this was something that changed how I was going to do my job as a leader. If *disharmomy* on a medical unit puts patients at risk, then my top job has to be *harmony*."

Linda Deering, Chief Nursing Executive, at Delnor Community Hospital

Deering began to focus on communication, relationships, and organizational culture. Recognizing that she did not know exactly where to begin, Deering convinced Delnor leaders to enlist the help of consultant Quint Studer (featured in Chapter 10).

One of Studer's first lessons was to communicate with everyone—patients, guests, and employees. "He engaged every single person in the hallway every day," Deering remembers. "I remember when he and I got into an elevator. For me, elevators are an infringement of your personal space. I thought, 'He's going to be quiet now.' " However, Studer talked with people in the elevator, too. Deering says the lesson was clear: Engage people at every opportunity, no excuses. She decided to try it.

"I came the next day, it was 10 minutes to 7 in the morning. I got in the elevator. And you know what? Gosh darn it, there was someone in the elevator! I didn't want to do it," Deering exclaims. "I wanted a cup of coffee. I actually started to rationalize: 'It's only 10 to 7, I'm not officially on duty yet.'" Nevertheless, she took Studer's lead and introduced herself. Deering's elevator-mates told her the nurses had been excellent, and she made it a point to pass along their compliments to the staff.

When Deering and others began offering praise, employees started to pay attention. Soon, the Delnor staff implemented a peer-recognition program called BOB (Best of the Best) Awards. Employees were given BOB Awards they could bestow when they saw a staff member making an exceptional effort. BOB recipients could cash in the awards for $5 gift certificates. "It was a little rough at first," Deering acknowledges. "We gave a lot of undeserved gift certificates for things like bringing cookies to work. But we had to look at it a year later and say, 'You know what? They're more joyful than before.'" As staff morale improved, employees began to raise their expectations and their achievement levels. Now Delnor staff members give out about 400 BOB Awards per month. Deering says they are well worth the expense.

Before the Delnor staff launched the cultural transformation, the hospital had a 25% annual turnover of nursing staff. "That's horrible," Deering says. "It wasn't horrible for our region at the time. But it's horrible. Think about it. That's one fourth of our nurses changing each year." Now, several years into the cultural transformation, Delnor enjoys an extraordinarily low turnover rate of 8%. (The national average is 20%.) Deering estimates that the lower turnover rate saves the hospital about $1.5 million a year. Patient satisfaction at Delnor has also improved—from a respectable 70th percentile ranking in the 1990s to an astounding 99th percentile now.

Following are some lessons the Delnor staff has learned about orchestrating a cultural transformation.

- *Train leaders, and keep training them.* "Of those of who have arrived in positions of management and leadership, very few of us have really had training on how to lead people effectively," Deering says. Delnor sponsors a 2-day leadership retreat four times a year. Participants learn new skills and set goals for the next quarter.
- *Don't underestimate the importance of leadership.* "When you have an effective team, you have an effective leader," Deering attests. "When you have a team that's struggling, you have a leader who's struggling." The Delnor staff learned to model the behavior they wanted others to adopt. "As a leader you can't ask your staff to engage in these behaviors unless you're doing them yourselves. And we weren't," Deering says. "I had to change too. I had to change the way I walked to meetings. I'm a marcher. I like to walk quickly, with purpose. I like to read on the way to meetings. I had my head down. I wasn't engaging people. I had to change." The changes had an effect. "When 75 leaders started acting a little nicer, a little softer, everyone noticed," Deering says.
- *Establish clear expectations, and don't set the bar too low.* "In health care we haven't always been an effectively run business," Deering says. "I think it's born out of 24/7 shifting. We tolerated very bad behaviors. I mean, I could tolerate a bad nurse on the night shift, because

continued

Box 9.1 PERSPECTIVES
Cultural Transformation at Delnor Hospital, *continued*

if I confront her what might happen? I might lose her. And if I lose her, who might have to take the night shift?" To turn things around, Delnor leaders asked employees to set standards for everyday behaviors such as answering the phone and greeting people in the hallway. "When you take the time to put the right behaviors down on paper and get everyone in the organization to commit to it in writing, you can enforce it throughout the organization," Deering explains.

- *Hold people accountable.* "I happened to be the first manager who fired someone for not following behavior standards," Deering says. "That changed the organization overnight. The word was out that if you don't follow the rules you might lose your job!" Another benefit of accountability is seeing clear results. "There is nothing more satisfying that seeing those results," Deering says. "And it will radically change the way I'm going to spend my time in the next quarter when I see results that aren't moving."
- *Don't hide behind excuses.* Previously, Delnor employees assumed nurse turnover was sustained by the high number of affluent nurses who could afford to leave their jobs and competition from doctors willing to pay top dollar for staff nurses. Now that turnover rates have dropped, they are forced to admit those were excuses. "Are we still in an affluent community?" Deering asks. "Of course we are. Has the competition changed? No! *We* changed. The truth is every system is perfectly designed to produce the results it is producing. I didn't like that because it meant I had to change my behavior. But when we changed as leaders, good things started happening."

vision and mission. However, taken to extremes, members' like-mindedness can cause organizations to become stagnant and unimaginative. In a rapidly changing industry such as health care, stability is a risky illusion that numbs the system to the need for continued evolution. From the perspective of complexity theory, the greatest risk to a complex system is a continued state of equilibrium (Pascale, 1999). Threats to the system—if not too overwhelming or explosive—stimulate change and improvement. A good example is Baptist Health Care in Pensacola, Florida. In the mid-1990s, in an attempt to save the hospital, organizational members launched a full-scale cultural overhaul. "We were in trouble," recalls Pam Bilbrey, now senior vice president of corporate development. With a "nothing to lose" philosophy, they began bold and innovative changes that catapulted the once-hobbling medical center to the top of the charts in patient satisfaction surveys (du Pré, in press).

- *Involve everyone.* Another step was to get everyone involved. Deering and her colleagues instituted a system of shared governance, allowing the people who carry out decisions to make the decisions. "We started putting decision making at the lowest level possible," Deering explains. "They know because they're doing the work. Decisions can't rest in the hands of a few leaders. It's got to be permeated in the organization."
- *Praise lavishly.* "We learned that criticism doesn't work," Deering says. "I think because we're scientists, by nature we're highly trained to see what's wrong. That's a good skill, but it doesn't work very well in raising the human spirit. Praise and recognition work. Take it down to a simple thing: 'You look good in lavender.' Oh yeah? I'm going to start wearing a lot more lavender."
- *Strive for excellence, and profits will follow.* Deering recalls when "the number one topic on the table was money." Organizational leaders met to discuss how they could increase the bottom line. "Now you know what the topic is? It's quality, patient satisfaction, or employee morale. When you focus on service, people, and quality, you're going to get volume and financials. Put your attention where it ought to be, and the rest will take care of itself."

Looking back over the Delnor transformation, Deering reflects on the personal and organizational changes that have occurred over the last 6 years. Although leadership has been important, she does not take all the credit. "I'm not an extraordinary leader," she insists. "I'm just an ordinary person surrounded by an organization full of great people. But I am trainable!"

Organizational theorists agree that diversity is valuable because it enhances the potential for creative problem solving. An extensive literature review (Milliken & Martins, 1996) supports that innovative thinking is enhanced when diverse people bring different viewpoints to bear on a problem.

Another advantage is that diverse employees are well suited to serve diverse consumers, possibly expanding the organization's clientele (Gardenswartz & Rowe, 1998). Employers who consider diverse applicants also have a wider selection, and thus a better chance of finding outstanding employees (Gardenswartz & Rowe, 1998). Overall, diversity is a valuable means of growth and expansion—both for the organization and for individuals within in it.

Diversity does present challenges. A diverse workforce can seem fragmented, with different members working toward different goals. And research shows that employees are often less satisfied and less likely to remain in highly

Box 9.2 THEORETICAL FOUNDATIONS
Model of Multiculturalism

Having established that health care is becoming more diverse and that there are advantages and challenges to diversity, the question is how to maximize the rewards and minimize the potential drawbacks. Evidence suggests that most health organizations have a ways to go before they truly honor diversity in its fullest sense.

The process of integrating diverse viewpoints in an organization is typically gradual. Taylor Cox, Jr. (1991) suggests that organizations develop along a continuum from **monolithic organizations** that recognize only one culture, with few minority members, to **plural organizations** with more minority members but continued pressure to conform, to **multicultural organizations** that integrate many diverse cultures and ideas.

Although organizations may hire people who are diverse, they often squelch diversity as soon as new employees walk in the door. Taylor (2001) calls these "diversity-toxic cultures." As he puts it:

> *Due to the pressure to conform, members who have high cultural distance from prevailing norms of the work culture tend to either leave the organization or modify their thinking—and their behavior—to achieve acceptance. The result is that apparent differences of cultural groups, such as an increasing presence of women, may represent only small differences in worldviews. (pp. 12–13)*

Health care, overall, is in a state of pluralism. Diversity is increasing, but full-scale acceptance is yet to come. Linda Larkey (1996) points out that discrimination operates beneath the surface in plural organizations. These "pseudoprogressive" organizations purport to honor diversity, and members may even believe they are. But subtle prejudices keep some people from excelling or advancing.

diverse workplaces (Milliken & Martins, 1996). One reason is that members of minority cultures often feel undervalued, as if their contributions and ideas are not considered important. A study of Hispanic employees found that perceived discrimination was their greatest work stressor and was associated with low job satisfaction and low commitment to the organization (Sanchez & Brock, 1996). Sanchez and Brock urge employers to be sensitive to signs of discrimination so they can avoid losing valuable employees and damaging workplace morale.

Research shows that people are likely to be stereotyped on the basis of their most visible differences—skin color, age, and sex (Milliken & Martins, 1996). Before they even open their mouths to share ideas, members of minority cultures may find that others have made judgments about their intelligence

A **glass ceiling** exists when women and minorities are excluded from management positions or are denied equal compensation for similar work. A study by the American College of Health Care Executives (2002) shows that, among health care managers, African Americans earn about 13% less than White managers who have the same education and experience. Women do not fare any better. Female health care executives earn about 19% less than their male counterparts—a gap that has grown rather than diminished in recent years (Tieman, 2002).

What Do You Think?

1. Have you ever been judged by your appearance before you had a chance to prove yourself?
2. In what ways do the organizations to which you belong honor diversity? In what ways do they squelch diversity?
3. Are you surprised by the salary disparities described here? Why or why not?
4. What are the implications for health communication if health care organizations do not value diversity?

Suggested Sources

Cox, T. H., Jr. (1991). The multicultural organization. *Academy of Management Executive, 5,* 34–47.

Cox, T. H., Jr. (2001). *Creating the multicultural organization: A strategy for capturing the power of diversity*. San Francisco: Jossey-Bass.

Cox, T. H., Jr., & Beale, R. L. (1997). *Developing competency to manage diversity: Readings, cases, and activities.* San Francisco: Berrett-Koehler.

and importance. Ironically, visible differences usually say far less about a person than "invisible" variables such as education level, length of employment, personality, and so on (Milliken & Martins, 1996). Sometimes organizations present the appearance of diversity on the surface, but actual differences are discouraged or intolerated. (See Box 9.2 for more on this.)

Implications

Treating organizations as cultures means considering the viewpoints of organizational members, not simply assuming they will perform tasks as if they are cogs in a machine. Cultural assumptions are embodied in written guidelines and in unspoken rules of interaction, all of which imply certain values and assumptions. Personal preferences also play a role, especially as people with diverse ideas come together to solve problems and establish goals.

Members of organizations (and the people they serve) are diverse in terms of race, gender, national origin, ethnicity, ability, and other factors. Diverse coworkers are likely to come up with new ideas, but they may initially feel uncomfortable together and must overcome their prejudices if everyone is to participate fully and feel valued within the organization.

The first step in encouraging diversity is to allow diverse people into the organization. The next section describes how women and minorities have slowly gained acceptance in medicine.

■ HISTORICAL PATTERNS OF ACCEPTANCE

This section examines historical patterns that have regulated the number of women and minorities in medicine. As you will see, the numbers are improving, but women and minorities still strive for equal treatment.

Female Physicians

In the book, *Woman as Healer*, Jeanne Achterberg (1991) describes women's place in medicine and society from ancient times to the modern day. Achterberg describes ancient cultures that believed women were skilled and intuitive healers, primarily because of their "cosmic link" to the earth and the birth of new life. The healing image of an Earth Mother was largely abandoned during the Middle Ages, however. Christianity depicted women as the embodiment of original sin and decreed that church positions be restricted to men. Women who continued to practice healing arts were often regarded as heretics and witches. Women were tortured and burned by the thousands when plagues ravaged Europe and women were accused of using witchcraft to spread the disease (Achterberg, 1991, p. 85). Women were further excluded from medicine during the 16th century with the advent of scientific medicine. Largely prohibited from academic pursuits, women were not seen as qualified caregivers because they lacked scientific knowledge (p. 99). Not until the 1900s were women allowed to adopt professional caregiver roles. Even then, they were mostly restricted to holistic medicine, alternative therapies, and subordinate roles (as nurses but not as doctors).

The first woman known to receive a medical degree was Elizabeth Blackwell, who graduated in 1849 from the Geneva Medical School of Western New York (Duffy, 1979). Ironically, she had to leave America to find a hospital willing to host her clinical training, and when she returned, was forced to open her own clinic because no hospital would allow her privileges.

By the middle of the 19th century, a few medical schools had begun accepting women applicants, and by 1859 about 300 women physicians had begun medical practices in America (Bonner, 1992). All were denied privileges in established hospitals and were forced to open their own clinics and hospitals, specializing mostly in homeopathic and herbal medicine.

By necessity, women physicians were allowed to practice during times of war. About 55 female doctors served in the U.S. Army during World War I (Bonner, 1992). However, women doctors lost professional ground during the Great Depression of the 1930s, when they were strongly discouraged from filling jobs men desperately wanted.

In 1970 the Women's Equity League filed a class action suit against all U.S. medical schools, accusing them of unfair discrimination. At the time, only about 9.2% of medical students in the United States were women (Waalen, 1997). Continued efforts by women's groups and civil rights leaders led to affirmative actions laws, requiring schools and businesses to accept qualified minority applicants. By 2002, 44.1% of medical students in the United States were women ("Educational Programs," 2002).

Building Equity

In the last 30 years women have gained significant entrance into medical communities. However, female doctors still make less money and are promoted less often than their male counterparts (Tesch, Wood, Helwig, & Butler, 1995). According to the AMA website, female physicians make about 60% what male doctors make (AMA, 2003b). This is partly because women typically specialize in lower paying specialties such as pediatrics and are vastly underrepresented in more specialized fields such as neurosurgery, oncology, and cardiology (AMA, 2001a). Lauren Picker (1995) reports that female physicians are 3 times as likely as male doctors to be pediatricians and only half as likely to be surgeons.

The numbers are not much more equitable in U.S. medical schools. Nationwide, male medical faculty are more likely to advance in the ranks. Although women make up 50.1% of entry-level professor positions, only 10.7% of full professors are female (AMA, 2000). In a study of one large university medical college, female medical professors were found to earn about 11% less than men in comparable positions, even adjusting for rank, specialty, and years in field (Wright et al., 2003). Almost one third of the female medical faculty reported being discriminated against, compared to 5% of men (Wright et al., 2003). Similar evidence suggests these numbers are not atypical. In the right atmosphere, however, the numbers can change. The Johns Hopkins University School of Medicine was able to increase the number of female associate professors from 4 to 26 within 5 years (Fried et al., 1996). The school increased women's participation in leadership, implemented equitable pay scales, increased awareness of gender-related stereotypes, and rescheduled meetings to conflict less with family life. The results benefited both male and female faculty. More convenient meeting times boosted attendance across the board. Women *and* men perceived their treatment to be more equitable than before, were satisfied with their opportunities for advancement, and rated themselves significantly more optimistic about their careers.

Communication Styles

Overall, research does not show dramatic differences between the way male and female caregivers communicate with patients. There are often slight differences, however. Women tend to display more interest in patients' life contexts and feelings, possibly because they are often trained to be primary caregivers (pediatricians, obstetricians/gynecologists, and so on) (Roter et al., 1997, Novack et al., 1997). Female physicians are more likely than men to suggest preventive health screenings (Novack et al., 1997), and female medical students are more likely than their male classmates to be egalitarian (believe all people are equal) and to support health services for people in poverty (Crandall et al., 1993).

Cultural expectations may affect how patients react to male and female caregivers. Verbal aggressiveness is often considered appropriate for men, but not for women. Studies show that female physicians who behave contrary to cultural expectations (as in being verbally aggressive) are often viewed negatively by patients, who consequently are less likely to follow the doctor's advice (Burgoon & Burgoon, 1990; Conlee, Amabisca & Vagim, 1995). The same is presumably true of male doctors who defy expectations.

Gender is only part of the story, though. Medical socialization, professional constraints, and personal style may mitigate differences between male and female speech. Some patients are surprised to find that there is little difference between the communication styles of some men and women doctors (Conlee et al., 1995).

Minorities in Medicine

The racial and ethnic diversity of America is underrepresented in the health professions. Although African Americans, Hispanics, and Native Americans together make up 25.7% of the U.S. population, only 6.6% of the country's physicians and 12% of the nurses are from these groups (American Medical Association, 2001b; "HHS Awards," 2003; U.S. Bureau of the Census, 2000). In some areas, the disparity is even more striking. In the Boston area, only 3.2% of physicians are African American or Hispanic American although those groups comprise 13% of the state's population (Powell, 2003). And the numbers are not improving. Only 37 of 600 physicians who graduated from Massachusetts medical schools in 2000 were Black or Hispanic (Peter, 2003). The numbers correspond to disturbing health statistics. In Boston, cancer death rates are 45% higher among African Americans than European Americans (Peter, 2003). This is not to say that White doctors intentionally let people of color die. A more reasonable explanation is that the social conditions and discrimination that make minorities at risk for health concerns also create disadvantages in medical settings and limit their opportunities to become medical professionals.

History A history of racial discrimination has affected patients as well as caregivers. African Americans were barred from most hospitals in the United

States well into the 1960s (Cassedy, 1991). They could neither be treated nor practice medicine alongside White citizens. Members of other minorities were also discouraged from becoming doctors and often had little in common with the physicians they were allowed to consult.

Of necessity, African Americans formed their own medical societies and hospitals. By 1910 the United States was home to nearly 100 hospitals and 7 medical schools catering to African-American citizens (Duffy, 1979). Denied membership in the AMA and other medical societies, African-American doctors formed their own. In 1895 they founded the National Medical Association. (The organization remains active with a current membership of 25,000).

African-American hospitals and universities suffered from meager funding and harsh criticism. Not until 1964 did the U.S. government ban segregation in federally funded hospitals and pass legislation in the name of affirmative action. No longer would federal money be used to build "separate but equal" facilities (Duffy, 1979).

Current Representation Slowly, the number of minority physicians grew. There were modest gains in the number of African-American, Native-American, Alaskan-American, Puerto Rican, and Hispanic students admitted to medical school in the 1990s (Barzansky, Jonas, & Etzel, 1995). But their numbers have never been comparable to the overall population. By 2000, the percentage of Native-American, Hispanic, and African-American medical students (14.6%) was slightly more than half that of the population overall (AMA, 2002). And members of those ethnic groups comprise 3.4% of full professors in U.S. medical schools (86.9% are White) (AMA, 2002; "Distribution," 2000). Efforts to increase minority enrollment in medical schools have been the subject of recent debates (see Box 9.3).

After a long wait, African Americans were able to take key posts in medical leadership in the 1990s. In 1992, Jocelyn Elders became the first African-American U.S. Surgeon General, and her successor, David A. Satcher, became the second. In 1998, the American Medical Association inaugurated its first woman president, Nancy W. Dickey. However, minority influence has continued to be conspicuously low in the AMA, which launched efforts in the 1990s to recruit minority doctors, acknowledging that less than a third of them were AMA members (Foubister, 1997).

Communication Effects The odds are that minority patients in the United States will be cared for by doctors whose race and cultures are different from their own. This is not necessarily a problem, but it can be. Levy (1985) observes that physicians may be more critical and less comfortable with patients of another race, or they may be overly paternal or condescending. Caregivers may also under- or overestimate cultural differences. As a result, they may consider behavior abnormal because it does not conform to their expectations or may

Box 9.3 ETHICAL CONSIDERATIONS
Is Affirmative Action Justified or Not?

Enrollment in U.S. medical schools has remained relatively constant in the last decade, but the number of applications has risen, heating up competition between would-be doctors. A particular point of contention is affirmative action.

Based on civil rights legislation passed in the 1960s, **affirmative action** requires publicly funded universities to give preference to minority applicants who meet admission requirements. Contrary to what many believe, affirmative action does not require acceptance of unqualified persons, nor does it set quotas requiring a certain number or percentage of minority members. Institutions are under no obligation to accept individuals who do not meet qualifications. However, if minority applicants meet the established criteria for admittance, they may be chosen even if nonminority applicants also meet or exceed the criteria. Affirmative action was designed to offset historic patterns of discrimination that limited opportunities for women and minorities and resulted in them being significantly underrepresented in professional positions.

Controversy over affirmative action has escalated in recent years when nonminority applicants who met (or exceeded) the minimum requirements for medical school admission were passed over in favor of minority candidates. In 2003, after three White students sued because they were not accepted into the University of Michigan, the U.S. Supreme Court ruled that the university can give minority applicants special consideration, but it cannot continue its policy of granting minority candidates a portion of the points needed for a favorable admission review (Newbart & Grossman, 2003).

Opponents of affirmative action argue that prospective doctors should be chosen only on the basis of their qualifications. In 1996 the California Board of Regents banned state schools from considering the race and ethnicity of university applicants. Courts in Texas also banned consideration of race and ethnicity after White students sued because they were denied admission to the University of Texas law school. In 1999 Florida governor Jeb Bush removed race from consideration in state university admission programs, effectively ending affirmative action in the state's higher education system.

People who favor affirmative action argue that the public is poorly served by physicians who do not reflect the diversity of the overall

perceive unhealthy irregularities as mere cultural differences (Daly, Jennings, Beckett, & Leashore, 1995). Caregivers may not be aware that they are acting differently or offensively. However, members of minority cultures may be especially sensitive to these overtures and may fear discrimination and humiliation more than most patients (Levy, 1985).

population. L. C. Bollinger (2003) argues that exposure to diverse classmates helps doctors become more open-minded and aware of cultural differences. A survey of medical students at Harvard and the University of California showed overwhelming agreement that sharing classes with diverse students would help them become better doctors (Whitla et al., 2003). A national board of advisors convened to study the issue recommended the continuation of affirmative action because the percentage of minority doctors in the United States is still low and because studies show that minority caregivers are especially willing and able to serve minority patients—the people who are currently least served by medicine and most at risk for health problems (Mitka, 1996a).

What Do You Think?

1. Do you feel medical schools should consider sex, race, and ethnicity when reviewing applicants? Why or why not?
2. How do you respond to the argument that affirmative action sometimes allows people to be accepted into medical school although others' credentials are higher?
3. How do you respond to the argument that affirmative action is needed to help the medical profession more closely reflect the concerns and backgrounds of patients?

Suggested Sources

Bollinger, L. C. (2003). The need for diversity in higher education. *Academic Medicine, 78*(5), 431–436.

Evelyn, J. (1998, April 16). In defense of diversity: Videoconference examines the anti-affirmative action movement. *Black Issues in Higher Education, 15,* 18.

Newbart, D., & Grossman, K. N. (2003, June 24). Court rules in the affirmative. *Chicago Sun-Times,* p. 6.

Whitla, D. K., Orfield, G., Silen, W., Teperow, C., Howard, C., & Reede, J. (2003). Educational benefits of diversity in medical school: A survey of students. *Academic Medicine, 78*(5), 460–466.

Implications

Health care is influenced by the social climate surrounding it. Civil rights advancements since the 1960s have brought unprecedented diversity to medicine. Women doctors are now present in numbers nearly equal to their portion of the population, but the proportion of minority doctors is still only half that of the population overall, and women and minorities still experience the lingering effects of discrimination. The challenges of communicating across racial and cultural lines are heightened by the importance of communicating effectively in medical situations and the relatively small number of minority physicians.

DIVERSE TYPES OF HEALTH CARE

Members of health organizations are not only diverse in terms of sex and race. They differ by profession as well. Many people think of medicine in terms of doctors. But doctors cannot meet every health care need. In fact, the expectation that they *should* do it all places an enormous burden on their shoulders. One solution is to expand people's notion of caregiving to include more than doctors. This section offers a brief overview of nursing and midlevel care. (Medicine is also becoming more diverse as alternative and complementary therapies gain popularity. A section on alternative and complementary medicine follows this one.)

Nurses

Nursing is unique in that it provides ongoing support for patients through periods of recovery and adjustment. Nurses typically spend more time with patients than doctors do and devote themselves more to patients' personal concerns. Nurses consider listening to be their most important communication skill (Cericola, 1999).

Registered nurses are the largest segment of health professionals, and 3 of 5 registered nurses work in hospitals (U.S. Bureau of Labor Statistics, 2003a).

Traditionally, nurses have been rewarded with personal satisfaction, but not much else. For much of the nation's history, nurses had little power or status in the health industry. They were often treated more as maids than as professional caregivers. And, although nurses worked long and unusual hours, their salaries were notoriously low.

Nursing Shortage A nationwide nursing shortage has been the most obvious impetus for recent changes. By 1989 there were at least 200,000 unfilled nursing jobs in the United States; three fourths of the nation's hospitals were short-staffed (Kleinman, 1989). In an effort to attract nurses, salaries were raised substantially, working hours and conditions were improved, and nurses were given new opportunities for advancement.

The nursing shortage of the 1980s and 1990s reflected the culmination of many factors. One was the women's movement, which had begun to expand women's career opportunities. Women began to pursue a variety of professions, including medicine. Between 1974 and 1986, the number of first-year college students aspiring to become nurses dropped by 75% (Green, 1988). At the same time nursing school enrollment plummeted, a growing elderly population increased demands on the health care system. Just when more nurses were needed, fewer people were interested. Nurses on the job were more overworked than ever, causing many of those already in the field to leave it.

The nursing shortage abated somewhat in the 1990s. Relief was short-lived, however. By 2000, experts estimated that health care organizations in the United States were understaffed by about 110,000 nurses (U.S. Department of Health and Human Services, 2002). That figure is expected to double by 2010.

There are a number of reasons for the current shortage. A comprehensive study by the U.S. Department of Health and Human Services and three other governmental agencies (U.S. Department of Health and Human Services, 2002) outlines the scope and causes of the current nursing shortage.

One reason is reduced funding of colleges and universities. At a rally in Olympia, Washington, nursing school officials protested because they must turn away hundreds of would-be nursing students per year because they cannot afford the faculty and facilities to train them ("Nurses Lobby," 2003). The situation is similar around the country. There were 26% fewer nursing graduates in 2000 than in 1995, partly because some nursing programs shut down and others were forced by financial pressures to limit enrollment (U.S Department of Health and Human Services, 2002).

Another factor is the increased need for nurses and other medical personnel. Between 1990 and 2000, the U.S. population increased by 14%, but the number of nurses increased by only 4.1% ("Final Report," 2002).

At the same time, the average age of U.S. residents is rapidly increasing, with corresponding demands on health care resources. Between 2000 and 2020, the need for health care services is expected to increase by about 40%. However, the number of available nurses is only expected to increase 6% a year until 2011, at which point the number of nurses is expected to decline, mostly because many nurses will themselves enter their retirement years (U.S. Department of Health and Human Services, 2002).

Fourth, many nurses have left the profession. About 490,000 registered nurses in the United States are not employeed as nurses (U.S. Department of Health and Human Services, 2002). Experts speculate that nurses have become discouraged by the demands of short-staffed medical units. Not only are nurses in short supply, but to cut costs, many hospitals have reduced the number of support staff. Nurses are often called on to fill the gaps (Apker, 2001). Stress is also elevated by the demands of caring for sicker patients. Despite growing pressures, nursing salaries plateaued in the 1990s, so nurses today earn little more than they did 10 years ago (U.S. Department of Health and Human Services, 2002).

Finally, men have not entered nursing at the rate once expected. Although men were attracted to nursing in the 1980s and 1990s, the numbers never got very high. Only about 5.9% of nurses in the United States are men ("Final Report," 2002).

The nursing shortage not only affects nurses and health care professionals. It also hurts patients. An extensive study of 799 hospitals by the U.S. Department of Health and Human Services revealed that patients in understaffed units are significantly more likely than others to have urinary tract infections, pneumonia, shock, and upper gastrointestinal bleeding, conditions that can often be averted or minimized with careful attention ("HHS Study Finds," 2001). Patients in understaffed units were also more likely to have extended hospital stays and less likely to be successfully resuscitated after cardiac arrest. The researchers concluded that understaffing costs health care organizations and patients.

In an effort to offset the nursing shortage, the federal government announced in 2003 that it would make available $3.5 million to help people from underprivileged backgrounds attend nursing school ("HHS Awards," 2003). Considering the outlook, this may help some, but not enough.

Nurse Practitioners and Physician Assistants

Many patients who visit their doctors for minor concerns or routine check-ups are now likely to be seen by midlevel providers instead. Two types of midlevel providers are nurse practitioners (NPs) and physician assistants (PAs), both of whom are specially trained and state licensed. (Another acronym associated with NPs is ACNP, which stands for acute care nurse practitioners.)

In the hierarchy of most medical enterprises, NPs and PAs are of equal status, about midway between that of doctors and nurses. The main difference is that PAs are trained in medical schools and NPs in nursing schools.

Restrictions limit what midlevel providers can prescribe and diagnose and require them to practice under the supervision of physicians. For minor health concerns, however, NPs and PAs function very much like doctors and are often employed in doctors' offices. They perform routines exams, do minor biopsies, suture cuts, and handle other minor concerns (Freeborn & Hooker, 1995). The use of midlevel providers is cost effective and helps offset the current shortage of general practitioners, especially in rural areas where there is a shortage of primary care physicians (Bergeron, Neuman, & Kinsey, 1999)

Research indicates patients are typically satisfied with midlevel practitioners, and many prefer their communication style to doctors'. NPs are usually able to spend more time with patients than doctors can (Courtney & Rice, 1997), and they tend to focus on social and personal concerns in addition to biomedical matters (Drass, 1988).

Implications

This review does not begin to cover the gamut of professional caregivers. The U.S. Bureau of Labor Statistics lists 58 categories of health care practitioners from audiologists to technicians, surgeons, aides, and therapists. Even a brief review illustrates the importance of teamwork between diverse professionals. Nurses often spend long amounts of time with patients and are concerned with their emotional and physical health. Midlevel providers such as nurse practitioners and physician assistants treat routine and minor health concerns much like a doctor would. The role of all these caregivers has changed in recent years, mostly because managed care organizations are emphasizing primary care. Although they still have a long way to go, nurses have been granted higher status and increased authority, and midlevel providers are accepting part of the responsibility for treating minor health concerns. The next section looks at another aspect of professional diversity, represented by the growing number of alternative and complementary care providers in the United States.

ALTERNATIVE AND COMPLEMENTARY CARE

Medical options such as acupuncture, meditation, and chiropractic—once considered quackery by conventional practitioners—are gaining some acceptance as complementary forms of care. As you will see, there are a number of reasons for this newfound acceptance. One result is that the culture of medical professionalism is quickly becoming more diverse. The following section describes alternative and complementary forms of medicine, factors fueling recent interest in them, and their advantages and drawbacks.

Definitions

The term **alternative medicine** has traditionally been applied to therapies that have not been scientifically researched and consequently approved by professional associations such as the AMA. Such therapies include everything from meditation, prayer, and herbal teas, to shark-cartilage serums. Popular types of alternative care include homeopathic and naturopathic medicine, chiropractic, and acupuncture. A brief glossary of terms that explains the basis of these and other types of care can be found in Box 9.4.

Some therapies long regarded as *alternatives* to conventional care are being accepted as *complements* to it. **Complementary medicine** is used, not instead of conventional medicine, but in addition to it. Doctors approve of complementary therapies and may even prescribe or provide them along with other forms of care. For instance, meditation is not a conventional means of treating cancer, but few (if any) oncologists would deny that it is useful if it promotes emotional well-being. In a similar way, therapies such as prayer, massage, and yoga are typically not considered unorthodox unless they are practiced to the exclusion of other therapies.

People interested in complementary medicine are typically dissatisfied with the words available to describe it. The term *complementary* seems to imply that science-based, institutional medicine is still the benchmark and other therapies are peripheral to it. In parts of the world such as Africa, Asia, and Latin America, people use the term *traditional medicine* (TM) instead of complementary or alternative medicine. However, *traditional* medicine seems to exclude recent innovations. Some prefer the term *holistic,* although

Box 9.4 Alternative and Complementary Medicine at a Glance

Acupuncture is believed to stimulate and balance the body's energy flow (chi) through the use of tiny needles inserted in the skin.

Aruveyda is based on ancient Indian practices including yoga, diet, and meditation.

Biofeedback involves learning to recognize the body's physiological states (like tension) and control them.

Chiropractic medicine focuses on the physical alignment of the spine, muscles, and nerves.

Herbal therapies use plant extracts such as chamomile, licorice, and St. John's Wort to treat ailments ranging from skin conditions to asthma and depression.

Holistic care emphasizes overall well-being (physical and emotional), with an emphasis on maintaining health, not just curing ailments.

Homeopathic medicine uses very small doses to escalate symptoms in an effort to stimulate the body's immune system. (By contrast, most mainstream medical care is allopathic, relying on remedies that counteract symptoms.) *Homeo* is derived from the Greek word meaning "same," and *allo* from the Greek word for "other."

Integrative medicine combines biomedical and naturopathic therapies.

Naturopathic medicine focuses on diet and the use of herbal therapies to help people maintain good health.

Oriental medicine includes therapies such as herbal remedies, acupuncture, and massage. It is based on establishing a healthy flow of energy through the body and achieving harmony between mind, body, spirit, and surroundings.

Osteopathic medicine is taught in traditional medical schools. This branch of medicine focuses on the muscular and skeletal system, treating the body as an integrated unit.

Reiki (pronounced RAY-kee), is based on the Japanese tradition of channeling energy through the healer's hands to increase the patient's spiritual strength, leading to better physical health.

others argue that not all therapies in this category are holistic. In fact, some are highly focused. At a preconference meeting on alternative and complementary medicine at the National Communication Association, I was part of an extended conversation on this issue. In the end, I think none of the delegates were entirely satisfied with the vocabulary available so far. For lack of a better term, I use the term *complementary* and the acronym *CAM* (complementary and alternative medicine) here.

Popularity

There are several reasons for the recent popularity of complementary medicine. First, Americans are receptive to the idea. About 40% report that they use CAM therapies such as acupuncture, massage, high-dose vitamins, and hypnosis (Astin, 1998). Complementary care is particularly popular among well-educated people with chronic health concerns like back pain (Astin, 1998). Acceptance is even greater in some areas of the world. WHO (2003b) reports that

- Herbs represent 30–50% of medicines consumed in China.
- In San Francisco, London, and South Africa 75% of people with AIDS use complementary medicine.
- Worldwide, herbal medicines are a $60 billion a year market that continues to grow.

Second, well-trained caregivers are becoming more plentiful. In Germany, the number of doctors trained to use natural remedies doubled from 5,400 to 10,800 between 1995 and 2000. In the United States, analysts expect the number of chiropractors to double between 1994 and 2010 and the number of oriental medicine and naturopathic practitioners to triple (Cooper & Stoflet, 1996). More than 50 colleges in the United States are devoted to chiropractic, oriental medicine, and/or naturopathic medicine (Cooper & Stoflet, 1996). Additionally, course work in complementary therapies is becoming available in some medical schools (Kronenberg, Mallory, & Downey, 1994). Chiropractors are now state licensed, and some states have begun licensing acupuncturists and others as well.

Third, research dollars are more available. In 1997, the U.S. Congress voted to fund an Office of Alternative Medicine as part of the National Institutes of Health (NIH). Although controversial, the new NIH office offers unprecedented funding for researchers interested in testing the efficacy of diverse therapies. It has already provided funding for research on the effects of Chinese herb therapies, biofeedback and music in the treatment of people with head injuries, and substances like shark cartilage that some believe diminish cancerous tumors.

Finally, many insurance companies and physicians are now giving the go-ahead to unconventional treatments. At least 60% of physicians surveyed have recommended complimentary therapies to their patients (Astin, 1998), and about 40% of HMOs now cover the cost of acupuncture and chiropractic ("Cancer Patients," 1997). Medicare and workers' compensation plans in all 50 states now reimburse chiropractic care (Cooper & Stoflet, 1996).

Advantages

There are several benefits of the growing popularity of complementary care. For one, complementary methods are typically low cost and low technology. If their usefulness can be substantiated, they stand to reduce health care costs. This is good news for insurance companies. It is also good for managed care organizations if people simultaneously maintain their involvement in conventional care (which they seem inclined to do). WHO is supporting research to see if low-cost herbal remedies can effectively treat malaria, AIDS, diabetes, and other conditions in impoverished areas of the world (WHO, 2003b).

Second, complementary methods are usually based on simple principles that may be more understandable and less frightening to patients than conventional medicine (Brown, Cassileth, Lewis, & Renner, 1994). Patients often feel they better understand and can even manage their own complementary care. Astin (1998) found that people who use CAM therapies choose them because they reflect their personal philosophy about health. For the most part, these people are not dissatisfied with conventional medicine, which suggests they will continue to seek both conventional and complementary care.

Third, complementary methods are usually more directed to health maintenance than is conventional medicine, which has traditionally focused on curing and treating. The new imperative to conserve health care resources and money makes prevention appealing.

Fourth, alternative practitioners often spend more time with their patients and develop closer relationships with them than do conventional practitioners. This may suit people who feel that conventional medical settings are too impersonal.

Finally, people may turn to alternative therapies if conventional methods offer little or no help. Symptoms of anxiety, for instance, which may not be cured by mainstream medicine, may be managed by relaxation and biofeedback. Concerning other supposedly incurable conditions, there is mixed evidence. Some (e.g., Dinur, 1997) report instances in which alternative medicine seems to cure diseases conventional medicine cannot. However, success is hard to document and tragic stories circulate as well.

Drawbacks

Many complementary therapies are nonthreatening. Attempts to improve energy, work, and relaxation, through minute traces of natural substances (as in homeopathy) are unlikely to hurt anyone. However, some therapies involve the use of herbs and other naturalistic products. Because herbs are considered dietary supplements rather than drugs, they are not regulated by the Food and Drug Administration (Capriottti, 1999). Consequently, many herbal remedies are not thoroughly researched or labeled before they go on the market. Research data is also limited because funding agencies have historically been reluctant to sponsor scientific investigation of unorthodox therapies. The three main dangers are that people will be hurt by natural remedies, that people will be fooled into paying for remedies that are not effective, and that the market for herbal remedies will endanger the survival of rare plants. These risks are described here.

First, significant health risks are associated with some natural therapies. Many medicines (conventional or not) are toxic. Prescribed to the wrong person or in the wrong amount, they can be deadly. Natural remedies have been known to cause lead poisoning, hepatitis, and renal failure (Brown et al., 1994). The herb germander, often included in herbal teas and tablets, has been linked to acute nonviral hepatitis. The herb ephedra, sold as a natural enhancement for bodybuilding, affects the heart and blood vessels and can cause dangerously high blood pressure. It has been linked to at least 17 deaths (Capriotti, 1999; WHO, 2003b).

Patients may also be swindled by alternative care therapies promoted with unverified claims. Cancer patients, particularly, are vulnerable to people who claim to provide the latest life-saving serum. Shark cartilage sells for as much as $115 per bottle although claims that it stops cancer have yet to be fully tested (Brown et al., 1994). Whether shark cartilage will be accepted as a medical breakthrough or labeled a quack cure is still unknown.

Finally, WHO warns that endangered plant species may be wiped out in the zeal to provide health benefits (and reap the financial awards) associated with high-demand herbal remedies (WHO, 2003b). Already, rain forests in Malaysia, Africa, and the Amazon have been endangered by harvesting efforts. Environmentalists urge world citizens to consider regulations, herbal farming, and ocean-based cultivation to protect the planet's wildlife.

Implications

Alternative and complementary care specialists focus primarily on lifestyle changes and natural remedies. These diverse therapies are gaining popularity based on public interest, an increase in trained care providers, new research, and acceptance by health plans and conventional practitioners.

Complementary care is appealing because it is relatively inexpensive, easy to understand, prevention oriented, and personal. Some people seek alternative and complementary care when they are not satisfied with the results or nature of conventional medicine. In the majority of cases, however, people who seek complementary care continue to see conventional practitioners as well.

Alternative care can be disadvantageous because the effects of some alternative therapies are not well understood, because people may be tricked into buying useless products, and because large-scale harvests of natural remedies threaten the environment. Although individuals may assume that natural products are not harmful, they can be deadly. All in all, it is a good idea to become knowledgeable about complementary care before pursuing it.

The next section examines the conflict that can sometimes result when people have diverse goals and diverse ways of thinking and behaving.

MANAGING CONFLICT

As you have seen, diversity comes in many forms. People are diverse in terms of gender, race, culture, and profession. Even people who grow up in the same community may have different views and goals. Diversity is a driving force behind innovation and growth. It is also a source of conflict. **Conflict** results when people perceive that some goals are incompatible with others.

Conflict is not necessarily negative, nor is it avoidable. To some extent, conflict is a natural product of diversity. One of the reasons diversity gives rise to new ideas is that people's ideas are different. Conflict is also inevitable in times of change, when new ideas conflict with established ways of doing things. Even relatively homogeneous organizations experience conflict.

Conflict is a natural component of health care, with its mix of professions and people. However, it is especially important to manage health-related conflict well because the goals of health care are so important and because the emotional intensity of medical settings can cause conflict to escalate out of control. This section looks at three different types of conflict common to health organizations: conflict of interest, violent conflict, and role conflict.

Definitions

Conflict of interest is internal and occurs when a person wishes to meet multiple objectives but meeting one objective means sacrificing another. In this section, you will see how doctors are being called on to provide quality care but, at the same time, cut costs. Some people fear that meeting one objective will mean sacrificing the other.

Conflict can also be interpersonal, as when some people's goals and objectives are different than other people's. As Linda Putnam and Marshall Scott Poole (1987) define it, **interpersonal conflict** occurs when people who depend on each other have conflicting goals, aims, and values that seem to stand in the way of accomplishing their objectives. This conflict can turn violent. In this section, you will see why health organizations are sometimes dangerous places to be, partly because anxious people perceive that caregivers are not doing everything they should, and partly because violent conflicts often land people in the hospital.

At another level, people may experience role conflict. A **role** is the way a person is expected to behave when performing certain functions within the culture. People often play multiple roles at the same time (i.e., friend, doctor, boss, subordinate). **Role conflict** occurs when a person is playing more than one role but the expectations for those roles conflict. For example, nursing home residents often regard their caregivers as surrogate family members (Hullett, McMillan, & Rogan, 2000). However, although caregivers typically consider emotional support to be the one of the most important parts of their job, emotional support is not often part of their official duties, and some facilities discourage caregivers from becoming too friendly with residents. Thus there is a conflict between what caregivers and residents feel is important and what the caregivers are rewarded for doing as employees (Hullett et al., 2000). In this section you will see how nurses struggle to be patient advocates at the same time they serve as subordinates to doctors and supervisors. The following discussion examines how each of these forms of conflict is actualized in health settings.

Conflict of Interest

Despite pressure to cut health care costs, physicians have a particular duty to tell the truth and to be as helpful as they can. In this regard, they are in a different position than most business people. To illustrate, if a sign in a restaurant windows says, "Best coffee in the world," you can easily judge for yourself whether the claim has merit. And it does not matter much either way. But claims made about more important services—like medical care or financial advice—*do* matter. The stakes are higher, and it is difficult to know if providers' claims are true. In those situations, it is important to know you can trust the source.

The legal term **fiduciary** refers to people such as doctors, attorneys, and bankers who are expected to uphold the public's trust. As Marc Rodwin (1995) explains it:

> Fiduciaries advise and represent others and manage their affairs. Usually they have specialized knowledge or expertise. Their work requires judgment and discretion. Often the party that the fiduciary serves cannot effectively monitor the fiduciary's performance. The fiduciary relationship is based on dependence, reliance, and trust. (paragraph 11)

Rodwin worries that doctors cannot truly be fiduciaries (trustworthy) while they are being pressured to make financial decisions that may not be in patients' best interest (also see Morreim, 1989). For example, imagine that physicians work for an organization that withholds a portion of their pay unless the care they prescribe for patients comes in under budget (a common practice in managed care organizations). Or imagine that physicians are paid on a capitation basis (a set amount per patient regardless of the care provided). When a doctor says treatment is not needed, is it the truth or a cost-cutting fiction? Patients who are aware of the pressure to cut costs may wonder.

Rodwin (1995) worries what will become of the patient–physician relationship if people cease to believe they can trust their doctors' advice. Furthermore, if people receive substandard care because their doctors are pressured to save money, who is to be held responsible—the physicians or the organizations that exert the pressure? There is no clear answer yet. The National Conference of State Legislatures reports that in 8 years, 900 state laws have been passed concerning managed care liability across the nation (NCSL, 2003). Most of the legislation is couched within a **patients' bill of rights** that specifies what actions people may take in contesting managed care decisions. Citizens of 45 states have the right to appeal managed care decisions before an external review board or to file grievances with an ombudsman. In 11 of those states, people have the right to sue managed care organizations. This is a departure from earlier malpractice laws, which applied almost entirely to physicians.

However, courts have been inconsistent in how they apply the new laws, and a proposed nationwide patients' bill of rights failed to get Congressional approval (Eversley, 2003).

If public trust in medical decisions is eroded, the quality of health communication will suffer. Distrustful patients may not take medical advice seriously, may feel it is not worth seeking care, and may blame caregivers for adverse outcomes even when the caregivers acted in good faith.

Violent Conflict

One reason communication in health organizations is so important—and so difficult—is because health care is a high-pressure atmosphere. It is characterized by emotional highs and lows. This is true for employees as well as for patients and their loved ones.

In some instances, working together in high-pressure situations can foster a sense of camaraderie and mutual support. Former nursing student, Frank Kelly (1996), remembers a particularly demanding shift during which he and a staff nurse were kept busy changing soiled bedclothes and attending to seizure patients. He recalls being inspired by the calm compassion of the other nurse:

> She had a quiet manner tending to the philosophical, and I found myself drawn to her astonishing patience . . . [She] never gave the slightest hint of annoyance . . . "If she can do it then so can I," was my thought. (p. 28)

Kelly was surprised at the end of the shift, when the nurse turned to him and said, "Your patience is wonderful . . . I couldn't keep going if it weren't for you" (p. 28). Without realizing it, they had been role models for each other.

Sometimes stressful situations turn ugly, however. Frustration can boil over, leading to hurt feelings and even violence. Of nurses surveyed, 2 out of 3 said they had been verbally abused by co-workers in the last year (Begany, 1995). About 16% reported being sexually harassed by physicians, and 6% said doctors had thrown objects at them.

More violent assaults occur in health care settings than in any other type of workplace (Elliott, 1997). According to an estimate by the U.S. Bureau of Labor Statistics, health care workers are 16 times more likely to be assaulted than employees in other industries. One reason is that people are worried and anxious. Another is that violence often culminates in a trip to the hospital. Emergency personnel and others are called upon to treat people who are violently out of control, are on drugs, or are victims of violence. Gang members and substance abusers may frequent health care facilities, either for treatment, to visit patients, or because they hope to steal drugs ("Guidelines for Preventing," 1997).

Security is a challenge in health care settings. Most hospitals and clinics are open to the public, some of them 24 hours a day. As a result, workers come and go at all hours, and so do visitors. This makes it difficult to know who is on the premises, if they are carrying weapons, and how agitated they may be.

Box 9.5 RESOURCES
More on Conflict Management

- Borisoff, D., & Victor, D. A. (1998). *Conflict management: A communication skills approach* (2nd ed.). Boston: Allyn & Bacon.
- Marcus, L. J. (1999). *Renegotiating health care: Resolving conflict to build collaboration.* San Francisco: Jossey-Bass.
- Spangle, M. (2003). *Negotiation: Communication for diverse settings.* Thousand Oaks, CA: Sage.

Communication Skill Builders: Defusing Violent Situations Skillful communication can sometimes defuse violent situations. Communication specialists help people learn to spot the warning signs that individuals may become violent, such as agitated movements and unusually loud or quiet speech. They can also help people develop communication strategies for conflict situations. Following are some communication techniques recommended by the Occupational Safety and Health Standards Association (OSHA). These are meant to reduce the sense of conflict between people.

- Keep people well informed so they do not wait anxiously.
- Listen patiently to people's concerns.
- Establish ground rules for discussions (such as no loud voices).
- Avoid making statements that might be interpreted as defensive or demeaning.

It is also recommended that employees keep an eye on each other, develop secret distress signals, and avoid being alone with agitated individuals. For additional resources on managing conflict, see Box 9.5.

Nurses' Role in Conflict

Nurses serve as patient advocates, meaning they seek to protect patients' interests and speak out for them when necessary. Because nurses often spend a great deal of time with patients, they are in a good position to monitor their overall health. At the same time, however, nurses play a subordinate role, obligated to follow instructions given by physicians and supervisors. The roles of patient advocate and subordinate are sometimes at odds. Consider the following scenario.

> The nurse takes a deep breath and walks into the hospital room. It should be a happy time—the patient is going home today. Instead, the patient looks worried and upset. He still feels ill and is scared to leave the hospital. Although his vital signs are strong, the nurse agrees. This patient is not ready to go home. The patient turns to her with tears in his eyes and asks, "Why are they sending me home?" The nurse doesn't know what to say.

In situations such as this, nurses are in a difficult position. They are not at liberty to criticize the doctor's decision in front of the patient. To do so would undermine the doctor–patient relationship, anger the doctor, and perhaps cause the nurse to be fired for insubordination (Begany, 1995; Marin, Sherblom, & Shipps, 1994). All the same, it is difficult for nurses to carry out orders when they believe patients' health is at risk. The dilemma is especially difficult to manage because patients often feel comfortable talking to their nurses, and nurses work hard to earn their patients' trust.

All in all, nurses say they often feel caught in the cross-fire. They are forced to carry out decisions that are not their own, but they often take the blame. Nine nurses, employed by nine different organizations, described frequent episodes in which physicians, peers, and patients took out their frustrations on the nurses by yelling at them, making them do scut work (unpleasant, menial tasks), blaming them for others' mistakes, and treating them as if they were ignorant or childlike (Smith et al., 1996). The nurses felt they might lose their jobs if they stood up for themselves, but they would be bullied if they were too accommodating. Said one: "It's as though if you are the least bit quiet, gentle, nonassertive, you're going to get your head knocked off" (p. 24). Overall, the nurses felt their viewpoints were not valued, despite their knowledge and experience. Said one: "I had the experience as a nurse of being voiceless, of having no voice" (p. 29).

In a study of 1,900 nurses, Mark Orbe and Granville King III (2000) found that nurses were distressed by role conflict when they observed colleagues putting patients at risk, but they feared they would be ignored or punished if they reported the bad behavior. In a number of cases, nurses were too afraid to report that colleagues were using or stealing drugs.

One option is for nurses (and other personnel) to participate more in clinical decision making. Nurses are typically more satisfied with their jobs when they are involved in decisions (Bucknall & Thomas, 1996; Ellis & Miller, 1993). In Orbe and King's (2000) study, nurses who felt they were supported by peers and supervisors were likely to report wrongdoing, which may save lives and protect the organization from lawsuits. By contrast, nurses who feel excluded are more apt to feel emotionally exhausted and to leave their jobs (Ellis & Miller, 1993). Some people feel that empowering nurses to make more routine decisions may relieve some of the strain on doctors (Beebe, 1995). However, others worry that it is risky for nurses to make decisions about patient care because they are less educated than doctors and because doctors are ultimately responsible for patients' well-being.

By long-standing convention, nurses do not challenge doctors' authority, and most doctors are not in the habit of asking nurses' opinions. This may stem partly from sex-role differences (historically, most doctors were men and most nurses were women), partly from educational differences, and partly from authority roles instilled in doctors as medical students (Sharf, 1984). Sex roles among health professionals are changing, and many nurses are now highly educated (some with master's and doctorate degrees). Based on traditional patterns of deference, however, doctors may still be insulted when other caregivers seem to question their authority.

Implications

Whether diversity results from different ideas, different types of people, or changing environments, it is likely to result in some degree of conflict. There is a potential conflict of interest between providing quality patient care and cutting costs. Even if physicians manage the conflict successfully, patients' trust may be damaged if they perceive that their doctors are not acting in their best interests. The intense emotions inherent in health settings can escalate to violence if people are already prone to violence or it they believe they (or their loved ones) are being neglected or mistreated. Finally, role conflict results when nurses are expected to speak on patients' behalf but also to follow orders without question. The following section provides suggestions for dealing effectively with multiple viewpoints in health organizations.

COMMUNICATION SKILL BUILDERS: INTEGRATING DIVERSE EMPLOYEES

Here are some suggestions for better integrating diverse employees into health care organizations:

- *Analyze your own biases.* At all levels of the organization, people should honestly take stock of their ideas and prejudices. Even unconscious assumptions can affect people's behavior and minimize the degree to which diverse members are accepted in the organization (Law, 1994).
- *Learn about other cultures.* Members of other cultures may have different accents, languages, and styles of dress. It is helpful to understand that they are different, not purposefully defiant (Law, 1994). It is also useful to remember that other cultures may have different concepts of time. Be explicit about your expectations.
- *Set a good example.* It is especially important for managers and supervisors to show that they honor diversity (Blank & Slipp, 1998). Not only does this contribute to job satisfaction and commitment, it also sets an example for people who may be unsure how to act around diverse coworkers and clients.
- *Make assumptions cautiously.* People sometimes misunderstand each other because they assume everyone thinks as they do. Blank and Slipp (1998) use the example of an Asian-American employee who works late and seems very satisfied with his job. Supervisors—unaware that this employee considers it unacceptable to refuse to work late or to show signs of discontent—are surprised when he leaves for another job. Members of some cultures may also consider it improper to make their accomplishments known or suggest themselves for raises or promotions (Blank & Slipp). Smart supervisors reward efforts, even when employees do not call attention to them.

- *Know the law.* It is illegal to discriminate on the basis of age, race, gender, or national origin. Become familiar with laws governing hiring procedures, job interviews, and employment termination.
- *Help people develop their skills.* The entire organization benefits when its members are equipped to do their jobs well and communicate effectively with others. Help all employees develop the skills necessary to succeed. Do not overlook basic communication skills, which may differ from culture to culture.
- *Make diversity a priority.* Odette Pollar (1998) suggests a communication audit to identify the organization's level of diversity, its strengths, limitations, and goals. Task forces and diversity awareness programs can be used to establish diversity as a primary objective, help people learn to behave respectfully, and exchange ideas in a cooperative and innovative way.
- *Implement a mentorship program.* To welcome new and marginalized employees into the organization, Max Messmer (1998) suggests the creation of mentoring programs in which long-standing employees team up with newer ones to show them the ropes and help them see that their input is important. Messmer says the program reduces training time, opens new lines of communication, establishes trusting relationships, and helps people become established in the organization when they might otherwise feel left out.
- *Do not be too sensitive.* When people make culturally insensitive remarks in your presence, explain why the statement is hurtful and show that there are no hard feelings (Grensing-Pophal, 1997). Most people do not mean to be offensive.
- *Celebrate diversity.* The true benefits of diversity occur when people do not consider it simply a difficulty to be managed or tolerated, but a rich asset to enjoy (Pollar, 1998).

SUMMARY

Organizational culture influences how people behave in health organizations. Culture is comprised of values and assumptions that are so familiar most people are no longer conscious of them. Nevertheless, the implications of culture are profound.

An important aspect of organizational culture is members' attitude toward diversity. Diversity can stimulate new ideas and improve the quality of care in health organizations. However, diversity can be threatening, and it is important to manage inevitable conflicts in a productive manner.

Historical patterns of discrimination are weakening somewhat, opening more doors for women and minority doctors. Although they are more prevalent in medicine than before, women and minorities are still likely to be passed over for promotions, and minority doctors and administrators are still comparatively rare.

Nurses have long played a significant role in health care, and they make up the largest segment of caregivers. Recent changes have increased the pay and status of nurses, although many of them still feel excluded from medical decisions. Nurses' communication is typically characterized by extended contact with patients and a concern with biopsychosocial issues. The nursing shortage makes it imperative that we consider how to help nurses function at top levels and feel that their efforts are valuable and well rewarded.

The emerging emphasis on staying healthy may place patients in contact with diverse caregivers including midlevel and complementary care providers. These caregivers typically devote time to talking about patients' lifeworld concerns. Moreover, their contributions may lighten doctors' loads.

Conflict is a natural result of change and diversity. It is particularly prevalent in health settings because people tend to be emotional and highly goal oriented. Physicians are likely to experience internal conflict as they try to reconcile treatment decisions with the pressure to save money. Health care employees of all types are exposed to higher-than-normal amounts of violent conflict. Communication can be a valuable tool in assessing and managing violent situations. Finally, role conflict makes it difficult for nurses to simultaneously perform the many functions expected of them.

Experts suggest that health organizations can become truly multicultural if they make diversity a priority, honestly assess personal and organizational barriers to cultural acceptance, develop knowledge and skills to communicate effectively, and work together to avoid hurt feelings and enjoy the benefits of diversity.

In closing, it is important to acknowledge that there is far more diversity than can be covered in one chapter or book. White males, who make up the largest contingent of physicians, differ from each other in personal preferences, family backgrounds, beliefs, and more. For the most part, personal differences are too numerous to describe on paper, and research about the communication behavior of different types of caregivers is still relatively scarce. However, an awareness of the diversity in health care may help put available health communication research into perspective.

KEY TERMS

health care organizations
organizational culture
integrated organization
monolithic organizations
plural organizations
multicultural organizations
glass ceiling
affirmative action
alternative medicine
complementary medicine
conflict
conflict of interest
interpersonal conflict
role
role conflict
fiduciary
patients' bill of rights

REVIEW QUESTIONS

1. What is the significance of regarding organizations as cultures rather than machines?
2. What are the advantages and challenges of diversity within an organization?
3. How do monolithic, plural, and multicultural organizations compare?
4. Describe the effects of a glass ceiling in health care organizations today.
5. What historical factors influenced women's acceptance as doctors?
6. As a general rule, how are female physicians' attitudes and communication styles different than men's?
7. Describe the history of African-American doctors in the United States.
8. How does affirmative action differ from the quota system?
9. What are some potential pitfalls when patients and caregivers are of different races? In your opinion, how can these best be avoided?
10. What historical factors have influenced nursing today?
11. What factors have led to the nursing shortage?
12. What are the effects of the nursing shortage?
13. What are two types of midlevel providers? How are they alike, and how are they different?
14. What is the difference between alternative medicine and complementary medicine?
15. What factors contribute to the popularity of alternative and complementary medicine? What are the potential advantages? Disadvantages?
16. What does it mean to say physicians are fiduciaries? How might the pressure to cut medical costs affect their fiduciary role?
17. Why is violence relatively common in health settings?
18. What are some communication tips useful in averting violent situations?
19. In what way do nurses experience role conflict?
20. According to Cox, what are the three levels of diversity in organizations?
21. What are some tips for managing diversity effectively?

CLASS ACTIVITY

Inventory of Personal Beliefs

Objective: One of the first techniques for honoring diversity is to analyze your own ideas and assumptions. Try to write freely in this exercise (you need not share your responses with anyone else). Write whatever comes to mind, even if your ideas are conflicting, and even if they reflect viewpoints you do not hold to be true. For instance, your first response to "old people" may be "grouchy," although you may not really believe old people are grouchy. Write it down anyway. The idea is to assess ideas society may have planted in your brain as well as those that you believe to be true.

Directions: Write down the first 10 words or phrases that occur to you describing people in each of the following categories. (To save time, you may focus on a set number of categories.)

Old people	Young people	Caucasians
Handicapped people	Children	African Americans
Doctors	Nurses	Hispanic Americans
Women	Men	Asian Americans

What Do You Think?

After you have listed your responses, consider the following questions. (You may discuss your answers to the following questions with classmates, but no one should be forced to share their word lists.)

1. Were you surprised by some of the words that popped into your head? If so, why?
2. Do you personally believe everything you wrote down?
3. Did any of your descriptions reflect societal views more than your own personal beliefs?
4. Do you think your behavior is affected by any of the ideas you wrote down? If so, how?
5. People generally rely on stereotypes when they have limited first-hand experience with people in a category. Was this true in your case?
6. Do you think being aware of stereotypes (even though you may not believe them) will help you become a more sensitive communicator?

CHAPTER 10

Leadership and Teamwork

Sam Hill was on duty at the Center for Advanced Medicine in Chicago one night when he saw an older woman leave the building. It was raining and dark outside, and no taxis were waiting at the curb. Hill, encouraged by the organization's mission of providing top-quality service, dashed out in the rain himself. While the woman stood under shelter, he ran down the street to find a taxi. "I practically had to stand in the middle of the road," he recalls. But the woman's gratitude made the trip worthwhile. Waving off her offer of a tip, he recalls, "I was just so glad I could help."

This story, told by Judy Schueler (2000) in an article about customer service in health care, illustrates how a well-defined mission can influence the way people communicate and behave in health care organizations.

Health care organizations are changing the way they do business. Changes in care delivery systems are accompanied by intense competition for clients and qualified employees. The principle change agent is communication.

Effective communication can improve satisfaction, earn clients' and employees' loyalty, save money, and stimulate change and innovation—goals health care organizations cannot afford to ignore. Health care leadership consultant, Quint Studer, articulated the need for a revised vision in an article published by the American Hospital Association in 2002. In the article Studer described a 1998 survey in which health care executives listed their strategies for organizational change. The executives listed technology, provider networks, and new services. "What didn't make the list?" Studer asked. "Not patient or employee satisfaction, nor leadership development. As a result, these goals did not receive attention or resources" (Studer, 2002, paragraph 1). He says this is a mistake.

Studer advocates creating "cultures of excellence" in which employee and client satisfaction are paramount and, although goals are clearly defined, leadership is dispersed throughout the organization. His ideas are catching on. Studer works with organizations around the country and has been named one of the Top 100 Most Powerful People by *Modern Healthcare* magazine (Romano, 2002). In Box 10.1, Studer shares additional insights about health care leadership.

As Quint Studer and others have recognized, health care is in a state of transition. In some ways this adds to the stress of communicating in health organizations, making it especially important to keep employees and clients informed and involved. At the same time, transition provides exciting opportunities to help reshape the system. Communication skills are put to the test as people from many disciplines come together to share ideas and establish new policies.

This chapter describes the conditions that make it necessary for health care organizations to break free of the slow-moving bureaucratic model in favor of more innovative leadership and teamwork. You will read about current issues, evolving ideas about leadership and teamwork, and ways communication specialists can help health organizations manage the challenges ahead. The chapter showcases the challenges, but also the opportunities, for communicating effectively in health care organizations. Throughout the chapter experts share their tips for working in teams, training new leaders, collaborating on creative solutions, developing a shared vision, evaluating existing rules, and managing crises.

CURRENT ISSUES

Health care has changed dramatically in the last few decades, primarily because of efforts to control costs. As you may recall from Chapter 2, in the 1970s insurance and governmental agencies began to limit the amounts they would pay for medical services. Health organizations were subsequently faced with a drastic loss of income unless they cut their own costs. Organizations unable to adapt quickly or efficiently enough closed their doors. Some 949 U.S. hospitals closed between 1980 and 1993 (American Hospital Association, 1994). Hospitals in minority neighborhoods were especially hard hit. Between 1990 and 1997, 70% of hospitals in predominantly African-American or Hispanic neighborhoods closed (Robert Wood Johnson Foundation, 2001).

Remaining organizations have reacted to funding limitations by consolidating, becoming more competitive and consumer oriented, and investing in employee retention. In each case, communication has become a valuable means of establishing and pursuing important goals.

Consolidation

Health organizations that once operated independently are now likely to be part of multicorporation enterprises. By the 1990s, more than half the hospitals in the United States had been bought by large corporations (Shortell, Gillies, & Devers, 1995). Many others merged with competitors or formed alliances with other health organizations. **Integrated health systems** are formed when local care providers collaborate to offer a spectrum of health services (Jennings & O'Leary, 1995). An integrated health system may include hospitals, outpatient surgery centers, doctors' offices, fitness centers, nursing homes, rehabilitation centers, hospices, and more (Slusarz, 1996). The idea is that, by sharing resources, these organizations can reduce their operating costs. As a

Box 10.1 PERSPECTIVES
Leaders Communicate With Purpose

As futurists continue to forecast a "perfect storm" brewing in health care (i.e., all industry challenges are converging toward an unprecedented crisis), I believe the reality is quite different. There has never been a more rewarding or exciting time to be a leader in this noble profession. In health care, we have great purpose, do worthwhile work, and have the opportu-

Quint Studer shares his ideas about innovative leadership with audiences around the country.

nity to make a difference. This passion is at the heart of all we do in health care. When leaders find ways to engage it and harness it in their organizations, the opportunity to shape great change is limitless.

I meet many highly effective leaders daily in my work with hospitals and health systems across the country. And I find that it is truly the good organizations that want to become great. Their leaders are committed to creating and sustaining a corporate culture that thrives on communication at all levels, so physicians and employees can live the organization's mission and vision daily in ways that meet and exceed patient expectations. In fact, I find that the strength of a hospital's culture correlates directly with the amount of compassion and caring that employees show for each other and patients.

Where does culture reside in an organization? Is it in the bricks and mortar? Or the technology we are so proud of? I believe the heart and soul of an organization lies in its people . . . from the receptionist who reaches out for the hand of a walk-in suicidal patient to the physician who goes in search of throat lozenges for a sick child at an all-night pharmacy.

Creating this kind of ownership requires goals that are aligned at every level (from housekeeper to CEO), accountability that is "hardwired" into the infrastructure of the organization, and tools that open channels of communication. The hospitals and systems I work with achieve this by setting goals and measuring progress in Five Pillars™: service, people, quality, finance, and growth. Leaders at these organizations align goals and performance objectives that cascade throughout the organization so there is a cohesive plan with benchmarks and tools to get there. Each employee knows the hospital's goals, where it is headed, how it is doing, and how well they as individuals are contributing.

These leaders also build service and operational excellence through the use of Nine Principles™: They commit to excellence; measure the important things; build a culture around service; create and develop leaders; focus on employee satisfaction; build individual accountability; align goals and values; communicate at all levels; and recognize and reward excellence.

Communicating with purpose (Principle #8) means using prescriptive tools and practices that convey a constant and consistent message to all employees about an organization's mission, vision, and values. Posting communication boards throughout the hospital, for instance, promotes a "no secrets" culture by graphing each department's progress toward organizational goals in service, quality, finance, people, and growth (i.e., the Five Pillars™).

I also recommend the use of *key words at key times.* There are many examples of how specific words, when used with patients, can proactively set patient expectations, demonstrate caring, and increase patient satisfaction. Perhaps the most compelling are the words, "Is there anything else I can do for you? I have time." Even busy nurses find that by anticipating patient needs, these words magically and dramatically reduce call lights. Then nurses find they actually do have more time to care for patients.

I also believe *effective unit rounding* is a key communication tool. It is the single most important thing a hospital can do to dramatically increase patient satisfaction and drive employee satisfaction. When nurse leaders round on their staff by talking to each person, for instance, their goal is to empower staff to help patients. They should ask five key questions: (1) a relationship-building question (e.g., How was your family vacation?), (2) Which systems are working well? (3) Who among the staff can I recognize?, (4) Who among the physicians can I recognize?, and (5) What can be improved? Then they must follow through by delivering needed improvements.

In my experience, *employee thank-you notes,* especially when sent to an employees' home, are another great way to communicate. Thank-you notes build the emotional bank account with employees by recognizing the good things leaders have seen and heard during rounding. Leaders

continued

Box 10.1 PERSPECTIVES
Leaders Communicate With Purpose, *continued*

can "manage up" their staff in this way, by sharing noteworthy accomplishments with their supervisors who can thank the employee. This is also a surprisingly powerful way to reduce employee turnover, one of the biggest challenges in health care today.

I also recommend that staff conduct *discharge phone calls* to patients 24 to 48 hours after they have left the hospital. This allows them to reconnect back to their sense of purpose (delivering quality care) and to the patient by demonstrating empathy, hearing the patient's perception of care, and improving clinical outcomes.

As one hospital CEO I know says, "We are in the life enhancement business." Just as students ask teachers to help cultivate their potential, patients come to our hospitals for help during pivotal events in their lives . . . whether a loved one has just been diagnosed with terminal cancer or a child is born. It is my greatest hope that the next generation of leaders in health care will reach out with sensitivity, skill, and compassion during such moments. Never underestimate the difference one individual can make.

—*Quint Studer, Studer Group*

About Quint Studer

Quint Studer, named one of the top 100 most powerful people by *Modern Healthcare* in 2002, began his career in a hospital staff position in 1984

result, they can offer health care at discount prices, either to members of their own health care plans or to managed care organizations that pay the system to provide care for their enrollees.

By joining forces health organizations may be more marketable and cost-efficient. But takeovers, mergers, and alliances present communication challenges. For one thing, long-standing competitors may find themselves working together. This challenges organizational members to form new relationships and find ways to integrate their ideas (Slusarz, 1996). Furthermore, as organizations become more complex, it is difficult to manage them by the old rules. Centralized decision making is inadequate to guide the efforts of highly diverse enterprises.

Competition

With health care dollars limited, health organizations have become more competitive. With capitated fees and limited reimbursements, organizations must and later became chief operating officer of Holy Cross Hospital in Chicago and president of Baptist Hospital, Inc., in Pensacola, Florida, before forming Studer Group in January 2000. Today, Studer Group coaches more than 250 hospitals and health systems nationwide to service and operational excellence. To learn more about these principles and practices in action at hospitals nationwide, visit www.studergroup.com.

Other Articles by Quint

Read excerpts of some of these articles online at www.studergroup.com. Full reprints are available at no charge by e-mailing allyson.holliday@studergroup.com.

Studer, Q. (2003, November). Communicating quality. *COR Healthcare Market Strategist,* published by COR Health.

Studer, Q. (2003, Summer). How healthcare wins with consumers who want more. *Frontiers of Health Services Management 19*(4), 3-16, published by the American College of Healthcare Executives.

Studer, Q. (2002, September). Back to the basics: Making service excellence a priority. *Trustee Magazine 55*(8), 7–10, published by the American Hospital Association.

Studer, Q. (2003, May/June). Sustaining the gains: Creating organizational alignment through accountability. *Press-Ganey Satisfaction Monitor,* published by Press-Ganey. Available online at www.pressganey.org/research/resources/satmon/text/bin/139.shtm.

anticipate as accurately as possible what health services their subscribers are likely to need (Azevedo, 1996). This requires that they collect and track information about community health and that they promote community health as much as possible. As you will see later in the chapter, communication specialists can help with this.

To be competitive, health systems must also keep the public up to date about the services they offer. Competition has led to a new emphasis on marketing and advertising. The AMA, which banned physician advertising in 1914, lifted the ban in 1975 under pressure from the U.S. Supreme Court, which felt that the ban restricted public information and physicians' livelihood (Kotler & Clarke, 1987). Although doctors have been somewhat reluctant to advertise aggressively themselves, many insurance companies and managed care organizations are avid advertisers, as are pharmaceutical companies, which spend more than $2 billion a year to advertise prescription drugs (Kane, 2003). (You will read more about this in Chapter 11.)

Box 10.2 ETHICAL CONSIDERATIONS
Should Health Organizations Advertise?

In 1914 the American Medical Association forbade physicians to advertise their services, asserting that commercialism had no place in medicine. The association felt it was unethical to promote medical services for the purpose of making money (Walt, 1997). That ban was lifted in 1975, and although doctors have not become conspicuous advertisers, many types of health care organizations do advertise.

Some people object to advertising medical services and products. Robert Boyd (1997), for one, argues that "media hype" has no place in health. He warns that it is confusing enough to keep up with medical research without being bombarded by sales pitches promoting various health products and services.

A related worry is that advertisers will exaggerate the benefits, but minimize the ill effects, of what they are selling. For example, prescription drug advertisements may lead people to expect miracle cures or may underrate the side effects of the products (Chaker, 1998). Patients may be disappointed when their doctors do not prescribe products they have seen advertised or may disregard warnings in light of the rosy pictures painted by advertisements. The argument is that patients do not have the expertise to know when advertisers are making exaggerated and inaccurate claims about health benefits. Moreover, seriously ill patients and their loved ones may be particularly vulnerable to advertisers' claims because they so badly want to believe a cure is possible (Irvine, 1991).

Others fear that health advertisements will alarm people and make them needlessly preoccupied with health issues. Alison Bass (1990) describes a hospital advertisement that shows a woman examining her breasts for lumps. The headline reads: "This woman just missed the cancer that will kill her" (p. 1). Bass concludes: "People who provide health care have begun playing on the very fears and anxieties they are supposed to alleviate" (p. 1).

There is also concern that advertising will damage the professional image of caregivers. Critics cringe at sales ploys that make health professionals seem silly or greedy. For example, some clinics now offer money-back guarantees if patients are not satisfied with the care they receive.

Although competition is fierce, "selling" medical services remains a controversial subject. For a discussion of the ethical issues involved, see Box 10.2.

Consumerism

Patients have choices in the health care marketplace. Choice is underlined not only by advertising and marketing efforts, but also by an unprecedented amount of health information available in the news media and on the Internet.

Health ethicist John La Puma (1998) wonders if free toasters will be the next marketing strategy.

People who support health advertising have a simple but compelling case as well. They feel that advertising is a useful way to let the public know what health products and services are available (Bass, 1990). Without advertisements, they argue, people may not be aware that certain treatments exist. Proponents of health advertising maintain that consumers are wise enough to be skeptical about advertisers' claims and avoid being taken in by misleading promises.

What Do You Think?

1. Should doctors be allowed to advertise their services? Why or why not?
2. Should other providers (hospitals, drug companies, rehabilitation centers, managed care organizations, etc.) be allowed to advertise? Why or why not?
3. If advertising is allowed, should there be any restrictions on what the ads may (or must) contain?

Suggested Sources

Bass, A. (1990, November 25). Health care marketing seeks gain from pain. *Boston Globe,* National/Foreign section, p. 1.

Boyd, R. S. (1997, June 21). Medical aids, media reports "a flood of confusing advice": Marketing hype, thirst for the news among causes of bewilderment. *Houston Chronicle,* p. 7.

Chaker, A. M. (1998, October 4). Anti-acne birth control pills cause conflicting viewpoints. *Wall Street Journal,* Business section, p. 2.

Irvine, D. H. (1991, March). The advertising of doctors' services. *Journal of Medical Ethics, 17,* 35–40.

Walt, D. (1997, March 17). Standing up for ethics. *American Medical News, 40,* 12–15.

In this context, patients are well-informed consumers motivated and capable enough to choose between different health services vying for their business.

As a result of these factors, health organizations must strive for consumer satisfaction. Putting the consumer first may require that managers relax protocol so that employees can accommodate consumers' needs. For instance, many medical centers have eliminated the paperwork that used to make hospital admissions a lengthy and frustrating process. Instead, they now obtain information over the phone in advance so people feel less hassled when they

Box 10.3 RESOURCES
More About Adapting to Changes in Health Care

- Coddington, D. C., Moore, K. D., & Fischer, E. A. (2001). *Strategies for the new health care marketplace: Managing the convergence of consumerism and technology.* San Francisco: Jossey-Bass.
- Geisler, E., Krabbendam, K., & Schuring, R. (2003). *Technology, health care, and management in the hospital of the future.* Westport, CT: Praeger.
- Leebov, W., & Scott, G. (2002). *The indispensable health care manager: Success strategies for a changing environment.* San Francisco: Jossey-Bass.

arrive for treatment. Others have authorized employees to reimburse patients for lost items or award gift certificates and coupons when they see fit.

Staffing Shortages

In the midst of other challenges, health care organizations are also struggling to attract and keep qualified personnel. As you read in Chapter 9, experts estimate that by 2010, U.S. health care organizations will be short-staffed by 220,000 registered nurses (U.S. Department of Health, 2002). Already, the shortage has topped 100,000. Consequently many health care organizations are doing whatever they can to attract and keep qualified personnel. This includes listening more closely to employees' needs, responding to their ideas, and involving them in collaborative efforts to create satisfying environments. (For additional resources about strategic changes in health care organizations, see Box 10.3.)

Implications

Health care is reacting to a new set of challenges: to conserve resources, to develop a clearer understanding of community health needs, and to attract and satisfy clients and employees. The next section examines some of the changes taking place in the health industry in response to these challenges. The most notable change is a shift from bureaucratic management to an emphasis on human resources.

CHALLENGING THE BUREAUCRACY

Like most businesses that developed during the Industrial Revolution, U.S. health organizations (especially large ones) adopted a bureaucratic model. A **bureaucracy** is a highly structured organization with a clear chain of command, centralized power, specialized tasks, and established rules for operation (Weber, 1946).

Over the years, the bureaucratic model has strengthened health care organizations in some ways and weakened them in others. The principle weakness—top-down leadership that is often insulated and slow moving—has become a liability few organizations can afford. A case in point is the U.S. Veterans Administration (VA). Although the VA is the second largest bureaucracy in the American government, its health system has launched an extensive effort to become less bureaucratic. Describing the VA's planned transformation, Vestal, Fralicz, and Spreier (1997) explain:

> The rigid, functionally focused, command-and-control culture that has long been a hallmark of VA must be replaced by one that values speed, flexibility, and the processes for delivering high-quality, cost-effective patient care. (p. 339)

An effort is underway to restructure the VA health system so employees are empowered to respond to consumers' needs, not simply to the dictates of the bureaucracy. Employees will be encouraged to think of ways to please customers, solve problems, work together in teams, and come up with innovative methods to improve care and conserve resources.

As in the VA, members of many health care organizations are considering new options. A few of those options are presented here. As you will see, future trends are still more easily defined by questions than answers, which means leaders and teams have a particularly challenging and exciting task ahead of them.

Hierarchies or Partnerships?

In a classic bureaucracy a strict hierarchy establishes who the bosses are. The organizational chart is vertical, meaning there are many layers of management, and managers at each level supervise a relatively small number of people (Hamilton & Parker, 1997). The old saying, "It's lonely at the top," is true in a vertical organization. Few people make it that far. Although top-level managers make most of the decisions, employees are encouraged to communicate mostly with those directly above and below them, meaning that top-level administrators typically have little contact with the majority of organizational members.

Advantages There are some advantages to a vertical hierarchy. Centralized authority provides stability and a common sense of purpose. This is important in health care organizations, which may have dozens of departments and different types of employees. Particularly with mergers and consolidations, it may be difficult to achieve a shared vision without strong leadership at the core. Moreover, a strict hierarchy reduces ambiguity. It is clear who has decision-making power. This is useful when making quick or important decisions.

In emergencies, for example, paramedics know exactly which procedures they are authorized to begin and which procedures require the approval of a supervisor or physician. This clarity can save time and prevent mistakes that inexperienced personnel might make. Likewise, appointed decision makers can help organizations reach decisions about marketing, new service lines, staffing, and other issues that cross departmental lines. Without clear management levels, divisions may be at odds with each other, unclear what agenda should prevail.

Disadvantages Centralized authority also has drawbacks. Nurse executive Ann L. Hendrich proposes that vertical health care organizations should consider a change of format. As she puts it: "Vertically structured organizations are often bureaucratic, expensive, and difficult to operate in a cost-driven, competitive environment. In the new market there will be two kinds of organizations—quick and dead" (quoted by Porter-O'Grady, Bradley, Crow, & Hendrich, 1997, paragraph 10).

As Hendrich points out, centralized decision making does not enable bureaucracies to change quickly or to accommodate unusual circumstances. Because people who carry out policies do not often have direct contact with decision makers, opportunities for change may be lost or delayed. This means organizations may perpetuate inefficient and costly procedures and miss opportunities to respond to emerging market needs.

Restricted communication limits organizational effectiveness, but it also frustrates employees. Human resource theorists have long observed that employees are more satisfied when they have a voice in the workplace (Blake & Mouton, 1964; Likert, 1961; McGregor, 1960). However, hierarchies inhibit an open and trusting exchange of information. Employees may be reluctant to discuss sensitive issues with people in positions of higher power, particularly since there is typically little opportunity to get to know (and trust) top-level leaders. Information may be filtered and distorted as it moves upward through the chain of command (Lee, 1993). For example, employees in the billing department may be reluctant to admit that the new computerized billing system they requested is not working well. Ironically, *because* power is centralized, the people at the top (who make the decisions) may be poorly informed or misinformed about day-to-day issues and client responses.

In short, innovation and problem solving are compromised when people are poorly informed or afraid to be honest. Considering that (under the right conditions) employees want to share ideas and have valuable suggestions to make, reserving power for top-level officials seems to present more problems than it solves.

Opportunities for Change Faced with the need to adapt more quickly than a bureaucratic framework allows, some health care organizations have eliminated one or more layers of middle management. The rationale is that, with fewer status differences and hierarchical levels, communication will flow more freely and organizational members will be better informed and more actively involved. (No doubt, another consideration is that it is less costly to employ fewer managers.)

In a decentralized, horizontal structure, organizational members have more peers and fewer managers. For example, perhaps you are a market research coordinator who used to report to the marketing supervisor, who reported to the director of marketing and public relations (PR), who reported to the vice president of strategic planning, who reported to the CEO, who reported to the board of directors. (Confusing, isn't it?) However, it has recently been declared that the marketing and PR departments will report directly to the vice president. This can be an exciting opportunity to present your ideas directly to top-level management, and perhaps you will now be more involved in making decisions that affect everyday operations.

Participative decision making (PDM) means people are involved in making the decisions they will be expected to carry out (Goldhaber, 1993). As previously mentioned, employees are usually more satisfied with their jobs, and more committed to staying with the organization, when they have input (Bucknall & Thomas, 1996; Ellis & Miller, 1993; McNeese-Smith, 1996; Miller et al., 1990; Nakata & Saylor, 1994).

However, simply removing a layer of management does not guarantee more or better communication. With PDM, the greatest influence lies with people who are able to express themselves clearly and win support for their ideas. While it is true that you (at least theoretically) have more access to top-level administrators and more voice in decision making, so do a lot of other people. You may find yourself either fighting for the spotlight or wondering how you should perform when you are suddenly *in* the spotlight. I remember being promoted to PR supervisor one week and being asked to make a presentation before the board of directors the next week. Although I was trained to give presentations, it was a tense week for me. I did not know how board meetings were conducted or what was expected of me. The pressure is especially great for people thrust into leadership roles without much communication training.

Nevertheless, organizations often expect people to assume leadership roles with little or no preparation. At a recent workshop I attended, Bob Murphy, vice president and chief operating officer of Baptist Hospital in Pensacola, Florida, quipped: "There's an old saying, 'What's the difference between a nurse on Friday and a nurse leader on Monday?' . . . A weekend to think about it!" The same is often true of personnel in other areas as well.

Murphy compares leadership to bull-riding in that, even if you know what you want to accomplish, it still takes a good deal of skill to be successful at it. "Bull-riding is a simple concept," Murphy exclaims, "'Hang on!' But that's hard to do isn't it?" The following section presents suggestions for cultivating leaders.

Communication Skill Builders: Training New Leaders The Leadership Institute at Baptist Hospital in Pensacola has become so popular that people travel from around the country to take part in workshops and benchmarking sessions. Here are some of the leadership lessons the Baptist staff shares with others:

- *Provide leadership training.* Involve midlevel and upper-level managers in day-long leadership training programs at least four times a year, and invite people throughout the organization to take part in series of briefer workshops. Also help people develop leadership experience by involving them in self-governance.
- *Keep no secrets.* If people are to be accountable as leaders, they must know where they stand and how the organization is performing. Make current financial records and satisfaction survey reports available to all employees so they can chart their successes and receive immediate market feedback on what works well and what does not.
- *Make organizational leaders accessible.* Avoid placing administrative officers in a far-off or segregated area. Encourage leaders to interact freely throughout the organization and share conversations, praise, and ideas.
- *Reward people for sharing ideas.* Develop a program that invites employees' suggestions and rewards them for submitting workable ideas that improve services, save money, and increase employee morale.
- *Respond to ideas.* Even when the ideas cannot be implemented, people want to know they have been heard. "We made a lot of mistakes when we began," Murphy confides. "We encouraged ideas, but 99 percent of the time, we didn't do anything with them." Now committees are in place to review ideas and respond quickly.
- *Celebrate successes.* Post thank-you letters and praise the people involved. Hold celebrations when the organization reaches key goals. Develop recognition programs to honor people who exceed expectations.

Authority Rule or Multilevel Input?

In bureaucratic language, **rational-legal authority** is based on "rationality, expertise, norms, and rules" (Miller, 1999, p. 13). In health care this translates to a reverence for those people who are most educated, have the most up-to-date knowledge, and hold the most impressive titles and credentials (Cadogan, Franzi, Osterweil, & Hill, 1999). Health care employees typically advertise their credentials right up front. Their name badges list their job titles, and very often their degrees and accreditations as well. For example, the initials CRNA behind a person's name stand for Certified Registered Nurse Anesthetist. Patients may not fully grasp the difference in credentials, but professionals probably do.

Advantages Most people would agree that health care is not a job for amateurs. The emphasis on education and experience is justified by the immense knowledge and responsibilities associated with providing top-quality care.

Attention to norms and rules helps assure that treatment is given in time-honored and consistent ways by people who are well qualified to provide it.

Disadvantages Status differences can cause rifts and intolerance. People without impressive titles (including patients) may be excluded from discussions even though they may have valuable information and ideas to share. Health care is often characterized by what Kreps (1990) calls **professional prejudice.** Some professions are considered more prestigious than others based on their training, their authority, or their place in the organization. For example, critical care nurses may be given higher status than maternal-child or psychiatric nurses (Smith, Droppleman, & Thomas, 1996). Nonclinical personnel may be given less credence than doctors and nurses. These prejudices can silence people with good ideas to share. They also can provoke animosity between co-workers and lead to turf battles in which one department or profession asserts that it is more important than another, thus more deserving of new equipment, pay raises, additional staff, or the like (Albrecht, 1982). Unfortunately, recent efforts to cut expenses and limit resources have aggravated this long-standing competitiveness in many institutions (Forte, 1997).

Opportunities for Change From a communication standpoint, there is value in education and seniority, but overlooking low-ranking employees is a mistake. Often, front-line employees are more familiar than anyone about clients' wishes and the organization's daily routines. Steve Miller, a worldwide manager at Shell Oil Company, emphasizes the need to treat members throughout the organization as intelligent change agents:

> In the past, the leader was the guy with the answers. Today if you're going to have a successful company, you have to recognize that no leader can possibly have all the answers. The leader may have a vision. But the actual solutions about how best to meet the challenges of the moment have to be made by the people closest to the action. (quoted by Pascale, 1999, p. 210)

Communication skills are essential to leaders in today's health care industry. Margaret Jobes and Amy Steinbinder (1996) advise that "leaders in new staff roles will no longer achieve power through position and title, but rather through the development of interpersonal skills" (paragraph 23).

We established earlier that participative decision making requires new skills and expectations, up-to-date knowledge, responsiveness, and recognition. It is also important that organizational leaders establish trusting relationships and provide employees the latitude to experiment with new ideas and programs. In other words, although it may look different, leadership is still important in horizontal organizations. As James Pepicello and Emmett Murphy (1996) put it, empowering organizational members "does not relieve leadership of its responsibility to lead" (paragraph 17). Leaders in horizontal organizations are charged with communicating the organization's overall goals, enabling organizational members to participate fully, and rewarding them for contributions.

Otherwise, employees may feel adrift and overwhelmed, particularly if they are accustomed to the close supervision provided within a vertical hierarchy (Porter-O'Grady, Bradley, Crow, & Hendrich, 1997). Research shows that employees are typically dissatisfied and unmotivated if they are unsure what is expected of them, if they lack the skills to perform new duties, or if they are discouraged by managers who do not seem to support organizational changes (Northouse & Northouse, 1985).

Communication Skill Builders: Managing by Collaboration In the article, "The View from the Middle," two midlevel managers in health care organizations suggest the following communication strategies for leaders in participative environments (Bachenheimer & DeKoven, 2003):

- *Be a leader* and *a team member.* As an organizational leader, you are responsible for providing direction, but you are also a team member who listens to and works alongside others.
- *Choose your words—and your medium—carefully.* Do not use e-mail to communicate praise, advice, criticism, or critical information. Discuss sensitive and important information face to face or over the telephone.
- *Make the most of meetings.* Plan meetings carefully, invite everyone to participate, listen actively, and follow up afterwards.
- *Invite ideas and follow up on them.* Bachenheimer and DeKoven urge leaders to follow up on everything—every promise, every conversation.
- *Invite solutions.* Create an environment in which people are encouraged to present solutions, not just describe problems.
- *Think and act positively.* Acknowledge challenges but present your organization in a positive light.
- *Praise people for their efforts.* Recognize those who try hard even if things do not go exactly as planned.

Specialized Jobs or Mission-Centered Expectations?

A **division of labor** means that workers have specific tasks to perform. No one person takes a project from beginning to end. This is the idea behind assembly lines. The assumption is that workers operate at maximum efficiency performing simple, repetitive tasks.

Of course, health organizations did not take medicine to the extreme of assembly line production. But they did adopt a division of labor. Whereas rural physicians traditionally performed the gamut of activities—from delivering babies, to keeping medical records, to performing surgeries, to collecting fees—health organizations during the Industrial Revolution began to separate these tasks (Reiser, 1978). Nurses were assigned specific duties such as giving injections, taking health history information, and so on. Bookkeeping and scheduling were taken over by staff members trained to perform those tasks. Physicians also began to specialize. Although almost all doctors in the 1800s were general practitioners, 1 in 4 doctors specialized in a particular type of medicine by 1929, and 3 out of 4 doctors were specialists by 1969 (Reiser, 1978).

Advantages As medical knowledge and the business of providing health care became more complex, specialization helped people develop expertise in different areas. The division of labor also helped maintain the image of caregivers as public servants rather than businesspeople. As health organizations evolved, doctors usually did not discuss fees with patients. Specially trained staff members took charge of financial details, leaving caregivers to (presumably) ignore monetary concerns in single-minded pursuit of better health for their patients.

Disadvantages A division of labor enabled health care professionals to become highly focused experts, but to a large extent, it also created boundaries between them. Members of one department or specialization were unlikely to communication or collaborate with professionals in another (Raffell & Raffell, 1989), and caregivers were largely excluded from health care management. Gradually, hospitals and clinics ceased to be run by doctors and were instead managed by people with backgrounds in business, management, and finance. This trend was supported by the complexity of new tax laws and business regulations, which made managing health care organizations more complicated. Although business expertise was welcome, many caregivers began to feel disconnected from policy decisions.

Another disadvantage is that people with specialized job duties are not likely to go beyond them. For example, any number of employees may walk past a spill in the hallway because it is not their job to clean it up.

Opportunities for Change Members of some organizations are realizing that top-quality care transcends the efforts of any one person or department. It is as important to work *together* as to work hard. For example, during a rather lengthy wait to see the doctor recently, a nurse assistant hurrying in and out noticed me. She stopped to apologize for the delay and explain that an emergency had disrupted the schedule. This simple gesture dispelled my irritation. I am sure it was not part of her job description to do this, but by making the extra effort, she improved my estimation of the entire experience. These sort of gestures are most likely in organizations in which leaders establish over achieving goals and reward employees for taking the initiative to satisfy clients' needs.

Communication Skill Builders: Promoting a Shared Vision Studer (2003a) compares an effective health care leader to the conductor of an orchestra whose job is to achieve the following:

- Establish goals for the performance.
- Keep everyone on the same page.
- Define the contribution of each individual.

In other words, a good organizational leader recognizes that harmony results from clear expectations and the coordinated performance of individuals. Although each person will make unique contributions, they must be in sync to be successful. We might add that good leaders also enable people to improvise when doing so will improve the group's performance.

At Missouri Baptist Medical Center, employees are encouraged to "make their patients' day" even when that requires going beyond their job descriptions. Therefore, when nurse assistant Leo Carter was caring for an elderly patient who was agitated and near death, Carter sought a means of soothing the man without restraining him. A fellow nurse remembered that the patient had been a symphony conductor. Leo ran to his car to get a clarinet, which he played quietly in the man's room. Stephen Lundin and colleagues (2002) describe what happened:

> As the soft, mellow notes drifted through the room, something happened. The old man stopped thrashing. He closed his eyes and smiled. Lying on his back, he raised his arms and began to wave them back and forth. Perhaps, deep in his mind, he was standing in a great concert hall once again, wearing coat and tails, with a baton in his strong hands, leading *his* orchestra. After a few minutes the old man's arms dropped slowly to his sides and he slept quietly through the night. (p. 93)

In short, when people are united by a strong mission but encouraged to go beyond traditional boundaries, unforeseeable circumstances become opportunities to make a difference.

Strictly by the Rules . . . or Not?

Ask people to define *bureaucracy* and they are apt to mention red tape. Bureaucracies are known for their paperwork. Nearly any task requires that a form be filled out, signed, and submitted to the appropriate people. Ask why and an employee is likely to pull out more paper in the form of written rules and procedures.

Advantages In some ways, paperwork and guidelines are well suited to health care. For one, careful records allow health care organizations (and oversight boards) to review care procedures and evaluate their efficacy and cost effectiveness. Additionally, written records keep teams members informed about patient care. Standardized forms help assure that information is recorded in a form others can quickly read and understand. This is crucial for managing medical emergencies and around-the-clock shift changes. Third, established policies reduce ambiguity and may give people a sense of security and predictability (Vestal et al., 1997). For example, clear rules for employee evaluation and advancement discourage favoritism and provide performance guidelines (Eisenberg & Goodall, 1997). Finally, people are less likely to overlook important information (or skip crucial steps) if they are following established procedures. Missing even a small detail can have tragic consequences when people's lives are at stake.

Disadvantages Adherence to written guidelines presents some disadvantages, however. People may be frustrated by what they see as needless amounts of paperwork. Nurses today say they spend almost as much time filling out paperwork as caring for patients. Established policies can also jeopardize customer service. Because few people have the authority to override policies when an unforeseen problem arises, the best an employee can do is request that a policy be reconsidered (which may take weeks or months) or refer the situation to someone higher on the ladder hoping it will eventually reach someone with authority to grant an exception (Hamilton & Parker, 1997). In the meantime, clients are likely to feel mistreated, share their grievances with others, and look for another organization more responsive to their needs. The emphasis on following written policies, asking specific questions, and filling out forms can also discourage open communication. Patients' input may be largely limited to the information requested on forms, where there is often little room to add comments not specifically requested (Thompson, 1996; Wyatt, 1995). Furthermore, professionals may rely on written communication more than face-to-face discussions. Although notes and charts are informative, they are a meager substitute for interactive discussions when it comes to making collaborative judgments.

Communication Skill Builders: Evaluating the Rules On reflection, good rules help organizations run smoothly and effectively. Paperwork, if used effectively, can improve communication. However, bad rules and needless red tape frustrate employees and clients. To separate the good from the bad, Irwin Press, one of the country's best known patient satisfaction experts, recommends that health care leaders take the following steps:

- *Ask employees to identify "really stupid rules."* "This is fun and focuses analytical attention on the often arbitrary nature of regulations" (Press, 2002, p. 42). By identifying what does not make sense, organizations can get rid of rules that impede performance.
- *Next, examine rules that make sense but do not work well.* For example, Press (2002) asks, is it necessary that nurses deliver meal trays? Could other staff members perform this task and free nurses to respond more quickly to patients' requests?
- *Remember that patients don't much care about the paperwork.* "No matter how firmly we argue that paperwork is a necessary part of care, patients don't see it this way. Paperwork is not the hands-on care that patients want or that they base their evaluations on" (Press, 2002, p. 39).
- *If the rules and paperwork are important, allow time and space to complete them.* Press (2002) urges leaders to analyze employees' job duties to make sure they are compatible. For example, it is unrealistic to expect an

employee to answer the phone, file reports, and simultaneously respond to others' needs. Frustration—and poor service—are likely to result. Instead, provide adequate time and space to complete necessary procedures and paperwork. If the regulations are important, make fulfilling them part of the job.

Implications

As hospitals and clinics began to spring up during the Industrial Revolution, many of them adopted a bureaucratic framework. Bureaucracy presents advantages and disadvantages relevant to health care. The advantages may include a sense of stability within the organization, clear expectations about performance, high standards embodied in well-established procedures, and respect for authority and experience. The disadvantages may include a communication gap between workers and decision makers, resistance to change, prejudice against people who do not occupy high-status positions in the organization, turf battles between different divisions, and separation from the organization's external environment. Because employees are typically divided into specialized work units, it may be difficult for them to understand other people's contributions or imagine new ways to do things.

Most of the issues surrounding bureaucratic management and change involve communication. Reshaping the health care system requires new skills and awareness. Skills such as leadership training, collaborative leadership, development of a shared vision, and self-evaluation become especially important.

The next section focuses on teamwork, an important part of the trend toward participative- and self-management and a long-standing component of health care organizations.

TEAMWORK

Simply defined, a **team** is "a set of individuals who work together to achieve common objectives" (Unsworth, 1996, p. 483). Teamwork is nothing new to health care. Doctors, nurses, technicians, clerks, and others have long relied on each other to reach common objectives. But the rules and reasons for teamwork are changing.

To apply the terminology of management guru Peter Drucker, health care teams used to function like baseball teams, but now they must act like doubles tennis partners. Drucker (1993) writes that (managerially speaking) a doubles tennis game is different than a baseball game. In baseball each player is assigned a position with a specific set of tasks to perform. The pitcher pitches, the catcher catches, the batter bats, and so on. The game is specialized and precise. Doubles tennis is different—faster, less precise. Players have basic positions but must always be poised to help each other, and there is scarcely time to stand still.

To flourish health care teams must function like tennis partners, argues Mary Fanning (1997). They must be ready for the unexpected and be prepared to help each other. Caregivers used to play their positions with little overlap (like baseball players). A patient might see a physical therapist, a nurse, a doctor, and a laboratory technician—but one at a time, never all together (Zimmermann, 1994). Technically, the caregivers were working toward the same goal, but they contributed in specialized ways, independently. The problem is that team members who do not communicate with each other are likely to drop the ball. Lack of communication can lead to duplicated efforts, costly (and sometimes life-threatening) delays, frustration, and wasted time. Teamwork can minimize the waste and frustration. However, like leadership, teamwork is not always easy to accomplish.

Advantages

One advantage of teamwork is that members are able to apply multiple perspectives to a problem, enhancing innovation and creativity. Some health care organizations are making the most of this with interdisciplinary teams made up of doctors, nurses, marketing specialists, financial experts, and others. These teams are uniquely qualified to design innovative programs that cut costs without sacrificing the quality of care (Farley & Stoner, 1989; Pepicello & Murphy, 1996). (See Box 10.4 for more about encouraging innovation in health care organizations.)

Interdisciplinary teamwork blurs the line between departments and presents new opportunities for diverse employees to take part in decision making (Green, 1994). One result is that doctors and nurses are again playing a major role in health care management (Pepicello & Murphy, 1996).

Another advantage is that teamwork reduces costly oversights that may occur when people are devoted to highly specialized tasks. Health care organizations can no longer afford (if ever they could) the oversights that result when team members do not communicate with each other. Ask any hospital employee about patients who have gotten "lost in the system." Usually, the story is that the patient is scheduled for a series of treatments or tests, but somewhere along the way everyone assumes the patient is with someone else—until they realize the poor soul has spent hours lying on gurney in the hallway. (I am told of a case, years ago, when a patient went up and down in the staff elevator for hours, with everyone assuming an escort was waiting at the next stop.) Bureaucracies are especially vulnerable to these kinds of oversights because many tasks do not fall squarely within the boundaries of any job description. Workers who concentrate on specialized tasks may not take the initiative to go beyond their borders (they may not even realize they should). Teamwork encourages people to look at the larger picture and pitch in, even with tasks that are not specifically assigned to them (Sullivan & Wolfe, 1996). For example, nurses who notice that lab results have not arrived on time may take the initiative to find out if tests were run and why results are

Box 10.4 THEORETICAL FOUNDATIONS A Model for Innovative Leadership

When writers for the *Harvard Business Review* interviewed 100 innovative business leaders they identified some common characteristics among them (Davenport, Prusak, & Wilson, 2003). For one, innovators are *idea scouts,* always looking for new ideas within the organization and outside it. They talk to people and really listen. They are also *tailors* who modify new ideas to suit the organization's needs, all the while inviting frequent and candid input from others. As the process continues, the best innovators are *promoters* who sell their ideas to people throughout the organization, communicating effectively and enthusiastically with top and middle management as well as front-line employees and clients. Finally, innovators are *experimenters.* They pilot and test new ideas on a small scale to prepare them for wider adoption. Importantly, innovators are *not* do-it-all-myself types. When an innovation has been tested and refined, they "get out of the way and let others execute" (Davenport, Prusak, & Wilson, 2003, p. 58). The implications for communication are clear: observe, listen, invite feedback, sell your ideas, experiment, and enable others.

What Do You Think?

1. In what ways are you an idea scout? Think of the best idea scout you know. How does he or she do it?
2. What steps might you follow to tailor ideas to a particular organization or group of people?
3. What skills are needed to promote new ideas?
4. Have you ever been part of (or coordinated) a pilot study or experimental program? Did you feel it was worthwhile? What did you learn during the process?
5. Why are skillful innovators not "do-it-myself" types when it comes to implementing widespread changes?

Suggested Sources

Davenport, T. H., Prusak, L. & Wilson, H. J. (2003). Who's bringing you hot ideas and how are you responding? *Harvard Business Review, 81*(2), 58–64, 124.

Preker, A. S., & Harding, A. (Eds.). (2003). *Innovations in health service delivery: The corporatization of public hospitals.* Washington, DC: World Bank.

delayed. This extra effort can save time and money in the long run (Sullivan & Wolfe, 1996).

Third, teamwork is well suited to biopsychosocial care. Some organizations are concluding that the best way to keep patients healthy is to pay attention to their broad range of concerns. As physician Alan R. Zwerner advises:

> The dog ate a 100-year-old patient's glasses, and she's not eligible for a covered pair for another year? Give her a pair. Free. It could prevent a fall that would break her hip. There is a reward for quality care, patient satisfaction, and doing the right thing at the right time. (quoted by Azevedo, 1996, paragraph 22)

Teams can help provide care that simultaneously addresses a variety of issues such as patients' personal resources, nutrition, exercise, psychological well-being, and more. The object is not to replace physicians with teams, but to help physicians provide broader care than they can provide alone. Frasier and colleagues assert that interdisciplinary care teams can provide more complex biopsychosocial care than could any one caregiver (Frasier, Savard-Fenton, & Kotthopp, 1983).

Finally, team members may benefit from their involvement with co-workers. Teamwork allows professionals to share the immense responsibilities of health care, provide mutual support, and learn from each other (Abramson & Mizrahi, 1996). For example, an ethics committee can help guide caregivers and family members and relieve some of the pressure that an individual making a difficult decision alone might face (Harding, 1994). This support may be especially important as health care employees deal with the stress and uncertainty of providing care while adjusting to industry changes.

Difficulties and Drawbacks

None of this means teamwork is easy. Although teamwork presents many advantages, it has potential disadvantages as well. For one thing, teamwork takes time. If a quick decision is needed, an individual may be better qualified to make it. Some nurses in Julie Apker's (2001) study appreciated opportunities to be part of shared governance teams. Others said that there was not enough time for it. Said one nurse: "I don't feel it's fair to give someone a project if they don't have time" (quoted by Apker, 2001, p. 125). Furthermore, especially if they are rushed or intimidated, team members may resort to **groupthink,** that is, going along with ideas they would not normally support (Janis, 1972).

Teamwork can be particularly difficult in health care organizations. Professionals from different disciplines often have very different ideas about health, which creates the potential for competition and conflict (Abramson & Mizrahi, 1996). A study of 320 doctors and nurses revealed that 73% of the physicians felt they collaborated well with nurses, but only 33% of the nurses agreed (Thomas, Sexton, & Helmreich, 2003). The discrepancy may lie in their different expectations. Whereas physicians were mostly satisfied with the communication, nurses reported feeling left out and intimated about expressing themselves freely with doctors. Busy schedules make it hard to schedule meetings, especially if the organization is not supportive in allowing time for teamwork. There is also a question of leadership. Doctors are accustomed to calling the shots, but dominating group interactions may defeat the purpose of teamwork (Frasier et al., 1983; Sharf, 1984).

Communication Skill Builders: Working on Teams

Considering the advantages and difficulties of effective teamwork, experts present the following suggestions to help team members communicate effectively.

- During meetings, minimize distractions and sit so all members can easily see each other (Sharf, 1984).
- Establish ground rules for attendance, discussions, and decision making (Farley & Stoner, 1989).
- Before trying to solve a problem, make sure group members agree on the nature, importance, and cause of the problem.
- Make an effort to understand each group member's background and expertise. Often, one group of professionals is not clear on what another group is trained to do. For example, doctors surveyed were not able to accurately describe the duties of social workers (Abramson & Mizrahi, 1996).
- Be aware that conflict is a natural part of group work. Group members who remain committed to the task often work through the conflict to achieve a mutual sense of accomplishment (Northouse & Northouse, 1985).
- Encourage all group members to contribute ideas (Sharf, 1984).
- Be willing to compromise (Sharf, 1984).
- Summarize group discussions out loud to clarify the group's viewpoints and perspectives (Sharf, 1984).

Implications

Interdisciplinary teams may help organizations bridge communication gaps between people in different departments and professions. Teamwork may reduce the oversights that occur when workers focus on only one aspect of a job. Interdisciplinary teams may also be well qualified to provide biopsychosocial care and to develop services that combine cost-efficiency and quality care. Team members may find comfort and support in working together. However, they will be challenged to overcome time constraints, professional differences, and the tendency to simply go along with what other members want.

ROLE OF COMMUNICATION SPECIALISTS

Communication is a valuable tool for handling the tremendous challenges and rewards associated with health care organizations today. Communication specialists can help organizations meet the following goals:

- To keep morale up in this time of change and uncertainty.
- To encourage employees to participate in decision making.
- To integrate ideas from different disciplines.
- To avoid oversights by working as teams.
- To keep the public informed about services and health issues.
- To better understand health-related behaviors and communication patterns.

The term **communication specialist** is used in a general sense to refer to people with expertise in communicating face to face, in small groups, with large audiences, and/or through mass media. Health organizations often hire people with communication backgrounds to be part of public relations, community relations, in-house communication, human resources, personnel, education, and patient advocacy departments. In addition, nonprofit and public institutions hire people to conduct health communication research, educate the public, and work one-on-one with professionals and clients. Let's look at a few of the contributions communication specialists are qualified to make in the health industry.

Reducing Uncertainty

Uncertainty is especially stressful in today's health care system. With so many changes occurring, people may worry about job security and other factors (Porter-O'Grady et al., 1997). One way to bolster workplace morale is to keep employees well informed. Research suggests that health care employees who do not feel informed about changes in their organizations are typically less satisfied than others (Salem & Williams, 1984).

Communication specialists can help reduce uncertainty by developing a free flow of information throughout the organization. For example, in-house newsletters help to make minor policy changes known (major changes should be announced in person). They also include brief announcements about employees' professional activities; news of births, deaths, and marriages; and information about services available to employees, such as counseling or daycare. Some organizations also create and distribute newsletters tailored to consumers, physicians, office staff personnel, and other groups with a stake in the organization.

Bridging Boundaries

Physical distance, status differences, professional outlooks, and different working hours may make it difficult for health care employees to communicate regularly with each other (Ray & Miller, 1990). However, employees are more likely to work as teams if they are familiar with their co-workers and the work they do. Communication specialists can help bridge organizational gaps by coordinating opportunities for employees to get to know each other. Interpersonal relationships may reduce status differences and make it easier for employees to work as team members.

Providing Social Support

Communication can be a way to soothe feelings and encourage social support. Nurses in Smith, Droppleman, and Thomas's (1996) study reported being demoralized by a lack of support among their co-workers. Feelings of isolation may be even worse for people such as home health personnel and physician marketers whose duties require them to work outside the organization most of the time. Developing social events and other activities that include these personnel may reduce their sense of isolation.

Building Skills

Communication skills training can help employees assume new roles in the organization and manage the inevitable conflicts involved in change and teamwork. Nursing professors Mary Farley and Martha Stoner (1989) encourage nurses who wish to assume leadership roles to develop their skills in negotiation, team building, facilitating discussions, and sharing ideas. A nurse quoted by Apker (2001) attests: "My job is 25% direct patient care, 50% collaboration with others, and 25% documentation of care" (p. 127). Nurses are not the only ones whose success relies on communication. Communication skills training can include these topics:

- Managing conflict.
- Facilitating meetings and discussions.
- Listening and showing empathy.
- Writing effective memos and press releases.
- Handling complaints.
- Making presentations.
- Speaking in public.
- Speaking with the media.

Even basic communication skills such as phone courtesy and message taking can have an important influence on the organization's success. Communication skills affect the performance of every employee, not just those in leadership roles. Chuck Appleby (1997) reminds health care organizations that "everything is marketing, from greeters to nurses to the way someone's bill is paid" (p. 58). Courtesy and listening skills are essential.

Working With the Media

Part of a health organization's mission is to keep people informed about health issues that concern them. This may involve publicizing a medical study, a new treatment option, warning signs of disease, a special program or event, an interesting occurrence, or some other noteworthy topic.

Wise public relations professionals go beyond issuing pat press releases. Charles Salmon and Charles Atkin (2003) write:

> Public relations in the health domain has moved beyond the traditional distribution of press releases to aggressively place guests on talk shows, regularly feed feature writers with compelling news stories, and creatively stage pseudo-events to attract journalistic attention. (p. 463)

When communication specialists work effectively with the media, they are in a good position to help the public and to meet organizational goals. Here are some tips for establishing good media relations suggested by Hartman, Gellert, Higgins, Maxwell, and Lowery (1994):

- Establish close working relationships with media professionals.
- Learn to recognize newsworthy topics.
- Write professional-quality features and news stories.
- Know and respect media deadlines.
- Understand media objectives (such as promoting exciting stories, human interest items, and local news).
- Supply the media with good story ideas.
- Recommend and arrange interviews with knowledgeable persons.

Health care and media organizations stand to benefit when they work together. I know this from experience. As a health reporter on a city newspaper, I was invited to cover many human interest stories by hospital public relations personnel who knew the value of positive publicity. In one instance I was able to interview an Argentinean woman whose sight was restored by cataract surgery after 15 years of blindness. I'll never forget the woman's expression when the bandages were removed from her eyes. She shrieked in glee, grinned at her reflection in a mirror, and joyfully kissed her (slightly embarrassed) doctor on both cheeks. Readers loved the story, and the medical center received calls from people interested in more information about cataract surgery. When I later accepted a position in health care public relations, I made it a point to supply the media with great story ideas, arrange interviews with medical experts, and make the medical center library available to reporters. Everyone benefited—the media, the medical center, and the public.

Being visible in the media is good for business and helpful in educating people about health matters. But it has another benefit as well. It boosts the morale of people in the organization (Johnson, 1994). Most people love recognition, and despite the tireless efforts of many health care professionals they are not often recognized or singled out for thanks.

Managing Crises

By their very nature, health organizations are apt to be part of crises. As Kathleen Fearn-Banks (1996) defines it, a **crisis** is "a major occurrence with a potentially negative outcome affecting an organization, company, or industry, as well as its publics, products, services, or good name" (p. 1). In health care, the crisis usually has an external origin: a natural disaster, an accident, or an outbreak of contagious disease. In such cases, health care organizations (especially hospitals and medical centers) may be called upon to explain the crisis and keep the public informed about it. In some cases the crisis originates within the organization—a fire, a baby kidnapped from the nursery, charges of extortion. In any case, it is important to have a well-developed plan for handling crises, collecting information, and making information available to members of the organization, the media, and the public.

Communication Skill Builders: Crisis Management Crisis management is a job for communication specialists, especially those in public relations. For a helpful guide to preparing a crisis plan and managing publicity during a crisis, see Fearn-Banks's (1996) book *Crisis Communication.* Following are a few tips from the book:

- Let people within the organization know what constitutes a crisis and who to contact at the first sign of crisis.
- Educate people in the organization about how to handle a crisis, including who talks to the media and when, and who to call for information.
- Develop a crisis communication box, including key phone numbers, emergency supplies like paper and pens, the names of designated spokespersons, and plans for accommodating members of the media.
- Develop good relationships with media professionals before a crisis occurs, and do not play favorites during a crisis.
- Designate a primary spokesperson for the organization (usually the CEO) and help that person decide what information to release and how.

Promoting Community Outreach and Health Education

People in health care organizations possess important information, and most are willing to share what they know. Communication specialists can help by organizing community events, preparing educational materials, and developing speakers' bureaus composed of people who are willing to speak before school, church, and civic groups or be interviewed by the media (Morris, 1989). Communication specialists can coordinate speakers' bureaus and help participants plan their presentations, perfect their delivery skills, and prepare audiovisual materials.

Marketing

Marketing is a broad term concerned with assessing and meeting consumer needs. Many people equate marketing with advertising, but that is only part of the picture (and some marketers do not advertise at all). Marketing personnel not only promote the organization but also work within it to help improve services and plan for the future. As Philip Kotler and Roberta Clarke (1987) explain it, "marketing involves the organization in studying the target market's needs and wants, designing appropriate products and services, and using effective pricing, communication, and distribution to inform, motivate, and service the market" (p. 36).

Marketing personnel draw upon communication skills to collect information about consumer needs and preferences, help design and propose health care services, and promote the organization to consumers. Some health organizations are integrating their marketing philosophy into everyday operations. For example, if a medical center prides itself on "caring for the whole family," it may examine its policies (such as visiting hours and family accommodations) to make sure it is living up to that philosophy. Additionally, marketing personnel and others can work with employees to make sure everyone shares the philosophy and displays it in the service they provide.

Many health organizations are adjusting their thinking to consider that they have many types of "customers." Patients are customers, but so are physicians, other organizations, and even the organization's own employees. Success requires that each of these groups be satisfied (Mitka, 1996b).

Advocating for Patients

Some health care organizations offer opportunities for **patient advocates** who represent patients' interests and serve as liaisons between patients and health professionals (Greene, 1997; Maleskey, 1984). Patient advocates may be hired by patients directly, but most of them are employed by hospitals.

Communication specialists may qualify to be patient advocates. The job usually involves talking one-on-one with patients and their families to help explain hospital procedures, make sure patients are receiving adequate information, and handle any complaints they may have. A patient advocate's role is not to provide medical information (that should be provided by clinical personnel) but to make sure patients are well informed and satisfied.

Another form of patient advocacy is less direct. Communication specialists can help develop written information that is easy to read and understand. This information may describe services offered by the organization or procedures patients should follow. By working with clinicians, communication specialists can help assure that information is accurate and understandable.

Researching Health Communication

As we appreciate the impact of health communication it becomes especially important to understand how such communication occurs and what effects it has. Health communication scholars are involved in studying communication patterns, cultural expectations, satisfaction levels, goals, treatment outcomes, and more. Many health communication researchers work for academic or nonprofit institutions. However, their work has influence in much larger sectors, especially since most health care practitioners appreciate that they can save time, money, frustration, and even *lives* by communicating more effectively. A good example is Gillespie's (2001) study of asthma patients for Jewish National Treatment and Research Center. Administrators at the center commissioned Gillespie to study and interview asthma patients to gain a better understanding of how the patient perceive asthma, their satisfaction with care issues, and what they do and do not tell their doctors. Using her talents as a researcher, Gillespie was able to help the staff better understand patients' concerns and decisions. In this way and others, health communication scholars can help identify effective communication strategies and help people become more sensitive to communication cues and preferences. Considering this, health communication researchers are most effective if their conclusions are "timely, accessible, and make intuitive sense to the practitioner" (Brown, Stewart, & Ryan, 2003, p. 141).

Health educators, campaign designers, marketing professionals, and others have integrated communication research into their everyday jobs. They use research to gauge audience needs, preferences, abilities, and reactions before embarking on new projects. As new programs and campaigns take shape, they conduct preliminary research to test their effectiveness. This groundwork can help professionals adapt to audiences and avoid launching projects that will be needlessly costly, counterproductive, or just plain ignored. Finally, after a new project or campaign, research can demonstrate its influence and effectiveness. (See Chapters 12 and 13 for more on this topic.)

Implications

Communication specialists have many roles in health care. They can assist with communication within an organization and help establish communication between the organization and the community. Communication is a valuable means of reducing uncertainty, establishing professional relationships, and developing a sense of belonging. Communication specialists can help organizational members improve their speaking, listening, and presentation skills and help people adapt to new roles within health care organizations. Effective media relations is important for sharing information and marketing services as well as for managing organizational crises. Marketing specialists are involved with assessing community needs and tailoring services to meet those needs. At the same time, scholars and researcher/practitioners are increasing our understanding and mastery of health communication. (For more about careers in health communication, see Box 10.5.)

Box 10.5 RESOURCES
More About Careers in Health Communication

See the following websites for information about communication-related careers in the health care industry.

- American College of Health Care Administrators: www.achca.org
- American College of Health Care Executives: www.ache.org
- American Society for Health Care Marketing and Public Relations: www.stratsociety.org
- Association of University Programs in Health Administration: www.aupha.org
- International Association of Business Communicators: www.iabc.com
- National Institute of Health Center of Excellence in Cancer Communication Research: hcrl.slu.edu
- Patient Advocate Foundation: www.patientadvocate.org
- Public Relations Society of America: www.prsa.org
- Public Service Advertising Research Center: www.psaresearch.com

SUMMARY

Bureaucratic elements are still evident in most health organizations, and it is doubtful that they can or should be completely abandoned. However, the need to contain costs, respond to changing consumer demands, and diversify services has led some health organizations to change their patterns of leadership and teamwork. Many are reshaping their bureaucratic structures to become more adaptive and innovative. The new emphasis is on participative decision making, employee input, patient satisfaction, and interdisciplinary teamwork.

The factors that make health care such a dynamic field also make its members vulnerable to stress and conflict. Communication specialists can help organizations manage the uncertainty of change, assess consumer needs, make information available to the public, manage crises, and enhance patient satisfaction.

KEY TERMS

integrated health systems
bureaucracy
participative decision making (PDM)
rational-legal authority
professional prejudice
division of labor
team
groupthink
communication specialist
crisis
patient advocates

REVIEW QUESTIONS

1. What advice does Quint Studer (Box 10.1) offer for leading with purpose?
2. What current issues affect communication in health care organizations?
3. Why are some health care organizations breaking free of the bureaucratic model?
4. In your opinion, should physicians advertise? If not, why not? If so, should their ads adhere to particular regulations or ethical guidelines?
5. What are advantages and disadvantages of a vertical hierarchy?
6. What is meant by participative decision making (PDM)? What are the advantages of PDM? The challenges?
7. What suggestions do experts offer for training organizational leaders?
8. In what ways is rational-legal authority advantageous in health care organizations? In what ways is it limiting? What is one alternative?
9. How can professional prejudice affect communication between health workers?
10. What communication skills are involved in collaborative leadership?
11. How does a division of labor make people more productive? In what ways does it interfere with communication? What are some ways to unite people in pursuit of a common vision?
12. What are the advantages and disadvantages of relying on standardized, written communication in health settings? What are some ways health care organizations can use written communication effectively without going overboard with paperwork?
13. What are the qualities exhibited by innovative leaders in Davenport and colleagues' (2003) study (Box 10.4)?
14. What are the advantages of teamwork in today's health care organizations? What factors make teamwork difficult to achieve?
15. What are some tips for making teamwork productive?
16. What are some functions communication specialists are qualified to perform in health organizations? What are some tips for handling crises effectively?

CLASS ACTIVITY

Mending a Breach of Trust

After 8 years as a nurse, Leah took a prestigious job as a hospital administrator. She was determined to be accessible and sympathetic to employees, and she told them this every chance she got. Eventually, employees who had come to distrust the administration began to open up to Leah.

But all of that changed in one day. At a high-level meeting, Leah mentioned something an employee had told her in confidence. The unintended disclosure resulted in strained relations between the employee and her immediate supervisor, who was also at the meeting.

Word got around and soon employees were incensed that Leah had encouraged them to confide in her and then betrayed that trust. During a break-room conversation between several aides, one remarked, "If one of the other administrators had done this, I wouldn't be nearly so mad. You expect it from them. But for Leah to do it is a slap in the face. She knew better." Someone else took Leah's side, saying, "She made a mistake, but Leah has been more receptive than all the other administrators put together. Compared to them, she's still the best leader in the whole organization."

What Do You Think?

1. What would you do at this point if you were Leah?
2. Why would the employees be angrier at Leah than at another administrator who behaved the same way?
3. If you were an employee, what would you say to Leah?
4. Would you trust Leah with confidential information again? If so, under what conditions?
5. Describe the relational contract (implied rules for the relationship) between Leah and the employees:
   a. What rules were inherent in the contract?
   b. How were they formed and agreed upon?
   c. What are the implications for breaking the contract?

Part Five

HEALTH IN THE MEDIA

CHAPTER 11

Health Images in the Media

Do What Hubby Tells You?

When a group of British researchers found that submissive women were slightly less likely to have heart attacks than other women, they prepared a media release they felt was accurate, interesting, and readable. Many media organizations ran the release or suitable portions of it. However, others misconstrued the study to mean that women should return to being housewives. Headlines about the study admonished, "Put Down That Rolling Pin Darling, It's Bad For Your Heart," and "Do What Hubby Says and You'll Live Longer. Professor's Shock Advice to Women." The researchers were discouraged by journalists' handling of the story, calling the supposed link between submissiveness and housewifery "bewildering." (Deary, Whiteman, & Fowkes, 1998)

The researchers in this example say they learned a valuable lesson: Where health is concerned, the mass media is both friend and foe. The publicity helped the scientists share valuable knowledge and promote their work. However, inaccuracies and exaggerations made them wonder if some of the stories did more harm than good.

This chapter examines health's presence in mass communication. **Mass communication** is the dissemination of messages from one person (or one group of persons) to large numbers of people via transmitting devices called media (Biagi, 1999). These media include television, radio, computers, newspapers, magazines, billboards, video games, and other ways of presenting information to large audiences. The effects are hard to judge. However, most people believe mass-media messages have significant influence, especially in places like the United States where media use is a regular part of most people's lifestyle (Signorielli, 1993).

As you will see, there is evidence that media messages encourage people to overeat, doubt their self worth, drink alcohol, smoke, and neglect physical activity. However, mass communication is irreplaceable for getting health information to large numbers of people. It may enable them to better understand their own health and experience more control over their lives. Used wisely, the media can promote knowledge and healthy behaviors.

The chapter is divided into four parts. The first three examine health images in advertising, news, and entertainment. The final section discusses media literacy. Researchers often identify an association between media use and various behaviors (such as overeating and drinking). Remember that this does not prove the media, or the media alone, *cause* these behaviors. Mass-mediated messages are only one of many influences on health. Their effects are likely to be lessened or exaggerated by a range of other factors including personal preferences, culture, social networks, and health status.

ADVERTISING

"This product may cause headaches, drowsiness, stomach upset, liver problems, heartbeat irregularities . . ." You may wonder why prescription drug advertisements seem to list more *dis*claimers than claims. The answer lies in Food and Drug Administration (FDA) antideception regulations. In 1985, the FDA ruled that pharmaceutical companies may advertise their products to the public. However, if the advertisements present potential benefits of a drug, they must report potentially harmful side effects as well. Thus, in the name of fairness, for every promise of relief you are likely to hear a list of disagreeable outcomes you might also experience. Selling drugs in public venues such as the mass media is called **direct-to-consumer** advertising, as compared to physician-marketing, in which drugs are marketed to doctors who, in turn, make patients aware of them as they perceive a need to do so.

By the FDA decree, a pharmaceutical ad that makes no *positive* claims need not present *negative* information either. Consequently, you see drug advertisements that present the name of a product such as Claritan, and invite you to ask your doctor about it, but they do not tell you what the product does. In these instances, advertisers apparently feel that you will recognize the drug by name, that the disclaimers would be so discouraging as to scare people away, or that you will be curious enough to ask about or research the drug.

Reaction to advertising pharmaceutical drugs and other health-related products has been mixed. From one standpoint, advertisements for needed products and services are beneficial. They make people aware of health options by describing potential remedies for indigestion, asthma, allergies, depression, muscle aches, and the like. Consumers exposed to advertising messages may benefit from knowing such treatment options exist (Calfee, 2002).

Second, active competition inspires product development. The public presumably benefits when companies strive to offer the most appealing products. John Calfee (2002) reports that drug companies encouraged by public interest in cholesterol-reducing drugs increased research and development of these drugs in the 1990s. By targeting people at moderate risk for heart attacks, the drug companies were able to open up a new market and at the same time motivate consumers to visit their doctors and initiate preventive measures.

Finally, advertisements sometimes educate consumers about health matters beyond the scope of particular products. When Kellogg's began advertising its All-Bran cereal as a high-fiber way to reduce cancer risk, the percentage of Americans aware of fiber's benefits rose from 8.5% to 32% (Calfee, 1998).

Other companies have since begun to promote health information relevant to their products.

Although health information is beneficial within limits, it also has drawbacks. For one, expensive advertising drives up the price of health products. The latest figures available show that prescription drug prices rose about 15% a year from 1997 to 2001 ("Prescription Drug Expenditures," 2002). One *New York Times* reporter observed that pharmaceutical advertising went from "literally nothing" to $2.33 billion a year (Kane, 2003), this at a time when 57% of Americans feel drug prices are too high ("Harris Interactive Study," 2003).

Second, physicians worry that patients are romanced by drug advertisements into believing that high-priced "designer" drugs are the best and that every condition can be cured ("Drug Marketing," 2003). As a result, consumers may squander money on unnecessary medications, overmedicate themselves, and feel disappointed when their doctors do not prescribe the drugs they see in the media (Harper, 1997).

Finally, some experts worry that Americans are developing an unhealthy preoccupation with their own health, based largely on the amount of health care products and information now surrounding them. "We're not exactly a nation of hypochondriacs. But we're close," writes Jennifer Harper (1997).

Even advertisements that seem unrelated to health care often affect people's health by influencing social expectations about how they should behave, what they should eat and drink, and how they should appear (Ivinski, 1997). The remainder of this section expands on this idea with a discussion of advertising's impact on nutrition, alcohol, and body image.

Nutrition

It's been called the "coach potato physique," characterized by soft bulges where muscle ought to be. Television viewing is not the only factor contributing to unhealthy eating habits and obesity, but research supports that it often has an adverse affect on people's knowledge of nutrition and their food preferences. The prevalence of TV commercials for fatty and sugary foods may have serious implications for health, considering that overweight people are at risk for heart disease, cancer, diabetes, and sudden death (Bray, 1998).

Television seems to offer a triple punch to good nutrition. People usually burn few calories while watching TV, they have a tendency to snack while watching, and the commercials usually encourage consumption of nonnutritious foods (Dennison, Erb, & Jenkins, 2002; Signorielli & Staples, 1997). As one study concludes, in the content of television commercials, "fruits and vegetables are virtually nonexistent" (Kotz & Story, 1994, paragraph 11).

Obesity Television viewing has been linked to obesity, especially among women. Larry Tucker and Marilyn Bagwell (1991) found that women who watched 3 or 4 hours of television a day were twice as likely to be obese as women who watched 1 hour or less per day. In another study, women's body mass was positively associated with television viewing and fast-food consumption (Jeffery & French, 1998). The effect was most notable among high-income women, perhaps because they could afford to indulge in fast food and were encouraged by commercials to do so.

Effects on Children Children are exposed to large numbers of food advertisements. More than half the commercials during Saturday morning programming are for food, mostly high-sugar cereals (Kotz & Story, 1994). In 52.5 hours of children's programs, Kotz and Story counted 564 food commercials and only 10 nutrition-related public service announcements (PSAs). They estimate that audiences saw an average of one food commercial per every 5 minutes of viewing. After comparing the commercials to USDA dietary recommendations for children, Kotz and Story concluded: "The diet depicted in Saturday morning television programming is the antithesis of what is recommended for healthful eating for children" (paragraph 11).

Other studies support that children who watch a lot of TV tend to have mistaken ideas about nutrition. Nancy Signorielli and Jessica Staples (1997) asked fourth and fifth graders to list their favorite foods and to point out which foods they thought were most nutritious from comparisons such as "soda or fruit juice" and "fruit roll-ups or fresh fruit" (p. 295). They found that the more television children watched, the more likely they were to prefer unhealthy foods and to overrate the nutritional value of those foods.

Activity Levels It should be noted that advertising is not entirely to blame for the obesity linked to TV viewing. Some research suggests that the content of television may be less important than the sedentary nature of viewing. Children who watch 4 or more hours of TV a day have significantly higher body fat and body weight than children who engage in more vigorous pastimes, even when their calorie intake is similar (Andersen, Crespo, Bartlett, Cheskin, & Pratt, 1998). However, the sedentary nature of television watching may lead to other unhealthy behaviors as well. Youngsters who watch a lot of television are more likely to smoke (Gidwani, Sobol, DeJong, Perrin, & Gortmaker, 2002). The researchers speculate that extensive television viewing substitutes for physical activities and social development that might otherwise help teens avoid peer pressure.

Overall, it seems that commercials have some influence on food preferences and knowledge of nutrition, especially among children. See Box 11.1 for a theoretical understanding of media effects on children.

Alcohol

If media messages influence the way people eat, they are also likely to influence the way they drink. A study of prime-time programs suggests alcoholic beverages are shown more than any other drink (Mathios, Avery, Bisogni, & Shanahan, 1998). Televised sports events feature about one and a half beer commercials per hour (Madden & Grube, 1994), many of them depicting drinkers surrounded by beautiful women, fun-loving friends, and exotic locales.

What's more, youth under age 21 may be exposed to more of these ads than adults are. According to a study at Georgetown University, underage radio listeners heard 8% more ads for beer, 11.6% more ads for malt liquor, and 14.5% more ads for distilled alcoholic beverages such as whiskey, vodka, and tequila than listeners over the legal drinking age (Elliott, 2003). Young people from minority cultures may be especially aware of such messages. African-American youth see about 66% more beer and ale magazine advertisements and 81% more ads for distilled beverages than other youth (Elliott, 2003). This is because alcohol companies buy heavily in magazines aimed at young, minority audiences and because they employ rappers and youthful-appearing spokespersons designed to catch the attention of young people of color. Says the director of an alcohol and drug recovery center in San Francisco: "The models they use in the ads have to be 21, but they're the youngest 21-year-olds you'll ever see" (quoted by Green, 2003, p. 1C).

Source of Knowledge By third grade, children typically know a lot about alcoholic beverages based on what they have seen advertised (Austin & Nach-Ferguson, 1995). What's more, children with brand-name knowledge (the ability to link brand names with certain types of alcohol) are more likely than others to try alcohol (Mastro & Atkin, 2002). The implication is that advertising has an influence on what children know, and perhaps on what they do, even when the ads are not intended for them.

Glamorized Images Excessive alcohol consumption poses several health threats. Heavy drinkers risk liver damage, hypertension, and strokes, and are more likely to hurt others (and to be hurt) in accidents and acts of violence (Nestle, 1997). Additionally, the babies of pregnant women who drink are at risk for low birth weight and fetal alcohol syndrome (Markowitz & Grossman, 1998). Considering these risks, beer companies are sometimes criticized for glamorizing alcohol consumption by portraying drinking episodes as fun and sexy (Parker, 1998).

Some people worry that beer ads showing "the good life" will affect young people's views about drinking. Research supports that lifestyle-oriented beer advertisements are more appealing to adolescents than ads focusing on product qualities like taste. Adolescents surveyed by Kathleen Kelly and Ruth Edwards (1998) preferred beer ads showing fun lifestyles, but this preference was not linked to the youths' intention to drink. Other research suggests young people (especially boys) *may* be more likely to drink if they find beer commercials appealing (Grube & Wallack, 1994; Slater et al., 1997).

Betty Parker (1998) studied college students' reactions to beer commercials. She found that some students considered the commercials unrealistic based on their own experiences, but others regarded the commercials as fairly accurate, and even as instructional guides for how to enjoy drinking.

Box 11.1 THEORETICAL FOUNDATIONS
Cultivation Theory and Social Comparison Theory

In a video about sexist images in advertising (*Killing Us Softly 3*), Jean Kilbourne observes that people frequently tell her they are not affected by the media. "Of course, they are usually standing there in their Gap t-shirt while they say this," she laughs.

The fact is that we are all affected by the media to varying extents. The two theories described here—cultivation theory and social comparison theory—consider how media messages influence our attitudes and expectations about the world.

Cultivation theory helps explain why children may be especially vulnerable to advertising messages. According to **cultivation theory,** people develop beliefs about the world based on a complex array of influences, including the media. Media influence is not uniform or automatic, but it is likely to be most profound if (a) media images are highly consistent, (b) people are exposed to large amounts of media, and (c) these people have a limited basis for evaluating what they see and hear (Gerbner, Gross, Morgan, & Signorielli, 1994). To clarify, consider that children have fewer experiences and less knowledge than adults. Because of this, they are less able to perceive that media images may be wrong or unrealistic. The same principle would hold true if you watched a documentary about a faraway land about which you knew very little. People familiar with that land might see inaccuracies in the documentary that you would be unable to identify.

The effect is compounded among high media users because not only is their exposure high, but the more time they spend tuned into mass media, the less opportunity they have to experience activities that might provide a basis for comparison. Researchers in Thailand found that children who watched TV more than their peers were more likely to think television portrayals were realistic and to want to be part of TV families (Jantarakolica, Komolsevin, & Speece, 2002). Children in the United States typically spend more time watching television than any activity except sleep, and viewing is highest among boys and minorities (Signorielli & Staples, 1997).

Social comparison theory helps explain why people yearn to emulate the models they see in the media. Proposed by Leon Festinger (1957), social comparison theory suggests that people judge themselves largely in comparison to others. Want to know if you are attractive, popular, healthy, or smart? The only answer may lie in how you stack up to the people around you.

Social comparisons can be useful when they enhance self-esteem or serve as the basis for reasonable self-improvement. However, they become dysfunctional when the comparison establishes an unrealistic standard (like being super-model thin or weight-lifter strong). Ironically, even those with super-model looks are not spared from criticism. When actress Alicia Silverstone appeared a few pounds heavier than usual at the Academy Awards in 1996, tabloids mocked her cruelly. In reference to her appearance in Batman and Robin, headlines taunted: "Batman and Fatgirl" and "Look Out Batman! Here Comes Buttgirl" (Schneider, 1996).

What Do You Think?

1. In what ways are you influenced by media messages?
2. If you are around children, what reactions do you observe as they are exposed to messages in the media?
3. How do you think we can minimize the effects of media images that establish unrealistic standards of attractiveness?

Suggested Sources

Buunk, B., & Gibbons, F. X. (1997). *Health, coping, and well-being: Perspectives from social comparison theory*. Mahwah, NJ: Lawrence Erlbaum.

Festinger, L. (1957). *A theory of cognitive dissonance*. Stanford, CA: Stanford University Press.

Gerbner, G. (1990). Advancing on the path of righteousness (maybe). In N. Signorielli & M. Morgan (Eds.), *Cultivation analysis: New directions in media effects research.* Newbury Park, CA: Sage.

Gerbner, G., Gross, L., Morgan, M., & Signorelli, N. (1994). *Living with television: The dynamics of the cultivation process.* In J. Bryant & D. Zillmann (Eds.), *Perspectives on media effects* (pp. 17–40). Hillsdale, NJ: Lawrence Erlbaum.

Kilbourne, J. (2000). *Killing us softly 3: Advertising's image of women.* Media Education Foundation.

Shanahan, J., & Morgan, M. (1999). *Television and its viewers: Cultivation theory and research.* Cambridge, UK: Cambridge University Press.

Suls, J. M., & Wheeler, L. (Eds.). (2000). *Handbook of social comparison: Theory and research.* New York: Plenum.

Programming Content Alcohol figures prominently in the TV programs during which beer commercials appear. Mathios and colleagues (1998) counted 555 alcohol incidents in 276 prime-time programs. In the programs, underage drinkers were usually portrayed as weak and unlikable. However, adult drinkers were often rich and attractive (especially those shown drinking wine). The authors suggest that these programs seem to discourage teen drinking at the same time they portray adult drinkers as positive role models. Combined with commercial images of fun-loving drinkers, these messages may be stiff competition for antidrinking campaigns.

The good news is that, although "responsible drinking" messages are far outnumbered by glamorous portrayals, they may have some influence as well. Itzhak Yanovitzky and Jo Stryker (2001) observed that, over time, binge drinking among youth decreased in the midst of news coverage about its harmful effects. The downturn is not likely to continue, however, unless the media can keep the dangers of binge drinking on the public agenda.

Body Images

Consumers are repetitiously warned by advertisers that their skin, weight, hair style, clothing, and teeth are "problem areas" requiring vigorous and immediate attention—at a price. Theorists call this **pathologizing the human body,** making natural functions seem weird and unnatural (Wood, 1999). In short, advertisers are accused of making people feel badly about themselves so they will be willing to pay for "needed" changes.

Adolescents are particularly susceptible to these messages (Kowalski, 1997). With the physical and social changes of adolescence comes a heightened self-consciousness that makes it easy to escalate (and capitalize on) teens' insecurity. Advertisers often encourage an obsessive concern with physical appearance, sometimes to the detriment of people's health and self-esteem.

"Advertisers realize that having your period is the grossest thing in the world, and they want to help," quips Ann Hodgman (1998, paragraph 6). "As long as Procter & Gamble can scare a teen into thinking that [a boy] can see her bulky maxi through her dress, she'll buy Always . . . If a teen wasn't obsessing about it before, Tampax wants her to start."

Advertisements aimed at teens are working, judging by sales figures and the number of products on the market. Teenagers in the United States spend about $70 billion annually on clothes (Williams, 2003). Additionally, teens are encouraged to buy (or convince their parents to buy) skin care creams, lotions, powders, perfume, makeup, shaving cream, shampoo, bath oil, mouthwash, toothpaste, and more. Bardbard (1993) points out that—aside from making teens feel unattractive without them—these products can be health risks when they cause rashes, hives, eye irritation, and other reactions.

Media images affect how we regard our bodies. For most people, it would be difficult and unhealthy to have a fashion model physique. Although the average American woman wears a size 12, the average fashion model wears a size 0 or 2 (Betts, 2002). And even they feel fat. Some 73% of female models are underweight by medical standards, but most of them wish they could be 20% thinner ("Models "R" Us, 1992). Advertisers are accused of establishing unrealistic standards for attractiveness, then raking in profits as people strive to measure up (Martin & Gentry, 1997).

Health Effects Unrealistic standards can have serious health consequences. Studies indicate that two thirds of women and one third of men are unhappy with their weight and body shape (see Rabak-Wagener, Eickhoff-Shemek, & Kelly-Vance, 1998).

Negative body image contributes to the number of people who starve themselves or eat excessively and then purge with vomiting or laxatives. About 8 million Americans (90% of them female) suffer from eating disorders, which may damage their hearts and livers, make their bones brittle, and even kill them (Ho, 2003). Although eating disorders often start in adolescence, they do not end there. Most women who die from eating disorders are older than 45 ("Disappearing Act," 1998). In fact, one reason children are likely to feel their bodies are inferior is because their parents are preoccupied about their own weight and appearance (Maynard, 1998).

Steroid abuse is another problem as people try to become more muscular and athletic. More than 1 million Americans (nearly half of them adolescents) have abused steroids (Yesalis, Barsukiewicz, Kopstein, & Bahrke, 1997; Yesalis, Kennedy, Kopstein, & Bahrke, 1993). The risks of steroid abuse include cardiovascular disease, liver damage, hair loss, sterility, aggressiveness, and depression.

Many people link eating disorders and steroid abuse to media exposure. In one year's time, health and bodybuilding magazines promoted about 311 products promising to stimulate muscle growth (Philen, Ortiz, Auerbach, & Falk, 1992). Many of the products promoted their similarity to steroids and were judged by experts to be either useless or potentially harmful. Other culprits are misleading diet books and websites that promise people will lose weight through unhealthy (and ineffective) means such as skipping meals or eating only one type of food (like popcorn or grapefruit). Michael Fumento (1998) reports that the only healthy, long-term way to lose weight is to eat less, eat healthy foods, and exercise more. Nevertheless, outlandish promotions like the Chocolate Lovers' Diet continue to make money for their creators.

Eternal Hope Why do people keep buying into what the media sells? There is some evidence that people are hopeful when they see idealized models and are optimistic that they can attain the same look. Philip Myers and Frank Biocca (1992) were surprised when female college students in their study reacted favorably to television programs and commercials featuring slender women. Immediately after viewing these images, most viewers were more elated than depressed, and they tended to consider *themselves* to be thinner than usual. The researchers concluded that media images make idealized body shapes

BOX 11.2 RESOURCES
More About Media Effects on Children

- Groesz, L. M., Levine, M. P., & Murnen, S. K. (2002, January). The effect of experimental presentation of thin media images on body satisfaction: A meta-analytic review. *International Journal of Eating Disorders, 31,* 1–16.
- Livingstone, S., & Bovill, M. (Eds.). (2001). *Children and their changing media environment: A European comparative study.* Mahwah, NJ: Lawrence Erlbaum.
- Sands, E. R., & Wardel, J. (2003). Internalization of ideal body shapes in 9–12 year old girls. *International Journal of Eating Disorders, 33*(2), 193–204.
- Von Feilitzen, C., & Carlsson, U. (1996). *Children and media: Image, education and participation.* Goteborg, Sweden: UNESCO.

seem attainable, causing an optimism that may later turn to disappointment because it is infeasible for most people to look like that.

Implications

There are advertisements everywhere you turn, each trying to exert its own influence. Advertising can be helpful if it provides useful information and leads to more affordable and better products. However, it may be harmful when it inspires unrealistic hopes and fears, promotes unhealthy behaviors, and creates artificial needs. Advertisements seem to influence people's perceptions about nutrition, drinking, and the perfect body. Children and adolescents may be especially susceptible to the ideas cultivated by persuasive media messages and the standards set by "idealized" models. For more about the media's effects on children, see Box 11.2.

NEWS COVERAGE

When America's Health Network announced it would show a live Internet broadcast of a woman giving birth in June 1998, more than 50,000 curious viewers logged on to witness the event (Charski, 1998). From births to cancer to overall fitness, health is news. Health issues comprise about 51% of national TV news and 7% of local TV news ("Health Ranks Fifth," 1998). Additionally, health is the topic of special-interest television channels, magazines, books, and radio advice programs.

Madge Kaplan, a health news reporter on the public radio program *Marketplace,* says covering health issues is "a rich, exciting and suspenseful journey" (Kaplan, 2003, paragraph 4). "My hope is that health care reporting stays closely tied to the central purpose of health care—service to patients. . . . This means we need to do a better job illustrating our story subjects' mulitidimensional character" (paragraph 13).

Medical innovations, public interest in health, and the threat of bioterrorism have made health big news. In Box 11.3, Vicki Freimuth, former director of communication at the Centers for Disease Control and Prevention, tells about the backstage efforts to supply media professionals with information during the anthrax and SARS threats.

Americans have access to more health information than ever before. The main criticism of health news is that, in the rush to provide the latest information, media professionals sometimes oversell scientific findings and overlook ongoing, everyday concerns. This section examines health news in terms of accuracy and sensationalism and discusses the advantages of media coverage. It concludes with a discussion of interactive technology, which is revolutionizing the way people get health information.

Accuracy

Although many media organizations do an admirable job of informing the public about health issues, a sizable number of health stories are misleading and exaggerated. When researchers compared 60 scientific studies to newspaper and magazine stories about them, they found 42 inaccuracies (Moyer, Greener, Beauvais, & Salovey, 1995). The most common news errors occur when writers overgeneralize the results of medical studies. For instance, a study of elderly women may be reported simply as a study about woman or the elderly, although the health concerns of these populations may be significantly different. Such inaccuracies are particularly troubling since it is often difficult for readers to verify scientific information for themselves. Of the news items studied by Moyer and colleagues, 35% did not cite the original story, and 53% gave incomplete or misleading citation information.

One worry is that overly optimistic news about medical research will give people false hopes. Jon Cohen (1997) quotes headlines in major publications suggesting an imminent cure for AIDS ("When AIDS Ends" in the *New York Times Magazine* and the "The End of AIDS?" in *Newsweek*). Cohen writes: "If treatments don't live up to unrealistic expectations, researchers fear a public backlash against medical science" (paragraph 2). Premature reports about cures for cancer raise the same fear (Arnst, 1998).

Sometimes news items seem to cater to commercial interests. In a study of magazines written for African-American women, researchers found 1,500 tobacco advertisements but only 9 articles about smoking as a cause of cancer (Hoffman-Goetz, Gerlach, Marino, & Mills, 1997). Considering that cancer is the leading cause of death among elderly African-American women, the researchers suggest that editorial decisions were made in advertisers' interest rather than readers'.

Box 11.3 PERSPECTIVES
Media Relations at the CDC

From 1996 through June 2003, I was the Director of Communication at the Centers for Disease Control and Prevention (CDC), the world's premier public health agency. My responsibilities included media relations and health communication. During those 7 years the CDC's visibility increased dramatically as a result of the anthrax attacks in the fall of 2001 followed by an intensified West Nile virus outbreak in the summer of 2002 and the introduction of a brand new virus, SARS, in the spring of 2003. CDC is the federal agency charged with protecting the health and safety of the American people. It is headquartered in Atlanta but has employees in 47 states and 45 countries across the world. Although CDC works on a broad array of health issues, it is best known for its epidemiology team, a group the media often refers to as "disease detectives," who are dispatched across the country and even around the world when a new outbreak is detected. CDC's history includes such well-known cases as HIV, toxic shock syndrome, Legionnaire's disease; and Ebola.

Vicki S. Freimuth, Ph.D.

This brief essay focuses on the media relations function in CDC's Office of Communication. A staff of nine professional media relations specialists has oversight of the press work for the entire agency even though each of CDC's 12 centers has its own communication office and small media relations staff. CDC is one of the agencies that reports to the Department of Health and Human Services (DHHS) so media relations also are coordinated through DHHS's Office of Public Affairs. In addition, CDC's work is highly interrelated with the health departments of individual states. Every outbreak happens locally and is commonly responded to locally. When the health problem exceeds local capacity or crosses several jurisdictional boundaries, the CDC is invited to assist.

Obviously such a complex network of involved agencies poses a *collaboration challenge.* CDC's media relations division responds to this challenge in a number of ways. First, the central office of communication led an effort across the agency to establish policies, procedures, and relationships to ensure coordination across all centers in the agencies. These policies address such issues as when press interviews need to be cleared at the agency level and at DHHS level, how upcoming events and activities will be communicated through these levels, and how centers will coordinate among themselves when issues cross their organizational lines.

Relationships are probably more important than policies for effective coordination. Communication between the central office and the centers occurs frequently. The central office is organized around a type of beat system so individual press officers work very closely with each center, developing relationships and an understanding of their issues.

Coordination with the state health departments focuses around an organization that CDC supports, the National Public Health Information Coalition (NPHIC), composed of the chief information officer for each of the 50 states. CDC communication staff attends their annual meeting, holds regular conference calls with them, and uses an e-mail list to quickly notify them of breaking news from the agency.

DHHS also has a set of policies and procedures that govern coordination between the cabinet level office of communication and all the agencies that report to it. In addition, multiple e-mails and phone calls occur between CDC and DHHS staff on a daily basis.

The second challenge I want to address is *responding to public health crises.* CDC mobilized to serve media during several crisis periods in the last 2 years. The crisis that taxed the agency the most was the anthrax attacks occurring in the wake of September 11. The media interest in these events was unprecedented. These attacks were the first major acts of bioterrorism the country experienced. Newsrooms deployed everybody to cover them. CDC experienced a torrent of inquiries from reporters, many of whom had never contacted the agency before. CDC communication staff took several steps to try to manage these events. First, we increased the hours of operation. Our normal 8:30 to 6:00 hours were increased to 14-hour days, seven days a week. Drawing on the media relations staff from the CDC centers, we tripled the size of the staff responding to the media and created two separate teams who split the week's hours. One team worked Sunday through Wednesday and the other worked Wednesday through Saturday. Every staff had to adapt to new schedules, sharing offices and computers, and quickly assimilating the events that had occurred during their three days off.

Second, we developed systems to manage the rapidly changing and expanding information that was being generated in response to the crisis. When the anthrax attacks began, there were only a handful of studies on naturally occurring anthrax. Protocols on laboratory testing, environmental sampling, diagnosis, and treatment had to be developed rapidly and disseminated to many audiences. The media staff had to be aware and knowledgeable of these issues as the press demanded the information as rapidly as it was created. Internal scientific briefings were held twice a day and these had to be covered by press officers and converted

continued

Box 11.3 PERSPECTIVES
Media Relations at the CDC, *continued*

to additional questions and answers and added to a rapidly expanding database that could be accessed electronically by other media staff to answer press questions.

Third, we developed approaches to try to get ahead of the demands from the media by holding daily telephone press briefings, which would regularly attract 100 key reporters with many more accessing the archived audio and written transcripts of these briefings. Fourth, in addition to the energy spent in responding to reporters' needs, we also had to read and analyze the output from the media. While CDC had a system for clipping and analyzing media coverage during routine operations, it could not handle the volume of coverage these attacks generated. More staff had to be devoted to the task of reading, analyzing, and creating brief summaries for media relations staff and key spokespeople.

It was more than 3 months before the interest in these attacks subsided enough to return to regular staffing levels. We were determined to use these experiences to create emergency response systems to respond more effectively the next time. We created the communication emergency response system, which consists of 10 teams, each with responsibility for either an audience such as the media or a function such as the Web. This system has been deployed successfully to manage the communication during the West Nile and SARS outbreaks.

The media team refined many of the approaches it created during the anthrax attacks. If some new disease is detected as was the case with SARS, CDC immediately holds a press conference, now simultaneously face-to face as well as via telephone, where a scientist shares what the agency knows now about the issue, what is unknown, and what the agency is doing to close that gap. A new state of the art press room has been established at CDC to accommodate these press conferences. Knowledge management information systems have been created to make the gathering and accessing of rapidly changing information more efficient. The expanded media relations staff, hastily assembled during the anthrax attacks, has been institutionalized so that it can be assembled in

Sensationalism

The media is also criticized for favoring sensational health news rather than useful information about everyday concerns. For example, mass media professionals traditionally give children's health low priority (Ludtke & Trost, 1998). When they do present pediatric health news, it usually involves dying children or rare diseases rather than everyday concerns such as safety and prevention (Prabhu, Duffy, & Stapleton, 1996). Furthermore, among all ages, accidental hours. The media relations Web page has been integrated with the overall CDC's Web information on emergencies so rapidly changing information such as case counts can be updated in one place and reporters will not be frustrated by conflicting information. The question and answer databases, used by media relations staff, also become the FAQs on the Web.

These two challenges are among many faced by the media relations staff at the CDC. They also are typical of professionals working in the role of gatekeepers between public agencies and the media.

—Vicki S. Freimuth, PhD, Department of Speech Communication and Grady College of Journalism, University of Georgia

About the Author

Vicki Freimuth (PhD, Florida State University, 1974) is a professor at the University of Georgia. Her major research interests center on health communication, specifically the role of communication in health promotion. Before joining the faculty at the University of Georgia, she served as director of communication at the Centers for Disease Control and Prevention (CDC). Prior to that position, she was professor and director of the health communication program at the University of Maryland. She is the author of *Searching for Health Information,* co-editor of *AIDS: Communication Perspectives* and numerous chapters and articles in communication and medical publications. Freimuth has received grants from several organizations, including the National Cancer Institute. She was selected as the first Outstanding Health Communication Scholar by the International Communication Association and the National Communication Association and was selected as the Woman of the Year at the University of Maryland in 1990. She has provided consultation to many organizations including the U.S. Agency for International Development, the World Health Organization, the World Bank, the National Cancer Institute, the National Eye Institute, and the Robert Wood Johnson Foundation.

and violent deaths get more than their share of news coverage, while deaths from cancer and heart disease, although more prevalent, receive less media attention (Frost, Frank, & Maibach, 1997).

In some instances, snappy headlines have little to do with scientific evidence. A study conducted for *Consumer Research Magazine* revealed that women's magazines like *Redbook, Mademoiselle, McCall's,* and *Better Homes and Gardens* published frightening health stories without documentation to back them up (Zipperer, 1997). Menacing headlines included, "Will Pollution Ruin Your

Chance of Having a Baby?" and "Is Your Lawn Making You Sick?" although there is little or no scientific evidence that the implied risks actually exist.

Advantages

Despite the criticisms, health news does offer several advantages. Media organizations are credited with increasing people's awareness about health. And even when medical news is not what scientists would wish, its presence keeps health on the public agenda and garners support for medical science (Deary, Whiteman, & Fowkes, 1998).

It should also be said that news writers are not entirely to blame for misleading health coverage. The fault lies partly with the nature of news and the nature of science. It is the nature of news to be unusual and recent (Taubes, 1998). The public is hungry for current and interesting information, and media organizations strive to provide it. However, it is the nature of science to be meticulous and cautious, weighing diverse evidence over long periods of time (Taubes, 1998). Consequently, news writers are at a disadvantage trying to cover scientific news accurately. The latest study may reach different conclusions than the study before it or after it. Science is full of reliable accounts that, for one reason or another, arrive at different conclusions. News writers who report up-to-date information from medical science are apt to find themselves presenting contradictory information at a later date.

Furthermore, reporters may be ill prepared to meet the extraordinary challenges health coverage presents. Medical terminology and statistical analyses make medical science difficult to understand and interpret, and comparatively few reporters are trained to do so (Ludtke & Trost, 1998). Although health is the fifth most common subject of local TV news (behind crime, weather, accidents, and human interest stories), 94% of local stations do *not* have designated health reporters. Instead, they rely on anchors or reporters who are available when stories arise ("Health Ranks Fifth," 1998). On the bright side, with many sources of health news available, the chances are greater that people can evaluate and compare information, judging for themselves what is credible and useful (Eng et al., 1998).

Communication Skill Builders: Presenting Health News

Here are some suggestions that Melissa Ludtke and Cathy Trost (1998) offer to help media news writers present fair coverage:

- *Favor the factual over the sensational and trendy.*
- *Do not allow ongoing issues to fade from coverage.* "Put a fresh face on coverage of long-standing health issues like asthma, lead poisoning and infant mortality" (paragraph 20).
- *Never rely on just one source.* Consult a number of experts; read a variety of reliable literature.

BOX 11.4 RESOURCES
Learning Opportunities for Health Journalists

If you are considering a career covering health news you may wish to become familiar with the following organizations and professional development opportunities.

- Association for Education in Journalism and Mass Communication: aejmc.org
- Broadcast Education Association: www.beaweb.org
- Foundation for American Communications: www.facsnet.org
- Henry J. Kaiser Media Fellowships for Health: www.kff.org/docs/fellowships/fih2000.html
- Knight Center for Specialized Journalism Fellowships: www.knightcenter.umd.edu
- Knight Science Journalism Fellowships: web.mit.edu/knight.science
- National Association of Broadcasters: www.nab.org
- National Press Foundation: www.nationalpress.org

- *Set the record straight.* If a health news item is revealed to be untrue or misleading, update the public.

Also see Box 11.4 for opportunities to develop your skills as a health news journalist.

In the next section we consider a relatively new medium in mass dissemination of health messages—the computer.

Communication Technology: Interactive Health Information

Predictions are that Americans will soon be using interactive "teleputers" to conduct research, play games, order take-out food, watch movies and television programs, correspond with people, and more (Biagi, 1999). These teleputers would combine the functions of computers, telephones, and televisions, making it easier than ever to send and receive information on nearly any topic. Computer use has already expanded to include the Internet and e-mail. Around the world, more than 580 million people use the Internet, and health information is one of the most popular search topics ("Global Internet Population," 2003).

Computer-based communication is more interactive than traditional mass media, meaning that it allows people to send and receive messages nearly simultaneously (Street, 1997). Rather than simply receiving mass-mediated messages, users can respond to them, ask questions, request more information, and choose how and when they wish to receive information. For example, individuals with cancer can communicate with others, review case studies, and experiment with computer simulations of various treatments such as radiation or chemotherapy (Manning, 1997).

Advantages Computerized communication has several advantages, according to the book *Health Promotion and Interactive Technology* (Street, Gold, & Manning, 1997):

- The opportunity for feedback and response improves the chances for effective communication.
- The interactive nature of computerized information makes it highly memorable and engaging. Children with asthma who took part in an interactive computer program about asthma subsequently displayed fewer symptoms, needed less medication, and required fewer visits to the emergency room than children exposed to printed materials (Krishna et al., 2003).
- Information is quickly available when consumers need or want it, accommodating different needs and schedules.
- To some extent, formats (graphics, color, print size) can be tailored to meet the needs of people with special needs and preferences.
- People have more control over what they receive. For instance, people may use computers as televisions, with the option to edit out commercials or portions of programs.
- Computer users can easily store information, replay items of interest, and forward information to others.

These advantages signal an empowerment on the part of media users that may affect their health knowledge and behaviors.

Drawbacks Computer-mediated communication is not without drawbacks, however:

- Although format changes are available, access for people with visual disabilities is still discouragingly limited. For example, only about 19% of health-related websites offer automated screen readers (Davis, 2002). These screen readers, run by computer software, allow people to hear a voice that reads the contents of the webpage and describes the graphics.
- Even when access is available, content may not be especially helpful. Among 36 websites designed to educate teenagers about sexually transmitted diseases, only 2 provided information on how to negotiate with partners for safer sex practices (Keller, Labelle, Karimi, & Gupta, 2002).
- Online communication typically occurs without touching or watching other human beings, which limits nonverbal feedback and may add to people's sense of isolation (Quittner, 1995).

- Access is limited to people who have computers and know how to use them. Most researchers agree that using computers has become a fairly simple process. However, underprivileged populations are usually the most in need of health information but the last to get information technology (Eng et al., 1998). Computer access is 3 times greater among Caucasian children in the United States than among African Americans and Hispanics (Rimal & Flora, 1997). The good news is that underprivileged persons tend to make good use of technology when it is made available to them (Eng et al.; Hawkins et al., 1997).
- Important messages may be lost in the vast amount of information available. (See the section on tailored health messages in Chapter 12.)
- Technology specialist Tony Gorry points out that more information and quicker access is not always beneficial. For some people, multimedia is "confusing, disturbing, and may in fact not be understood" ("Reflections," 1997, p. 224).
- It is difficult to govern the content of computer-based information. Hundreds of fraudulent health products are already for sale via the World Wide Web ("Web Sweep Finds," 1997). These and other health scams cost Americans about $27 billion a year (Kowalski, 1997).

Communication Skill Builders: Using the Internet

Because there is reliable and unreliable health information on the Internet, experts offer the following suggestions:

- Do not trust information if there is no author or sponsor or if the name given is not well known.
- Look for another source if the sponsors are trying to sell a product rather than offer free information. Plenty of websites make reliable health information available free.
- Do not rely on information if it is dated, references are missing, or references do not seem legitimate.
- Keep in mind that legitimate health practitioners do not speak in terms of "secret formulas" or "miraculous cures." Only con artists use such language (Kowalski, 1997).
- Do not be convinced by case studies of "actual" satisfied customers. An isolated case does not prove a product's effectiveness, and this may not be an actual customer (Kowalski, 1997).
- Do your own research. Read medical journal articles. Ask health professionals.
- Read the fine print very carefully. Look for disclaimers and vague wording.
- Report suspicious claims to the Federal Trade Commission, Better Business Bureau, or state attorney general's office (Kowalski, 1997).

Implications

Research shows that media organizations sometimes distort scientific findings, favor sensational stories over more useful information, and allow advertisers to influence editorial content. Although some of these shortfalls can be improved, others are inherent in the effort to provide up-to-date coverage of medical science. All in all, consumers may do well to approach media news with a healthy skepticism, but they should also keep in mind that the media can be valuable sources of health information (Deary et al., 1998).

People with access to computers are now able to tap into abundant sources of health information, communicate quickly with others, and tailor information to suit their needs. The challenge is to make technology available to the people who most need it, help people distinguish between reliable and unreliable information, and continue to find ways to make important information known to large numbers of people.

ENTERTAINMENT

Medical settings have long been popular fare for entertainment programs. Shows like *Marcus Welby* and *M*A*S*H* were forerunners of today's popular medical dramas. This section examines how medical care and health issues are portrayed in entertainment programming, commercial influences on entertainment, and the possibilities for pro-social programming.

Portrayals of Health-Related Behaviors

The mad scientist cackles as he prepares his next victim. The music rises, the lights dim . . . Characterizations like this are fun, but they are also suggestive. People base their perceptions of mental illness and other health concerns partly on fictional portrayals. In her book, *Mass Media Images and Impact on Health,* Signorielli (1993) reviews how health is depicted in the media. Her analysis of the literature suggests that today's media decision makers are more sensitive to health issues than in the past, but portrayals of many health-related behaviors are still distorted. This section examines how mental illness, disabilities, sex, and violence are depicted in entertainment programming.

Mental Illness One media distortion is the portrayal of mentally ill persons as violent and dangerous. Traditionally, about 72% of mentally ill characters in prime-time programs are prone to violence (Willwerth, 1993). In reality, only about 11% of mentally ill persons are violent, which is roughly equal to the proportion of violent people in the overall population. James Willwerth attests: "In reality, most mentally ill patients are withdrawn, frightened and passive" (paragraph 6). Nevertheless, media programs are fond of featuring diabolically insane characters. Laurel Fruth and Allan Padderud (1985) identify a long-standing soap opera traditional of depicting mentally ill characters as "tense, cold, dangerous individuals" (p. 387).

Disabilities Television also tends to perpetuate stereotypes about people with physical disabilities. Persons with physical disabilities are vastly underrepresented in TV programs, and when they are depicted, their disabilities are usually the focus of attention (Signorielli, 1993). In short, people with disabilities are not usually portrayed as "normal" persons on TV.

Disabilities are more common in the movies than on television, especially since the 1970s. Stephen Safran (1998) reports that the number of characters with disabilities in Academy Award–winning movies has risen dramatically over the years. In the 1990s, disabilities were depicted in 43% of the movies that won Best Picture, Best Actor, or Best Actress awards. Notable were the amputee Lieutenant Dan in *Forrest Gump,* the wheelchair-bound hero in *Coming Home,* and the mute musician in *The Piano.* According to Safran's study, psychiatric disorders are proportionately overrepresented in award-winning movies, whereas few children with physical or intellectual disabilities have been depicted. Although portrayals are still somewhat distorted, Safran (1998) predicts that increased visibility will help persons with disabilities gain more public acceptance.

Overall, the goal of many health advocates is to portray people with physical and mental disabilities as relatively normal (which they are). Ironically, although entertainment programs tend to depict mental illness as more dangerous than it is, the next section shows how programs downplay the dangers associated with sex and violence.

Sex The exact amount of sex on television depends on who is counting. Some groups say sexual content has decreased in recent years, at least during prime time. Others, such as the Henry J. Kaiser Family Foundation, say sex is more visible than ever. According to statistics released by the Kaiser Foundation, two thirds of evening TV shows depict sex, and sexual intercourse is suggested in about one of every seven shows (Stanley, 2003).

Daytime programs and movies are even more explicit. In 50 hours of soap operas, researchers noted 333 instances of sexual activity (Greenberg & Woods, 1999). In soap operas and movies, the majority of sex occurs between unmarried partners. In soap operas, viewers see unmarried couples engage in sex about 1.5 to 1.8 times per hour (Greenberg & Woods, 1999). In R-rated movies with teenaged characters, sex between unmarried partners outnumbers sex between married partners 32 to 1 (Greenberg, Brown, & Buerkel-Rothfuss, 1993).

Sex is treated differently depending on the program format. Situation comedies tend to treat sex as something funny or whimsical, not as a serious act with potentially harmful consequences (Larson, 1991; Shidler & Lowry, 1995). In dramas, sexual acts are most often portrayed in association with violent crimes (Signorielli, 1993), while music videos tend to show sex in association with alcohol consumption (DuRant et al., 1997). Overall, the idea that sex can be risky in everyday life, for average persons, is not evident.

On the bright side, shows such as *Seventh Heaven* and *Gilmore Girls* are praised for depicting young people talking about sex in responsible ways with their parents and friends. Condoms are often mentioned when sex is depicted in daytime television (Stepp, 2003), and soap operas have ventured to include more talk about rape and HIV than most programs (Greenberg & Busselle, 1996).

Violence Violence has become the norm in television programming. No matter what time you watch TV, you are likely to see violence in two out of three programs (Smith, Nathanson, & Wilson, 2002). The movies are no better. Even the previews are violent. About 75.7% of movie previews include violence, and 56% show sexuality (Oliver & Kalyanaraman, 2002).

One criticism of media violence is that the effects are so unrealistic. People run through machine gun fire unscathed. They are shot or stabbed but continue to perform like athletes. Evil characters die, but heroes seldom do. George Gerbner (1996) calls it happy violence: "'Happy violence' is cool, swift, painless, and always leads to a happy ending, so as to deliver the audience to the next commercial in a receptive mood" (paragraph 10).

In the fast-paced world of entertainment, violence is popular, but lengthy recoveries are considered boring. A case in point involves the police drama *NYPD Blue.* In the first episode, a police officer is critically wounded by a bullet and goes into a coma. By the second episode, however, he is back on the beat. Silver (1993) protests: "What about the weeks of physical therapy?" (paragraph 5).

Most researchers agree that there is a link between violence in the media and violence in real life. As the first generations to grow up with television have reached adulthood, the evidence is convincing that children exposed to media violence are more likely than others to engage in violent behavior themselves (Huesmann, Moise-Titus, Podolski, & Eron, 2003; Wartella, 1996).

Of course, not everyone reacts to media violence in the same way, and it is difficult to isolate media effects among the many factors that influence people (Gunter, 1994). Researchers suggest that male children are more likely than females to imitate violence (Huesmann, Lagerspetz, & Eron, 1984), and people are more likely to imitate media violence that seems justified than violence they perceive to be senseless or unfair (based on Paik and Comstock's 1994 review of 217 studies). Furthermore, media violence often causes people to feel afraid and to overestimate the threat of violence in their environment (Nabi & Sullivan, 2001; Romer, Jamieson, & Aday, 2003).

Several initiatives were launched in the 1980s and 1990s to help limit young people's exposure to media violence. The music recording industry agreed to a system of warning labels and parental consent requirements on music with violent and sexually explicit lyrics (Powell, 1985). A television rating system was begun to identify shows that might be inappropriate for young audiences. And since 1998, televisions sold in the United States must be equipped with a computerized V-chip (V for violence) that allows adults to restrict programs that can be viewed on that television (Silver & Geier, 1996). The computerized chip reads the show's rating, which must be encoded in the broadcast signal. These are steps toward reducing violence, but many feel they are not strict enough. Controversy continues to surround rating decisions. The most common complaint is that TV programs rated acceptable for youthful audiences are still very violent (Dreazer, 1998).

Portrayals of Health Care Situations

What most people "know" about the interior of a surgery unit or doctors' lounge they learned from television. Medical dramas like *ER* seem to offer a backstage pass to medicine. During these programs, areas usually off limits to the public are open for inspection, or at least it seems that way. In some ways, medical dramas are likely to give people mistaken impressions about the way medical work is done.

Medical Miracles Based on television portrayals, it may seem that heroic rescues and miraculous recoveries are the norm. Kimberly A. Neuendorf (1990) calls the tendency to portray doctors as "all-powerful and all-good" the "Marcus Welby syndome." Health crises arise and are resolved on TV in 30-minute or 1-hour segments, compared to the weeks or months often required to resolve real-life medical conditions.

One group of researchers (Diem, Lantos, & Tulsky, 1996) studied instances of CPR (cardiopulmonary resuscitation) in TV episodes. On television, CPR was usually administered to children and young adults, and most of them recovered fully and quickly. Some even regained full health in a matter of minutes. In everyday life, however, CPR is most often used to help elderly persons having heart attacks, and it only saves 2% to 30% of actual patients (many of whom will have lasting disabilities). Susan Diem and co-authors conclude that television medical dramas encourage people to believe in miracles that are not likely to occur.

Entertainment and Commercialism

It is usually easy to tell the difference between a commercial and a television program or movie. But what if a commercial looks like entertainment, or commercial messages are subtly embedded in entertainment programming?

Entertainomercials Journalists have coined the term **entertainomercials** to characterize sales pitches that resemble entertainment programming ("Entertainomercials," 1996). A classic example involves Joe Camel, the former cartoon-like mascot of Camel cigarettes. R. J. Reynolds Tobacco Company introduced the colorful, sunglass-wearing camel in their 1988 advertising. Although the company insisted the animated character was not meant to capture children's interest, it had that effect. Sales of Camel cigarettes to children rose from $6 million per year to $476 million per year (DiFranza et al., 1991). Within a few years, research revealed that children were as familiar with Joe Camel as with Mickey Mouse (Fischer, Schwartz, Richards, & Goldstein, 1991). Under public and legal pressure, Reynolds ceased using images of Joe Camel in 1997, after a 10-year run (Vest, 1997).

Product Placement The tobacco industry is also involved in another type of commercial/entertainment blend called product placement. **Product placement** means that a sponsor pays (with cash, props, services, or so on) to have a product or brand name included in a movie, television program, video game, or other form of entertainment (Babin & Carder, 1996). The Federal Communication Commission forbids television studios from selling promotional exposure within programs, but the rule is only loosely enforced, and most product placements are allowed in movies (Stanley, 1998).

Notable examples of product placement include the Reese's Pieces in *E.T.* (Babin & Carder, 1996), the Ford Explorers in *Jurassic Park* (Darlin, 1995), and Wheaties cereal in the *Rocky* movies (Babin & Carder, 1996). All resulted from deals between moviemakers and marketers.

Product placements become forms of health communication when they concern the way people think or behave concerning health issues. This may range from an emphasis on fast food and cigarettes to athletic gear. A particular concern arises when product placements are used to dodge restrictions on conventional advertising. Again, tobacco products are a striking example. Tobacco industry documents obtained in the 1990s suggest companies secretly reward actors and producers to prominently display their cigarettes in the movies (Basil, 1997). Stars including Sean Connery, Sylvester Stalone, Paul Newman, and Clint Eastwood have allegedly accepted expensive cars and jewelry in return for smoking brand-name cigarettes on the big screen.

Promoting cigarettes in this way violates several restrictions: (a) the prohibition on advertising tobacco on radio, TV, or in the movies, (b) the ban on celebrity endorsements, and (c) federal law requiring health warnings on all tobacco packages and advertisements (Basil, 1997). These restrictions, initiated in the 1960s, are based on medical evidence that tobacco products are serious health hazards (Jacobson, Wasserman, & Anderson, 1997).

Public concern has become even more intense in light of evidence that secondhand smoke is hazardous and that nicotine is addictive (Gibson, 1997). All 50 states and many private citizens have filed suits against tobacco companies, charging that they have unethically manipulated the public, suppressed information about tobacco risks while making cigarettes even more addictive, and marketed their products to children (Jacobson et al., 1997). Tobacco companies are charged with making enormous profits while states and citizens bear the immense emotional and financial burdens of tobacco-related illnesses. The tobacco industry has agreed to pay states at least $206 billion in damages ("New York," 1998). As the next section shows, some people have decided to fight fire with fire, using the product placement strategy to promote recommended health behaviors. See Box 11.5 for ethical issues related to health images in entertainment programs.

Pro-Social Programming

Subtle messages may be embedded in programs, not to sell products but to educate or persuade people regarding health matters. Efforts to benefit the public using an entertainment format are known as **pro-social programming.** Entertainment producers today are likely to be lobbied by health advocates urging them to incorporate health messages in their scripts, props, and story lines (Montgomery, 1990). The Hollywood, Health & Society program helps entertainment writers portray health issues in accurate and informative ways. The program is sponsored by the CDC and the University of Southern California's Annenberg Norman Lear Center. Medical experts and Hollywood insiders provide tip sheets about health issues and offer story ideas and scripts to incorporate health information in entertainment programming. From the website (entertainment.usc.edu/hhs), entertainment writers can find information about topics ranging from AIDS, to bat bites, to car seats, to suicide, and West Nile Fever.

A similar program is offered by the Entertainment Industries Council, which sponsors a website (eiconline.org) and publishes a guidebook useful in depicting AIDS, alcohol, and drugs in entertainment programming ("The Sensitive Screenwriter," 1994). The council suggests terminology to accurately convey the dangers of high-risk behaviors. For example, it cautions against using the term "hard drugs" because it incorrectly implies that drugs that are not "hard" are relatively harmless. The book also recommends that characters be shown using seat belts and other safety devices.

In the United States, comic books and video games are popular ways to educate children about health. A series of Spiderman comics was released in which the superhero cautions against substance abuse (Parrott, 1995). The video game *Rex Ronan—Experimental Surgeon* takes players through a smoker's body, and *Packy and Marlon* depicts two elephants who attend a summer diabetes camp and must choose between various foods and activities (Lieberman, 1997).

In some countries, entertainment programs have been designed specifically to promote healthy behaviors. In Poland, people who regularly watch a television series designed to promote healthy behaviors subsequently score higher on health knowledge surveys and feel more able to control health risks (Chew, Palmer, Slonska, & Subbiah, 2002). Likewise, Mexico, India, Turkey, and Kenya have developed soap operas to promote family planning, respect for women, safer sex, and other issues (Brown & Singhal, 1990).

Box 11.5 ETHICAL CONSIDERATIONS
Is the Entertainment Industry Responsible for Health Images?

Does the entertainment industry have a responsibility to promote healthy behaviors? Some claim that entertainment writers and producers behave irresponsibly when they consistently portray unhealthy and unrealistic images of life and health.

One way the media distorts reality is by showing unhealthy and violent behaviors without the natural consequences (Gerbner, 1996). People are shot with guns but continue to run and fight. Others overeat but appear to be slender and healthy nevertheless (Brown & Walsh-Childers, 1994). Another way the media often misrepresent health is depicting ill (especially mentally ill) individuals as dangerous, corrupt, and antisocial (Signorielli, 1993).

Taking the concept of reality TV to new extremes, some programs have begun staging medical tests as public forms of entertainment. For example, on a television program in the United Kingdom, fathers were invited to air their suspicions about their partners' infidelity. The results of paternity tests on the men's children were announced on the air (English, Critchley-Romano, Sheather, & Sommerville, 2002). Medical ethicists observe that the United States has set a precedent for this type of reality-shock programs. Whereas documentaries about giving birth and undergoing surgery may be educational, programs like the one just described are meant only to shock and entertain. Some question the ethics of using medical procedures as entertainment and violating the privacy of nonconsenting participants (such as the men's children).

Some people argue that the entertainment industry need not offer such a shocking or distorted view of reality. They challenge Hollywood to create engrossing yet realistic programming. Going one step further, some people advocate pro-social program programming to educate people while they are entertained.

On the other side of the issue people argue that entertainment programming should not be harnessed to a social agenda. They feel that artistic creativity is compromised when writers and producers must

Impact of Persuasive Entertainment

Before becoming too optimistic (or perturbed) about the prospects for incorporating messages within entertainment, it is important to ask: Do messages in entertainment programs have any effect?

Some theorists believe media images affect the way people view society, but not necessarily the way they view themselves personally. **Social adaptation theory** suggests people evaluate messages considering how useful the information adhere to social guidelines. Moreover, they say, it is difficult to know whose agenda should prevail. When health professionals disagree (as they often do) about specific guidelines for healthy living, is it entertainers' job to decide which viewpoints should be represented? If the industry is held to a standard of realism, they wonder what will become of fantasy themes and movies made famous by earlier generations, at a time when different social expectations prevailed.

What Do You Think?

1. Does entertainment programming influence people's behavior? For instance, would people be more likely to use condoms if they saw their favorite characters talking about them in television programs or movies?
2. Should entertainers consider how their programs might influence audience members?
3. Do you think it is irresponsible of the entertainment industry to misrepresent the natural consequences of violent and otherwise unhealthy behavior?
4. Do you think it would diminish the entertainment value of your favorite movies and TV shows if they showed healthy behaviors or realistic consequences?
5. Do you believe programs designed specifically to promote healthy behaviors would be popular in the United States? Do you think such programs should be created? Why or why not?

Suggested Sources

Brown, W. J., & Singhal, A. (1990). Ethical dilemmas of pro-social television. *Communication Quarterly, 38,* 268–280.

Faden, R. R. (1987). Ethical issues in government sponsored public health campaigns. *Health Education Quarterly, 14,* 27–37.

is likely to be in their lives (Perse, Nathanson, & McLeod, 1996). In this regard, entertainment may have an edge over news. Leslie Snyder and Ruby Rouse (1995) found that people perceived entertainment portrayals to be more relevant to their lives than news items, probably because entertainment episodes tend to be more intimate and vivid. Snyder and Rouse's study revealed that movies and television programs increased people's perception of personal AIDS risk, while news coverage decreased their sense of being personally vulnerabile. The researchers concluded that the dramatic nature of entertainment programming often makes it seem up-close and personal, whereas news seems to depict what happens to "other people."

Concerning product placement, there are a few (but not many) striking success stories. After a character on *The Young & the Restless* saved a child using CPR techniques he "learned at the Red Cross," the Red Cross received thousands of calls from interested people (Drum, 1997). When a product placement deal put James Bond behind the wheel of a BMW Z3 roadster in *Goldeneye,* the car maker had to put anxious buyers on waiting lists ("Let Us Put," 1996). Likewise, the sales of Reese's Pieces reportedly rose 65% after the release of *E.T.,* which depicted them as the favorite snack of a lovable outer space creature (Babin & Carder, 1996).

Success stories aside, most product placements seem to do no more than increase brand-name recognition. College students who watched *Rocky III* or *Rocky V* were not able to name many of the products within the movies, but they were reasonably successful at recognizing those brands when presented with a list of 75 possibilities (Babin & Carder, 1996). Recognition seemed to depend on how prominently the brand name was displayed and how integral it was to the plot. (It is presumably easier to overlook or forget products that seem irrelevant to the overall storyline.) Babin and Carder found no evidence that viewers' attitudes toward the products had been significantly affected.

Implications

Although entertainment is not usually meant to provide health information, it frequently depicts medical scenes and health issues. Based on these depictions, people may perceive that mentally ill and disabled persons are very different from other people and may even be dangerous. Audiences may get the idea that sex and violence are less risky than they are and that medical miracles can save almost anyone. Finally, commercials and entertainment are sometimes intertwined, either for commercial or pro-social purposes.

■ MEDIA LITERACY

This chapter concludes where it began, with the reminder that the media's influence is by no means uniform. People are affected differently and to varying extents. Perhaps the best defense against excessive or negative media influence is the ability to analyze messages logically (Austin & Meili, 1994). This is a central tenet of media literacy.

Media literacy is defined as awareness and skills that allow a person to evaluate media content in terms of what is realistic and useful (adapted from Potter, 1998). According to Dorothy Singer and Jerome Singer's (1998) overview, media literate individuals are aware that advertisers are apt to highlight (and even exaggerate) the attractive aspects of their products and downplay the disadvantages. They evaluate the creator's intent and try to figure out what is not being said and why. Media literate individuals are also skillful at identifying portrayals that are unrealistic or have been enhanced by special effects. Overall, media literate individuals tend to evaluate the message in terms of fairness and appropriateness, weighing ideas for themselves.

Teaching Media Literacy

Media literacy instruction usually involves an informative, an analytic, and an experiential stage. Arli Quesada and Sue Summers (1998) have described these stages well, and the discussion here is based on their work.

In the **informative stage** participants in media literacy programs learn to identify different types of messages (persuasive, informative, and entertaining) and different types of media (television, radio, newspapers, and so on). They learn about the strengths and limitations of various media. For example, Internet resources are vast and accessible, but some sources are not trustworthy. Participants also learn about production techniques and special effects.

In the **analytic stage** participants are invited to discuss their perceptions of media in general and of specific media messages. In this stage they typically deconstruct messages with guidance from a trained leader. **Deconstructing** a message means breaking it down into specific components such as key points, purpose, implied messages, production techniques, and goals. For instance, beer commercials often present a social reality in which drinking is fun and sexy. In deconstructing a beer commercial (or any other media message), participants try to identify the message's purpose, what information is missing from it, and how it compares to their own social reality. They might conclude that beer companies make drinking look fun to sell their products, but the reality is something more than or different from what the commercials show. Finally, in the **experiential stage,** media literacy programs challenge participants to write their own news stories, design ads, perform skits, and participate in other creative efforts to help them understand the process and demystify the way media messages are created.

Media literacy skills have been taught successfully to people of different ages. In one study, third graders watched a 28-minute video about advertising techniques and took part in guided discussions (Austin & Johnson, 1997). Following this brief exercise, they were more likely than other children to identify commercials as sales pitches, to see them as less realistic, and to judge for themselves whether the behaviors depicted were appropriate and desirable.

A similar project helped college students critique fashion advertisements, noting how extremely thin or muscular the models were (Rabak-Wagener et al., 1998). The students were challenged to redesign the ads using models of different body sizes, ages, ethnicities, and physical abilities. They were consequently less likely to believe people should look like supermodels and were more satisfied with their own bodies.

Media literacy can be taught at home when parents help children understand aspects of the media messages they encounter. This is known as **parental**

mediation. Adults are often able to make children aware of inaccuracies and discrepancies in media messages. For example, "Why does this program show thin people eating fattening foods?" (Austin, 1995) or "Is the violence shown in this program realistic?" (Nathanson & Yang, 2003). Research suggests that children get maximum benefits from media (while minimizing unfavorable influences) when their parents (a) limit media exposure, (b) choose programs with care, (c) watch, listen, or read alongside them, and (d) discuss program content with them (Austin, 1993; Austin, Roberts, & Nass, 1990; Singer & Singer, 1998).

Although the research about media literacy is encouraging overall, it does not suggest a cure-all. Some stereotypes persist, even when people have explicitly been told they are not valid. College students who watched a movie about a mentally ill murderer were more negative in their assessment of mentally ill persons than students who viewed an unrelated film (Wahl & Lefkowits, 1989). This was true even when the students saw a message stating that violence is not a characteristic of mental illness. The authors conclude that awareness and information campaigns will not be entirely successful at counteracting negative media portrayals.

Implications

To some extent, people can control how the media influences them. Media literacy is the ability to analyze messages to judge if they are realistic, appropriate, and relevant. Media literacy skills can be taught by informing people about media goals and techniques, helping them learn to analyze what they see and hear, and encouraging them to become creative message producers themselves. Although media literacy cannot completely eliminate media effects, research suggests people of all ages can use it with reasonable success.

■ SUMMARY

Whether you regard the media as friend or foe, mass-mediated messages are an important component of health communication. The distinction in this chapter between advertising, news, and entertainment is useful for explanatory purposes, but do not forget that actual media exposure involves a great deal of blending and juxtaposing. For instance, a news story about eating disorders may be followed by an advertisement featuring unnaturally thin models. Such clashes are common, and contradictions of this nature may mitigate the effects of health-conscious messages.

Although it is difficult to say to what degree people's actions are affected by advertising, significant influence is suggested by the number of people who eat the unhealthy food advertisers promote, drink the beverages they sell, and strive to emulate supermodels. Based on cultivation theory, children and adolescents may be especially susceptible to advertising messages because their frame of reference is limited. Social comparison theory suggests people strive to measure up to "idealized" characters in the media, even when the ideals are far from attainable. Sometimes advertisers make natural conditions (such as the presence of body hair) seem bad or unnatural (pathological) so people will pay money to change them. Although advertising offers many advantages, it can be harmful if it encourages poor nutrition, drug and alcohol abuse, or an unhealthy reliance on cosmetics and fad diets.

News coverage of health issues is important to share valuable knowledge. However, news audiences should remember that scientific findings are usually tentative, news stories tend to focus on unusual concerns, and coverage may be influenced by the desire to please advertisers or attract new audiences.

Interactive technology combines elements of mass media with interpersonal communication. Participants are able to access information written for mass audiences, but they have the option of responding, asking questions, making requests, and choosing what information they wish to receive. The challenge now becomes securing computer access and discriminating between reliable and unreliable information.

Entertainment portrayals may influence what people believe about medical care, risky behavior, and people with disabilities. Sex and drugs are shown mostly for entertainment value, not as serious subjects with health consequences. In reality, medical miracles are less common than on television, medical professionals are more diverse, and medicine is more bureaucratic.

Do not be surprised if the food, drinks, cigarettes, vehicles, and props in your favorite movie were put in purposefully to please advertisers. Although product placements may not look like commercials, advertisers go to great expense hoping that they will function like commercials. Health advocates use the same tactic to insert health messages into some entertainment programs, a practice known as pro-social programming.

Finally, media literacy allows people some control over how media messages affect them. Wise consumers learn to distinguish between reliable and unreliable information by critiquing media messages to determine their purposes, strengths, and limitations.

KEY TERMS

- mass communication
- direct-to-consumer
- cultivation theory
- social comparison theory
- pathologizing the human body
- entertainomercials
- product placement
- pro-social programming
- social adaptation theory
- media literacy
    - informative stage
    - analytic stage
    - deconstructing
    - experiential stage
- parental mediation

REVIEW QUESTIONS

1. In what ways are pharmaceutical drug advertisements beneficial? In what ways can they be harmful?
2. How does television viewing seem to affect children's eating habits and knowledge of nutrition?
3. Based on cultivation theory, why are children particularly susceptible to media messages?
4. In what ways do advertisers pathologize the human body?
5. Using social comparison theory, explain why and how people are influenced by "ideal" people portrayed in the media.
6. In what ways are health news items frequently distorted in the mass media?
7. What are the advantages and disadvantages of health news coverage in the mass media?
8. What are some suggestions for reporters covering health topics?
9. What are some advantages and drawbacks of using interactive computer technology to educate people about health?
10. Name some tips for avoiding health scams and for using the Internet wisely.
11. How are mentally ill people typically portrayed on television and in the movies? Are these portrayals accurate?
12. How is sex portrayed in different forms of programming?
13. In what ways are violent media images typically unrealistic?
14. What steps have been taken to limit young people's exposure to media violence?
15. How might people be misled by media images of health care situations?
16. How does promoting cigarettes in the movies violate advertising regulations?
17. Name some examples of pro-social programming.
18. Describe the steps in teaching media literacy.

CLASS ACTIVITY

Building Media Literacy

Bring a song, video clip, or page from a newspaper or magazine to class. Analyze elements of the messages using the following questions suggested by Quesada and Summers (1998). Keep in mind that there are no "right" answers. Opinions will differ. The object is to develop personal awareness and become skilled at analyzing media messages.

- Whose point of view is expressed in the message?
- Is the creator an expert on the topic?
- Is the information fact or opinion—or a mixture of both?

- Is the message supported with facts and examples? If so, are they believable?
- Who is the intended audience?
- Are the vocabulary, tone, illustrations, and other media elements appropriate for the intended audience?
- Are there inconsistencies in the information presented?
- What is not being told and why?
- Do you think the message is realistic? Why or why not?
- Will the message influence your behavior? Why or why not?
- If you were creating the message, what would you do differently?

CHAPTER 12

Planning Health Promotion Campaigns

Do You Want to See Something Gross?

This headline reflects the powerful impact of audience analysis. It was designed by a group of seventh graders to catch the attention of students in their school. Intrigued by the headline, students view photographs of bacteria growing on items they touch everyday and read information about the value of hand washing. The campaign caught the students' attention, and more. It won a national award. (See Box 12.1 more on the campaign.)

As you will see in this chapter, different audiences have different preferences. Designing health promotion messages that are both advantageous and audience oriented is a multistage process.

Health-promoting behaviors are those that "enhance health and well-being, reduce health risks, and prevent disease" (Brennan & Fink, 1997, p. 157). These behaviors include lifestyle choices, medical care, prevention efforts, and activities that foster an overall sense of well-being.

Health promotion campaigns are efforts to influence large numbers of people to engage in health-promoting behaviors (Backer & Rogers, 1993). These efforts may involve the use of many communication channels, from face-to-face communication to mass media. The term **health promoter** includes anyone involved in the process of creating and distributing health promotion messages. This includes volunteers in the community, employees of nonprofit health agencies, public relations and community relations professionals, production artists, media decision makers, and more. As this list suggests, health promotion offers diverse career opportunities for communication specialists. This chapter considers the challenges of promoting health behaviors among diverse members of the population. It opens with a brief overview of health campaigns, describing some particularly notable ones. The chapter then guides the reader through the first four stages of designing a health promotion campaign:

Step 1: Defining the Situation and Potential Benefits

Step 2: Analyzing and Segmenting the Audience

Step 3: Establishing Campaign Goals and Objectives

Step 4: Selecting Channels of Communication

Steps 5 through 7 in designing and implementing a campaign are covered in the next chapter. Keep in mind that it is important to know all the steps before you actually begin. Although evaluating and refining the campaign is the final step, you must consider from the beginning how you will accomplish those goals later on. (The steps in these chapters are based on recommendations by Brown and Einsiedel, 1990, and reflect an abbreviated version of the steps recommended by the CDC [Donovan, 1995].)

BACKGROUND ON HEALTH CAMPAIGNS

"Live long and prosper," the Vulcan salutation on *Star Trek,* seems to say it all. A long and healthy existence—isn't that what life is all about? You might think so. But it turns out that Vulcan logic is not always able to explain human behavior, as Mr. Spock discovered.

Early health campaigns were designed with the confidence that humans want nothing so much as their own health and longevity. From that viewpoint it follows that, if people know a behavior is unhealthy, they will not act that way. Likewise, they should go to great lengths to pursue health-enhancing outcomes. Seen this way, persuasion was not an issue. All people needed was reliable information. The motivation to comply with it was presumably already there, as innate as the animal instinct for survival.

Motivating Factors

Influencing human behavior is not that simple. People are motivated by a number of factors that make them more or less receptive to health information and more or less motivated to change their behavior. Sometimes people do things they know to be unhealthy because the behavior is inexpensive, convenient, socially rewarding, or fun (Brown & Einsiedel, 1990). For instance, research indicates people may drink alcoholic beverages even though they believe them to be unhealthy because they are reluctant to give up the social ritual of drinking with friends (Brennan & Fink, 1997). Conversely, people sometimes change their behavior without knowing much about the change or the reasons for it. They may try a behavior (like taking vitamins) simply because someone in authority tells them to, or because the change seems interesting, easy, fashionable, and so on. In these instances, knowledge may *follow* behavior change.

Research has not always been encouraging about health campaigns' actual effects. Campaigns have been criticized for naively seeking to change people's behavior without changing their circumstances (Green, 1996) and for assuming that knowledge reaches and affects all people equally (Brown & Walsh-Childers, 1994).

In reality, campaigns may raise awareness, but unless the recommended behaviors are compatible with people's beliefs and are supported within their social networks, campaigns are unlikely to change people's behavior (Ratzan,

BOX 12.1 PERSPECTIVES
Gross! Wash Your Hands

You need not have a Madison Avenue address or a huge budget to design a top-quality health campaign. A group of seventh graders in Nebraska recently made the news by creating a national award-winning multimedia campaign to get kids in their school to wash their hands more.

Goodrich Middle School students Irina Sulejmanovic, Kam McKinney, and Kristen Benson (left to right, front row) celebrate the success of their handwashing campaign with science teacher, Jennifer Kiser (back left) and principal, Dr. Bess Scott (back right). *Photo by James Kegley.*

The students designed a multimedia campaign with the headline, "Do You Want to See Something Gross?" featuring pictures of bacteria cultures found on common items. They created their own DVD movie, a computer slide presentation, t-shirts, bookmarks, and posters in multiple languages.

So impressive was the campaign that its creators—science students at Goodrich Middle School in Lincoln and their teacher, Jennifer Kiser—earned $2,000 for their school and an all-expense-paid trip to

Washington, D.C., where they were honored at a reception overlooking the White House.

The award and student campaign are part of a national program called *Healthy Schools, Healthy People—It's a SNAP,* sponsored by the Soap and Detergent Association, the Centers for Disease Control and Prevention, and the U.S. Department of Health and Human Services. SNAP stands for the *School Network for Absenteeism Prevention,* an initiative to engage middle school students as peer educators and leaders in a "stay-healthy" movement.

As participants in *SNAP,* the Lincoln Middle School class downloaded an online tool kit that provides facts and statistics about the benefits of hand washing. Here the students and Mrs. Kiser describe the process of creating and implementing the campaign.

Question: Why were you interested in creating this campaign?

Kam McKinney: We had learned about bacteria and viruses and how they relate to us, how we become exposed to different diseases and I wanted to know what I could do to stay healthy. We were interested in this project as a class because it was different from reading about bacteria, it was actually hands-on and gave us the opportunity to apply what we already knew to learn things we did not know.

Question: How did you know what types of campaign messages would appeal to students in your school?

McKinney: We felt the campaign messages needed to attract the attention of middle school students. Our bacterial culture pictures really got the attention of the students in the building because it was growing on the things they were touching regularly. We felt the I-movie was something that was new and innovative, yet different from just reading the information. We also felt that giving students tools such as saying your "ABC's" or singing "Happy Birthday" twice while washing their hands was an easy way to remember how long they should wash.

Question: What was your biggest challenge in creating and implementing the campaign?

Irina Sulejmanovic: The largest challenge was creating a survey that would give us good data for our campaign ads. We spent many nights after school tallying the data to make sure that we were properly informing our students about what was happening with hand washing and the spread of diseases in our school.

continued

BOX 12.1 PERSPECTIVES
Gross! Wash Your Hands, *continued*

Question: How do you know if the campaign messages worked?

Kristen Benson: We know that almost all of the student population uses the hand sanitizer on their way into the lunchroom. We are hoping to see an increase in students attending school and a decrease in students who are ill. We will be doing some follow-up data to check these things out.

Question: What advice do you have for other health campaign managers?

Mrs. Kiser: I think the most important tool for anyone who is managing a campaign is the students. When students are given ownership of something they go above and beyond what we as teachers could ever imagine they could do. It is pretty amazing!

For More Information:

- For a free program tool kit and information about the *SNAP* program and sponsors, visit www.itsasnap.org.
- For more about the Goodrich Middle School campaign, go to Goodrich.lps.org/stories/storyReader$133.

Payne, & Massett, 1994). Health promoters have discovered they cannot simply educate people about health and presume they will adjust their lifestyles accordingly. A range of factors must be taken into account. This means the promoter must know the audience, and consider not just why audience members should act in recommended ways, but also why they may find it difficult to do so.

Exemplary Campaigns

This section describes five exemplary health promotion campaigns. Each provides an inspiring lesson for promoters. Together, these examples illustrate that health promoters must often do more than simply give out information if they are to succeed. Sensitivity to audience needs, problem-solving skills, assessment, and careful planning and follow-through are required as well.

Go to the Audience A health promoter interviewed by a student of mine once said, "You can't talk to people where you wish they were. You have to talk to them where they really are." His words characterize one quality of good campaigners: *They know their audiences well and design campaigns to suit those audiences.*

A case in point is an HIV-prevention effort in rural Alabama. Roger Myrick (1998) describes how a local campaign director became personally acquainted with community members, church leaders, and business people. Realizing that many high-risk members of the community lived in a low-income housing project, the local director organized a neighborhood event. He set up tents on a nearby sports field and offered free food, door prizes, and music by a popular disc jockey. Crowds of people attended, were informed about HIV and AIDS, and were offered free testing. Myrick reports that the project was successful because it was entertaining, educational, and consistent with community values.

Another exemplary campaign was designed to reach elderly African-American women, who are at high risk for breast cancer but are often unable to afford cancer screening and are hard to reach via traditional media. The campaigners noted that the women they most wanted to reach had a favorite place for swapping stories and sharing information—the beauty salon (Forte, 1995). With this in mind, they arranged for salons in Los Angeles to show an educational video about breast cancer throughout the day. The video featured African-American women and emphasized that they are at high risk for cancer. Salon clients were also given pamphlets about breast cancer and were offered free mammograms at a local clinic or in a mobile unit scheduled to visit the salon on a regular basis. According to Deirdra Forte, the beauty of this program was that "by showing the video where African-American women already exchange information and socialize, they are more likely to understand and accept the benefit of mammography" (paragraph 22). The campaign was honored as one of the year's best by the U.S. Department of Health and Human Services.

Take Action Another lesson is that health promotion comes in many forms, and *sometimes actions are as important as words.* When the leaders of an extensive heart health campaign in New York City realized that preschoolers in the area received 40% of their daily saturated fat from whole milk served at school, they put down their pens for a while and rolled up their sleeves (Shea, Basch, Wechsler, & Lantigua, 1996; Wechsler & Wernick, 1992). In addition to public education, community involvement, and a multimedia campaign, the health promoters convinced schools to serve low-fat milk. The program won awards for its open-eyed, innovative approach.

Measure Your Success The value of combining media exposure, community outreach, and scientific research was demonstrated by the Minnesota Heart Health Program (MHHP), which was one the most extensive health campaigns in American history (Luepker et al., 1994). It was conducted for 13 years (1980–1993) and involved nearly half a million people in the upper Midwest (Luepker et al.). The goal of MHHP was to lower heart-disease risk factors (cholesterol, high blood pressure, and smoking) and increase heart-healthy behaviors such as exercise. It included an extensive mass media campaign, educational programs in schools, and the involvement of local organizations.

What made MHHP extraordinary was its dedication to charting the health outcomes of people exposed to campaign messages. It is a good example of how to *establish goals and measure your success.* Researchers monitored people's behavior over a period of years and compared people touched by the campaign to people in other communities. Over time, they found modest but significant decreases in high blood pressure, high cholesterol, and smoking in communities involved in the program (Luepker et al., 1994). There was also a notable increase in physical activity among female school children involved in the heart-healthy education programs (Kelder, Perry, & Klepp, 1993).

Encourage Social Support An award-winning program called the 90-Second Intervention is being used to lower Americans' risk of high blood pressure (Fishman, 1995). The intervention program is based on the principle that *recruiting social support for healthy behaviors increases the likelihood that people will stick to them.* The 90-Second Intervention was designed because many Americans (about 50 million) are at risk for high blood pressure, but compliance with medical advice is notoriously low, mostly because people with high blood pressure feel OK most of the time so they do not perceive a reason to change their lifestyle or continue medication. (Despite the lack of symptoms, high blood pressure can lead to strokes, heart disease, and kidney disease.)

The campaign planners reasoned that people would be more likely to follow medical advice (1) if their doctors were not the only ones imploring them to eat right, exercise, and stay on medication and (2) if they received daily encouragement. Therefore, they designed a simple intervention program that takes place in the doctor's office. During a check-up, the doctor asks the patient to call a loved one and ask that person to commit to becoming a "health partner." The partner's role is to exercise with the patient, help maintain a healthy diet, and so on. The genius of the plan is that it makes healthy behaviors socially rewarding. The health partner and patient both benefit from the healthy activities they enjoy together, and the doctor is no longer the only one concerned about the problem. The 90-second phone call is presumably well worth the effort.

Implications

Successful health promotion recognizes that people do not necessarily change their behaviors because they are presented with new health information. As you will see in this chapter and the next, even award-winning campaigns sometimes have small or hard-to-evaluate effects. Campaigners must take into account the concerns, habits, and preferences of the people they wish to influence. Campaigns with the best chance of succeeding talk to people where they are, whether it is the beauty salon, athletic field, or doctor's office. They make it practical for people to adopt healthy behaviors, even if it means changing public policy or offering free treatment. Good health campaigns are thorough and backed by long-term commitment. Furthermore, they speak with many voices, including the concerned tones of loved ones, the calm assurance of experts, and the printed and recorded messages of mass media. Here are four principles embodied by the campaigns just described:

- Know your audience.
- Take action when words are not enough.
- Establish goals and measure your success.
- Encourage social support for healthy behaviors.

PLANNING A HEALTH CAMPAIGN

To illustrate the steps in planning a health campaign, imagine that the staff of a university sports recreation department has asked you to help recruit new participants. Specifically, they would like to increase the number of people who go to the campus gym in their free time to take part in basketball and aerobics. The recreation department will not benefit financially from the added enrollment, but the staff wishes to increase participation because physical activity improves people's health. In accepting this project, you take on the role of health promoter. The rest of the chapter guides you through the initial steps of creating a campaign. The hypothetical sports recreation campaign is admittedly a small-scale effort, but many influential campaigns are aimed at small audiences, and improving health habits among even a small group is a momentous goal. Furthermore, the steps given apply well to large and small campaigns.

Step 1: Defining the Situation and Potential Benefits

If you are like many people, your first instinct is to post fliers and send a story about the recreation program to the campus newspaper. Those may be effective steps, but before you begin, take the advice of professional campaign planners and do some preliminary research to assess potential benefits and the current situation (Nowak & Siska, 1995).

Benefits At this stage, you should be interested in learning what benefits (if any) your efforts might achieve. Following are some questions you might research:

- Would these behaviors (aerobics and basketball) actually improve people's health?
- Would everybody benefit from these activities?
- Are there some people who would not benefit?
- Are there alternative ways to get the same benefits?

Answers to these questions can be obtained by reading published literature and talking with experts in the field. Such preliminary research will prepare you to share useful knowledge with others and may help you decide if the project is worthwhile.

Current Situation Assuming that you find reasonable evidence to believe that people might benefit from basketball and aerobics, the next step is to assess the current situation. Following are some questions to guide your preliminary research. The same questions will be useful later in guiding audience analysis. Remember that experts, program leaders, current participants, and nonparticipants are all valuable sources of information. In addition to these general questions, you may want to add some specific questions relevant to your campaign.

- How many people currently participate in the recommended behavior?
- What types of people participate and for what reasons? (Of interest is demographic information such as age, sex, and income, as well as cultural, personal, social, or personality variables that might be relevant.)
- What are the strengths and weaknesses of the program (from the perspective of participants and nonparticipants)?
- What types of people do not participate?
- What are their reasons for not participating?
- What factors are most important to participants and nonparticipants (e.g., cost, convenience, social interaction)?
- Do people consider the potential benefits of this behavior important? Why or why not?
- Are there any conditions under which nonparticipants might participate?
- How do the people in your audience usually receive information (i.e., fliers, newspaper, radio, e-mail)?
- Through what channels do they prefer to get information?
- What information sources do they trust?

Preliminary answers to your questions may surprise you. You may find, for instance, that current sports recreation participants are not primarily concerned about health benefits. They go to the gym because their friends are there and they enjoy the social aspects of aerobics and basketball. Or you might find that some people will not participate no matter how healthy physical activity is because they are afraid of looking foolish on the basketball court or out of shape in aerobics classes. Perhaps recreational programs are scheduled when many people cannot attend them. If these factors are important, simply educating people about the health benefits of exercise may not do much good.

Diverse Motivations Keep in mind that health concerns are not people's only motivation. People are most receptive to options that satisfy them on many levels (intellectual, emotional, personal, social, etc.). In assessing the situation, it is important not to assume that everyone is motivated in the same way as you. Consider (and ask about) the diversity among people who might participate in the sports recreation program. Your audience is probably not just traditional college students (a diverse group in itself), but international students, middle-aged and elderly students, experienced students and newcomers, university faculty and staff members, and maybe even community members and children.

In Step 2, you will attempt to learn about your audience and choose a portion of it to target. Being sensitive to diverse beliefs and motivations can help you understand why people behave as they do. This understanding is crucial to your success as a health promoter.

Step 2: Analyzing and Segmenting the Audience

After assessing the health benefits and the current situation at the sports recreation department, you are ready to analyze the audience. This will involve asking a larger number of people many of the questions you asked in preliminary research.

Audience research may seem an unnecessary step, but experienced campaign planners know better. Audience analysis allows health promoters to collect important data about people's behaviors and preferences. Additionally, it helps them identify a target audience and determine how best to reach and motivate that audience. Edward Maibach and Roxanne Parrott (1995) applaud promoters for considering the audience's needs before they determine campaign goals. As they put it, audience-centered analysis "means that health messages are designed primarily to respond to the needs and situation of the target audience, rather than to the needs and situation of the message designers or sponsoring organizations" (p. 167).

Data Collection There are several ways to learn about potential audience members. Preexisting databases are a good place to start (Salmon & Atkin, 2003). For example you might request demographics about the student body and usage statistics from the intramural department.

You should also find out more specific information about the target audience's beliefs, values, and habits. This section describes the comparative advantages of using interviews, questionnaires, and focus groups to learn about the people you wish to influence.

Interviews Interviews are a useful way to collect information. In an **interview,** one person asks another person questions, either in person or over the phone. Here are different interview strategies and the advantages and limitations of each (based on Frey, Botan, Friedman, & Kreps, 1991).

- **Highly scheduled interviews.** Interviewers are given specific questions to ask and are not allowed to make comments or ask additional questions. This helps minimize the interviewers' influence on respondents' answers, but it does not allow for follow-up questions or clarifications. Answers are typically brief, but easy to tally and compare.

- **Moderately scheduled interviews.** Interviewers are given a set of questions but are allowed to ask for clarification and additional information as they see fit. These interviews are more relaxed and conversational, but less precise, than highly scheduled interviews.
- **Unscheduled interviews.** Interviewers are given a list of topics but are encouraged to phrase questions as they wish and to probe for more information when it seems useful and appropriate. These interviews are useful for collecting information about respondents' feelings, but they do not yield answers that can be easily compared or tallied.

Questionnaires Questionnaires are another popular way to collect audience information because they can be administered to large numbers of people in less time than it would take to interview them. A **questionnaire** asks respondents to write down their answers to a list of questions. In general, written responses are more limited than interview responses, but people may be more willing to answer sensitive questions in writing, especially if surveys are conducted anonymously.

Communication Skill Builders: Designing a Questionnaire Here are some guidelines for designing an effective questionnaire (based on Arnold & McClure, 1989; Frey et al., 1991).

- *Keep it brief.* People are most likely to complete the questionnaire if it is no longer than one page.
- *Seek immediate response.* If people take time to complete the survey right away, the response rate will be higher.
- *Collect demographic information.* Demographic information includes age, sex, income, college major, occupation, and the like. Ask respondents to select the appropriate responses from a list of all possibilities. (These are called **fixed alternative questions.**) This will make it easy for respondents to answer and easy for you to count and compare answers.
- *Ask about knowledge and behaviors.* A mixture of open and closed questions will yield the most useful information. **Open questions** allow respondents to express ideas in their own words (e.g., How do you feel about basketball and aerobics?). **Closed questions** require very brief answers (e.g., Do you prefer basketball or aerobics?).
- *Pilot (pretest) the questionnaire.* Try the questionnaire on a few people before making a full set of copies. Ask them to indicate if any questions are confusing or leading, if the fixed alternative questions include all possible answers, and if they can think of other questions that should be added.

- *Allow for anonymity.* If you think people may wish to respond anonymously, provide a way for them to fill out questionnaires privately and submit them without revealing their identity (as in a drop box or through the mail).

Focus Groups A third option for collecting information is the use of focus groups. A **focus group** involves a small number of people who respond to questions posed by a moderator (Berko, Wolvin, & Curtis, 1993). The moderator encourages group members to speak openly on topics relevant to the campaign. Members' comments are usually recorded so they can be studied later. Focus groups are useful for learning the target audience's feelings about an issue. Lisa Goldman and Stanton Glantz (1998) used focus groups to gauge the effectiveness of various strategies used in antismoking campaigns. Kim Witte (1997) used focus groups to ask teenage mothers about the impact of peer pressure and education on young people's sexual behavior.

Whether you use surveys, questionnaires, or focus groups, it is important to think carefully about whom you include. Choosing people to include is called **sampling** the population. Interviews and surveys allow you to collect information from a large number of people. Make sure your sample reflects the diversity in the population you are considering. By contrast, focus group members are usually chosen because they are members of a target group (like nontraditional students or freshmen). Too much diversity can make it hard to develop a focused discussion. Just be careful not to assume that focus group responses reflect the views of the population overall.

Communication Skill Builders: Conducting Focus Groups Experts offer the following tips for conducting effective focus groups (based on Greenbaum, 1991; Katcher, 1997):

- Determine what type of information you most want to collect. Bruce Katcher (1997) advises: "You must be clear from the outset what you really want to learn from the participants and how you will use the information" (paragraph 7). For example, are you more interested in the opinions of people who already use the sports recreation center or people who are not yet involved?
- Design a list of open questions to get the information you most want.
- Appoint (or hire) a facilitator to lead the focus group discussion. A good facilitator helps people feel comfortable expressing their opinions, allows everyone to contribute to the discussion and does not influence members' responses. Many experts recommend using a facilitator not associated with the promotion effort because focus group members may feel more comfortable voicing criticisms and because the facilitator may be more objective.
- Choose 7 to 10 people from your target audience to make up the focus groups.

Box 12.2 RESOURCES
Careers in Health Education and Promotion

If you are considering a career educating people about healthy behaviors, you might wish to become acquainted with the following organizations and programs:

- American Public Health Association: www.apha.org
- Area Health Education Centers: www.nationalahec.org/main/ahec.asp
- Center for Disease Prevention and Control Division of Health Communication: www.cdc.gov/od/oc/hcomm/aboutdivision.html
- National Institutes of Health: www.nih.gov
- Social Marketing Institute: www.social-marketing.org
- Society for Public Health Education: www.sophe.org

- Recruit people who share similar characteristics relevant to your program. For instance, it is more effective to conduct separate focus groups with people who use the workout facilities and those who do not. Too much diversity among participants makes it difficult to develop key ideas and may discourage some people from participating.
- Arrange to conduct the focus group in a conference room or another comfortable area. (It is customary to provide refreshments for focus group participants.)
- Arrange to unobtrusively audiotape and videotape the session (with participants' permission).
- Review the information collected.
- Consider conducting multiple focus groups with different members of your target audience.

Segmenting the Audience The next step is to use the data you have collected to identify a target audience. Following are some questions to consider:

- Who is currently involved (and not involved) in the recommended activity?
- What are people's reasons for participating (or not)?
- Who stands to benefit from the recommended behaviors?
- Who is in most need of these benefits?
- Who might reasonably be expected to adopt these behaviors?
- Is there anyone who should *not* be encouraged to participate?

Remember that some campaigns do more harm than good by recommending behaviors inappropriate for the audience. For example, vigorous exercise is not right for everybody. As you consider who should receive information about the sports recreation program, it may be tempting to target everyone possible. However, research suggests that appealing to an entire population at one time does not usually pay off. Because people tend to evaluate information based on its relevance to them, a broad message may seem too general for anyone to take personally (Slater, 1995). Furthermore, tastes differ, and what appeals to one group does not necessarily appeal to others. Messages that try to satisfy everyone very often become so generic they do not interest anyone. The odds are that, even on small campuses, the population is varied enough to make audience segmentation preferable.

Segmenting the audience means identifying specific groups who are alike in important ways and whose involvement is important to the purpose of the campaign (Slater, 1995). As you attempt to segment the audience, avoid grouping people based on superficial attributes. Characteristics such as race and income are not reliable indicators of how people think and behave (Williams & Flora, 1995). People within those categories may have very divergent viewpoints. Identifying groups on the basis of similar goals and experiences is harder to do, but more productive.

Be open to unexpected combinations. For instance, freshmen and university staff members may be alike in that they feel out of place at the campus gym. Where the campaign is concerned, this similarity may be more important than the differences between these groups. Based on these similarities, you might decide that both freshman and staff members would respond more enthusiastically to personal invitations than to bulletin board notices.

It is sometimes difficult to decide where to draw the line in segmenting an audience. Nurit Guttman (1997) describes the dilemma of choosing between a small audience of high-need individuals and a large audience whose needs are less severe. There is no definitive rule for choosing, but health promoters who are sensitive to audience needs and health benefits are most likely to make reasonable judgments.

Based on your audience analysis, you might decide to target your sports recreation campaign toward people new on campus (students, staff, or both), to community members, or to nontraditional students. You might find that current participants do not reflect the racial and ethnic diversity on campus, or that the current membership is mostly men or women, or that people with disabilities are not as involved as they could be. Consequently, you might direct the campaign toward groups that are currently underutilizing the sports recreation program or those people who have the greatest need of the benefits it offers. And do not forget the current participants. Maybe their involvement can be improved. The possibilities are numerous, making it especially important to research the audience before choosing a segment of it to target.

Audience as a Person Once a target audience has been identified, Lefebvre et al. (1995) recommend imagining the audience as a single person, complete "with name, gender, occupation, and lifestyle" (p. 221). With this "person" in mind, they pose the following questions for consideration:

- What is important to this person?
- What are the person's feelings, attitudes, and beliefs about the behavior change (including perceived benefits and barriers)?
- What are his or her media habits?

Lefebvre and co-authors say that imagining the audience as a person is useful in focusing the campaign and in creating messages that seem personal and immediate.

Audience Profiles Every audience, and every audience member, is unique, but some overall characteristics may help guide your efforts. Here is some information that may be useful to you as you attempt to understand your target audience.

Young Audiences The age of your target audience may have some affect on how members perceive health messages. Although it is difficult to make generalizations about adult audiences, the developmental stages of youth often have relatively predictable effects on children and teenagers.

Children are an important audience. As Erica Weintraub Austin (1995) points out, it is easier to prevent bad habits than to break them. Sending consistent messages to children early on may prevent them from developing unhealthy behaviors. Adults are in a good position to help. Evidence supports that children are strongly influenced by adults. On the bright side, they tend to follow their parents' advice (Henriksen & Jackson, 1998). However, children often seek to emulate adult behaviors—even the unhealthy ones. Glantz (1996) cautions that portraying behaviors such as smoking as "adult-only" may actually make them seem more appealing to youngsters.

Adolescents often believe they are unlike other people and that others do not understand them (this is called **personal fable**). Consequently, they are likely to assume health warnings do not apply to them (Greene, Rubin, Hale, & Walters, 1996). Teenagers also tend to be extremely self-conscious and feel that people are scrutinizing their appearance and behavior (this is called **imaginary audience**). This makes them sensitive to peer pressure and social approval, which can work for or against health promotion efforts (Greene et al., 1996). Researchers emphasize the importance of peer support for healthy behaviors. Austin (1995) reminds promoters that teens' immediate social concerns may outweigh their long-term health considerations. In Austin's words, adolescents may "care more that smoking will make their breath smell bad than that they could develop cancer" (p. 115).

Sensation-Seekers In the 1990s, *Rolling Stone* magazine ran an advertisement that proclaimed, "Why Women Find a Little Prick Attractive." Beside the headline is a photograph of a beautiful woman in a black teddy. In smaller type below, the reader learns that the prick is a small mark on a man's finger where he has drawn blood to verify he is not HIV-infected (Ivinski, 1997). The advertisement touts an at-home HIV test. It concludes: "And if the woman in your life is having any doubts—don't worry. That little prick is sure to satisfy her."

As you might imagine, "The Little Prick" ad drew considerable comment. At least one critic considered it irresponsible to portray a serious subject such as HIV in such a whimsical (some would say tasteless) manner. As Pamela Ivinksi (1997) expressed it:

> Using sex to sell a test that determines whether someone has contracted a virus that's often transmitted during sex, and then subtly implying in the copy that the user shouldn't worry because he'll probably test negative, and he can use that fact to attract women for more sex, is a little bit creepy, not to mention misleading and even cynical. (paragraph 8)

The advertisement's creators acknowledged that the ad was not for everyone, but argued that it was shocking and sexy enough to make young men pay attention to an important topic.

Adolescents and young adults are more likely than others to be high **sensation-seekers,** meaning they enjoy new and intense experiences (Everett & Palmgreen, 1995; Zuckerman, 1994). The danger with high sensation-seekers is that risky behaviors appeal to them. Not only are they less likely than others to take precautions, they are more apt to be in dangerous situations in the first place. For instance, high sensation-seekers typically have more sexual partners than other people do, but they are less likely to use condoms (Sheer & Cline, 1995). The intense messages that sensation-seekers enjoy may be too much for most audiences, making it difficult to target high-risk individuals without offending others. (For ethical considerations about health promotion, see Box 12.3.)

Underinformed Audiences In their article "Lessons From the Field," three noted health promotion specialists urge campaign designers not to overlook marginalized members of society. They write:

> Conducting communication research within diverse ethnic/racial/underserved communities will be especially important in the future. Attention to these audiences is a necessity, not a nicety. . . . Working with an audience for the first time inevitably brings frustrations as one discovers that principles applied successfully in the past with other populations do not necessarily fit in other contexts. Our experience has been that the potential payoff is worth the initial frustration. (Edgar, Freimuth, & Hammond, 2003, p. 627)

Box 12.3 ETHICAL CONSIDERATIONS The Politics of Prevention—Who Should Pay?

Health promotion may seem like a win-win situation. If people can be encouraged to prevent disease and injuries, they will enjoy better health and the nation's health costs will be kept under control. How far should we carry this line of reasoning? Should people who work hard to be healthy get cut-rate health care? Should they be given advantages when competing for jobs? If people knowingly engage in unhealthy behaviors, should society help pay for their medical bills?

Experts estimate that Americans pay more than $100 billion each year to treat injuries and diseases that are largely preventable (Johnson & Bootman, 1995). The expense eats up tax money and leads to hikes in health insurance rates. As Daniel Wikler (1987) puts it, "The person who takes risks with his [or her] own health gambles with resources which belong to others" (p. 14). Some theorists argue that people who continue risky behavior (like smoking, overeating, or driving without seatbelts) when they know it is bad for them should pay from their own pockets when their behavior leads to medical expenses.

In a related issue, some feel that companies that profit from selling unhealthy products should pay part of the health bill. State and federal governments have sought damages from tobacco companies in the last decade, charging that it is unfair for tobacco companies to make huge profits while others foot the enormous bill of treating tobacco-related illnesses. Around the world, about 11,000 people die every day from tobacco-related illnesses—totaling nearly 5 million a year (WHO, "Health Impact," n.d.). The expense is magnified by the impact on society. In general, smokers cut 13 to 14 years off their life expectancy (MMWR, 2003). Experts estimate that smoking cost Americans $150 billion between 1995 and 1999 in terms of medical expenses and lost productivity (MMWR, 2003). Some companies now refuse to hire smokers or people who are extremely overweight because they are at greater health risk, and thus likely to cost the company more money in health benefits and sick leave. Similarly, some insurance companies offer a discount to people who do not smoke and those who remain accident-free or complete informational programs such as defensive driving courses.

On the other side of the issue, some worry that government and employers are becoming too much involved in people's lifestyle decisions. Some charge that groups like Mothers Against Drunk Driving (MADD) are taking a good thing too far by seeking to punish people for drinking even small amounts of alcohol (DiLorenzo & Bennett, 1998). Similarly, policy analyst Will Crawford (1997) warns that the government may soon be telling people what to eat in the name of controlling obesity. Some people say that increasing the "sin taxes" on alcohol and tobacco will hurt consumers, not companies, and they are afraid the taxes will be extended to cover snack foods and other not-so-healthy items. All in all, opponents of tighter health requirements say you cannot control the risks people take without controlling their freedom to choose.

What Do You Think?

1. Should people who knowingly take health risks pay more for health insurance? Should they be denied insurance? Should they be denied health services?
2. Should people be required by law to engage in healthy practices (like being immunized or exercising regularly)?
3. Should it be against the law to sell or advertise products known to have a high health risk? Does it matter if such products are addictive?
4. Do you agree with the rationale behind many states' seatbelt and motorcycle helmet laws—that people who neglect safety precautions not only endanger their own lives, but increase the trauma and expense for everybody?
5. In your opinion, which of the following behaviors (if any) should be grounds for denying or limiting health benefits? On what criteria do you make your judgments?
   - Smoking
   - Engaging in unprotected sex
   - Exceeding the speed limit
   - Snow skiing
   - Neglecting to exercise regularly
   - Overeating
   - Playing football
   - Rescuing accident victims
6. If a person has a family history of a disease, should he or she be required by society to take extra health precautions?

Suggested Sources

Califano, J. A. (1994). Revealing the link between campaign financing and deaths caused by tobacco. *Journal of the American Medical Association, 272,* 1217–1218.

Crawford, W. (1997, October). Taxing for health? *Consumers' Research Magazine, 80,* 34.

Faden, R. R. (1987). Ethical issues in government sponsored public health campaigns. *Health Education Quarterly, 14,* 27–37.

continued

Box 12.3 ETHICAL CONSIDERATIONS
The Politics of Prevention—Who Should Pay? *continued*

Goodman, L. E., & Goodman, M. J. (1986, April). Prevention—How misuse of a concept undercuts its worth. *Hastings Center Report, 16,* 26–38.

Gostin, L. O., Arno, P. S., & Brandt, A. M. (1997). FDA regulation of tobacco advertising and youth smoking: Historical, social, and constitutional perspectives. *Journal of the American Medical Association, 277,* 410–419.

Veatch, R. M. (1980). Voluntary risks to health. *Journal of the American Medical Association, 243,* 50–55.

Wikler, D. (1987). Who should be blamed for being sick? *Health Education Quarterly, 14,* 11–25.

Unfortunately, people most in need of health resources and information are often the least likely to benefit from health information campaigns. (See Box 12.4 for more on the knowledge gap hypothesis.)

The challenge for health promoters is to come up with specialized and innovative means of disseminating information to people most in need of it. For example, Satya Krishnan (1996) recommends that clinics educate people with low reading skills by showing instructional health videos in their waiting rooms.

As you complete Step 2, it may seem that you have already done a lot of work and you still do not know what the campaign will involve. Your hard work will not go to waste. Research shows that campaigns launched without a clear understanding of the audience, current situation, and potential benefits are often frustrating to create and ineffective at reaching their goals. With a target audience in mind, you are ready for Step 3.

Step 3: Establishing Campaign Goals and Objectives

By this point you should have a fairly clear impression of the sports recreation department, its potential benefits, and the people you most want to reach with your campaign. Collecting and analyzing data has prepared you to establish goals for your campaign.

Goals state in clear, measurable terms exactly what you hope to achieve with the campaign. You might consider the following questions:

- What exactly do you want people to start/stop/continue doing?
- If the goal is a behavior, when (and for how long) should it occur?
- How will you know if your campaign has been successful?

Box 12.4 THEORETICAL FOUNDATIONS
The Knowledge Gap Hypothesis

The **knowledge gap hypothesis** proposes that people with plentiful information resources (such as newspapers, televisions, computers, and well-informed friends and advisors) are likely to know more and to continue learning more than people with fewer information resources (Tichenor, Donohue, & Olien, 1970). Income and education are highly linked to resource availability and media habits. Consequently, people of high socioeconomic status tend to be knowledge rich, and people of low status tend to be knowledge poor. The gap remains even when less educated persons are highly motivated to learn the information (Viswanath, Kahn, Finnegan, Hertog, & Potter, 1993). New information often increases the knowledge gap rather than diminishing it. In other words, the people who already know a lot learn more, and the others fall farther behind.

Unfortunately, people who are information poor are often most in need of health information. William Brown (1992) reports that members of minority cultures in the United States are at highest risk for contracting AIDS, but they are less informed than others about AIDS and perceive themselves to be less vulnerable than others.

There are several reasons underprivileged persons are hard to reach with health messages. One barrier is ethnic. Underprivileged audiences tend to be disproportionately comprised of people from minority cultures. They may be skeptical about mainstream messages, either because they seem irrelevant or because they mistrust the sources. For example, African Americans trust media outlets (magazines, television stations, and radio stations) owned by African Americans more than they trust other media (Holden, 1998; "Study Reveals," 1998).

Second, underprivileged people are more likely than others to rely on television instead of newspapers and magazines (Engelberg, Flora, & Nass, 1997). Partly because print sources are more detailed, newspaper readers are typically more knowledgeable than TV viewers. Thus, underprivileged persons' media habits often put them at a disadvantage.

Third, underprivileged audiences may have different priorities. A high-tech AIDS message was perceived negatively by African Americans, who felt that science and technology cause people to lose jobs (Walters, Walters, Kern-Foxworth, & Priest, 1997). Other research shows that people worried about violence and hunger may feel long-term health issues are the least of their worries (Holtgrave, Tinsley, & Kay, 1995).

Finally, underprivileged audiences are more likely to trust interpersonal sources (like friends and health professionals) than they are to trust messages in mainstream media (Engelberg et al., 1997). This makes it difficult to reach underprivileged people in large numbers.

Relevant to the sports recreation campaign, you may decide that your goal is to sign up 40 freshmen in 3 months. Or perhaps you have decided to focus on students with disabilities or newcomers. Your goal may be to get at least 20 current participants to bring an individual from one of those groups to an event.

Make sure your goals are oriented to the overall purpose of the campaign. For instance, if people participate in aerobics only once, will there be health benefits? If not, it may be important to set a goal for continued participation—perhaps attendance once a week for at least 2 months. Think ahead about how you will assess the campaign's effects. This may involve follow-up surveys or sign-up sheets to keep track of participation. Setting measurable goals allows you (and others) to determine if the campaign has been a success. It is important to set meaningful and realistic goals and to consider in advance how you will test the effectiveness of your campaign.

Health promoters are increasingly being held accountable for their efforts (McGrath, 1995). **Accountability** means demonstrating how the results of a project compare to the money and time invested in it. For example, a medical center reorganized its marketing and public relations department because patient surveys consistently showed that people chose the medical center based on their doctors' advice, not on advertising. The hospital did not completely discontinue advertisements (employee surveys showed the ads raised workplace morale), but the medical center redirected part of its effort into marketing services directly to physicians.

Step 4: Selecting Channels of Communication

A **channel** is a means of communicating information, either directly (in person) or indirectly (through media like TV or radio or computers). To select the best channels for your campaign, consider what channels your target audience uses most and trusts most.

Sometimes channel selection is limited by time or money. Your sports recreation enrollment effort will probably not involve full-color magazine ads or sophisticated television commercials. Nevertheless, as a health promoter, you should be familiar with all types of channels. Moreover, do not assume too quickly that a channel is out of your reach. For example, you may not produce television commercials, but you might book appearances on local television talk shows.

Channel Characteristics You should also consider the advantages and limitations of different channels. Experts suggest that channels for a health campaign be evaluated in terms of reach, specificity, and impact (Schooler, Chaffee, Flora, & Roser, 1998). **Reach** refers to the number of people who will be exposed to a message via a particular channel. **Specificity** refers to how accurately the message can be targeted to a specific group of people. **Impact** is how influential a message is likely to be.

Television has a larger and more diverse audience than any other medium (Warner, 1987). As such, it has immense reach. However, because the audience is so large and diverse, it is hard to tailor messages to particular viewers. Thus, television has low specificity (although that is changing somewhat with the creation of special-interest cable and satellite programs). Radio stations and large-circulation newspapers and magazines also have broad reach.

Although it may be tempting to aim for the broadest reach possible, it is advisable to focus on your target audience. Exposure that is broader than necessary can waste resources and contribute to information overload, making it difficult for people to identify which messages are most important and relevant to them (Rees, 1994). One solution is to use channels like magazines and direct mail that have high specificity. Magazines are often marketed to people with specific interests such as health, family, entertainment, automobiles, hobbies, travel, and so on (Biagi, 1999). Direct mail is sent directly to people at their homes or businesses. Direct mail is inexpensive compared to mass media and offers more assurance that campaign messages are actually reaching target audience members, even people who do not use traditional media much (Dignan, Michielutte, Jones-Lighty, & Bahnson, 1994).

Impact is usually related to arousal and involvement. **Arousal** refers to how emotionally stimulating and exciting a message is (Schooler et al., 1998). Interactive computer programs are a good example. They are very engrossing, with colorful graphics, moving images, and sound (Street & Rimal, 1997). **Involvement** is the amount of mental effort required to understand a message (Parrott, 1995). Interpersonal communication is high involvement. It requires a great deal of thought and action. Thus, health professionals, family members, and friends tend to have high impact. Newspapers are also high-involvement channels because people must read and use their imaginations. Television is low involvement because viewers passively observe the sounds and sights displayed for them.

Greater involvement usually means more attention to detail, more evaluation of the message, longer memory of it, and a greater likelihood to act on it (Petty & Cacioppo, 1981). In short, people usually pay closer attention when using high-involvement channels like reading and talking, and this affects how much they are influenced by the information. Surveys show that people who use high-involvement channels are usually better informed about health than people who rely on low-involvement channels like television (for literature review, see Parrott, 1995).

Communication Technology: Using Computers to Narrow Messages We often speak of *broadcasting* messages to large audiences. Messages in the mass media draw people's attention to health topics. However, there are advantages to *narrowcasting* as well.

Narrowcasting, or tailored communication, is designed to meet the specific needs of individual consumers. Matthew Kreuter and colleagues (1999) use the example of a doctor's visit to treat high cholesterol. As usual, the physician offers advice on diet and exercise, but this time the doctor also provides a printout tailor-made for you:

> It seems like the cold weather has been keeping you from walking every day like you had hoped to in your physical activity plan. Did you know that many of the local malls open early in the winter for walkers? Crestwood Mall is the one closest to your house, and it opens for walkers at 6:30 every morning. Mall walking might also help with your recent lack of motivation. You've been struggling with exercise because your walking partner moved away, and this might be a way for you to meet some new people, and not feel like you're exercising alone. (Kreuter, Farrell, Olevitch, & Brennan, 1999, p. 2)

The information might also include healthy recipes suited to your family's preferences and tips for finding healthy food in the local supermarket.

Before receiving tailored health messages, people typically fill out questionnaires about their health, habits, preferences, and environments. The questions go beyond simple demographics such as age and sex (Rimal & Adkins, 2003). For example, if the goal is to help older adults avoid harmful falls, the questions may ask about the presence of stairs, handrails, and rugs, and the need to do lawn work and home repairs (Kreuter et al., 1999). This information is entered into computer databanks (either online or in the doctor's office) that produce individualized profiles and suggestions. For example, the tailored response might suggest ways to reorganize one's home to minimize the chance of falling and community resources to help with riskier activities such as house painting and snow shoveling (Kreuter et al., 1999). It is also possible to key in information about an individual's education and literacy level, so that the resulting printout is usable and comprehensible, perhaps showing mostly pictures and diagrams if the client is not proficient at reading (Bernhardt & Cameron, 2003).

The idea is that people are more likely to act on customized information than to sift through data that may or may not apply to them or that may exceed their comprehension level. Kreuter and colleagues (1999) compare tailored health messages to a realtor who provides a list of homes that meet a client's wishes rather than a realtor who says, "Here's a street map of our entire city. By going up and down all the streets, you're sure to find something that meets your needs" (p. 4).

Multichannel Campaigns As you have seen, there are advantages to broadcasting and narrowcasting. Many times, the best chance of making a difference is to reach people through several channels (Flay & Burton, 1990). Multichannel efforts are important because people have different communication patterns and preferences. What appeals to some people may not appeal to others. For example, Richard Street Jr. and Timothy Manning (1997) found that women who were highly interested in breast cancer preferred to get information about it through an interactive, multimedia computer program. However, women who were less interested preferred to watch a videotape about breast cancer, presumably because it required less effort. In this study, women learned about the same amount from both formats.

BOX 12.5 RESOURCES
More on Tailored Health Communication

Following are some sources on designing and using narrowcast messages.

- *Annals of Behavioral Medicine* special issue on tailored health messages, September 2000.
- Kreuter, M., Farrell, D., Olevitch, L., & Brennan, L. (1999). *Tailoring health messages: Customizing communication with computer technology.* Mahwah, NJ: Lawrence Erlbaum.
- National Cancer Institute's Online Guide to Creating Tailored Health Messages. *Health message tailoring: First cut.* Dino.nci.nih.gov/public/glassman/TailoringGuide.
- Science Panel on Interactive Communication and Health. *Wired for health and well-being: The emergence of interactive health communication.* (1999, April). Washington, D.C.: U.S. Department of Health and Human Services, U.S. Government Printing Office. Available online at www.health.gov/scipich/pubs/finalreport.htm.

Other researchers suggest that culture may affect channel preferences. Traditional Hispanics typically consider health an intimate topic, not to be discussed outside one's close social network (Alcalay & Bell, 1996). African Americans often get health messages and health-related assistance at church. The 635 African-American churches included in one study sponsored a total of 1,804 outreach programs, offering such services as food, shelter, substance abuse counseling, and AIDS education (Thomas, Quinn, Billingsley, & Caldwell, 1994). The researchers suggest that health promoters work with churches when trying to reach and assist African Americans.

Mass-mediated and interpersonal channels are also complementary in that the media messages typically influence what people think about and talk about (see Rogers & Dearing, 1988), but people do not simply buy into everything the media says. They are also likely to be influenced by discussions with neighbors and family members. The phrase **diffusion of innovations** refers to the process through which new information is filtered and passed along throughout a community (Rogers, 1983). Researchers suggest that some community members act as opinion leaders, who have credibility by virtue of their expertise or social standing. Often, opinion leaders pass along new ideas or information from the media to other people. In this way, media messages may influence people indirectly whether they use the media or not. The process by which people relay media messages to others is called **two-step flow** (Brosius & Weimann, 1996; Lazarsfeld, Berelson, & Gaudet, 1948). For example, physicians can be powerful change agents. In the 1990s, citizens of Milwaukee were warned via pamphlets and news stories that lead pipes might be poisoning the water in their homes. Although inundated with information, the people at highest risk (poorer residents living in older homes) did not perceive their risk to be any higher than others and were relatively unwilling to take precautions (Griffin & Dunwoody, 2000). However, these residents *did* respond when their doctors told them they were personally at risk.

SUMMARY

The success of a public health campaign depends on how well it interests and motivates the audience. It is unrealistic to think every audience member will react in the same way. People are motivated by a variety of factors, and they have different ideas about what is interesting or important.

People are inclined to pay more attention to messages that seem relevant to them. Therefore, campaigns directed at "everyone" may not pique the interest of anyone. Health campaign success stories show that it is important to know the audience well, take positive action, establish clear goals, measure your success, and make behaviors socially rewarding.

The first step in creating a health campaign is to research potential benefits of the campaign. Find out who stands to gain, who is already behaving according to campaign recommendations, and what alternatives exist.

The second step is to choose a target audience. Interviews, questionnaires, and focus groups are useful ways to learn about potential audience members—what they like, what they know, how they typically behave, what they consider important, and more. You may wish to choose to target people in great need or those who are most likely to respond to the campaign. Keep in mind that it is typically difficult to reach audiences who are culturally different from the mainstream. However, considering the knowledge gap hypothesis, these audiences are often the most in need of health information and assistance.

With a target audience in mind, the third step in creating a health campaign is to establish goals and objectives. Goals should be clear and measurable so that the campaign's effects can be accurately assessed.

Fourth, health promoters select channels through which to communicate campaign messages. Channels typically differ in terms of reach, specificity, and impact. Often, the best campaigns make use of several channels. All in all, the media play an important role in promoting health issues, but media impact is limited without interpersonal reinforcement.

KEY TERMS

health-promoting behaviors
health promotion campaigns
health promoter
interview
highly scheduled interviews
moderately scheduled interviews
unscheduled interviews

questionnaire
- fixed alternative questions
- open questions
- closed questions

focus group
sampling
segmenting an audience
personal fable
imaginary audience
sensation-seekers
knowledge gap hypothesis
goals
accountability
channel
- reach
- specificity
- impact
    - arousal
    - involvement

narrowcasting
diffusion of innovations
two-step flow

REVIEW QUESTIONS

1. Name some of the factors that influence people's behavior.
2. What job duties are communication specialists qualified to perform in the field of health promotion?
3. What are four qualities of good campaigns (as illustrated by the exemplary campaigns in this chapter)?
4. What questions might you address as you research the current situation and potential benefits of a health campaign?
5. Why is it important to select a target audience?
6. What are three types of interviews? How do they compare?
7. Provide some guidelines for designing an effective questionnaire.
8. What is the difference between an open and closed question?
9. Give some guidelines for conducting effective focus groups.
10. Why is sampling important?
11. What are some questions to consider when segmenting an audience?
12. What are some factors to keep in mind if your target audience includes children? If it includes adolescents?
13. What type of health promotion messages are likely to appeal to high sensation-seekers?
14. Do you believe people should pay more for health insurance if they engage in risky or unhealthy behaviors? Why or why not?
15. Using the knowledge gap hypothesis, explain why people of low socioeconomic status are often underinformed about health issues.
16. What factors make it particularly difficult to influence underprivileged persons with conventional promotion efforts?
17. What are some questions to consider when determining campaign goals?
18. Explain how channels differ in terms of reach, specificity, and impact.
19. Describe the process of creating narrowcast messages. What are the advantages of narrowcasting?
20. Why are multichannel efforts recommended?

CLASS ACTIVITY

Focus Group Exercise

Imagine that the class is planning to conduct a focus group discussion concerning an upcoming health campaign.

1. Choose a health-related topic that affects everyone in the audience (e.g., drinking enough water, getting sufficient sleep, walking, or jogging).
2. Brainstorm what topics and questions you might present for focus group members to discuss.
    - Remember to ask questions that will reveal the group's current behaviors, motivations, reservations, attitudes, and knowledge about the topic.
    - Keep in mind that questions should be phrased in neutral terms to avoid influencing participants' responses.
3. Now pretend the class is the focus group.
4. Choose one or two members of the class to facilitate the focus group discussion, and one or two members to take notes (note-takers may take part in the group discussion).
    - Remember that facilitators should encourage everyone to participate.
    - They should ask neutral follow-up questions to probe for information.
    - Note-takers should keep a record of the comments made. (Brief notes will do.)
5. Have the facilitators lead a group discussion based on the questions the class has suggested.
6. When time is up, have the facilitators and note-takers summarize what was said.

What Do You Think?

1. Did the focus group discussion reveal useful information?
2. Were you surprised by comments made?
3. Did most people agree or were there a variety of opinions?
4. Did you feel the focus group accurately represented the concerns of most college students?
5. Do you think focus groups are a good way to assess audience needs and interests? Why or why not?
6. How would you improve focus group interactions in the future?

CHAPTER 13

Designing and Implementing Health Campaigns

An adolescent on a city street pulls back an orange curtain and quotes a tobacco industry document proposing to use ice cream trucks to promote the sale of drugs.

The TV spot described above, like other messages of the *truth* campaign, is simple and direct. In another, a young man reveals a tobacco industry plan to target gay and homeless persons. The plan was called Subculture and Urban Marketing—Project SCUM for short.

The *truth* campaign's website introduces the concept this way:

> We called ourselves truth because we knew we'd never have to make this stuff up. It's all in there like some kind of messed up soap opera. The tobacco industry was required to make all these documents available to us, the public, so we can figure out for ourselves what's going on—and what's been going on for a while. All we have to do is pull back the curtain and show it. Kinda like a mutant Vanna White. (www.thetruth.com)

As part of the largest anti-tobacco campaign ever aimed at young audiences, the *truth* campaign has drawn the attention of both researchers and adolescents. The rebellious, youth-oriented nature of the ads makes them appealing to the target audience, youth ages 12 to 17. A report in the *American Journal of Public Health* reveals that teens' awareness of anti-tobacco messages nearly doubled in the first 10 months of the *truth* campaign. Youths exposed to *truth* campaign messages were significantly less likely than others to consider smoking "cool" and more likely to believe that tobacco companies lie to sell their products (Farrelly, Healton, Davis, Messeri, & Haviland, 2002).

By contrast, evidence shows that the "Think. Don't Smoke" campaign led by the Philip Morris tobacco company had a boomerang effect. Youths exposed to that campaign were slightly *more* likely than others to begin smoking in the next year (Farrelly et al., 2002). Analysts suggest that the Philip Morris ads do not damage the reputation of the tobacco industry in youth's eyes. In fact, the industry looks more respectable because of the messages (Farrelly et al., 2002). Following this study, some public health advocates asked Philip Morris to remove the PSAs from television ("Legacy Today Urged," 2002). (Philip Morris PSAs continue to run.)

Like many health promotion efforts today, the *truth* campaign is based on social marketing. **Social marketing** means that campaign designers apply the principles of commercial advertising to pro-social campaigns such as health promotion efforts (Lefebvre & Flora, 1988). The rationale is that many of the techniques used to sell goods and services work equally well when promoting healthy lifestyles. From a social marketing perspective, health-related behaviors have a price tag of sorts. They "cost" something, either in terms of money, time, energy, or some other investment. Although the cost does not translate into profits for the health promoter, the promoter is a salesperson of sorts, who tries to keep the cost as low as possible and convince people that the "price" of the recommended behavior is worth paying.

Because the concern in social marketing is primarily with what the "consumer" needs, health promoters make a great effort to understand the audience, assess its needs, and target specific people *truth* campaign designers clearly understood their audience. Matthew Farrelly and colleagues (2002) write:

> The "truth" brand builds a positive, tobacco-free identity through hard-hitting advertisements that feature youths confronting the tobacco industry. This rebellious rejection of tobacco and tobacco advertising channels youths' need to assert their independence and individuality, while countering tobacco marketing efforts. (paragraph 2)

Social marketing is also devoted to using multiple channels and conducting follow-up research to measure the success of campaign efforts. This process is exemplified by the Partnership for a Drug-Free America (PDFA), which has won many awards by applying the expertise of advertising professionals to the antidrug campaign. (See Box 13.1 for more about PDFA's efforts.)

PDFA is one of many groups devoted to improving public health. Also involved in this effort are the Ad Council, the American Heart Association, the American Lung Association, the Muscular Dystrophy Association, and others. Chapter 12 provided a guide through the first four stages of creating a health campaign to increase participation in a university sports recreation program:

Step 1: Defining the Situation and Potential Benefits

Step 2: Analyzing and Segmenting the Audience

Step 3: Establishing Campaign Goals and Objectives

Step 4: Selecting Channels of Communication

The process continues in this chapter with a description of key theories and techniques to create health promotion campaigns. The hypothetical sports recreation campaign helps illustrate how a health promotion effort comes together. Keep in mind that the same steps apply to campaigns of various sizes on any number of health topics.

This chapter begins by introducing five influential models of behavior change: the health belief model, social cognitive theory, the embedded behaviors model, the theory of reasoned action, and the transtheoretical model. It goes on to describe the three final stages in campaign development:

Step 5: Designing Campaign Messages

Step 6: Piloting and Implementing the Campaign

Step 7: Evaluating and Maintaining the Campaign

THEORIES OF BEHAVIOR CHANGE

The theories described here emphasize that people make lifestyle decisions based on a complex array of factors including personal perceptions, skills, social pressure, convenience, and more. Each theory described has earned considerable respect among health communication scholars and health promoters. Space is not available to discuss each theory in great detail, but this introduction should help orient the reader to the rich theory behind health campaign efforts and provide opportunities for further investigation. Applying these theories to health campaigns can have a positive effect—at least sometimes. Keep in mind that theories are only guiding principles, not magic formulas. No one theory works all of the time, or with every audience.

Health Belief Model

The **health belief model** proposes that people base their behavior choices on five primary considerations (Rosenstock, 1960; Stretcher & Rosenstock, 1997). Namely, people are most motivated to change their behaviors if they believe that

- they will be adversely affected if they do not change,
- the adverse effects will be considerable,
- behavior change will be effective in preventing the undesired outcome,
- the effort and cost of preventive behavior is worthwhile, and
- they are moved to action by a novel or eye-opening occurrence such as a brush with danger, a compelling warning message, or an alluring incentive.

In short, motivation is based on an individual's perception of personal susceptibility, serious consequences, worthwhile benefits, justifiable costs, and cues to actions.

The health belief model emphasizes that motivation is a complex process. Considering the factors just outlined, it seems naive to assume people will change simply because someone tells them to do so. A campaign message may be a cue to action, but unless someone has reason to believe the recommended behavior is useful and worthwhile, and will prevent an outcome that is otherwise likely to occur, the recommendation will probably not be motivation enough.

BOX 13.1 PERSPECTIVES
Unselling Drugs With Madison Avenue Know-How

Advertising agencies are usually interested in selling products and services—and they're very good at it. But Ginna Marston had a different idea. What if the top advertisers in the country tried to "unsell" something? Namely, illegal drugs.

In 1986 she helped launch the nonprofit Partnership for a Drug-Free America (PDFA). A former advertising professional herself, Marston was optimistic that, given the chance, professionals around the country would apply their talents to the anti-drug effort.

"At the time, a lot of people were looking at the end results of drug abuse—addiction, crime, and things like that," Marston explains. "We said, 'One thing we can do from a communication standpoint is start at the front end of the problem.' Considering that drug use is initially a choice, maybe we can influence people before they start."

Ginna Marston

From the beginning, the aim was simple and clear. "We try to make drugs seem uncool, unwise, less normal, and more consequential," says Marston. The idea was to promote this message with help from leading market researchers, copywriters, designers, producers, media decision makers, and others. By combining their talents and resources, Marston and her associates hoped to create and distribute anti-drug messages as carefully researched and appealing as multimillion-dollar campaigns—but without the cost.

Industry professionals answered the call. Marston marvels at how willing people were to set aside their professional rivalries and work together. "It was unprecedented in our business, having all these ad agencies working together on the same campaign," she explains. "You see creative directors from some of the top agencies in the country. Usually they're competitors, but they sit elbow to elbow reviewing ideas. It's really something."

From its first media release (the now famous "This is your brain on drugs" fried-egg series), PDFA was able to capture audiences' interest. The secret of the campaign's success, says Marston, is careful research and clearly focused messages. From PDFA headquarters in New York City, Marston serves as executive vice president, founding member, and director of program development, working with 30 paid staff members to research drug abuse trends, establish campaign goals, meet with concerned citizens and community leaders, and coordinate the efforts of volunteers across the country.

No idea gets off the ground without careful research beforehand. The PDFA staff uses focus groups, surveys, and interviews to collect the viewpoints of experts, drug users, potential drug users, national and community leaders, and others. They attend community meetings where they

Partnership for a Drug-Free America

DIRECTOR: ADAM REED
TITLE: "CORONER MOSAIC"

LENGTH: 30 SECONDS
ISCI CODE: DETV-4268

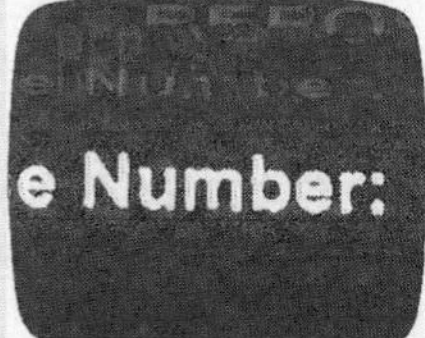

CORONER VO: Autopsy Report,

Case number

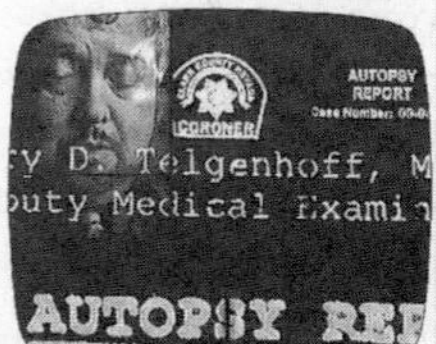

zero, zero, dash...

The body's that of a well-developed, well nourished adult Caucasian female.

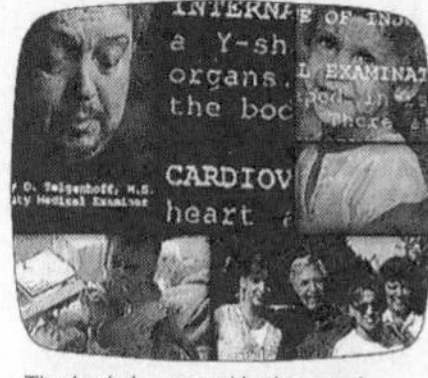

The body is opened in the usual manner with a y-shaped incision.

The lungs are 910 grams together.

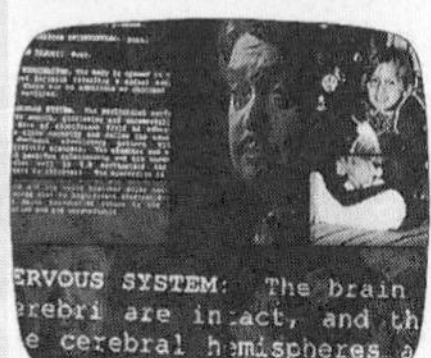

The brain is 1,460 grams.

The pericardial surfaces of the 280 gram heart are smooth, glistening and unremarkable.

It is my opinion that the death of Danielle C. Heird

is due to acute drug intoxication.

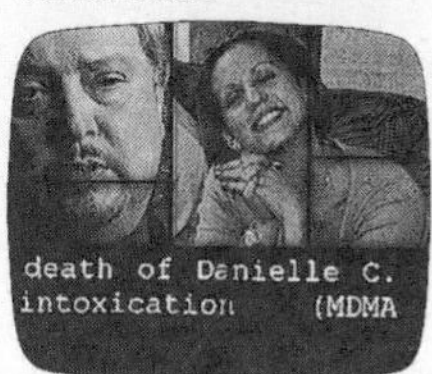

The only drug present in her system,

was ecstasy.

continued

BOX 13.1 PERSPECTIVES
Unselling Drugs With Madison Avenue Know-How, *continued*

talk to people battling drug addiction. They also interview young people to see how they feel about drugs and what they know.

The research helps to identify target audiences and develop clear strategies for reaching them. That clarity is reflected in the ads PDFA creates. "The better spots are those where there is a single message," Marston reflects. "We're concerned with whether the message is clear and: Does it make sense? Is it meaningful and credible to our target audience?"

Keeping in touch with audience members has earned PDFA a valued reputation, Marston says. "We have the kind of credibility that you only get over the long run when people know you're listening to them and telling the truth."

"A lot of people assume drug abuse is an epidemic in inner cities and there's nothing we can do," Marston says. "We found that most of these inner-city kids had *negative* feelings about drug use. They had seen what drugs could do and they didn't like them. They knew the facts and figures about drugs. They wanted something positive—a show of support."

When PDFA identified the drug Ecstasy as an emerging threat, the staff asked industry professionals to create a series of messages that shows how deadly the drug can be. As with all PDFA efforts, the Partnership's Creative Review Committee (made up of industry executives) reviewed the ideas and helped refine the best ones. They eventually approved production of the "Coroner's Mosaic" series shown here.

PDFA has also joined the White House effort to unsell marijuana and is working with the Robert Wood Johnson Foundation on a campaign to change attitudes about drug treatment. "It's not enough to stop children from experimenting with drugs," Marston says. "We have to encourage families with a problem to get the help they need."

PDFA devotes a great deal of research to assessing the effects of campaign messages. Often, they use a pretest-posttest design, tracking drug abuse in a particular area before and after campaign messages are released there. The object is to see who is exposed to campaign messages and if those messages make a difference.

To people who are interested in careers such as hers, Marston recommends an education in public health. She says many public health programs now incorporate mass media strategies in the curriculum, appreciating how powerful the media can be. "It's been a positive experience for me," Marston says, "working with people in the industry to change society for the better."

For example, if you are trying to increase participation in your university's sports recreation program, you might consider how strongly members of your target audience believe the benefits you propose would actually help them. Let's say your audience analysis reveals a number of statements such as, "I know exercise is good for people. But I'm young and healthy. I don't have to worry about that yet." According to the health belief model, people who feel this way will not be motivated to seek the benefits proposed because they simply do not believe they need those benefits. Your job as a promoter is to either (1) convince them they do need the benefits proposed or (2) appeal to them on the basis of another need (such as their desire to look good, meet people, or win awards).

Conversely, if people do not know about the benefits of exercise, your role is to educate them. Knowledge does not assure behavior change, but it is an important foundation for it. Research shows that people sometimes change their behavior without being well informed. However, these people are less likely to maintain the new behavior than others, especially if the change requires effort or discomfort (Valente, Paredes, & Poppe, 1998).

The health belief model is a widely used and studied theory of health-related behavior change. On the whole, researchers suggest it provides a useful framework for assessing audiences and organizing campaigns (Kohler, Grimly, & Reynolds, 1999). However, people are affected to varying degrees by the components named in the model. People who do not change their behaviors usually perceive that it would be too difficult or costly to do so. On the other hand, people are most likely to make changes if they feel personally at risk. To appreciate the factors that influence individual perception, campaign designers should also review theories that focus on cognitive, environmental, and social influences.

Social Cognitive Theory

Returning to the sports recreation campaign, imagine that everything seems to be in your favor. People are aware of the recreation program. They know about the benefits. They even feel they would benefit personally. Yet they do not plan to participate. This may seem very puzzling. What's a health promoter to do?

A promoter familiar with social cognitive theory would consider the environment. **Social cognitive theory** holds that people make decisions considering the interplay of internal and environmental factors (Bandura, 1986, 1994). **Internal factors** include knowledge, skills, emotions, habits, and so on. **Environmental factors** include social approval, physical environment, institutional rules, and the like. According to the theory, people are most comfortable when internal and environmental factors are in sync. This may explain why changing people's minds (the goal of most campaigns) does not necessarily change their behavior (Maibach & Cotton, 1995). Without corresponding changes in people's environments, behavioral change is unlikely. In your campaign, people may not participate in recreational activities because of environmental factors—others might laugh at them, the hours are not convenient, or they do not know anyone at the gym.

Social concerns sometimes outweigh personal concerns, even when the behavior in question is particularly risky. For instance, research indicates people sometimes wish to use condoms during sex, and plan to use them, but abandon their intentions because they are too embarrassed to bring up the subject (Edgar, 1992). Especially between new partners, it may seem more socially acceptable for sex to "just happen" than to talk about it in advance. Social considerations of this sort reflect the influence of environmental factors. Significantly, people who *do* insist on condom use are typically good communicators—skilled at asserting themselves, understanding other people's feelings, self-disclosing, and managing conflict (Edgar, 1992; Monahan, Miller, & Rothspan, 1997). The implication is that communication skills can help people overcome environmental challenges.

Let's apply social cognitive theory to your sports recreation campaign. If you find that people in your target audience want to participate in recreational activities but are reluctant to do so, your job may be to help them develop new skills, improve the social atmosphere at the gym, suggest different hours, or make other changes that reduce the risk of participating.

Overall, social cognitive theory suggests that health promoters must do more than make people aware of health risks. They must do what they can to make healthy behaviors practical and socially acceptable. It is also important to teach people communication skills such as empathy, assertiveness, and effective self-disclosure, which may build their confidence enough to try new behaviors.

Embedded Behaviors Model

The embedded behaviors model (Booth-Butterfield, 2003) is similar to social cognitive theory in that it recognizes internal and external influences on health-related behavior. However, the embedded behaviors model also includes consideration of the behavior itself: its frequency, complexity, familiarity or novelty, and links to other behaviors. In short, the **embedded behaviors model** suggests that behaviors are enduring to the extent that they are an integral part of an individual's lifestyle or self-image and are supported by internal and external factors.

Some behaviors, such as switching to a salt substitute, are relatively easy to change because the change does not alter one's lifestyle and because equally desirable alternatives are available. However, other behaviors (such as tobacco use) may be extremely difficult to give up. In a study of teen smoking, Melanie Booth-Butterfield (2003) reports that "Smoking is much more complex than simply buying cigarettes and smoking them" (p. 179). Some teen smokers say they feel a sense of belonging around others who smoke (although they typically insist peer pressure has not influenced them). They report that their cigarettes become like friends who are "always there" (p. 178) and that smoking is a way to manage their moods by relieving boredom and either soothing or energizing them.

Theory of Reasoned Action

The **theory of reasoned action (TRA)** is based on the assumption that people are rational decision makers. They do not just *happen* to behave one way or another. Instead, they make decisions and deliberate choices based on two primary considerations: (1) how strongly they believe a behavior will lead to positive outcomes and (2) the perceived social implications of performing that behavior (Ajzen & Fishbein, 1980).

TRA is similar to social cognitive theory in that both consider personal and social influences. However, TRA is more global in focus. Its predictive power lies in assessing the attitudes and behaviors of large numbers of people (Ajzen & Fishbein, 1980). Because TRA is designed to make generalizations, its founders do not consider it necessary (or even helpful) to focus on specifics such as personality, rules, or emotions. The effects of these variables tend to even out over large numbers of people. By the same token, TRA does not assume that small changes will make much difference overall. As Ajzen and Fishbein put it, "Changing one or more beliefs may not be sufficient to bring about change in the overall attitude" (p. 81).

It may seem that the macrolevel focus of TRA is not very helpful in planning your sports recreation campaign. Indeed, your target audience may be too small to make broad generalizations very useful. But TRA is of interest theoretically because it suggests that people make behavior changes based on their *overall* beliefs and perceptions. Small changes may not have much effect if they are outweighed by larger concerns. For example, imagine that a new study suggests it is healthy for men to wear panty hose to protect their skin from the sun. Do you suppose you could get the men on your campus to do so? Probably not. Their belief in the health benefits of panty hose is probably outweighed by their desire to be socially acceptable. Luckily for you, physical exercise *is* widely accepted, and you are likely to have a good chance of getting new participants for the sports recreation program. In your case, small changes may make a difference because what you propose is already in line with people's overall intentions.

Transtheoretical Model

In analyzing the audience for your sports recreation campaign, imagine that you find some people *want* to exercise, but many of them are not doing so. You may even find that people *plan* to go to the gym but do not make it there. This is an important finding because it helps you understand your audience's state of mind. According to the **transtheoretical model,** people may not proceed directly from thinking about a problem to changing their behavior (Holtgrave et al., 1995; Prochaska & DiClemente, 1983; Prochaska, DiClemente, & Norcross, 1992).

Instead, they tend to change in stages. According to the model, change typically involves the following five stages:

Precontemplation: Not aware of a problem.

Contemplation: Thinking about a problem.

Preparation: Deciding to take action.

Action: Making a change.

Maintenance: Sticking to the change for 6 months or more.

The implication is that people react differently to health promotion efforts depending on their current stage. Information that gets attention is called for when people are unaware of a problem. But skills training and encouragement may be more useful for those already prepared to make a change. Furthermore, people who have already adopted the recommended behavior should be encouraged to continue it.

For example, the AIDS quilt project is effective partly because it does not push directly for behavior change. Instead, the project stimulates interest by involving people firsthand in an emotionally moving display about AIDS. Participants in the traveling quilt project report an increased interest in information about AIDS and safer sex practices (Knaus, Pinkleton, & Austin, 2000). In other words, many move from precontemplation to contemplation.

Another component of the transtheoretical model is the observation that people do not simply change from one stage to another like pieces on a chess board. Change is a process characterized by a range of activities including consciousness raising, self-reevaluation, changes in social opportunities, and increased or diminished relational support. (For a more thorough description of these factors, see Prochaska, Johnson, & Lee, 1998).

From this perspective, people choose options by weighing the relative pros and cons among a complex array of considerations. For example, Alan DeSantis (2002) describes the camaraderie in a cigar shop in which the regulars meet to smoke and drink, seemingly impervious to the antismoking messages of loved ones and media campaigns, and even to the smoking-related death of their comrade.

> Within days, and sometimes hours, after wives and children have implored their husbands and fathers to quit smoking, the local press has reported on the "latest findings from the *New England Journal of Medicine*" or *20/20* has broadcasted its latest investigative report on the hazards of cigar smoking, the regulars at the cigar shop light back up with only the smell of cigar smoke on their minds. (DeSantis, p. 169)

DeSantis details how cigar shop regulars—who highly value their get-togethers—rationalize their habit through collective arguments that cigar smoking is poorly understood by the medical establishment, is actually no more dangerous than mowing the lawn or driving on the freeway, and is actually beneficial in that it relieves their stress. Members regularly tell of cigar smokers (such as George Burns and Milton Berle) who lived long lives and of health advocates who died young. Everyone in the shop knows the story of a heart surgeon who stopped by one day and reportedly said, through a "relaxing" exhale, "Now how can that be bad for you?" (p. 185).

The cigar shop study illustrates the difficulty of changing behaviors embedded in social and environmental contexts. It also emphasizes that change is not automatic or linear. The stages described are only a general guide. People may remain in one stage indefinitely, lose interest, or skip steps.

Considering change as a stage-based process reveals some key challenges and opportunities for health campaign managers. One challenge is that people do not simply overhaul their behavior as soon as they hear new information (Maibach & Cotton, 1995). Change agents must be sensitive to barriers and motivations as well. Second, the transtheoretical model reveals why prevention efforts are particularly challenging. Campaign planners are wise to seek incremental change rather than radical transformations (Prochaska, Johnson, & Lee, 1998). Pushing for too much change can be counterproductive. Edward Maibach and David Cotton (1995) report that inundating audience members with messages inappropriate to their stage of change may actually discourage them from proceeding. Rather than accelerate the change process, they may avoid the issue entirely. Considering that 70% to 80% of people in high health-risk populations are not ready to change their behavior (DiClemente et al., 1991), this is a serious consideration.

The transtheoretical model presents opportunities for important contributions as well. Without motivational health campaigns, members of at-risk populations are likely to "remain stuck in the early stages" (Prochaska, Johnson, & Lee, 1998, p. 64). Therefore the potential for making positive change is profound. Likewise, the model suggests that changes, once made, must be supported. Effective campaigns are not simply one-shot affairs, but ongoing programs that support change and commitment.

Implications

The health belief model proposes that decisions are based on perceived need, value, and opportunity. Outside influences are instrumental, but motivation ultimately comes from within. Because the health belief model is based almost entirely on perceptual factors, it presents a challenge to researchers and campaign planners. In keeping with the theory, they must conduct careful audience analysis to gauge audience response to health messages.

Social cognitive theory observes that people are unlikely to make choices that are not consistent with both internal and external factors. Successful health promotion sometimes requires changing the environment and people's minds.

The embedded behaviors model and theory of reasoned action include consideration of social implications. Behaviors are embedded, thus not easily changed, to the extent that they are interwoven with a person's lifestyle and

BOX 13.2 THEORETICAL FOUNDATIONS
Synopsis of Behavior Change Theories

Embedded behaviors model: The likelihood for behavior change is related to the behavior itself—how frequent, complex, familiar, or novel it is and how interwoven it is with other valued behaviors.

Health belief model: People are more or less motivated to change their behavior based on their perception of personal susceptibility, serious consequences, worthwhile benefits, justifiable costs, and cues to actions.

Language expectancy theory: People evaluate, and are variably influenced by, messages considering how they compare to expectations. Messages are especially influential when they are more desirable than expected.

Extended parallel process model: People evaluate threatening messages, first, to determine if they are personally at risk, and second, to judge whether they can prevent a harmful outcome. If they perceive a risk but do not feel they can avoid a bad outcome, they are likely to avoid the issue.

Social cognitive theory: People make decisions considering the interplay of internal factors such as skills and knowledge and environmental factors such as environment and social approval.

Theory of reasoned action: People make rational and deliberate choices based on how strongly they believe a behavior will lead to positive outcomes and the perceived social implications of performing that behavior.

Transtheoretical model: People tend to change in stages ranging from precontemplation, to contemplation, preparation, action, and maintenance.

beliefs. Changing a behavior at the price of sensory, personal, social, and cultural rewards is unlikely unless a realistic and pleasing alternative exists. The theory of reasoned action challenges campaign planners to balance perceived risks against social expectations.

The transtheoretical model holds that people typically advance through a series of stages in which they think about a problem, consider what to do about it, and decide whether to take action. If they change their behavior, they may or may not maintain the change over time. From this perspective, it is important to consider what stage best describes target audience members because they are likely to react to information differently depending on their state of mind.

It is important to point out that health promotion efforts need not be restricted to any one theory or to one-way communication. The theories described here support that people are not simply passive recipients who can (or should) be told what to do. Ratzan et al. (1994), among others, encourage health promoters to engage people in cooperative dialogues about health. This two-way communication is expected to help health promoters and the public better understand and assess health concerns, develop options that make sense in everyday life, and promote a sense of trust, openness, and cooperation.

It is also important to consider the ethical ramifications of health promotion. Although promoters mean well, their efforts can needlessly alarm people, scapegoat segments of the population, and stigmatize ill or disabled persons. (See Box 13.3 for more on the ethical concerns of health promotion.)

DESIGNING AND IMPLEMENTING A CAMPAIGN

This section discusses the three final stages in developing a health campaign: designing campaign messages, piloting and implementing the campaign, and evaluating and maintaining the effort.

Step 5: Designing Campaign Messages

The first step in designing an effective campaign is to carefully review the data collected during preliminary research and audience analysis. Campaign messages should be designed considering the audience's needs, the benefits of the proposed behavior, the goals of the campaign, and the communication channels to be used (see Chapter 12 for a review of these steps). Holtgrave and colleagues (1995) recommend that campaign designers determine what aspect of the problem is most important to the target audience, and then make that the focal point of the campaign. The next sections provide guidance in selecting a personality for the campaign and deciding what approach to take.

Choosing a Voice Every campaign message has a voice. It may seem masculine, feminine, young, old, friendly, casual, stern, or so on. The voice embodies the mood and personality of the campaign.

Just as Lefebvre et al. (1995) recommend that you imagine the target audience as a person with a name, gender, occupation, and lifestyle, it is useful to imagine your campaign as a person. Here are some questions to consider in finding that voice:

- What is the campaign's personality and mood?
- Is this an authority figure or a friend?
- Is this a logical or an emotional person?
- Is this the sort of person to whom the audience is likely to respond?

Even when words appear in print, the tone of the message gives the reader a sense of who is "talking" and what type of relationship the writer wishes to

Box 13.3 ETHICAL CONSIDERATIONS
Three Issues for Health Promoters to Keep in Mind

Health promoters are faced with several ethical considerations. They must decide how to warn audiences without needlessly frightening them. They must be careful not to blame people for ill health, while at the same time encouraging people to prevent any illnesses they can. All the while, they must walk a fine line between making people concerned about illness and making them worried sick.

Timing

When early evidence of a health risk surfaces, is it better to warn the public right away or wait for more conclusive evidence? This question poses a dilemma for health promoters. On the one hand, researchers suggest people are wary of premature announcements that are later shown to be inaccurate. Health news writer Alan Rees (1994) contends that "the average individual is caught in a withering crossfire of conflicting health messages and is inclined to disregard them all" (paragraph 7). For example, the public was long urged to increase their exposure to sunlight to ensure sufficient amounts of Vitamin D. Now people are encouraged to avoid sunlight to lower their risk of skin cancer (Parrott, 1995). Conflicting messages such as these may confuse people and cause them to ignore health advisories.

On the other hand, it may take months or years to compile conclusive evidence. All the while, people may be exposed to health risks they might have avoided. People are likely to be angry if health officials are aware of potential risks yet do not warn the public.

Scapegoating

It is difficult to know where the responsibility for personal health lies. For example, if children are not vaccinated, (a) is it the parents' fault for not bringing them to a doctor, (b) the government's fault for not providing neighborhood health services, (c) the city's fault for not providing better public transportation to the health unit, or (d) health officials' fault for not educating parents about the need for immunization? Although all of these factors probably contribute to the problem, part of a health promoter's job is to identify what conditions most need improvement. In doing so, however, it is easy to **scapegoat** (blame one person or group for the whole problem).

Scapegoating presents an ethical dilemma. It makes sense to focus attention on the condition or people with the greatest chance of making a difference. The typical health promotion message cannot describe all the factors that contribute to a problem. However, focusing on one aspect or group of people may seem to place blame (Burdine, McLeroy, & Gottlieb, 1987). For example, a campaign that admonishes parents to bring their children in for vaccinations may alienate parents who do not have transportation to the public health unit and cannot afford private care. These parents may feel frustrated and criticized, and they may resent promoters' efforts. Second, people not held to blame may feel the problem is no longer their responsibility. Ruth Faden (1987) asserts that government promotes the idea that people are personally responsible for their health partly because this lets government off the hook. There is little imperative to make sweeping social changes or health care reform if it seems that health is solely the product of voluntary lifestyle changes.

Evidence fuels both sides of the debate, suggesting that personal choices and empowerment are important to health, but at the same time, personal efforts are often constrained by environmental factors beyond individuals' control (such as money to afford medical care or sanitary living conditions). Health promoters may find themselves trying to identify key objectives without ignoring that every objective is intertwined with others.

Stigmatizing

Prevention is the process of avoiding undesirable outcomes. People wear helmets to avoid head injuries, they are immunized to avoid diseases, and so on. Typically, the worse the potential outcome, the more people will try to prevent it. Health promoters try to motivate people by showing them how bad undesirable outcomes can be.

The dilemma is that, in portraying some *conditions* as undesirable, promoters may stigmatize some *people* as undesirable. Guttman (1997) warns that campaigners' good intentions sometimes backfire when they make people so frightened of diseases that they avoid the people who have them. For instance, an image of a child with a disability may be frightening enough to make children observe safety rules, but how are they likely to feel about children with disabilities? The same dilemma applies to AIDS publicity. People may become so frightened that they overprotect themselves by avoiding people who have AIDS.

What Do You Think?

1. Should health promoters release information about potential health risks immediately or wait for more conclusive evidence?
    a. How long is it reasonable to wait?
    b. What constitutes conclusive evidence?

continued

BOX 13.3 ETHICAL CONSIDERATIONS
Three Issues for Health Promoters to Keep in Mind, *continued*

2. Can you think of a way to promote public health without seeming to place the blame on certain people or groups?
3. Do you think it is possible to warn people about health hazards without stigmatizing people who have already been affected?

Suggested Sources

Burdine, J. N., McLeroy, K. B., & Gottlieb, N. H. (1987). Ethical dilemmas in health promotion: An introduction. *Health Education Quarterly, 14,* 7–9.

Faden, R. R. (1987). Ethical issues in government sponsored public health campaigns. *Health Education Quarterly, 14,* 27–37.

Guttman, N. (1997). Ethical dilemmas in health campaigns. *Health Communication, 9,* 155–190.

Guttman, N., & Ressler, W. H. (2001, April–June). On being responsible: Ethical issues in appeals to personal responsibility in health campaigns. *Journal of Health Communication, 6*(2), 117–136.

Leask, J., & Chapman, S. (2002, February). "The cold hard facts:" Immunization and vaccine preventable diseases in Australia's newsprint media. *Social Science & Medicine, 53*(3), 445–457.

Musham, C., & Trettin, L. (2002, August). Bringing health services to the poor through social marketing: Ethical issues. *Journal of Health Care for the Poor and Underserved, 13*(3), 280–287.

Rees, A. M. (1994). Consumer enlightenment or consumer confusion? *Consumer Health Information Source Book, 4,* 10–11.

establish with the reader. Lefebvre et al. (1995) describe how carefully Nike considered the presentation of its "Just do it" advertising slogan. They say the creators decided not to use an exclamation mark after the statement and not to have an announcer say it aloud. "The concern was that the wrong voice, the wrong delivery, and the wrong inflection could have doomed the ads for many viewers" (Lefebvre et al., p. 224).

Of course, the source is even more apparent when the audience can see or hear a spokesperson deliver the message. Research suggests that messages have more impact when the target audience trusts the spokesperson and thinks the spokesperson is capable and attractive (Atkin, 1979).

Well-known spokespeople have potential drawbacks, however. Overly attractive or controversial people may distract viewers from the actual message (Salmon & Atkin, 2003). Moreover, famous spokespeople may behave in ways that contradict or cloud health campaign messages. For example, when Mark McGwire broke the major league home run record in 1998 even people who did not follow baseball knew about it. In the subsequent media coverage, it was revealed that McGwire had used androstenedione, a dietary supplement meant to speed muscle development. About 24% of the people who heard about his use of androstenedione wanted to learn more about, and about 22% said they would like to try it (Brown, Basil, & Bocarnea, 2003). In Australia, a pharmaceutical company paid a well-known soccer star the equivalent of $123,000 to stop smoking. He didn't. Fortunately for the promoters, the publicity surrounding the failed attempt increased sales of nicotine replacement therapies nonetheless (Chapman & Leask, 2001).

There is also some evidence that audiences are most likely to believe people who are similar to them, an effect called **source homophily** (Rogers, 1973). For example, African-American women who watched a breast care video were twice as likely to perform breast self-exams when the video was moderated by an African-American woman as when the moderator was a White or Hispanic woman (Anderson & McMillion, 1995).

The source of a message can affect how audiences interpret it. Typically, aggressive messages have high impact if they come from sources perceived to be competent and respectable. However, aggressive messages from negatively evaluated sources are not likely to change people's minds (Buller, Borland, & Burgoon, 1998). One study suggests that audiences respond favorably when spokespersons defy stereotypes, as when a young woman presents an aggressive, logical argument about condom use (Perse et al., 1996).

Celebrities can be effective spokespersons, especially if the audience identifies strongly with them. On the day basketball star Magic Johnson announced he had HIV (November 14, 1991), the National AIDS Hotline received 10 times as many calls as usual. After the extensive news coverage, public knowledge about HIV transmission increased, especially among young people, and the number of people seeking HIV tests increased dramatically (Casey et al., 2003). After studying public reaction to the announcement, William Brown and Michael Basil (1995) concluded that people reacted so strongly because they felt they knew Magic Johnson.

Spokespersons may be especially important when the audience is not highly interested in the topic. Evidence suggests that less interested individuals are likely to judge information on a superficial level, perhaps by how entertaining it is or how much they like the spokesperson (Petty & Cacioppo, 1986). If the announcement is not interesting and appealing, they may ignore it altogether.

Designing the Message In designing an effective health campaign message, it is important to consider audience expectations and the role of logic, emotion, and novelty.

Audience Expectations A message is only effective if the target audience responds to it. In a study of messages promoting early screening for prostate cancer, Juanne Nancarrow Clarke (1999) found that nearly all the messages embodied themes of male sexuality, machoism, and brotherhood. Although these messages may appeal to some men, others are probably turned away by an image they do not feel applies to them.

Language expectancy theory holds that people are influenced by messages that are more desirable than they expected based on cultural norms and circumstances (Siegel & Burgoon, 2002; Burgoon, 1989). If a speaker held in high regard delivers a message that is even better (e.g., more appropriate, useful, or skillful) than expected, listeners are apt to change their attitudes and behaviors in response. By the same token, a speaker who is regarded unfavorably may change people's mind through language choice and behaviors that exceed the audience's expectations.

For example, David Buller and colleagues (2000) found that parents of elementary school students responded favorably to a highly intense message about sun protection *if* the message presented an acceptable solution. The messages began by describing the problem in intense language: "A bad sunburn is embarrassing. So is the peeling skin that follows a sunburn. Worse than peeling skin and redness are the deadly problems which can follow these annoyances . . ." (p. 273). Readers were then presented with a solution (using sunscreen year-round). The authors speculate that this message was effective because it was arousing enough to be memorable and because it provided a clear, culturally appropriate solution. On the other hand, a highly intense message without a promising solution might dissuade audience members from changing their attitudes or behaviors.

Based on language expectancy theory, audiences may react differently to highly intense messages depending on what they expect to hear and who is delivering the message. This is important to keep in mind as you consider the following research about logical and emotional appeals.

Logical and Emotional Appeals A **logical appeal** attempts to educate audiences and demonstrate a clear link between a behavior and a result. For example, it is logical to eat less if that will result in greater health and a longer life. An **emotional appeal** may suggest that people should feel a certain way regarding their health or their behaviors. For example, they should be frightened if they are exposed to AIDS, proud if they have quit smoking, or guilty if they are endangering others. If the emotions are rewarding, they are called **positive affect** (affect is another word for emotion). If they are undesirable emotions, they are called **negative affect.** Campaigns encourage people to strive for positive outcomes and avoid negative ones. Research quoted in this section describes the usefulness and the limitations of various emotional appeals.

Positive Affect Appeals Campaigns may promote positive emotional rewards in the form of popularity, a sense of accomplishment, honor, fun, or happiness. For example, a nutrition information program helped people feel confident and optimistic about their ability to reduce fat intake (Chew, Palmer, &

Kim, 1998). These people were subsequently more concerned about nutrition than others and were more likely to monitor their diets. The researchers concluded that providing nutrition information was not very helpful unless people felt empowered to make a difference.

Campaigns may also inspire positive affect because the messages themselves are pleasant or entertaining. For instance, the audience may enjoy the music, humor, graphics, or the attractiveness of a spokesperson featured in a campaign message (Monahan, 1995). Research shows that pleasant messages hold people's attention, but people may not take these messages as seriously as fearful ones (Monohan, 1995).

Negative Affect Appeals Some campaigns attempt to motivate people by making them feel anxious, fearful, or guilty. Kim Witte (1995) proposes that, if people are not at all anxious about a health topic they probably are not motivated to learn about it or to take action. However, if they are overly anxious, they may wish to avoid the subject. The **extended parallel process model** (Witte, 1997) proposes that people evaluate a threatening message, first, to determine if they are personally at risk, and second, to judge whether they can prevent a harmful outcome. If they perceive a risk but do not feel they can avoid a bad outcome, they are likely to soothe their anxiety by avoiding the issue.

Jerold Hale and James Price Dillard (1995) calculate that about 26% of PSAs use fear appeals. Their effectiveness varies. For instance, women responding to a cancer screening campaign said they would not like to hear messages that escalated their fears about cancer or mammography (Marshall, Smith, & McKeon, 1995). They were already frightened by these topics, and they wanted clear information. However, Murray Millar and Karen Millar (1998) found that people who were not anxious about health risks were not very interested in prevention information. Intense messages might get their attention.

Guilt, a feeling of remorse about having done something wrong, is a strong emotion. Consequently, it is a useful tool for advertisers and health campaigners. Bruce Huhmann and Timothy Brotherton (1997) assert that people typically feel sorry or ashamed when they have behaved badly, especially when others are hurt by their actions. Advertisers who bring these feelings to the surface, and offer a way to make retributions, may find that people are willing to cooperate to soothe their consciences. Huhmann and Brotherton found that 1 in 20 magazine advertisements included a guilt appeal, ranging from, "I wish I had started saving for my children's college education when they were young" to "Last night, two million children in the U.S. went to bed hungry." Relevant to health promotion, a study about antismoking efforts concluded that it is an effective strategy to warn smokers that secondhand smoke can harm loved ones (Goldman & Glantz, 1998). Appealing to smokers' sense of responsibility is sometimes more effective than warning them about their own health risks.

Overall, negative affect is a popular component of persuasive messages, but it must be used carefully. Research suggests that messages aimed at highly anxious or fearful people should help them develop a sense of confidence and control (or they are likely to avoid the messages). However, messages aimed at unanxious people should encourage them to become somewhat concerned (or they are likely to ignore the messages). All the while, campaigners must consider the ethical implications of influencing people's emotions, especially to the extent of making them feel extremely fearful or ashamed.

Novel and Shocking Messages Novel messages tend to catch people's attention and stick in their memory (Parrott, 1995). Some messages are **novel** (new or different) without being **shocking** (intense or improper). For instance, posting health warnings in public restrooms is an effort to use an unexpected format to reinforce the risks of smoking and drinking during pregnancy. It is a novel approach, but not particularly shocking.

At other times, novel messages may be shocking, either because they deal with topics not usually discussed in public or because they are purposefully controversial so they will attract attention. One difficulty surrounding AIDS awareness is that health promoters must deal with delicate issues like premarital sex and anal intercourse. Particularly when AIDS first became a health concern, these were not socially acceptable topics for mass media campaigns.

Where AIDS is concerned, it is still difficult to balance decorum with the need for public awareness. In 1994, controversy arose concerning a poster campaign in New York City. The posters (which were hung in subway terminals) read "Young, Hot, Safe!" and showed images of homosexual couples kissing while holding condoms, gloves, and spermicide ("Controversy Heats Up," 1994). Some people felt the posters were indecent, while others argued that they communicated an important message to a high-risk group. At any rate, the posters were eventually removed from the subways.

Shocking or intense messages may be especially appealing to high sensation-seekers, who often find mild messages boring and are apt to engage in risky behaviors (Zuckerman, 1994). In Maureen Everett and Philip Palmgreen's (1995) study of college students, high sensation-seekers responded favorably to anti-cocaine PSAs featuring heavy metal music and vivid, complex visuals. Overall, they remembered more about these PSAs than others and rated themselves less likely to use cocaine in the future. Likewise, novel antidrug PSAs shown on television were shown to be successful with sensation-seeking adolescents (Donohew, Lorch, & Palmgreen, 1998).

One difficulty about using novel images to attract attention is that the novelty wears off (Walters et al., 1997). Relying on novelty may mean becoming ever more risque. All in all, it is hard to know where to draw the line.

Step 6: Piloting and Implementing the Campaign

It is important to pilot (pretest) a campaign before launching it full-scale. **Piloting** usually involves selecting members from the target audience to review

BOX 13.4 RESOURCES
More About Designing Health Campaigns

For guidance on creating your own health campaign, visit the following websites.

- The Community Tool Box: http://ctb.ku.edu
- The American Public Health Association: http://www.apha.org
- www.Healthbehavior.com
- http://www.social-marketing.com/HELinks.html
- The CDC offers a CD-ROM tutorial for health communication planning and evaluation. Contact the CDC at (404) 639-7290 for details.
- The National Cancer Institute offers free copies of its *Making Health Communication Programs Work: A Planner's Guide* in print and on CD-ROM. To order a copy, call 1-800-4-CANCER or visit cancer.gov/publications.

the campaign materials and comment on them. Salmon and Atkin (2003) say early feedback is crucial:

> The feedback from the audience can reveal whether the tone is too righteous (admonishing unhealthy people about their incorrect behavior), the recommendations too extremist (rigidly advocating unpalatable ideas of healthy behavior), the execution too politically correct (staying within tightly prescribed boundaries of propriety to avoid offending overly sensitive authorities and interest groups), and the execution too self-indulgent (letting creativity and style overwhelm substance and substantive content). (p. 453)

Some questions to consider include these (adapted from Donohew, 1990):

- Are written messages easy to read and understand?
- Are recorded messages easy to understand?
- Do messages seem relevant and important?
- Are the messages appealing? Why or why not?
- Is the spokesperson effective?
- Does the information seem controversial or offensive?

It may be useful to survey people before and after they are exposed to the campaign materials to see if there is any change in their knowledge, attitudes, and intentions. When possible, it is also advisable to survey people a week or month after they are initially exposed to campaign materials to see how much they remember and whether message effects are still present. Remember to allow time to refine campaign messages based on the results of pretesting. Planning ahead will improve the campaign's likelihood of success.

Once campaign messages have been created, piloted, and refined, it is time to distribute them through the chosen channels. In some cases (as with one-on-one communication and community presentations), health promoters have direct contact with audience members. With the majority of channels, however, health promoters must rely on others to share their messages. For instance, editors and news directors choose what PSAs to publicize and when, and what topics to cover in the news. On a social level, community opinion leaders focus on some issues more than others, affecting what the people around them think and believe. People such as these, who decide what information will be publicized and how, are known as gatekeepers. **Gatekeepers** decide what messages will reach the public (Shoemaker & Reese, 1991).

Good campaigners employ a variety of communication channels to help ensure that messages make it to target audience members through one gate or another. The wise health promoter realizes the importance of gatekeepers, includes them in campaign planning, and considers their point of view. John McGrath (1995) observes that media gatekeepers are bound by multiple pressures (e.g., operating budgets, audience demands, and time constraints). The promoter who gets to know gatekeepers personally and makes it easy for them to pass along information has a better chance of getting through to an audience.

Step 7: Evaluating and Maintaining the Campaign

A campaign is not over when it has been released to the public. Effective health promotion requires that campaign managers evaluate the success of the project, help audience members maintain any positive changes they may have made, and refine and develop future campaign messages.

Evaluation The effects of a campaign may be evaluated in several ways. A **pretest–posttest design** means that campaigners survey people before the campaign is released, then survey them again afterward (Wimmer & Dominick, 1997). The survey may indicate if people's attitudes, knowledge, or actions have changed since the campaign was conducted. Keep in mind that if changes have occurred, they may or may not be the result of campaign exposure.

To evaluate the impact of the *truth* campaign, researchers conducted telephone surveys with 6,897 youth ages 12 to 17 before the campaign began (Farrelly et al., 2002). The survey participants were chosen to represent teens in different ethnic and racial groups, urban and nonurban areas, and areas with and without other anti-tobacco campaigns. The youth were asked to indicate their level of agreement or disagreement with statements about the tobacco industry, the social acceptability of smoking, and their intention to smoke within the next year. In follow-up interviews after the campaign's release, 10,692 youth were asked if they remembered seeing any anti-tobacco campaigns, and if so, what they remembered about them. They also answered the same set of questions about perceptions of the tobacco industry, the social acceptability of smoking, and their intention to smoke in the next year. To factor out as many intervening variables as possible, researchers statistically controlled for such factors as the number of parents in the household, amount of television viewing, the presence of smokers in the household, and parental messages about smoking. With the data collected, researchers were able (1) to gauge the extent to which target audience members saw and remembered the campaign and (2) to compare youth attitudes before and after the campaign.

Another way to evaluate a campaign's success is to study actual behavior changes such as the number of people who sign up for basketball or the number of hospital admissions or calls to a hotline.

These evaluation techniques are useful, but it is always difficult to know precisely what effects a campaign has had. For one thing, the campaign is not the only factor influencing people's attitudes and behavior. They may be affected by personal experiences, news stories, or other occurrences. Imagine trying to evaluate the impact of an AIDS awareness program that happened to coincide with Magic Johnson's public announcement that he had HIV. Second, campaigns often have indirect effects. For instance, the campaign may have reached influential members of the community, who in turn spread the word to others. Thus, people who were not exposed to campaign messages personally may be affected by them. Third, sometimes the success of a health campaign is reflected in what does *not* occur over the long run. For example, the coordinators of a drug-free program in elementary schools may not know if they have been successful until the children involved are adolescents or adults, by which time they will have been influenced by many other factors as well. When undesired behaviors do not occur, it is difficult to know how many people might have adopted those behaviors if not for the campaign.

Sometimes health campaigns have unintended or undesirable consequences. Audiences may be so turned off by the message that they actively avoid the subject or lose trust in the sender. Here is an extreme example. When I was in college, the 1936 film *Reefer Madness* made a comeback—not as the frightening documentary it was originally designed to be but as a comedy. College students flocked to the local midnight movie to see the jerky-action black-and-white film. In the film, young people smoke what the narrator (a high school principal) calls "demon weed" and immediately become shaky, wild-eyed, and demented. They listened to "evil jazz" music and become serial killers—threats so incredulous to young audiences in the 1980s that the movie dialogue was often drowned out by their laughter. We can only imagine the extent that the outdated movie damaged the credibility of antidrug messages at the time.

For better or worse, sometimes the best campaigners can do is evaluate the reach (number of people exposed to campaign messages) and specificity (the type of people exposed to the campaign). For this purpose, promoters can survey audience members and keep track of when and where campaign messages are publicized.

Maintenance Maintaining behaviors that have been positively influenced by a campaign involves continued encouragement and skills training. Keep in

BOX 13.5 RESOURCES
More About Assessing the Impact of Health Campaigns

The following sources offer excellent advice about measuring the affect of your campaign.

Hornik, R. C. (Ed.). (2002). *Public health communication: Evidence for behavior change*. Mahwah, NJ: Lawrence Erlbaum.

Murray-Johnson, L., & Witte, K. (2003). Looking toward the future: Health message design strategies. In T. L. Thompson, A. M. Dorsey, K. I. Miller, & R. Parrott (Eds.), *Handbook of health communication* (pp. 473–495). Mahwah, NJ: Lawrence Erlbaum.

mind that people are most apt to continue new behaviors if they fully understand the benefit of doing so (Valente et al., 1998). Because some people try new behaviors without fully understanding them first, do not assume that people who begin a behavior are fully educated about it. Encouragement, incentives, and continued skills training can help people overcome setbacks they are likely to encounter (Maibach & Cotton, 1995).

SUMMARY

Social marketers conduct extensive audience analysis and strive to create messages with the same appeal as commercial messages. The results of social marketing are measured, not in sales figures or profit margins, but in public awareness and improved health. These outcomes are often realized in subtle ways over long periods of time, but social marketers work hard to gauge the success of their efforts and apply what they learn to future campaigns.

Theories of behavior change explain the conditions under which people are likely to make lifestyle changes. The overall message is that behavior is influenced by a complex array of factors, and campaign designers who fail to consider and accommodate audience members' beliefs and opportunities may be ineffectual or even harmful. In designing campaign messages health promoters should consider audience needs, campaign goals, and benefits of the recommended behavior. Campaign messages have different voices ranging from stern to casual and friendly. Often, the spokesperson influences the way the message is perceived. Research suggests that people typically respond most favorably to spokespersons who are similar to them, likable, and attractive. A celebrity may be an effective spokesperson or a public liability.

Campaign messages often have a logical and an emotional appeal. Some campaigns motivate audiences through positive affect such as the promise of pleasure and happiness. Negative affect appeals may induce people to change by stirring up feelings of anxiety, fear, and guilt. According to the extended parallel process model, anxiety is a powerful motivator except when the threat is so overwhelming people would rather avoid the issue. Novel and shocking messages typically create interest, but they may be controversial.

It is recommended that health promoters pilot new campaigns before implementing them. Testing campaign messages on sample audience members can reveal unanticipated reactions and ambiguities in time to improve the messages before they are publicly released. Finally, health promoters should evaluate campaigns once they are released, apply what they have learned to future efforts, and compare the results with their stated goals.

KEY TERMS

social marketing
health belief model
social cognitive theory
- internal factors
- environmental factors

embedded behaviors model
theory of reasoned action (TRA)
transtheoretical model
scapegoat
source homophily
language expectancy theory
logical appeal
emotional appeal
- positive affect
- negative affect
- extended parallel process model (EPPM)
- guilt

novel messages
shocking messages
piloting
gatekeepers
pretest–posttest design

REVIEW QUESTIONS

1. What do you think of the *truth* campaign? Has it influenced the way you regard the tobacco industry? What is appealing (or unappealing) about the campaign to you?
2. According to the health belief model, what five criteria affect people's decision to make behavior changes?
3. Explain what role internal and environmental factors play in social cognitive theory. What internal and environmental factors influence your health-related behavior?
4. According to the embedded behaviors model, what factors influence how likely people are to change particular behaviors? What behaviors are embedded in your lifestyle? What would it take to change those behaviors?
5. What factors influence people's behavior according to the theory of reasoned action?

6. What are the stages of change in the transtheoretical model? What can result if campaigners expose audience members to messages inconsistent with their stage of change?
7. What are the implications of blaming (scapegoating) people for engaging in risky health behaviors?
8. What are some questions to consider when choosing a "voice" and "personality" for your campaign?
9. What is meant by source homophily?
10. What factors should you keep in mind when choosing a spokesperson?
11. In what circumstances are positive affect messages usually effective?
12. Explain the extended parallel process model as it relates to negative affect appeals.
13. What types of audiences are likely to respond favorably to shocking or intense messages?
14. What are some questions to consider when piloting campaign materials?
15. What role do gatekeepers play in health promotion efforts?
16. Why is it often difficult to accurately assess the impact of a health campaign?

CLASS ACTIVITY

Evaluating Messages

Bring recordings or copies of health-related commercials or PSAs to class. Analyze the messages in small groups or as a class. Consider the following questions:

1. How would you describe the voice or personality of each message?
2. Who do you think the target audience is, and why? Are you a member of the target audience?
3. What is the central message of each advertisement or PSA?
4. How do the different messages compare to each other?
5. Do you think the messages are effective? Which do you prefer and why?
6. Why do you think the creators chose the graphics and words they did?
7. What are the health-related implications of these messages?

References

About 11 million children below the age of five die every year. (2002, September 7). *The Economist.*

Abrams, J. (2003, May 1). Major global AIDS bill approved by House. The Associated Press. Retrieved online September 12, 2003, from LexisNexis.

Abramson, J. S., & Mizrahi, T. (1996). When social workers and physicians collaborate: Positive and negative interdisciplinary experiences. *Social Work, 41,* 270–281.

Achterberg, J. (1991). *Woman as healer.* Boston: Shambhala.

Ackerknecht, E. H. (1968). *A short history of medicine.* New York: Ronald Press.

Adams, R. J., & Parrott, R. (1994, February). Pediatric nurses' communication of role expectations to parents of hospitalized children. *Journal of Applied Communication Research, 22,* 36–47.

Adelman, M. B., & Frey, L. R. (1997). *The fragile community: Living together with AIDS.* Mahwah, NJ: Lawrence Erlbaum.

AIDS conference: Number of U.S. AIDS cases remains stable after recent declines. (2002, August 5). *AIDS Weekly.* Retrieved online from July 19, 2003, through LexisNexis.

Ajzen, I., & Fishbein, M. (1980). *Understanding attitudes and predicting behavior.* Englewood Cliffs, NJ: Prentice Hall.

Al-Anon.Org. (2003). Retrieved online August 3, 2003, from www.al-anon.org/mkbody.html

Albrecht, T. L. (1982). Coping with occupational stress: Relational and individual strategies of nurses in acute health care settings. In M. Burgoon (Ed.), *Communication yearbook 6* (pp. 832–849). Beverly Hills, CA: Sage.

Albrecht, T. L., & Adelman, M. B. (1987). Communicating social support: A theoretical perspective. In T. L. Albrecht & M. B. Adelman (Eds.), *Communicating social support* (pp. 18–39). Newbury Park, CA: Sage.

Albrecht, T. L., & Halsey, J. (1991). Supporting the staff nurse under stress. *Nursing Management, 22,* 60–64.

Alcalay, R., & Bell, R. A. (1996). Ethnicity and health knowledge gaps: Impact of the California *Wellness Guide* on poor African American, Hispanic, and Non-Hispanic White women. *Health Communication, 8,* 303–330.

Allman, J. (1998). Bearing the burden or baring the soul: Physicians' self-disclosure and boundary management regarding medical mistakes. *Health Communication, 10,* 175–197.

American College of Healthcare Executives (ACHE). (2002). A race/ethnic comparison of career attainments in healthcare management. Retrieved online August 12, 2003, from www.ache.org

American Hospital Association. (1994). *Hospital closures, 1980 through 1993, a statistical profile.* Chicago, IL: Health Care Information Resources Group.

American Medical Association. (2000). Table 8: Medical school faculty distribution of U.S. medical school faculty by gender and rank. Retrieved online August 9, 2003, from www.ama-assn.org/ama/pub/article/171-203.html

American Medical Association (2001a). Table 15: Percent distribution of female physicians by age and specialty. Retrieved online August 9, 2003, from www.ama-assn.org/ama/pub/article/171-7134.html

American Medical Association (2001b). Total physicians by race/ethnicity. Retrieved online August 9, 2003, from www.ama-assn.org/ama/pub/article/168-187.html

American Medical Association. (2002). Racial and ethnic backgrounds of medical students—total enrollment. Retrieved online August 6, 2003, from www.ama-assn.org/ama/pub/print/article/168-191.html

American Medical Association. (2003a). Low literacy has a high impact on patients' ability to follow doctors' orders. Retrieved July 30, 2003, from www.ama-assn.org/ama/pub/print/article/4197-7395.html

American Medical Association. (2003b). Table 11: Income/total by year. Retrieved online August 9, 2003, from www.ama-assn.org/ama/pub/article/171-206.html

Amundsen, D. W., & Ferngren, G. B. (1983). *The clinical encounter.* Dordrecht: D. Reidel.

And the Effie goes to truth®. (2003, June 4). PR Newswire Association. Retrieved online July 31, 2003, from http://www.prnewswire.com

Andersen, R. E., Crespo, C. J., Bartlett, S. J., Cheskin, L. J., & Pratt, M. (1998). Relationship of physical activity and television watching with body weight and level of fatness among children: Results from the Third National Health and Nutrition Examination Survey. *Journal of the American Medical Association, 279,* 938–942.

Anderson, A. (1996). Nurse–physician interaction and job satisfaction. *Nursing Management, 27,* 33–36.

Anderson, J. O., & Geist Martin, P. (2003). Narratives and healing: Exploring one family's stories of cancer survivorship. *Health Communication, 15*(2), 133–143.

Anderson, R. B., & McMillion, P. Y. (1995). Effects of similar and diversified modeling on African American women's efficacy expectations and intentions to perform breast self-examination. *Health Communication, 7,* 327–344.

Angell, M. (1997, September 18). The disputed editorial (reproduced online from the *New England Journal of Medicine*). ABCNEWS.COM (Online). Available: www.abcnews.aol.com/sections/living/DailyNews/nejmedit1015.html

Apker, J. (2001). Role development in the managed care era: A case in hospital-based nursing. *Journal of Applied Communication Research, 29*(2), 117–136.

Appleby, C. (1997). Speed dialing. *Hospitals & Health Networks, 71,* 58–60.

Arnold, W. E., & McClure, L. (1989). *Communication training and development.* Prospect Heights, IL: Waveland Press.

Arnst, C. (1998, May 18). Of mice, men, and cancer cures. *Business Week, 3578,* 44.

Ashley, B. M., & O'Rourke, K. D. (1997). *Health care ethics: A theological analysis* (4th ed.). Washington, DC: Georgetown University Press.

Astin, J. A. (1998). Why patients use alternative medicine: Results of a national study. *Journal of the American Medical Association, 279,* 2548–2553.

Atkin, C. K. (1979). Research evidence on mass mediated health communication campaigns. In D. Nimmo (Ed.), *Communication Yearbook III* (pp. 655–668). New Brunswick, NJ: Transaction Books.

Auslander, W. F., Thompson, S. J., Dreitzer, D., & Santiago, J. V. (1997). Mothers' satisfaction with medical care: Perceptions of racism, family stress, and medical outcomes in children with diabetes. *Health and Social Work, 22,* 190–199.

Austin, E. W. (1993). Exploring the effects of active parental mediation of television content. *Journal of Broadcasting & Electronic Media, 37,* 147–158.

Austin, E. W. (1995). Reaching young audiences: Developmental considerations in designing health messages. In E. Maibach & R. L. Parrott (Eds.), *Designing health messages* (pp. 114–144). Thousand Oaks, CA: Sage.

Austin, E. W., & Johnson, K. K. (1997). Immediate and delayed effects of media literacy training on third graders' decision making for alcohol. *Health Communication, 9,* 323–350.

Austin, E. W., & Meili, H. K. (1994). Effects of interpretations of televised alcohol portrayals on children's alcohol beliefs. *Journal of Broadcasting & Electronic Media, 38,* 417–435.

Austin, E. W., & Nach-Ferguson, B. (1995). Sources and influences of young school-age children's general and brand-specific knowledge about alcohol. *Health Communication, 7,* 1–20.

Austin, E. W., Roberts, D. F., & Nass, C. I. (1990). Influences of family communication on children's television-interpretation processes. *Communication Research, 17,* 545–564.

Ayres, J., & Hopf, T. (1995). An assessment of the role of communication apprehension in communicating with the terminally ill. *Communication Research Reports, 12,* 227–234.

Azevedo, D. (1996). Taking back health care: Doctors must work together. *Medical Economics, 73,* 156–162.

Babin, L. A., & Carder, S. T. (1996, May). Viewers' recognition of brands placed within a film. *International Journal of Advertising, 15,* 140–151.

Babrow, A. S. (1992). Communication and problematic integration: Understanding diverging probability and value, ambiguity, ambivalence, and impossibility. *Communication Theory, 2,* 95–130.

Babrow, A. (2001). Uncertainty, value, communication, and problematic integration. *Journal of Communication, 51*(3), 553–573.

Bachenheimer, E. A., & DeKoven, M. (2003). The view from the middle. *Healthcare Executive, 18*(2), 73–74.

Backer, T. E., & Rogers, E. M. (1993). Introduction. In T. E. Backer & E. M. Rogers (Eds.), *Organizational aspects of health communication campaigns: What works?* (pp. 1–9). Newbury Park, CA: Sage.

Balas, E. A., Jaffrey, F., Kuperman, G. J., Boren, S. A., Brown, G. D., Pinciroli, F., & Mitchell, J. A. (1997). Electronic communication with patients: Evaluation of distance medicine technology. *Journal of the American Medical Association, 278,* 152–160.

Baldwin, D. A. (1995). How I made medicine fun again. *Medical Economics, 72,* 153–156.

Baldwin, D. C., Jr., Daugherty, S. R., Rowley, B. D., & Schwarz, M. D. (1996). Cheating in medical school: A survey of second-year students at 31 schools. *Journal of the Association of American Medical Colleges, 71*(3), 267–273.

Baldwin, D. M. (2003). Disparities in health and health care: Focusing on efforts to eliminate unequal burdens. *Online Journal of Issues in Nursing, 8*(1), 2.

Balint, J., & Shelton, W. (1996). Regaining the initiative: Forging a new model of the patient–physician relationship. *Journal of the American Medical Association, 275,* 887–892.

Baltes, M. M., & Wahl, H. (1996). Patterns of communication in old age: The dependence-support and independence-ignore script. *Health Communication, 8,* 217–231.

Bandura, A. (1986). *Social foundations of thought and action: A social cognitive approach.* Englewood Cliffs, NJ: Prentice Hall.

Bandura, A. (1994). Social cognitive theory of mass communication. In J. Bryant & D. Zillmann (Eds.), *Media effects: Advances in theory and research* (pp. 61–90). Hillsdale, NJ: Lawrence Erlbaum.

Barber, K. R., Shaw, R., Folts, M., Taylor, K., Ryan, A., Hughes, M., Scott, V., & Abbott, R. R. (1998). Differences between African American and Caucasian men participating in a community-based cancer screening program. *Journal of Community Health, 23,* 441.

Bardbard, L. (1993, November). Cosmetics and reality. *FDA Consumer, 27,* 32–33.

Barnard, A. (2003, January 22). Doctors brace for changes on patient privacy. *Boston Globe,* National/Foreign, p. A1.

Barnes, M. K., & Duck, S. (1994). Everyday communicative contexts for social support. In B. R. Burleson, T. L. Albrecht, & I. G. Sarason (Eds.), *Communication of social support: Messages, interactions, relationships, and community* (pp. 175–194). Thousand Oaks, CA: Sage.

Barrett, B. (2003). Alternative, complementary, and conventional medicine: Is integration upon us? *Journal of Alternative and Complementary Medicine, 9*(3), 417–427.

Barzansky, B., Jonas, H. S., & Etzel, S. I. (1995). Educational programs in U.S. medical schools, 1994–1995. *Journal of the American Medical Association, 274,* 716–723.

Basil, M. D. (1997). The danger of cigarette "special placements" in film and television. *Health Communication, 9,* 191–198.

Bass, A. (1990, November 25). Health care marketing seeks gain from pain. *Boston Globe,* National/Foreign section, p. 1.

Bates, D. W., & Komaroff, A. L. (1996). A cyberday in the life. *Journal of the American Medical Association, 275,* 753–755.

Baur, C. (2000). Limiting factors on the transformative powers of e-mail in patient–physician relationships: A critical analysis. *Health Communication 12*(3), 239–259.

Beach, W. A. (2002). Between dad and son: Initiating, delivering, and assimilating bad cancer news. *Health Communication, 14*(3), 271–298.

Beach, W. A., & Japp, P. (1983). Storifying as time-traveling: The knowledgeable use of temporally structured discourse. In R. N. Bostrom (Ed.), *Communication yearbook 7* (pp. 867–889). New Brunswick, NJ: Transaction Books.

Beagan, B. L. (2003). Teaching social and cultural awareness to medical students. *Academic Medicine, 78*(6), 605–614.

Bean-Mayberry, B. A., Chang, C. C., McNeil, M. A., Whittle, J., Hayes, P. M., & Scholle, S. H. (2003). Patient satisfaction in women's clinic versus traditional primary care cares in the Veterans Administration. *Journal of General Internal Medicine, 18*(3), 175–181.

Beck, C. S., & Ragan, S. L. (1992). Negotiating interpersonal and medical talk: Frame shifts in the gynaecologic exam. *Journal of Language and Social Psychology, 11,* 47–61.

Beck, C., Ragan, S. L., & du Pré, A. (1997). *Partnership for health: Building relationships between women and health caregivers.* Mahwah, NJ: Lawrence Erlbaum.

Becker, G., & Newsom, E. (2003). Socioeconomic status and dissatisfaction with health care among chronically ill African Americans. *American Journal of Public Health, 93*(5), 742–748.

Beckman, H. B., & Frankel, R. M. (1984). The effect of physician behavior on the collection of data. *Annals of Internal Medicine, 101,* 692–696.

Beebe, S. A. (1995). Nurses' perception of beeper calls: Implications for resident stress and patient care. *Archives of Pediatrics & Adolescent Medicine, 149,* 187–191.

Begany, T. (1995). Do you get the respect you deserve? *RN, 58,* 32–33.

Bensing, J. M., Kerssens, J. J., & van der Pasch, M. (1995). Patient-directed gaze as a tool for discovering and handling psychosocial problems in general practice. *Journal of Nonverbal Behavior, 19,* 223–242.

Ben-Sira, Z. (1980). Affective and instrumental components in the physician–patient relationship: An additional dimension of interaction theory. *Journal of Health and Social Behavior, 7,* 170–180.

Ben-Sira, Z. (1990). Primary care practitioners' likelihood to engage in a biopsychosocial approach: An additional perspective on the doctor–patient relationship. *Social Science and Medicine, 31,* 565–576.

Bergeron, J., Neuman, K., & Kinsey, J. (1999). Do advanced practice nurses and physician assistants benefit small rural hospitals? *Journal of Rural Health, 15*(2), 219–232.

Bergstrom, M. J., & Holmes, M. E. (2000). Lay theories of successful aging after the death of a spouse: A network text analysis of bereavement advice. *Health Communication, 12*(4), 377–406.

Bergstrom, M. J., & Nussbaum, J. F. (1996). Cohort differences in interpersonal conflict: Implications for the older patient–younger care provider interaction. *Health Communication, 8,* 233–248.

Berko, R. M., Wolvin, A. D., & Curtis, R. (1993). *The business of communicating* (5th ed.). Madison, WI: Brown & Benchmark.

Bernard, L., Lavellee, C., Gray-Donald, K., & Delisle, H. (1995). Overweight in Cree schoolchildren and adolescents associated with diet, low physical activity, and high television viewing. *Journal of the American Dietetic Association, 95,* 800–802.

Bernhardt, J. M., & Cameron, K. A. (2003). Accessing, understanding, and applying health communication messages: The challenge of health literacy. In T. L. Thompson, A. M. Dorsey, K. I. Miller, & R. Parrott (Eds.), *Handbook of health communication* (pp. 583–605). Mahwah, NJ: Lawrence Erlbaum.

Bethea, L. S., Travis, S. S., & Pecchioni, L. (2000). Family caregivers' use of humor in conveying information about caring for dependent older adults. *Health Communication, 12*(4), 361–376.

Betts, K. (2002, March 31). The tyranny of skinny, fashion's insider secret. *New York Times,* p. 1, section 9.

Beyers, M. (1996, February 15). The value of nursing. *Hospitals & Health Networks, 70,* 52.

Bhopal, R. (1998, June 27). Spectre of racism in health and health care: Lessons from history and the United States. *British Medical Journal, 7149,* 1970–1973.

Biagi, S. (1999). *Media/impact: An introduction to mass media.* Belmont, CA: Wadsworth.

Bille, D. A. (1981). The approach to health care in three American minorities. In D. A. Bille (Ed.), *Practical approaches to patient teaching* (pp. 85–94). Boston: Little, Brown & Company.

Blake, R., & Mouton, J. (1964). *The managerial grid.* Houston: Gulf.

Blank, R., & Slipp, S. (1998, July). Managers' diversity workbook. *HR Focus, 75,* S7–S8.

Bochner, S. (1983). Doctors, patients and their cultures. In D. Pendleton & J. Hasler (Eds.), *Doctor–patient communication* (pp. 127–138). London: Academic Press.

Bohm, D. (1980). *Wholeness and the Implicate Order.* London: Routledge & Kegan Paul.

Bollinger, L. C. (2003). The need for diversity in higher education. *Academic Medicine, 78*(5), 431–436.

Bonner, T. N. (1992). *To the ends of the earth. Women's search for education in medicine.* Cambridge, MA: Harvard University Press.

Bonsteel, A. (1997, March–April). Behind the white coat. *The Humanist, 57,* 15–19.

Boodman, S. (1997, February 25). Silent doctors more likely to be sued; malpractice study suggests that physicians' manner affects patients' readiness to go to court. *Washington Post,* p. WH9.

Booth-Butterfield, M. (2003). Embedded health behaviors from adolescence to adulthood: The impact of tobacco. *Health Communication, 15*(2), 171–184.

Booth-Butterfield, M., Anderson, R., & Booth-Butterfield, S. (2000). Adolescents' use of tobacco, health locus of control, and self-monitoring. *Health Communication, 12*(2), 137–148.

Borisoff, D., & Victor, D. A. (1998). *Conflict management: A communication skills approach* (2nd ed.). Boston: Allyn & Bacon.

Botta, R. A., & Dumlao, R. (2002). How do conflict and communication patterns between fathers and daughters contribute to or offset eating disorders? *Health Communication, 14*(2), 199–219.

Bottorf, J. L., Gogag, M., & Engelberg-Lotzkar, M. (1995). Comforting: Exploring the work of cancer nurses. *Journal of Advanced Nursing, 22,* 1077–1084.

Bowen, D. J., Singal, R., Eng, E., Crystal, S., & Burke, W. (2003). Jewish identity and intentions to obtain breast cancer screening. *Cultural Diversity and Ethnic Minority Psychology, 9*(1), 78–87.

Bowker, J. (1996). Cancer, individual process, and control: A case study of metaphor analysis. *Health Communication, 8,* 91–104.

Boyd, R. S. (1997, June 21). Medical aids, media reports 'a flood of confusing advice': Marketing hype, thirst for the news among causes of bewilderment. *Houston Chronicle,* p. 7.

Bradac, J. J. (2001). Theory comparison, uncertainty reduction, problematic integration, uncertainty management, and other curious constructs. *Journal of Communication, 51*(3), 456–476.

Bradford, E. W. (1995, December 11). Don't sabotage your own malpractice defense. *Medical Economics, 72,* 143–145.

Brady, M. J., & Cella, D. F. (1995, May 30). Helping patients live with their cancer. *Patient Care,* pp. 41–49.

Braithwaite, D. O. (1996). "Persons first": Expanding communicative choices by persons with disabilities. In E. B. Ray (Ed.), *Communication and disenfranchisement: Social health issues and implications* (pp. 449–464). Mahwah, NJ: Lawrence Erlbaum.

Braithwaite, D. O., & Harter, L. M. (2000). Communication and the management of dialectic tensions in the personal relationships of people with disabilities. In D. O. Braithwaite & T. L. Thompson (Eds.), *Handbook of communication and people with disabilities: Research and applications* (pp. 17–36). Mahwah, NJ: Lawrence Erlbaum.

Braithwaite, D. O., & Thompson, T. L. (Eds.). (2000). *Handbook of communication and people with disabilities: Research and applications.* Mahwah, NJ: Lawrence Erlbaum.

Braithwaite, D. O., Waldron, V. R., & Finn, J. (1999). Communication of social support in computer-mediated groups for people with disabilities. *Health Communication, 11,* 123–151.

Branch, W. T., Arky, R. A., Woo, B., Stoeckle, J. D., Levy, D. B., & Taylor, W. C. (1991). Teaching medicine as a human experience: A patient–doctor relationship course for faculty and first-year medical students. *Annals of Internal Medicine, 114,* 482–489.

Branch, W. T., & Malik, T. K. (1993). Using 'windows of opportunities' in brief interviews to understand patients' concerns. *Journal of the American Medical Association, 269,* 1667–1668.

Brashers, D. E., & Babrow, A. S. (1996). Theorizing health communication. *Communication Studies, 47,* 237–251.

Brashers, D. E., Haas, S. M., & Neidig, J. L. (1999). The patient self-advocacy scale: Measuring patient involvement in health care decision-making interactions. *Health Communication, 11*(2), 97–121.

Bray, G. A. (1998). Obesity: A time bomb to be defused. *The Lancet, 352,* 160.

Brennan, P. F. (1996, October). The future of clinical communication in an electronic environment. *Holistic Nursing Practice, 11,* 97–105.

Brennan, P. F., & Fink, S. V. (1997). Health promotion, social support, and computer networks. In R. L. Street Jr., W. R. Gold, & T. Manning (Eds.), *Health promotion and interactive technology: Theoretical applications and future directions* (pp. 157–169). Mahwah, NJ: Lawrence Erlbaum.

Bresolin, L. B. (1999). Health literacy. *Journal of the American Medical Association, 281*(6), 552.

Brody, H. (1987). *Stories of sickness.* New Haven, CT: Yale University.

Brody, H., & Bonham, V. L. Jr. (1997). Gag rules and trade secrets in managed care contracts: Ethical and legal concerns. *Archives of Internal Medicine, 157,* 2037–2043.

Brosius, H., & Weimann, G. (1996). Who sets the agenda? Agenda-setting as a two-step flow. *Communication Research, 23,* 561–580.

Brotman, S., Ryan, B., & Cormier, R. (2003). The health and social service needs of gay and lesbian elders and their families in Canada. *Gerontologist, 43*(2), 192–202.

Brown, H., Cassileth, B. R., Lewis, J. P., & Renner, J. H. (1994). Alternative medicine—or quackery? *Patient Care, 28,* 80–90.

Brown, J. B., Stewart, M., & Ryan, B. L. (2003). Outcomes of patient–provider interaction. In T. L. Thompson, A. M. Dorsey, K. I. Miller, & R. Parrott (Eds.), *Handbook of health communication* (pp. 141–161). Mahwah, NJ: Lawrence Erlbaum.

Brown, J. B., Weston, W. W., & Stewart, M. (1995). The first component: Exploring both the disease and the illness experience. In M. Stewart,

J. B. Brown, W. W. Weston, I. R. McWhinney, C. L. McWilliam, & T. R. Freeman (Eds.), *Patient-centered medicine: Transforming the clinical method* (pp. 31–43). Thousand Oaks, CA; Sage.

Brown, J. D., & Einsiedel, E. F. (1990). Public health campaigns: Mass media strategies. In E. B. Ray & L. Donohew (Eds.), *Communication and health: Systems and applications* (pp. 153–170). Hillsdale, NJ: Lawrence Erlbaum.

Brown, J. D., & Walsh-Childers, K. (1994). Effects of media on personal and public health. In J. Bryant & D. Zillmann (Eds.), *Media effects: Advances in theory and research* (pp. 389–415). Hillsdale, NJ: Lawrence Erlbaum.

Brown, S. J. (1995, May 15). Rethink how medical schools pick 'best' students. *American Medical News, 19,* 29.

Brown, W. J. (1992). Culture and AIDS education: Reaching high-risk heterosexuals in Asian-American communities. *Journal of Applied Communication Research, 20,* 275–291.

Brown, W. J., & Basil, M. D. (1995). Media celebrities and public health: Responses to "Magic" Johnson's HIV disclosure and its impact on AIDS risks and high-risk behaviors. *Health Communication, 7,* 345–370.

Brown, W. J., Basil, M. D., & Bocarnea, M. C. (2003). The influence of famous athletes on health beliefs and practices: Mark McGwire, child abuse prevention, and androstenedione. *Journal of Health Communication, 8*(1), 41–57.

Brown, W. J., & Singhal, A. (1990). Ethical dilemmas of prosocial television. *Communication Quarterly, 38,* 268–280.

Bruck, L. (1996, September). Today's issues in tax exemption. *Nursing Homes, 45,* 43–46.

Bryan, G. T. (1991). Physicians and medical education. *Journal of the American Medical Association, 266,* 1407–1408.

Buchholz, B. (1992, January-February). Psyching yourself: How to prepare for medical procedures. *Arthritis Today, 6*(1), 20–24.

Buckman, R., Lipkin, M,. Jr., Sourkes, B. M., Toole, S. W., & Talarico, L. D. (1997). Strategies and skills for breaking bad news. *Patient Care, 31,* 61–78.

Bucknall, T., & Thomas, S. (1996). Critical care nurse satisfaction with level of involvement in clinical decisions. *Journal of Advanced Nursing, 23,* 571–577.

Buller, D. B., Borland, R., & Burgoon, M. (1998). Impact of behavioral intention on effectiveness of message features: Evidence from the family sun safety project. *Human Communication Research, 24,* 433–453.

Buller, D. B., Burgoon, M., Hall, J. R., Levine, N., Taylor, A. M., Beach, B., Buller, M. K., & Melcher, C. (2000). Long-term effects of language intensity in preventive messages on planned family solar protection. *Health Communication, 12*(3), 261–275.

Burdine, J. N., McLeroy, K. B., & Gottlieb, N. H. (1987). Ethical dilemmas in health promotion: An introduction. *Health Education Quarterly, 14,* 7–9.

Burgoon, M. (1989). The effects of message variables on opinion and attitude change. In J. Bradac (Ed.), *Messages in communication science: Contemporary approaches to the study of effects* (pp. 129–164). Newbury Park, CA: Sage.

Burgoon, M. H., & Burgoon, J. K. (1990). Compliance-gaining and health care. In J. P. Dillard (Ed.), *Seeking compliance: The production of interpersonal influence messages* (pp. 161–188). Scottsdale, AZ: Gorsuch Scarisbrick.

Burleson, B. R. (1990). Comforting as social support: Relational consequences of supportive behaviors. In S. Duck & R. C. Silver (Eds.), *Personal relationships and social support* (pp. 66–82). London: Sage.

Burleson, B. R. (1994). Comforting messages: Significance, approaches, and effects. In B. R. Burleson, T. L. Albrecht, & I. G. Sarason (Eds.), *Communication of social support: Messages, interactions, relationships, and community* (pp. 3–28). Thousand Oaks, CA: Sage.

Buunk, B., & Gibbons, F. X. (1997). *Health, coping, and well-being: Perspectives from social comparison theory.* Mahwah, NJ: Lawrence Erlbaum.

By the numbers (1900 and 1995 demographic, economic data compared). (1995, August 28). *U.S. News & World Report, 119,* 83.

Byck, R. (1986). *The encyclopedia of psychoactive drugs: Treating mental illness.* New York: Chelsea House.

Cadogan, M. P., Franzi, C., Osterweil, D., & Hill, T. (1999). Barriers to effective communication in skilled nursing facilities: Differences in perception between nurses and physicians. *Journal of the American Geriatrics Society, 47,* 71–75.

Calfee, J. E. (1998, April). How advertising informs to our benefit. *Consumers' Research Magazine, 81,* 13–18.

Calfee, J. E. (2002, Fall). Direct-to-consumer advertising of prescription drugs: Evaluating regulatory policy in the United States and New Zealand. *Journal of Public Policy & Marketing, 21*(2), 174.

Califano, J. A. (1994). Revealing the link between campaign financing and deaths caused by tobacco. *Journal of the American Medical Association, 272,* 1217–1218.

Campbell-Heider, N., & Hart, C. A. (1993). Updating the nurse's bedside manner. *Image: Journal of Nursing Scholarship, 25,* 133–139.

Cancer patients try many forms of alternative therapy. (1997, August 11). *Cancer Weekly Plus,* pp. 6–7.

Candib, L. M. (1994). Reconsidering power in the clinical relationship. In E. S. More & M. A. Milligan (Eds.), *The empathic practitioner: Empathy, gender, and medicine* (pp. 135–155). New Brunswick, NJ: Rutgers University.

Cantanzarite, E. (1992). *Managing the chemically dependent nurse: A guide to identification, intervention, and retention.* Chicago: American Hospital Association.

Capossela, C., Warnock, S., & Miller, S. (1995). *Share the care: How to organize a group to care for someone who is seriously ill.* New York: Fireside.

Capriotti, T. (1999, February 1). Exploring the 'herbal jungle.' *MedSurg Nursing, 8,* 53.

Cardello, L., Ray, E. B., & Pettey, G. R. (1995, Winter). The relationship of perceived physician communicator style to patient satisfaction. *Communication Reports, 8,* 27–37.

Carter, W. H., Schill, M. H., & Wachter, S. M. (1998). Polarisation, public housing and racial minorities in U.S. cities. *Urban Studies, 35,* 1989.

Casey, M. K., Allen, M., Emmers-Sommer, T., Sahlstein, E., Degooyer, D., Winters, A. M., Wagner, A. E., & Dun, T. (2003). When a celebrity contracts a disease: The example of Earvin "Magic" Johnson's announcement that he was HIV positive. *Journal of Health Communication, 8*(1), 249–256.

Cassedy, J. H. (1991). *Medicine in America: A short history.* Baltimore, MD: Johns Hopkins University Press.

Cassell, E. J. (1991). *The nature of suffering.* New York: Oxford.

Cawyer, C. S., & Smith-du Pré, A. (1995). Communicating social support: Identifying supportive episodes in an HIV/AIDS support group. *Communication Quarterly, 43,* 243–258.

Cecil, D. W. (1998). Relational control patterns in physician-centered clinical encounters: Continuing the conversation. *Health Communication, 10,* 125–150.

Cegala, D. J., & Broz, S. L. (2003). Provider and patient communication skills training. In T. L. Thompson, A. M. Dorsey, K. I. Miller, & R. Parrott (Eds.), *Handbook of health communication* (pp. 95–119). Mahwah, NJ: Lawrence Erlbaum.

Cegala, D. J., McClure, L., Marinelli, T. M., & Post, D. M. (2000). The effects of communication skills training on patients' participation during medical interviews. *Patient Education and Counseling, 41,* 209–222.

Cegala, D. J., McGee, D. S., & McNeilis, K. S. (1996). *Components of patients' and doctors' perceptions of communication competence during a primary care medical interview.* Paper presented at the annual meeting of the Speech Communication Association, San Antonio.

Cegala, D. J., Post, D., & McClure, L. (2001). The effects of patient communication skills training on the discourse of elderly patients during a primary care interview. *Journal of the American Geriatrics Society, 49,* 1505–1511.

Centers for Disease Control and Prevention. (2002). National health expenditures. Retrieved online September 9, 2003, from www.cdc.gov/nchs/fastats/hexpense.html

Centers for Disease Control and Prevention. (2003, April 17). Comparative causes of annual deaths. Retrieved online July 18, 2003, from www.cdc.gov/tobacco/research_data/health_consequences/andths.htm

Cericola, S. A. (1999). Communication skills: The art of listening. *Plastic Surgical Nursing, 19*(1), 41–42.

Chaker, A. M. (1998, October 4). Anti-acne birth control pills cause conflicting viewpoints. *Wall Street Journal,* Business section, p. 2.

Chamberlain, M. A. (1994). New technologies in health communication: Progress or panacea? *American Behavioral Scientist, 38,* 271–285.

Chapman, S., & Leask, J. A. (2001, December). Paid celebrity endorsement in health promotion: A case study from Australia. *Health Promotion International, 16*(4), 333–338.

Charles, C., Goldsmith, L. J., Chambers, L., Haynes, R. B., & Gauld, M. (1996). Provider–patient communication among elderly and nonelderly patients in Canadian hospitals: A national survey. *Health Communication, 8,* 281–302.

Charmaz, K. (1987). Struggling for a self: Identity levels of the chronically ill. In J. Roth & P. Conrad (Eds.), *Research in the sociology of health care.* (pp. 283–321). Greenwich, CT: JAI Press.

Charski, M. (1998, June 29). Now on the Net: Live birth. Next: the operating room. *U.S. News & World Report, 124,* 36.

Chatterjee, P. (2003). Spreading the word about HIV/AIDS in India. *The Lancet, 361*(9368), 1526–1527.

Chesebro, J. W. (1982). Illness as a rhetorical act: A cross-cultural perspective. *Communication Quarterly, 30,* 321–331.

Chesler, M. A., & Barbarin, O. A. (1984). Difficulties of providing help in a crisis: Relationships between parents of children with cancer and their friends. *Journal of Social Issues, 40,* 113–134.

Chew, F., Palmer, S., & Kim, S. (1998). Testing the influence of the health belief model and a television program on nutritional behavior. *Health Communication, 8,* 227–246.

Chew, F., Palmer, S., Slonska, Z., & Subbiah, K. (2002, May/June). Enhancing health knowledge, health beliefs, and health behavior in Poland through a health promoting television program series. *Journal of Health Communication, 7*(3), 179–196.

Children in developing world bear the burden of cancer. (2003, March 18). *Cancer Weekly, 125.* Retrieved online July 19, 2003, from LexisNexis.

Choi, N. G. (1996). The never-married and divorced elderly: Comparison of economic and health status, social support, and living arrangement. *Journal of Gerontological Social Work, 26,* 3–25.

Clancy, C. (1995). Managed care: Jekyll or Hyde? *Journal of the American Medical Association, 273,* 338–339.

Clarke, J. N. (1999). Prostate cancer's hegemonic masculinity in select print mass media depictions (1974–1995). *Health Communication, 11*(1), 59–74.

Clements, B. (1996). Talk is cheaper than three extra office visits. *American Medical News, 39,* 17–20.

Cline, R. J. W., & Boyd, M. F. (1993). Communication as threat and therapy: Stigma, social support, and coping with HIV infection. In E. B. Ray (Ed.), *Case studies in health communication* (pp. 131–148). Hillsdale, NJ: Lawrence Erlbaum.

Coddington, D. C., Moore, K. D., & Fischer, E. A. (2001). *Strategies for the new health care marketplace: Managing the convergence of consumerism and technology.* San Francisco: Jossey-Bass.

Cohn, F., Harrold, J., & Lynn, J. (1997). Medical education must deal with end-of-life care. *Chronicle of Higher Education, 43,* A56.

Cohen, J. (1997). The media's love affair with AIDS research: Hope vs. hype. *Science, 275,* 298–299.

Cohen, S., & Wills, T. A. (1985). Stress, social support, and buffering hypothesis. *Psychological Bulletin, 98,* 310–357.

Comprehensive survey of working women's health issues. (1998, May–June). *Public Health Reports, 113,* 196.

Conan, N. (2002, April 12). Medical privacy. National Public Radio's Talk of the Nation. Transcript retrieved online August 31, 2003, from LexisNexis.

Conlee, C. J., Amabisca, W., & Vagim, N. N. (1995). *Gender differences for patient satisfaction: The clash between medical socialization and patient expectations.* Paper presented at the annual meeting of the Speech Communication Association, San Antonio.

Conlee, C. J., Olvera, J., & Vagim, N. N. (1993, Winter). The relationships among physician nonverbal immediacy and measures of patient satisfaction with physician care. *Communication Reports, 6,* 25–33.

Conrad, C. (1994). *Strategic organizational communication: Toward the twenty-first century.* New York: Holt, Rinehart & Winston.

Conrad, P. (1988). Learning to doctor: Reflections on recent accounts of the medical school years. *Journal of Health and Social Behavior, 29,* 323–332.

Controversy heats up over subway's safer sex ads. (1994, February 7). *AIDS Weekly, 9,* 9–10.

Cooney, E. (2003). Resident physicians hope limits on grueling hours won't compromise patient care, education. *Telegram & Gazette* (Massachusetts), Health, p. C1.

Cooper, R. A., & Stoflet, S. J. (1996). Trends in the education and practice of alternative medicine clinicians. *Health Affairs, 15,* 226–237.

Cooper-Patrick, L., Gallo, J. J., Gonzalez, J. J., Vu, H. T., Power, N. R., Nelson, C., & Ford, D. E. (1999). Race, gender, and partnership in the patient–physician relationship. *Journal of the American Medical Association, 282*(6), 583.

Corbin, J., & Strauss, A. L. (1988). Experiencing body failure and a disrupted self image. In J. Corbin & A. L. Strauss (Eds.), *Unending work and care: Managing chronic illness at home* (pp. 49–67). San Francisco: Jossey-Bass.

Cottingham, J. (1992). Cartesian dualism: Theology, metaphysics, and science. In J. Cottingham (Ed.), *The Cambridge companion to Descartes* (pp. 236–257). Cambridge, MA: Cambridge University Press.

Council on Ethical and Judicial Affairs, American Medical Association. Ethical issues in managed care. (1995). *Journal of the American Medical Association, 273,* 330–335.

Coupland, N., Coupland, J., & Giles, H. (1991). *Language, society & the elderly.* Oxford, UK: Blackwell.

Coupland, N., Coupland, J., Giles, H., & Coupland, D. (2003, March). *Language, society, and the elderly: Discourse, identity, and aging* (Language in Society, No. 18). Malden, MA: Blackwell.

Courtney, R., & Rice, C. (1997, February). Investigation of nurse practitioner–patient interactions: Using the nurse practitioner rating form. *Nurse Practitioner, 22,* 46–53.

Coward, D. D. (Fall, 1990). The lived experience of self-transcendence in women with advanced breast cancer. *Nursing Science Quarterly, 3*(3), 162–169.

Cowart, D., & Burt, R. (1998). Confronting death: Who chooses, who controls? *The Hastings Center Report, 28,* 14–24.

Cox, T. H. (1991). The multicultural organization. *Academy of Management Executive, 5,* 34–47.

Cox, T. H., Jr. (2001). *Creating the multicultural organization: A strategy for capturing the power of diversity.* San Francisco: Jossey-Bass.

Cox, T. H., Jr., & Beale, R. L. (1997). *Developing competency to manage diversity: Readings, cases, and activities.* San Francisco: Berrett-Koehler.

Crandall, S. J., George, G., Marion, G. S., & Davis, S. (2003). Applying theory to the design of cultural competency training for medical students: A case study. *Academic Medicine, 78*(6), 588–594.

Crandall, S. J., Volk, R. J., & Loemker, V. (1993). Medical students' attitudes toward providing care for the underserved: Are we training socially responsible physicians? *Journal of the American Medical Association, 269,* 2519–2523.

Crawford, B. L., Taylor, L. S., Siepert, B. S., & Lush, M. (1996). The imperative of outcome analysis: An integration of traditional and nontraditional outcome measures. *Journal of Nursing Care Quality, 10,* 33–40.

Crawford, W. (1997, October). Taxing for health? *Consumers' Research Magazine, 80,* 34.

Croft, J. B., Giles, W. H., Pollard, R. A., Keenan, N. L., Casper, M. L., & Anda, R. F. (1999). Heart failure survival rate among older adults in the United States. *Archives of Internal Medicine, 159,* 505.

Cross, M. L., Wright, S. W., Wrenn, K. D., Ishihara, K. K., Socha, C. M., & Higgins, J. P. (1996). Interaction between the trauma team and families: Lack of timely communication. *American Journal of Emergency Medicine, 14,* 548–550.

Cutrona, C. E., & Suhr, J. A. (1994). Social support communication in the context of marriage: An analysis of couples' supportive interactions. In B. R. Burleson, T. L. Albrecht, & I. G. Sarason (Eds.), *Communication of social support: Messages, interactions, relationships, and community* (pp. 113–135). Thousand Oaks, CA: Sage.

Daly, A., Jennings, J., Beckett, J. O., & Leashore, B. R. (1995). Effective coping strategies of African Americans. *Social Work, 40,* 240–248.

Daniels, D. Y. (1996, October). An open ICU. *RN, 59,* 30–33.

Darlin, D. (1995, November 6). Junior Mints, I'm gonna make you a star. *Forbes, 156,* 90–93.

Daumit, G. L., Hermann, J. A., Coresh, J., & Powe, N. R. (1999). Use of cardiovascular procedures among Black persons and White persons. *Annals of Internal Medicine, 130*(3), 173–182.

Davenport, T. H., Prusak, L., & Wilson, H. J. (2003). Who's bringing you hot ideas and how are you responding? *Harvard Business Review, 81*(2), 58–64, 124.

Davis, J. J. (2002, July/September). Disenfranchising the disabled: The inaccessibility of Internet-based health information. *Journal of Health Communication, 7,* 355–367.

Dean, V. C. (1997). Physician satisfaction reflects changes in health care landscape. *Journal of Family Practice, 45,* 319–321.

Deary, I. J., Whiteman, M. C., & Fowkes, F. G. R. (1998). Medical research and the popular media. *The Lancet, 351,* 1726–1727.

Demographics and the 2000 census. (2002, January 30). Health Policy Tracking Service. Retrieved online August 1, 2003, from LexisNexis.

Dennis, B. P., & Small, E. B. (2003). Incorporating cultural diversity in nursing care: An action plan. *Association of Black Nursing Faculty Journal, 14*(1), 17–25.

Dennison, B. A., Erb, T. A., & Jenkins, P. L. (2002, June). Television viewing and television in bedroom associated with overweight risk among low-income preschool children. *Pediatrics, 109*(6), 1028–1035.

DeSantis, A. D. (2002). Smoke screen: An ethnographic study of a cigar shop's collective rationalization. *Health Communication, 14*(2), 167–198.

Desloge, R. (1997, October 20). Optometry school sets sights on elderly vision loss. *St. Louis Business Journal* (Online). Available: www.amcity.com//stlouis/stories/102097/focus7.html

DiClemente, C. C., Prochaska, J. O., Fairhurst, S. K., Velicer, W. F., Velasquez, M., & Rossi, J. S. (1991). The processes of smoking cessation: An analysis of precontemplation, contemplation and preparation stages of change. *Journal of Consulting and Clinical Psychology, 59,* 295–304.

Diem, S. J., Lantos, J. D., & Tulsky, J. A. (1996). Cardiopulmonary resuscitation on television: Miracles and misinformation. *New England Journal of Medicine, 334,* 1578–1582.

DiFranza, J. R., Richards, J. W., Paulman, P. M., Wolf-Gillespie, N., Fletcher, C., Jaffe, R. D., & Murray, D. (1991). RJR Nabisco's cartoon camel promotes Camel cigarettes to children. *Journal of the American Medical Association, 266,* 3149–3153.

Dignan, M. B., Michielutte, R., Jones-Lighty, D. D., & Bahnson, J. (1994). Factors influencing the return rate in a direct mail campaign to inform minority women about prevention of cervical cancer. *Public Health Reports, 109,* 507–511.

DiLorenzo, T. J., & Bennett, J. T. (1998, May). The U.S. is becoming a nanny state. *USA Today Magazine, 126,* 12–15.

DiMatteo, M. R. (1979). Nonverbal skill and the physician–patient relationship. In R. Rosenthal (Ed.), *Skills in nonverbal communication:*

Individual differences (pp. 104–134). Cambridge, MA: Oelgeschlager, Gunn, & Hain.

DiMatteo, M. R., McBride, C. A., Shugars, D. A., & O'Neil, E. H. (1995). Public attitudes toward dentists: A U.S. household survey. *Journal of the American Dental Association, 126,* 1563–1571.

Diminitz, J. A. (1998). Race, treatment, and survival among colorectal carcinoma patients in an equal-access medical system. *Journal of the American Medical Association, 280,* 1122.

Dinur, E. (1997, January). In praise of alternative medicine. *College Health, 45,* 183–186.

Disappearing act. (1998, November 2). *Time,* p. 110.

Distribution of U.S. medical school faculty by rank and ethnicity. (2000). American Medical Association. Retrieved online August 6, 2003, from www.ama-assn.org/ama/pub/print/article/168-1536.html

Do, T.-P., & Giest, P. (2000). Embodiment and dis-embodiment: Identity transformation and persons with physical disabilities. In D. O. Braithwaite & T. L. Thompson (Eds.), *Handbook of communication and people with disabilities: Research and applications* (pp. 49–65). Mahwah, NJ: Lawrence Erlbaum.

Donnelly, J. (2003, January 26). Lives lost; none of them had to die. *Boston Globe,* p. 1.

Donohew, L. (1990). Public health campaigns: Individual message strategies. In E. B. Ray & L. Donohew (Eds.), *Communication and health: Systems and applications* (pp. 136–170). Hillsdale, NJ: Lawrence Erlbaum.

Donohew, L., Lorch, E. P., & Palmgreen, P. (1998). Applications of a theoretic model of information exposure to health interventions. *Human Communication Research, 24,* 454–468.

Donovan, R. J. (1995). Steps in planning and developing health communication campaigns: A comment on CDC's framework for health communication. *Public Health Reports, 110,* 215–217.

Douglas, C. (1994). The barber trembles. *British Medical Journal, 309,* 545.

Dow, J. P., Jr. (1996). Pushing the rock. *Radiologic Technology, 68,* 184.

Dowling, C. G. (1997, February). Through the ages, artists and doctors have confronted the mysteries of anatomy. *Life, 20,* 48–56.

Drass, K. A. (1988). Discourse and occupational perspective: A comparison of nurse practitioners and physician assistants. *Discourse Processes, 11,* 163–181.

Dreazer, Y. (1998, June 22). Report hits quality of children's TV, adequacy of rating system. *Buffalo News,* p. 5A.

Dreidger, S. D. (1996, December 2). Critical care: 'We are sending people home quicker and sicker.' *Macleans, 109,* 52.

Drucker, P. F. (1993). *Post-capitalistic society.* New York: HarperCollins.

Drug marketing: DTC ads influence majority of consumers, say doctors. (2003, January 20). *Advertising Age, 74*(3), 6.

Drum, D. (1997, November 17). Product placement matures into placement of nonprofit causes. *Variety, 369,* S27–S28.

Duffy, J. (1979). *The healers: A history of American medicine.* Urbana, IL: University of Illinois Press.

Duggleby, W. (2003). Helping Hispanic/Latino home health patients manage their pain. *Home Healthcare Nurse, 21*(3), 174–179.

du Pré, A. (1998). *Humor and the healing arts: Multimethod analysis of humor use in health care.* Mahwah, NJ: Lawrence Erlbaum.

du Pré, A. (2002). Accomplishing the impossible: Talking about body and soul and mind during a medical visit. *Health Communication, 14*(1), 1–22.

du Pré, A. (in press). Making empowerment work: Medical center soars in satisfaction ratings. In E. B. Ray (Ed.), *Case studies in health communication* (2nd ed.). Mahwah, NJ: Lawrence Erlbaum.

du Pré, A., & Beck, C. S. (1997). "How can I put this?": Exaggerated self-disparagement as alignment strategy during problematic disclosures by patients to doctors. *Qualitative Health Research, 7,* 487–503.

du Pré, A., & Ray, E. B. (in press). Comforting episodes: Transcendent experiences of cancer survivors. In L. Sparks, D. O'Hair, & G. L. Kreps (Eds.), *Cancer communication and aging.* Cresskill, NJ: Hampton Press.

DuRant, R. H., Rome, E. S., Rich, M., Allred, E., Emans, S. J., & Woods, E. R. (1997). Tobacco and alcohol use behaviors portrayed in music videos: A content analysis. *American Journal of Public Health, 87,* 1131–1135.

Dyer, J. (1996). *In a tangled wood: An Alzheimer's journey.* Dallas, TX: Southern Methodist University Press.

Eastman, J. K., Eastman, K. L., & Tolson, M. A. (1997). The ethics of managed care: An initial look at physicians' perspectives. *Marketing Health Services, 17,* 26–40.

Eaton, L., & Dyer, O. (2003, March 15). African women at high risk of death in pregnancy. *British Medical Journal, 326,* 567.

Eaton, L. G., & Tinsley, B. J. (1999). Maternal personality and health communication in the pediatric context. *Health Communication, 11,* 75–96.

Ebell, M. H., Smith, M., Kruse, J. A., Drader-Wilcox, J., & Novak, J. (1995). Effect of race on survival following in-hospital cardiopulmonary resuscitation. *Journal of Family Practice, 40,* 571–577.

Edelstein, L. (1967). *Ancient medicine.* Baltimore, MD: Johns Hopkins University Press.

Edgar, T. (1992). A compliance-based approach to the study of condom use. In T. Edgar, M. A. Fitzpatrick, & V. S. Freimuth (Eds.), *AIDS: A communication perspective* (pp. 47–67). Hillsdale, NJ: Lawrence Erlbaum.

Edgar, T., Freimuth, V., & Hammond, S. L. (2003). Lessons learned from the field on prevention and health campaigns. In T. L. Thompson, A. M. Dorsey, K. I. Miller, & R. Parrott (Eds.), *Handbook of health communication* (pp. 625–636). Mahwah, NJ: Lawrence Erlbaum.

Educational programs in U.S. medical schools, 2001–2002. (2002, September 4). *Journal of the American Medical Association, 288*(9), 1067–1072.

Edwards, H., & Noller, P. (1998). Factors influencing caregiver–care receiver communication and the impact on the well-being of older care receivers. *Health Communication, 10,* 317–342.

Eggly, S. (2002). Physician–patient co-construction of illness narratives in the medical interview. *Health Communication, 14*(3), 339–360.

Eisenberg, E. M., & Goodall, H., Jr. (2004). *Organizational communication: Balancing creativity and constraint.* New York: Bedford/St. Martin's.

Eisenberg, E. M., & Goodall, H. I., Jr. (1997). *Organizational communication: Balancing creativity and constraint* (2nd ed.), New York: St. Martin's Press.

Elliott, P. P. (1997, December). Violence in health care: What nurse managers need to know. *Nursing Management, 28,* 38–42.

Elliott, S. (2003, April 4). Changes requested in ads for youth. *New York Times,* p. 5C.

Ellis, B. H., & Miller, K. I. (1993). The role of assertiveness, personal control, and participation in the prediction of nurse burnout. *Journal of Applied Communication, 17,* 327–342.

Ely, J. W., Levinson, W., Elder, N. C., Mainous, A. G., III, & Vinson, D. C. (1995). Perceived causes of family physicians' errors. *Journal of Family Practice, 40,* 337–344.

Emanuel, E. J., & Dubler, N. N. (1995). Preserving the physician–patient relationship in the era of managed care. *Journal of the American Medical Association, 273,* 323–329.

Emanuel, E. J., & Emanuel, L. L. (1995). Four models of the physician–patient relationship. In J. D. Arras & B. Steinbock (Eds.), *Ethical issues in modern medicine* (4th ed., pp. 67–76). Mountain View, CA: Mayfield.

Emanuel, E. J., & Emanuel, L. L. (1998, May 16). The promise of a good death. *The Lancet, 351,* S21–S29.

Employment status and managed care involvement of physicians by gender, 2001. American Medical Association. Retrieved September 4, 2003, from www.ama-assn.org/ama/pub/article/171-1840.html

Eng, T. R., Maxfield, A., Patrick, K., Deering, M. J., Ratzan, S. C., & Gustafson, D. H. (1998). Access to health information and support. *Journal of the American Medical Association, 279,* 1371.

Engelberg, M., Flora, J. A., & Nass, C. I. (1997). AIDS knowledge: Effects of channel involvement and interpersonal communication. *Health Communication, 7,* 73–91.

English, V., Critchley-Romano, G., Sheather, J., & Sommerville, A. (2002). Medicine as entertainment. *Journal of Medical Ethics, 28*(5), 327–328.

Entertainomercials. (1996, November 4). *Forbes, 158,* 322–323.

Erdman, L. (1993). Laughter therapy for patients with cancer. *Journal of psychosocial oncology, 11,* 55–67.

Evans, R. L., & Connis, R. T. (1995). Comparison of brief group therapies for depressed cancer patients receiving radiation treatment. *Public Health Reports, 110,* 306–312.

Evelyn, J. (1998, April 16). In defense of diversity: Videoconference examines the anti affirmative action movement. *Black Issues in Higher Education, 15,* 18.

Everett, M. W., & Palmgreen, P. (1995). Influences of sensation seeking, message sensation value, and program context on effectiveness of anticocaine public service announcement. *Health Communication, 7,* 225–248.

Eversley, M. (2003, March 9). Norwood revives patients' bill: Few in Congress willing to sign on. *Atlanta Journal-Constitution,* p. 4A.

Expert group stresses that unsafe sex is primary mode of transmission of HIV in Africa. (2003, March 14). World Health Organization. Retrieved online July 19, 2003, from www.who.int/mediacentre/statements/2003/statement5/en

Fabre, J. (1997). Hip, hip, Hippocrates: Extracts from The Hippocratic Doctor. *British Medical Journal, 315,* 1669–1670.

Faden, R. R. (1987). Ethical issues in government sponsored public health campaigns. *Health Education Quarterly, 14,* 27–37.

Fagin, L., Carson, J., Lear, J., De Villiers, N., Bartlett, H., O'Malley, P., West, M., Mcelfatrick, S., & Brown, D. (1996). Stress, coping and burnout in mental health nurses: Findings from three research studies. *International Journal of Social Psychiatry, 42,* 102–111.

Falk, A., Hanson, B. S., Isacsson, S., & Ostergren, P. (1992). Job strain and mortality in elderly men: Social network support, and influence as buffers. *American Journal of Public Health, 82,* 1136–1139.

Fanning, M. M. (1997). A circular organization chart promotes a hospital-wide focus on teams. *Hospital & Health Services Administration, 42,* 243–264.

Farber, N. J., Novack, D. H., & O'Brien, M. K. (1997). Love, boundaries, and the patient–physician relationship. *Archives of Internal Medicine, 157,* 229–294.

Farley, M. J., & Stoner, M. H. (1989). The nurse executive and interdisciplinary team building. *Nursing Administration Quarterly, 13,* 24–30.

Farrelly, M., Healton, C. G., Davis, K. C., Messeri, P., & Haviland, M. L. (2002, June). Getting to the truth: Evaluating national tobacco countermarketing campaigns. *American Journal of Public Health, 92*(6), 901–907.

Fearn-Banks, K. (1996). *Crisis communication: A casebook approach.* Mahwah, NJ: Lawrence Erlbaum.

Feeling comfortable in a hospital. (1995, February). *Consumer Reports, 60,* 84–85.

Felty, D. W., & Jones, M. B. (1998). Human services at risk. *Social Services Review, 72,* 192–208.

Female teen market is hotter than ever. (1993, Winter). *Media Report to Women, 21,* 8.

Ferguson, J. A., Weinberger, M., Westmoreland, G. R., Mamlin, L. A., Segar, D. S., Greene, J. Y., Martin, D. K., & Tierney, W. M. (1998). Racial disparity in cardiac decision making: Results from patient focus groups. *Archives of Internal Medicine, 158,* 1450–1453.

Ferguson, T. (1997, November–December). Health care in cyberspace: Patients lead a revolution. *The Futurist, 31*(6), 29–34.

Festinger, L. (1957). *A theory of cognitive dissonance.* Stanford, CA: Stanford University Press.

Final report of RN survey. (2002, March). American Association of Critical-Care Nurses. Retrieved online August 8, 2003, from www.aacn.org

Financial impact of low health literacy could be as high as billions annually. (2003, May 7). American Medical Association. Retrieved online September 9, 2003, from www.ama-assn.org/ama/pub/article/4197-7398.html

Finney, J. W., Brophy, C. J., Friman, P. C., Golden, A. S., Richman, G. S., & Friman, A. F. (1990). Promoting parent–provider interaction during young children's health-supervision visits. *Journal of Applied Behavioral Analysis, 23,* 207–213.

Fischer, P. M., Schwartz, M. P., Richards, J. W., Jr., & Goldstein, A. O. (1991). Brand logo recognition by children aged 3 to 6 years: Mickey Mouse and Old Joe the Camel. *Journal of the American Medical Association, 266,* 3154–3158.

Fisher, J. A. (1994). *The plague makers.* New York: Simon & Schuster.

Fisher, J. D., Goff, B. A., Nadler, A., & Chinsky, J. M. (1988). Social psychological influences on help seeking and support from peers. In B. H. Gottlieb (Ed.), *Marshaling social support: Formats, processes, and effects* (pp. 267–304). Newbury Park, CA: Sage.

Fisher, S. (1984). Institutional authority and the structure of discourse. *Discourse Processes, 7,* 201–224.

Fishman, T. (1995). The 90-second intervention: A patient compliance mediated technique to improve and control hypertension. *Public Health Reports, 110,* 173–178.

Fitzpatrick, M. A., & Vangelisti, A. (2001). Communication, relationships, and health. In W. P. Robinson & H. Giles (Eds.), *The new handbook of language and social psychology* (pp. 505–530). Chichester, England: John Wiley & Sons.

Flay, B. R., & Burton, D. (1990). Effective mass communication strategies for health campaigns. In C. Atkin & L. Wallack (Eds.), *Mass communication and public health* (pp. 129–146). Newbury Park, CA: Sage.

Flores, G., Abreu, M., Olivar, M. A., & Kastner, B. (1998). Access barriers to health care for Latino children. *Archives of Pediatric & Adolescent Medicine, 152,* 1119.

Fontana, A., & McLaughlin, M. (1998). Coping and appraisal of daily stressors predict heart rate and blood pressure levels in young women. *Behavioral Medicine, 24,* 5–17.

Ford, L. A., Babrow, A. S., & Stohl, C. (1996). Social support messages and the management of uncertainty in the experience of breast cancer: An application of problematic integration theory. *Communication Monographs, 63,* 189–208.

Ford, L. A., & Yep, G. A. (2003). Working along the margins: Developing community-based strategies for communicating about health with marginalized groups. In T. L. Thompson, A. M. Dorsey, K. I. Miller, & R. Parrott (Eds.), *Handbook of health communication* (pp. 241–261). Mahwah, NJ: Lawrence Erlbaum.

Forte, D. A. (1995). Community-based breast cancer intervention program for older African women in beauty salons. *Public Health Reports, 110,* 179–183.

Forte, P. S. (1997, May–June). The high cost of conflict. *Nursing Economics, 15,* 119–123.

Foubister, V. (1997). Advisory panel encourages minority doctor involvement. *American Medical News, 40,* 24.

Frampton, S., Gilpin, L., & Charmel, P. (Eds.). (2003). *Putting patients first: Designing and practicing patient-centered care.* San Francisco: Jossey-Bass.

Frankel, R. M. (1984). From sentence to sequence: Understanding the medical encounter through microinteractional analysis. *Discourse Processes, 7,* 135–170.

Frankel, R. M., & Beckman, H. B. (1989). Conversation and compliance with treatment recommendations: An application of micro-interactional analysis in medicine. In L. Grossberg, B. J. O'Keefe, & E. Wartella (Eds.), *Rethinking communication: Vol. 2. Paradigm exemplars* (pp. 60–74). Newbury Park, CA: Sage.

Frasier, P. Y., Savard-Fenton, M., & Kotthopp, M. E. (1983). The education of primary care residents in team health care delivery. In T. L. Thompson & R. L. Byyny (Eds.), *Primary and team health care education* (pp. 126–133). New York: Praeger.

Freeborn, D. K., & Hooker, R. S. (1995). Satisfaction of physician assistants and other nonphysician providers in a managed care setting. *Public Health Reports, 110,* 714–720.

Frey, L. R., Botan, C. H., Friedman, P. G., & Kreps, G. L. (1991). *Investigating communication: An introduction to research methods.* Englewood Cliffs, NJ: Prentice Hall.

Fried, L. P., Francomano, C. A., MacDonald, S. M., Wagner, E. M., Stokes, E. J., Carbone, K. M., Bias, W. B., Newman, M. M., & Stobo, J. D. (1996). Career development for women in academic medicine: Multiple interventions in a department of medicine. *Journal of the American Medical Association, 276,* 898–906.

Friedman, H. S., & DiMatteo, M. R. (1979). Health care as an interpersonal process. *Journal of Social Issues, 35,* 1–11.

Frost, K., Frank, E., & Maibach, E. (1997). Relative risk in the news media: A quantification of misrepresentation. *American Journal of Public Health, 87,* 842–845.

Fruth, L., & Padderud, A. (1985). Portrayals of mental illness in daytime television. *Journalism Quarterly, 62,* 384–387, 449.

Fumento, M. (1998, January–February). Living off the fat of the land: The only people benefiting from diet books are the authors. *Washington Monthly, 30,* 40–42.

Gabbard-Alley, A. S. (1995). Health communication and gender: A review and critique. *Health Communication, 7,* 35–54.

Gabbard-Alley, A. S. (2000). Explaining illness: An examination of message strategies and gender. In B. B. Whaley (Ed.), *Explaining illness* (pp. 147–170). Mahwah, NJ: Lawrence Erlbaum.

Gadacz, T. R. (2003). A changing culture in interpersonal and communication skills. *The American Surgeon, 69*(6), 453–458.

Galinsky, M. J., Schopler, J. H., & Abell, M. D. (1997). Connecting group members through telephone and computer groups. *Health and Social Work, 22,* 181–189.

Gamble, V. N. (1997). Under the shadow of Tuskegee: African Americans and health care. *American Journal of Public Health, 87,* 1773–1778.

Gamlin, R. (1999). Sexuality: A challenge for nursing practice. *Nursing Times, 95*(7), 48–50.

Gardenswartz, L., & Rowe, A. (1998, July). Why diversity matters. *HR, 75,* S1–S3.

Garfinkel, H. (1967). *Studies in ethnomethodology.* Cambridge: Polity Press/Basil Blackwell.

Garrison, F. H. (1929). *An introduction to the history of medicine* (4th ed.). Philadelphia, PA: W. B. Saunders.

Gearon, C. J. (2002). Planetree (25 years older). *Hospitals & Health Networks, 76*(10), 40–43.

Geisler, E., Krabbendam, K., & Schuring, R. (2003). *Technology, health care, and management in the hospital of the future.* Westport, CT: Praeger.

Geist, P., & Dreyer, J. (1993). The demise of dialogue: A critique of medical encounter dialogue. *Western Journal of Communication, 57,* 233–246.

Geist, P., & Gates, L. (1996). The poetics and politics of recovering identities in health communication. *Communication Studies, 47,* 218–228.

Gerbner, G. (1990). Advancing on the path of righteousness (maybe). In N. Signorielli & M. Morgan (Eds.), *Cultivation analysis: New directions in media effects research.* Newbury Park, CA: Sage.

Gerbner, G. (1996, Fall). TV violence and what to do about it. *Nieman Reports, 50,* 10–12.

Gerbner, G., Gross, L., Morgan, M., & Signorielli, N. (1994). Growing up with television: The cultivation perspective. In J. Bryant & D. Zillmann (Eds.), *Media effects: Advances in theory and research* (pp. 17–41). Hillsdale, NJ: Lawrence Erlbaum.

Getting old is a pain. (2003, August). *National Geographic* (unnumbered Geographica supplement).

Gibson, B. (1997, Spring). An introduction to the controversy over tobacco. *Journal of Social Issues, 53,* 3–11.

Gidwani, P. P., Sobol, A., DeJong, W., Perrin, J. M., & Gortmaker, S. L. (2002, September). Television viewing and initiation of smoking among youth. *Pediatrics, 110*(3), 505–508.

Giles, H., Ballard, D., & McCann, R. M. (2002). Perceptions of intergenerational communication across cultures: An Italian case. *Perceptual and Motor Skills, 95,* 583–591.

Gillespie, S. R. (2001). The politics of breathing: Asthmatic Medicaid patients under managed care. *Journal of Applied Communication Research, 29*(2), 97–116.

Gillioti, C. M. (2003). Medical disclosure and decision-making: Excavating the complexities of physician–patient information exchange. In T. L. Thompson,

A. M. Dorsey, K. I. Miller, & R. Parrott (Eds.), *Handbook of health communication* (pp. 163–181). Mahwah, NJ: Lawrence Erlbaum.

Giuffrida, A., & Torgerson, D. J. (1997). Should we pay the patient? Review of financial incentives to enhance patient compliance. *British Medical Journal, 315,* 703–707.

Glantz, S. A. (1996). Editorial: Preventing tobacco use—the youth access trap. *American Journal of Public Health, 86,* 156–158.

Glass, R. M. (1996). The patient–physician relationship: JAMA focuses on the center of medicine. *Journal of the American Medical Association, 275,* 147–148.

Global Internet population grows an average of four percent year-over-year. (2003, February 20). *PR Newswire.* Retrieved online July 19, 2003, from LexisNexis.

Goffman, E. (1963). *Stigma: Notes on the management of spoiled identity.* Englewood Cliffs, NJ: Prentice Hall.

Goffman, E. (1967). *Interaction ritual.* New York: Pantheon Books.

Goffman, E. (1974). *Frame analysis: An essay on the organization of experience.* New York: Harper Colophon.

Goldhaber, G. M. (1993). *Organizational communication* (6th ed.). Dubuque, IA: Wm. C. Brown.

Goldman, L. K., & Glantz, S. A. (1998). Evaluation of antismoking advertising campaigns. *Journal of the American Medical Association, 279,* 772–778.

Goldsmith, D. J. (1994). The role of facework in supportive communication. In B. R. Burleson, T. L. Albrecht, & I. G. Sarason (Eds.), *Communication of social support: Messages, interactions, relationships, and community* (pp. 29–49). Thousand Oaks, CA: Sage.

Goode, E. E. (1993, February 15). The cultures of illness. *U.S. News & World Report, 114,* 74–76.

Goodkin, K., Fletcher, M. A., & Cohen, N. (1995). Clinical aspects of psychoneuroimmunology. *The Lancet, 345,* 183–185.

Goodman, L. E., & Goodman, M. J. (1986, April). Prevention—how misuse of a concept undercuts its worth. *Hastings Center Report, 16,* 26–38.

Gorawara-Bhat, R., Gallagher, T. H., & Levinson, W. (2003). Patient–provider discussions about conflicts of interest in managed care: Physicians' perceptions. *American Journal of Managed Care, 9*(8), 564–571.

Gordon, E. J., Leon, J. B., & Sehgal, A. R. (2003). Why are hemodialysis treatments shortened and skipped? Development of a taxonomy and relationship to patient subgroups. *Nephrology Nursing Journal, 30*(2), 209–217.

Gostin, L. O. (1995). Informed consent, cultural sensitivity, and respect for persons. *Journal of the American Medical Association, 274,* 844–845.

Gostin, L. O., Arno, P. S., & Brandt, A. M. (1997). FDA regulation of tobacco advertising and youth smoking: Historical, social, and constitutional perspectives. *Journal of the American Medical Association, 277,* 410–419.

Gotcher, J. M. (1995). Well-adjusted and maladjusted cancer patients: An examination of communication variables. *Health Communication, 7,* 21–33.

Govindarajan, A., & Schull, M. (2003). Effect of socioeconomic status on out-of-hospital transport delays of patients with chest pain. *Annals of Emergency Medicine, 41*(4), 481–490.

Grant, C. J., III, Cissna, K. N., & Rosenfeld, L. B. (2000). Patients' perceptions of physicians' communication and outcomes of the accrual to trial process. *Health Communication, 12*(1), 23–39.

Green, F. (2003, June 20). Booze ads target Black teens, report finds. *San-Diego Union-Tribune,* p. C1.

Green, J. (1996, September 15). Flirting with suicide. *New York Times Magazine,* p. 39.

Green, J. O., & Burleson, B. R. (Eds.). (2003). *Handbook of communication and social interaction skills.* Mahwah, NJ: Lawrence Erlbaum.

Green, K. C. (1988, January). Who wants to be a nurse? *American Demographics, 10,* 46–49.

Green, R. (1994, Summer). Healthcare public relations shift gears. *Public Relations Quarterly, 39,* 33–36.

Greenbaum, T. L. (1991, September). Outside moderators maximize focus group results. *Public Relations Journal, 47,* 31–33.

Greenberg, B. S., Brown, J. D., & Buerkel-Rothfuss, N. L. (1993). *Media, sex, and the adolescent.* Cesskill, NY: Hampton Press.

Greenberg, B. S., & Busselle, R. (1996, June–July). What's old, what's new: Sexuality on the soaps. *SIECUS Report, 24,* 14–16.

Greenberg, B. S., & Woods, M. G. (1999). The soaps: Their sex, gratifications, and outcomes. *Journal of Sex Research, 36*(3), 250.

Greene, J. (1997, May 5). What a little arm-twisting can do: The role of the patient advocate. *Hospitals & Health Networks, 71,* 39–40.

Greene, K., Rubin, D. L., Hale, J. L., & Walters, L. H. (1996). The utility of understanding adolescent egocentrism in designing health promotion messages. *Health Communication, 8,* 131–152.

Greene, M. G., Adelman, R. D., & Majerovitz, S. D. (1996). Physician and older patient support in the medical encounter. *Health Communication, 8,* 263–279.

Greenfield, S., Kaplan, S., & Ware, J. E. (1985). Expanding patient involvement in care. *Annals of Internal Medicine, 102,* 520–528.

Grensing-Pophal, L. (1997, Spring). Dealing with diversity in the workplace: Learn how to keep differences from being divisive. *Nursing, 27,* 78.

Griffin, R. J., & Dunwoody, S. (2000). The relation of communication to risk judgment and preventive behavior related to lead in tap water. *Health Communication, 12*(1), 81–107.

Grissett, N. I., & Norvell, N. K. (1992). Perceived social support, social skills, and quality of relationships in bulimic women. *Journal of Consulting and Clinical Psychology, 60,* 293–299.

Groesz, L. M., Levine, M. P., & Murnen, S. K. (2002, January). The effect of experimental presentation of thin media images on body satisfaction: A meta-analytic review. *International Journal of Eating Disorders, 31,* 1–16.

Grube, J. W., & Wallack, L. (1994). Television beer advertising and drinking knowledge, beliefs, and intentions among school children. *American Journal of Public Health, 84,* 254–259.

Guidelines for preventing workplace violence for health care and social service workers. (1997, March–May). *Prairie Rose, 66,* 11a–18a.

Gunter, B. (1994). The question of media violence. In J. Bryant & D. Zillmann (Eds.), *Media effects: Advances in theory and research* (pp. 163–211). Hillsdale, NJ: Lawrence Erlbaum.

Guttman, N. (1997). Ethical dilemmas in health campaigns. *Health Communication, 9,* 155–190.

Guttman, N., & Ressler, W. H. (2001, April–June). On being responsible: Ethical issues in appeals to personal responsibility in health campaigns. *Journal of Health Communication, 6*(2), 117–136.

Haas, S. (2002). Social support as relationship maintenance in gay male couples coping with HIV or AIDS. *Journal of Social and Personal Relationships, 18*(1), 87–111.

Hale, J. L., & Dillard, J. P. (1995). Fear appeals in health promotion campaigns: Too much, too little, or just right? In E. Maibach & R. L. Parrott (Eds.), *Designing health messages* (pp. 65–80). Thousand Oaks, CA: Sage.

Hall, M. A., & Berenson, R. A. (1998, March 1). Ethical practice in managed care: A dose of realism. *Annals of Internal Medicine, 128,* 395–402.

Hamilton, C., & Parker, C. (1997). *Communicating for results: A guide for business & the professions* (5th ed.). Belmont, CA: Wadsworth.

Hanh, B. A. (1995). Children's health: Racial and ethnic differences in the use of prescription medications. *Pediatrics, 95,* 727–732.

Hanlon, J. M. (1996, April). Teaching effective communication skills. *Nursing Management, 27,* 48B–50B.

Harding, J. (1994). The role of organizational ethics committees. *Physician Executive, 20,* 19–24.

Haring, T. G., & Breen, C. G. (1992). A peer-mediated social network intervention to enhance the social integration of persons with moderate and severe disabilities. *Journal of Applied Behavior, 25,* 319–333.

Harper, D. C., & Wadsworth, J. S. (1992). Improving health care communication for persons with mental retardation. *Public Health Reports, 107,* 297–302.

Harper, J. (1997, September 15). Information overload may be making some Americans sick. *Insight on the News, 13,* 40–41.

Harris interactive study on prescription drug prices, hospital costs and doctors' fees. (2003, June 13). *PR Newswire.* Retrieved online July 9, 2003, from LexisNexis.

Harrison, R., Clayton, W., & Wallace, P. (1996). Can telemedicine be used to improve communication between primary and secondary care? *British Medical Journal, 313,* 1377–1380.

Hart, C., & Chesson, R. (1998). Children as consumers. *British Medical Journal, 316,* 1600–1603.

Hartman, N. S., Gellert, G. A., Higgins, K. V., Maxwell, R. M., & Lowery, R. (1994). Training health professionals to use the media. *Journal of the American Medical Association, 272,* 1002–1003.

Harwood, J., & Sparks, L. (2003). Social identity and health: An intergroup communication approach to cancer. *Health Communication, 15*(2), 145–159.

Haug, M. R. (1996). The effects of physician/elder patient characteristics on health communication. *Health communication, 8,* 249–262.

Hawkins, R. P., Pingree, S., Gustafson, D. H., Boberg, E. W., Bricker, E., McTavish, F., Wise, M., & Owens, B. (1997). Aiding those facing health crises: The experience of the CHESS project. In R. L. Street, Jr., W. R. Gold, & T. Manning (Eds.), *Health promotion and interactive technology: Theoretical applications and future directions* (pp. 79–102). Mahwah, NJ: Lawrence Erlbaum.

Hawthorne, P. (2003, April 20). Dying to get AIDS drugs to all. *Time Europe.* Retrieved online July 27, 2003, from www.time.com/time/europe/hero/zackieachmat.html

Health and income equity. (nd). University of Washington and Health Alliance International. Retrieved online from July 19, 2003, from http://depts.washington.edu/eqhlth

Health economics: Soaring healthcare premiums seen as threat to managed care. (2003, July 14.) *Health & Medicine Week,* p. 56.

Health literacy overview. (2003). American Medical Association. Retrieved online July 30, 2003, from www.ama-assn.org/ama/pub/printcat/8577.html

Health Privacy Project. (2003). Myths and facts about the HIPAA privacy rule. U.S. Department of Health and Human Services. Retrieved online August 31, 2003, from www.healthprivacy.org

Health promotion glossary. (1998). World Health Organization. Retrieved online July 30, 2003, from www.who.int/hpr/ncp/support.documents.shtml

Health ranks fifth on local TV news. (1998). *Public Health Reports, 113,* 296–297.

Hearing and older people. (1998). National Institute on Aging (Online). Available: www.aoa.dhhs.gov/aoa/pages/agepages/hearing.html

Helman, C. G. (1985). Communication in primary care: The role of patient and practitioner explanatory models. *Social Science and Medicine, 20,* 923–931.

Henriksen, L., & Jackson, C. (1998). Anti-smoking socialization: Relationship to parent and child smoking status. *Health Communication, 10,* 87–102.

Herbert, J. (1997). Stress, the brain, and mental illness. *British Medical Journal, 315,* 530–536.

Herselman, S. (1996). Some problems in health communication in a multicultural clinical setting: A South African experience. *Health Communication, 8,* 153–170.

HHS [Health and Human Services] awards nearly $3.5 million to promote diversity in the nursing workforce. (2003, June 2). *U.S. Newswire.* Retrieved August 8, 2003, from LexisNexis.

HHS [Health and Human Services] study finds strong link between patient outcomes and nurse staffing in hospitals. (2001, April 20). U.S. Department of Health and Human Services. Retrieved online September 4, 2003, from newsroom.hrsa.goy

Hines, S. C. (2001). Coping with uncertainties in advance care planning. *Journal of Communication, 51*(3), 498–513.

Ho, D. (2002, January 18). Eli Lilly settles charges of violating the privacy of Prozac patients. Associated Press, Business News. Retrieved online August 31, 2003, from LexisNexis.

Ho, D. (2003, April 28). College students with eating disorders. *Tufts Daily.* Retrieved online July 19, 2003, from LexisNexis.

Hodgman, A. (1998, May 25). Burb's eye-view. *Brandweek, 39,* 38.

Hoffman-Goetz, L., Gerlach, K. K., Marino, C., & Mills, S. L. (1997). Cancer coverage and tobacco advertising in African-American's popular magazines. *Journal of Community Health, 22,* 261–270.

Hofmann, J. C., Wenger, N. S., David, R. B., Teno, J., Connors, A. F., Desbiens, N., Lynn, J., & Phillips, R. S. (1997). Patient preferences for communication with physicians about end-of-life decisions. *Annals of Internal Medicine, 127,* 1–12.

Holden, J. (1998, October). The ring of truth. *American Demographics, 20,* 14.

Holland, J. C., & Zittoun, R. (1990). Psychosocial issues in oncology: A historical perspective. In J. C. Holland & R. Zittoun (Eds.), *Psychosocial aspects of oncology* (pp. 1–10). New York: Springer-Verlag.

Holleman, W. L., Holleman, M. C., & Moy, J. G. (1997, February 1). Are ethics and managed care strange bedfellows or a marriage made in heaven? *The Lancet, 349,* 350–351.

Holmes, O. W. (1891). *Medical essays: 1842–1882.* Boston, MA: Houghton Mifflin.

Holtgrave, D. R., Tinsley, B. J., & Kay, L. S. (1995). Encouraging risk reduction: A decision-making approach to message design. In E. Maibach & R. L. Parrott (Eds.), *Designing health messages: Approaches from communication theory and public health practice* (pp. 24–40). Thousand Oaks, CA: Sage.

Hornberger, J., Itakura, H., & Wilson, S. R. (1997). Bridging language and cultural barriers between physicians and patients. *Public Health Reports, 112,* 410–418.

Hornik, R. C. (Ed.). (2002). *Public health communication: Evidence for behavior change.* Mahwah, NJ: Lawrence Erlbaum.

How is your doctor treating you? (1995, February). *Consumer Reports, 60,* 81–89.

Huesmann, L. R., Lagerspetz, K., & Eron, L. D. (1984). Intervening variables in the TV violence-aggression relation: Evidence from two countries. *Developmental Psychology, 20,* 746–775.

Huesmann, L. R., Moise-Titus, J., Podolski, C., & Eron, L. D. (2003). Longitudinal relations between children's exposure to TV violence and their aggressive and violent behavior in young adulthood: 1977–1992. *Developmental Psychology, 39*(2), 201–221.

Hufford, D. J. (1997). Gender, culture and experience: A painful case. *Southern Folklore, 54,* 114–123.

Huhmann, B. A., & Brotherton, T. P. (1997, Summer). A content analysis of guilt appeals in popular magazine advertisements. *Journal of Advertising, 26,* 35–45.

Hullett, C. R., McMillan, J. J., & Rogan, R. G. (2000). Caregivers' predispositions and perceived organizational expectations for the provision of social support to nursing home residents. *Health Communication, 12*(3), 277–299.

Hummert, M. L., Gartska, T. A., & Shaner, J. L. (1997). Stereotyping of older adults: the role of target facial cues and perceiver characteristics. *Psychology and Aging, 12,* 107–114.

Hummert, M. L., Gartska, T. A., Shaner, J. L., & Strahm, S. (1995). Judgments about stereotypes of the elderly: Attitudes, age associations, and typicality ratings of young, middle-aged, and elderly adults. *Research on Aging, 17,* 168–189.

Hummert, M. L., & Nussbaum, J. F. (Eds.). (2001). *Aging, communication, and health.* Mahwah, NJ: Lawrence Erlbaum.

Hummert, M. L., Nussbaum, J. F., & Wiemann, J. M. (1992). Communication and the elderly: Cognition, language, and relationships. *Communication Research, 19,* 413–422.

Hummert, M. L., & Shaner, J. L. (1994). Patronizing speech to the elderly as a function of stereotyping. *Communication Studies, Summer, 45,* 145–158.

Hyde, M. J. (1993). Medicine, rhetoric, and euthanasia: A case study in the workings of a postmodern discourse. *Quarterly Journal of Speech, 79,* 201–224.

Hymes, D. H. (1962). The ethnography of speaking. In T. Gladwin & W. C. Sturtevant (Eds.), *Anthropology and human behavior* (pp. 13–53). Washington, DC: Anthropological Society of Washington.

Interview: Zachie Achmat. (2003, July 25). *Currier International.* Retrieved online July 25, 2003, from www.courierinternational.com/interview/avec/Achmat.htm

Intrieri, R. C., Kelly, J. A., Brown, M. M., & Castilla, C. (1993). Improving medical students' attitudes toward and skills with the elderly. *The Gerontologist, 33,* 373–378.

Irvine, D. H. (1991, March). The advertising of doctors' services. *Journal of Medical Ethics, 17,* 35–40.

Irvine, D. M., & Evans, M. G. (1995). Job satisfaction and turnover among nurses: Integrating research findings across studies. *Nursing Research, 44,* 246–253.

Ivinski, P. A. (1997, September–October). Test case: Sex and humor in pharmaceutical advertising. *Print, 51,* 44–46.

Jacobson, P. D., Wasserman, J., & Anderson, J. R. (1997, Spring). Historical overview of tobacco legislation. *Journal of Social Issues, 53,* 75–95.

Jadad, A. R., & Rizo, C. A. (2003). I am a good patient believe it or not. *British Medical Journal, 326*(7402), 1293–1294.

Jahn, M. (1997). Model programs for defusing physician stress. *Medical Economics, 74,* 127–132.

Janis, I. (1972). *Victims of groupthink* (2nd ed.). Boston: Houghton Mifflin.

Jantarakolica, K., Komolsevin, R., & Speece, M. (2002). Children's perception of TV reality in Bangkok, Thailand. *Asian Journal of Communication, 12*(1), 77–99.

Jarrett, N., & Payne, S. (1995). A selective review of the literature on nurse–patient communication: Has the patient's contribution been neglected? *Journal of Advanced Nursing, 22,* 72–78.

Jecker, N. S., Carrese, J. A., & Pearlman, R. A. (1995). Caring for patients in cross-cultural settings. *Hastings Center Report, 25,* 6–15.

Jeffery, R. W., & French, S. A. (1998). Epidemic obesity in the United States: Are fast foods and television viewing contributing? *American Journal of Public Health, 88,* 277–280.

Jenkins, C. L. (1997, Summer). Women, work, and caregiving: How do these roles affect women's well-being? *Journal of Women & Aging, 9,* 27–45.

Jennings, M. C., & O'Leary, S. J. (1995). The role of managed care in integrated delivery networks. In S. B. Goldsmith (Ed.), *Managed care* (pp. 11–20). Gaithersburg, MD: Aspen.

Jobes, M., & Steinbinder, A. (1996). Transitions in nursing leadership roles. *Nursing Administration Quarterly, 20,* 80–84.

Johnson, B. (1994, April). Prove public relations affects the bottom line. *Public Relations Journal, 50,* 40–41.

Johnson, J. A., & Bootman, J. L. (1995). Drug-related morbidity and mortality: A cost-of-illness model. *Archives of Internal Medicine, 155,* 1949–1956.

Jones, D., Gill, P., Harrison, R., Meakin, R., & Wallace, P. (2003). An exploratory study of language interpretation services provided by videoconferencing. *Journal of Telemedicine and Telecare, 9*(1), 51–56.

Jordan, S. R. (2001). *The immune spirit: A story of love, loss, and healing.* Deerfield Beach, FL: Health Communications Inc.

Joseph, J. (1998, February 19). The ethics of an AIDS study. ABCNEWS.COM (Online). Available: www.abcnews.aol.com/sections/living/Daily News/aidspregnant_0218.html

Joyce, M. L. (1994). The graying of America: Implications and opportunities for health marketers. *American Behavioral Scientist, 38,* 341–351.

Kadushin, G., & Egan, M. (1997, August). Educating students for a changing health care environment: An examination of health care practice course content. *Health and Social Work, 22,* 211–222.

Kagawa, S. M., & Kassim-Lakha, S. (2003). A strategy to reduce cross-cultural miscommunication and increase the likelihood of improving health outcomes. *Journal of the Association of American Medical Colleges, 78*(6), 577–587.

Kai, J. (1996). Parents' difficulties and information needs in coping with acute illness in preschool children: A qualitative study. *British Medical Journal, 313,* 987–990.

Kakai, H. (2002). A double standard in bioethical reasoning for disclosure of advanced cancer diagnosis in Japan. *Health Communication, 14*(3), 361–376.

Kalichman, S. C., Benotsch, E. G., Weinhardt, L., Austin, J., Luke, W., & Chauncey, C. (2003). Health-related Internet use, coping, social support, and health indicators in people living with HIV/AIDS. *Health Psychology, 22*(1), 111–116.

Kamwendo, G., & Kamowa, O. (1999). HIV/AIDS and a return to traditional cultural practices in Malawi. In K. R. Hope Sr. (Ed.), *AIDS and development in Africa: A social science perspective* (pp. 165–184). New York: Haworth.

Kane, C. (2003, February 20). Advertising: BBDO Worldwide enters the lucrative category of marketing prescription drugs to consumers. *New York Times,* Section C, Page 4, Column 1.

Kaplan, M. (2003). Reporting on the business of health care. *Nieman Reports, 57*(1), 24–25.

Kaplan, R. M. (1997). Health outcomes and communication research. *Health Communication, 9,* 75–82.

Katcher, B. (1997). Getting answers from a focus group: Focus groups must be well conceived and conducted if they are to yield useful data. *Folio: The Magazine for Magazine Management, 25,* 222.

Kate, N. T. (1997, September). And taking care. *American Demographics, 19,* 42.

Katz, J. (1984). *The silent world of doctor and patient.* New York: The Free Press.

Katz, J. (1995). Informed consent: Ethical and legal issues. In J. D. Arras & B. Steinbock (Eds.), *Ethical issues in modern medicine* (4th ed., pp. 87–97). Mountain View, CA: Mayfield.

Katz, R. (1997, October 13). Health TV launch on cable is test tube for consumers. *Media Week, 7,* 8.

Kearney, M. (1978). Spiritualist healing in Mexico. In P. Morley & R. Wallis (Eds.), *Culture and curing* (pp. 19–39). Pittsburgh, PA: University of Pittsburgh Press.

Kelder, S. H., Perry, C. L., & Klepp, K. (1993). Community-wide youth exercise promotion: Long-term outcomes of the Minnesota Heart Health Program and the Class of 1989 study. *Journal of School Health, 63,* 218–223.

Keller, S. N., Labelle, H., Karimi, N., & Gupta, S. (2002). STD/HIV prevention for teenagers: A look at the Internet universe. *Journal of Health Communication, 7*(4), 341–353.

Kelly, F. (1996, April). Taking time to talk. *Nursing Times, 92,* 28.

Kelly, K. J., & Edwards, R. W. (1998, Spring). Image advertisements for alcohol products: Is their appeal associated with adolescents' intention to consume alcohol? *Adolescence, 33,* 47–59.

Kelly, K. S., Soderlund, K., Albert, C., & McGarrahan, A. G. (1999). Social support and Chronic Fatigue Syndrome. *Health Communication, 11*(1), 21–34.

Kenny, R. W. (2001). Toward a better death: Applying Burkean principles of symbolic action to interpret family adaptation to Karen Ann Quinlan's coma. *Health Communication, 13*(4), 363–385.

Kenny, R. W. (2002). The death of loving: Maternal identity as moral constraint in a narrative testimonial advocating physician assisted suicide. *Health Communication, 14*(2), 243–270.

Kirkham, S. R. (1998). Nurses' descriptions of caring for culturally diverse clients. *Clinical Nursing Research, 7,* 125–146.

Kjellstrand, C. M. (1998). Age, sex, and race inequality in renal transplantation. *Archives of Internal Medicine, 148,* 1305–1309.

Klass, P. (1987). *A not entirely benign procedure: Four years as a medical student.* New York: Putnam.

Kleinman, A., Eisenberg, L., & Good, B. (1978). Culture, illness, and care: Clinical lessons from anthropological and cross-cultural research. *Annals of Internal Medicine, 88,* 251–258.

Kleinmann, L. (1989, February). Code blue. *Health, 21,* 68–73.

Kline, K. N., & Mattson, M. (2000). Breast self-examination pamphlets: A content analysis grounded in fear appeal research. *Health Communication, 12*(1), 1–21.

Knaus, C. S., Pinkleton, B. E., & Austin, E. W. (2000). The ability of the AIDS quilt to motivate information seeking, personal discussion, and preventive behavior as a health communication intervention. *Health Communication, 12*(3), 301–316.

Knight, J. A. (1981). *Doctor-to-be: Coping with the trials and triumphs of medical school.* New York: Appleton-Century-Crofts.

Kohler, C. L., Grimley, D., & Reynolds, K. (1999). Theoretical approaches guiding the development and implementation of health promotion programs. In J. M. Raczynski & R. J. DiClemente (Eds.), *Handbook of health promotion and disease prevention* (pp. 23–49). New York: Kluwer Academic/Plenum.

Komaroff, A. L., & Fagioli, J. (1996). Medical assessment of fatigue and chronic fatigue syndrome. In M. A. Demitrack & S. E. Abbey (Eds.), *Chronic fatigue syndrome: An integrative approach to evaluation and treatment* (pp. 154–181). New York: Guilford.

Koplan, J. P. (2002). The small world of global health. *The Mount Sinai Journal of Medicine, 69*(5), 291–298.

Korsch, D. M., & Negrete, V. F. (1972). Doctor–patient communication. *Scientific American, 227,* 66–74.

Korsch, D. M., & Negrete, V. F. (1981). Doctor–patient communication. In G. Henderson (Ed.), *Physician–patient communication* (pp. 29–40). Springfield, IL: Charles C. Thomas.

Kotler, P., & Clarke, R. N. (1987). *Marketing for health care organizations.* Englewood Cliffs, NJ: Prentice Hall.

Kotz, K., & Story, M. (1994). Food advertisements during children's Saturday morning television programming: Are they consistent with dietary recommendations? *Journal of the American Dietetic Association, 94,* 1296–1300.

Kowalski, K. M. (1997, October). On guard against health rip-off. *Current Health, 24,* 6–11.

Krakauer, E. L., & Truog, R. D. (1997, May–June). Mistrust, racism, and end-of-life treatment. *Hasting Center Report, 27,* 23–25.

Kramer, H., & Kramer, K. (1993, March–April). *Psychology Today, 26,* 26–27.

Kreps, G. L. (1990). Applied health communication research. In D. O'Hair & G. L. Kreps (Eds.), *Applied communication theory and research* (pp. 313–330). Hillsdale, NJ: Lawrence Erlbaum.

Kreps, G. L. (2003). The impact of communication on cancer risk, incidence, morbidity, mortality, and quality of life. *Health Communication, 15*(2), 161–169.

Kreps, G. L., & Thornton, B. C. (1992). *Health communication: Theory & practice* (2nd ed.). Prospect Heights, IL: Waveland Press.

Kreuter, M., Farrell, D., Olevitch, L., & Brennan, L. (1999). *Tailoring health messages: Customizing communication with computer technology.* Mahwah, NJ: Lawrence Erlbaum.

Krishna, S., Francisco, B. D., Balas, E. A., Konig, P., Graff, G. R., & Madsen, R. W. (2003). Internet-enabled interactive multimedia asthma education program: A randomized trial. *Pediatrics, 111*(3), 503–510.

Krishnan, S. P. (1996). Health education at family planning clinics: Strategies for improving information about contraception and sexually transmitted diseases for low-income women. *Health Communication, 8,* 353–366.

Kroll, T., Beatty, P. W., & Bingham, S. (2003). Primary care satisfaction among adults with physical disabilities. The role of patient–provider communication. *Managed Care Quarterly, 11*(1), 11–19.

Kroll, J., Rothert, M., Davidson, W. S., III, Schmitt, N., Holmes-Rovner, M., Padonu, G., & Reischl, T. M. (2000). Predictors of participation in health care at menopause. *Health Communication, 12*(4), 339–360.

Kronenberg, F., Mallory, B., & Downey, J. A. (1994). Rehabilitation medicine and alternative therapies: New worlds, old practices. *Archive of Physical Medicine and Rehabilitation, 75,* 928–929.

Krug, P. (1998). Where does physician-assisted suicide stand today? *Association of Operating Room Nurses Journal, 68,* 869.

Kubler-Ross, E. (1969). *On death and dying.* New York: Macmillan.

Kundrat, A. L., & Nussbaum, J. F. (2003). The impact of invisible illness on identity and contextual age. *Health Communication, 15*(3), 331–347.

Kulich, K. R., Berggren, U., & Hallberg, I, R.-M. (2003). A qualitative analysis of patient-centered dentistry in consultations with dental phobic patients. *Journal of Health Communication, 8*(2), 171–187.

Laframboise, D. (1998). When home is the hospital. *Chatelaine, 71,* 26–31.

Laine, C., & Davidoff, F. (1996). Patient-centered medicine: A professional evolution. *Journal of the American Medical Association, 275,* 152–155.

Laitinen, P. (1994). Elderly patients' and their informal caregivers' perceptions of care given: The study-control ward design. *Journal of Advanced Nursing, 20,* 71–76.

Lamberg, L. (1996). Knitting up the raveled sleeve of care: Role of sleep and effects of its lack examined. *Journal of the American Medical Association, 276,* 1205–1207.

Lambert, B. L., Street, R. L., Cegala, D. J., Smith, D. H., Kurtz, S., & Schofield, T. (1997). Provider–patient communication, patient-centered care, and the mangle of practice. *Health Communication, 9,* 27–43.

Landsdale, D. (2002). Touching lives: Opening doors for elders in retirement communities through e-mail and the Internet. In R. W. Morrell (Ed.), *Older adults, health information, and the World Wide Web* (pp. 133–151). Mahwah, NJ: Lawrence Erlbaum.

La Puma, J. (1998). *Managed care ethics: Essays on the impact of managed care on traditional medical ethics.* New York: Hatherleigh Press.

Larkey, L. K. (1996). Toward a theory of communicative interactions in culturally diverse workgroups. *Academy of Management Review, 21,* 463–491.

Larson, R. (1998, August 3). Wealth, education help Americans live longer. *Insight on the News, 14,* 40.

Larson, S. G. (1991). Television's mixed messages: Sexual content on "All My Children." *Communication Quarterly, 39,* 156–163.

Law, D. (1994, January 15). Making diversity work. *Restaurants & Institutions, 104,* 84–86.

Lazarsfeld, P., Berelson, B., & Gaudet, H. (1948). *The people's choice.* New York: Columbia University Press.

Leape, L. L., Hilborne, L. J., Bell, R., Kamberg, C., & Brook, R. H. (1999). Underuse of cardiac procedures: Do women, ethnic minorities, and the uninsured fail to receive needed revascularization? *Annals of Internal Medicine, 130,* 183.

Leask, J., & Chapman, S. (2002, February). "The cold hard facts:" Immunization and vaccine preventable diseases in Australia's newsprint media. *Social Science & Medicine, 53*(3), 445–457.

Lee, F. (1993). Being polite and keeping MUM: How bad news is communicated in organizational hierarchies. *Journal of Applied Social Psychology, 23,* 1124–1149.

Leebov, W., & Scott, G. (2002). *The indispensable health care manager: Success strategies for a changing environment.* San Francisco: Jossey-Bass.

Lefebvre, R. C., Doner, L., Johnston, D., Loughrey, K., Balch, G. I., & Sutton, S. M. (1995). Use of database marketing and consumer-based health communication in message design: An example for the Office of Cancer Communications' "5 a Day for Better Health" program. In E. Maibach & R. L. Parrott (Eds.), *Designing health messages: Approaches from communication theory and public health practice* (pp. 217–246). Thousand Oaks, CA: Sage.

Lefebvre, R. C., & Flora, J. A. (1988). Social marketing and public health intervention. *Health Education Quarterly, 15,* 299–315.

Legacy today urged Philip Morris to pull it's "Think. Don't Smoke" ads based on research showing the ads make kids more likely to smoke. (2002, June 29). American Legacy Foundation. Retrieved July 4, 2003, from http://pressroom.americanlegacy.org

Lehman, D. R., Ellard, J. H., & Wortman, C. B. (1986). Social support for the bereaved: Recipient's and provider's perspectives on what is helpful. *Journal of Consulting and Clinical Psychology, 54,* 438–446.

Lepper, H. S., Martin, L. R., & DiMatteo, M. R. (1995). A model of nonverbal exchange in physician–patient expectations for patient involvement. *Journal of Nonverbal Behavior, 19,* 207–222.

Leserman, J. (1981). *Men and women in medical school: How they change and how they compare.* New York: Praeger.

Let us put you in the movies. (1996, September 16). *Brandweek, 37,* S3–S9.

Levin, A. (1998). Evidence-based medicine gaining supporters. *Annals of Internal Medicine, 128,* 334–336.

Levinsky, N. (1995). The doctor's master. In J. D. Arras & B. Steinbock (Eds.), *Ethical issues in modern medicine* (4th ed., pp. 116–119). Mountain View, CA: Mayfield.

Levinson, W., Roter, D. L., Mullooly, J. P., Dull, V. T., & Frankel, R. M. (1997). Physician–patient communication: The relationship with malpractice claims among primary care physicians and surgeons. *Journal of the American Medical Association, 277,* 553–559.

Levy, D. R. (1985). White doctors and Black patients: Influence of race on the doctor–patient relationship. *Pediatrics, 75,* 639–643.

Lewis, M., & Haviland-Jones, J. M. (Eds.). (2000). *Handbook of emotions.* New York: Guilford Press.

Liao, S. S., Schensul, J., & Wolffers, I. (2003). Sex-related health risks and complications for interventions with hospitality women in Hainan, China. *AIDS Education and Prevention, 15*(2), 109–121.

Lieberman, D. A. (1997). Interactive video games for health promotion: Effects on knowledge, self-efficacy, social support, and health. In R. L. Street, Jr., W. R. Gold, & T. Manning (Eds.), *Health promotion and interactive technology: Theoretical applications and future directions* (pp. 103–120). Mahwah, NJ: Lawrence Erlbaum.

Lief, H. I., & Fox, R. C. (1963). Training for "detached concern" in medical students. In H. I. Lief, V. F. Lief, & N. R. Lief (Eds.), *The psychological basis of medical practice.* New York: Harper & Row.

Likert, R. (1961). *New patterns of management.* New York: McGraw-Hill.

Lindberg, D. A. B. (2002). Older Americans, health information, and the Internet. In R. W. Morrell (Ed.), *Older adults, health information, and the World Wide Web* (pp. 13–19). Mahwah, NJ: Lawrence Erlbaum.

Lingard, L., Garwood, K., Schryer, C., & Spafford, M. (2003). "Talking the talk:" School and workplace genre tension in clerkship care presentations. *Medical Education, 37*(7), 612–620.

Lippy, C. H., & Williams, P. W. (1988). *Encyclopedia of the American religious experience.* New York: Charles Scribner's Sons.

Living with cancer. (1997, September). *Harvard Health Letter, 22,* 4–5.

Livingstone, S., & Bovill, M. (Eds.). (2001). *Children and their changing media environment: A European comparative study.* Mahwah, NJ: Lawrence Erlbaum.

Löffler, W., Kilian, R., Toumi, M., & Angermeyer, M. C. (2003). Schizophrenic patients' subjective reasons for compliance and noncompliance with neuroleptic treatment. *Pharmacopsychiatry, 36*(3), 105–112.

Lombardo, F. A. (1997). If you don't befriend your patients, your competitors will. *Medical Economics, 74,* 121–124.

Longino, C. F. (1997, December). Beyond the body: An emerging medical paradigm. *American Demographics, 19,* 14–18.

Ludtke, M., & Trost, C. (1998). Covering children's health. *American Journalism Review, 20,* 81–88.

Luepker, R. V., Murray, D. M., Jacobs, D. R., Jr., Mittelmark, M. B., Bracht, N., Carlaw, R., Crow, R., Elmer, P., Finnegan, J., Folsom, A. R., Grimm, R., Hannan, P. J., Jeffrey, R., Lando, H., McGovern, P., Mullis, R., Perry, C. L., Pechacek, T., Pirie, P., Sprafka, J. M., Weisbrod, R., & Blackburn, H. (1994). Community education for cardiovascular disease prevention: Risk factor changes in the Minnesota Heart Health Program. *American Journal of Public Health, 84,* 1381–1393.

Lumsdon, K. (1996, February 5). A kinder, gentler ER. *Hospitals & Health Networks, 70,* 43–45.

Lund, C. C. (1995). The doctor, the patient, and the truth. In J. D. Arras & B. Steinbock (Eds.), *Ethical issues in modern medicine* (pp. 55–57). Mountain View, CA: Mayfield.

Lundin, S. C., Christensen, J., Paul, H., & Strand, P. (2002). *Fish! Tales: Real-life stories to help you transform your workplace and your life.* New York: Hyperion.

MacDonald, M. (1981). *Mystical bedlam: Madness, anxiety, and healing in seventeenth-century England.* Cambridge, MA: Cambridge University.

Madden, P. A., & Grube, J. W. (1994). The frequency and nature of alcohol and tobacco advertising in televised sports, 1990 through 1992. *American Journal of Public Health, 84,* 297–299.

Maibach, E. W., & Cotton, D. (1995). Moving people to behavior change: A staged social cognitive approach to message design. In E. Maibach & R. L. Parrott (Eds.), *Designing health messages* (pp. 41–64). Thousand Oaks, CA: Sage.

Maibach, E. W., & Parrott, R. L. (Eds.). (1995). *Designing health messages.* Thousand Oaks, CA: Sage.

Majerovitz, S. D., Greene, M. G., Adelman, R. D., Brody, G. M., Leber, K., & Healy, S. W. (1997). Older patients' understanding of medical information in the emergency department. *Health Communication, 9,* 237–252.

Maleskey, G. (1984, January). Meet the patient advocate: These troubleshooters help hospitals respond to patients' needs. *Prevention, 36,* 134–139.

Malinksi, V. M. (Ed.). (1986). *Explorations on Martha Rogers' science of unitary human beings.* Norwalk, CT: Appleton-Century-Crofts.

Malinowski, M. J. (1996). Capitation, advances in medical technology, and the advent of a new era in medical ethics. *American Journal of Law & Medicine, 22,* 331–360.

Mangan, K. S. (1996, November 15). A medical school changes its curriculum to increase the emphasis on care and compassion. *Chronicle of Higher Education, 43,* A12–A13.

Manning, T. (1997). Interactive environments for promoting health. In R. L. Street Jr., W. R. Gold, & T. Manning (Eds.), *Health promotion and interactive technology: Theoretical applications and future directions* (pp. 67–78). Mahwah, NJ: Lawrence Erlbaum.

Marantz, P. R. (1990). Blaming the victim: The negative consequence of preventive medicine. *American Journal of Public Health, 80,* 1186–1187.

Marcus, L. J. (1999). *Renegotiating health care: Resolving conflict to build collaboration.* San Francisco: Jossey-Bass.

Marin, M. J., Sherblom, J. C., & Shipps, T. B. (1994). Contextual influences on nurses' conflict management strategies. *Western Journal of Communication, 58,* 201–228.

Markowitz, S., & Grossman, M. (1998). Alcohol regulation and domestic violence toward children. *Contemporary Economic Policy, 16,* 309–320.

Marks, L. I. (1998). Deconstructing locus of control: Implications for practitioners. *Journal of Counseling and Development, 76,* 251–260.

Marshall, A. A., Smith, S. W., & McKeon, J. K. (1995). Persuading low-income women to engage in mammography screening: Source, message, and channel preferences. *Health Communication, 7,* 283–300.

Marshall, R. F. (2003, July 20). Not a clean bill of health. *Newsday,* p. F06.

Marston, R. Q. (1992). The Robert Wood Johnson Foundation Commission on Medical Education: The sciences of medical practice, summary report. *Journal of the American Medical Association, 268,* 1144–1145.

Martin, M. C., & Gentry, J. W. (1997, Summer). Stuck in the model trap: The effects of beautiful models in ads on female pre-adolescents and adolescents. *Journal of Advertising, 26,* 19–33.

Marwick, C. (1997). Proponents gather to discuss evidence-based medicine. *Journal of the American Medical Association, 278,* 531–532.

Maslach, C. (1982). *Burnout: The cost of caring.* Englewood Cliffs, NJ: Prentice Hall.

Mastro, D. E., & Atkin, C. (2002). Exposure to alcohol billboards and beliefs and attitudes toward drinking among Mexican American high school students. *Howard Journal of Communications, 12*(2), 129–151.

Mathios, A., Avery, R., Bisogni, C., & Shanahan, J. (1998). Alcohol portrayals on prime-time television: Manifest and latent messages. *Journal of Studies on Alcohol, 59,* 305–310.

Matthews, A. K. (1998). Lesbians and cancer support: Clinical issues for cancer patients. *Health Care for Women International, 1993,* 193–203.

Mattson, M., & Roberts, F. (2001). Overcoming truth telling as an obstacle to initiating safer sex: Clients and health practitioners planning deception during HIV test counseling. *Health Communication, 13*(4), 343–362.

Maynard, C. (1998, September). How to make peace with your body. *Current Health 2,* 66–71.

McCague, J. J. (2001, May 21). On today's older patients. *Medical Economics, 78*(10), 104.

McConatha, D. (2002). Aging online: Toward a theory of e-equality. In R. W. Morrell (Ed.), *Older adults, health information, and the World Wide Web* (pp. 21–41). Mahwah, NJ: Lawrence Erlbaum.

McCormick, T. R., & Conley, B. J. (1995). Patients' perspectives on dying and the care of dying patients. *Western Journal of Medicine, 163,* 236–243.

McCue, J. D. (1995). The naturalness of dying. *Journal of the American Medical Association, 273,* 1039–1044.

McDermott, J. (1995). The first step (universal coverage is foundation for health care reform). *Journal of the American Medical Association, 273,* 251–254.

McGee, D. S., & Cegala, D. J. (1998). Patient communication skills training for improved communication competence in the primary care medical consultation. *Journal of Applied Communication Research, 26,* 412–430.

McGrath, J. (1995). The gatekeeping process: The right combinations to unlock the gates. In E. Maibach & R. L. Parrott (Eds.), *Designing health messages* (pp. 199–216). Thousand Oaks, CA: Sage.

McGregor, D. (1960). *The human side of enterprise.* New York: McGraw-Hill.

McNeese-Smith, D. (1996). Increasing employee productivity. *Hospital & Health Services Administration, 41,* 160–175.

McWhinney, I. (1989). The need for a transformed clinical method. In M. Stewart & D. Roter (Eds.), *Communicating with medical patients: Vol. 9 Interpersonal communication* (pp. 25–40). Newbury Park, CA: Sage.

Medical records; the growing threat to patient privacy. (2001, November 28). *San Diego Union-Tribune,* p. B-8.

Medicare. (2003). Covering health issues: Source book for journalists. Retrieved September 4, 2003, from www.allhealth.org/sourcebook2002/index.html

Merriam-Webster WWWebster Dictionary. (1990). Merriam-Webster Inc. Available http://www.m-w.com/cgi-bin/dictionary

Messmer, M. (1998, September). Mentoring: Building your company's intellectual capital. *HR Focus, 75,* 511–512.

Metts, S., & Manns, H. (1996). Coping with HIV and AIDS: The social and personal challenges. In E. B. Ray (Ed.), *Communication and disenfranchisement: Social health issues and implications* (pp. 347–364). Mahwah, NJ: Lawrence Erlbaum.

Millar, M. G., & Millar, K. (1998). Processing messages about disease detection and health promotion behaviors: The effects of anxiety. *Health Communication, 10,* 211–226.

Miller, J. F. (2000). *Coping with chronic illness: Overcoming powerlessness.* Philadelphia: F. A. Davis.

Miller, K. I. (1999). *Organizational communication: Approaches and processes* (2nd ed.). Belmont, CA: Wadsworth.

Miller, K. I., Birkholt, M., Scott, C., & Stage, C. (1995). Empathy and burnout in human service work: An extension of the communication model. *Communication Research, 22,* 123–147.

Miller, K. I., Ellis, B. H., Zook, E. G., & Lyles, J. S. (1990). An integrated model of communication, stress, and burnout in the workplace. *Communication Research, 17,* 300–326.

Miller, K. I., Stiff, J. B., & Ellis, B. H. (1988). Communication and empathy as precursors to burnout among human service workers. *Communication Monographs, 55,* 250–265.

Miller, P. (1997, July). Support systems of nurses recovering from chemical dependency: A pilot study. *Holistic Nursing Practice, 11,* 56–70.

Miller, V., & Jablin, F. (1991). Information seeking during organizational entry: Influences, tactics, and a model of the process. *Academy of Management Review, 16,* 92–120.

Milliken, F. J., & Martins, L. L. (1996). Searching for common threads: Understanding the multiple effects of diversity in organizational groups. *Academy of Management Review, 21,* 402–433.

Mishler, E. G. (1981). The social construction of illness. In E. B. Mishler, L. R. Amarasingham, S. D. Osherson, S. T. Hauser, N. E. Waxler, & R. Leim (Eds.), *Social contexts of health, illness, and patient care* (pp. 141–168). Cambridge: Cambridge University Press.

Mishler, E. G. (1984). *The discourse of medicine: Dialectics of medical interviews.* Norwood, NJ: Ablex.

Mitka, M. (1996a, August 26). Coalition presses to preserve affirmative action in medicine. *American Medical News, 39,* 1–4.

Mitka, M. (1996b). Marketing doesn't have to be your worst nightmare. *American Medical News, 39,* 18–21.

Models 'R' Us. (1992). *Psychology Today, 25,* 11.

Monahan, J. L. (1995). Thinking positively: Using positive affect when designing health messages. In E. Maibach & R. L. Parrott (Eds.), *Designing health messages* (pp. 81–98). Thousand Oaks, CA: Sage.

Monahan, J. L., Miller, L. C., & Rothspan, S. (1997). Power and intimacy: On the dynamics of risky sex. *Health Communication, 9,* 303–322.

Montgomery, K. (1990). Promoting health through entertainment television. In C. Atkin & L. Wallack (Eds.), *Mass communication and public health* (pp. 114–128). Newbury Park, CA: Sage.

Moore, J. R., & Gilbert, D. A. (1995). Elderly residents: Perceptions of nurses' comforting touch. *Journal of Gerontological Nursing, 21*(6), 6–13.

Moore, L. G., Van Arsdale, P. W., Glittenberg, J. E., & Aldrich, R. A. (1987). *The biocultural basis of health: Expanding views of medical anthropology.* Prospect Heights, IL: Waveland Press.

Moore, L. W., & Miller, M. (2003). Older men's experiences of living with severe visual impairment. *Journal of Advanced Nursing, 43*(1), 10–18.

Morbidity and Mortality Weekly Report (MMWR)—Annual smoking-attributable mortality. (2003, April 12). Retrieved online July 18, 2003, from www.cdc.gov/tobacco/research_data/economics/mmwr5114.highlights.htm

Morell, V. W., Sharp, P. C., & Crandall, S. J. (2002). Creating study awareness to improve cultural competence: Creating the critical incident. *Medical Teacher, 24*(5), 532–534.

Morreim, E. H. (1989). Fiscal scarcity and the inevitability of bedside budget balancing. *Archives of Internal Medicine, 149,* 1012–1015.

Morrell, R. W. (Ed.). (2002). *Older adults, health information, and the World Wide Web.* Mahwah, NJ: Lawrence Erlbaum.

Morris, F. E. (1989, Spring). Getting results from a corporate speakers bureau. *Public Relations Quarterly, 34,* 14–15.

Morse, J. M., & Proctor, A. (1998). Maintaining patient endurance: The comfort work of trauma nurses. *Clinical Nursing Research, 7,* 250–274.

Mosby's medical, nursing, and allied health dictionary (4th ed.). (1994). St. Louis, MO: Mosby-Year Book, Inc.

Moyer, A., Greener, S., Beauvais, J., & Salovey, P. (1995). Accuracy of health research reported in the popular press: Breast cancer and mammography. *Health Communication, 7,* 147–161.

Moynihan, R., Christ, G., & Silver, L. G. (1998). AIDS and terminal illness. *Social Casework: The Journal of Contemporary Social Work,* 380–387.

Muirhead, G. (1994, November 21). The MO of HMO pharmacists. *Drug Topics, 138,* 47–49.

Mulac, A., & Giles, H. (1996). "You're only as old as you sound": Perceived vocal age and social meanings. *Health Communication, 8,* 199–215.

Murquia, A., Peterson, R. A., & Zea, M. C. (2003). Use and implications of ethnomedical health care approaches among Central American immigrants. *Health & Social Work, 28*(1), 43–51.

Murray-Johnson, L., & Witte, K. (2003). Looking toward the future: Health message design strategies. In T. L. Thompson, A. M. Dorsey, K. I. Miller, & R. Parrot (Eds.), *Handbook of health communication* (pp. 473–495). Mahwah, NJ: Lawrence Erlbaum.

Musham, C., & Trettin, L. (2002, August). Bringing health services to the poor through social marketing: Ethical issues. *Journal of Health Care for the Poor and Underserved, 13*(3), 280–287.

Muskin, P. R. (1998). The request to die: Role for a psychodynamic perspective on physician-assisted suicide. *Journal of the American Medical Association, 279,* 323–328.

Myers, P. N., & Biocca, F. A. (1992, Summer). The elastic body images: The effect of television advertising and programming on body image distortions of young women. *Journal of Communication, 42,* 108–133.

Myrick, R. (1998). In search of cultural sensitivity and inclusiveness: Communication strategies used in rural HIV prevention campaigns. *Health Communication, 10,* 65–86.

Nabi, R. L., & Sullivan, J. L. (2001). Does television viewing relate to engagement in protective action against crime? A cultivation analysis from a theory of reasoned action perspective. *Communication Research, 28*(6), 802–825.

Naeem, A. G. (2003). The role of culture and religion in the management of diabetes: A study of Kashmiri men in Leeds. *Journal of the Royal Society of Health, 123*(2), 110–116.

Nakata, J. A., & Saylor, C. (1994). Management style and staff nurse satisfaction in a changing environment. *Nursing Administration Quarterly, 18,* 51–57.

Nathanson, A. I., & Yang, M.-S. (2003, January). The effects of mediation content and form on children's reponses to violent television. *Human Communication Research, 29*(1), 111–134.

National Conference of State Legislatures (NCSL). (2003, August 7). Managed care. Retrieved online August 12, 2003, from www.ncsl.org/programs/managed.htm

National Vital Statistics Report. (2002, December 19), 51(3), 33. National Center for Health Statistics.

Nelkin, D., & Gilman, S. L. (1991). Placing blame for devastating disease. In A. Mack (Ed.), *In time of plague: The history and social consequences of lethal epidemic disease* (pp. 39–56). New York: New York University Press.

Nemeth, S. A. (2000). Society, sexuality, and disabled/able bodied romantic relationships. In D. O. Braithwaite & T. L. Thompson (Eds.), *Handbook of communication and people with disabilities: Research and applications* (pp. 37–48). Mahwah, NJ: Lawrence Erlbaum.

Nestle, M. (1997, March–April). Alcohol guidelines for chronic disease prevention: From prohibition to moderation. *Nutrition Today, 32,* 86–92.

Neuendorf, K. A. (1990). Health images in the mass media. In E. B. Ray & L. Donohew (Eds.), *Communication and health: Systems and applications* (pp. 111–135). Hillsdale, NJ: Lawrence Erlbaum.

Newbart, D., & Grossman, K. N. (2003, June 24). Court rules in the affirmative. *Chicago Sun-Times,* p. 6.

Newman, M. A. (1986). *Health as expanding consciousness.* St. Louis, MO: C. V. Mosby.

Newman, M. A. (1995). *A developing discipline: Selected words of Margaret Newman.* New York: National League for Nursing Press.

Newman, M. A. (2000). *Health as expanding consciousness* (2nd ed.). Boston, MA: Jones & Bartlett.

New York deal between four tobacco companies and 46 states. (1998, November 30). *Time International,* p. 14.

Nichols, J. D. (2003, February). Lawyer's advice on physician conduct with malpractice cases. *Clinical Orthopaedics and Related Research, 407,* 14–18.

Nickens, H. W., & Cohen, J. J. (1996). On affirmative action. *Journal of the American Medical Association, 275,* 572–575.

Norcross, W. A., Ramirez, C., & Palinkas, L. A. (1996). The influence of women on the health care–seeking behavior of men. *Journal of Family Practice, 43,* 475–480.

Northouse, P. G., & Northouse, L. L. (1985). *Health communication: A handbook for health professionals.* Englewood Cliffs, NJ: Prentice Hall.

Novack, D. H., Suchman, A. L., Clark, W., Epstein, R. M., Najberg, G. E., & Kaplan, C. (1997). Calibrating the physician: Personal awareness and effective patient care. *Journal of the American Medical Association, 278,* 502–510.

Nowak, G. L., & Siska, M. J. (1995). Using research to inform campaign development and message design. In E. Maibach & R. L. Parrott (Eds.), *Designing health messages: Approaches from communication theory and public health practice* (pp. 169–185). Thousand Oaks, CA: Sage.

Nurses lobby to address nursing shortage. (2003, February 10). *PR Newswire.* Retrieved online August 8, 2003, from LexisNexis.

Nussbaum, J. F., & Coupland, J. (Eds.). (2004). *Handbook of communication and aging research* (2nd ed.). Mahwah, NJ: Erlbaum.

Nussbaum, J. F., Pecchioni, L., Grant, J. A., & Folwell, A. (2000). Explaining illness to older adults: The complexities of the provider–patient interaction as we age. In B. B. Whaley (Ed.), *Explaining illness* (pp. 171–194). Mahwah, NJ: Lawrence Erlbaum.

Nussbaum, J. F., Pecchioni, L. L., Robinson, J. D., & Thompson, T. L. (2000). *Communication and aging* (2nd ed.). Mahwah, NJ: Lawrence Erlbaum.

Nussbaum, J. F., Ragan, S., & Whaley, B. (2003). Children, older adults, and women: Impact on provider–patient interaction. In T. L. Thompson, A. M. Dorsey, K. I. Miller, & R. Parrott (Eds.), *Handbook of health communication* (pp. 183–204). Mahwah, NJ: Lawrence Erlbaum.

Nussbaum, J. F., Thompson, T., & Robinson, J. D. (1989). *Communication and aging.* Cambridge, MA: Harper & Row.

Nyinah, S. (1997). Cultural practices in Ghana. *World Health, 50*(2), 22–24.

O'Connell, B., Bailey, S., & Pearce, J. (2003). Straddling the pathway from paediatrician to mainstream health care: Transition issues experienced in disability care. *Australian Journal of Rural Health, 11*(2), 57–63.

O'Connor, S. J., Shewchuk, R. M., & Carney, L. W. (1994, Summer). The great gap: Physicians' perceptions of the way patient service quality expectations fall short of reality. *Journal of Health Care Marketing, 14,* 32–40.

Ogawa, T., Taguchi, N., & Sasahara, H. (2003). Assessing communication skills for medical interviews in a postgraduate clinical training course at Hiroshima University Dental Hospital. *European Journal of Dental Education, 7*(2), 60–65.

O'Leary, S. C. B., Federico, S., & Hampers, L. C. (2003). The truth about language barriers: One residency program's experience. *Pediatrics, 111*(5), 1100.

Oliver, M. B., & Kalyanaraman, S. (2002). Appropriate for all viewing audiences? An examination of violent and sexual portrayals in movie previews featured on video rentals. *Journal of Broadcasting & Electronic Media, 46*(2), 283–299.

Olson, L. G., & Ambrogetti, A. (1998). Working harder—working dangerously? Fatigue and performance in hospitals. *Medical Journal of Australia, 168,* 614–616.

Optenberg, S. A., Thompson, I. M., Friedrichs, P., Wojcik, B., Stein, C. R., & Kramer, B. (1995). Race, treatment, and long-term survival from prostate cancer in an equal-access medical care delivery system. *Journal of the American Medical Association, 274,* 1599–1606.

Orbe, M. P., & King, G., III. (2000). Negotiating the tension between policy and reality: Exploring nurses' communication about organizational wrongdoing. *Health Communication, 12*(1), 41–61.

Oregon begins paying for assisted suicide. (1998, December 9). *Academic universe* (vol. 2.). Mealey Publications. Lexis Nexis database.

Ornish, D., Scherwitz, L. W., Billings, J. H., Gould, K. L., Merritt, T. A., Sparler, S., Armstrong, W. T., Ports, T. A., Kirkeeide, R. L., Hogeboom, C., & Brand, R. J. (1998). Intensive lifestyle changes for reversal of coronary heart disease. *Journal of the American Medical Association, 280,* 2001.

Orr, R. D. (1996). Transcultural medical care. *American Family Physician, 53,* 2004–2007.

Pachter, L. M. (1994). Culture and clinical care: Folk illness beliefs and behaviors and their implications for health care delivery. *Journal of the American Medical Association, 271,* 690–694.

Paget, M. A. (1993). On the work of talk: Studies in misunderstandings. In A. D. Todd & S. Fisher (Eds.), *The social communication of doctor–patient communication* (2nd ed., pp. 107–126). Norwood, NJ: Ablex.

Paik, H., & Comstock, G. (1994). The effects of television violence on antisocial behavior: A meta-analysis. *Communication Research, 21,* 516–546.

Parednia, D. A., & Allen, A. (1995). Telemedicine technology and clinical applications. *Journal of the American Medical Association, 273,* 483–489.

Parker, B. J. (1998, Spring). Exploring life themes and myths in alcohol advertisements through a meaning-based model of advertising experiences. *Journal of Advertising, 27,* 97–112.

Parkes, C. M. (1998). The dying adult. *British Medical Journal, 316,* 1313–1315.

Parrott, R. L. (1995). Motivation to attend to health messages: Presentation of content and linguistic considerations. In E. Maibach & R. L. Parrott (Eds.), *Designing health messages: Approaches from communication theory and public health practice* (pp. 7–23). Thousand Oaks, CA: Sage.

Pascale, R. T. (1999). Leading from a different place: Applying complexity theory to tap potential. In J. A. Conger, G. M. Spreitzer, & E. E. Lawler III (Eds.), *The leader's change handbook: An essential guide to setting direction and taking action* (pp. 195–220). San Francisco: Jossey-Bass.

Pasternack, A. (1997, September 20). Why the phone company may be your best strategic partner. *Hospitals & Health Networks, 71,* 32–35.

Pearson, J. C., & Nelson, P. E. (1991). *Understanding and sharing* (5th ed.). Dubuque, IA: Wm. C. Brown.

Peeno, L. (1998, March 9). What is the value of a voice? *U.S. News & World Report, 124,* 40–44.

Pendleton, D., Schofield, T., Tate, P., & Havelock, P. (1984). *The consultation: An approach to learning and teaching.* Oxford: Oxford University Press.

Pepicello, J. A., & Murphy, E. C. (1996). Integrating medical and operational management. *Physician Executive, 22,* 4–9.

Perry, B. (2002, November). Growth and satisfaction: "I became a nurse because I wanted to help others." *Canadian Business and Current Affairs, 98*(10), not paginated.

Perse, E. M., Nathanson, A. I., & McLeod, D. M. (1996). Effects of spokesperson sex, public announcement appeal, and involvement in safe-sex PSA's. *Health Communication, 8,* 171–189.

Peter, J. (2003, June 16). Pilot launched to increase diversity in medical field. Associated Press. Retrieved online August 8, 2003, from LexisNexis.

Pettegrew, L. S., & Turkat, I. D. (1986). How patients communicate about their illness. *Human Communication Research, 12,* 376–394.

Petty, R. E., & Cacioppo, J. T. (1986). *Communication and persuasion: Central and peripheral routes to attitude change.* New York: Springer.

Petty, T., & Cacioppo, J. T. (1981). *Attitudes and persuasion: Classic and contemporary approaches.* Dubuque, IA: Wm. C. Brown.

Philen, R. M., Ortiz, D. I., Auerbach, S. B., & Falk, H. (1992, August 26). Survey of advertising for nutritional supplements in health and bodybuilding magazines. *Journal of the American Medical Association, 268,* 1008–1011.

Pick, S., Givaudan, M., & Poortinga, Y. H. (2003). Sexuality and life skills education: A multistrategy intervention in Mexico. *American Psychologist, 58*(3), 230–234.

Picker, L. (1995, February). Where are the women doctors? *Town & Country Monthly, 149,* 113.

Pickering, A. (1995). *The mangle of practice: Time, agency, and science.* Chicago: University of Chicago Press.

Pincus, C. R. (1995). Why medicine is driving doctors crazy. *Medical Economics, 72,* 40–44.

Pollar, O. (1998, December). A diverse workforce requires balanced leadership. *Workforce, 77,* S4–S5.

Porter-O'Grady, T., Bradley, C., Crow, G., & Hendrich, A. L. (1997, Winter). After a merger: The dilemma of the best leadership approach for nursing. *Nursing Administration Quarterly, 21,* 8–19.

Potter, J. E. (2002). Do ask, do tell. *Annals of Internal Medicine, 137*(5), 341–343.

Potter, W. J. (1998). *Media literacy.* Thousand Oaks, CA: Sage.

Powell, J. H. (2003, June 17). Goal: More minority docs: Representation lacks for races suffering more. *Boston Herald,* p. 28.

Powell, S. (1985, October 28). What entertainers are doing to your kids. *U.S. News & World Report, 99,* 46–49.

Prabhu, N. P., Duffy, L. C., & Stapleton, F. B. (1996). Content analysis of prime-time television medical news: A pediatric perspective. *Archives of Pediatric & Adolescent Medicine, 150,* 46–50.

Preker, A. S., & Harding, A. (Eds.). (2003). *Innovations in health service delivery: The corporatization of public hospitals.* Washington, DC: World Bank.

Prescription drug expenditures in 2001: Another year of escalating costs. (2002, May 6). National Institute for Health Care Management and Research and Educational Foundation. Retrieved online July 9, 2003, from www.nihcm.org

Press, I. (2002). *Patient satisfaction: Defining, measuring, and improving the experience of care.* Chicago: Health Administration Press.

Probst, J. C., Greenhouse, D. L., & Selassie, A. W. (1997). Patient and physician satisfaction with an outpatient care visit. *Journal of Family Practice, 45,* 418–426.

Prochaska, J. O., & DiClemente, C. C. (1983). Stages and processes of self-change of smoking: Toward an integrative model of change. *Journal of Consulting and Clinical Psychology, 51,* 390–395.

Prochaska, J. O., DiClemente, C. C., & Norcross, J. C. (1992). In search of how people change applications to the addictive behaviors. *American Psychologist, 47,* 1102–1114.

Prochaska, J. O., Johnson, S., & Lee, P. (1998). The transtheoretical model of behavior change. In S. A. Shumaker, E. B. Schron, J. K. Ockene, & W. L. McBee (Eds.), *The handbook of behavior change* (2nd ed.), pp. 59–84. New York: Springer.

Prostate Cancer in Michigan, Michigan Department of Public Health Cancer Registry. (1993). State of Michigan, Department of Public Health.

Public, physicians voice positive views of profession. (1996). *American Medical News, 39,* 62.

Putnam, L., & Poole, M. S. (1987). Conflict and negotiation. In F. Jablin, L. Putnam, K. Roberts, & L. Porter (Eds.), *Handbook of organizational communication* (pp. 549–599). Newbury Park, CA: Sage.

Putnam, S. M., Stiles, W. B., Jacob, M. C., & James, S. A. (1985). Patient exposition and physician explanation in initial medical interviews and outcomes of clinic visits. *Medical Care, 23,* 74–83.

Query, J. L., Jr., & Wright, K. (2003). Assessing communication competence in an online study: Toward informing subsequent interventions among older adults with cancer, their lay caregivers, and peers. *Health Communication, 15*(2), 203–218.

Quesada, A., & Summers, S. L. (1998, January). Literacy in the cyberage: Teaching kids to be media savvy. *Technology & Learning, 18,* 30–36.

Quesenberry, C. P. (1997). Choice of a personal physician and patient satisfaction in a health maintenance organization. *Journal of the American Medical Association, 278,* 1596–1599.

Quittner, J. (1995, April 17). Back to the real world. *Time, 145,* 56–57.

Rabak-Wagener, J., Eickhoff-Shemek, J., & Kelly-Vance, L. (1998, July). The effect of media analysis on attitudes and behaviors regarding body image among college students. *Journal of American College Health, 47,* 29–35.

Rabinowitz, E. (2003). Simpler all around. Lightening doctors' administrative load can improve relationships. *Healthplan, 44*(2), 26–29.

Raffel, M. W., & Raffel, N. K. (1989). *The U.S. health system: Origins and functions* (3rd ed.). New York: Wiley.

Ragan, S. L. (1990). Verbal play and multiple goals in the gynaecological exam interaction. *Journal of Language and Social Psychology, 9,* 67–84.

Ragan, S. L., Wittenberg, E., & Hall, H. T. (2003). The communication of palliative care for the elderly cancer patient. *Health Communication, 15*(2), 219–226.

Ramirez, A. J., Graham, J., Richards, M. A., Cull, A., & Gregory, W. M. (1996). Mental health of hospital consultants: The effects of stress and satisfaction at work. *The Lancet, 347,* 724–729.

Ratzan, S. C., Payne, J. G., & Massett, H. A. (1994). Effective health message design. *American Behavioral Scientist, 38,* 294–309.

Rawlins, W. K. (1989). A dialectical analysis of the tensions, functions, and strategic challenges of communication in young adult friendships. *Communication Yearbook, 12,* 157–189.

Rawlins, W. K. (1992). *Friendship matters: Communication, dialectics, and the life course.* New York: Aldine De Gruyter.

Ray, E. B. (1983). Identifying job stress in a human service organization. *Journal of Applied Communication Research, 11,* 109–119.

Ray, E. B., & Miller, K. I. (1990). Communication in health-care organizations. In E. B. Ray & L. Donohew (Eds.), *Communication and health: Systems and applications.* Hillsdale, NJ: Lawrence Erlbaum.

Rees, A. M. (1994). Consumer enlightenment or consumer confusion? *Consumer Health Information Source Book, 4,* 10–11.

Reflections on health promotion and interactive technology: A discussion with David Gustafson, Jack Wennberg, and Tony Gorry. (1997). In R. L. Street Jr., W. R. Gold, & T. Manning (Eds.), *Health promotion and interactive technology: Theoretical applications and future directions* (pp. 221–236). Mahwah, NJ: Lawrence Erlbaum.

Regan-Smith, M. G., Obenshain, S. S., Woodward, C., Richards, B., Zeitz, H. J., & Parker, A. S. Jr. (1994). Rote learning in medical schools. *Journal of the American Medical Association, 272,* 1380–1381.

Reilly, D. R. (2003, Winter). Not just a patient: The dangers of dual relationships. *Canadian Journal of Rural Medicine, 8*(1), not paginated.

Reilly, P. (1987). *To do no harm: A journey through medical school.* Dover, MA: Auburn House.

Reinhardt, J. P. (Ed.). (2001). *Negative and positive support.* Mahwah, NJ: Lawrence Erlbaum.

Reiser, S. J. (1978). *Medicine and the reign of technology.* Cambridge, MA: Cambridge University Press.

Rhodes, S. D., Yee, L. J., & Hergenrather, K. C. (2003). Hepatitis A vaccination among young African American men who have sex with men in the deep south: Psychosocial predictors. *Journal of the American Medical Association, 95*(4), 31S–36S.

Rimal, R. (2000). Closing the knowledge–behavior gap in health promotion: The mediating role of self-efficacy. *Health Communication, 12*(3), 219–238.

Rimal, R. N., & Adkins, D. A. (2003). Using computers to narrowcast health messages: The role of audience segmentation, targeting, and tailoring in health promotion. In T. L. Thompson, A. M. Dorsey, K. I. Miler, & R. Parrott (Eds.), *Handbook of health communication* (pp. 497–513). Mahway, NJ: Lawrence Erlbaum.

Rimal, R. N., & Flora, J. A. (1997). Interactive technology attributes in health promotion: Practical and theoretical issues. In R. L. Street Jr., W. R. Gold, & T. Manning (Eds.), *Health promotion and interactive technology: Theoretical applications and future directions* (pp. 19–38). Mahwah, NJ: Lawrence Erlbaum.

Rimal, R. N., Ratzan, S. C., Arnston, P., & Freimuth, V. S. (1997). Reconceptualizing the "patient": Health care promotion as increasing citizens' decision-making competencies. *Health Communication, 9,* 61–74.

Ringel, M. (1997, December). Patients: Why some press on while others give up. *Business & Health, 15,* 14–18.

Robertson, D. W. (1996). Ethical theory, ethnography, and differences between doctors and nurses in approaches to patient care. *Journal of Medical Ethics, 22,* 292–299.

Robertson, T. (1999, March 26). Michigan jury gets Kevorkian case: Defendant cites civil rights leaders. *Boston Globe,* p. A3.

Robert Wood Johnson Foundation. (2001). National program project report on urban hospital closing, mergers, and other reconfigurations. Retrieved online August 13, 2003, from www.rwjf.org/reports/grr/0208054.htm#

Robinson, J. D. (2003). An interactional structure of medical activities during acute visits and its implications for patients' participation. *Health Communication, 15*(1), 27–58.

Roche, W. P., III, Scheetz, A. P., Dane, F. C., Parish, D. C., & O'Shea, J. T. (2003). Medical students' attitude in a PBL curriculum: Trust, altruism, and cynicism. *Journal of the Association of American Medical Colleges, 78*(4), 398–402.

Rodwin, M. A. (1995). Strains in the fiduciary metaphor: Divided physician loyalties and obligations in a changing health care system. *American Journal of Law & Medicine, 21,* 241–257.

Rodwin, M. A. (1998, March). Conflicts of interest and accountability in managed care: The aging of medical ethics. *Journal of the American Geriatrics Society, 46,* 338–341.

Rogers, E. M. (1973). *Communication strategies for family planning.* New York: The Free Press.

Rogers, E. M. (1983). *Diffusion of innovations* (3rd ed.) New York: The Free Press.

Rogers, E. M., & Dearing, J. W. (1988). Agenda-setting research: Where has it been, where is it going? In J. A. Anderson (Ed.), *Communication yearbook* (11th ed., pp. 555–593). Newbury Park, CA: Sage.

Rogers, M. E. (1986). Science of unitary human beings. In V. M. Malinski (Ed.), *Explorations of Martha Rogers' science of unitary human beings* (pp. 3–14). Norwalk, CT: Appleton-Century-Crofts.

Romano, M. (2002, August 26). 100 most powerful. *Modern Healthcare, 32*(34), 6–15.

Romer, D., Jamieson, K. H., & Aday, S. (2003, March). Television news and the fear of crime. *Journal of Communication, 53*(1), NA.

Rook, K. S. (1995). Support, companionship, and control in older adults' social networks: Implications for well-being. In J. F. Nussbaum & J. Coupland (Eds.), *Handbook of communication and aging* (pp. 437–463). Mahwah, NJ: Lawrence Erlbaum.

Rosenberg, J. (1996). When patients die. *American Medical News, 39,* 14–18.

Rosenstock, I. M. (1960). What research in motivation suggests for public health. *American Journal of Public Health, 50,* 295–301.

Rosenthal, S. L., Lewis, L. M., Succop, P. A., Burklow, K. A., Nelson, P. R., Shedd, K. D., Heyman, R. B., & Biro, F. M. (1999). Adolescents' views regarding sexual history taking. *Clinical Pediatrics, 38*(4), 227–233.

Rossiter, C. M., Jr. (1975). Defining "therapeutic communication." *Journal of Communication, 25*(3), 127–130.

Roter, D., & Hall, J. A. (1992). Improving talk through interventions. *Doctors talking with patients/patients talking with doctors: Improving communication in medical visits.* Westport, CT: Auburn House.

Roter, D. L., Hall, J. A., & Katz, N. R. (1988). Patient–physician communication: A descriptive summary of the literature. *Patient Education and Counseling, 12,* 99–119.

Roter, D. L., Stewart, M., Putnam, S. M., Lipkin, M. Jr., Stiles, W., & Inui, T. S. (1997). Communication patterns of primary care physicians. *Journal of the American Medical Association, 277,* 350–357.

Rowe, S., & Toner, C. (2003). Dietary supplement use in women: The role of the media. *Journal of Nutrition, 133*(6), 2008S–2009S.

Ruppert, R. A. (1996, March). Caring for the lay caregiver. *American Journal of Nursing, 96,* 40–46.

Ryan, E. B., & Butler, R. N. (1996). Communication, aging, and health: Toward understanding health provider relationships with older clients. *Health Communication, 8,* 191–197.

Ryff, C. D., & Singer, B. H. (Eds.). (2001). *Emotion, social relationships, and health.* New York: Oxford.

Sadler, C., & Marty, F. (1997). *Members of the family: Socialization of Hospice volunteers.* Paper presented at the annual meeting of the National Communication Association in Chicago.

Safran, S. P. (1998). Disability portrayal in film: Reflecting the past, directing the future. *Exceptional Children, 64,* 227–238.

Salem, P., & Williams, M. L. (1984). Uncertainty and satisfaction: The importance of information in hospital communication. *Journal of Applied Communication Research, 12,* 75–89.

Salmon, C. T., & Atkin, C. (2003). Using media campaigns for health promotion. In T. L. Thompson, A. M. Dorsey, K. I. Miller, & R. Parrott (Eds.), *Handbook of health communication* (pp. 449–472). Mahwah, NJ: Lawrence Erlbaum.

Sanchez, J. I., & Brock, P. (1996, June). Outcomes of perceived discrimination among Hispanic employees: Is diversity management a luxury or a necessity? *Academy of Management Journal, 39,* 704–719.

Sanders, L. (2003). The ethics imperative. *Modern Healthcare, 33*(11), 46.

Sands, E. R., & Wardel, J. (2003). Internationalization of body types of 9–12 year old girls. *International Journal of Eating Disorders, 33*(2), 193–204.

Scharlach, A. E. (1994). Caregiving and employment: Competing or complementary roles? *The Gerontologist, 34,* 378–385.

Schein, E. H. (1986). *Organizational culture and leadership.* San Francisco: Jossey-Bass.

Scherz, J. W., Edwards, H. R., & Kallail, K. J. (1995). Communicative effectiveness of doctor–patient interactions. *Health Communication, 7,* 163–177.

Schneider, K. S. (1996, June 3). Mission impossible. *People Weekly, 45,* 64–72.

Schooler, C., Chaffee, S. H., Flora, J. A., & Roser, C. (1998). Health campaign channels: Tradeoffs among reach, specificity, and impact. *Health Communication Research, 24,* 410–432.

Schopler, J. H., & Galinsky, M. J. (1993). Support groups as open systems: A model for practice and research. *Health and Social Work, 18,* 195–207.

Schueler, J. (2000, October). Customer service through leadership: The Disney way. *Training & Development, 54,* 10, 26.

Schulman, K. A., Berlin, J. A., Harless, W., Kerner, J. F., Sistrunk, S., Gersh, B. J., Dubé, R., Taleghani, C. K., Burke, J. E., Williams, S., Eisenberg, J. M., & Escarce, J. J. (1999). The effect of race and sex on physicians' recommendations for cardiac catheterization. *New England Journal of Medicine, 340,* 618–626.

Schulz, R., Scheckler, W. E., Moberg, D. P., & Johnson, P. R. (1997). Changing nature of physician satisfaction with health maintenance organization and fee-for-service practices. *Journal of Family Practice, 45,* 321–331.

Schwade, S. (1994, December). Hospitals with the human touch. *Prevention, 46,* 92–99.

See the enemy. (1993, December 24). *Rolling Stone,* p. 6.

The sensitive screenwriter. (1994, February). *Harper's Magazine, 288,* 20–21.

Shanahan, J., & Morgan, M. (1999). *Television and its viewers: Cultivation theory and research.* Cambridge, UK: Cambridge University Press.

Shapiro, R. S., Tym, K. A., Eastwood, D., Derse, A. R., & Klein, J. P. (2003). Managed care, doctors, and patients: Focusing on relationships, not rights. *Cambridge Quarterly of Healthcare Ethics, 12*(3), 300–307.

Sharf, B. F. (1984). *The physician's guide to better communication.* Glenview, IL: Scott, Foresman.

Shea, S., Basch, C. E., Wechsler, H., & Lantigua, R. (1996). The Washington Heights-Inwood Healthy Heart Program: A 6-year report from a disadvantaged urban setting. *American Journal of Public Health, 86,* 166–171.

Sheehan, K. H., Sheehan, D. V., White, K., Leibowitz, A., & Baldwin, D. C. (1990). A pilot study of medical student 'abuse.' *Journal of the American Medical Association, 263,* 533–537.

Sheer, V. C., & Cline, R. J. W. (1995). Individual differences in sensation seeking and sexual behavior: Implications for communication intervention for HIV/AIDS prevention among college students. *Health Communication, 7,* 205–224.

Shelton, D. L. (1997, April 15). Mistrust of doctors lingers after Tuskegee; many Blacks remain wary—and underserved—a quarter-century after infamous syphilis study. *Washington Post,* p. WH8.

Shidler, J. A., & Lowry, D. T. (1995). Network TV sex as a counterprogramming strategy during a sweeps period: An analysis of content and ratings. *Journalism & Mass Communication Quarterly, 72,* 147–157.

Shoemaker, P. J., & Reese, S. D. (1991). *Meeting the message: Theories of influences on mass media content.* New York: Longman.

Shortell, S. M., Gillies, R. R., & Devers, K. J. (1995). Reinventing the American hospital. *Milbank Quarterly, 73,* 131–160.

Siegel, J. T., & Burgoon, J. K. (2002). Expectancy theory approaches to prevention: Violating adolescent expectations to increase the effectiveness of public service announcements. In W. D. Crano & M. Burgoon (Eds.), *Mass media and drug prevention: Classic and contemporary theories and research* (pp. 163–186). Mahwah, NJ: Lawrence Erlbaum.

Signorielli, N. (1993). *Mass media images and impact on health.* Westport, CT: Greenwood Press.

Signorielli, N., & Staples, J. (1997). Television and children's conceptions of nutrition. *Health Communication, 9,* 289–302.

Silver, H. K. (1982). Medical students and medical school. *Journal of the American Medical Association, 247,* 309–310.

Silver, H. K., & Glicken, A. D. (1990). Medical student abuse: Incidence, severity, and significance. *Journal of the American Medical Association, 263,* 527–532.

Silver, M. (1993, September, 20). Sex, violence and the tube: The fall lineup has more of the first, less of the second. Most of the good TV is aimed at kids. *U.S. News & World Report, 115,* 76–79.

Silver, M., & Geier, T. (1996). Ready for prime time? *U. S. News & World Report, 121,* 54–61.

Singer, D. G., & Singer, J. L. (1998). Developing critical viewing skills and media literacy in children. *Annals of the American Academy of Political and Social Science, 557,* 164–179.

Skolnick, A. (1990). Christian scientists claim healing efficacy equal if not superior to that of medicine. *Journal of the American Medical Association, 264,* 1379–1381.

Slack, P. (1991). Responses to plague in early Modern Europe: The implications of public health. In A. Mack (Ed.), *In time of plague: The history and social consequences of lethal epidemic disease* (pp. 111–132). New York: New York University Press.

Slater, M. D. (1995). Choosing audience segmentation strategies and methods for health communication. In E. Maibach & R. L. Parrott (Eds.), *Designing health messages: Approaches from communication theory and public health practice* (pp. 186–198). Thousand Oaks, CA: Sage.

Slater, M. D., Rouner, D., Domenech-Rodriguez, M., Beauvais, F., Murphy, K., & Van Leuven, J. K. (1997). Adolescent responses to TV beer ads and sports content/context: Gender and ethnic differences. *Journalism & Mass Communication Quarterly, 74,* 108–122.

Slusarz, M. J. (1996). From fried rice to sushi: To market an integrated delivery system throw out the old menu. *Journal of Health Care Marketing, 16,* 12–15.

Smith, D. H. (1998). Interviews with elderly patients about side effects. *Health Communication, 10,* 199–209.

Smith, D. H., & Pettegrew, L. S. (1986). Mutual persuasion as a model for doctor–patient communication. *Theoretical Medicine, 7,* 127–146.

Smith, M., Droppleman, P., & Thomas, S. P. (1996, January–March). Under assault: The experience of work-related anger in female registered nurses. *Nursing Forum, 31,* 22–33.

Smith, R. C., & Hoppe, R. B. (1991). The patient's story: Integrating the patient- and physician-centered approaches to interviewing. *Annals of Internal Medicine, 115,* 470–477.

Smith, S. L., Nathanson, A. I., & Wilson, B. J. (2002). Prime-time television: Assessing violence during the most popular viewing hours. *Journal of Communication, 52*(1), 84–111.

Smith-du Pré, A., & Beck, C. S. (1996). Enabling patients and physicians to pursue multiple goals in health care encounters: A case study. *Health Communication, 8,* 73–90.

Snyder, L. B., & Rouse, R. A. (1995). The media can have more than an impersonal impact: The case of AIDS risk perceptions and behavior. *Health Communication, 7,* 125–145.

Solomon, R. (1996). Coping with stress: A physician's guide to mental health in aging. *Geriatrics, 51,* 46–50.

Soule, K. P., & Roloff, M. E. (2000). Help between persons with and without disabilities from a resource theory perspective. In D. O. Braithwaite &

T. L. Thompson (Eds.), *Handbook of communication and people with disabilities: Research and applications* (pp. 67–83). Mahwah, NJ: Lawrence Erlbaum.

South, D. (1997). All I really need to know about medicine I learned from my patients. *Patient Care, 31*, 238–240.

Spangle, M. (2003). *Negotiation: Communication for diverse settings.* Thousand Oaks, CA: Sage.

Sparks, L., O'Hair, H. D., & Kreps, G. L. (Eds.) (in press). *Cancer communication and aging.* Creskill, NJ: Hampton Press.

Spear, S. (2003, April). Where there's hope, there's change. *Journal of Environmental Health, 65*(8), 26–28.

Spector, R. E. (1979). *Cultural diversity in health and illness.* New York: Appleton-Century-Crofts.

Stanley, A. (2003, February 5). It's a fact of life: Prime-time shows are getting sexier. *New York Times,* p. E1.

Stanley, T. L. (1998, August 10). Wanted: Ally McBeal. *Brandweek, 39,* 32.

Stepp, L. S. (2003, February 5). On television, safer sex—and more of it. *Washington Post,* p. C01.

Stivers, T. (2002). Presenting the problem in pediatric encounters: "Symptoms only" versus "candidate diagnosis" presentations. *Health Communication, 14*(3), 299–338.

Street, R. L., Jr. (1990). Dentist–patient communication: A review and commentary. In D. O'Hair & G. L. Kreps (Eds.), *Applied communication theory and research* (pp. 331–351). Hillsdale, NJ: Lawrence Erlbaum.

Street, R. L., Jr. (1992). Analyzing communication in medical consultations. *Medical Care, 30,* 976–988.

Street, R. L., Jr. (1997). Health promotion and technology. In R. L. Street, Jr., W. R. Gold, & T. Manning (Eds.), *Health promotion and interactive technology: Theoretical applications and future directions* (pp. 1–18). Mahwah, NJ: Lawrence Erlbaum.

Street, R. L., Jr. (2003). Communication in medical encounters: An ecological perspective. In T. L. Thompson, A. M. Dorsey, K. I. Miller, & R. Parrot (Eds.), *Handbook of health communication* (pp. 63–89). Mahwah, NJ: Lawrence Erlbaum.

Street, R. L., Jr., & Buller, D. B. (1987). Nonverbal response patterns in physician–patient interactions: A functional analysis. *Journal of Nonverbal Behavior, 11,* 234–253.

Street, R. L., Jr., & Buller, D. B. (1988). Patients' characteristics affecting physician–patient nonverbal communication. *Human Communication Research, 15,* 60–91.

Street, R. L., Jr., Gold, W. R., & Manning, T. (Eds.). (1997). *Health promotion and interactive technology: Theoretical applications and future directions.* Mahwah, NJ: Lawrence Erlbaum.

Street, R. L., Jr., & Manning, T. (1997). Information environments in breast cancer education. In R. L. Street Jr. W. R. Gold, & T. Manning (Eds.), *Health promotion and interactive technology: Theoretical applications and future directions* (pp. 121–139). Mahwah, NJ: Lawrence Erlbaum.

Street, R. L., Jr., & Millay, B. (2001). Analyzing patient participation in medical encounters. *Health Communication, 13*(1), 61–73.

Street, R. L., Jr., & Rimal, R. N. (1997). Health promotion and interactive technology: A conceptual foundation. In R. L. Street Jr., W. R. Gold, & T. Manning (Eds.), *Health promotion and interactive technology: Theoretical applications and future directions* (pp. 1–18). Mahwah, NJ: Lawrence Erlbaum.

Street, R. L., Jr., Voigt, B., Geyer, C., Manning, T., & Swanson, G. P. (1995). Increasing patient involvement in choosing treatment for early breast cancer. *Cancer, 76,* 2275–2285.

Stretcher, V. J., & Rosenstock, I. M. (1997). The health belief model. In K. Glanz, F. M. Lewis, & B. K. Rimer (Eds.), *Health behavior and health education* (pp. 41–59). San Francisco: Jossey-Bass.

Stroebe, M. S. (Ed.) (2001). *Handbook of bereavement research: Consequences, coping, and care.* Washington, DC: American Psychological Association.

Studer, Q. (2002, September). Back to the basics: Making service excellence a priority. *AHA* [American Hospital Association] *Trustee Magazine, 55*(8), 7–10. Retrieved online August 13, 2003, from www.hospitalconnect.com/DesktopServlet.

Studer, Q. (2003a, July). Thoughts from Quint. Retrieved online August 13, 2003, through the Studer Group website available at www.studergroup.com/$spindb.query.articles3.studview.142

Studer, Q. (2003b, Summer). How healthcare wins with consumers who want more. *Frontiers of Health Services Management, 19*(4), 3–16.

Studer, Q. (2003c, May/June). Sustaining the gains: Creating organizational alignment through accountability. *Press-Ganey Satisfaction Monitor.* Retrieved online September 22, 2003, from www.pressganey.org/research/resources/satmon/text/bin/139.shtm

Studer, Q. (2003d, November). Communicating quality. *COR Healthcare Market Strategist.* Santa Barbara, CA: COR Health.

Study reveals Blacks trust Black media most and magazines have highest trust level of all. (1998, November 2). *Jet, 94,* 57.

Suchman, A. L., Markakis, K., Beckman, H. B., & Frankel, R. (1997). A model of empathic communication in the medical interview. *Journal of the American Medical Association, 277,* 678–683.

Sullivan, G. H., & Wolfe, S. (1996). When communication breaks down. *RN, 59,* 61–64.

Suls, J. M., & Wheeler, L. (Eds.). (2000). *Handbook of social comparison: Theory and research.* New York: Plenum.

Swiderski, R. M. (1976). The idiom of diagnosis. *Communication Quarterly, 24,* 3–11.

Taira, D. A., Safran, D. G., Seto, T. B., Rogers, W. H., & Tarlov, A. R. (1997). The relationship between patient income and physician discussion of health risk behaviors. *Journal of the American Medical Association, 278,* 1412–1418.

Tardy, C. H. (1994). Counteracting task-induced stress: Studies of instrumental and emotional support in problem-solving contexts. In B. R. Burleson, T. L. Albrecht, & I. G. Sarason (Eds.), *Communication of social support: Messages, interactions, relationships, and community* (pp. 71–87). Thousand Oaks, CA: Sage.

Tarrant, C., Windrige, K., Boulton, J., Baker, R., & Freeman, G. (2003, June 14). How important is personal care in general practice? *British Medical Journal (Clinical Research Edition), 326,* 1310.

Taubes, G. (1998). Telling time by the second hand. *Technology Review, 101,* 76–78.

Taylor, S. E. (1982). Hospital patient behavior: Reactance, helplessness, or control? In H. S. Friedman & M. R. DiMatteo (Eds.), *Interpersonal issues in health care* (pp. 209–232). New York: Academic Press.

Taylor, S. E., Falke, R. L., Mazel, R. M., & Hilsberg, B. L. (1988). Sources of satisfaction and dissatisfaction among members of cancer support groups. In B. H. Gottlieb (Ed.), *Marshaling social support: Formats, processes, and effects* (pp. 187–208). Newbury Park, CA: Sage.

Tervalon, M. (2003). Components of culture in health for medical students' education. *Academic Medicine, 78*(6), 570–576.

Tesch, B. J., Wood, H. M., Helwig, A. L., & Butler, A. N. (1995). Promotion of women physicians in academic medicine: Glass ceiling or sticky floor? *Journal of the American Medical Association, 273,* 1022–1026.

Thomas, E. J., Sexton, J. B., & Helmreich, R. L. (2003). Discrepant attitudes about teamwork among critical care nurses and physicians. *Critical Care Medicine, 31*(3), 956–959.

Thomas, S. B., Quinn, S. C., Billingsley, A., & Caldwell, C. (1994). *American Journal of Public Health, 84,* 575–579.

Thompson, C. B. (1996, October). Research to support holistic nursing taxonomies. *Holistic Nursing Practice, 11,* 31–38.

Thompson, T. L. (1984). The invisible helping hand: The role of communication in the health and social service professions. *Communication Quarterly, 32,* 148–161.

Thompson, T. L. (1990). Patient health care: Issues in interpersonal communication. In E. B. Ray & L. Donohew (Eds.), *Communication and health: Systems and applications* (pp. 27–50). Hillsdale, NJ: Lawrence Erlbaum.

Thompson, T. (1996). Allowing dignity: Communicating with the dying. In E. B. Ray (Ed.), *Communication and disenfranchisement: Social health issues and implications* (pp. 387–404). Mahwah, NJ: Lawrence Erlbaum.

Thorpe, K., & Loo, P. (2003). Balancing professional and personal satisfaction of nurse managers: Current and future perspectives in a changing health care system. *Journal of Nurse Management, 11*(5), 321–330.

Thorwald, J. (1962). *Science and secrets of early medicine* (translated by R. Winston & C. Winston). New York: Harcourt, Brace & World.

Tichenor, P. J., Donohue, G. A., & Olien, C. N. (1970). Mass media flow and differential growth in knowledge. *Public Opinion Quarterly, 34,* 159–170.

Tieman, J. (2002, January 14). Exec pay gap grows between the sexes. *Modern Healthcare, 32,* 12.

Todd, A. D. (1984). The prescription of contraception: Negotiations between doctors and patients. *Discourse Processes, 7,* 171–200.

Todd, A. D. (1989). *Intimate adversaries: Cultural conflict between doctors and women patients.* Philadelphia: University of Philadelphia Press.

Trends and indicators in the changing health care marketplace. (2002). Kaiser Family Foundation. Retrieved September 4, 2003, from www.kff.org

Trix, F., & Psenka, C. (2003). Exploring the color of glass: Letters of recommendation for female and male medical faculty. *Discourse & Society, 14*(2), 191–220.

Troth, A., & Peterson, C. C. (2000). Factors predicting safe-sex talk and condom use in early sexual relationships. *Health Communication, 12*(2), 195–218.

Tucker, C. M., Herman, K. C., Pedersen, T. R., Higley, B., Montrichard, M., & Ivery, P. (2003). Cultural sensitivity in physician–patient relationships: Perspectives of an ethnically diverse sample of low-income primary care patients. *Medical Care, 41*(7), 859–870.

Tucker, L. A., & Bagwell, M. (1991). Television viewing and obesity in adult females. *American Journal of Public Health, 81,* 908–911.

TV fitness programs are helping viewers stay fit and healthy. (1997, April 21). *Jet,* p. 16.

Twaddle, A. C., & Hessler, R. M. (1987). *A sociology of health* (2nd ed.). New York: Macmillan.

Uba, L. (1992). Cultural barriers to health care for Southeast Asian refugees. *Public Health Reports, 107,* 544–548.

Ulrich, C. M., Soeken, K. L., & Miller, N. (2003). Ethical conflict associated with managed care: Views of nurse practitioners. *Nursing Research, 52*(3), 168–175.

UN report cites global Internet growth despite economic woes. (2002, November 18). *USAToday.com.* Retrieved online September 10, 2003, from www.usatoday.com/tech/news/2002-11-18-global-net_x.htm

Unsworth, C. (1996). Team decision-making in rehabilitation. *American Journal of Physical Medicine & Rehabilitation, 75,* 483–486.

Urba, S. (1998). Sometimes the best thing I do is listen. *Medical Economics, 75*(9), 167–170.

U.S. Bureau of the Census Profile of Older Americans (1997). Administration on Aging. [Online]. Available: www.aoa.dhhs.gov/aoa/stats/profile/

U.S. Bureau of the Census. (2000). Profile of general demographic characteristics. Retrieved online August 6, 2003, from factfinder.census.gov/servlet

U.S. Bureau of Labor Statistics. (2003a). BLS career information: Nurse. Retrieved online August 11, 2003, from www.bls.gov/k12/sci_004t.htm#Jobs

U.S. Bureau of Labor Statistics. (2003b). Health services 2002–2003: Career guide to industries. U.S. Bureau of Labor. Retrieved online September 9, 2003, from www.bls.gov/oco/cgs035.htm

U.S. Department of Health and Human Services. (2002). Projected supply, demand, and shortages of registered nurses. Health Resources and

Services Administration, Bureau of Health Professions, National Center for Health Workforce Analysis.

Valente, T. W., Paredes, P., & Poppe, P. R. (1998). Matching the message to the process: The relative ordering of knowledge, attitudes, and practices in behavior change research. *Human Communication Research, 24,* 366–385.

Vanderford, M. L., Jenks, E. B., & Sharf, B. F. (1997). Exploring patients' experiences as a primary source of meaning. *Health Communication, 9,* 13–26.

van der Pal-de Bruin, K. M., de Walle, H. E., de Rover, C. M., Jenninga, W., Cornel, M. C., de Jong-van den Berg, L. T., Buitendijk, S. E., & Paulussen, T. G. (2003). Influence of educational level on determinants of folic acid use. *Paediatric and Perinatal Epidemiology, 17*(3), 256–263.

Veatch, R. M. (1980). Voluntary risks to health. *Journal of the American Medical Association, 243,* 50–55.

Veatch, R. M. (1983). The physician as stranger: The ethics of the anonymous patient–physician relationship. In E. E Shelp (Ed.), *The clinical encounter: The moral fabric of the patient–physician relationship* (pp. 187–207). Dordrecht: D. Reidel.

Veatch, R. M. (1991). *The patient–physician relation: The patient as partner, Part 2.* Bloomington: Indiana University Press.

Vest, J. (1997, July 21). Joe Camel walks his last mile. *U.S. News & World Report, 123,* 56.

Vestal, K. W., Fralicx, R. D., & Spreier, S. W. (1997). Organizational culture: The critical link between strategy and results. *Hospital & Health Services Administration, 42,* 339–365.

Viswanath, K., Kahn, E., Finnegan, J. R., Hertog, J., & Potter, J. D. (1993). Motivation and the knowledge gap: Effects of a campaign to reduce diet-related cancer risk. *Communication Research, 20,* 546–563.

Voelker, R. (1994). New trends aimed at healing by design. *Journal of the American Medical Association, 272,* 1885–1887.

Voelker, R. (1995). Speaking the language of medicine and culture. *Journal of the American Medical Association, 273,* 1639–1642.

Von Feilitzen, C., & Carlsson, U. (1996). *Children and media: Image, education and participation.* Goteborg, Sweden: UNESCO.

Waalen, J. (1997). Women in medicine: Bringing gender issues to the fore. *Journal of the American Medical Association, 277,* 1404–1405.

Wahl, O. F., & Lefkowits, J. Y. (1989). Impact of a television film on attitude toward mental illness. *American Journal of Community Psychology, 17,* 521–528.

Waitzkin, H. (1991). *The politics of medical encounters: How patients and doctors deal with social problems.* New Haven, CT: Yale University Press.

Walker, K. L., Arnold, C. L., Miller-Day, M., & Webb, L. M. (2002). Investigating the physician–patient relationship: Examining emerging themes. *Health Communication, 14*(1), 45–68.

Walt, D. (1997, March 17). Standing up for ethics. *American Medical News, 40,* 12–15.

Walters, T. N., Walters, L. M., Kern-Foxworth, M., & Priest, S. H. (1997). The picture of health? Message standardization and recall of televised AIDS public service announcements. *Public Relations Review, 23,* 143–159.

Warner, K. E. (1987). Television and health education: Stay tuned. *American Journal of Public Health, 77,* 140–142.

Wartella, E. A. (1996). The context of television violence. Paper presented at the annual meeting of the Speech Communication Association in San Antonio.

Wartik, N. (1996). Learning to mourn. *American Health, 15,* 76–81.

Watzlawick, P., Beavin, J. H., & Jackson, D. D. (1967). *Pragmatics of human communication.* New York: W. W. Norton.

Wear, D. (2003). Insurgent multiculturalism: Rethinking how and why we teach culture in medical education. *Academic Medicine, 78*(6), 549–554.

Weaver, R. R. (2003). Informatics tools and medical communication: Patient perspectives of "knowledge coupling" in primary care. *Health Communication, 15*(1), 59–78.

Web sweep finds false health advertisements. (1997, November 17). *AIDS Weekly Plus,* 21–22.

Weber, M. (1946). *From Max Weber: Essays in sociology.* New York: Oxford University Press.

Wechsler, H., & Wernick, S. M. (1992). A social marketing campaign to promote low-fat milk consumption in an inner-city Latino community. *Public Health Reports, 107,* 202–207.

Weech-Maldonado, R., Morales, L. S., Elliott, M., Spritzer, K., Marshall, G., & Hays, R. D. (2003). Race/ethnicity, language, and patients' assessments of care in Medicaid managed care. *Health Services Research, 38*(3), 789–808.

Weingarten, R. (2003). Brazil's mental health adventure. *Psychiatric Rehabilitation Journal, 26*(3), 303–305.

Weisman, E., & Hagland, M. (1994). Built-in care: One hospital sees the future in patient-centered design. *Hospitals & Health Networks, 68* (22), 54–58.

West, C. (1984). Medical misfires: Mishearings, misgivings, and misunderstandings in physician–patient dialogues. *Discourse Processes, 7,* 107–134.

West, C. (1993). "Ask me no questions . . ."—an analysis of queries and replies in physician–patient dialogues. In A. D. Todd & S. Fisher (Eds.), *The social organization of doctor–patient communication* (2nd ed., pp. 127–157). Norwood, NJ: Ablex.

Weston, W. W., & Brown, J. B. (1989). The importance of patients' beliefs. In M. Stewart & D. Roter (Eds.), *Communicating with medical patients: Vol. 9. Interpersonal Communication* (pp. 77–85). Newbury Park, CA: Sage.

Weston, W. W., & Lipkin, M., Jr. (1989). Doctors learning communication skills: Developmental issues. In M. Stewart & D. Roter (Eds.), *Communicating with medical patients: Vol. 9. Interpersonal communication* (pp. 43–57). Newbury Park, CA: Sage.

Whaley, B. (1999). Explaining illness to children: Advancing theory and research by determining message content. *Health Communication, 11,* 185–193.

Whaley, B. B. (2000). Explaining illness to children: Theory, strategies, and future inquiry. In B. B. Whaley (Ed.), *Explaining Illness* (pp. 195–207). Mahwah, NJ: Lawrence Erlbaum.

What her friends did when she was dying. (1997, March). *Redbook, 188,* 73–78.

While managed care is still unpopular, hostility has declined. (2002, October 22). *PR Newswire,* Financial News. Retrieved September 4, 2003, from LexisNexis.

White, A. D. (1925). *A history of the warfare of science with theology in Christendom* (vol. 2). New York: D. Appleton. (originally published in 1896).

White, R., & Cunningham, A. M. (1991). *Ryan White: My own story.* New York: Signet.

Whitla, D. K., Orfield, G., Silen, W., Teperow, C., Howard, C., & Reede, J. (2003). Educational benefits of diversity in medical school: A survey of students. *Academic Medicine, 78*(5), 460–466.

Whitten, P., Sypher, B. D., & Patterson, J. D., III. (2000). Transcending the technology of telemedicine: An analysis of telemedicine in North Carolina. *Health Communication, 12*(2), 109–135.

Wikler, D. (1987). Who should be blamed for being sick? *Health Education Quarterly, 14,* 11–25.

Williams, A., & Nussbaum, J. F. (2001). *Intergenerational communication across the life span.* Mahwah, NJ: Lawrence Erlbaum.

Williams, C. (2003, June 30). Retailers find profits in catering to teens. *Post and Courier,* p. 16E. Charleston, SC.

Williams, D. R., Yan, Y., Jackson, J. S., & Anderson, N. B. (1997). Racial differences in physical and mental health: Socio-economic status, stress and discrimination. *Journal of Health Psychology, 2,* 335–352.

Williams, J. E., & Flora, J. A. (1995). Health behavior segmentation and campaign planning to reduce cardiovascular disease risk among Hispanics. *Health Education Quarterly, 22,* 36–48.

Williams, M. V., Parker, R. M., Baker, D. W., Parikh, N. S., Pitkin, K., Coates, W. C., & Nurss, J. R. (1995). Inadequate functional health literacy among patients at two public hospitals. *Journal of the American Medical Association, 274,* 1677–1672.

Williams, S. A. (1997, June). The relationship of patients' perceptions of holistic nursing caring to satisfaction with nursing care. *Journal of Nursing Care Quality, 11,* 15–29.

Willing, R. (1999, April 14). Kevorkian sentenced to 10–25 years. *USA Today,* p. 1A.

Wills, T. A. (1985). Supportive functions of interpersonal relationships. In S. Cohen & S. L. Syme (Eds.), *Social support and health* (pp. 61–82). Orlando, FL: Academic Press.

Willwerth, J. (1993, February 15). It hurts like crazy. *Time, 141,* 53.

Wilson, K. (2003). Therapeutic landscapes and the First Nations people: An exploration of culture, health and place. *Health & Place, 9*(2), 83–93.

Wimmer, R. D., & Dominick, J. R. (1997). *Mass communication research* (5th ed.). Belmont, CA: Wadsworth.

Winchester, T. A. (2003). Teaching communication skills to nursing home certified nursing assistants. *Geriatric Nursing, 24*(3), 178–181.

Witte, K. (1995). Fishing for success: Using the persuasive health message framework to generate effective campaign messages. In E. Maibach & R. L. Parrott (Eds.), *Designing health messages* (pp. 145–166). Thousand Oaks, CA: Sage.

Witte, K. (1997). Preventing teen pregnancy through persuasive communications: Realities, myths, and the hard-fact truths. *Journal of Community Health, 22,* 137–154.

Witte, K., & Zmuidzinas, M. (1993). The impact of relational dimensions of risk communication on infertility patients' risk perceptions. *Southern Communication Journal, 58,* 308–317.

Woloshin, S., Bickell, N. A., Schwartz, L. M., Gany, F., & Welch, H. G. (1995). Language barriers in medicine in the United States. *Journal of the American Medical Association, 273,* 724–729.

Women the most active online audience for health information. (2003). *Datamonitor, M2Presswire.* Retrieved online August 1, 2003, from LexisNexis.

Wood, C. S. (1979). *Human sickness and health: A biocultural view.* Mountain View, CA: Mayfield.

Wood, J. (1999). *Gendered lives* (3rd ed.). Belmont, CA: Wadsworth.

Woottin, R. (1996). Telemedicine: A cautious welcome. *British Medical Journal, 313,* 1375–1377.

World Health Organization (WHO) (n.d.). Health Impact. Retrieved online July 18, 2003, from www.who.int/tobacco/health_impact/en

World Health Organization. (1948). Preamble to the Constitution of the World Health Organization. Official Records of the World Health Organization, no. 2, p. 100. Retrieved online September 7, 2003, from www.who.int/about/definition/en

World Health Organization. (2002a). Active ageing: A policy framework. Retrieved online July 19, 2003, from http://www.who.int/hpr/ageing/ActiveAgeingPolicyFrame.pdf

World Health Organization. (2002b). Report on the global HIV/AIDS epidemic 2002. Retrieved online July 19, 2003, from www.unaids.org/barcelona/presskit/barcelona%20report/contents_html.html

World Health Organization. (2003a). About HIV/AIDS. Retrieved online September 12, 2003, from www.who.int/hiv/abouthiv/en

World Health Organization. (2003b). Traditional medicine: WHO fact sheet No. 134. Retrieved online July 18, 2003, from www.who.int/mediacentre/factsheets/2003/en/print.html

World Health Organization. (2003c). Update 83—One hundred days into the outbreak. Retrieved online July 19, 2003, from www.who.int/csr/don/2003_06_18/en

Wright, A. L., Schwindt, L. A., Bassford, T. L., Reyna, V. F., Shisslak, C. M., St. Germain, P. A., & Reed, K. L. (2003). Gender differences in academic advancement: Patterns, causes, and potential solutions in one U.S. College of Medicine, *Academic Medicine, 78*(5), 500–508.

Wright, K. (2002). Social support within an on-line cancer community. An assessment of emotional support, perceptions of advantages and disadvantages, and motives for using the community from a communication perspective. *Journal of Applied Communication Research, 31*(3), 195–209.

Wyatt, J. C. (1995). Hospital information management: The need for clinical leadership. *British Medical Journal, 311,* 175–178.

Wynia, M. K., VanGeest, J. B., Cummins, D. S., & Wilson, I. B. (2003). Do physicians not offer useful services because of coverage restrictions? *Health Affairs, 22*(4), 190–197.

Yamba, C. B. (1997). Cosmologies in turmoil: Witchfinding and AIDS in Chiawa, Zambia. *Africa, 67,* 200–223.

Yanovitzky, I., & Stryker, J. (2001, April 2). Mass media, social norms, and health promotion efforts: A longitudinal study of media effects on youth binge drinking. *Communication Research, 28*(2), 208–239.

Yep, G. A. (1992). Communicating the HIV/AIDS risk to Hispanic populations: A review and integration. *Hispanic Journal of Behavioral Sciences, 14,* 403–420.

Yep, G. A. (1993). HIV/AIDS in Asian and Pacific Islander communities in the U.S.: A review, analysis, and integration. *International Quarterly of Community Health Education, 13,* 293–315.

Yesalis, C. E., Barsukiewicz, C. K., Kopstein, A. N., & Bahrke, M. S. (1997, December). Trends in anabolic-androgenic steroid use among adolescents. *Archives of Pediatrics & Adolescent Medicine, 151,* 1197–1206.

Yesalis, C. E., Kennedy, N. J., Kopstein, A. N., & Bahrke, M. S. (1993, September 8). Anabolic-androgenic steroid use in the United States. *Journal of the American Medical Association, 270,* 1217–1221.

Young, A., & Flower, L. (2002). Patients as partners, patients as problem-solvers. *Health Communication, 14*(1), 69–97.

Young, M., & Klingle, R. S. (1996). Silent partners in medical care: A cross-cultural study of patient participation. *Health Communication, 8,* 29–54.

Zimmermann, S. (1994). Social cognition and evaluations of health care team communication effectiveness. *Western Journal of Communication, 58,* 116–141.

Zimmermann, S., & Applegate, J. L. (1994). Communicating social support in organizations: A message-centered approach. In B. R. Burleson, T. L. Albrecht, & I. G. Sarason (Eds.), *Communication of social support: Messages, interactions, relationships, and community* (pp. 50–70). Thousand Oaks, CA: Sage.

Zipperer, R. (1997, February). Bias and beauty tips? *Consumers' Research Magazine, 80,* 35.

Zook, E. (1993). Diagnosis HIV/AIDS: Caregiver communication in the crisis of terminal illness. In E. B. Ray (Ed.), *Case studies in health communication* (pp. 113–128). Hillsdale, NJ: Lawrence Erlbaum.

Zook, R. (1997, April). Handling inappropriate sexual behavior with confidence: Here are nine tips for keeping the boundaries clear. *Nursing, 27,* 65.

Zuckerman, M. (1994). *Behavioral expressions and biosocial bases of sensation seeking.* Cambridge, UK: Cambridge University Press.

Credits

FIGURE 2.1 from The *New Handbook of Language and Social Psychology,* W. Peter Robinson and Howard Giles, 2001. ©John Wiley & Sons Limited. Reproduced with permission.

BOX 6.4 Copyright ©2003 by *The Voyager,* the student newspaper at the University of West Florida. Reprinted by permission from *The Voyager* and Ms. Davis.

BOX 9.1 Photo courtesy of Linda Deering.

BOX 10.1 Text and photo courtesy of Quint Studer.

BOX 11.3 Photo courtesy of Vicki S. Freimuth.

BOX 12.1 Photo by James Kegley, reprinted with permission.

BOX 13.1 Photo courtesy of Ginna Marston.

BOX 13.1 Printed with permission from Partnership for a Drug-Free America®.

Author Index

Abell, M.D., 78, 182, 183
Abbott, R.R., 147
Abrams, J., 20
Abramson, J.S., 291, 292
Abreau, M., 148
Achterberg, J., 246
Ackerknecht, E.H., 30
Adams, R.J., 158
Aday, S., 326
Adelman, M.B., 174, 178, 217
Adelman, R.D., 60–61, 161
Adkins, D.A., 360
AIDS Conference 2002, 205
Ajzen, I., 372
Al-Anon Organization, 182
Albert, C., 180
Albrecht, T.L., 108, 110, 174, 178
Alcalay, R., 361
Aldrich, R.A., 27, 225
Allen, A., 79
Allen, M., 381
Allman, Joyce, 104
Amabisca, W., 248
Ambrogetti, A., 93
American College of Health Care Executives, 245
American Hospital Association 1994, 271
American Medical Association (AMA), 142, 247, 248
Amundsen, D.W., 26, 29–30
Anda, R.F., 147, 148
Andersen, R.E , 308
Anderson, J.O., 176, 179
Anderson, J.R., 328
Anderson, N.B., 147–148
Anderson, R., 175
Anderson, R.B., 381
Angell, M., 129, 139
Angermeyer, M.C., 125
Apker, J., 253, 291, 294
Appleby, C., 294
Armstrong, W.T., 109
Arno, P.S., 356
Arnold, W.E., 348
Arnst, C., 315
Ashley, B.M., 127, 129
Association for Community Health Improvement, 166
Astin, J.A., 257, 258
Atkin, C., 295, 309, 347, 380, 385
Auerbach, S.B., 313
Auslander, W.F., 147
Austin, E.W., 309, 332, 333, 334, 352, 374
Austin, J., 183
Avery, R., 308
Ayres, J., 179
Azevedo, D., 275, 291

Babin, L.A., 328, 332
Babrow, A.S., 197, 198
Bachenheimer, E.A., 284
Backer, T.E., 338
Bagwell, M., 307
Bahnson, J., 359
Bahrke, M.S., 313
Bailey, S., 156
Baker, D.W., 21, 141, 142
Baker, R., 7, 122
Balas, E.A., 77, 322
Balch, G.I., 377, 380
Baldwin, D.C., 92, 93, 109–110
Baldwin, D.M., 147
Balint, J., 40, 66, 71
Ballard, D., 160, 165
Baltes, M., M., 161
Bandura, A., 174, 371
Barber, K.R., 147
Bar-David, G., 187–188
Bardbard, L., 312
Barnard, A., 100, 101, 102
Barnes, M.K., 174, 176, 179
Barrett, B., 18
Barsukiewicz, C.E., 313
Bartlett, S.J., 308
Barzansky, B., 249
Basch,C.E., 343
Basil, M.D., 328, 381
Bass, A., 276, 277
Bates, D.W., 76
Baur, C., 77, 79
Beach, B., 382
Beach, W.A., 132,199
Beagan, B.L., 228
Beale, R.L., 245
Bean-Mayberry, B.A., 144
Beatty, P.W., 156
Beauvais, J., 315
Beavin, J.H., 58
Beck, C., 61, 71, 144, 227
Beckett, J.O., 250
Beckman, H.B., 57, 59, 60, 70, 125, 126
Beebe, S.A. , 264
Begany, T., 264
Bell, R., 145
Bell, R.A., 361
Benotsch, E.G., 183
Bensing, J.R., 69
Ben-Sira, Z., 97, 98
Benson, K., 340, 342
Berelson, B., 361
Berenson, R.A., 51
Bergeron, J., 254
Berggren, U., 69
Bergstrom, M.J., 163, 180
Berko, R.M., 349
Berlin, J.A., 149
Bernhardt, J.M., 142, 360
Bethea, L.S., 71
Betts,K., 313
Beyers, M., 58
Bhopal, R., 146
Biagi, S., 305, 321, 351, 359
Bilbrey, P., 242
Bille, D.A., 28, 210, 211, 225
Billings, J.H., 109
Billingsley, A., 361
Bingham, S., 156
Biocca, F., 313
Bisogni, C., 308
Blackburn, H., 343, 344
Blackwell, E., 246
Blake, R., 280
Blank, R., 265
Boberg, E.W., 238, 323
Bocarnea, M.C., 381
Bochner, S., 21, 58, 141, 143
Bohm, D., 214, 216
Bollinger, L.C., 251
Bonner, T.N., 34, 237, 246, 247
Bonsteel, A., 90, 92, 93, 103, 105, 222

Boodman, S., 57
Booth-Butterfield, M., 175, 372
Booth-Butterfield, S., 175
Bootman, J.L., 354
Boren, S.A., 77
Borisoff, D., 263
Botan, C.H., 347
Botta, R.A., 180
Bottorf, J.L., 177
Boulton, J., 7, 122
Bovill, M., 314
Bowen, D.J., 218
Bowker, J., 123
Boyd, M.F., 217, 219
Boyd, R.S., 276, 277
Bracht, N., 343, 344
Bradac, J.J., 198
Bradford, E.W., 104
Bradley, C., 280, 284, 293
Brady, M.J., 177
Braithwaite, D.O., 155, 166, 176, 183
Branch, W.T., 70, 94, 97, 110
Brand, R.J., 109
Brandt, A.M., 356
Brashers, D.E., 71, 197
Bray, G.A., 307
Breen, C.G., 180
Brennan, L., 359–360
Brennan, M., 359–360
Brennan, P.F., 338, 339
Bresolin, L.B., 142
Bricker, E., 238, 323
Brody, G.M., 161
Brody, H., 218
Brook, R.H., 145
Brophy, C.J., 71
Brosius, H., 361
Brotherton, T.P., 383
Brotman, S., 145
Brown, G.D., 77
Brown, H., 258, 259
Brown, J.B., 132, 298
Brown, J.D., 325, 330, 339
Brown, S., 89
Brown, W.J., 329, 331, 357, 381
Broz, S., 121
Bruck, L., 48
Bryan, G.T., 89
Buchholz, B., 159
Buckman, R., 176
Bucknall, T., 105, 264, 281
Buerkel-Rothfuss, N.L., 325
Buller, D.L., 382
Buller, M.K., 382
Burdine, J.N., 379, 380
Burgoon, J.K., 124, 248, 382
Burgoon, M., 124, 248, 381, 382
Burke, J.E., 149
Burke, W., 218
Burleson, B.R., 174, 178, 184
Burt, R., 192, 193
Burton, D., 360
Busselle, R., 326
Butler, A.N., 247
Buunk, B., 311
Bycke, R., 209

Cacioppo, J.T., 359, 381
Cadogan, M.P., 282
Caldwell, C., 361
Calfe, J.E., 306
Califano, J.A., 355
Cameron, K.A., 360
Campbell-Heider, N., 238, 239
Candib, L.M., 110, 140
Cantanzarite, E., 110
Capossela, C., 188
Capriotti, T., 258, 259
Cardelo, L., 124
Carder, S.T., 328, 332
Carlaw, R., 343, 344
Carney, L.W., 62
Carlsson, U., 314
Carrese, J.A., 203
Carter, W.H., 147
Casey, M.K., 381
Caspter, M.L., 147, 148
Cassedy, J.H., 33, 34, 35, 37, 211, 237, 249
Cassell, E.J., 222
Cassileth, B.R., 258
Cawyer, C.S., 217
Cecil, D.W., 12, 130
Cegala, D.J., 14, 66, 115, 121, 122, 134–135
Cella, D.F., 177
Centers for Disease Control (CDC), 15
Cericola, S.F., 252
Chaffee, C., 358
Chaker, A.M., 276, 277
Chamberlain, M.A., 78, 79
Chang, C.C., 144
Chapman, S., 380, 381
Charles, C., 123, 161
Charmaz, K., 132, 135
Charmel, P., 76
Charski, M., 314
Chatterjee, P., 206
Chauncey, C., 183
Cheskin, L.J., 308
Chesler, M.A., 175, 179, 180, 199
Chew, F., 329, 382–383
Chinsky, J.M., 182, 199
Choi, N.G., 180
Christ, G., 187
Christensen, J., 286
Cissna, K.N., 7, 122, 123
Clancy, C., 151
Clark, W., 99, 103
Clarke, J.N., 382
Clarke, R., 297
Clarke, R.N., 275
Clements, B., 126
Cline, R.J.W., 217, 219, 353
Coates, W.C., 21, 141
Coddington, D.C., 278
Cohen, J., 315
Cohen, N., 11
Cohen, S., 173
Cohn, F., 189
Comstock, G., 326
Conan, N., 100, 101,102
Conlee, C.J., 123, 248
Conley, B.J., 179, 190, 191
Connis, R.T., 182
Connors, A.F., 191
Conrad, C., 239
Conrad, P., 93, 94
Cooney, E., 95
Cooper, R.A., 257
Cooper-Patrick, L., 44, 141, 149
Corbin, J., 135
Coresh, J., 146
Cormier, R., 145
Cottingham, J., 33
Cotton, D., 371, 375, 388
Council on Ethical and Judicial Affairs, 151
Coupland, D., 165
Coupland, J., 162, 165
Coupland, N., 162, 165
Courtney, R., 254
Coward, D.D., 216
Cowart, D., 192–193
Cox, T.H. Jr., 244, 245
Crandall, S.J., 141, 228, 248
Crawford, B.L., 12
Crawford, W., 354, 355
Crespo, C.J., 308
Critchley-Romano, G., 330
Croft, J.B., 147, 148
Cross, M.L., 181
Crow, G., 280, 284, 293
Crow, R., 343, 344
Crystal, S., 218
Cull, A., 14, 108, 109, 126
Curtis, R., 349
Cutrona, C.E., 177

Daly, A., 250
Daniels, D.Y., 181
Darlin, D., 328
Daumit, G.L., 146
Davenport, T.H., 290, 300
David, R.B., 191
Davidoff, F., 94
Davidson, W.S., 121
da Vinci, L., 9, 31
Davis, B., 157
Davis, J.J., 322
Davis, K.C., 365, 386

Davis , S., 228
Dean, V., 98
Dean, V.C., 51
Dearing, J.W., 361
Deary, I.J., 305, 320, 324
Deering, M.J., 218
Degooyer, D., 381
Deinard, Amos, 212
DeJong, W., 308
DeKoven, M., 284
Dennis, B.P., 229
Dennison, B.A., 307
Deering, L., 240–242
Derse, A.R., 51
DeSantis, A.P., 374
Desbiens, N., 191
Descartes, René, 31, 33
Desloge, R., 163
Devers, K.J., 271
Dickey, N.W., 249
DiClemente, C.C., 373–374, 375
Diem, S.J., 327
DiFranza, J.R., 328
Dignan, M.B., 359
Dillard, J.P., 383
DiMatteo, M. R., 70, 89, 97, 226
Diminitz, J.A., 148
Dinur, E., 258
Dominick, J.R., 386
Doner, L., 377, 380
Donnelly, J., 204
Donohew, L., 384, 385
Donohue, G.A., 357
Donovan, R.J., 339
Douglas, C., 29
Dowling, C.J., 31
Downey, J.A., 257
Drader-Wilcox, J., 146
Drass, K.A., 58, 89, 254
Dreazer, Y., 327
Dreitzer, D., 147
Dreyer, J., 69, 105
Droppleman, P., 105, 264, 283, 294
Drucker, P.F., 288
Drum, D., 332
Druyer, J., 69
Dubé, R., 149
Duck, S., 174, 176, 179
Duffy, J., 29, 34, 246, 249
Duffy, L.C., 318
Duggleby, W., 219
Dull, V.T., 50, 58
Dumlao, R., 180
Dun, T., 381
Dunwoody, S., 362
du Pré, A., 60, 61, 71, 73, 97, 144, 216, 227, 242
DuRant, R.H., 326
Dyer, J., 191, 194
Dyer, O., 204

Eastman, J.K., 16, 50
Eastman, K.L., 16, 50
Eastwood, D., 51
Eaton, L., 204
Eaton, L.G., 121
Ebell, M.H., 146
Edelstein, L., 26
Edgar, T., 353, 372
Edwards, H., 195, 196
Edwards, H.R., 120
Edwards, R., 309
Egan, M., 21
Eggly, S., 133
Eickhoff-Shemek, J., 313
Einsiedal, E.F., 339
Eisenberg, E.M., 69, 286
Eisenberg, J.M., 149
Eisenberg, L., 203, 211
Elder, N.C., 96, 104
Elders, J., 249
Ellard, J.H., 177, 179
Elliott,M., 149
Elliott, P.P., 262
Elliott, S., 309
Ellis, B.H., 108, 109, 110, 264, 281
Elmer, P., 343, 344
Ely, J.W., 96, 104
Emanuel, E.J., 49, 68, 190, 191, 223, 224
Emanuel, L.L., 68, 190, 191, 223, 224
Emmers-Sommer, T., 381
Eng, T.R., 218, 320, 323
Engelberg, M., 148, 357
Engelberg-Lotzkar, M., 177
English, V., 330
Epstein, R.M., 99, 103
Erb, T.A., 307
Erdman, L., 194
Eron , L.D., 326
Escare, J.J., 149
Etzel, S.I., 249
Evans, M.G., 103
Evans, R.L., 182
Evelyn, J., 251
Everett, M.W., 353, 384
Eversley, M., 262

Faden, R.R., 331, 355, 379, 380
Fagioli, J., 209
Falk, A., 180
Falk, H., 313
Fanning, M.M., 289
Farber, N.J., 61, 62
Farley, M.J., 289, 292, 294
Farrell, D., 359–360
Farrelly, M., 365, 366, 386
Fearn-Banks, K., 296
Federico, S., 149
Felty, D.W., 41

Ferguson, J.A., 148
Ferguson, T., 19, 62, 173, 182, 183
Ferngren, G., 26, 29–30
Festinger, L., 310
Fink, S.V., 338, 339
Finn, J., 183
Finnegan, J., 343, 344
Finnegan, J.R., 357
Finney, J.W., 71
Fischer, E.A., 278
Fischer, P.M., 328
Fishbein, M., 372
Fisher, J.A., 199, 223
Fisher, J.D., 182, 199
Fisher, S., 61, 132
Fishman, J., 344
Fitzpatrick, M.A., 42–44, 45
Flay, B.R., 360
Fletcher, C., 328
Fletcher, M.A., 11
Flexner, A., 37
Flora, J.A., 323, 351, 357, 358, 366
Flores, G., 148, 149
Flower, L., 67–68
Folsom, A.R., 343, 344
Folts, M., 147
Fontana, A., 11
Ford, D.E., 44, 141, 149
Ford, L.A., 165–166, 197, 198
Forte, D.A., 343
Foubister, V., 249
Fowkes, F.G.R., 305, 320
Fox, R.C., 108
Fralicx, R.D., 279, 286
Frampton, S., 76
Francisco, B.D., 322
Frank, E., 319
Frankel, R.M., 12, 50, 57, 58, 59, 60, 70, 125, 126
Franzi, C., 282
Frasier, P.Y., 291, 292
Freeborn, D.K., 98, 254
Freeman, G., 7, 122
Freimuth, V., 315, 319, 353
French, S.A., 308
Frey, L.R., 217, 347, 348
Fried, L.P., 247
Friedman, H.S., 211, 213, 226
Friedrichs, P., 148
Friman, A.F., 71
Friman, P.C., 71
Frost, K., 319
Fruth, L., 325
Fumento, M., 313

Gabbard-Alley, A.S., 144
Gadacz, T.R., 91
Galinsky, M.J., 78, 181, 182, 183
Gallagher, T.H., 50
Gallo, J.J., 44, 141, 149

Gamble, V.N., 147
Gamlin, R., 145
Gardenswartz, L., 243
Garfinkel, H., 212
Garrison, F.H., 26
Gartska, T.A., 160
Garwood, K., 86–87, 88, 113
Gates, L., 133
Gaudet, H., 361
Gay and Lesbian Medical Association, 166
Gearon, C.J., 76
Geier, T., 327
Geisler, E., 278
Geist, P., 69, 105, 133
Gellert, G.A., 295
Gentry, J.W., 313
George, G., 228
Gerbner, G., 310, 311, 326, 330
Gerlach, K.K., 315
Gersh, B.J., 149
Geyer, C., 120
Gibbons, F.X., 311
Gibson, B., 328
Gidwani, P.P., 308
Gilbert, D.A., 69
Giles, H., 160, 162, 163, 165
Giles, W.H., 147, 148
Gillespie, S. R., 18, 50, 120, 125, 298
Gillies, R.R., 271
Gillioti, C.M., 129
Gilman, S.L., 213, 217
Gilpin, L., 76
Giuffrida, A., 127
Givaudan, M., 205
Glantz, S.A., 349, 383
Glass, R.M., 227
Glicken, A.D., 92
Glittenberg, J.E., 27, 225
Goff, B.A., 182, 199
Goffman, E., 131, 135, 217
Gogag, M., 177
Gold, W.R., 322
Golden, A.S., 71
Goldhaber, G.M., 281
Goldman, J., 101
Goldman, L.K., 349, 383
Goldsmith, D.J., 196, 199
Goldstein, A.O., 328
Gonzalez, J.J., 44, 141, 149
Good, B., 203, 211
Goodall, H.I., 286
Goode, E.E., 204, 212
Goodkin, K., 11
Goodman, L.E., 356
Goodman, M.J., 356
Gorawara-Bhat, R., 50
Gordon, E.J., 125
Gorry, T., 323
Gortmaker, S.L., 308
Gostin, L.O., 65, 356
Gotcher, J.M., 178, 179
Gottlieb, N.H., 379, 380
Gould, K.L., 109
Govindarajan, A., 148
Graff, G.R., 322
Graham, J., 14, 108, 109, 126
Grant, C.J., 7, 122, 123
Green, F., 309
Green, J., 339
Green, J.O., 184
Green, K.C., 253
Green, R., 289
Greenbaum, T.L., 349
Greenberg, B.S., 325, 326
Greene, J., 297
Greene, M.G., 60–61, 161
Greene, J.Y., 148
Greene, K., 231–232, 352
Greener, S., 315
Greenfield, S., 71
Greenhouse, D.L., 97, 104, 105, 123
Gregory, W.M., 14, 108, 109, 126
Grensing-Pophal, L., 266
Griffin, B., 239
Griffin, R.J., 362
Grimly, D., 371
Grimm, R., 343, 344
Grissett, N.I., 180
Groesz, L.M., 314
Gross, L., 310, 311
Grossman, K.N., 250, 251
Grossman, M., 309
Grube, J.W., 309
Gunter, B., 326
Gupta, S., 322
Gustafson, D.H., 218, 238, 323
Guttman, N., 351, 379, 380

Haas, S., 145
Hagland, M., 74
Hale, J.L., 383
Hall, J.R., 382
Hall, M.A., 51
Hallberg, I.R., 69
Halsey, J., 108
Hamilton, C., 279, 287
Hammond, S.L., 353
Hampers, L.C., 149
Hanh, B.A., 146
Hanlon, J.M., 109
Hannan, P.J., 343, 344
Hanson, B.S., 180
Harding, A., 290
Harding, J., 291
Haring, T.G., 180
Harless, W., 149
Harper, D.C., 155–156
Harper, J., 307
Harrold, J., 189
Hart, C., 158
Hart, C.A., 238, 239
Harter, L., 155
Hartman, N.S., 295
Harwood, J., 131
Hass, S.M., 71
Haug, M.R., 194
Havelock, P., 58, 70
Haviland, M.L., 365, 386
Haviland-Jones, J.M., 184
Hawkins, R.P., 238, 323
Hawthorne, P., 207
Hayes, P.M., 144
Hays, R.D., 149
Health, C.G., 365
Healton, C.G., 386
Healy, S.W., 161
Helman, C.G., 118
Helmreich, R.L., 291
Helwig, A.L., 247
Hendrich, A.L., 280, 284
Henriksen, L., 352
Herbert, J., 11
Hermann, J.A., 146
Herman, K.C., 149
Herselman, S., 23
Hertog, J., 295
Hessler, R.M., 35, 37
Higgins, J.P., 181
Higgins, K.V., 295
Higley, B., 149
Hilborne, L.J., 145
Hill , T., 282
Hines, S.C., 198
Ho, D., 102, 313
Hodgman, A., 312
Hoffman-Goetz, L., 315
Hoffman, J.C., 191
Hogeboom, C., 109
Holden, J., 357
Holland, J.C., 213
Holleman, N.C., 51
Holleman, W.L., 51
Holmes, O.W., 223
Holmes-Rovner, M., 121
Holtgrave, D.L., 377
Holtgrave, D.R., 357, 373–374
Hooker, R.S., 98, 254
Hope, K.R. Sr., 207
Hoppe, R.B., 70, 97, 133, 227
Hopf, T., 179
Hornberger, J., 154
Howard, C., 251
Huesmann, L.R., 326
Hufford, D.J., 223, 227
Hughes, M., 147
Huhmann, B.A., 383
Hullett, C.R., 260
Hummert, M.L., 160, 165

Hyde, M.J., 189
Hymes, D.H., 85

Irvine, D.H., 103, 276, 277
Isaacson, S., 180
Ishihara, K., 181
Itakura, H., 154
Ivery, P., 149
Ivinski, P.A., 353

Jackson, C., 352
Jackson, D.D., 58
Jacob, M.C., 133
Jacobson, P.D., 328
Jadad, A., 122, 123
Jaffe, R.D., 328
Jaffrey, F., 77
Jahn, M., 105
James, S.A., 133
Jamieson, K.M., 326
Janis, I., 291
Jantarakolica, K., 310
Japp, P., 132
Jarrett, N., 60
Jecker, N.S., 203
Jefferey, R.W., 308
Jeffrey, R., 343, 344
Jenkins , C.L., 185
Jenkins, P.L., 307
Jennings, J., 250
Jennings, M.C., 271
Jobes, M., 283
Johnson, S., 374, 375
Johnson, B., 295
Johnson, J.A., 354
Johnson, K.K., 333
Johnson, P.R., 98
Johnston, D., 377, 380
Jonas, H.S., 249
Jones, D., 155
Jones-Lighty, D.D., 359
Joseph, J., 139
Joyce, M.L., 163, 185

Kadushin, G., 21
Kagawa, S.M., 91
Kahn, E., 357
Kai, J., 158
Kakai, H., 64, 65
Kalichman, S.C., 183
Kallail, K.J., 120
Kalyanaraman, S., 326
Kamberg, C., 145
Kamowa, O., 205
Kamwendo, G., 205
Kane, C., 275, 307
Kaplan, C., 99, 103
Kaplan, M., 314–315
Kaplan, R.M., 19, 68
Kapland, S., 71
Karimi, N., 322
Kassim-Lakha, S., 91
Kastner, B., 148
Katcher, B., 349
Kate, N.T., 185
Katz, J., 36, 59, 65, 127, 129, 130
Kay, L.S., 357, 373–374, 377
Kearney, M., 225
Keenen, N.L., 147, 148
Kelder, S.H., 344
Keller, S.N., 322
Kelly, F., 262
Kelly, K., 180, 309
Kenny, R.W., 193
Kelly-Vance, J., 313
Kern-Foxworth, M., 357, 384
Kerner, J.F., 149
Kerssens, J.J., 69
Kilbourne, J., 310, 311
Kilian, R., 125
Kim, S., 382–383
King, G., 264
Kinsey, J., 254
Kirkeeide, R.L., 109
Kirkham, S.R., 228
Klass, P., 92–93
Klein, J.P., 51
Kleinman, A., 203, 211
Kleinman, L., 252
Klepp, K., 344
Knaus, C.S., 374
Knight, J.A., 94
Kohler, C.L., 371
Komaroff, A.L., 76, 209
Komolsevin, R., 310
Konig, P., 322
Koplan, J.P., 207–208
Kopstein, A.S., 313
Korsch, D.M., 57, 80
Korsey, A.M., 129
Kotler, P., 275, 297
Kotthopp, M.E., 291
Kotz, K., 307, 308
Kowalski, K.M., 312, 323
Krabbendam, K., 278, 312, 323
Krakauer, E.L., 148
Kramer, B., 148
Kramer, H., 188
Kramer, K., 188
Kreps, G., 8, 12
Kreps, G.L., 71, 72-73, 104, 126, 165, 177, 226, 283, 347
Kreuter, M., 359–360
Krishna, S., 322
Kroll, T., 156
Kroll, J., 121
Kronenberg, F., 257
Krug, P., 192, 193
Kruse, J.A., 146
Kubler-Ross, E., 195
Kulich, K.R., 69
Kundrat, A.L., 131, 156
Kuperman, G.J., 77
Kurtz, S., 134–135

Labelle, H., 326
Laframboise, D., 184–186, 187–188
Lagerspetz, K., 326
Laine, C., 66, 94
Laitinen, P., 123
Lamberg, L., 93
Lambert, B.L., 134–135
Lando, H., 343, 344
Lansdale, D., 164–165
Lantigua, R., 343
Lantos, J.D., 327
La Puma, J., 51, 277
Larkey, L.K., 244
Larson R., 40
Larson, S.G., 325
Law, D., 265
Lazarsfeld, P., 361
Leape, L.L., 148
Leashore, B.R., 250
Leask, J., 380
Leaske, J.A., 381
Leber, K., 161
Lee, F., 280
Lee, P., 374, 375
Leebov, W., 278
Lefebvre, R.C., 352, 366, 377, 380
Lefkowits, J.Y., 334
Lehman, D.R., 177, 179
Leibowitz, A., 92, 93
Leon, J.B., 125
Lepper, H.S., 97
Levin, A., 208
Levine, M.P., 314, 341
Levine, N., 382
Levinsky, N., 150, 151
Levinson, W., 50, 96, 104
Levy, D.R., 94, 209, 249, 250
Lewis, J.P., 258
Lewis, M., 184
Liao, S.S., 205
Lieberman, D.A., 329
Lief, H.I., 108
Likert, R., 280
Lindberg, D.A.B., 164
Lingard, L., 86–87, 88, 113
Lipkin, M., Jr., 99, 176
Lippy, C.H., 226
Lister, J., 35
Livingstone, S., 314
Loemaker, V., 141, 248
Löffler, W., 125
Lombardo, F.A., 226, 227
Longino, C.F., 10, 18

Loo, P., 14
Lorch, E.P., 384
Loughrey, K., 377, 380
Lowery, R., 295
Lowry, D.T., 325
Ludtke, M., 318, 320
Luepker, V.L., 343, 344
Luke, W., 183
Lumsdon, K., 75
Lund, C.C., 64, 65
Lundin, S.C., 286
Lush, M., 12
Lyles, J.S., 110, 281
Lynn, J., 189

MacDonald, M., 213
Madden, P.A., 309
Madsen, R.W., 322
Maibach, E.W., 319, 347, 371, 375, 388
Mainous, A.G., 96, 104
Majerovitz, S.D., 60–61, 161
Maleskey, G., 297
Malik, T.K., 70, 97, 110
Malinksi, V.M., 216
Malinowski, M.J., 150, 151
Mallory, B., 257
Mamlin, L.A., 148
Mangan, K.S., 94
Manning, T., 120, 322, 360
Manns, H., 174
Marantz, P., 218
Marcus, L.J., 263
Marin, M.J., 264
Marinelli, T.M., 122
Marino, C., 315
Marion, G.S., 228
Markakis, K., 60, 70
Markowitz, S., 309
Marks, L.I., 174
Marshall, A.A., 383
Marshall, G., 149
Marshall, R.F., 49
Marston, R.Q., 90
Martin, D.K., 148
Martin, L.R., 97
Martin, M.C., 313
Martins, L.L., 243–244, 245
Marty, F., 195
Marwick, C., 208
Maslach, C., 106, 108, 126
Massett, H.A., 339, 377
Mastro, D.E., 309
Mather, C., 34
Mathios, A., 308, 312
Matthews, A.K., 145
Mattson, M., 181
Maxfield, A., 218
Maxwell, R.M., 295
Maynard, C., 313
Mazur, L., 188
McCague, J.J., 160–161
McCann, R.M., 160, 165
McClure, L., 122, 348
McConatha, D., 164
McCormick, T.R., 176, 179, 189, 190, 191
McCue, J.D., 189, 194
McDermott, J., 40
McGarrahan, A.G., 180
McGee, D.S., 122
McGovern, P., 343, 344
McGrath, J., 358, 386
McGregor, D., 280
McGwire, M., 381
McKeon, J.K., 383
McKinney, K., 340, 341
McLeod, D.M., 331, 381
McLeroy, K.B., 379, 380
McMillan, J.J., 260
McMillion, P.Y., 381
McNeil, M.A., 144
McNeese-Smith, D., 281
McTavish, F., 238, 323
McWhinney, I., 211
Meili, H.K., 332
Melcher, C., 382
Merriam-Webster, 146
Merrit, T.A., 109
Messeri, P., 365, 386
Messmer, M., 266
Metts, S., 173, 174, 178, 180
Michielutta, R., 359
Millar, K., 383
Millar, M.G., 383
Millay, B., 59
Miller, J.F., 184
Miller, K.I., 108, 109, 110, 129, 198, 199, 264, 281, 282
Miller, L.C., 372
Miller, M., 156
Miller, N., 51
Miller, S., 188, 283
Miller, P., 110
Miller, V., 85
Milliken, F.J., 243–244, 245
Mills, S.L., 315
Mishler, E., 85, 117, 118
Mitchell, J.A., 77
Mitka, M., 251, 297
Mizrahi, T., 291, 292
Moberg, D.P., 98
Moise-Titus, J., 326
Monahan, J.L., 372, 383
Montgomery, K., 329
Montrichard, M., 149
Moore, J.R., 69
Moore, K.D., 278
Moore, L.G., 27, 225
Moore, L.W., 156
Morales, L.S., 149
Morell, V.W., 228
Morgan, M., 310, 311
Morreim, E.H., 150, 151, 261
Morrell, R.W., 165
Morris, F.E., 296
Morse, J.M., 57
Mouton, J., 280
Moy, J.G., 51
Moyer, A., 315
Moyniham, R., 187
Muirhead, G., 98
Mulac, A., 160, 163
Mullis, R., 343, 344
Mullooly, J.P., 50, 58
Murnen, S.K., 314, 341
Murphy, B., 281
Murphy, E., 283
Murphy, E.C., 289
Murquia, A., 229
Murray, D., 328
Murray-Johnson, L., 7
Musham, C., 380
Muskin, P.R., 193, 196
Myers, P.N., 313
Myrick, R., 343

Nabi, R.L., 326
Nach-Ferguson, B., 309
Nadler, A., 182, 199
Naeem, A.G., 217
Najberg, G.E., 99, 103
Nakat, J.A., 281
Nass, C.I., 334, 357
Nathanson, A.I., 326, 331, 334, 381
National Conference of State Legislature, 261
Negrete, V.F., 57, 80
Neidig, J.L., 71
Nelkin, D., 213, 217
Nelson, C., 44, 141, 149
Nelson, P., 5
Nemeth, S.A., 155
Nestle, M., 309
Neuendorf, K.A., 327
Neuman, K., 254
Newbart, D., 250, 251
Newman, M.A., 214, 215, 216
Nichols, J.D., 14
Noller, P., 195, 196
Norcross, J.C., 373–374
Norcross, W.A., 185
Northouse, L.L. , 59, 69, 292
Northouse, P.G., 59, 62, 292
Norvell, N.K., 181
Novack, D.H., 61, 62, 99, 103, 104, 108, 109–110, 248
Novak, J., 146
Nowak, G.L., 345
Nurss, J.R., 21, 141

Nussbuam, J.F., 49, 131, 159, 160, 161, 163, 164, 165
Nyinah, S., 219

Obenshain, S.S., 90, 91
O'Brien, M.K., 61, 62
O'Connell, B., 156
O'Connor, S.J., 62
Ogawa, T., 88, 91
O'Hair, H.D., 165
O'Leary, S.C.B., 149
O'Leary, S.J., 271
Olevitch, L., 359–360
Olien, C.N., 357
Olivar, M.A., 148
Oliver, M.B., 326
Olson, L.G., 93
Olvera, J., 123
Optenberg, S.A., 148
Orbe, M., 264
Orfield, G., 251
Ornish, D., 109
O'Rourke, K.D., 127, 129
Orr, R.D., 203
Ortiz, D.I., 313
Ostergreen, P., 180
Osterweil, D., 282
Owens, B., 238, 323

Pachter, L.M., 212
Padderud, A., 325
Padonu, G., 121
Paget, M.A., 61
Paik, H., 326
Palinkas, L.A., 185
Palmer, S., 329, 382–383
Palmgreen, P., 384
Paredes, P., 371, 388
Parednia, D.A., 79
Parikh, N.S., 21, 141
Parker, A.S., Jr., 90, 91
Parker, B.J., 309
Parker, C., 279, 287, 309
Parker, R.M., 21, 141
Parkes, C., 194
Parrott, R.L., 129, 158, 329, 347, 359, 378, 384
Pascale, R. T., 5, 242
Pasternack, A., 79
Patrick, K., 218
Patterson, J.D., 77, 78
Paulman, P.M., 328
Payne, J.G., 339, 377
Payne, S., 60
Pearce, J., 156
Pearlman, R.A., 203
Pearson, J.C., 5
Pechacek, T., 343, 344
Pecchioni, L.L., 71, 163, 164, 165
Pedersen, T.R., 149
Peeno, L., 51
Pendelton, D., 58, 70
Pepicello, J.A., 283, 289
Perrin, J.M., 308
Perry, B., 190–191
Perry, C.L., 343, 344
Perse, E.M., 331, 381
Peter, J., 248
Peterson, C.C., 180
Peterson, R.A., 229
Pettegrew, L.S., 62, 68
Pettey, G.R., 124
Petty, R.E., 359
Petty, R.T., 381
Petty, T., 359
Philen, R.M., 313
Phillips, R.S., 191
Pick, S., 205
Pickering, A., 135
Pinciroli, F., 77
Pincus, C.R., 105, 108
Pingree, S., 238, 323
Pinkleton, B.E., 374
Pirie, P., 343, 344
Pitkin, K., 21, 141
Podolski, C., 326
Pollar, O., 266
Pollard, R.A., 147, 148
Poole, M.S., 260
Poortinga, Y.H., 205
Poppe, P.R., 371, 388
Porter-O'Grady, T., 280, 284, 293
Ports, T.A., 109
Post, D.M., 122
Potter, J., 144–145
Potter, J.D., 357
Potter, W.J., 332
Powe, N.R., 146
Powell, S., 326
Powell, J.H., 248
Power, N.R., 44
Prabhu, N.B., 318
Pratt, M., 308
Preker, A.S., 290
Press, I., 287
Priest, S.H., 384
Probst, J.C., 97, 104, 105, 123
Prochaska, J.D., 373–374, 375
Prochaska, J.O., 374
Proctor, A., 57
Prusak, L., 290
Putnam, L., 260
Putnam, S.M., 133

Query, J.L., Jr., 188
Quesada, A., 333, 336
Quesenberry, C.P., 123
Quinn, S.C., 361
Quittner, J., 322

Rabinowitz, E., 49
Rabak-Wagener, J., 313, 333
Raffell, M.W., 35, 36, 37, 285
Raffell, N.K., 35, 36, 37, 285
Ragan, S.L., 49, 61, 90, 91, 108, 159, 190
Ramirez, A.J., 14, 108, 109, 126
Ramirez, C., 185
Ratzan, S.C., 80, 218, 339, 342, 377
Rawlins, W.K., 58
Ray, E.B., 107, 216, 294
Reede, J., 251
Rees, A.M., 359, 378, 380
Reese, S.D., 386
Regan-Smith, M.G., 90
Reilly, D.R., 224
Reilly, P., 93
Reinhardt, J.P., 184
Reischl, T.M., 121
Reiser, S.J., 38, 284, 285
Renner, J.H., 258
Ressler, W.H., 380
Reynolds, K., 371
Rhodes, S.D., 145
Rice, C., 254
Rich, M., 326
Richards, B., 90, 91
Richards, J.W., Jr., 328
Richards, M.A., 14, 97, 104, 105, 108, 109, 123, 126
Richman, G.S., 71
Rimal, R.N., 68, 175, 323, 359, 360
Ringel, M., 124, 125
Rizo, C., 122, 123
Roberts, D.F., 334
Roberts, F., 181
Robertson, D.W., 89, 105
Robertson, T., 192, 193
Robert Wood Johnson Foundation, 90, 271
Robinson, J.D., 120, 161, 163, 164, 165
Rodwin, M.A., 261
Rogan, R.G., 260
Rogers, E.M., 338, 361, 381
Rogers, M.E., 216
Rogers, W.H., 141
Roloff, M.E., 156
Romano, M., 270
Rome, E.S., 326
Romer, D., 326
Rook, K.S., 180
Rosenberg, J., 194
Rosenfeld, L.B., 7, 122, 123
Rosenstock, I.M., 367
Rosenthal, S.L., 145
Roser, C., 358
Rossiter, C.M., Jr., 209
Roswin, M.A., 51

Roter, D.L., 11, 44, 50, 58, 60, 97, 141, 226, 248
Rothert, M., 121
Rothspan, S., 372
Rouse, R., 331
Row, S., 14
Rowe, A., 243
Ruppert, R.A., 186, 187, 188
Ryan, A., 147
Ryan, B., 145
Ryan, B.L., 298
Ryan, E.B., 160, 162
Ryff, C.D., 184

Sadler, C., 195
Safran, D.G., 141
Safran, S., 325
Sahlsten, E., 381
Salem, P., 293
Salmon, C.T., 38, 295, 347, 380
Salovey, P., 315
Sanchez, J.I., 244
Sanders, L., 16
Sands, E.R., 314
Santiago, J.V., 147
Sasahara, H., 88, 91
Satcher, D.A., 249
Savard-Fenton, M., 291
Saylor, C., 281
Scharlach, A.E., 185
Scheckler, W.E., 98
Schein, E.H., 237, 239
Schensul, J., 205
Scherwitz, L.W., 109
Scherz, J.W., 59, 120
Schmitt, N., 121
Schneider, K.S., 311
Schofield, T., 58, 134–135
Scholle, S.H., 144
Schooler, C., 358
Schopler, J.H., 78, 181, 182, 183
Schryer, C., 86–87, 88, 113
Schueler, J., 270
Schull, M., 148
Schulman, K.A., 149
Schulz, R., 98
Schuring, R., 278
Schwade, S., 75
Schwartz, M.P., 328
Scott, C., 198, 199
Scott, G., 278
Scott, V., 147
Segar, D.S., 148
Sehgal, A.R., 125
Selassie, A.W., 97, 104, 105, 123
Seto, T.B., 141
Sexton, J.B., 291
Shanahan, J., 308, 311
Shaner, J.L., 160
Shapiro, R.S., 51
Sharf, B.F., 292
Sharp, P.C., 228
Shaw, R., 147
Shea, S., 343
Sheather, J., 330
Sheehan, D.V., 92, 93
Sheehan, K.H., 92, 93
Sheer, V.C., 353
Shelton, D.L., 40, 66, 71, 129
Sherblom, J.C., 264
Shewchuk, R.M., 62
Shidler, J.A., 325
Shipps, T.B., 264
Shoemaker, P.J., 386
Shortell, S.M., 271
Siegel, J.T., 382
Sieport, B.S., 12
Signorelli, N., 305, 307, 308, 310, 311, 324, 325, 326, 330
Silen, W., 251
Silver, H.K., 92
Silver, L.G., 187
Silver, M., 326, 327
Singal, R., 218
Singer, B.H., 184
Singer, D.G., 14, 332–333, 334
Singer, J.L., 14, 332–333, 334
Singhal, A., 329, 331
Sistrunk, S., 149
Skolnick, A., 225
Slack, P., 213
Slater, M.D., 309, 351
Slipp, S., 265
Slonska, Z., 329
Slusarz, M.J., 271, 274
Small, E.B., 229
Smith, D.H., 68, 134–135, 161
Smith, M., 105, 146, 264, 283, 294
Smith, R.C., 70, 97, 133, 227
Smith, S.L., 326
Smith, S.W., 383
Smith-duPre, A., 71, 217
Snyder, L., 331
Sobol, A., 308
Socha, C.M., 181
Soderlund, K., 180
Soeken, K.L., 51
Solomon, R., 160, 161
Sommerville, A., 330
Soule, K.P., 156
Sourkes, B.M., 176
South, D., 143
Spafford, M., 86–87, 88, 113
Spangle, M., 263
Sparks, L., 131, 165
Sparler, S., 109
Spear, S., 204
Spector, R.E., 209
Speece, M., 310
Sprafka, J.M., 343, 344
Spreier, S.W., 279, 286
Stage, C., 198, 199
Stanley, A., 325
Stanley, T.L., 328
Staples, J., 307, 308
Stapleton, F.B., 318
Stein, C.R., 148
Steinbinder, A., 283
Stepp, L.S., 326
Stewart M., 132, 298
Stiff, J.B., 108, 109
Stiles, W.B., 133
Stivers, T., 103
Stoeckle, J.D., 94
Stoflet , S.J., 257
Stohl, C., 197, 198
Stoner, M.H., 289, 292, 294
Story, M., 307, 308
Strahm, S., 160
Strand, P., 286
Strauss, A.L., 135
Street, R.L., Jr., 59, 64, 79, 120, 123, 134–135, 321, 322, 359, 360
Stretcher, V.J., 367
Stroebe, M.S., 184
Stryker, J., 312
Studer, Q., 270, 272–275, 285–286, 300
Subbiah, K., 329
Suchman, A.L., 60, 70, 99 ,103
Suhr, J., 177
Sullivan, G.H., 289, 291
Sullivan, J.L., 326
Suls, J.M., 311
Summers, S.L., 333, 336
Sutton, S.M., 377, 380
Swanson, G.P., 120
Swiderski, R.M., 222, 225
Sypher, B.D., 77, 78

Taguchi, N., 88, 91
Taira, D.A., 141
Talarico, L.D., 176
Taleghani, C.K., 149
Tardy, C.H., 174
Tarlov, A.R., 141
Tarrant, C., 7, 122
Tate, P., 58, 70
Taubes, G., 320
Taylor, A.M., 382
Taylor, K., 147
Taylor, L.D., 176
Taylor, S.E., 62
Taylor, W.C., 94
Teno, J., 191
Teperow, C., 251
Tervalon, M., 228
Tesch, B.J., 247
Thieriot, Angelica, 75
Thomas, E.J., 291

Thomas, S., 105, 264, 281
Thomas, S.B., 361
Thomas, S.P., 283, 294
Thompson, I.M., 148
Thompson, S.J., 147
Thompson, T., 8, 80, 161, 211, 287
Thompson, T.L., 29, 129, 155, 163, 164, 165, 166
Thornton, B., 8, 12
Thornton, B.C., 165
Thorpe, K., 14
Thorwald, J., 25, 26
Tichenor, P.J., 357
Tierney, W.M., 148
Tinsley, B.J., 357, 377
Tinsley, B.R., 373–374
Todd, A., 61
Todd, A.D., 126, 212, 222
Tolson, M.A., 16, 50
Toner, C., 14
Toole, S.W., 176
Torgerson, D.J., 127
Toumi, M., 125
Travis, S.S., 71
Trettin, L., 380
Trost, C., 318, 320
Troth, A., 180
Truog, R.D., 148
Tucker, C.M., 149
Tucker, L., 307
Tulsky, J.A., 327
Turkat, I.D., 62
Twaddle, A.C., 35, 37
Tym, K.A., 51

Uba, L., 203, 210, 211, 217, 223
Ulrich, C.M., 51
UN Report, 19
Unsworth, C., 288
Urba, S., 84
U.S. Bureau of Labor Statistics, 15, 252, 262
U.S. Bureau of the Census, 21, 159
U.S. Department of Health and Human Services, 253, 254

Vagim, N.N., 123, 248
Valente, T.W., 371, 388
Van Arsdale, P.W., 27, 225
Vanderford, M.L., 131
van der Pal-de Bruin, K.M., 14
van der Pasch, M., 69
Vangelisti, A., 42–44, 45
Veatch, R.M., 64, 65, 224, 356
Vest, J., 14, 328
Vestal, K.W., 279, 286
Victor, D.A., 263
Vinson, D.C., 96, 104
Viswanath, K., 357
Voelker, R., 75
Voigt, B., 120
Volk, R.J., 141, 248
Von Feilitzen, C., 314
Vu, H.T., 44, 141, 149

Waalen, J., 247
Wachter, S.M., 147
Wadsworth, J.S., 155–156
Wagner, A.E., 381
Wahl, H., 161
Wahl, O.F., 334
Waitzkin, H., 118
Waldron, V.R., 183
Walker, K.L., 60
Wallack, L., 309
Walsh-Childers, K., 330, 339
Walt, D., 276, 277
Walter, L.M., 384
Walters, T.N., 357, 384
Wardel, J., 314
Ware, J.E., 71
Warner, K.E., 359
Warnock, S., 188
Wartik, N., 175
Wasserman, J., 328
Watzlawick, P., 58
Wear, D., 228
Weaver, R.R., 111–112
Weber, M., 279
Wechsler, H., 343
Weech-Maldonado, R., 149
Weimann, G., 361
Weinberger, M., 148
Weingarten, R., 228
Weinhardt, L., 183
Weintraub, E., 352
Weisbrod, R., 343, 344
Weisman, E. Hagland, 74
Wenger, N.S., 191
Wernick, S.M., 343
West, C., 60, 61
Westmoreland, G.R., 148
Weston, W.W., 99, 132
Whaley, B., 49, 159
Wheeler, L., 311
White, A.D., 28, 29, 30, 213, 226
White, K., 92, 93
Whiteman, M.C., 305, 320, 324
Whitla, D.K., 251
Whitten, P., 77, 78
Whittenberg, E., 190
Whittle, J., 144
WHO 1948, 4, 210
WHO 2002, 165, 205
WHO 2003, 19–20, 257, 258, 259
Wiemann, J.M., 160
Wikler, D., 354, 356
Williams, A., 165
Williams, C., 312
Williams, D.R., 123, 144, 147–148
Williams, G., 13
Williams, J.E., 351
Williams, M.L., 293
Williams, M.V., 21, 141
Williams, P.W., 226
Williams, S., 149
Willing, R., 192, 193
Wills, T.A., 173, 177
Willwerth, J., 324
Wilson, B.J., 326
Wilson, H.J., 290, 300
Wilson, K., 210
Wilson, S.R., 154
Wimmer, R.D., 386
Winchester, T.A., 91
Windrige, K., 7, 122
Winters, A.M., 381
Wise, M., 238, 323
Witte, K., 7, 124, 349, 383
Wojcik, B., 148
Wolfe, S., 289, 291
Wolf-Gillespie, N., 328
Wolffers, I., 205
Woloshin, S., 155
Wolvin, A.D., 349
Woo, B., 94
Wood, C.S., 219
Wood, H.M., 247
Wood, J., 312
Woods, M.J., 325
Woodward, C., 90, 91
Woottin, R., 77
World Health Organization (WHO), 20
Wortman, C.B., 177, 179
Wrenn, K.D., 181
Wright, A.L., 247
Wright, K., 185, 188
Wright, S.W., 181
Wyatt, J.C., 287
Wynia, M.K., 50

Yamba, C.B., 216–217
Yang, M.-S., 334
Yanovitzky, I., 312
Yep, G. A., 148, 165–166
Yesalis, C.E., 313
Young, A., 57, 67–68
Young, M., 12

Zea, M.C., 229
Zeitz, H.J., 90, 91
Zimmerman, S., 178, 289
Zipperer, R., 319
Zittoun, R., 213
Zmuidzinas, M., 124
Zook, E.G., 62, 108, 199
Zuckerman, M., 353, 384
Zwerner, Alan R., 291

Subject Index

Abuse, medical student, 92, 94
Access to health care, 148, 150–151
Accommodate, 162
Accountability, 358
Action-facilitating support, 177
Acupuncture, 37, 255, 256, 257
Ad Council, 366
Adolescents. *See also* Children
  and alcohol advertisements, 309, 312
  and body image, 312
  health campaigns for, 352, 353, 365, 384, 386–387
    sensation seeking and, 353
    smoking and, 372–373
Advance-care directives, 191
Advance-care planning, 198
Advertising. *See also* Health information; Health promotion campaigns
  alcoholic beverages, 308–309, 311
  antideception regulations, 306
  benefits of, 306–307
  and body image, 312–314
  drawbacks of, 307
  effect on children, 308
  and entertainment, 327–329
  ethics of, 276–277
  physicians, 275
  product placement in, 328–329
  sensationalism in, 353
  tobacco products, 327–329
Affirmative action, 250, 251
Africa
  AIDS/HIV deaths in, 205
  sexual practices in, 205
    witchcraft in, 216
African Americans
  access to technology, 323
  dissatisfaction with health care, 148, 209
  health promotion campaigns channeled to, 343, 361
  high risk of ill health among, 147–148
  knowledge of health issues, 147, 148, 357
  life expectancy, 146
    media messages to, 309
  medical care for, 146–147
  and medical decision-making, 148–149
  medical practice among, 237, 248–249
  and racial segregation, 38
  social implications of disease in, 216
Age. *See also* Adolescents; Children; Elderly, the
  communication with children, 158–159
  communication with older adults, 159, 161, 164–165
  health promotion campaign audience, 352
Ageism, 159–160, 161
AIDS and HIV
  and global health concerns, 205
  health news on, 315
  health promotion campaign on, 343, 374, 381, 384
  number of people infected with, 20
  social support for, 180
  as stigma, 145, 217
  as taboo, 206
  treatment, 206, 207
Alaskan-Americans, 249
Alcohol use, 308–309, 311
Alternative medicine, 18. *See also* Complementary and alternative medicine (CAM))
Alzheimer's disease, 186, 187
America
  Colonial America, 33–34
  rise of orthodox medicine in, 35–38
  twentieth-century health care in, 38–39
American Association for Health Education, 20
American Communication Association, 20
American Heart Association, 366
American Lung Association, 366
American Medical Association (AMA), 249, 276
Analytic stage, 333
Ancient times, 25–28
Anthrax attacks, 317–318
Anti-drug message, 369–370
Anti-tobacco campaign, 365, 386–387
Arousal, 359
Artists, Renaissance, 31
Aruveyda, 256
Asian cultures, harmony perspective on health, 210–211
Asian Americans
  and mental illness, 203–204
  and physician authority, 223
Ask Me 3 program, 142–143
Assertiveness
  patient, 81, 120–121
  physician, 59–60
Attentiveness, caregiver, 122–123
Audience for health promotion campaigns, 347–353, 356
Autonomy, professional, 97–98

Baby boomers, 160
Baptist Health Care (Pensacola, Florida), 242
Barber surgeons, 29
Beer advertisements, 308–309, 333
Behavior changes, theories of
  embedded behaviors model, 372–373
  health belief model, 367, 371
  overview, 375–377
  social cognitive theory, 371–372
  theory of reasoned action, 373
  transactional model, 373–375
Bergan Mercy Medical enter (Omaha, Nebraska), 75
Biofeedback, 256
Biomedical model
    characteristics of, 10–11
  and low socioeconomic status, 141
  organic perspective, 208
  and time constraints, 97

Biopsychosocial model
  characteristics of, 11–12
  harmony perspective, 210, 211
  and Hippocrates, 28
  and nursing school curriculum, 89
  and teamwork, 291
Blocking, 60–61
Body image, 312–314
Bureaucracy
  defined, 278–279
    division of labor, 284–285
    hierarchical, 279–280
    multilevel input in, 283–284
    partnerships in, 280–281
    rational-legal authority in, 282–283
  rules and procedures, 286–287
Burnout, 106, 109–110. *See also* Stress and burnout

Camel cigarettes, 327–328
Cancer. *See also* Illness
  and alternative medicine, 259
  "survivor," vs. "victim," 131
Capitation, 47, 48. *See also* Managed care
Career opportunities in health industry, 14–15
Caregiver perspective
  and death and dying, 189
  managed care, 46–47
  patient perspective vs., 116–119
Caregivers. *See also* Nurses; Patient-caregiver communication; Physicians
  and changing populations, 21
  and consumerism, 226–227
  lay caregivers, 184–188, 195
  mechanic role of, 222–223
  medical mistakes by, 104
  minorities, 248–249, 252
  nurse practitioners, 254
  partnership with patients, 227
  paternalism in, 223, 224
  physician assistants, 254
  professional pressures on, 96–99
  psychological influences on, 99, 103–105
  shortage of, 278
  as spiritual figures, 223, 225, 225–226
  stress and burnout of, 105–111
Cartesian dualism, 31, 33
Case presentation, 86
Cash-for-compliance programs, 127
Catholic church, 28–30
Celebrities as spokespersons, 381
Centers for Disease Control and Prevention (CDC), 316–318, 319, 341
  Health Communication Key, 20
Central States Communication Association, 20
Channel, 358
Channels of communication, 358–362
Chi, 210
Children. *See also* Youth
  advertising's impact on, 308, 309
  communication with, 158–159
  impact of media on, 310
  and media literacy, 333–334
China, 205–206
Chiropractic, 37, 255, 256, 257
Christian church, 29–30
Christian magic, 29–30
Christian Science Church, 225
Chronic fatigue syndrome (CFS), 180
Cigar shop study, 374–375
Closed questions, 348
Coaching patients, 71
Co-authoring, 74
Collaborative communication, 66–71
Colonial America, 33–34
Comic books, 329
Commercialism in entertainment programs, 327–329
Commercials. *See* Advertising
Communication. *See also* Health communication; Patient-caregiver communication
  defined, 5
    gender differences in, 248
  implications, 10
  and interdependence, 7
  and personal goals, 6–7
  process and, 5–6
  and sensitivity, 7–8
  and shared meaning, 8
Communication accommodation theory, 162
Communication deficits, 108–109
Communication skills training, 121, 282, 294
Communication specialists, 17–18, 293–298
Communication techniques
  allowing emotions, 178–179
  avoiding burnout, 109–110
  communicating with children, 159
  conducting focus groups, 349–350
  coping with death, 194–195
  cultivating dialogue, 69–71
  cultural competence, 229
  defusing violent situations, 263
  designing a questionnaire, 348–349
  evaluating the rules, 287–288
  healthcare organization crisis management, 296
  integrating diverse employees, 265–266
  keeping social networks alive, 180–181
  managing by collaboration, 284
  patient techniques, 80–81
  promoting a shared vision, 285–286
  reaching marginalized populations, 165–166
  supportive listening, 178
  surmounting status barriers, 143
  teamwork, 292
  training new leaders, 281–282
  using the Internet, 323
Communication technology. *See* Technology
Community outreach, 296–297
Competition, 97, 274–276
Complementary and alternative medicine (CAM)
  acceptance of women and minorities, 255
  advantages of, 257–258
  definitions, 255–256
  drawbacks to, 258–259
  popularity of, 257
  types of, 256
Complexity theory, 242
Compliance, patient, 12, 125–126
Computers, 321–323, 359–360
Confidentiality, 49–50
Conflict
  conflict of interest, 260, 261–262
  and diversity, 259–260, 267
  interpersonal, 260
  management of, 259–265
  role conflict, 260, 263–265
  stress and burnout, 107–108
  violent conflict, 262–263
Conflict of interests, 260, 61–62
Consent, patient, 124, 126–130
Consumerism, 226–227, 276–278
Consumers. *See* Advertising
Contingent personal identity, 132
Convergence, 162
Cooperation, patient, 124, 125–126
Co-payment, 45
Coping, 174–175, 183
Coping strategies. *See also* Social support
    and locus of control, 174–175
  death and dying, 191, 194–195
  and social support, 176–177, 183

Cost-cutting. *See also* Managed care
  competition, 274–276
  consolidation, 271, 274
  effects of, 15–18, 98
  managed care and, 41–42
    reform efforts, 41
CPR (cardiopulmonary resuscitation), 327
Crisis, 175–176. *See also* Social support
Crisis management in health care organizations, 296
Cultivation theory, 310, 334–335
Cultural competence, 228–229
Cultural differences, population changes, 21
Cultural display rules, 8
Cultural diversity and expectations
  caregiver role, 222–223, 225–226, 227
    and coping strategies, 175
  and ideas about health, 208–212, 230
  misunderstandings, 203–204
  and patient-caregiver communication, 58
  and patient-caregiver roles, 219–228, 227, 230
  reasons for considering, 204–208, 230
  social implications of disease, 212–219
Cultural integration, 239
Culture, 204. *See also* Cultural diversity and expectations
Current issues in health care, 15–22, 271, 274–278
Curriculum for caregiver training, 89–91
CVS Pharmacy, 100

Death and dying
  advance-care directives, 191
  coping with, 191, 194–195
  death with dignity perspective, 190–191
  emotional support, 201–202
  euthanasia, 192
  life-at-all-costs perspective, 189–190
  media coverage of, 318–319
  physician-assisted suicide, 192–193
  resources on, 196
  social support, 188–195
Death with dignity, 190–191
Deconstructing a message, 333
Delnor Community Hospital (Geneva, Illinois), 239, 240–242
Dentistry training, 89
Department of Health and Human Services (DHHS), 316, 317
Depersonalization, 106
Detached concern, 108
Diagnosis-related groups (DRGs), 41
Dialogue, 69–71
Diffusion of innovations, 361
Directives, 60
Direct mail, 359
Disabilities, persons with
  communication tips for interacting with, 156, 158
  and handicapped hangtags, 157
  media portrayal of, 325
  and normalcy, 176
  overcoming self-consciousness of, 169
  treatment of, 155–156, 167
Discrimination. *See also* Stereotypes
  age, 159–160
    impact on health, 147–148
  and sexual orientation, 145
    and workplace morale, 245
Disease. *See also* Illness
  caused by germs, 35–36
  colonial America, 33–34
  as a curse, 213, 216–217
  illness vs., 33
  social implications of, 212–213, 216–217
  spiritualist perspective of, 29
  as stigma, 217–218
Dispositions, patient, 120–121
Distrust of medical establishment, 147
Divergence, 162
Diversity. *See also* Cultural diversity and expectations; Diversity in organizations
  age differences, 158–165
  disabilities, 155–158
  gender differences, 143–144
  language differences, 149, 152–155
    population shifts, 21
  race, 146–149
  sexual orientation, 144–146
  status differences, 140–143
Diversity in organizations. *See also* Complimentary and alternative medicine (CAM)
  acceptance of women and minorities, 246–252
  advantages of, 239, 242–243
  challenges to, 243–245
  communication techniques, 265–266
  conflict management, 259–265
  multiculturalism, 244, 245
  organizational culture, 238–239, 242–246
  and personal beliefs, 268–269
  types of health care, 252–255
Division of labor, 284–285
Doctors. *See* Physicians
Doorknob disclosures, 74
Doublebind, 108
Drug companies. *See* Pharmaceutical companies
Drug use,
  by medical professionals, 105, 106, 107
  "unselling", 368–370
Dualism, mind-body, 31, 33

Earnings of health care workers, 245
East Carolina University (ECU) School of Medicine, 77
Eastern Communication Association, 20
Eating disorders, 180, 313
Egypt, medicine in ancient, 25–28
Elderly
  accommodating behaviors with, 162–163
  and ageism, 159–160, 161
    changing attitudes toward, 160–161
  communication patterns of, 161, 164
  and communication technology, 164–165
    stereotypes of, 160
Eli Lilly pharmaceuticals, 100
Embedded behaviors model, 372–373, 375–376
Emotional adjustment, 174
Emotional appeal, 382
Emotional concerns
    and biopsychosocial model, 11
  caregiver maturity, 99, 103
  caregiver stress, 108
  caregiver time constraints, 97
  and physician-centered communication, 60
    Voice of Lifeworld, 118
Emotional contagion, 198–199
Emotional exhaustion, 106
Emotional "hot buttons," 99, 103
Emotional support, 178–179, 180, 201–202
Empathic communication model of burnout, 108

Empathic concern, 198
Empathy, 198, 198–199
Entertainment Industries Council, 329
Entertainment programs
entertainomercials in, 327–328
impact of, 330–332
portrayal of disabilities in, 325
portrayal of health care situations in, 327
portrayal of mental illness in, 324–325
pro-social programming in, 329
product placement in, 328–329
responsibility for health images on, 330, 331
sex in, 325–326
violence in, 326–327
Entertainomercials, 327–328
Environmental factors, 371
Environmental restructuring, 72–76
E-quality theory of aging, 164
Esteem support, 177
Ethical considerations, 6,13
advertising, 276–277
affirmative action, 250, 251
allocation of health resources, 150–151
as component of health communication, 16–17
health images in entertainment industry, 330, 331
health promotion campaigns, 354–356, 378–380
hospital experience, 13
informed consent, 128–129
managed care, 51
physician role, 224
privacy regulations, 100–103
questions to ask when considering, 17
therapeutic privilege, 64
Ethics. *See also* Ethical considerations
Hippocratic Oath, 26, 27, 224
Ethnic differences. *See* Cultural diversity and expectations
European Renaissance, 30–31, 33
Euthanasia, 192
Evaluating health campaigns, 386–387
Evidence-based medicine (EBM), 208
Experiential stage, 333
Explicate order, 214
Extended parallel process model, 376, 383
External locus of control, 175
Faith healers, 225
Family and Medical Leave Act (1993), 185
Family members as source of support, 180, 181
Fatalistic cultures, 175
Fear appeals, 383
Fee-for-service, 46
Feelings versus evidence, 118
Fetishes, 30
Fiduciary, 261
Fixed alternative questions, 348
Flexner Report (1910), 37
Focus group, 349–350
Folk healing, 211
Folk medicine, 34, 35, 36
Food and Drug Administration (FDA), 258, 306
Free enterprise and medicine, 39
Friends as source of support, 180

Gag rules, 50
Gatekeepers, 386
Gay and lesbian patients, 144–145
Gender differences, 143–144, 248
Generalist care, 229
Germ theory, 35
Glass ceiling, 245
Global health concerns, 205. *See also* Cultural diversity and expectations
Global health needs, 19–20
Glossolalia, 225–226
Goals
health promotion campaign, 356, 358
personal, 6–7
Goba, the, 216
Goodrich Middle School (Lincoln, Nebraska), 340–342
Government-funded programs, 41
Government regulation, 98, 100–103
Grieving, 175
Griffin Hospital (Derby, Connecticut), 74
Groupthink, 291
Guilt, 383

Handicapped handtags, 157
Handwashing health promotion campaign, 340–342
Harmony perspective, 210–211, 212, 230
Harvard Medical School, 37, 94
Health
defined, 4
effect of body image on, 313
factors influencing ideas about, 3–4
harmony perspective of, 210–211, 212, 230
media's effects on, 305–307
organic perspective of, 209–210, 211–212, 230
Health belief model, 367, 371, 375, 376
Health campaigns. *See* Health promotion campaigns
Health care organizations. *See also* Cost-cutting; Diversity in organizations
as bureaucracies, 278–288
career opportunities in, 14–15
communication specialists in, 293–298
consumer satisfaction of, 276–278
current issues in, 15–22, 271, 274–278
effective communication in, 14
teamwork in, 288–289, 291–292
types of, 237
Health care reform, 41. *See also* Cost-cutting
Health communication. *See also* Patient-caregiver communication
defining, 8–9
everyday instances of, 3
importance of, 12–15
Health Communication Around the World, 20
Health education, 296–297
Health industry. *See* Health care organizations
Health information. *See also* Health promotion campaigns
advertising, 306–309, 312–314
entertainment programs, 324–332
news, 314–315, 318–321
via interactive technology, 321–323
Health insurance. *See also* Managed care
cost-cutting and, 15
and free enterprise, 39
and managed care, 40
Health Insurance Portability and Accountability Act (HIPAA) (2003), 100–103
Health literacy, 12, 14, 141–143
Health maintenance organization (HMO), 46–47, 48, 98. *See also* Managed care
Health professionals. *See* Caregivers; Nurses; Physicians
Health promoter, 338

Health-promoting behaviors, 338
Health promotion campaigns
  analyzing audience for, 347–350
  anti-tobacco, 365
  behavior change theories used for, 366–367, 371–377
  behavioral changes through, 339, 342
  defined, 338
  designing, 338–339, 377, 380–384
  establishing goals and objectives for, 356, 358
  ethical considerations, 354–356, 378–380
  evaluating, 386–387
  exemplary campaigns, 338, 340–342, 342–345
  focus group exercise on, 364
  identifying the situation and potential benefits for, 345–347
  and knowledge gap, 357
  maintaining, 387–388
  piloting and implementing, 384–386
  segmenting the audience, 350–353, 356
  selecting channels of communication for, 358–362
  and social marketing, 366
  stages of creating, 366, 367
Health resources, allocation of, 150–151
Health self-efficacy, 174–175
Herbal remedies, 37, 256, 257, 258, 258–259
Heterosexism, 144
Hierarchical bureaucracies, 279–281
Highly scheduled interviews, 347–348
Hills, Karen, 188
Hippocrates, 25, 26–28, 34
Hippocratic Oath, 26, 27, 224
Hispanic Americans
  access to technology, 323
    and cultural differences, 229
  health promotion campaigns channeled to, 361
    impact of perceived discrimination on, 244
    language barriers of, 149, 154
    in medical professions, 248, 249
History of medicine. *See* Medicine, history of
HMOs. *See* Health maintenance organizations
Holistic medicine, 255–256
Hollywood, Health & Society program, 329
Homeopathic medicine, 255, 256
Homosexuality, 144–145
Hospice care, 190–191
Hospitals. *See also* Health care organizations
  closing of, 271
  personal experience in, 13
Humor, 71

Identity
  and illness, 130–132
  and medical school, 92
  and narratives, 132–133
Illiteracy, 141, 142
Illness. *See also* Disease
  cultural viewpoints on, 208–212, 230
  disease vs., 33
  opportunities for growth and change through, 214–217
  and personal identity, 130–132
  verifying, 31, 32
Imaginary audience, 352
Imhotep, 25–26
Impact, 358
Impassioned care, 229
Implicate order, 214
India, 204, 205–206, 206, 217
Industrialization, 35
Informational support, 177
Informative stage, 333
Informed consent, 124, 126–130, 138
Instrumental support, 177
Insurance deductible, 44–45. *See also* Health insurance
Insurance premium, 44. *See also* Health insurance
Integrated health systems, 271
Integrated organization, 239
Integrative health theory, 134–135
Integrative medicine, 256
Interdependent communicators, 7
Internal factors, 371
Internal locus of control, 174
International Association of Business Communicators, 20
International Communication Association, 20
Internet, 323
Interpersonal conflict, 260
Interpreters, 154–155
Interruptions, conversational, 59
Interview, 347–348
Involvement, 359

Joe Camel advertisement, 327–328
John Hopkins University School of Medicine, 37, 247
Journals, health communication, 80
"Just do it" advertising slogan, 380

Kaleidoscope model of health communication, 40, 42–44, 45
Kashmiri men, 217
Kevorkian, Jack, 192
Kiser, Jennifer, 340, 342
Knowledge coupling, 111–112, 113
Knowledge gap hypothesis, 357

Language barriers, 152–155
Language differences, 149, 154–155
Language expectancy theory, 376, 382
Latinos. *See* Hispanic Americans
Lay caregivers, 184–188, 195
Leadership
  authority rule, 282–283
  breaches of trust in, 300–301
  bureaucratic, 278–288
  division of labor, 284–285
  hierarchical, 279–281
  innovative leadership characteristics, 290
  multilevel input, 283–284
  participative decision making, 281, 283–284
  perspective by Quint Studer, 272–274
  rules and procedures for, 286–287, 286–288
  training new leaders, 281–282
  transition in, 270–271
Legislation
  Family and Medical Leave Act (1993), 185
  managed care liability, 261–262
  privacy regulations, 100
Lesbianism, 144–145
Life-at-all-costs perspective, 189–190
Life expectancy, 189
  cultural differences, 204–205
  and race, 146
Listening, supportive, 178
Literacy
  health, 141–143
  illiteracy, 141, 142
Locus of control, 174–175
Logical appeal, 382
Low socioeconomic status, 21, 140–141, 166–167

Magazines, 359
Magic, 29–30
Maintenance, health campaign, 387–388

Male nurses, 253
Managed care
  caregiver perspective on, 46–47
  consumer's perspective on, 44–46
  cost-cutting and, 15–16, 41–42
    defined, 41, 44
  ethical considerations, 51
  factors giving rise to, 39–41
  liability, 262–263
  organization's perspective, 47–48
  and professional autonomy, 97–98
  pros and cons of, 48–50
  terminology, 48
Management. *See* Leadership
Marketing for health care organizations, 297
Marston, Ginna, 368–370
Mass communication, 305. *See also* Mass media
Mass media, 14. *See also* Entertainment programs; Health information
  alcohol advertisements, 308–309, 311
    communication specialists working with, 295–296
  health stories in the news, 314–315, 318–321
  impact of, 305
  influence of, 310–311, 334–335
  media literacy, 332–334
  media relations at the CDC, 316–318, 319
  sensationalism in, 318–320
  television's impact on nutrition, 307–308
Maturity, caregiver, 99, 103
Media. *See* Mass media
Media literacy, 14, 332–334, 336–337
Medicaid, 41
Medical associations, 249. *See also* American Medical Association (AMA)
Medical environments, 74–76
Medical instruments, sterilizing, 35–36
Medical mistakes, 104
Medical models, 67–68. *See also* Biomedical model; Biopsychosocial model
Medical research, 208
Medical school
  cultural competence taught in, 228
  curriculum, 89–91
  implications, 95–96
  minorities in, 249
  reform efforts, 37, 94–95
  and rise of conventional medicine, 36
  socialization process, 91–94
  student communication patterns, 86–88
  student selection, 88–89
  women in, 246, 247
Medical spiritualism, 28–29
"medical student abuse", 92, 94
Medicare, 41
Medicine, history of
  ancient Egypt, 25–28
  colonial America, 33–34
  European Renaissance, 30–31, 33
  medieval Europe, 28–30
  twentieth century, 38–39
Medieval Europe, 28–30
Meditation, 255
Medline database, 78
Mental illness
  and cultural expectations, 203–204
  media portrayal of, 324–325, 334
  social taboos of, 213
Mexican-American cultures, 211. *See also* Hispanic Americans
Mexico, 205
Michelangelo, 31
Midlevel providers, 254–255
Mind-body dualism, 31, 33
Minnesota Heart Health Program, 343–344
Minorities. *See also* Cultural diversity and expectations
  access to medical care, 148
  discrimination of, 244–245
  distrust of medical establishment, 147
  as health care workers, 21, 237, 248–249, 252
  high risk for diseases, 147–148
  knowledge of health issues, 147, 148
Mistakes, medical, 104
Model of collaborative interpretation (CI), 67–68
Moderately scheduled interviews, 348
Monolithic organizations, 244
Morality of prevention, 218
Mothers Against Drunk Driving (MADD), 354
Motivation, behavior change and, 367, 371
Movies, 114, 325, 328, 332. *See also* Entertainment programs
Multichannel campaigns, 360–362
Multiculturalism, 244. *See also* Cultural diversity and expectations
Multicultural organizations, 244
Muscular Dystrophy Association, 366
Music, warning labels on, 326

Narratives, patient, 132–133, 136
Narrowcasting, 359–360
National Accreditation Council for Graduate Medical Education, 95
National AIDS Hotline, 381
National Communication Association, 20
National Institutes of Health (NIH), 257
National Medical Association, 249
National Public Health Information Coalition (NPHIC), 317
Native Americans, 33–34, 210, 211, 225, 249
Natural therapies, 258–259
Naturopathic medicine, 255, 256
Navajo cultures, 210
Negative affect, 382, 383–384
News, health information in, 314–315, 318–321
Nike, 380
90-Second Intervention health campaign, 344
Noncompliance, patient, 125–126
Non-English speakers, 149, 152–155
Nonverbal communication, 69–70
Normalcy, 176
Novel messages, 384
Nurse practitioners, 254
Nurses. *See also* Patient-caregiver communication
  communication skills training for, 294
  communication styles, 58, 60
  communication with children, 158
  generalist care by, 229
  helpfulness of, 13
  impassioned care by, 229
  male, 253
  patient evaluation of, 123
  resistant care by, 228–229
  and role conflict, 263–265
  satisfaction of, 105
  shortage of, 252–254, 278
  status of, 238–239, 252
  stress among, 107–108, 109, 110
  and teamwork, 291–292

Nursing school programs, 89, 112, 253
Nurturing support, 177–181
Nutrition, advertising's impact on, 307–308

Obesity and advertising, 307–308
Odawa aboriginal communities, 210
Office of Alternative Medicine, 257
Ojibway aboriginal communities, 210
Older adults. *See* Elderly
Open questions, 348
Organic perspective, 208–210, 211–212, 230
Organizational culture, 238–246
Organizations, 20. *See also* Health care organization
Oriental medicine, 256
Orthodox medicine, rise of, 35–38
Orthodox practitioners, 35
Osteopathy, 37, 256
Outcomes model, 68
Overaccommodation, 162
Overempathizing, 198–199
Overhelping, 196
Overinforming, 196–198
Oversupporting, 195–199

Parental mediation, 333–334
Parental responsibility for vaccinations, 378–379
Participative decision making (PDM), 281
Partnership for a Drug-Free America (PDFA), 366, 368–370
Pasteur, Louis, 35
Paternalism, 223, 224
Pathologizing the human body, 312
Patient advocates, 297
Patient-caregiver communication. *See also* Communication techniques
  caregiver gender differences, 248
  class activity on improving, 231–233
  collaborative, 66–71
  doorknob disclosures, 74
  environmental factors in, 72–76
  importance of, 12–14, 57–58
  lack of, 57
  and minority cultures, 249–250
  and patient compliance, 126
  patient techniques, 80–81
  physician-centered, 58–61, 63–66
  positive experience with, 72, 73
  and race, 148–149
  and therapeutic privilege, 64, 65
  transgressions in, 61, 62
Patient perspective
  consent, 124, 126–130
  cooperation, 124, 125–126
  managed care, 44–46
  satisfaction, 122–124
  socialization, 115–119
  uncertainty of, 116, 117
Patients. *See also* Patient-caregiver communication
  in biomedical model, 11
  blaming, 218
    empowerment of, 18–19
  factors influencing communication patterns of, 119–121
    "good," 63
  narratives of, 132–133
  partnership with caregivers, 227
  and personal identity, 130–132
  as victims, 218–219
Patient's bill of rights, 261
Patronize, 60
Patronizing behavior, 61, 63
Personal fable, 352
Personal goals, 6–7
Personal identity. *See* Identity
Perspective, 11
Perspectives. *See also* Caregiver perspective; Patient perspective
  AIDS in Africa, 206, 207
  health promotion campaign, 340–342
  patient uncertainty, 116, 117
  positive experience with a dentist, 72, 73
  "sick in the head," 32
  substance abuse among physicians, 106, 107
  "unselling" drugs, 368–370
Pharmaceutical companies
  advertising by, 275, 276, 307
  antideception regulations for, 306
Philip Morris tobacco company, 365
Physical disabilities, 325
Physician assistants, 254
Physician-assisted suicide, 192–193
Physician-centered communication, 58–61, 63–66
Physicians. *See also* Caregivers; Medical school
  advertising, 275
  authority of, 36
  and biomedical model, 10–11
  and biopsychosocial model, 11
  minority, 237, 249
  in the movies, 114
  patient evaluation of, 122–124
  status differences, 238–239
  stereotypes influencing judgment of, 149
  and teamwork, 291–292
  women, 237, 246–248
Piloting a health promotion campaign, 384–385
Placebo effect, 226
Planetree, 75, 76
Plural organizations, 244
Population changes, 21, 35, 253
Positive affect, 382–383
Power differences between patients and physicians, 61, 63
Preferred provider organization (PPO), 47, 48. *See also* Managed care
Prejudice, 141
Prescription drug advertising. *See* Pharmaceutical companies
Pretest-posttest design, 386
Prevention, 18, 218
Primary care doctors, 40. *See also* Physicians
Principle of verification, 31, 32
Privacy
  regulations on, 98, 100–103
  and telemedicine, 79
Problematic integration, theory of, 196, 197–198
Problem-based learning (PBL), 91
Problem solving, 174
Product placement, 328–329, 332
Professional autonomy, 97–98
Professional influences
  competition, 97
  loss of autonomy, 97–98
  time constraints, 96–97
Professional prejudice, 283
Project Scum (Subculture and Urban Marketing), 365
Pro-social programming, 329
Psychological influences on caregivers, 99, 103–105. *See also* Stress and burnout
Public health campaigns. *See* Health promotion campaigns
Public Relations Society of America, 20
Puerto Ricans, 249
Purging practices, 28, 34

Questionnaire, 348
Questions, 60, 70

Race. *See* Minorities
Racial segregation, 38
Racism, 146, 149

Radiologists, 109
Rational/empirical approach, 27
Rational-legal authority, 282–283
Reach, 358
Reduced sense of personal accomplishment, 106–107
Reiki, 256
Reimbursement, 46
Reimbursement rates, 41
Religio-empirical approach, 26
Renaissance philosophy, 30–31, 33
Research
  evidence-based medicine, 208
  health communication, 298
  and rise of orthodox medicine, 36
Resistance, 136
Resistance care, 228–229
Resources
    conflict management, 263
    coping and social support, 184
  culture and health, 209
  death and dying, 196
  health communication careers, 299
  health communication journals, 80
  health education careers, 350
  health promotion campaigns, 385, 388
  managed care, 46
  media effects on children, 314
    organizations and websites, 20
  Planetree model, 76
    tailored health communication, 361
  using narrowcast messages, 361
Restored self, 132
Rite of passage, 94
R.J. Reynolds Tobacco Company, 327–328
Robert Wood Johnson Foundation, 370
Role
  collaboration between, 220–222
    and consumerism, 226–227
  defined, 220, 260
  family member, 220, 221
  patients, 220
    Thai customs, 220, 221
Role conflict, 260, 263–265
Rote learning, 90
Rules and policies, 286–288
Russian culture, 204

Safe-sex options, 179–180
Salaried physicians, 98
Salvaged self, 132
Sampling, 349
SARS (severe acute respiratory syndrome), 19–20, 318
Satisfaction
  caregiver, 103–105
    patient, 122–124
Scapegoat, 378
Scapegoating, 378–379
Scott, Bess, 340
Scut work, 92
Sectarian medicine, 37
Sectarians, 35
Segmenting the audience, 350–351
Self-doubt among caregivers, 103
Sensationalism in the media, 318–320
Sensitivity, 7–8
Sex
  media portrayal of, 325–326
  used for advertising, 353
Sex education, 156
Sex roles, 264
Sexually transmitted diseases, 205
Sexual orientation, 144–146, 167
Shamans, 225
Shocking messages, 384
Skills training. *See* Communication skills training
Sleep deprivation, 93
Smoking, 372–373. *See also* Tobacco industry
SNAP (School Network for Absenteeism Prevention), 341
Soap and Detergent Association, 341
Social adaptation theory, 330–331
Social cognitive theory, 371–372, 375, 376
Social comparison theory, 310–311, 335
Social identities, 130
Socialization
    medical students, 85–88, 91–94
  patient, 115–119
Social network support, 179–181
Social support
  action-facilitating support, 177
  benefits of, 173
  communication specialists, 294
  coping, 174–175, 183
  coping strategies, 176–177
  crisis, 175–176
  death and dying experiences, 188–195
  defined, 174
  emotional support, 178–179
  and health promotion campaigns, 344
  healthcare workplace, 294
  lay caregiving, 184–188
  normalcy, 176
  nurturing support, 177–181
  oversupport, 195–199
  scenarios of, 173
  social network support, 179–181
  support groups, 181–182
  supportive listening, 178
  virtual communities, 182–183
Socioeconomic status (SES), 140–141, 166–167
Soul, the, 31, 33
Source homophily, 381
Southern Appalachians, 225
Southern States Communication Association, 20
Spanish-speaking families, 149, 152–155
Speaking in tongues, 225–226
Specialists, 40
Specialization, 38–39
Specificity, 358
Speech community, 85, 88
Spiritualism, medical, 28–29
Spiritualists, caregivers as, 223, 225–226
Stereotypes, 149
  defined, 159
  the elderly, 160
    physicians impacted by, 149
Steroid abuse, 313
"stick in the head", 32
Stigma, 217–218
Stigmatizing, 379
St. Jude Children's Research Hospital, 13
Storytelling, 132–133
Stress and burnout
  causes, 107–109
  implications, 110–111
  and lay caregiving, 185–188
  substance abuse, 105, 106, 107
  suicide rate, 105
  terminology, 106–107
Stress-related disorders, 148
Studer, Quint, 240, 272–275
Subculture and Urban Marketing (Project Scum), 365
Substance abuse, 105, 106–107, 110
Sulejmanovic, Irina, 340, 341
Supernatural forces, 216–217, 225
Supernormal identity, 132
Support groups, 181–183
Supportive listening, 178
Surgeons, stress among, 109
Surgery, medieval, 29
Syphilis, 128

Team, 288
Teamwork, 288–289, 291–292

Technology, 21, 36
computer-mediated health information, 321–323
knowledge coupling, 111–112
narrowcasting, 359–360
and older adults, 164–165
telemedicine, 76–79
using the Internet, 323
virtual communities, 182–183
Telemedicine
advantages of, 77–78
defined, 76
disadvantages of, 78–79
examples of, 76, 77
Teleputers, 321
Television rating system, 326–327
Television viewing. *See also* Entertainment programs
alcohol beverage advertising on, 312
and nutrition, 307–308
sedentary nature of, 308
sex on, 325
violence on, 326–327
Tertiary identity, 131
Thai culture, 220, 221
Theoretical foundations
behavior change theories, 376
communication as collaborative interpretation, 67
cultivation theory, 310
explanation, 9
integrative health model, 134–135
Kaleidoscope Model of health communication, 42–44
knowledge gap hypothesis, 357
medical student communication patterns, 86–88
model for innovative leadership, 290
model of collaborative interpretations (CI), 67–68
model of multiculturalism, 244, 245
social comparison theory, 310–311
theory of health as expanded consciousness, 214–217
theory of problematic integration, 197–198
Theories, behavior change, 366–367, 371–377
Theory of health as expanded consciousness, 214–217
Theory of problematic integration, 196, 197–198
Theory of reasoned action (TRA), 373, 375–376, 376
Therapeutic privilege, 64, 65
"Think. Don't Smoke" campaign, 365
Time constraints, 96–97
Timing of health promotion campaigns, 378
Tobacco industry, , 354
entertainomercials and, 327–328
health campaigns against, 354, 365, 386–387
product placement and, 328–329
Touch, 69
Traditional medicine (TM), 255
Transactional communication, 58
Transgressions, 60, 62, 63
Transtheoretical model, 373–375, 376
Truth campaigns, 365–366
Tuskegee Syphilis Study, 127
Two-step flow, 361

Uncertainty
employee, 293
patient, 116, 117
United Kingdom, 204
Unscheduled interviews, 348
U.S. Department of Health and Human Services, 341

V-chip, 327
Verbal encouragement, 70–71
Vertical hierarchies, 279–280
Victimization, 218–219
Video games, 329
Violence in the media, 324–325, 326–327
Violent conflict, 262–263
Virtual communities, 182–183
Voice of Lifeworld, 115–118
Voice of Medicine, 85, 116–117

Wealth, health and, 40
Websites, 20
Western Reserve Medical School, 37
Western States Communication Association, 20
Williams, Gwynné, 13
Witchcraft, 216–217
Withdrawal and resentment, medical student, 93
Women
colonial American, 34
communication styles of, 248
earnings, 245
equity for, 247
health promotion campaigns channeled to, 343, 360
historical role in medicine, 246–247
physicians, 237
Workload, 109

Yang, 210
Yin, 210
Youth. *See* Adolescents; Children